Entrepreneur MAGAZINE'S

ULTIMATE

HOMEBASED BUSINESS HANDBOOK

How To Start, Run and Grow Your Own Profitable Business

JAMES STEPHENSON

EP
Entrepreneur Press

Managing editor: Jere L. Calmes
Cover design: Beth Hansen-Winter
Composition and production: Eliot House Productions

This publication is designed to provide accurate and authoritative information in regard to the subject matter covered. It is sold with the understanding that the publisher is not engaged in rendering legal, accounting, or other professional services. If legal advice or other expert assistance is required, the services of a competent professional person should be sought.

Library of Congress Cataloging-in-Publication Data

Stephenson, James, 1966–
    The ultimate homebased handbook: how to start, run, and grow your own profitable business/by James Stephenson.
        p. cm.
    Includes bibliographical references.
    ISBN 1-932531-02-5
    1. Homebased businesses—management—Handbooks, manuals, etc. 2. New business enterprises—Management—Handbooks, manuals, etc. 3. Small business—Management—Handbooks, manuals, etc. 4. Success in business—Handbooks, manuals, etc. I. Title.
    HD62.38.S678 2004
    658'.0412—dc22

                                                                    2004045557

Printed in Canada

10 09 08 07 06 05   10 9 8 7 6 5 4 3 2

Contents

Acknowledgments

I WOULD NOT HAVE BEEN ABLE TO WRITE THIS book without the help of all of the top businesspeople that I have had the pleasure of working with through the years. They have graciously shared their business wisdom and knowledge with me. Thank you. I would also like to thank Jere Calmes and Entrepreneur Press for providing the opportunity to share this book with you, and my wife Pamela for her continued encouragement and support. I extend thanks to Karen Billipp. This is the third book that Karen and I have worked on together, and because of her valuable contributions, perceptive insights, and incredible eye for detail, the readers and I have greatly benefited. Thank you, I am grateful.

Introduction

A S THE NAME SUGGESTS, A HOME BUSINESS IS a business venture that you operate from a homebased location. This certainly does not mean that you have to spend your time working exclusively in your home for your business to be classified as a home business. Any business that is operated or substantially managed from a residential location is classified as a home business, including:

- Professionals such as dentists that set up homebased practices
- Consultants that manage their businesses from home, but spend the majority of their working time at their clients' locations
- Service repair technicians that work from mobile vans and trucks, but store equipment and tools at home
- People manufacturing or assembling products in the garage or creating craft products in the basement at home

In a nutshell, if your home address is the same as the address your business uses, then you are operating a homebased business.

You are in good company. According to the U.S. Small Business Administration (SBA), more than 750,000 new business ventures are started each year, with the vast majority of homebased business enterprises started by first-time entrepreneurs. Wow, that adds up to a lot of people taking a gigantic leap of faith! But it does beg the questions: Where do you find all the need-to-know information? Like, how do you get started? Where do you find customers? How do you manage your new home business enterprise?

These questions and hundreds more are answered in great detail in this book. The *Ultimate Homebased Business Handbook* was specifically developed for the thousands of people that start a home business each week and for the thousands more that are considering starting a home business venture in the near future. The *Ultimate Homebased Business Handbook* provides first-time, and even seasoned, entrepreneurs with all the vital information that they need to start, run, and grow their own profitable businesses from the comforts of home. The information is presented in an easy-to-use, understandable, step-by-step format that acts as a road map to guide readers effortlessly through the entire process of starting a homebased business.

GETTING STARTED

My objective in creating the *Ultimate Homebased Business Handbook* was to give people that want to start their own home business a time machine that would enable them to flash forward into the future to see how their dreams of home business ownership became a successful and profitable reality. So you may be wondering where is this time machine? You are looking at it. That's right, this book. I can call this book a time machine because over the years I have owned and operated some successful home business ventures and some not so successful home business ventures. And as the old saying goes, "If I knew then what I know now, I would have done things much differently." Obviously, it's too late for me to go back and do things differently, but I do know now what I wished I'd known then. That is why I refer to this book as a time machine. The information featured in this book covers the steps you need to take to succeed and the actions that you should avoid so that 10 years from now you are not saying "I wish I knew then what I know now." Once again, the information and advice featured in this book are based on my own business and sales experience and on the experiences of the many successful businesspeople that I have had the pleasure of working with over the years and that have graciously shared their infinite business wisdom and knowledge with me.

HOW TO USE THIS BOOK

The biggest compliment that you can pay to me is by writing in this book. In fact, if you have read the book completely and did not utilize any of the checklists or worksheets, and did not jot notes in the margin, then I have failed miserably in my objectives in writing it. This is a workbook and should be used as such. It is not a book that should be taking a restful nap on a dusty shelf. Use it incrementally through all phases of getting your new home business rolling, including:

- Identifying your personal strengths and weaknesses
- Setting attainable and realistic goals
- Identifying the right new home business idea
- Choosing the right legal structure
- Developing a workable business plan
- Finding the money needed to start, operate, and grow your business
- Designing and organizing a superproductive home workspace

- Creating a marketing plan that's guaranteed to find and keep customers for life
- Managing the day-to-day operations like a pro

WHAT YOU WILL DISCOVER INSIDE

I have attempted to maintain a sense of order in this book by putting specific information in what I feel is the logical chapter, though out of order in the true sense of an A to Z, step-by-step format. I chose this format because of the sheer amount of information contained in the *Ultimate Homebased Business Handbook*, the largest and most comprehensive book available on the subject of starting and operating a home business. For instance, in Chapter 3, Financial Issues, you will find information dealing with the financial aspects of starting and operating a home business—securing start-up funding, establishing business bank accounts, the various payment options available to your customers, and small business tax information. Sometimes I have also included relevant financial issues in other chapters to help explain the specific topic being discussed.

I strongly advise you to read each and every chapter in this book, even if you feel the information featured does not apply to your particular situation or the type of business you intend to start. I say this because in each chapter there are literally hundreds of Web resources, business ideas, and valuable marketing tips. Overall, after completing this book, you will have acquired the following information:

- *Help to identify the right new home business for you.* Information in the book has been specifically developed to guide you effortlessly through the process of knowing what the right new home business for you is. Also included is a bonus chapter featuring 99 great home business start-up ideas, as well as information on 99 terrific home franchise opportunities.
- *Answers for all of those tough financial and legal questions.* Far too many business books leave you with more questions than answers in terms of the financial and legal issues that you need to understand to start and run a home business. In this one, you will discover information on legal business structures, how to finance

your new business, the permits and licenses that you will need, and how to make sure that Uncle Sam gets his portion of the pie, but not before you have gotten yours.

- *How to develop business and marketing plans.* You will learn how to develop your own business and marketing plans step by step, from where to start research to how you can use your plans to secure business start-up and growth capital. And, of course, plans will act as a road map leading you to home business success and profits.

- *Learn how to set up and organize your home workspace.* If you have never designed, planned, and equipped a home workspace before, you will be glad to know that I have a few times. I have included lots of tips and ideas that are sure to save you money and help you put together workspace (even on a tight budget) that will still prove to be efficient and productive.

- *Tips that will show you how to build a better business team.* No one person can build a successful business on his own, it requires a business team comprised of people that understand your goals and that are dedicated to making sure that you reach these goals. Here you will discover who the key players should be, why you need them, and how to recruit them onto your business team.

- *The quick and easy route for home business management.* One of the most difficult aspects of operating a home business is the hands-on, day-to-day management that is required to keep the ship on its course. A great deal of attention has been paid to providing information that allows you to spend less time managing your business and more time creating opportunities for new business and enjoying the personal rewards this affords.

- *Surefire ways to find and keep customers.* Without customers you have no business, so the importance of finding and keeping customers cannot be overstated. Included here are the tools that you need to conduct customer research and create a target customer profile, the strategies that will take you to your cus-

tomers, the words and actions that will make them buy, and the incredible customer service tips that will keep them coming back for life.

- *Uncovering selling secrets that the pros use.* Deep in the core of the earth you will find a chamber. In that chamber you will find a chest. Locked away in that chest are the selling secrets that the pros have used for centuries to win big every time. Guess what? I found the key, unlocked the chest, and at great risk to my personal safety swiped these closely guarded selling secrets while no one was watching. Best of all, I have included these selling secrets in this book for you to use freely so that you too can win big every time, just like the pros.

- *Advertising that gets the results that you want and need.* One of the biggest marketing challenges that home business owners face is determining the type of advertising that will give them the biggest bang for their precious marketing buck. Inside you will learn what type of advertising gets the results you need and want—without putting a second mortgage on your home to pay for it.

- *What you need to know to get on the Internet and start doing business there.* Consumers spend billions every month purchasing products and services online. There you will learn how to build, maintain, and market a professional e-commerce Web site that will help you secure your piece of the very lucrative Internet pie.

CHECKLISTS AND WORKSHEETS

Throughout the *Ultimate Homebased Business Handbook,* you will find many helpful checklists, worksheets, and forms that you can use as featured. Alternately, you can use these as a template. With your computer and a basic word processing program, customize each checklist, worksheet, or form to create ones that are relevant to your home business, products, services, or marketing objectives. You will also find many helpful examples, such as a sample press release, target customer profile sheet, and media questionnaire, just to mention a few. Their purpose is to help explain visually information that is being featured and to give you a useful tool for you business that will save time and money. Worksheets and checklists can prove invaluable when setting up a new business, especially if this is your first time. Therefore, I encourage you to take advantage of these useful tools.

HOME BUSINESS RESOURCES

As you read through the *Ultimate Homebased Business Handbook* you will notice that hundreds of business-related resources have been included in the text and at the end of each chapter. The resources featured throughout the book include both American and Canadian business associations, government agencies, private corporations, individuals, Web sites, books and publications, products, services, and lots more. However, you will find that these business resources fall into three main categories: associations, books, and Web sites.

Association Resources

At both the end of the book and at the end of each chapter, you will find association resources and listings. I have endeavored to locate and list important nonprofit business and industry associations, as well as government agencies, to help guide you through important business and marketing activities. Organizations like the American Home Business Association and government agencies like the Copyright Office are listed with full contact information and Web sites addresses. The purpose of these listing is to allow you to visit their Web sites or contact them directly to receive valuable publications and information. There are hundreds of association and agencies listed throughout this book, many of which you will find extremely helpful when you are establishing your home business, operating your home business, and marketing your products or services. In many cases, especially with government agencies, there are free programs in place to help entrepreneurs from every walk of life succeed in starting their own businesses. I encourage you to use these valuable resources so that you can take advantage of these programs, thereby greatly increasing your odds of enjoying long-term, profitable business success.

Book Resources

You will also find a suggested additional reading list at the end of each chapter featuring relevant books and publications. Once again, the purpose of this list is not to promote or endorse any one author, book title, publisher, or program. The book resources are there to give you a research tool for finding additional information and advice about the specific information that was featured in the chapter. Likewise, the suggested reading list is not meant to inspire you to run out and spend hundreds of dollars on new books and publications, though investments made in products that can assist you to become a better business operator and marketer are without question wise business and personal investments. However, once again, do not feel compelled to purchase these titles. If you find a title that interests you, start your search at the local library and take it for a information test drive first, so to speak. Afterward, if you feel that you cannot live without it, buy a copy so that you will have a constant research and advice companion handy on your own bookshelf whenever the need for it arises.

Web Resources

Throughout this book and at the end of each chapter, you will find numerous useful online Web resources, which are highlighted with a computer icon. The purpose of these Web resources is not to promote or endorse any one particular company, product, service, individual, Web site, agency, or organization. The Web resources are there to give you an additional research tool so that you have an avenue to learn more about the information featured, without having to spend your valuable time having to research and find this information yourself. For instance, you might be interested in finding a home business insurance agent or broker. Inside you will find online resources featuring that information. Or perhaps you need further information about desktop software applications. Once again, you will find this resource information here. The hundreds of Web resources featured throughout this book are incredible research tools: they enable you to quickly explore and compile further data and information about specific home business information, ideas, or topics painlessly and in a matter of moments. All of the Web resources featured were active links at the time of writing the book. However, over time some organizations, agencies, and businesses can change their domain, close shop, or alter the products or services they handle. In an effort to ensure that the links remain active for the long term I have endeavored to find reputable businesses, organizations, and individuals to feature as Web resources.

Entrepreneur Magazine's Ultimate Homebased Business Handbook is the most authoritative and comprehensive home business start-up book available today. It gives you the answers to all of the questions that you have about starting, operating, and growing your own home business for long-term profitable success. Harness

CHAPTER 1

Why Start a Home Business?

SHOULD YOU START A HOME BUSINESS? MAYBE you should, or maybe you shouldn't. That's likely not what you were expecting to hear or what you wanted to hear. But the truth is that while some people are destined to succeed at operating their own business, others are not and will fail in business.

Not every person is suited for starting and operating a business—not because they are afraid, not because they do not want to succeed, and certainly not because they are stupid—mainly because starting and operating a home business is hard work, much harder than the vast majority of new entrepreneurs realize. In fact, it is not uncommon for home business owners to work in excess of 60 hours per week—week in and week out with little time off and for much less financial compensation than most are willing to admit. And other statistics suggest that four out of every five businesses will fail within the first five years of operation, making for a very bleak forecast.

Personally, I think that the numbers of business failures actually may be skewed to a degree. If a person starts a business and a year later decides to close the business because, as it turns out he or she does not enjoy being self-employed, would that be classified as a business failure? Statistically yes, but in reality I do not believe this example would constitute a business failure. They may be guilty of not fully understanding what they were getting into or not taking enough time to rationalize their decision to start a business in the first place, but definitely not of failing. Besides, success and failure are relative terms. As explained above, a person that starts a business and decides to close the business after a year because he doesn't like being self-employed may very well consider the experience fulfilling and a success. Another person in similar circumstances may consider the event to be one of the greatest failures of her life. It is relative to each person's individual situation, goals, and way of thinking. In reality, failing in business or in some other area is not about the fact that you tried something new that didn't work out. Failing is wanting to do something but never giving it a whirl. You cannot succeed if you do not try.

Still, why do so many new businesses fail? For many reasons. That said, most business failures can be traced to three main problems—lack of proper research, lack of proper planning, and lack of money—with the last the main culprit. Additional reasons why businesses fail include:

* Lack of business skills
* Starting the business for the wrong reasons
* Bad business idea, product, or service

- Lack of self-confidence
- Events beyond the control of the owner
- No support structure
- Underestimating the strength and resolve of competitors
- Mismatched expectations
- Health or other personal issues

If you decide to start a home business, there is no question that it will be successful and you will reach all of your personal and financial goals. I can say this unconditionally because you have two secret weapons on your side: Your determination to make it happen, and the information contained in this book. For me personally, the rewards of being self-employed far outweigh the risks, hard work, and other potential disadvantages. I believe that this is a very fair and objective assessment because I have started businesses that have been successful and businesses that have not, as is true of most entrepreneurs that stick with it long enough. Of course, at the end of the day you want more checks on your scorecard in the win column then the loss column, especially from a financial perspective. So if you are the type of person that longs for independence, wants to control your future, and can stomach a certain degree of risk without pulling out your hair in the process, then there is a better than average chance that you have what it takes to start and operate your own home business.

However, before you hang out the "open for business sign," make sure that you want to start a business for the right reasons, not the wrong ones. Quitting your job and starting your own home business because you hate your boss is definitely a wrong reason. As soon as you cool down, you'll probably realize that, providing it's not too late. Starting your own home business because you want to buy a really neat $100,000 sports car is also a wrong reason. If you don't believe me, give it a try. Starting your own home business because you have a good idea, want the potential to improve your lifestyle, and have the focus and determination to see it through to the end are very good reasons. It's true, especially if you have thought out the entire process, weighed advantages against disadvantages, and still feel the same a day, week, month, or even years later.

THE ADVANTAGES OF STARTING A HOME BUSINESS

There are many advantages associated with starting your own home business.

You Are Your Own Boss

Without question the greatest lure for starting and running a business is the fact that you become your own boss. Of course, this is only partly true for the simple reason that your customers will always be the true boss of your business. I have been self-employed in various ventures for a number of years, with the majority being operated from my home. For me the lure of self-employment is the freedom, hands down. It's not so much the potential to generate a substantial income or the ability to grow equity, but simply the sense of freedom and independence that being the boss affords.

You Have the Potential to Earn More Money

While it may not be a good reason to start a business solely on the prospect of making big bucks. It is true that the majority of people do have the potential to make more money owning and operating a business than they do working for a paycheck. Why? If for no other reason, simple duplication. When you work for someone else, there is only you and so many hours in the day to work for an hourly wage or a commission. However, when you operate a business, you can duplicate yourself by hiring employees and sales people to increase revenues, you can duplicate your customers and find more to purchase your goods or services, you can duplicate your business model and open in new geographical areas, and you can duplicate and expand the number of products that you sell. Once you have built a business that is generating revenues and profits, duplicating what works can greatly increase your personal income and equity.

You Can Create Your Own Working Environment

Having the ability to create your own work environment and the ability to be flexible in how you operate the business are two more of the major advantages of starting and operating a business from home. Operating a home business will give you the ability to spend less time commuting and more time with your family. You can set your own work hours. You can walk the dog at noon, pick the kids up after school, be at home to let the TV repairperson in, and do a host of other personal activities on your schedule.

You Can Take Advantage of Tax Benefits

Operating a business from home also qualifies you for any number of the tax benefits associated with operating a business, even if you work a regular job and only operate your business part time. As soon as you open for business, a portion of your utility bills are tax deductible against business revenues, a portion of your transportation costs equal to the percentage that your car is used for business are tax deductible, and even this book that you just purchased is an allowable deduction for educational purposes. Start your own business and you'll get back the $20 or so that you paid for this book against your business revenues. Not even 25 pages in and you are already making money.

DISADVANTAGES OF STARTING A HOME BUSINESS

This books should come with an audio soundtrack. At the precise moment you reach this point, the menacing music would start. In scary movie terms, it's just before the axe falls. In this case, the axe is the disadvantages associated with starting and operating your own home business. Like the advantages, there are many.

Financial Risks

Without question, the biggest disadvantage to starting your own home business, or any business for that matter, is the potential that you will lose your financial investment and possibly damage your credit rating should the business fail. Unfortunately, financial risks can also affect your family. If disaster strikes, there will be no money to pay the bills, put food on the table, or pay for that super cool bicycle in the window of the sports shop. Financial risks also extend into other areas of your life, including the potential to earn less income than you currently

are, the need to pay for the health care once covered by your employer's program, and the problem of business loans and leases that you are still on the hook for financially after the business has failed.

Pressure

When you own and operate a business, there is little if any support system in place to help share the workload, worry, and daily strains of running a business. And small business owners wear many hats. One day you are an accounting expert, the next day a customer service expert, the following day an advertising expert, and the list goes on and on. To make matters worse, there is no escape. If things get to a snapping point at work, you simply call in sick and take a day off to recharge your batteries. But when you operate your own business, this option is not so easy. Who will answer the phones? Who will sell the products or services? Who will meet with clients that are not so happy? Once you have made the decision to jump into business with both feet, there is no going back. The pressure will be there day after day. It gets you, or you learn to manage it.

Finding and Keeping Customers

An often overlooked aspect of starting and operating a business is the customers. Not only must you find them and convince them that yours is the best business for them to give their hard-earned money to, you must also work twice as hard to keep them as you did to get them in the first place. The work never stops. The minute your let your guard down and a customer out of your sight, there will be a competitor with arms wide open to take them and take their money. I say that customers are a disadvantage only because many people never fully understand that it is customers that pay the bills, provide the income, and keep the business rolling. Without them, there is no business.

Hard Work

If you have any allergies whatsoever to hard work, you will definitely consider this a disadvantage to starting your own business. As previously mentioned, small business owners as a rule work incredibly hard and have super long hours. It is not uncommon to put in more than 60, or even 70 hours, a week, day in and day out, year round, with little more than the occasional weekend off. You might wonder why work so hard, why not just pace yourself and work as needed? The answer is simple. If it were that easy, everyone would be in business for himself or herself. Once again it comes back to two main issues—no support structure and finding and keeping customer. So reread the information above and you will have your answer about why you need to work hard and long hours if you plan on staying in business. Hard work is especially important for new start-ups with no track record of reliability and performance.

WHAT DOES IT TAKE TO SUCCEED?

Success never happens by accident. Success is a combination of ambition, research, planning, goal setting, hard work, persistence, and the support of others. It requires never losing sight of why you are doing something and what you want to achieve, which will eventually lead you to success. At which point, if you are like most successful people, you will start searching for your next big challenge with the enthusiasm and focus that made you successful in the first place.

I stress again that success is a relative term. Your definition of business success may be to start and operate a business that generates an extra $1,000 per month to help offset the cost of putting the kids through college, while the next person's definition of success might be to expand his small home business into an international business concern employing hundreds and generating millions.

The key to knowing what it takes to succeed is really knowing your own personal definition of success, what you want to achieve, and then putting a plan in place to make it happen. Never get caught up in someone else's definition of success. That is like keeping up with the proverbial Jones—where will it end and even if it does end, how will you know? Besides, who cares what someone else thinks that you should be doing or what you need to do to be successful?

There are, however, certain things that are required to succeed in businesses large or small. Without them you will never obtain success, no matter what your definition of success is. You have to want to be in business. You have to enjoy what you are doing. You have to be persistent. You have to have clear goals. And you have to be prepared to work hard and smart to achieve your goals and ultimately succeed on your own terms and by your own definition.

25 Common Characteristics Shared by Successful Entrepreneurs

Regardless of your definition of success, there are, oddly enough, a great number of common characteristics that are shared by successful businesspeople. See the Entrepreneur Characteristics Checklist (see Figure 1.1) featured. You can place a check beside each characteristic that you feel that you possess to see how you stack up. Even if you do not have all of these characteristics, don't fret. Most can be learned with practice and by developing a winning attitude, especially if you set goals and apply yourself through strategic planning to reach those goals in incremental and measurable stages. That said, here are some of the most common characteristics shared by successful entrepreneurs.

THE HOME BUSINESS MUSTS

Like any activity you pursue there are certain musts that are required in order to be successful in a chosen activity. To legally operate a vehicle on public roadways, one must have a driver's license; to excel in sports, one must train and practice; to retire comfortably, one must become an informed investor and actively invest for retirement. If your goal is success in business, then the formula is no different. There are certain musts that have to be fully developed, implemented, and managed in order for your business to succeed. There are many business musts, but featured in this chapter are what I believe to be some of the more important musts that are required to start, operate, and grow a profitable home business. Many of the ideas and much of the information discussed here are also featured in other chapters, but that is only because of the importance and positive effects that these ideas can have on your business.

FIGURE 1.1 Entrepreneur Characteristics Checklist

❏ Successful entrepreneurs have a strong desire to take control and guide their futures.

❏ Successful entrepreneurs are not afraid to work hard and put in long hours to achieve their personal and business goals.

❏ Successful entrepreneurs are outgoing and very optimistic about what the future holds for their businesses and themselves personally.

❏ Successful entrepreneurs are very self-confidant in their abilities.

❏ Successful entrepreneurs set goals, develop an action plan to reach their goals, and reward themselves when goals (big and small) have been reached and exceeded.

❏ Successful entrepreneurs are well adapted to handle stress and welcome challenges.

❏ Successful entrepreneurs are ambitious almost to a fault.

❏ Successful entrepreneurs are not procrastinators, but proactive in their approach to getting jobs and tasks completed in full, correctly, and on time.

❏ Successful entrepreneurs have a competitive spirit by nature.

❏ Successful entrepreneurs are accountable, accepting personal responsibility for their decisions and actions.

❏ Successful entrepreneurs like to take charge, lead others, and delegate.

❏ Successful entrepreneurs are independent thinkers and workers.

❏ Successful entrepreneurs enjoy taking calculated risks and understand that in the absence of risk, success is seldom if ever achieved.

❏ Successful entrepreneurs communicate well with other people and respect everyone's right to their own opinion even when they disagree.

❏ Successful entrepreneurs are proficient time managers and develop time-saving systems to squeeze the most productivity out of each day.

❏ Successful entrepreneurs work at maintaining good mental and physical health.

❏ Successful entrepreneurs are persistent and not easily discouraged.

❏ Successful entrepreneurs are organized.

❏ Successful entrepreneurs think and react logically and not emotionally.

❏ Successful entrepreneurs are knowledge hungry and never stop looking for ways to become better in all areas of business.

❏ Successful entrepreneurs have realistic expectations.

❏ Successful entrepreneurs are great planners and plan for every aspect of business and marketing.

❏ Successful entrepreneurs are proficient problem solvers and decisive decision makers.

❏ Successful entrepreneurs keep an open mind, are flexible, and are adaptable to change when change is beneficial.

❏ Successful entrepreneurs know how to handle criticism, especially if there is a message within that they can learn from.

Do What You Love

What you get out of your business in the form of personal satisfaction, financial gain, stability, and enjoyment will be the sum of and a direct result of what you put into your business. So if you do not enjoy what you are doing, in all likelihood it is safe to assume that will be reflected in the success of your business—or subsequent lack of success. In fact, if you do not enjoy what you are doing then chances are you will be horribly miserable.

Most people start a business because they want to do something they enjoy, have control over their future, have the ability to make decisions, and build a stable financial foundation for their family. Basically, the business that you start or purchase should be your dream. This is not to say there will not be bad days when you dislike what you are doing, but by and large the good days should outnumber the bad. The best way to guarantee this is to start a business that involves something that you really enjoy. If you enjoy sailing, find a niche in the sailing industry that is not being filled and start a business that will service that niche. If you enjoy selling, make sure that your business is sales-oriented and revolves around personal interaction. And, if you enjoy working with your hands, consider a homebased manufacturing business or a business in which you provide services. The old adage "Do what you love and the money will follow" is great advice, especially coupled with solid research and planning.

Take What You Do Seriously

You cannot expect ever to be effective and successful in business unless you truly believe in your business and in the goods and services that you sell. Far too many home business owners fail to take their businesses seriously, mainly because of the misconceived notion that a real business needs a real location such as a retail storefront or commercial office space. This outlandish notion could not be further from the truth. According to the National Association of Home Based Businesses, more than 50 million people in the United States work from a home office or workspace in some capacity on a full-time or part-time basis. And not surprisingly, almost 30 million are self-employed, owning and operating a home business venture. In fact, home business enterprises create more jobs and employ more people annually in the United States than any other business classification or industry sector.

Your home business is not merely a hobby and should not be treated as such, even if you operate the business part-time or seasonally. Starting a home business requires the input of three very valuable assets—a considerable investment of money at start-up and along the way to grow the business, a substantial investment of time initially to start the business and to manage and ensure continued growth, and a significant investment of one's personal energy at start-up and for the life of the enterprise. All three are extremely valuable commodities that should never be wasted or taken lightly. Take your home business seriously and in return you will reap all of the lifestyle benefits, financial rewards, and long-term security that business ownership can provide to the serious business owner.

Plan Everything

I won't say that failing to plan means that you're planning to fail because few people consciously set out to fail in business. But I will say that many people do not properly plan, generally for two reasons. First, they're lazy and do not want to commit the time, money, and energy that is required to properly develop various business, marketing, and financial plans. Second, many people are intimidated by the planning process because of their lack of understanding. Both hurdles are easily overcome. In the first case, there are no shortcuts in business. You will greatly increase your odds of succeeding if you plan for success. In the second case, read books about business planning, or contact the U.S. Small Business Administration (SBA) and inquire about business planning courses and programs offered in your local area or online. Likewise, contact home business associations and make inquiries about business planning courses and programs.

Planning every aspect of your home business is not only a must, but also builds habits that every home business owner should develop, implement, and maintain. The act of business planning is so important because it requires you to analyze each business situation, research and compile data, and make conclusions based mainly on the facts as revealed through the research and your assumptions or hopes. Business planning also serves a second function, which is having your goals and how you will achieve them on paper; you can use the plan that you create both as map to take you from point A to Z and as a yardstick to measure the success of each individual plan or segment within the plan. This is not to say that every plan you create for your small business must be a hefty tome chock full of statistics, but the basics must be covered. Enough information must be revealed so that you can develop business, marketing, and growth strategies. Key plans include a business plan, marketing plan, advertising plan, sales plan, and financial forecasts and plans.

Be a Wise Money Manager

The lifeblood of any business enterprise is cash flow. You need it to buy inventory, pay for services, promote and market your business, repair and replace tools and equipment, and pay yourself so that you can continue to work. Therefore, all home business owners must become wise, and when required frugal money managers to ensure that the cash keeps flowing, and the bills get paid. There are two aspects to wise money management—the money you receive from clients in exchange for your goods and services you provide, and the money you spend on inventory, supplies, wages, and other items required to keep your business operating. The first aspect of wise money management is taking your billing procedures seriously, making sure that you get paid for what you sell—in full and on time. There are never any exceptions to this rule. In the second aspect of wise money management, smart home business owners know when and where to economize and when and where to spend extra loot. They know that spending more money on a telephone system with more business functions is a wise expenditure and that spending less on disposable pens imprinted with your name is also a smart and frugal business move. They know that spending money on business products such as professional artwork for advertising that can be used over and over again is a very wise investment and spending money on products that can only be used once or on a very limited basis is a poor and ultimately costly decision. Top entrepreneurs know that in order to compete in today's extremely competitive business environment, every purchase they make must be an investment in disguise, one that will have a beneficial impact on their business.

Ask for the Sale

A home business entrepreneur must always remember that marketing, advertising, or promotional activities are completely worthless, regardless of how clever, expensive, or perfectly targeted they are, unless one simple thing is accomplished—ask for the sale. This is not to say that being a great salesperson, advertising copywriting whiz, or a public relations specialist isn't a tremendous asset to your business. However, all of these skills will be for naught if you do not actively ask people to buy what you are selling.

Home business owners do not have to be sales and marketing geniuses to be successful. In fact, you will win more times than not by following one simple rule—always ask for the sale. In all of your advertising, ask people to buy. In your booth at the trade show, ask people to buy. In all of your signage, ask people to buy. In all of your promotional materials, ask people to buy. During sales presentations, ask people to buy. On your Web site, ask people to buy. The last eight words that you say to a prospect or current customer should be "How do you want to pay for that?" Few people will offer you their hard-earned money without being asked to. This simple, yet time-tested and proven-to-work, business premise can easily mean the difference between success and failure. Therefore, every time you are talk about your business, products, or services to prospects or current customers personally or via any promotional activity you must always ask for the sale.

It's All about the Customer

Your home business *is not* about the products or services that you sell. Your home business *is not* about the prices that you charge for your goods and services. Your home business *is not* about your competition and how to beat them. Your business *is* all about your customers, period. After all, your customers are the people that will ultimately decide if your business goes boom or goes bust. Everything you do in business must be customer focused, including your policies, warranties, payment options, operating hours, presentations, advertising and promotional campaigns, and Web site. In addition, you must know who your customers are inside out and upside down. You have to know what they need, the problems they have that must be solved, where the majority of them are based, how much money they want to spend for what you sell, and how often they want to buy what you have to sell. Everything you do in business must be for the benefit of your customers and potential customers and no one else.

Become a Shameless Self Promoter

One of the greatest myths about personal or business success is that eventually your business, personal abilities, products, or services will get discovered and be embraced by the masses who will beat a path to your door to buy what you are selling. But how can this happen if no one knows who you are, what you sell, and why they should be buying? Self-promotion is one of the most beneficial, yet most underutilized, marketing tools that the majority of home business owners have at their immediate disposal. Become a shameless promoter of your business and the goods or services you sell by creating unique promotions on a regular basis and constantly seeking publicity. Build a network of people that believe strongly enough in you and your business that they too will become supporters and shamelessly help spread the word for you via word-of-mouth advertising and referrals. Never stop asking everyone you come into contact with for new business.

Success never happens by accident or by a lucky break; success is always the result of planning, smart and hard work, and tireless promotion of your products. You must become a portable advertisement for your business, a walking and talking example of what your business does and sells. So finely tuned and refined is your ability as a portable advertisement that in less than 30 seconds you can explain what you do and how others benefit. And most importantly, the people that you speak to instantly understand your advertisement and associate you with your business and the goods and service you provide. In addition, as a portable advertisement for your business, you are always armed with information, promotional items, business cards, and samples.

Project a Positive Business Image

You have but a passing moment to make a positive and memorable impression on people with whom you intend to do business. Home business owners must go out of their way and make a conscious effort always to project the most professional business image possible. The majority of home business owners do not have the advantage of elaborate offices or elegant storefronts and showrooms to wow prospects and impress customers. Instead, they must rely on imagination, creativity, and attention to the smallest detail when creating and maintaining a professional image for their home business.

It is wise to budget and spend extra to have business cards, stationery, and sales materials, such as catalogs and brochures, printed on high quality paper that is rich in texture and heavy to the touch. Likewise, the visual appearance of the inside and outside of your home and home office, your car or van, signage promoting your business, product displays and packaging, corporate logo, company uniform, and all forms of advertising must also be professionally developed and maintained with a high-impact, positive business image in mind. The more you strive to create a professional business image, the more likely your prospects will see your business as credible, overlooking the fact that it is small and operated from a home office location. However, keep in mind when developing your business image that consistency is the main objective. Once you have created the image you want to create and be remembered for, be sure to use it in all areas of your business. This includes a consistent color scheme, logo, sales messages, and promotional campaign. By consistently using a unified message and theme, people will begin to associate these things with your business and with the products and services you sell. Consistency is the foundation of branding.

Level the Playing Field with Technology

You might operate a small business from home, but that certainly doesn't mean you should not make every effort to streamline your operation by effectively using and applying technology into your business operations. Take advantage of current technology and new technologies as they become available to level the playing field with your larger competition. Technology allows you to access a larger base of potential customers. Create a Web site, and use it for marketing and communication purposes. Install an integrated telephone system with features such as voice mail, call forwarding, and fax on demand options. Use wireless devices such as cell phones, PDAs, and beepers to stay in constant contact with clients, prospects, and your business team. Use laptop computers for presentations, and have your own virtual presentation created and placed on CD-ROM for use as a powerful sales and marketing tool. Create and maintain an electronic mail list sending prospects and customers the latest news and information about your business. Take advantage of smart multiuse office products like printers that also scan and copy documents. Use digital cameras and user-friendly desktop software programs to create colorful and descriptive product brochures and catalogs. And, most important, never stop learning about new technologies, how they work, and how they can be integrated into your home business to make your operation seem taller, larger, and wider. Never think that you should wait to invest into technologies because of the myth that as what you purchase will be obsolete as soon as you do. Few products such as computers ever become obsolete; they only improve over time as new technological capabilities are introduced.

Build a Top-Notch Business Team

No one person can build a successful business alone. It is a task that requires a team that is as committed as you to the business and its success. Your business team consists of family members, friends, suppliers, business alliances, employees, sub-contractors, industry and business associations, local government and the community, and, most importantly, your customers. All have a say in how your business will function and a stake in your business future. Remove just one element and there is a better than average chance that your business will collapse like a house of cards.

With so much at stake, it stands to reason that you should go out of your way to build the strongest business team that you can possibly muster. Your team should be composed of people that share your vision of the future and believe in your ability to make it happen. A common challenge facing home business operators is the lack of a support system in place, people who can assist in growing the business and help out in its day-to-day operations. In most cases mid-to large-size corporations have the benefit and advantage of having in-house or on-hand support staff that the majority of small business owners cannot afford, either in employee wages or service retainers. These people can include in-house public relations staff, sales and marketing specialists, bookkeepers and accountants, lawyers, and financial analysts. So it is important that you take the time now, while your business is small, to build a top-notch team of true believers to ensure that your business is here for today and in the future.

Become Known as an Expert

When you have a problem that needs to be solved, do you seek just anyone's advice? Or do you seek an expert in the field to help solve your particular problem? Obviously, you want the most accurate information and assistance that you can get. You naturally seek an expert to help solve your problem. You call a plumber when the hot water tank leaks, a real estate agent when it's time to sell your home, or a dentist when you have a toothache. Therefore, it only stands to reason that the more you become known for your expertise in your business, the more people will seek you out to tap into your expertise, creating more selling and referral opportunities. In effect, becoming known as an expert is another style of prospecting for new business, just in reverse. Instead of finding new and qualified people to sell to, these people seek you out for your expertise.

Becoming an expert is not as difficult as you might think. By virtue of starting a business to a certain degree you are already an expert the moment that you sell your first product or service. You can also position yourself and business as an expert in your particular field by speaking at public and business functions on your specialty, writing a book or articles for magazines, newsletters, and newspapers, or by becoming a source of expert opinion for local media to call when they need information in the area of your specialty. The more widely you become known as an expert in your particular field, the more people will seek you out for help and the more people that others will refer to you.

Create a Competitive Advantage

A home business must have a clearly defined unique selling proposition. This is nothing more than a fancy way of asking the vital question, "Why will people choose to do business with you or purchase your product or service instead of doing business with a competitor and buying his product or service?" In other words, what one aspect or combination of aspects is going to separate your business from its competitors? Will it be better service, longer warranty, better selection, longer business hours, more flexible payment options, lowest price, or a combination of all of these? Your competitive advantage must be beneficial to consumers, exclusive to your business, and simplistic in nature. You should be able to sum up your unique selling proposition in one clearly defined sentence that makes customers say, "I understand why I should buy from you." Your competitive advantage is the reason why people choose to buy your products or services instead of a competitors. In fact, every entrepreneur needs a competitive advantage to survive in today's highly competitive, global business environment.

Because of the importance of your competitive advantage in positioning your business, products, or services in the marketplace, it should be used as the anchor for all of your promotional activities and should be thought of as your main marketing tool. You will also need to develop a message to describe your competitive advantage. This message should be brief, to the point, easy to understand, and, above all, clearly state why people should do business with you and not the competition.

Invest in You

Successful entrepreneurs share a common denominator that transcends all types of business ventures and every industry sector – they never stop investing in products, services, information, and education that will make them better, smarter, and more productive businesspeople. They know and believe that every dollar they invest in educational activities and items that are geared to make them better, more productive, and more innovative in business and marketing will pay back tenfold or greater. These investments will also give them a much-needed advantage in today's extremely competitive global business environment.

Top entrepreneurs buy and read business and marketing books, magazines, reports, journals, newsletters, and industry publications, knowing that these resources will improve their understanding of business and marketing functions and skills. They join business associations and clubs and network with other skilled business people to learn their secrets of success and help define their own goals and objectives. Top entrepreneurs attend business and marketing seminars, workshops, and training courses, even if they have already mastered the

subject matter of the event. They do this because they know that education is an ongoing process that never ends. There are always ways to do things better, in less time, and with less effort. They invest in home office and business equipment and technology to improve their business and marketing efficiency. Equipment such as a comfortable office chair, a fast computer, professional software, and multi-function telephone systems and printers, increases productivity and profitability. In short, top entrepreneurs never stop investing in the most powerful, effective, and best business and marketing tool at their immediate disposal—themselves.

Be Accessible

We live in a time when we all expect our fast food lunch at the drive-through to be ready in mere minutes, our dry cleaning to be ready for pick-up on the same day, our pizza delivered in 30 minutes or it's free, and our investment advisors to be no further away than a telephone call. You see the pattern developing—you must make it as easy as you can for people to do business with you, regardless of the home business you operate. By being accessible, your prospects will thank you by purchasing and your customers will thank you by purchasing more and more frequently. You must remain cognizant of the fact that few people will work hard, go out of their way, or be inconvenienced just for the privilege of giving you their hard-earned money. The shoe is always on the other foot. It is up to you to work hard and earn your customer's business and to make it as easy as possible for them to do business with you, the first time and every time. Making it easy for people to do business with you means that you must be accessible and knowledgeable about your products and services. You must be able to provide customers with what they want, when they want it. Accessibility means never dodging telephone calls, skipping meetings or appointments, or employing other procrastination techniques aimed at making things convenient for you rather than your and customers and prospects. Accessible means telling your prospects and customers in advance the hours and days that you can be reached and how they can reach you. It means never letting them down. If you make it difficult for people to do business with you, expect that they will choose to do business with people who do make it easy for them to get what they want, and when they want it.

Build a Rock Solid Reputation

A good reputation is unquestionably one of the home business owner's most tangible and marketable assets. Acquiring a rock solid reputation is an absolute home business must. All business is built on sales, and if you're not selling your goods or services, then you will not be in business long. It's that simple. One of the main reasons that people choose not to buy is risk. What if the product is not delivered on time? What happens if the product breaks or the repair service does not fix the problem? Or, what happens if what you got is far less than what you were expecting?

Fast food chain restaurants are perfect examples of why building a rock solid reputation is essential for business success. Seldom is the food the best, but customers know exactly what they will get in return for their money. This is because fast food restaurant chains spend time, money, and energy creating reputations for fast service, affordable prices, and clean environments. They're not promoting the lowest prices, the fanciest interiors, or exotic menus.

To build a rock solid reputation, it is the sum of the parts that equals the whole. You must provide great customer service, you must sell products and services that people need, you must always deliver on time and on budget, you must guarantee what you sell, you must provide value, and above all you must keep your promises and exceed your customers' expectations. Once again, it is the sum of all the parts, that goes into creating a rock solid reputation. Consistency in terms of how you operate your business, deliver products and services, and treat your customers will level the playing field with larger competitors, even if they have lower prices, faster service, or a broader selection. Few people refer friends to a business that sells inferior products at low prices. But many will refer a business that has treated them fairly and met their expectations, even if it did not have the lowest price or is not the biggest player.

Sell Benefits

Pushing product features is for inexperienced or wannabe entrepreneurs. Selling the benefits associated with owning and using the products and services you carry is what sales professionals worldwide focus on to create buying excitement and to sell, sell more, and sell more frequently to their customers. Your advertising, sales presentations, printed marketing materials, product packaging, Web site, newsletters, trade show exhibit, and signage are vital. Every time and every medium used to communicate with your target audience must always be selling the benefits associated with using and owning your product. A treadmill may have 30 features, but the true benefit to the user is the fact that if you buy and use the treadmill on a regular basis, you will be more physically fit. In this case, it is a proven fact that people who exercise are more physically fit than those people who do not. This information can then be translated into exciting selling terms, such as you will lose weight, you will become more healthy, you will enjoy increased self-confidence, and you might even live longer. All of which are the potential benefits of buying and using a treadmill. A built-in radio, a wider track surface, or larger color selection are features, but not the true benefits of the product. Also drop the long-winded explanations about what your business does or sells and develop a high-impact, mini sales-pitch to replace it. Keep the pitch short, simple, and directly to the point, which should be what you sell and the biggest benefit your customers receive. Clearly demonstrate to prospects how your product will benefit them and you will sell more.

Get Involved

Always go out of your way to get involved in the community that supports your business. You can do this in many ways, such as pitching in to help local charities or the food bank, becoming involved with your church, organizing community events, and getting involved in local politics. Or, you can join associations and clubs that concentrate on programs and policies designed to improve the local community. If you look beyond responsibilities of business owners to help support their local communities, it is a fact that people like to do business with people they know, like, and respect, and they also like to refer other people to these businesses. Therefore, get involved in your community and you will open many new doors in terms of networking, prospecting, referrals, and increased selling opportunities, which can have an enormous beneficial long-term effect on your business.

One of the primary building blocks for successful businesses is the investment of time, money, and energy in the people and community that supports the business. It's being a good corporate or business citizen, and is a responsibility shared by all business owners. In terms of building a positive business image and loyal customer base, no marketing effort can match getting involved with and giving back to the community that supports your business and helps to build your success.

Grab Attention

One way for small business owners to stand out in the ever increasingly competitive business world is to develop a strategy of always aiming to grab the attention of your target audience. Every business, marketing, promotional, and publicity activity you engage in must be designed and implemented in a way that grabs and holds the attention of the target audience long enough for them to form a positive image of your business. You have to create print advertisements that leap off the page screaming "Look at me." Your car, job site, and trade show signage must grab so much attention that people who turn to read it run the risk of getting whiplash. Your radio advertisements must make people turn up the volume at the mere mention of your business name, products, or services. And your networking style at meetings and events must have people mentioning your business name in a positive way to others, even days, weeks, and months after you spoke.

In short, if you want to stand out in today's business environment, everything you do to market or promote your business must be aimed at grabbing your target audience's attention. Small business owners cannot waste time, money, and energy on promotional activities aimed at building awareness solely through long-term, repeated exposure. If you do, chances are you will go broke long before this goal is accomplished. Instead, every promotional activity you engage in free or paid, must put money back in your pocket so that you can continue to grab more attention and grow your business.

Master the Art of Negotiations

The ability to negotiate effectively is unquestionably a skill that every home business owner must make every effort to master. It is perhaps second in importance only to asking for the sale in terms of home business musts. In business, negotiation skills are used daily. You negotiate with prospects and clients to sell more goods and services and for a higher price. You negotiate with your suppliers to receive a lower cost per unit or better payment and delivery terms. You negotiate with your bank to secure lines of operating capital, lower credit card merchant rates, and no-fee banking services. You may even find yourself negotiating with your family and friends about personal activities such as missed vacations or late meals because your business is swamped and time is at a premium.

Always remember that mastering the art of negotiation means that your skills are so finely tuned that you can always orchestrate a win-win situation. These win-win arrangements mean that everyone involved feels they have won, which is really the bases for building long-term and profitable business relationships. You cannot expect customers, employees, business alliances, and suppliers to be loyal to your brand, treat you with respect, and believe in your business unless you strive to build situations and relationships in which they all stand to win. In addition from a financial perspective, learning the art of negotiations can increase the average small business owner's bottom-line profits by 5 percent or more annually, based on nothing more than selling your products for 2.5 percent more and paying suppliers 2.5 percent less.

Design Your Workspace for Success

Carefully plan and design your home office workspace to ensure maximum personal performance and productivity and to project professionalism for visiting clients. If at all possible, resist the temptation to turn a corner of the living room or your bedroom into your office. Ideally, you'll want a separate room with a door that closes to keep business activities in and family members out, at least during prime business and revenue generating hours of the day. A den, spare bedroom, or converted garage are all ideal candidates for your new home office. Once this workspace is designed, keep what makes you money such as your telephone and computer the closest, and get rid of the stuff that doesn't make you money, the sports section of the newspaper, and the trophy you won. Basically, eliminate clutter and streamline your office to allow you to work productively and efficiently at all tasks and projects.

Success and productivity in the home office is often a result of having the right tools to do the job. Therefore, make an investment in business equipment and supplies that will enable you to be 100 percent effective and productive. Having to remove your client files from the kitchen table every time a family member wants to eat is not making the best use of your time. Ensure that your office and workspace are ergonomically designed for maximum productivity. Ergonomic and medical experts agree that this can increase productivity and quality of work by as much as 20 percent per annum. Invest in books that will explain the finer points of ergonomics such as chair and seating position, eyes and lighting, upper body position and monitor and keyboard. Proper ergonomic office design and layout will create a healthy and productive work environment.

Get and Stay Organized

Getting and staying organized is somewhat subjective. It depends on whom you ask. Some home business owners are perfectly comfortable and productive working in and surround by utter chaos. Clearly these people are in the minority. The vast majority of homebased entrepreneurs, myself included, need to be working in an organized environment with a regular routine in order to be efficient and productive in our day-to-day business life. So it makes sense that you should strive to get your home office, work routine, and business planning organized from the start and keep it that way. In fact, you should develop

systems and routines for just about every single business activity. Small things such as creating a to-do list at the end of each business day will help keep you on top of important tasks to tackle the following day. Creating a single calendar to work from, not multiple sets for individual tasks or jobs will also ensure that jobs are completed on schedule and appointments kept. Incorporating family and personal activities into your work calendar is critical so that you work and plan from a single calendar. Carefully planning out-of-office client meetings in blocks, such as an entire morning, afternoon, or the day will reduce the time wasted driving back and forth or with dead time in between appointments. Using color-coded client and prospect files will help to prioritize your work. Establishing a primary workstation in your home office for working on key, money-making projects and a secondary workstation for lesser projects such as mail sorting, filing, and general administrative work will also keep you organized and productive.

Take Time Off

The temptation to work around the clock is very real for the home business owner. After all, you do not have a manager telling you it's time to go home because they can't afford the overtime pay. Every person working from home must take time to establish a regular work schedule that includes time to stretch your legs and take lunch breaks, one full day each week away from the business, and scheduled vacations. Create the schedule as soon as you have made the commitment to start a home business. Of course, every now and then you will have to deviate from your work schedule to include a few late nights and the occasional Sunday afternoon, which is perfectly fine. But you do not want to get caught in the trap of working around the clock, 12, 14, or even 18 hours a day for extended periods of time.

There are real reasons for establishing and sticking to a work schedule. Firstly, your family life will crash if you spend too much time working and not enough time with your family. No business is worth that level of personal cost. Secondly, you will begin to suffer from burn out, which is counterproductive as it leaves you doing much less, but taking much longer to do it. You must also learn to say no, regardless of how difficult saying it can be. Saying yes too often is one of the biggest challenges faced by home business owners, and one of the most difficult to overcome and correct. We all say yes because we want to please clients, business alliances, and family. But usually at the end of the day all that is accomplished is spreading ourselves too thin, not getting the important moneymaking business tasks done properly. Few people near the end of their life reflect fondly on the times they spent working around the clock and foregoing everything else that life has to offer. Wouldn't you prefer to reflect on the good times spent with family, friends, and life's adventures? Make it a personal goal to stay fit and healthy. If you do not feel good physically or mentally, it is very difficult to be 100 percent effective and productive. Eat right, get lots of sleep, and maintain a regular physical exercise program.

Limit the Number of Hats You Wear

It is difficult for most business owners not to take a hands-on approach. They try to do as much as possible and tackle as many tasks as possible in their business. The ability to multitask, in fact, is a common trait shared by successful entrepreneurs. However, once in a while you have to stand back and look beyond today to determine what is in the best interests of your business and yourself over the long run. Often, by analyzing what is best for your business in the long term, you will discover that farming out some business and marketing tasks that would be better handled by an expert is a wise decision.

Without question there is a cost associated with paying others to do work that could be completed in-house. Outsourcing can be especially difficult for home business owners with limited capital. But the cost of trying to do something that you know little, if anything, about could be substantially higher. There is the potential for lost sales and lost customers or for not getting the desired results. For example, if prospecting or lead generation is not your forte, but presenting and closing the sale is, then hire professional telemarketers and direct marketers to solicit and collect qualified leads for you to present to and close. In almost all situations, you'll find that by sticking to your specialty you'll generate far more revenue and profit than you will spend on farming out some of your more unproductive tasks.

Constant Follow-Up

Constant contact, follow-up, and follow through with customers, prospects, and business alliances should be the mantra of every home business owner, new or established. Constant and consistent follow-up enables you to turn prospects into customers, increase the value of each sale and buying frequency from existing customers, and build stronger business relationships with suppliers and your core business team. Follow-up is especially important with your existing customer base, as the real work begins after the sale. It is easy to sell a prospect or service, but it takes effort and hard work to retain a customer for life. In fact, according to the U.S. Small Business Administration (SBA) more than of 60 percent of consumers stop doing business with a company because they feel they are being ignored and forgotten after the original sale. Couple that startling statistic with the fact that it costs ten times as much to find and sell to a new customer as it does to sell to existing customers. So you see why the real work begins after the sale—the work of building and maintaining a lifetime business relationship with your customers.

Never allow yourself the illusion that once you have made a sale, it's over, because it isn't. The real work is in regular follow-up, great customer service, and maintaining a close working relationship with your customer for life. What you do once you make a sale determines the true lifetime value of the sale. Develop a system that enables you to follow up with prospects and customers on a regular basis. Keep in touch with them by mail, telephone, fax, e-mail, and personal visits. Let them know that you are always thinking of them and encourage them to call you to ask for help, advice, and suggestions—or just to say hello.

RESOURCES

Associations
American Association of Home-Based Businesses (AAHBB)
PO Box 10023

Rockville, MD 20849
www.aahbb.org

American Home Business Association
4505 Wasatah Boulevard South
Salt Lake City, UT 84124
(800) 664-2422
www.homebusiness.com

National Association of Home Based Businesses
10451 Mill Run Circle, Suite 400
Owings Mills, MD 21117
(410) 363-3698
www.usahomebusiness.com

National Association of Women Business Owners (NAWBO)
830–1100 Wayne Avenue
Silver Spring, MD 20910
(301) 608-2590
www.nawbo.org

Small Office Home Office Business Group (SOHO)
2255B Queen Street East, Suite 3261
Toronto, ON M4E 1G3
(800) 290-7646
www.soho.ca

Women Business Owners of Canada
20 York Mills Road, Suite 100
York Mills, ON M2P 2C2
www.wboc.ca

Young Entrepreneurs Association (YEA)
720 Spadina Avenue, Suite 300
Toronto, ON M5S 2T9
(888) 639-3222
www.yea.ca

📖 Suggested Reading

Barnett, Rebecca. *Winning Without Losing Your Way: Character-Centered Leadership.* Bowling Green, KY: Winning Your Way Inc., 2003.

Barrett, Niall. *The Custom Home Office: Building a Complete Workspace.* Newtown, CT: Taunton Press, 2002.

Gleeson, Kerry. *The Personal Efficiency Program: How to Get Organized to Do More Work in Less Time.* New York: John Wiley & Sons, 2000.

Silber, Lee T. *Self-Promotion for the Creative Person: Get the Word Out About Who You Are and What You Do.* New York: Crown Publishing, 2001.

Stephenson, James. *The Ultimate Small Business Marketing Guide: Over 1,500 Great Marketing Tricks that Will Drive Your Business Through the Roof!* Irvine, CA: Entrepreneur Press, 2003.

Von Oech, Roger. *A Whack on the Side of the Head: How You Can Be More Creative.* New York: Warner Books, 1998.

🖥 Web Sites

Brian Tracy International, www.briantracy.com: Sales and motivational expert. Provides coaching, information, products, programs, and services.

Entrepreneur Online, www.entrepreneur.com: Small business information, products, and services portal.

Ergonomics Online, www.ergonomics.org: Ergonomics information, articles, industry links, and resources.

Guerrilla Marketing Online, www.gmarketing.com: Small business marketing tips, information, seminars, books, and links.

International Customer Service Association, www.icsa.com: The ICSA offers members information, products, services, and education aimed at improving customer service skills and relationship building.

Organized Times, www.organizedtimes.com: Information, advice, tools, and services aimed at getting the home office organized and productive.

Work At Home Parent, www.work-at-home-parent.com: Information, advice, products, services, and additional resources for parents working from a home office.

Work Spaces, www.workspaces.com: Information, advice, and links on setting up, organizing, and furnishing a home office.

CHAPTER 2

What Type of Home Business Should You Start?

WHAT TYPE OF HOME BUSINESS SHOULD you start? Ultimately, there is only one person who knows the answer for sure: You. Once you have decided that you want to start your own home business or are leaning toward starting your own home business, the next step is to decide what type of business to start. There are many factors that will weigh on your decision, and some of these factors weigh much more than others, including:

- Taking stock of your personal situations
- Suitability of your home for business
- Your wants
- Your experiences and special skills
- The income you need
- Your personal and financial goals
- Additional resources available
- The money needed to start a business
- Finding a good match

Owning and operating a business is very much a balancing act—you often have to make personal compromises and almost always have to make financial compromises to get the business up and running to a point to where it will generate an income and profit. As with anything in life that is worthwhile, sacrifices must be made along the way in order to build a successful business enterprise. However, if the sacrifices result in you losing focus or hating the business

that you started, chances are you will be miserable and ultimately the business will fail. Therefore, while weighing all factors might seem to be unproductive or hackneyed, it is critical in the business planning process. Without it you might start or purchase a business that is totally wrong for you. More detailed information about starting your business, and related topics can be found in later chapters. This section gives the highlights of other chapters, but it has been specifically designed to assist you in deciding on the right home business start-up.

Taking Stock of Your Personal Situation

One of the most important factors to consider prior to starting or purchasing a home business is to analyze carefully your reasons for starting a business and to consider the effect this decision will have on you and your family. Regardless of what you may think, there is no such thing as a business that can be operated solely by one person. Running even a small home business requires a team effort, and family members often make up a larger piece of the team than you think. Consider the following questions on the Taking Stock of Your Personal Situation Worksheet (see Figure 2.1) to determine what you feel is important to you and your family. If many of the important aspects of your or your

FIGURE 2.1 Taking Stock of Your Personal Situation Worksheet

Describe why you want to be self-employed and operate your own home business.

_____

_____

Are you dissatisfied with your current job or career? If so, why?

_____

_____

Do you want your family to be included in the decision-making process when selecting the right home business?

_____

_____

Do you want your family to support your business decisions? Why?

_____

_____

Do you want to spend more time with your family?

_____

_____

Are you prepared to miss family vacations and special events because of business commitments?

_____

_____

Do you want family members to participate actively in the business? If so, what are their individual feelings on the subject?

_____

_____

family's lives cannot be satisfied by your choice, the home business being considered may not be appropriate for you. (You may want to expand this list to include questions or issues that are specific to your family and your situation.)

Remember your answers and thoughts are for the purpose of collecting data to help you determine what new home business venture is right for you and your family. If you rank wanting to spend more time with your family as very important to you, then a business that keeps you in the home office would be a better choice then one that requires you to be visiting clients or working on job sites. Also, keep in mind that when you start a business, you are making decisions for more than yourself, so it is vital to include your family members in the decision-making process. That said, never assume that family members will have the same excitement as you about starting or working in the business. This decision must be left up to each individual. Additional information about family-related issues in the home business is featured in Chapter 8, Building Your Business Team.

Is Your Home Suitable for a Business?

Is your residence a good place to start and operate a home business? Lots of people decide to start a home business without giving this question much thought, but you should. Not every residence is a suitable location for a business. In fact, in some municipalities in the United States and Canada local zoning laws prohibit home business ventures entirely. Therefore, long before you invest substantial amounts of cash to get your new home business venture rolling, you should determine if your residence is the right location for operating a business and if the venture will be legal. Considerations in terms of setting up a business in your home include:

- Zoning regulations
- Space requirements
- Access for employees and clients
- Neighbors and neighborhood issues
- Suitable and adequate parking
- Privacy for yourself and family
- Adequate storage space for business needs
- Security issues
- Laws involving employees working from your home
- Safety issues
- Special insurance needs
- Pollution concerns in the forms of noise and odor
- Mechanical requirements, including electrical and phone lines

Additional information about setting up your home business workspace, legal issues, and employees can be found in Chapters 7, 4, and 8, respectively. There is no side-stepping this issue. If your residence is not a suitable location for running a business you have a few choices: move, make whatever changes are necessary to ensure that your home is the right location, or do not start a home business. You do not want to invest large amounts of time and money in starting or purchasing a business venture only to discover that a business cannot be run from your home.

What Do You Want to Do?

Another factor influencing your choice is doing something that you really enjoy doing. Without question, potential profit should be a motivation for starting your own business, and working hard at it. But enjoyment, pride, and self-fulfillment must also factor into the business mix. If you cannot enjoy what you are doing, money will be of little comfort. It is important to give what you really want to do some careful consideration. Once you have decided to invest substantial capital there is a good chance you will be operating your business for a long time.

You can be a little creative in terms of doing what you enjoy doing. For instance, if you enjoy carpentry, you can look at providing more than just carpentry services. You can also train others to become carpenters, write books or articles about carpentry, or sell carpentry-related products and services to other carpentry fanatics. One way that you can focus on what you might enjoy is to create categories, and match other criteria such as income and capital available, to fine tune your list of potential business start-ups or acquisitions. The list below does not include every category, so you may want to expand it. Likewise, the businesses featured under each category are for example purposes only. Once again, you will want to expand them once you have created your own category(s).

You enjoy helping others, then consider:

- Non-medical home care
- Wedding / event planner
- House inspector
- Catering

You are creative, then consider:

- Interior decoration
- Photography
- Homebased crafts
- Desktop publishing

You enjoy working with children, then consider:

- Homebased day care
- Birthday party planner
- Educational tutor
- Nanny service

You enjoy working with computers and technology, then consider:

- Mobile computer repair
- Web site design and maintenance
- E-commerce
- Software programmer

You enjoy working with your mind, then consider:

- Public relations
- Accounting and financial planning
- Advertising
- Consulting in your specialty

You enjoy selling, then consider:

- Independent sales agent
- Business broker
- Direct sales
- Import/export

You enjoy working with transportation, then consider:

- Driving instructor
- Automotive detailing
- Mobile auto inspections
- Delivery service

You enjoy the outdoors and adventure, then consider:

- Sailing instructor
- Tour guide
- Fitness instructor
- Outdoor or sports instruction

You enjoy working with your hands then consider:

- Homebased manufacturing business
- Cabinetmaking
- Home improvement business
- Small engine repair

You enjoy working with pets, then consider:

- Dog walking service
- Pet grooming
- Pet photography
- Pet trainer

The purpose of this exercise is to identify what it is that you really enjoy doing in broad terms so that you can then consider home business ventures that fall into the broad category and eliminate those that do not. For instance, if you enjoy working with your hands, skip home businesses that will keep your rump planted in a chair in front of a computer. Be true to what you really want to do, and look at opportunities that will enable you to work with your hands. At the same time you might also want to make a list of the things that you dislike doing so that you do not inadvertently start a home business that has some elements you enjoy and some you do not. In time the least enjoyable ones will quickly overshadow the enjoyable elements and you might begin to really dislike your business. With that in mind, in order of priority, use the Things You Dislike Doing Worksheet (see Figure 2.2) to list ten things you dislike doing.

FIGURE 2.2 **Things You Dislike Doing Worksheet**

1. _____
2. _____
3. _____
4. _____
5. _____

6. _____
7. _____
8. _____
9. _____
10. _____

What Experience and Special Skills Do You Have?

What are the special skills that you currently have, and how can these skills be applied to the new business venture? While you certainly do not have to possess all the skills necessary for running a home business, identifying your personal strengths and weaknesses prior to starting a business is logical and enables you to correct weaknesses and build upon your strengths. The Special Skills Checklist (see Figure 2.3) featured below is a good starting point for identifying your strengths and weaknesses in terms of common business skills.

FIGURE 2.3   Special Skills Checklist

Your ability to work independently is:

❑ Strong   ❑ Fair   ❑ Poor

Comments: _____

Your research skills are:

❑ Strong   ❑ Fair   ❑ Poor

Comments: _____

Your planning skills are:

❑ Strong   ❑ Fair   ❑ Poor

Comments: _____

Your sales and marketing skills are:

❑ Strong   ❑ Fair   ❑ Poor

Comments: _____

Your customer services skills are:

❑ Strong   ❑ Fair   ❑ Poor

Comments: _____

Your ability to lead/delegate is:

❑ Strong   ❑ Fair   ❑ Poor

Comments: _____

Your communications skills are:

❑ Strong   ❑ Fair   ❑ Poor

Comments: _____

Your ability to think logically is:

❑ Strong   ❑ Fair   ❑ Poor

Comments: _____

Your problem solving skills are:

❑ Strong   ❑ Fair   ❑ Poor

Comments: _____

Your record/bookkeeping skills are:

❑ Strong   ❑ Fair   ❑ Poor

Comments: _____

Your competitive spirit is:

❑ Strong   ❑ Fair   ❑ Poor

Comments: _____

Your organization skills are:

❑ Strong   ❑ Fair   ❑ Poor

Comments: _____

Your time management skills are:

❑ Strong   ❑ Fair   ❑ Poor

Comments: _____

Your risk assessment skills are:

❑ Strong   ❑ Fair   ❑ Poor

Comments: _____

Your computer/software skills are:

❑ Strong   ❑ Fair   ❑ Poor

Comments: _____

Your Internet skills are:

❑ Strong   ❑ Fair   ❑ Poor

Comments: _____

Your listening skills are:

❑ Strong   ❑ Fair   ❑ Poor

Comments: _____

Your ability to handle stress is:

❑ Strong   ❑ Fair   ❑ Poor

Comments: _____

| FIGURE 2.3 | **Special Skills Checklist,** continued |

Your ability to stay focused is:

❏ Strong ❏ Fair ❏ Poor

Comments: _____

Your networking skills are:

❏ Strong ❏ Fair ❏ Poor

Comments: _____

Your ability to set goals are:

❏ Strong ❏ Fair ❏ Poor

Comments: _____

Your money management skills are:

❏ Strong ❏ Fair ❏ Poor

Comments: _____

Your financial budgeting skills are:

❏ Strong ❏ Fair ❏ Poor

Comments: _____

Your public speaking skills are:

❏ Strong ❏ Fair ❏ Poor

Comments: _____

Your decision-making abilities are:

❏ Strong ❏ Fair ❏ Poor

Comments: _____

How Much Income Do You Need?

The amount of income that you need personally to keep food on the table and the bills paid is another factor that will directly affect your decision on what type of business that you start or if, in fact, you should be starting any business at all. Let's face it, if you need to earn $75,000 per year just to make ends meet, it makes little sense to start a window washing business. Yes, perhaps it is true that in ideal situations you could earn $75,000 per year operating a window washing business, but at the same time, it is not a realistic expectation.

The second income issue is how much money do you want to earn; that is, how ambitious are you? Once again, realistic expectations must come into play. When all is said and done, the business that you want to start must have the potential to generate a profit or at least generate an income sufficient to maintain your lifestyle, even if that lifestyle is a little leaner than you are currently enjoying. The harsh reality of working long hours for a less than minimum wage is that in time you will lose interest in your business. When that happens, the business will almost certainly begin to falter, if not fail. Therefore, you must be relatively sure that the business has the

potential to generate enough income to live on in the short-term, but it must also have the potential to match your income goals in the longer term.

Income does not have to factor into the business start-up equation for everyone. If you want and need to earn only a little money from a part-time or retirement business, you still want to make sure that the business you start can break even, but the income equation will not factor as heavily as other issues.

Use the Income Needs Worksheet (see Figure 2.4) to identify how much income you need to live, as well as the income that you would like to earn.

Additional information about paying yourself a salary from your home business can be found in Chapter 3, Financial Issues.

What Are Your Goals?

The only way to know if a home business venture has the potential to meet or exceed your short-term and long-term personal and financial goals is to know exactly what your goals for the future are. Given that few of us have a photographic memory or instant recall, we must rely on recording important information so that we can use it as a yardstick to measure progress and a motivational boost when

FIGURE 2.4	Income Needs Worksheet

How much income do you need per year?

❏ $0–$15,000   ❏ $15,000–$30,000   ❏ $30,000–$45,000

❏ $45,000–$60,000   ❏ $60,000–$75,000   ❏ $75,000+

How much income do you want to earn per year?

❏ $30,000–$60,000   ❏ $60,000–$90,000   ❏ $90,000–$120,000

❏ $120,000–$150,000   ❏ $150,000–$200,000   ❏ $200,000+

needed. Consequently, the best way to identify your goals is to create a document listing your and your family's goals and expectations. Keep the list close so that you can use it when it is necessary to make business, personal, and financial decisions. If the effect of your decision means sacrificing a short-term or long-term personal or financial goal, it is safe to assume this is not a wise decision.

Personal Goals

Starting a business has to do with your personality and what you want to achieve in life. Whether your goals are grandiose or small, they are important to you. Personal goals might include the desire to travel the world, be more physically fit, work less, attain more education, find a partner and start a family or even quit smoking. Personal goals have a great effect on the type of business you start simply because if the business does not assist you in reaching your goals, it is not the right business for you. For instance, if one of your personal goals is to take time every year to travel extensively, a seasonal home-based business such as operating a lawn maintenance service in a northern climate would be a wise start-up choice, while a home business that requires daily hands-on management such as a commercial office cleaning service would not be such a wise start-up choice. Using the Defining Your Personal Goals Worksheet (see Figure 2.5), list your short-term and long-term personal goals.

FIGURE 2.5	Defining Your Personal Goals

In order of priority, list your short-term (1–5 years) personal goals:

1. _____
2. _____
3. _____
4. _____
5. _____

In order of priority, list your long-term (10+ years) personal goals:

1. _____
2. _____
3. _____
4. _____
5. _____

Financial Goals

Much like personal goals, financial goals must also be considered when choosing a business start-up. Financial goals can include stashing away enough money to put the kids through college, paying off the mortgage over a fixed period of time, buying a vacation home, or amassing enough wealth to retire comfortably by age 55. Once again, the home business you choose must provide you the opportunity to meet your financial goals. If it does not, you will be getting into the wrong business. Using the Defining Your Financial Goals Worksheet (see Figure 2.6) list your short-term and long-term financial goals.

| FIGURE 2.6 | Defining Your Financial Goals Worksheet |

In order of priority, list your short-term (1–5 years) financial goals:

1. _____
2. _____
3. _____
4. _____
5. _____

In order of priority, list your long-term (10+ years) financial goals:

1. _____
2. _____
3. _____
4. _____
5. _____

Family Goals

You may also want to consider the goals of your entire family. These can have an effect on the type of home business that you choose. For instance, if your spouse wants to return to school in the near future to complete a degree, perhaps dreams of business ownership should be held off for a few years so that you can provide a stable income and benefit base until others in your family have achieved some of their goals. Once again, all goals must be prioritized in order of importance so that you can create a action plan regarding how you will go about working toward and reaching each goal. Using the Defining Your Family Goals Worksheet (see Figure 2.7) list your short-term and long-term family goals.

| FIGURE 2.7 | Defining Your Family Goals Worksheet |

In order of priority, list your family members' short-term (1–5 years) goals:

1. _____
2. _____
3. _____
4. _____
5. _____

In order of priority, list your family members' long-term (10+ years) goals:

1. _____
2. _____
3. _____
4. _____
5. _____

Additional Resources Available

Available additional resources can also greatly influence your decision on selecting one particular home business. These additional resources are for the most part things, and things are much easier to acquire than true ambition to succeed. Therefore, while additional resources can play an important role in choosing the right business start up, you must not, for example, let the fact that you do not have a computer or computer skills stop you from starting a business.

What existing resources do you have or have access to that can be utilized in the business? You may be surprised by what you may have kicking around the house that can be helpful and even more surprised by the amount of money you can save in business start-up and operation costs by utilizing any and all of your existing resources, including the resources of friends and family. Use the Resource Checklist (see Figure 2.8) below to help identify the resources that you have or can easily acquire. Add and delete from this list to meet your specific needs.

FIGURE 2.8 **Resource Checklist**

Do you have computer equipment and software that can be used in the business? ❑ Yes ❑ No

Comments: _____

Do you have a good contact base of people within the local or business industry for networking and business generation purposes? ❑ Yes ❑ No

Comments: _____

Do you have suitable transportation for the new business?

❑ Yes ❑ No

Comments: _____

Do you have general office equipment and fixtures that can be used in the business? ❑ Yes ❑ No

Comments: _____

Do you have access to a resource library and the Internet for business research and planning purposes? ❑ Yes ❑ No

Comments: _____

Are there business clubs and associations in your local community that you can join? ❑ Yes ❑ No

Comments: _____

Do you know any professionals or current business owners that can assist you with business decisions? ❑ Yes ❑ No

Comments: _____

These are only a few examples of existing resources that you may currently have or have access to. Carefully consider what information, equipment, and research you need to start and operate your business, and then compile a list of what is needed. Write any existing resources you have beside the needed item or information. Start thinking about family and people that you know who might have the resources that you lack.

Do You Have the Money to Start a Business?

One of the more important factors affecting your decision about which home business to start or purchase is "How much money is needed to start the business?" Do you have or have access to the money required? Do you then have or have access to additional money for working capital for the day-to-day operations of the business? Beyond start-up capital, working capital is needed to achieve positive cash flow. Unless you are purchasing an operating business, I have yet to come across a business opportunity that can be started today and generate a profit tomorrow. Every new business venture requires financing beyond the initial start-up costs in order to achieve positive cash flow, and, believe me, a lot of time can pass before a business shows a profit or even breaks even. Consider all the money you need and why it is needed:

- You need money to start or purchase the business.
- You need money to pay for the equipment and fixtures needed to operate the business.
- You need money to purchase initial inventory.
- You need money to buy consumables such as office supplies for use in the business.
- You need money to pay yourself an income until the business generates enough to cover your income requirements.
- You need money to pay fixed operating costs such as utilities, insurance, taxes, telephone, and your Web site until the business breaks even or produces a profit.
- You need money to pay employees and professionals providing services to your business.
- You need money to pay for advertising and marketing materials.

As you can see, every business needs money not only to get rolling, but also to stay rolling. Cash flow is king. Unfortunately, one of the most common errors entrepreneurs make when starting a business is not calculating the true start-up investment needed to reach positive cash flow. More information about raising capital and financing for your home business start-up is in Chapter 3, Financial Issues. At the end of this chapter you will also find a Home Business Start-Up Costs Estimator (see Figure 2.10) that you can use to assist you in calculating the amount of money needed to start your business. There is also a Fixed Monthly Overhead Calculator (see Figure 2.11) to assist you in calculating the money needed to pay the monthly businesses bills.

Finding a Good Match

Finally, the home business that you choose must be a compatible match. You must be well-suited to start and operate that particular business. Although you may have a great understanding and interest in one specific home business, that certainly does not ensure that the business is a good match for you. Finding a good match is really the result of combining all of the information previously discussed. Asking yourself the questions featured on the Finding a Good Match Worksheet (see Figure 2.9)

FIGURE 2.9 **Finding a Good Match Worksheet**

You can copy this worksheet and complete information for each home business that you are considering.

Type of Business: _____

Do I have the full support of my family to start or purchase this home business? ❏ Yes ❏ No

Comments: _____

Is my home a suitable location for this business? ❏ Yes ❏ No

Comments: _____

Do I have the financial resources needed to start or purchase this business? ❏ Yes ❏ No

Comments: _____

Do I have enough money to support this business and pay the bills until the business can generate an income and profit?

❏ Yes ❏ No

Comments: _____

Can this business potentially generate the income that I need to live? ❏ Yes ❏ No

Comments: _____

Can this business potentially generate the income that I would like to earn? ❏ Yes ❏ No

Comments: _____

Am I physically healthy enough to handle the potential physical strains of starting and running this business? ❏ Yes ❏ No

Comments: _____

Am I mentally healthy enough to handle the potential mental stresses of starting and running this business? ❏ Yes ❏ No

Comments: _____

Does operating this business still allow me the ability to reach my personal goals? ❏ Yes ❏ No

Comments: _____

FIGURE 2.9   Finding a Good Match Worksheet, continued

Does operating this business still allow me the ability to reach my financial goals?   ❏ Yes   ❏ No

Comments: _____

Do I have experience in this type of business, product, or service, and industry in which the business operates?   ❏ Yes   ❏ No

Comments: _____

Do I possess any special skills that can be utilized in this business?   ❏ Yes   ❏ No

Comments: _____

Are there any special certificates or educational requirements to start and operate this business? If so, are these readily available to me?   ❏ Yes   ❏ No

Comments: _____

Would I enjoy and have fun operating this business?

❏ Yes   ❏ No

Comments: _____

Does this business opportunity match my personality type?

❏ Yes   ❏ No

Comments: _____

Does this business match my level of maturity?   ❏ Yes   ❏ No

Comments: _____

Can I see myself still excited about this business years from now?

❏ Yes   ❏ No

Comments: _____

Can I commit to this business long-term, and am I prepared to work hard to succeed?   ❏ Yes   ❏ No

Comments: _____

Is this the type of business that I initially envisioned as a self-employment venture that would be suitable and a good match for me?   ❏ Yes   ❏ No

Comments: _____

will you help to determine if the business that you want to start is well suited to you.

WHAT ARE YOUR HOME BUSINESS OPTIONS?

The businesses that can be started and operated from a homebased location are nearly limitless, and expanding each day as new technologies and products are developed. However, before looking at specific home businesses, you first have to decide whether you will:

1. start a new home business from scratch.
2. purchase and operate an existing business.
3. purchase and operate a home franchise business.
4. purchase and operate a business opportunity from home.

But, before you decide what type of home business to start or purchase, you should first decide the time that you are prepared to commit to your new business. Not everyone will be able to start a full-time home business, nor does everyone want to make a full-time commitment to a home business.

Therefore, you have to identify your objectives relating to your goals and other issues featured earlier in this chapter to decide whether you will operate a full-time, part-time, seasonal, or retirement home business. Each option has its own unique set of advantages and disadvantages, depending on your objectives.

A Full-Time Home Business

The first option is to start a business that requires a 100 percent, full-time effort. As the commitment would suggest, a full-time venture is also the type of home business with the most risk and the most rewards. Risks come in the form of your initial financial investment, suspension of current employee benefits when you jump ship, and no guarantee of steady income, contributing spouses or partners excluded. On the other side of the coin there are also rewards that can be garnered from putting forth a full-time as opposed to a part-time or seasonal effort. These rewards can include the potential to make more money than you can at your job, or by operating on a part-time basis. Another reward comes because you are pursuing your dream on a full-time basis; you have assumed full control of your future and are prepared to work hard to ensure that your business dreams come to fruition. The majority of home business start-ups can be operated on a part-time basis, and outside of a few seasonal choices almost all can be operated on a full-time basis. However, some home business start-ups cannot be run with a part-time effort because of the nature of the business. A few of these would include:

- Property/house inspector
- Business broker
- Mobile on-call computer repair business
- Pest control

Again, your decision to operate your new business on a full-time basis will largely be determined by your financial situation, the type of business that you start, and your own risk-reward assessment.

A Part-Time Home Business

Your second option is to start a moonlighting business that requires a consistent part-time effort to operate. By consistent, I mean at least ten hours every week, week in, week out, on a year-round basis. You might also decide to transition from your current job, devoting more time to your new business each week, and decreasing the time at your current job. Of course, for this you need a good relationship with your current employer who would approve of this working arrangement.

Unlike the leap of faith that a full-time effort requires, part-timers can enjoy the best of both worlds while making the transition to a full-time business in due course. The advantages include keeping some income rolling in from your current job, taking advantage of current health program and employee benefits, and building your business over a longer period of time, which generally gives it a more stable foundation. You can also spread out your initial investment in the business over a longer period of time, which may negate the need to borrow money to finance needed equipment. Running a home business part-time allows you to test the waters without risking it all. By all, I mean money, your current job, and self-confidence. If it turns out that you are not the type of person who is comfort-

able with owning and operating a business, you have risked little and still have the security of your job to return to on a full-time basis. Once again, most home business ventures can be operated with a part-time effort. Examples include:

- Vending route
- Web site design and maintenance
- Wedding/event planner
- Commercial office cleaning

A Seasonal Home Business

The third option is to start a seasonal business that operates for only a few months a year. As the name suggests, seasonal businesses usually run during one specific season, although they may combine two seasons. Even though a business is seasonal, it can still be operated with a full-or part-time effort, although the majority are run full-time to maximize revenues and profits over the normally short season.

The potential to earn a very good living working only part of the year is real. I know entrepreneurs that are not only doing it, but also enjoying their time off to pursue other interests. Two very successful business people come to mind, both operating seasonal businesses from their homes. One with a wood lot spends the summer splitting logs into firewood and the fall delivering wood, and takes the remainder of the year off to travel. The second operates a kayak tour business for only four months a year, but generates enough revenue to comfortably enjoy other interests for the remaining eight months. When I say successful and comfortable, I mean that both draw in the six-figure range annually from their seasonal businesses.

A seasonally operated home business is suited to people that want to follow other interests, but are prepared to work very hard and smart to ensure that they can strike the balance that is required to do so. The balance is financial and time management, focus, planning, and setting measurable targets to make sure they can stay the required course. Many home business ventures can be operated with a full-time or part-time effort, but this is not the situation with all seasonal business ventures. In fact, you have to select the venture that you want to operate seasonally carefully conducting all the necessary research to ensure viability. Home business ventures that could be operated on a seasonal basis include:

- Christmas trees sales/holiday decorating service
- Pool cleaning and maintenance in northern climates
- Preparing personal income tax returns
- A summertime-only homebased day care

A Retirement Home Business

The fourth option is to start a retirement business, which can be operated full-time, part-time, or even seasonally if it meets your personal, financial, and business criteria. Retirement businesses have become extremely popular in the past decade for a number of reasons. First, the cost of living has dramatically increased, far outpacing wages in most cases. The result is lots of people heading into retirement needing little bit of extra income to cover expenses and provide a adequate lifestyle. This situation is especially common among people that started families later in life and still have children attending school or living at home. (Though perhaps once they hit 30 it's time to give them a gentle nudge out the door, and quickly change the locks.) Second, people are living longer and healthier now than in decades past—65-,70-, even 75-year-olds are seeking new challenges because they have the spirit, drive, and health to do so. Perhaps the biggest change here is attitude. The days of sitting on a porch in a rocking chair growing old are gone. People want to be vibrant and active, and operating your own business is a way to stay active physically and mentally.

Finally, many people have sacrificed their own personal dreams and goals so that family members and children can live theirs. Once everything is settled and secured, they want to take up the challenge and follow those dreams of business ownership that they have been putting off for years. At the end of the day, there are a host of reasons to start and operate a retirement business. And with shifting demographics and the huge number of baby boomers set to retire over the next 20 years, if you choose to start a retirement business, you'll be in the company of many other eager, if not slightly graying, entrepreneurs. Do keep in mind though that in both the United States and Canada, people over the age of 65 that start and operate an income producing business can face incremental decreases in Social Security benefits, depending on the amount of income earned and their age. Therefore, before getting your retirement business rolling, check with your accountant to see how these regulations will affect your individual situation. Examples of a retirement business include:

- Manufacturing woodcrafts
- Reselling new and used goods on eBay
- Freelance photography or writing
- Consulting

STARTING A NEW HOME BUSINESS FROM SCRATCH

As mentioned previously, there are four basic options for getting into a home business. Your first option is to start a new home business from scratch. This means a business that is not a franchise, a business opportunity, or a currently operating business, but a brand new business from the idea through operating the business. The single most important word of advice about a new business start-up is not to get caught trying to be too creative or innovative in terms of the business you start. In other words, do not try to reinvent the wheel. Follow the KISS formula, which means *keep it simple stupid* or, for the politically correct, *keep it simple silly*. I mention this because being the first to do anything burns money and plenty of it. Why? Because nobody will know what you have, how it works, what it will do for them, why they need it, and most of all, why they should buy it from you? Therefore, to introduce your great new thing, get consumers to take notice, and then convince them that they cannot live without it is an uphill battle that takes time, energy, and once again, plenty of money. If consumers already know, like, need, and purchase what you have to sell most of your job is already done for you. You can then concentrate your marketing efforts on telling consumers why your business is the right one from which to purchase what they already know, use, and need. You do this by adding value, making guarantees, providing incredible service, and a host of other business building activities. Your precious marketing money should not be used to introduce something new into the marketplace where you have to educate consumers about what it is and why they need it. Instead, your precious marketing money should go toward creating unique selling propositions that can be used to separate your business from competitors, thus winning consumer confidence and their business.

Where Can You Find Home Business Start-Up Ideas?

Fortunately, home business ideas are easy to come by because they are everywhere—in your community, in books and magazines, on the Internet, and from friends. Chapter 18, Home Business Start-Up Ideas and Home Franchise Opportunities, features 99 start-up ideas. Perhaps one of these ideas might even be right for you. But if not, don't fret. There are numerous sources that you can tap to start identifying home businesses that you can start from scratch.

Books

There are many books that focus on home business start-up ideas. Visit your local library, and check out a few. Or go to your local bookstore to purchase books on the topic. Of course, this is not to say that business start-up books are the definitive word on the subject and that you will definitely find a business to start from one. They are, however, a good launching point so that you will have a complete understanding of the sheer number of start-ups, as well as a few details about the business so that you can begin to narrow the field. You might even want to pick up a copy of my first book, *Entrepreneur's Ultimate Start-Up Directory* (Entrepreneur Press). *The Ultimate Start-Up Directory* features 1,350 great start-up ideas representing more than 30 industries, such as retail, manufacturing, advertising, sports, recreation, travel, and transportation and includes hundreds of home business opportunities. *The Ultimate Start-Up Directory* is available online from Entrepreneur Press, www.entrepreneurpress.com; Amazon, www.amazon.com; Barnes and Noble, www.barnesandnoble.com; and at bookstores across the United States, Canada, and many other countries. The book is also found at most public and school libraries in the United States and Canada.

The Internet

The Internet is another great place to find home business start-up ideas. There are a plethora of Web sites devoted to home businesses, business start-ups, and general business information from which to draw ideas. Best of all, much of this information can be acquired for free, at least in the early stages of research when selecting a few for your short list. The resources section at the end of this chapter features numerous home business and business opportunity Web sites where you can log on to start searching for home business ideas.

Current Job

If you like what you are currently doing, perhaps you can look at turning your job into your new home business start-up and maybe land your current employer as your first client. The idea is not as crazy as it may seem to be on the surface. Talk to your employer and find out what his or her plans are for the future of the business. Maybe he or she wants to slow down, sell out, or outsource some of the work? You never know unless you ask. If turning to your current employer is not in the cards and you still want to pursue a business start-up doing what you are currently doing, then go for it. Why not take advantage of the skills and knowledge you have worked hard to acquire? However, do it ethically. Do not try to lure clients away from your employer while you're still employed, and never compromise your current employer's intellectual or proprietary properties for your gain in your own business. These actions always have a way of catching up to the perpetrators.

Friends

You can ask friends and family members about what they think are good home business start-up ideas. Of course, be cautious here. You do not want to pursue someone else's dreams; you just want a few suggestions to get the creative juices flowing. Open discussions with friends and family members on home business start-up topics are a good idea. Usually, friends and family members will pull no punches because they care about your future.

Community

Another option is to take a look around your community at businesses that are currently or could be operated from a homebased location. See if they are successful and if those types of businesses interest you. The advantage of this method is that you can see the business in operation, talk to its customers, and check out its advertising, Web site, and other marketing material to get a good understanding of the business and the advantages and disadvantages associated with operating such a venture.

Hobbies and Interests

Starting a business based on one of your hobbies or interests is yet another way to get rolling in your own home business. You just need to make sure that the business idea is sound and has the potential to flourish and that the choice is more than an emotional attachment. A benefit of starting a business from a hobby is that you know the subject well, which can be used as a powerful marketing tool in terms of saleable expertise.

The Advantages of Starting a Home Business from Scratch

Those who feel the need to blaze trails rather than walk familiar turf will be pleased to know that there are numerous advantages to starting your own home business from scratch as opposed to purchasing an existing business, franchise, or business opportunity. Perhaps the biggest advantage, and one that is very attractive to many entrepreneurs that choose this route, is the fact that you can get started with little money, and the money that you do need can often be borrowed against credit cards, as a personal line of credit, or from a family member with moderately deep pockets. Depending on the venture you start and the equipment and supply needs of the business, you can often get into business for less than $1,000. You can almost always start something with good potential for less than a $10,000 initial investment. Additional advantages of starting a home business from scratch would include:

- The majority of your investment in the business is usually partially secured by inventory or equipment. Thereby, if things do not work out,

these assets can be sold to recoup a portion of the money invested in the start-up. Contrast this with a franchise, wherein you will be out the franchise fee and other related intangible start-up costs, or an existing business, wherein a portion of the purchase price will go toward paying for goodwill, which is lost if the business ultimately fails.

- When you start a home business from scratch, you are not buying into someone else's problems, which can be the case with some existing business purchases. The purchase may sound great, the equipment and inventory list may be impressive, and the financials may appear to be in order, but until you are actually operating the business, you don't know what skeletons might be hiding in the closet.

- Starting a business from scratch allows you to have full control over the venture and independence from managing influences that are often found in franchise arrangements and some business opportunities. In addition the growth and expansion potential for a start-up is excellent and not limited geographically or by agreement.

The Disadvantages of Starting a Home Business from Scratch

In a perfect world, I would tell you that there are no disadvantages to starting a home business from scratch, but this is not a perfect world. In fact, according to the SBA the highest percentage of business failures is in the new business start-up category, businesses that have been started from scratch by a first owner. This fact can be attributed to many factors, but at the core are the usual three suspects—lack of research, lack of planning, and lack of financial resources. The major disadvantages with starting a home business from scratch are, unfortunately, the things that attract first-time entrepreneurs to starting a business from scratch: low investment, little regulation, and quick and easy to get started. This combination can be a recipe for business disaster because you can literally have a business start-up idea today and be open for business tomorrow, which leave little, if any, time for two of the three main business killers: research and planning. Additional disadvantages to starting a home business from scratch include:

- You will be heading into 100 percent uncharted waters because you cannot be entirely sure that the business will prosper. If you have no previous experience in the venture, you have no system of checks and balances in place to measure progress, beyond your research and business and marketing plans.
- Unlike buying an operating business, there are no existing revenues to help pay for or offset fixed operating costs. You have to build the business to the breakeven point and profitability from scratch.
- Unlike purchasing a franchise or existing business, there is no road map that clearly identifies the steps that need to be taken to get the business started, operational, manageable, and profitable.

BUYING AN EXISTING HOME BUSINESS

A second option is to purchase a business that is currently operational and run the business from your home, regardless of whether the current owner is operating the business from a storefront, commercial office, or home. You will, however, still want to make sure that the business you purchase is suited to be a home business and, more importantly, suited to being run from your home. For people that want instant results and do not want to invest the time required to start a business and find customers from scratch, buying a currently operating business might be the best choice. If you choose this route to get into business, know that your approach to selecting the business, analyzing the potential, and planning for the future is no less involved than when starting a business from scratch. In fact, it may even be more involved because buying an operating business usually means investing a larger amount of money into the venture. It warrants extremely careful consideration, research, and planning to limit or minimize financial risk. So you will still need to research the marketplace, create a target customer profile, identify competitors, and develop business and marketing plans as you would

for any business. In addition, the purchase agreement is not a document that should be drafted and executed in the absence of professional help. Enlist a lawyer and accountant with experience in business purchase agreements to advise you on all aspects of buying a business, especially if a considerable amount of money will be changing hands. The following are a few tips about buying an operating business:

- Ask the current owner for a customer list and talk to customers randomly, asking if they are happy with the goods or services, the level of customer service provided, and the price. Also ask them what they would like to see changed and why? Check with your local chapter of the Better Business Bureau to make sure that the business does not have any unresolved complaint issues outstanding.
- Have the current owner supply you with the audited financial statements for the business going back at least five years or the entire time the business has been operating if less than five years.
- Talk to current suppliers to find out about payment history, amount of goods or services ordered, warranties, and deliveries.
- If the purchase is for a substantial amount of money, you may want to hire a business consultant to conduct a valuation of the business to make sure that you are paying fair market value in relation to profit potential. You can conduct your own valuation of the business. Tips about how to valuate a business are included in Chapter 11, Managing Your Home Business in the Selling Your Business section.
- All agreements and contracts that the current owner has with clients, suppliers, and manufacturers, should be transferable and stay with the business upon transition to a new owner without fee.
- Make sure that you have a noncompetition clause built into the sale agreement. Noncompetition clauses preclude the past owner from starting a similar type of business or selling similar goods and services within a set geographic area, generally within the same

state, and for a fixed period of time, generally five years.

- And finally, make sure that the current owner of the business stays on after the sale for a reasonable amount of time for training and to help in the transition.

Where Can You Find an Existing Business for Sale?

Once you have made the decision that you want to purchase a business that is currently operating, you have many options about where you can begin looking for the business that meets all of your criteria. Business brokers, real estate agents, newspapers, the Internet, and specialty business publications are the best places to start searching because these are a few of the main vehicles used to market and sell going business concerns.

Business Broker

The first stop is to contact an independent business broker, because these are the people who specialize in the sale of operating businesses and the resale of franchises. Business brokers have access to thousands of businesses that are currently for sale and can perform detailed searches for you with the information you supply. Best of all, the business broker will do all of this legwork and more for free because the vendor pays the business broker a commission when the business is sold. The International Business Brokers Association, located online at www.ibba.org, contains links to more than 1,100 independent business brokers around the world.

Realtor

Many business owners sell their business using a local real estate broker to market their business. Therefore, contacting a local realtor is also a good way of finding out what types of business are currently for sale. Even if nothing is currently available that meets your criteria, your realtor will keep his or her eyes open until the right opportunity comes along. Consult your local telephone book to find real estate agents and brokers in your area that specialize in business and commercial property sales.

Newspaper

Another option is to check the classified section under the heading *Business for Sale* or *Business Opportunities* in your local newspapers. Some business owners opt to save business broker and real estate broker commission fees and market their own business. You may even want to run your own advertisement describing the type of business that you want to purchase and let business owners call you.

Internet

The Internet is full of business-for-sale portals and Web sites, which makes it a great place for gathering information about what types of businesses might be available for sale, where they are located, and at what cost. The downside to shopping for a business, franchise, or business opportunity on the Internet is the fact that the Web does cater to a global audience so there is no guarantee that you will find the type of business you want for sale in your local area. Of course, if you are thinking about starting or purchasing a business that operates purely on the Internet this is probably the best place to search for the right opportunity. Biz Buy Sell, located online at www.bizbuysell.com, is billed as the Internet's largest business-for-sale portal, with over 20,000 listings.

Specialty Publications

There are also a number of specialty publications on the market that cater solely to businesses-for-sale and commercial listings. Check your local newsstand for availability. You can also log onto www.tradepub.com, which lists hundreds of specialty publications indexed by subject.

The Advantages of Buying an Existing Home Business

For the vast majority of entrepreneurs who choose to purchase a business that is operational, the number-one advantage for doing so is the fact that the business is generating revenue. The business may not be generating a profit and may not even be generating enough to pay you a wage, but revenue means cash flow. In business, cash flow is king! Cash flow enables you to keep the business machine running and at the same time promote your goods and services so that you can keep your current customers and attract new customers. Additional advantages for purchasing an operational business include:

- When you buy a operating business, the current customers come with it, and with rejuvenated management, it is often very easy to increase sales by as much as twice current levels by doing nothing more then convincing current customers to purchase more and more frequently.
- When you buy a business that is operating, you can make it part of the purchase agreement that the current owners stays on for a fixed period of time to provide training and for transitional help.
- When you purchase an operating business, you can often negotiate terms, meaning you pay a portion of the purchase price up front and the balance in installments or balloon payments. The advantage of buying on terms is that it gives you the ability to pay the installments out of business revenues. In effect, you will actually be purchasing the business for no more than your down payment. Of course, you may be working for free for a while if the money that would normally be paying your wages goes to paying off the balance of the purchase.

The Disadvantages of Buying an Existing Home Business

Without question, the number-one disadvantage associated with buying an operating business is the fact that you do not completely know what you are purchasing, even if you check out the business, the current owners, the customers, and the suppliers. There is always the potential for disaster. To put it put differently, potentially you may be purchasing someone else's problem. *Caveat emptor* (let the buyer beware) is very much the order of the day when you purchase an operational business. Therefore, do what is required to make sure that you do not inadvertently buy someone else's problem when you purchase what you think is your dream business. Additional disadvantages can include:

- Nine times out of ten it will cost more to purchase an existing business than it would to start

the same business from scratch. This is usually because when you purchase an operating business, you pay a premium for the things that a new start-up does not have, such as customers and, therefore, goodwill, a proven management system, and other valuable business assets such as trade accounts, merchant payment systems, vendors, trained employees, and lots more.
- Purchasing operating businesses can be very expensive, especially for entrepreneurs with limited investment funds. You would probably be hard pressed to find a decent operating business that has much potential for sale for under $20,000. While $20,000 of investment capital will easily fund hundreds of different home business start-ups ideas from scratch.

BUYING A HOME BUSINESS FRANCHISE

A third homebased business option is to purchase a franchise that can be operated/managed from a residential location. You could purchase either a new franchise, meaning that no other person has operated the franchise before, or you can purchase a resale franchise that is currently operating. Franchises can cost anywhere from a low of about $20,000, once you include franchise fees, start-up costs, inventory, and equipment, to well into the seven figure range for internationally known franchise operations. Purchasing and operating a franchise is a great option for people that want a proven management system, initial and ongoing training and support, and the benefits associated with branded names and products. However, if you choose to purchase a franchise, you still have to take the same precautions that you would when starting or purchasing any other type of business.

Do not be fooled into thinking that if you purchase a franchise you will be guaranteed success. Franchises, like any other type of businesses, fail; there is no franchisor that I am aware of that provides a 100 percent guarantee that you will stay in business and profit. It is, of course, in the franchisor's best interests to make sure that your business is successful and profitable so that they can continue to expand the brand through franchising into new geographical areas. For that reason, most franchisors provide very good training and support services to all of their franchisees. Before buying a homebased franchise you should:

- Make sure that the type of business that the franchisor is engaged in is something you want to do and think you would enjoy. A good match is still a key requirement for success, whether the business is a franchise or not.
- Check out the franchisor and talk to currently operating franchisees.
- Have your lawyer go over the franchisor's Uniform Franchise Offering Circular (UFOC), which is discussed later in this section.
- Conduct your own market research to make sure that the local market will support the franchise and that the franchisor's research, statements, and forecasts are correct.
- Become a customer of the franchise to make sure that you like and believe in the products or services being sold.

Where Can You Find Home Business Franchises for Sale?

Much like finding business start-up ideas and operating businesses for sale, franchise opportunities can be found everywhere and cover just about every type of business imaginable. In fact, at the time of writing, there are well in excess of 2,500 franchise opportunities available in the United States and Canada. Granted, not all are suited or can be operated from a homebased location, but many can. So where can you find home business franchises for sale? You should begin your search in the following places:

- *Franchise magazines and books.* Entrepreneur Media Inc., publishes an annual magazine, now in its 25th year, featuring the best franchises indexed by industry. The magazine is available at newsstands nationwide or www.entrepreneur.com.
- *Franchise associations* such as The American Franchisee Association, www.franchisee.org, International Franchise Association, www.franchise.org, and the Canadian Franchise Association (CFA), www.cfa.ca.
- *Internet search engines and directories* submitting "Franchise for Sale" or "Franchise Opportunity"

keyword searches and Web sites such as Franchise Zone, www.franchise-zone.com.
- *Local commercial real estate brokers and independent business brokers*, such as International Business Brokers www.ibb.com.
- *Newspaper and magazine classified advertisements.*
- *Talking to existing franchisees* inside and outside of your local area.

Chapter 18, Home Business Start-Up Ideas and Home Franchise Opportunities, features 99 franchise opportunities that can be operated from home. Many of the franchises featured in this chapter are nationally known chains with reputable management teams and multiple franchise units in operation. The name of the franchise is given as well as contact information and a brief synopsis detailing the franchisor's business activities.

The Advantages of Buying a Home Business Franchise

There are a great number of advantages associated with purchasing a homebased franchise, especially for people that want the security of a supportive team, proven management systems, and the benefits of branding on a large-scale basis. You have the combined strength of many franchisees as opposed to the possible weaknesses of one independent small business. The combined strengths can help lower costs by purchasing goods and services in bulk, reach a broader audience through collective advertising, and have an online presence managed through the head office, so you do not have to maintain and update your Web site. A few additional advantages include:

- Franchises are often a good business start-up choice for people who have never owned, operated, or even managed a small business. They come with a complete operations manual and a proven management system. All you have to do is follow the steps as outlined, and there is a better than average chance your business will succeed.
- Franchisees provide initial and ongoing training, support, and education to maximize the

potential for success and profitability. Again, this is very beneficial for people with little or no business experience.

- Once the decision has been made to proceed with the franchise, almost all small homebased franchises can be started within a few weeks and generate cash flow in less than one month.

The Disadvantages of Buying a Home Business Franchise

Unfortunately, there are also disadvantages associated with purchasing a homebased franchise. You have to decide if the advantages outweigh the disadvantages. Refer to your earlier analysis of your personal situation, goals, and possible good business matches prior to making the decision to purchase. A few disadvantages associated with purchasing and operating a home franchise include:

- When you own and operate a franchise, you have much less control and independence in all areas of your business then you do in a non franchise business. This is because one of the doctrines of the franchise model is conformity through consistent brand management. In fact, some of the more independent types reading this would find operating a franchise no more than managing someone else's business.
- Monthly advertising and royalty fees are two more disadvantages of the franchise business option, especially if fees are fixed and not calculated on a percentage of total gross sales. For instance, business may be down for a few months in a row, but if your royalty and advertising fees are fixed, you are still required to pay the full fees. Through the good times and bad, almost all franchises require that you pay monthly royalties or fees.
- A potentially big disadvantage of buying a franchise, especially for entrepreneurs with ambitious growth plans, is the fact that franchises can be extremely limiting in terms of growth, unless a master or area franchise is purchased, which can substantially increase the total initial investment. Basically, if you want to expand geographically, your options are to purchase another franchise area if available,

buy out another franchisee, or purchase a master or area franchise. All these options dramatically increase your overall investment.

Glossary of Common Franchise and Franchise Agreement Terms

If you decide that purchasing a franchise is the right new business enterprise for you, you will need to understand basic franchise terminology and their practical applications. Below is a glossary of common franchise and franchise agreement terms. However, prior to signing on the dotted line and purchasing a franchise, be sure to have a qualified lawyer experienced in franchise agreements to go over the details section by section with you. Good legal advice does not come cheap; it could, however, save you immeasurable heartache and financial hardship should the agreement or partnership not meet your expectations and fail.

Franchise

A business that offers to an individual, group of people, or company a set range of products or services and specific and valuable intellectual properties, defined by geographic boundaries known as a unit or area, for said individual, group of people, or company to purchase and operate that franchise unit or area in the manner set forth by the franchisor. A franchise is governed by a franchise agreement, which spells out the details of the business activities, relationship, mutual expectations, and financial obligations between the franchisee and franchisor. Examples of well-known franchise operations include McDonalds, Jani King, and Pillar-to-Post Home Inspection Services.

Franchisor

The person, people, or legal entity that owns the right to sell franchises for a specific business model, products, and/or services. Often a successful business will choose to grow its business by duplicating its original business operations and model and offering the duplicated business for sale to be purchased by qualified people, otherwise known as a franchisee, to manage the satellite business unit or area and to market the franchisor's specific product or service lines.

Franchisee

The franchisee is a person, group of people, or company that owns one or more franchise units or franchised operating areas. As a rule of thumb, the franchisee also manages the day-to-day operations of the franchise or hires managers or assistants to operate each franchise, if more than one is owned. Franchisees come from all walks of life, all ages, and all experiences.

Uniform Franchise Offering Circular (UFOC)

The Uniform Franchise Offering Circular is often referred to as a disclosure document. This mandatory document created by the franchisor and presented to the potential franchisee provides background information in numerous categories about the franchisor, as well as a copy of the proposed agreement listing all details and financial obligations between the franchisor and the franchisee. The franchise agreement will outline the following information, some of which is explained in greater detail in this chapter:

- Lists and defines all the parties involved in the agreement
- Lists and defines all financial transactions between parties
- Lists and defines all terms of the franchise agreement including franchisor's obligations, franchisee's obligations, opening for business dates, renewal of the agreement, assignment of the agreement, and termination of the agreement
- Lists and defines all of the equipment, supplies, and inventory that is included or needed and how these items will be procured and from whom
- Lists and defines the geographical territory the franchise agreement covers
- Lists and defines all advertising and marketing plans and activities
- Lists and defines all aspects of initial and ongoing training and education

Pro Forma

The pro forma details the franchisor's complete financial situation, including profit and loss statements, balance sheets and cash flow statements or projections, and asset and liability statements. Ideally, potential franchisees want financial information on both individual franchisee owned and operated units, as well as financial information and details of company owned and operated units. Reliance on tangible financial information is always preferred over financial projections, when available.

Minimum Capital Required

The minimum amount of money that will be required to purchase and operate the franchise. Although the total investment to purchase and start up a franchise might be $25,000, you are not always required to have the total investment amount. Some of the total investment may be financed or paid to the franchisor in installment payments. Many franchise agreements also have a minimum net worth clause in order for potential franchisees to qualify. This clause adds to the financial stability of the organization as a whole and is for the protection of the franchisor and existing franchisees. To calculate your net worth, add up all of your assets as well as all of your liabilities (debts) and subtract your liabilities from your assets to get your total net worth.

Franchise Fee

The franchise fee refers to the amount of money that you must pay the franchisor to purchase a single franchise, multiple franchises, or a master franchise area. The franchise fee almost always excludes the additional costs of inventory, equipment, operating capital, start-up costs, and initial marketing costs. Franchisors use the one-time, up-front franchise fee to cover costs associated with marketing individual franchise units or areas and finding qualified franchisees to purchase and operate these units or areas.

Total Investment

The total investment generally includes the up-front franchise fee, start-up fees, inventory, marketing, supplies, and equipment required to purchase and start the franchise. The total investment amount will be segmented by category costs, as in the basic example below.

Franchise fee	$10,000
Start-up fees and permits	$1,150

Initial inventory	$4,500
Equipment and supplies	$2,750
Initial marketing	$2,675
Total investment	$21,075

Remember, the total investment costs should be that: an all-inclusive number taking into account all fees and expenditures required to purchase and start the franchise, excluding ongoing maintenance fees, marketing, salaries, and product and services purchases once the franchise is operational.

Royalty Fees

The royalty fee is a monthly, or sometimes quarterly, fee that the franchisee pays directly to the franchisor for each franchise the franchisee owns and operates. Royalty fees can be a fixed amount such as $250 per month with a built-in cost of living or inflation index clause that automatically increases the royalty fee annually on the anniversary of the franchise agreement by the amount stated in the index clause. Or royalty fees can be based on a percentage of the franchisee's total gross or net revenues, such as 7.5 percent of gross monthly revenues or 12 percent of net monthly revenues, which may be calculated as total sales minus the total costs of products sold. Generally, royalty fees average between 5 and 10 percent of the franchisee's gross monthly revenues and are payable for each franchise the franchisee owns and operates.

Advertising Fees

Not to be confused with the royalty fee, the advertising or marketing fee is the amount of money a franchisee pays to the franchisor each month in exchange for a communal-based (regional and/or national) advertising program for the benefit of all franchisees and the franchisor. The advertising fee can be a fixed amount or based on a percentage of the franchisees total monthly revenues. Typically, the advertising or marketing fee is between 1.5 and 3 percent of the franchisee's gross monthly revenues, often with a set minimum and maximum figure, such as not to go below $200 per month or exceed $600 per month. Additional marketing materials and supplies generally fall under the authorized supplier section of the franchise agreement, which is highlighted later.

Company Owned Units

This term refers to areas or units (as defined by being a franchise) that are owned and operated by the franchisor and not a franchisee. Company owned units are still operated in the same manner as franchisee owned and operated units. The number of company or franchisor owned and operated units greatly vary, from one to all but one of the total number of franchised units or areas. Depending on the size of the franchisor, company owned and operated units often also serve as the head office for administration of all franchises and for centralized training of new franchisees.

Exclusive and Protected Territory

This refers to the franchise area, which is almost always defined by geographic boundaries such as a subdivision, city, county, state, or country. The franchisee retains the sole and exclusive right to operate the franchise under the terms and for the amount of time indicated in the franchise agreement. In the protected territory, the franchisor cannot sell any more franchises, although this does not mean that a competing franchise or independent business cannot operate in the franchise territory. The franchisor cannot prevent nor do they have control over competition opening in each franchise area.

Master Franchise

A master franchise is an agreement that covers multiple franchise units or areas. The master franchise holder may select to sell individual franchise units to new franchisees under the direction of the franchisor. Or the master franchise holder may opt to hold and develop each franchise unit within the master franchise area gradually over time with revenues generated by the first, and subsequent operating franchise units in the master franchise area. Owning a master franchise area or the right to develop a master franchise area is often a franchisee's best opportunity for long-term growth and increased revenues through the collection of franchise and maintenance fees or through opening and operating multiple franchise units within the master franchise area.

Conversion Franchise

Not overly common, a conversion franchise is a special class of franchise enabling existing independent businesses to join a franchise program. For example, if you owned and operated an existing cleaning service and wanted to convert your business to a nationally known cleaner there are some franchisors that have conversion programs in place to allow the transformation to take place. Be aware, however, that in most conversion situations, franchise purchase fees and other expenses still apply and must be paid by the new franchisee, even if they have a successful business track record and the needed equipment and supplies.

Operations Manual

Once you have purchased a franchise, you will receive the franchisee operations manual from the franchisor. This manual includes all information on systems, training, products, and procedures that are required to operate your franchise. The operations manual is the heart of the franchise as it contains specific intellectual materials, the combined experience of the franchisor and franchisees, and marketing methods that provide competitive advantages in the marketplace. In most homebased franchise situation, you are in fact purchasing access to a specific range of products for resale, training and knowledge on the delivery of specialized services, or a combination of these and the franchisors operations manual, which is best described as a roadmap to get your business started, operating, and growing.

Training

Training refers to the amount of initial training and ongoing training that the franchisee receives from the franchisor. The methods include live hands-on training at the franchisor's location, video or audio tape training, a print training manual, or a combination. The purpose of initial and ongoing training is to ensure that every franchisee knows how to operate the business, the products' or service's unique aspects and benefits, and to maintain consistency in the operations, corporate image, and delivery to consumers of the business, products, or services.

Franchisor Support

Support is in two main areas—the support structure between franchisee and franchisor and the support structure between franchisor and each franchisee's customers. Support between the franchisee and franchisor can be very inclusive or completely lacking. Typically, franchisor support will include areas such as marketing and advertising campaigns, Web site maintenance, centralized accounting, and ongoing training. Support to franchisee's customers typically includes such features as a centralized customer service help desk, product or workmanship warranty underwriting, and research and development in terms of sourcing new products and services or improving existing products and services.

Authorized Suppliers

In the majority of franchise agreements, you will find that franchisees must purchase products and services for resale and/or consumption through the franchisor directly or through a fanchisor authorized supplier. This is done for two reasons—to maintain consistency throughout the organization and to create an additional revenue and control center for the franchisor. Generally, authorized suppliers extend to all business activities and include products and services such as products for resale, printed marketing materials, couriers and other service providers, and office or job equipment.

BUYING INTO A HOME BUSINESS OPPORTUNITY

The final home business option is to purchase a business opportunity that can be operated from a homebased location. *Business opportunity* is a broad term that covers many different money making opportunities, including sales agent, distributor, direct sales, multi-level marketing, and vending. There are major differences between starting a business from scratch, purchasing an operating business, purchasing a franchise, and purchasing a business opportunity. When you purchase a business opportunity, it is not like starting a business from your own idea because someone else has come up with the idea and generally has combined that idea into a package with the equipment, inventory, and operations manual required for running the business. A business opportunity is not like a franchise, even though training and an operations manual might be included with the purchase, because there are no royalty fees or franchise fees to pay. You are on your own, although you may or may not be required to purchase inventory for resale from a distributor. Legally, you are not required to do so if you choose not to. Buying a business opportunity is not like purchasing an operational independent business because business opportunities are always sold as a new opportunity without proven customers or cash flow. So now that you know what a business opportunity is not, you may be wondering what a business opportunity is. Business opportunities can be many things including the following:

- *Multi-Level Marketing (MLM).* Most people are familiar with multi-level marketing, either because they have given it a whirl, or because they have had a friend or family member try to recruit you into their down line at some point. Multi-level marketing is selling goods or services directly to consumers, but the true focus of the business is recruiting people into your down line because recruiters retain a percentage of the down line sales. As your down line expands, so does your opportunity to make more money.

- *Direct Sales.* Selling cosmetics, health and fitness products, software, vitamins, cookware, and fashion accessories directly to consumers via the Internet, in-home parties, classified advertisements, and out of your home or car is classified as a business opportunity. An example would be Mary Kay Cosmetics.

- *Vending.* Vending is also classified as a business opportunity if you purchase a vending package, which generally includes vending machine(s), initial inventory for the machines, an operations manual, and guaranteed placement of the vending machine(s) that you purchase. Guaranteed placement means that the machine(s) will be installed in a retail, warehouse, or factory environment, but with no guarantee that the location(s) will be good or profitable.

These examples are only three of the numerous business opportunities that are available. Homebased business opportunities can cost as little as a few hundred dollars or as much as $20,000. As a rule of thumb, most are under or in the range of $5,000, which includes the basic equipment, operations manual, and initial inventory needed to start the business.

Where Do You Find Home Business Opportunities?

Like other types of home business operations featured in this chapter, the ways to find home business opportunities are nearly unlimited. The first place to look is in your local newspaper under the "Business Opportunities" classified section. Generally you'll find that there is no shortage of opportunities listed for sale, some legitimate and others suspect at best. You can also log onto the Internet and conduct a "Business Opportunities" keyword search on any of the major search engines and search directories. These keyword searches will return hundreds, if not thousands, of matches. At the end of this chapter in the Resources section, you will find numerous Web sites that feature business opportunities for sale and business opportunity information. A third, and perhaps the best, way to find a legitimate business opportunity is to ask friends and family members if they or someone they know is involved in a successful opportunity. The best aspect of using this method is that you can find out firsthand—without the marketing hype of the business opportunity seller—if indeed the opportunity has merit and can be financially viable. Finally, look around your community to see what business opportunities people are engaged in. Get out and talk to a few. Ask if they are happy, or if they are looking to sell. Again, there is no shortage of home business ideas, franchises, or opportunities. The key is to find one that matches your criteria and has the potential to meet your goals.

The Advantages of Buying a Home Business Opportunity

The biggest advantage of a business opportunity is cost. Most are cheap to purchase and start. Some can be started for only a few hundred dollars, affording entrepreneurs with a determination to succeed but with no money an opportunity to get into business and see if they have what it takes to succeed. Additional advantages associated with purchasing a homebased business opportunity include:

- Just about every business opportunity available has been specifically designed to be operated or managed from a homebased location, which is great for people looking for a home business. It eliminates the guesswork about whether the business can be operated from home.
- Business opportunities are very quick to start and get rolling. As a matter of fact, you can find and purchase one today and be open for business tomorrow. Most can also be operated part-time, nights, weekends, or even seasonally, enabling you to keep your job until the business is self-supporting and can provide you with an income.
- Perhaps the biggest lure of business opportunities for many people is the fact that almost all require no business experience to operate. Those that do have a learning curve that can be mastered in hours or days, instead of weeks or months.

The Disadvantages of Buying a Home Business Opportunity

The number-one disadvantage of purchasing a business opportunity is that you have to be extremely cautious when you do purchase any business oppor-

tunity. There are lots of business opportunity scams out there operated by slick con artists eager to get their hands on your money. Let's be logical, is anyone in their right mind really going to pay you $2,000 a week to stuff envelops at home or pay you $500 a day to assemble simple toys in your basement? There are additional disadvantages associated with purchasing and operating a business opportunity.

- Because business opportunities are not franchises or licenses, you do not receive a protected geographical territory, which means that you may very well be competing against numerous other business people operating exactly the same business opportunity as you, selling the exact same products or services as you, and operating within the same geographical territory as you.
- Business opportunities for the most part offer little, if any, real growth potential. There are exceptions to the rule, but for the most part business opportunities are very limited in terms of growth and profit potential.
- The majority of business opportunities offer little if any initial training and almost none provide ongoing support. Once you have paid for the opportunity, you are for all intents and purposes on your own, left to your own devices.

HOME BUSINESS START-UP COSTS ESTIMATOR

The Home Business Start-Up Costs Estimator (see Figure 2.10) is very comprehensive. Many items on the list will not be needed for every home business

FIGURE 2.10 Home Business Start-Up Costs Estimator

Type of Business Start-Up: _____

Section 1. General Start-Up Costs	Quantity	$Unit Cost	$Total Cost
❏ Business/Name Registration	____	$_____	$_____
❏ Business Incorporation	____	$_____	$_____
❏ Legal Fees	____	$_____	$_____
❏ Accounting Fees	____	$_____	$_____

FIGURE 2.10   Home Business Start-Up Costs Estimator, continued

Section 1. General Start-Up Costs	Quantity	$Unit Cost	$Total Cost
❏ Consultant Fees	_____	$_____	$_____
❏ Bank Account(s) Set-Up Charges	_____	$_____	$_____
❏ Merchant Account (credit card) Charges	_____	$_____	$_____
❏ Business Association Memberships	_____	$_____	$_____
❏ Industry Association Memberships	_____	$_____	$_____
❏ Professional Association Memberships	_____	$_____	$_____
❏ Distributor/Licensing Fees	_____	$_____	$_____
❏ Insurances			
1. _____	_____	$_____	$_____
2. _____	_____	$_____	$_____
3. _____	_____	$_____	$_____
4. _____	_____	$_____	$_____
❏ Special Training and Certificates	_____	$_____	$_____
❏ Other Permits	_____	$_____	$_____
❏ Trademarks, Copyrights, and Patents	_____	$_____	$_____
❏ Deposits	_____	$_____	$_____
❏ Other _____	_____	$_____	$_____
❏ Other _____	_____	$_____	$_____
		Section 1. Subtotal	$_____

Section 2. Office Furniture and Equipment Costs	Quantity	$Unit Cost	$Total Cost
❏ Desktop Computer	_____	$_____	$_____
❏ Desktop Computer Monitor	_____	$_____	$_____
❏ Notebook Computer	_____	$_____	$_____
❏ Printer	_____	$_____	$_____
❏ Software Programs			
1. _____	_____	$_____	$_____
2. _____	_____	$_____	$_____
3. _____	_____	$_____	$_____
4. _____	_____	$_____	$_____
❏ Photocopier	_____	$_____	$_____
❏ Digital Camera	_____	$_____	$_____
❏ Scanner	_____	$_____	$_____
❏ Telephone	_____	$_____	$_____
❏ Cellular Telephone	_____	$_____	$_____
❏ Pager	_____	$_____	$_____

FIGURE 2.10   Home Business Start-Up Costs Estimator, continued

Section 2. Office Furniture and Equipment Costs	Quantity	$Unit Cost	$Total Cost
❏ Fax Machine	_____	$_____	$_____
❏ Electronic Organizer	_____	$_____	$_____
❏ Desk	_____	$_____	$_____
❏ Chair	_____	$_____	$_____
❏ File Cabinet	_____	$_____	$_____
❏ Bookcase	_____	$_____	$_____
❏ Client Seating	_____	$_____	$_____
❏ Lighting	_____	$_____	$_____
❏ Shredder/Waste Receptacles	_____	$_____	$_____
❏ Small Office Equipment (staplers, etc.)	_____	$_____	$_____
❏ General Office Supplies (paper, etc.)	_____	$_____	$_____
❏ Reference Books/Directories	_____	$_____	$_____
❏ Other _____	_____	$_____	$_____
❏ Other _____	_____	$_____	$_____
		Section 2. Subtotal	$_____

Sections 3. Office Renovation Costs	Quantity	$Unit Cost	$Total Cost
❏ Building/Inspection Permits	_____	$_____	$_____
❏ New/Upgrades to Mechanicals	_____	$_____	$_____
❏ Fire/Security Alarms	_____	$_____	$_____
❏ Communications Upgrades	_____	$_____	$_____
❏ General Construction	_____	$_____	$_____
❏ Finish Carpentry	_____	$_____	$_____
❏ Windows/Doors	_____	$_____	$_____
❏ Paint/Wall Covering	_____	$_____	$_____
❏ Window Coverings	_____	$_____	$_____
❏ Flooring	_____	$_____	$_____
❏ Built-ins	_____	$_____	$_____
❏ Decorations	_____	$_____	$_____
❏ Other _____	_____	$_____	$_____
❏ Other _____	_____	$_____	$_____
		Section 3. Subtotal	$_____

Section 4. Inventory Costs	Quantity	$Unit Cost	$Total Cost
❏ Initial Product Orders			
1. _____	_____	$_____	$_____
2. _____	_____	$_____	$_____

FIGURE 2.10   Home Business Start-Up Costs Estimator, continued

Section 4. Inventory Costs	Quantity	$Unit Cost	$Total Cost
3. _____	_____	$_____	$_____
4. _____	_____	$_____	$_____
5. _____	_____	$_____	$_____
6. _____	_____	$_____	$_____
7. _____	_____	$_____	$_____
8. _____	_____	$_____	$_____
9. _____	_____	$_____	$_____
10. _____	_____	$_____	$_____
❏ Product Packaging	_____	$_____	$_____
❏ Product Samples	_____	$_____	$_____
❏ Product Shipping Supplies	_____	$_____	$_____
❏ Point of Purchase Displays	_____	$_____	$_____
❏ Other _____	_____	$_____	$_____
❏ Other _____	_____	$_____	$_____
		Section 4. Subtotal	$_____

Section 5. Web Site and E-Commerce Costs	Quantity	$Unit Cost	$Total Cost
❏ Domain Registration	_____	$_____	$_____
❏ Web Site Design	_____	$_____	$_____
❏ Content	_____	$_____	$_____
❏ Specialized Software			
1. _____	_____	$_____	$_____
2. _____	_____	$_____	$_____
3. _____	_____	$_____	$_____
4. _____	_____	$_____	$_____
❏ Special Equipment	_____	$_____	$_____
❏ Search Engine Submission Fees			
1. _____	_____	$_____	$_____
2. _____	_____	$_____	$_____
3. _____	_____	$_____	$_____
4. _____	_____	$_____	$_____
❏ Online Payment Systems	_____	$_____	$_____
❏ Online Shopping Cart	_____	$_____	$_____
❏ Other _____	_____	$_____	$_____
❏ Other _____	_____	$_____	$_____
		Section 5. Subtotal	$_____

FIGURE 2.10   **Home Business Start-Up Costs Estimator,** continued

Section 6. Marketing and Promotion Costs	Quantity	$Unit Cost	$Total Cost
❏ Initial Research/Planning Budget	_____	$_____	$_____
❏ Initial Advertising Budget	_____	$_____	$_____
❏ Advertising and Promotional Specialties	_____	$_____	$_____
❏ Printed Promotional Literature			
1. _____	_____	$_____	$_____
2. _____	_____	$_____	$_____
3. _____	_____	$_____	$_____
4. _____	_____	$_____	$_____
❏ Signage			
1. _____	_____	$_____	$_____
2. _____	_____	$_____	$_____
3. _____	_____	$_____	$_____
4. _____	_____	$_____	$_____
❏ Trade Show/Event Marketing Booth	_____	$_____	$_____
❏ Other _____	_____	$_____	$_____
❏ Other _____	_____	$_____	$_____
		Section 6. Subtotal	$_____

Section 7. Business Identity Costs	Quantity	$Unit Cost	$Total Cost
❏ Logo Design	_____	$_____	$_____
❏ Desktop Publishing/Design Fees	_____	$_____	$_____
❏ Business Cards	_____	$_____	$_____
❏ Stationery Package	_____	$_____	$_____
❏ Receipts/Invoices	_____	$_____	$_____
❏ Printed Specialties (pens, etc.)	_____	$_____	$_____
❏ Uniforms	_____	$_____	$_____
❏ Other _____	_____	$_____	$_____
❏ Other _____	_____	$_____	$_____
		Section 7. Subtotal	$_____

Section 8. Transportation Costs	Quantity	$Unit Cost	$Total Cost
❏ Vehicle Purchase	_____	$_____	$_____
❏ Vehicle Lease/Loan Down Payment	_____	$_____	$_____
❏ Specialty Accessories (toolbox, etc.)			
1. _____	_____	$_____	$_____
2. _____	_____	$_____	$_____

FIGURE 2.10 Home Business Start-Up Costs Estimator, continued

Section 8. Transportation Costs	Quantity	$Unit Cost	$Total Cost
3. _____	_____	$_____	$_____
4. _____	_____	$_____	$_____
❑ Insurance	_____	$_____	$_____
❑ Registration	_____	$_____	$_____
❑ Signage	_____	$_____	$_____
❑ Other _____	_____	$_____	$_____
❑ Other _____	_____	$_____	$_____
		Section 8. Subtotal	$_____

Section 9. Specialized Equipment Costs	Quantity	$Unit Cost	$Total Cost
1. _____	_____	$_____	$_____
2. _____	_____	$_____	$_____
3. _____	_____	$_____	$_____
4. _____	_____	$_____	$_____
5. _____	_____	$_____	$_____
6. _____	_____	$_____	$_____
7. _____	_____	$_____	$_____
8. _____	_____	$_____	$_____
		Section 9. Subtotal	$_____

Calculating Total Start-Up Costs

Section 1. General Start-Up Costs	$_____
Section 2. Office Furniture and Equipment Costs	$_____
Section 3. Office Renovation Costs	$_____
Section 4. Inventory Costs	$_____
Section 5. Web Site and E-Commerce Costs	$_____
Section 6. Marketing and Promotion Costs	$_____
Section 7. Business Identity Costs	$_____
Section 8. Transportation Costs	$_____
Section 9. Specialized Equipment Costs	$_____
Total Start-Up Costs	$_____
Reserve Fund (10%)	$_____
Estimated Number of Months Required to Reach Breakeven _____ x Fixed Monthly Overhead Costs	$_____
Total Capital Needed to Start the Business	$_____

start-up, especially part-time or basic ventures. Therefore, only complete the items that will be needed for the business that you want to start and leave the rest of the items on the form blank. You may also find that you have to add items to suit your start-up. If you are considering more than one home business start-up, you can remove this worksheet from the book, photocopy it, and complete it for each start-up. Or you can use this start-up costs estimator form as a guideline and create your own on your computer using any basic word processing or

accounting program. Regardless of how you utilize the estimator, the value of knowing how much money will be required to start your home business cannot be overestimated.

FIXED MONTHLY OVERHEAD CALCULATOR

Do you want to know how much money you will need every month to cover your fixed business operating costs and wages? Of course you do, and you can by using this fixed monthly overheads calculator (see Figure 2.11) for start-ups that your are

FIGURE 2.11   Fixed Monthly Overhead Calculator

Type of Business Start-Up: _____

Section 1. General Office Expenditures	Quantity	$Unit Cost	$Total Cost
❑ Loan and Interest Repayments	___	$___	$___
❑ Bank Charges	___	$___	$___
❑ Credit Card Fees	___	$___	$___
❑ Merchant Card Fees	___	$___	$___
❑ Business Taxes	___	$___	$___
❑ Business Permits and Registrations	___	$___	$___
❑ Additional Utilities	___	$___	$___
❑ Insurances			
1. _____	___	$___	$___
2. _____	___	$___	$___
3. _____	___	$___	$___
4. _____	___	$___	$___
❑ Workers' Compensation	___	$___	$___
❑ Equipment Leases/Loans/Rentals			
1. _____	___	$___	$___
2. _____	___	$___	$___
3. _____	___	$___	$___
4. _____	___	$___	$___
❑ Equipment Repairs	___	$___	$___
❑ Alarm Monitoring	___	$___	$___
❑ Off-Site Storage Costs	___	$___	$___
❑ General Office Supplies	___	$___	$___
❑ Postage	___	$___	$___

| FIGURE 2.11 | Fixed Monthly Overhead Calculator, continued |

Section 1. General Office Expenditures	Quantity	$Unit Cost	$Total Cost
❑ Courier/Delivery	___	$_____	$_____
❑ Cleaning/Maintenance	___	$_____	$_____
❑ Other _____	___	$_____	$_____
❑ Other _____	___	$_____	$_____
		Section 1. Subtotal	$_____

Section 2. Communications Expenditures	Quantity	$Unit Cost	$Total Cost
❑ Telephone	___	$_____	$_____
❑ Toll Free Line	___	$_____	$_____
❑ Facsimile Line	___	$_____	$_____
❑ Internet Connection	___	$_____	$_____
❑ Cellular Telephone	___	$_____	$_____
❑ Answering Service	___	$_____	$_____
❑ Pager	___	$_____	$_____
❑ Two-Way Radio	___	$_____	$_____
❑ Communications Equipment Lease	___	$_____	$_____
❑ Other _____	___	$_____	$_____
❑ Other _____	___	$_____	$_____
		Section 2. Subtotal	$_____

Section 3. Wages and Fees	Quantity	$Unit Cost	$Total Cost
❑ Personal Wages	___	$_____	$_____
❑ Employees			
1. _____	___	$_____	$_____
2. _____	___	$_____	$_____
3. _____	___	$_____	$_____
4. _____	___	$_____	$_____
❑ Employee Benefits			
1. _____	___	$_____	$_____
2. _____	___	$_____	$_____
3. _____	___	$_____	$_____
4. _____	___	$_____	$_____
❑ Accounting Fees	___	$_____	$_____
❑ Legal Fees	___	$_____	$_____
❑ Consultant Fees	___	$_____	$_____
❑ Business Association Fees	___	$_____	$_____
❑ Industry Association Fees	___	$_____	$_____

FIGURE 2.11 **Fixed Monthly Overhead Calculator,** continued

Section 3. Wages and Fees	Quantity	$Unit Cost	$Total Cost
❑ Professional Association Fees	_____	$_____	$_____
❑ Specialty Membership Fees	_____	$_____	$_____
❑ Other _____	_____	$_____	$_____
❑ Other _____	_____	$_____	$_____
		Section 3. Subtotal	$_____

Section 4. Marketing Expenditures	Quantity	$Unit Cost	$Total Cost
❑ Yellow Pages	_____	$_____	$_____
❑ Newspaper Display Ads	_____	$_____	$_____
❑ Newspaper Classified Ads	_____	$_____	$_____
❑ Magazine	_____	$_____	$_____
❑ Radio	_____	$_____	$_____
❑ Television	_____	$_____	$_____
❑ Business Directories	_____	$_____	$_____
❑ Fliers	_____	$_____	$_____
❑ Direct Mail	_____	$_____	$_____
❑ Telemarketing	_____	$_____	$_____
❑ Trade Shows/Seminars	_____	$_____	$_____
❑ Public Relations	_____	$_____	$_____
❑ Outdoor Advertising	_____	$_____	$_____
❑ Contests	_____	$_____	$_____
❑ Promotional Giveaways	_____	$_____	$_____
❑ Product Samples	_____	$_____	$_____
❑ Sponsorships	_____	$_____	$_____
❑ Surveys/Polls/Research	_____	$_____	$_____
❑ Customer Appreciation/Gifts	_____	$_____	$_____
❑ Graphic Design/Copy Fees	_____	$_____	$_____
❑ Other _____	_____	$_____	$_____
❑ Other _____	_____	$_____	$_____
		Section 4. Subtotal	$_____

Section 5. Web Site and E-Commerce Expenditures	Quantity	$Unit Cost	$Total Cost
❑ Server/Host/Web Master	_____	$_____	$_____
❑ Maintenance	_____	$_____	$_____
❑ Content/Plug-In Fees			
1. _____	_____	$_____	$_____
2. _____	_____	$_____	$_____

FIGURE 2.11   **Fixed Monthly Overhead Calculator,** continued

Section 5. Web Site and E-Commerce Expenditures	Quantity	$Unit Cost	$Total Cost
3. _____	_____	$_____	$_____
4. _____	_____	$_____	$_____
❏ Internet Advertising			
1. _____	_____	$_____	$_____
2. _____	_____	$_____	$_____
3. _____	_____	$_____	$_____
4. _____	_____	$_____	$_____
❏ Search Engine	_____	$_____	$_____
❏ Paid Placements	_____	$_____	$_____
❏ Software/Web Tool Licenses			
1. _____	_____	$_____	$_____
2. _____	_____	$_____	$_____
3. _____	_____	$_____	$_____
4. _____	_____	$_____	$_____
❏ Online Payment System Fees	_____	$_____	$_____
❏ Order Fulfillment Fees	_____	$_____	$_____
❏ Equipment Leases/Loans	_____	$_____	$_____
❏ Equipment Maintenance	_____	$_____	$_____
❏ Other _____	_____	$_____	$_____
❏ Other _____	_____	$_____	$_____
		Section 5. Subtotal	$_____

Section 6. Transportation Expenditures	Quantity	$Unit Cost	$Total Cost
❏ Lease/Loan Payment	_____	$_____	$_____
❏ Fuel	_____	$_____	$_____
❏ Insurance	_____	$_____	$_____
❏ Repairs	_____	$_____	$_____
❏ Licensing/Registration	_____	$_____	$_____
❏ Parking	_____	$_____	$_____
❏ Cleaning	_____	$_____	$_____
❏ Other _____	_____	$_____	$_____
❏ Other _____	_____	$_____	$_____
		Section 6. Subtotal	$_____

Section 7. Miscellaneous Expenditures	Quantity	$Unit Cost	$Total Cost
❏ Travel	_____	$_____	$_____
❏ Entertainment	_____	$_____	$_____

FIGURE 2.11 **Fixed Monthly Overhead Calculator,** continued

Section 7. Miscellaneous Expenditures	Quantity	$Unit Cost	$Total Cost
❏ Uniforms/Dry Cleaning	_____	$_____	$_____
❏ Subscriptions			
1. _____	_____	$_____	$_____
2. _____	_____	$_____	$_____
3. _____	_____	$_____	$_____
4. _____	_____	$_____	$_____
❏ Charitable Donations	_____	$_____	$_____
❏ Other _____	_____	$_____	$_____
❏ Other _____	_____	$_____	$_____
		Section 7. Subtotal	$_____

Calculating Total Fixed Monthly Overhead Expenditures	
Section 1. General Office Expenditures	$_____
Section 2. Communications Expenditures	$_____
Section 3. Wages and Fees	$_____
Section 4. Marketing Expenditures	$_____
Section 5. Web Site and E-Commerce Expenditures	$_____
Section 6. Transportation Expenditures	$_____
Section 7. Miscellaneous Expenditures	$_____
Fixed Monthly Overheads—Grand Total	$_____

considering so that you will have a good idea about the amount of net sales that must be generated to cover wages and operating expenses. Likewise, once you have started a home business you can also complete this form to keep track of your fixed operating costs on a monthly basis. Much like the start-up costs estimator, the overhead costs estimator is very comprehensive and not all home businesses will have every expense listed. Complete only the items that are relevant to your particular business and leave the balance of the items on the list blank. The fixed monthly overhead costs estimator can be removed from the book and photocopied. Or you can use this one as a guideline and create your own on a computer using any basic word processing or accounting program.

RESOURCES

⌨ Associations

The American Franchisee Association
53 W. Jackson Boulevard, Suite 205
Chicago, IL 60604
(312) 431-0545
www.franchisee.org

American Home Business Association
4505 Wasatah Boulevard South
Salt Lake City, UT 84124
(800) 664-2422
www.homebusiness.com

Canadian Franchise Association (CFA)
2585 Skymark Avenue, Suite 300

Mississauga, ON L4W 4L5
(800) 665-4232
www.cfa.ca

International Franchise Association (IFA)
1350 New York Avenue NW, Suite 900
Washington, DC 20005-4709
(202) 628-8000
www.franchise.org

U.S. Small Business Administration (SBA)
409 Third Street SW
Washington, DC 20416
(800) 827-5722
www.sba.org

Suggested Reading

Caffey, Andrew A. *Franchise & Business Opportunities.* Irvine, CA: Entrepreneur Media Inc., 2002.

Edwards, Paul, and Sarah Edwards. *The Best Home Businesses for the 21st Century: The Inside Information You Need to Know to Select a Home-Based Business That's Right for You.* New York: J.P. Tarcher, 1999.

Huff, Priscilla Y. *The Self-Employed Woman's Guide to Launching a Home-Based Business: Everything You Need to Know About Getting Started on the Road to Success.* Roseville, CA: Prima Publishing, 2002.

Lesonsky, Rieva. *Ultimate Book of Franchises: From the Experts at Entrepreneur Magazine.* Irvine, CA: Entrepreneur Press, 2004.

Sander, Jennifer, and Peter Sander. *Niche and Grow Rich: Practical Ways of Turning Your Ideas Into a Business.* Irvine, CA: Entrepreneur Press, 2003.

Stansell, Kimberly. *Bootstrapper's Success Secrets: 151 Tactics for Building Your Business on a Shoestring Budget.* Franklin Lakes, NJ: Career Press, 1997.

Stephenson, James. *Entrepreneur's Ultimate Start-Up Directory: 1350 Great Business Ideas!* Irvine, CA: Entrepreneur Press, 2001.

Walters, Lilly, and Martha Campbell Pullen. *You Can Make Money from Your Hobby: Building a Business Doing What You Love.* Nashville, TN: Broadman and Holman Publishing, 1999.

Web Sites

Business Know-How, www.businessknowhow.com: Small business information, advice, tools, and services.

Business Opportunities Classified Online, www.boc online.com: Online business opportunities portal listing hundreds of business opportunities indexed by category.

Canadian Business Service Center, www.cbsc.org: Canadian equivalent of the SBA.

Entrepreneur Online, www.entrepreneur.com: Online small business resource center providing entrepreneurs with information, advice, products, services, and resources.

Family Business Magazine Online, www.familybusi nessmagazine.com: Information, tips, articles, and advice about starting and operating a family business.

Franchise Times Magazine Online, www.franchise times.com: Electronic and print magazine providing readers with the latest franchise news, information, products, services, and industry resources.

Franchise Zone, www.franchise-zone.com: Online franchise opportunities directory indexed by type of franchise.

Home Based Business Opportunities, www.home-based-business-opportunities.com: Online directory service featuring hundreds of homebased and small business opportunities listings.

Home Business Magazine, www.homebusiness mag. com: Online magazine with information, advice, tools, and links for home business owners.

Home Business Report Magazine Online, www.home businessreports.com: Electronic and print magazine providing readers with the latest home business opportunities, news, information, and industry resources.

Home-Based Working Moms, www.hbwm.com: A professional association and online community for parents that work from home.

Home Working, www.homeworking.com: Information, advice, services, and support by and for people working from home.

Power Home Biz, www.powerhomebiz.com: Online information, advice, and tools for home business owners.

Small Business Now, www.smallbusinessnow.com: Small business information, advice, tools, products, services, and links of interest.

Small Business Opportunities Magazine Online, www.sbomag.com: Electronic and print magazine providing readers with the latest small business opportunities news, information, and industry resources.

U.S. Business Advisor, www.usbusinessadvisor.gov: U.S. Business Advisor is sponsored by the SBA and offers free information and links to other small business Web sites and service providers.

CHAPTER 3

Financial Issues

FINANCIAL ISSUES FACING THE NEW HOME business owner are many and varied, but certainly manageable if you take the time to identify your personal financial requirements and the financial requirements of your new venture. Home business owners must also educate themselves on a great number of financial issues, such as banking, record keeping, payment processing, money management, and small business taxation. Throughout this book, you will find additional information about financial issues facing the homebased business owner, especially in Chapter 11, Managing Your Home Business.

The first step that needs to be taken prior to getting your business going is to take stock of your personal financial situation to determine your net worth, and the amount of income that you need to generate each month to pay your family bills. Knowing your own personal financial situation is a critical factor because it will enable you to determine how much money you yourself can afford to put toward starting the business, how much you will have to borrow, and how much income you need to draw from your new business.

TAKING STOCK OF YOUR PERSONAL FINANCES

To help take stock of your personal finances complete the Personal Assets and Liabilities Worksheet (see Figure 3.1) as well as the Family Monthly Expense Worksheet (see Figure 3.2). The first, Personal Assets and Liabilities, will aid you in calculating your financial net worth and the second, Family Monthly Expenses, in calculating how much income you need to earn each month. However, you might want to complete both columns of the income worksheet. The first column identifies subsistence income level, the minimum amount you need to pay your personal bills. It has no fat. The second column is used to identify a comfortable income level, the amount you need to maintain your current lifestyle.

MAKING THE RIGHT FINANCIAL TRANSITION INTO YOUR OWN BUSINESS

Once you have determined your net worth and the income you need to pay your personal bills each month, you will be in a better position to identify the best financial transition into your new business. First, looking at your personal net worth, are you in a financial position to start the business you want to start? If so, are you prepared to risk the money you have to start the business? Only you know the answer for sure, especially on the second question. If you are not in a position to start a new business, you must identify how to raise the money needed, which is discussed later in this chapter.

FIGURE 3.1 Personal Assets and Liabilities Worksheet

Description	Assets Value	Liabilities Outstanding Balance
Real estate	$_____	$_____
Personal effects (furniture, electronics, etc.)	$_____	$_____
Automobile(s)	$_____	$_____
Cash in bank accounts	$_____	NA
Retirement saving plans	$_____	NA
Stocks	$_____	$_____
Personal loans	NA	$_____
Lines of credit	NA	$_____
Credit cards	NA	$_____
Totals	$_____	$_____

Total Assets $_____
Minus Total Liabilities $_____
Personal Net Worth $_____

FIGURE 3.2 Family Monthly Expenses Worksheet

Housing Expenses	Subsistence	Comfortable
Mortgage or rent	$_____	$_____
Common property fees	$_____	$_____
Utilities	$_____	$_____
Telephone, cable, and Internet	$_____	$_____
Property insurance	$_____	$_____
Property taxes	$_____	$_____
Property maintenance	$_____	$_____

Transportation Expenses	Subsistence	Comfortable
Auto loans or leases	$_____	$_____
Fuel and oil	$_____	$_____
Licensing	$_____	$_____
Maintenance	$_____	$_____
Insurance	$_____	$_____

FIGURE 3.2   Family Monthly Expenses Worksheet, continued

Personal Expenses	Subsistence	Comfortable
Food	$ _____	$ _____
Clothing	$ _____	$ _____
Pets	$ _____	$ _____
Health care	$ _____	$ _____
Dental	$ _____	$ _____
Insurances	$ _____	$ _____
School	$ _____	$ _____
Retirement plans	$ _____	$ _____
Entertainment	$ _____	$ _____
Recreation and hobbies	$ _____	$ _____
Memberships and subscriptions	$ _____	$ _____
Church	$ _____	$ _____
Credit card payments	$ _____	$ _____
Total expenses per month	$ _____	$ _____
Less other income	− $ _____	$ _____
(Spouse, investment income, or pensions)		
After tax income needed per month	$ _____	$ _____
After tax income needed per year (above number X 12 months)	$ _____	$ _____

The second consideration in making the right financial transition into your new business is of income. Does the business venture that you intend on starting have the potential to satisfy your income needs? If so, do you have enough money, or access to money, to live on until the business is capable of providing an adequate income? Once again, only you know the answers. However, one viable option is to start your new business part time while maintaining a part-time income at your current job or another job until the business is capable of supporting your entire income requirements. Additional information about making a transition into a home business can be found in Chapter 2, What Type of Home Business Should You Start, under What Are Your Home Business Options?, where you will find information about full-time, part-time, seasonal, and retirement businesses.

FINDING MONEY TO START YOUR NEW HOME BUSINESS VENTURE

Once you have taken stock of your own personal financial situation, the next step is to identify where the needed business funding will come from and what must be done to secure this funding. But, before you think about how you will finance your new business, you must first understand the three types of capital generally required to start, operate, and grow a business.

Capital

Heads up, if this is your first foray into the world of business ownership, you should know that there are generally three types of capital required to start or purchase a business—start-up capital, working capital, and growth capital. All three are important and serve their own function, but if you do not have or lack access to the first two, you would be well-advised to keep saving until you can satisfy these financing requirements. Or alternately, find a source that is willing to put up the capital needed with few demands in terms of when they want it back. Then the business has the opportunity to become stable and prosper.

Start-Up Capital

This is the money that you use to start a business or purchase an existing business or franchise. Start-up capital is needed to purchase equipment, office furniture, to meet legal requirements, to pay for training, and to purchase initial inventory. There are ways of limiting the start-up capital that you may need to get the business rolling, as you will see later in this section, but you will require some money to start or purchase a business.

Working Capital

This is the money that is needed to pay all the bills and give yourself an income until the business reaches the breakeven point. I believe that working capital is the most important, especially in the absence of adequate cash flow, which is almost always the situation with new business start-up. More than one entrepreneur has lost his or her start-up investment in a new business venture because a lack of operating capital prevented the business from reaching positive cash flow. Beyond start-up investment, working capital is needed to achieve positive cash flow. This should be the mantra of every entrepreneur thinking about starting a business.

Growth Capital

The third type of capital is growth capital, the money needed should you decide to expand your business. The reason growth capital is generally required to grow a business is that many entrepreneurs have tried unsuccessfully to expand from their current cash flow in their businesses and failed. Using cash flow places enormous financial strain on the current business and expanded business, ultimately starving both of adequate funding to stay operational.

That said, growth capital is the least important of the three, especially if your plans are not aimed at growing your business, but rather maintaining it. Lack of growth capital can become problematic for all business owners when forces beyond your control take effect. These forces can include competitors, government regulations, and general economic conciliations. For instance, you may not want to grow, but new competition that opens in your market and takes business away may necessitate growth in your own business, if for no other reason just to survive and remain viable.

Personal Savings

The next step is figuring out where the money will come from. Perhaps the best way to finance your new home business venture is by using your own personal cash savings or tapping your own personal investments. There are many reasons why I feel that this is the best way to fund your business. You stay in control of how, when, and why funds are distributed. You do not have to satisfy a doubting banker's or investor's questions and often very involved requirements. You will not feel anxious about whether or not you can get the proper funding. You do not have to worry about debt accumulation. There is no bank or investor loan and interest repayment to make each month. To fund your home business start-up personally the money can come from your bank savings account, investment certificates, retirement funds, mutual funds and stocks, or insurance policies. Be aware, however, that in some cases money that you remove from fixed certificates or retirement investments may be subject to additional personal income tax or specific penalties for early withdrawal or cancellation of the investment. It is always wise to consult with a financial planner prior to cashing, selling, or redeeming any personal investment or certificates. Also keep in mind that depending on the investment you want to liquidate you might actually be earning a higher rate of return than the interest rate that you can secure for a business start-up loan. Again, check with your financial planner and investigate all financing options and avenues available to you before cashing in investments to fund your business start-up.

You can also liquidate or borrow against other personal assets to fund a business start-up or purchase. You could, for example, sell or borrow against your boat, recreational vehicle, cottage, or antiques. At the end of the day, you will have to decide to what lengths you are prepared to go in personally financing your business ambitions. While some people are comfortable using savings and assets to fund a business dream, others are not. Only you and your family members can make that decision and commitment.

Government Business Loans

In the United States and Canada there are government programs in place to assist people in starting a new business or to provide growth funding for existing small businesses. In the United States these programs are administered thought the SBA. In Canada most small business financial aid and incentive programs are administered through the Business Development Bank of Canada. There are three financial assistance programs offered by the SBA that will be of particular interest to small business owners—Business Loans Program, Investment Programs, and Bonding Program.

1. *SBA's Business Loan Program.* These programs are available to new business enterprises with start-up funding loaned from microlending institutions (participating banks and credit unions) and guaranteed in full or part by the government. There are various levels of qualification for the Business Loans Program so check with your local SBA office for more details and to see if you qualify.
2. *SBA's Investment Program.* This program is aimed at supplying new business ventures with funding and existing small- to medium-sized businesses with venture capital that can be used to fuel growth and expansion. There are various programs available and qualifications to meet, so contact your local SBA office for details.
3. *SBA's Bonding Program.* The SBA also offers a Security Bond Guarantee (SBG) program which provides small and minority contractors with the opportunity to bid on supply and service contracts. Contact your local SBA office for details.

It should be noted that even though these government programs are in place in the United States and Canada to assist the funding needs for new and existing small business ventures, they in no way guarantee securing financial assistance. Each application is based on the potential of the venture and the people that will be managing the business. Therefore, all the usual steps are required, such as a complete business and marketing plan, if you intend to pursue government small business funding.

United States

U.S. Small Business Administration (SBA)
Financial Programs
409 Third Street SW
Washington, DC 20416
(800) 827-5722
www.sba.gov/financing/

Canada

Business Development Bank of Canada
BDC Building
5 Place Ville Marie, Suite 400
Montreal, Quebec H3B 5E7
(877) 232-2269
www.bdc.ca

Private Investors

Start-up funds can also come from private investors, but start-up financing almost always comes with strings attached. The private investor may want an incredibly high rate of interest on money loaned. The private investor may want an equity position within the business, perhaps as much as 51 percent to ensure having a controlling interest. The private investor may want to work in the business, which could lead to problems if he brings no special skills that can be capitalized upon or if your personality types prove to be combative instead of conducive. Of course, a private investor may want a combination of these conditions for funding. Therefore, if you go looking for private investors to help you float your business dream, you must be prepared to make sacrifices, such as the amount of control you want over decisions, how funding is spent, and how revenues and profits are divided. A word of caution: Don't let the fact that a person, group of people, or business is willing to throw money into your venture cloud your good judgment. Think long term, even if the prospect of fast start-up cash is tempting in the short term. If you decide to take in a private investor who wants to remain silent in the business, outside of the occasional progress meeting and so forth, then a good match between you is of less concern. However, if the private investor will be taking a more hands-on role in the business or working on a day-to-day basis, effectively making him a partner, there are more issues to consider, such as:

- You will want a lawyer to write or look over the investment and partnership agreement, and you may also want an accountant to look over the financial aspects of the deal to ensure your best interests.
- All parties should share a similar excitement for the business or concept and have similar future goals and ambitions, both personally and for the business.
- The private investor should have specific experiences and access to additional resources that can be utilized in the business.
- Both parties should live in close geographical proximity. If not, travel time and costs can quickly become problematic.

The most common way that people find investors to help finance a business start-up, expansion, or product invention is by placing a classified advertisement in their local newspapers or an industry magazine. This is true of basic deals in which small amount of capital are sought, generally less than $50,000 and almost always under $100,000. You might also want to talk to your accountant, because people looking to invest in businesses will often ask accountants to keep their ears open for interesting possibilities. You can also go online to any number of venture capital Web sites that have listings of entrepreneurs or venture capitalists that are seeking to invest in new and existing businesses.

Many of these venture capitalists are known as business angels. They are generally wealthy entrepreneurs with tons of previous business experience and provide capital in return for being part of a growing successful business. Business angels are somewhat different from your average private investor. They prefer to invest in businesses that have a successful operating track record or that have a great potential for profit because of a unique product, protected intellectual property, or verifiable market demand. The benefits of building investor relationships with business angels are numerous: Most are experienced and can be a useful addition to your business team, and they can supply low-risk capital quickly, void of the usual need for immediate principal and interest repayments.

Of course, as is the case with any partnership, there are also drawbacks, which can include a controlling interest in the business in the angel's favor, and large profit demands. Seeking out a private investor to fund your home business start-up has been proven to work, in fact, work very well provided that caution and sound judgment are practiced by all parties involved.

- Venture Directory Online, www.venturedirectory.com
- V Finance, www.vfinance.com
- NVST Inc., www.nvst.com
- National Venture Capital Association, www.nvca.org
- Canadian Venture Capital Association, www.cvca.ca

Borrowing from Family and Friends

Another way to fund your start-up is to ask well-heeled family members or friends for a loan. The downside to borrowing money from a family member or friend is the fact that although your intentions to pay back the money are, I am sure, 100 percent sound, the unfortunate fact is that many new business ventures fail. If your business venture were to fail, would you still be able to pay back the loan? If not, the relationship could be damaged beyond repair. On the other hand, many extremely successful business ventures have been built upon money that was loaned to the operator by friends and family members. One such success story that comes to mind is the three men who created the board game Trivial Pursuit. They hit up friends and family members to invest in their idea and issued *Love Stock* in the company in exchange for development and start-up money. The last time I heard, an initial

FIGURE 3.3 Sample Promissory Note

This loan agreement is by and between:

Borrower

Name _____   Address _____

City _____ State_____ Zip _____ Tel _____

Borrower (if more than one)

Name _____   Address _____

City _____ State_____ Zip _____ Tel _____

Lender

Name _____   Address _____

City _____ State_____ Zip _____ Tel _____

Lender (if more than one)

Name _____   Address _____

City _____ State_____ Zip _____ Tel _____

(Borrower's (s) name here) _____, jointly and severally, promise to pay (lender's name here) _____, the sum of $ _____, bearing interest at the rate of _____% per annum, and payable in _____ equal and consecutive monthly installments, commencing on the _____ day of each and every month thereafter until paid, with a final installment of $ _____, on the _____ day of _____, 20_____, upon which the loan shall be repaid in full with no further principal or interest amounts owing.

_____ _____   _____ _____
Borrower's Signature   Date   Borrower's Signature   Date

_____ _____   _____ _____
Lender's Signature   Date   Lender's Signature   Date

_____ _____   _____ _____
Witnessed by   Date   Witnessed by   Date

$1,000 investment made by these folks at start-up, is now worth about $3 million and climbing. If you decide to borrow from friends or family to fund your business, treat the transaction as you would if you were borrowing from a bank. Have a promissory note drawn up and signed (see Figure 3.3), noting the entire details of the agreement. Stick to your repayment schedule like glue so that you can keep friends and family just that, friends and family.

Bank Loans

Entrepreneurs with a good credit rating also have the option of applying for a business start-up loan through banks and credit unions. The business loan can be secured, meaning it is guaranteed with some other type of investment, such as a guaranteed investment certificate. Alternately, the loan can be unsecured, and the funds are advanced because of your credit worthiness. The advantage of a secured loan is that the interest rate is generally lower, often as much as 2 to 4 percent. The disadvantage of a secured loan is that many first-time entrepreneurs do not have investments or the resources to secure the loan; otherwise, they would be able to finance the start-up with the fixed investment.

Another option is to talk to your bank or trust company about setting up a secured or unsecured line of credit. Secured lines of credit also enjoy a much lower interest rate than unsecured credit lines. An advantage of a line of credit over a standard business loan is that you only have to repay interest based on the account line balance and not the principal. For example, a $30,000 line of credit fully extended with a per annum interest rate of 5 percent would require minimum monthly payments of $125 (5% x $30,000 divided by 12 months = $125). Of course, you would not be paying down the principal of the line of credit. But this flexibility is exactly what new business start-ups need: breathing space to get established and grow without the pressure of repaying high principle and interest loans every month in the early stages. If you decide to seek a business loan or line of credit, go armed with a bulletproof business and marketing plan. Bankers want to know that they are investing in sound and well-researched ideas that have the potential to succeed. Listed below are a few financial institutions with small business loan programs.

- Bank of America, www.bankofamerica.com
- Wells Fargo, www.wellfargo.com
- Royal Bank, www.royalbank.com/sme/
- Key Bank, www.key.com
- Business Finance, www.businessfinance.com

Credit Cards

Truth be known, probably more home business ventures have been started with the aid of credit cards than with any other financing. The obvious drawback here is that many credit cards have very high annual interest rates, some as much as 20 percent. This makes them a less than attractive home business financing option if you cannot pay off the balance for an extended period, but certainly it's a viable financing option just the same. If you have made the rounds to securing funding to start your business without any luck, and still feel confident about your business idea and the potential for the business to succeed, then chances are you will have to use your credit cards to get started. However, if this is the funding path you choose, try to pay off your credit cards to a zero balance while you are still working. Doing so leaves you carrying less debt, with lower monthly obligations, and the opportunity to borrow more money against the cards to start your business.

Shop for credit cards with the lowest interest charges and no annual fees and cards that reward purchases with air miles or redeemable shopping points. I would also suggest that you apply for credit cards that are specifically for small business use, such as the Visa Small Business Card. Business credit cards generally charge a lower annual interest rate and include useful small business features such as multi-cards for employees, online bookkeeping and access, business travel features, business insurance options, and no extra charges for cash advances. The following are a few popular choices for small business credit cards.

- MasterCard Business, www.mastercardbusiness.com
- Visa Small Business, www.usa.visa.com/business
- American Express Small Business, www.americanexpress.com
- Advanta Business Credit Cards, www.advanta.com
- Citi Bank CitiBusiness, www.citibank.com

Barter

Bartering your way into business is yet another option for the more creative entrepreneurial set. Barter clubs for small business owners have become extremely popular over the past decade, especially with the advent of the Internet, which allows goods and services to easily be exchange, without cash changing hands, and all with the simple click of a mouse. The premise behind barter is very basic: You offer the goods or services that you sell in exchange for goods and services that you need to operate or promote your business. For instance, if you operate a cleaning service and need printed fliers, you might barter office cleaning services with your local printer in exchange for a few thousand promotional fliers advertising your cleaning service, which can then be distributed throughout your local community to attract new business. Bartering will not supply all of the money that you need to start and operate your new homebased business, but it can greatly reduce the amount of hard cash that you need. Listed below are online barter clubs for small business owners.

- First Canadian Barter Exchange, www.barterfirst.com
- National Trade Association, www.ntatrade.com
- VIP Barter, www.vipbarter.com
- International Trade Exchange, www.itex.com
- Trade Away, www.tradeaway.com

Leasing and Renting

Leasing or renting equipment is another financing strategy that will not completely fund your entire start-up, but like barter it can greatly reduce the amount of hard cash that you need to get things rolling. First, you should understand the difference between leases and renting before you apply either cash-saving method to your business situation. When you rent equipment or tools, you do not take ownership in any form, you simply pay the going rental rate for the amount of time that you need the equipment and return the equipment when you no longer require it. When you lease, you also do not own the equipment, but you are legally bound to pay for a portion of the entire value of the equipment plus interest through scheduled lease payments, which are generally each month.

The benefits to new start-ups that rent or lease equipment, tools, or fixtures are that you do not need a lot of money up front, enabling you to save your precious money for other business building activitie such as marketing. An additional benefit of renting or leasing equipment is the fact that in most cases the total rental or lease payment is a 100 percent business expense, as opposed to a sliding scale of depreciation on owned equipment for tax purposes. When the lease or rental term is over, you can upgrade to a new model without having to worry about selling or trading in the old one, or simply turn it in and not replace the equipment if it is no longer required.

- GE Asset Funding, www.gesmallbusiness.com
- Alpha Lease, www.alphalease-equipment-leasing.com
- Lease Source, www.leasesource.net
- Optima Leasing Advisors, www.optimaleasing.com
- Lease-it, www.leaseit.biz.com

Credit Terms from Suppliers and Associates

Another way to bootstrap your way into business is to ask your new suppliers for a revolving credit account that gives you up to 90 days to pay for goods and services you need to operate your business, or that can be resold to customers for a profit. Keep in mind though that more times than not asking nicely will not work, you have to demonstrate to your suppliers that you are a worthy credit risk. This is usually accomplished by the supplier conducting a credit check on you, or through some sort of security guarantee that you provide. If your credit history is good, in some cases you can establish revolving credit accounts with suppliers that will give you up to 90 days to pay for goods, which in turn can be sold within that timeframe to generate revenues for your business and repay your suppliers. This is a favorite shoestring financing trick for many home business owners simply because it works. Where there is a will, there is a way.

PROVIDING CUSTOMERS WITH PAYMENT OPTIONS

In today's super competitive business environment, consumers have come to expect payment options, so a steadfast *cash only* payment policy is no longer acceptable. Instead, the majority of business owners must now provide customers with numerous purchase payment options—cash, check, debit card, credit card, financing options, and leasing options. The downside to most of these payment options are the fees charged back to the business—account fees, transactions fees, fixed monthly and annual equipment rentals fees, and in the case of credit cards a merchant user fee based on a percentage of the total sales value. Payment processing fees and commissions must be viewed as a cost of doing business in the 21st century, and not a reason not to provide these payment options to customers. Consumers expect, or more so correctly demand, choices on how they will pay for their purchases. If you elect not to provide payment options that meet their needs, in all likelihood they will go to one of your competitors that do offer purchase payment options that do meet their needs. You can recoup fees and commissions by including them in product and service costs when calculating pricing formulas. In most cases, the higher volume of sales from offering more purchase payment options will offset fees and commissions charged.

Cash

Cash is still the best way to get paid for your goods or services. Cash is instant. There is no processing time required. As fast as the cash comes in, you can use it to fuel growth in your business, buy more goods for resale, or pay expenses and wages to keep your business floating. There is, however, one major downside. Cash is very risky, especially for home business owners because of its proximity to you and to your family members, should you get robbed. Cash is also risky because if you lose it there is no paper transaction as proof. Collecting from your insurance company could prove difficult.

Even if you prefer not to receive cash, there will still be people that want to pay cash for their purchases. For this reason, you should purchase a good quality safe and get in the habit of making daily bank deposits during daylight hours. Additionally, make sure that you keep a low profile in terms of who you talk to about accepting cash. This should include family members, especially children.

Credit Cards

It is getting more and more difficult not to offer to customers a credit cards option, especially for business owners selling consumer goods and services. In fact, the vast majority of consumers have replaced paper money all together in favor of plastic.

The downside from a business owner's perspective is twofold. First, there are merchant fees that the

credit card company charges every time a consumer uses a credit card to pay for a purchase from your business. The merchant fee ranges from 1 to 8 percent of the total sales value, based on your arranged deal with the credit card service provider. One way to reduce the merchant rate for credit cards is to check with your local Chamber of Commerce or other small business association in your area to inquire if they provide association members with reduced credit card merchant rates. Often business associations like the Chamber of Commerce negotiate lower merchant rates with banks and credit card companies, based on the number of people who use the service. The second downside is that it takes time to process the transaction. So the cash is not available to you for a day to a week, although the time that it takes credit card companies to deposit money into a merchant's bank account has been reduced and continues to improve.

Despite these two relatively minor problems, the fact remains that if you plan on selling goods and services to consumers, you will need to accept credit cards. If you choose not to, your sales and bottom-line profits will suffer because many consumers will seek out competitors that do accept credit cards if you do not. Here are the major merchant accounts:

- Visa Financial Services, www.visa.com
- MasterCard, www.mastercard.com
- Discover Card, www.discovercard.com
- American Express, www.amercianexpress.com
- Charge Cardservices, www.charge.com
- USA Merchant Account, www.usa-merchant account.com
- Merchant Account Express, www.merchantex press.com
- Monster Merchant Account, www.monstermer chantaccount.com
- Merchant Systems, www.merchant-systems. com

Debit Cards

The majority of home business owners probably will not need to offer customers a debit card payment option unless they retail goods or services at trade show, seminars, and other direct selling events. In the event that you will be selling goods and services directly to consumers, it would be wise to set up a debit payment system with your bank so that you can offer consumers a debit card payment option along with your other payment options.

Be aware that there is a cost associated with providing debit-card payment options. First, you will need to purchase or rent the debit card processing equipment, which will set you back about $40 per month for a debit terminal connected to a conventional telephone line or about $100 per month for a cellular debit terminal; in both situations there is also the cost of the telephone service. There is also a transaction fee charged by the bank and payable by you every time there is a debit card transaction. Currently, this fee ranges from 10 cents to 50 cents per transaction, based on variables such as dollar value and frequency of use. Most banks and credit unions offer their business clients debit card equipment and services. Therefore, if you feel that offering debit-card payment options will help to increase sales, contact your bank to make arrangements to get the process up and running.

Paper and Electronic Checks

Paper and electronic checks are two other purchase payment options you might want to consider offering your customers. E-checks are especially helpful if you will be selling goods and services online or through the mail. Electronic checks work much like being paid in cash or by a debit card because once the purchase and payment amount have been verified, the funds are directly deposited into your bank account electronically. If you decide to also accept paper checks for purchases, make sure that you ask for picture identification and list the customer's driver's license number on the back of the check. Here are a few e-check payment services, which you can learn more about by logging on to their Web sites:

- Advanced Payment Solutions, www.eadvancedpaymentsolutions.com
- Internet E Checks, www.internet-e-checks.com
- Pay By Check, www.paybycheck.com
- E Check Processing, www.e-checkprocessing.com
- Alpha Check Express, www.alphacheckexpress.com

Financing and Leasing Plans

Other payment options that many consumers want are financing and leasing options, especially for expensive purchases or when buying specialized equipment. Fortunately, from a home business owner's perspective, offering customers financing and leasing options is very easy. All that is required is to establish an account with any one of a number of retail financing or leasing services that provide various consumer financing options and for just about any purchase imaginable. Featured below are the Web sites for a few retail financing and leasing services.

Retail Financing Services

- GE Consumer Financing, www.geconsumerfinancing.com
- Household Business Program, www.household.com
- Citi Retail Services Program, www.citifinancial.com
- Bank One Business Program, www.bankone.com
- Chase, www.chase.com

Retail Leasing Services

- GE Asset Funding, www.gesmallbusiness.com
- Alpha Lease, www.alphalease-equipment-leasing.com
- Lease Source, www.leasesource.net
- Optima Leasing Advisors, www.optimaleasing.com
- Lease-it, www.leaseit.biz.com

In-House Financing Options

In-house financing is yet another payment option that you may want to extend to your customers. At some point, if your customers operate their own businesses, it will be inevitable that they will want to establish a revolving trade account with your business payable 30, 60, or 90 days after purchase. In-house financing means that you are, in effect, loaning the money to your customers to make purchases from your business. If they do not pay for the purchase, you have to try and get them to pay by making demands, hiring a collection agency, or by taking them to small claims court. The steps involved in extending credit should revolve around the following:

1. Create a standard credit policy that includes acceptance and denial guidelines.
2. Develop a standard business credit application and a consumer credit application if you plan on extending credit to nonbusiness customers.
3. Conduct credit and reference checks from information supplied by customers on their credit applications.
4. Approve or decline based on credit and reference checks, and any extenuating circumstances.
5. If approved, establish an initial credit limit, along with an increase schedule should customer's credit worthiness remain in good standing.
6. If declined, work with customer to help find other ways to secure credit from a third party.
7. Bill customers on time as scheduled, keeping a watch for telltale signs of trouble.
8. Reward customers that continue to pay on time and in full with gifts, special discounts, or value-added rewards.
9. Develop a collection policy, schedule, and action plan for delinquent and nonpayment accounts.

Additional information about extending credit, credit checks, credit applications, collection agencies, and small claims courts can be found in Chapter 11, Managing Your Home Business.

TAXATION AND THE HOME BUSINESS

Operating a business from home, even a small, part-time venture has tax advantages, but with that comes the disadvantage—loads of bookkeeping paperwork and complicated tax forms to complete, especially if you have employees, are incorporated, or import and export goods. Like personal income, business earnings are taxed by multiple layers of government. In the United States these layers include the federal, state, and municipal governments. The same also holds true for Canada. Your business is taxed federally, provincially, and at the municipal level. The other constant in terms of

business taxation is that there are no constants, other than change.

The best information that you can obtain about small business and income taxation will come directly from the source. The source in the United States is the Internal Revenue Service, and in Canada the Canada Customs and Revenue Agency. Both are the government agencies that oversee federal business and income taxation.

A good accountant and bookkeeper can also help you navigate the seemingly uncharted taxation waters. And, there are also books specifically developed to help the small business owner understand and prepare tax forms. Two excellent books on small business taxation are, *Small Time Operator*, by Bernard B. Kamoroff, Bell Springs Publishing, and, *Top Tax Ideas for Small Business: How to Survive in Today's Tough Tax Environment*, by Thomas J. Stemmy, Entrepreneur Press. Both books are available online at Amazon, www.amazon.com, or Barnes and Noble, www.barnesandnoble.com, as well as at book retailers across the country. The investment into such books can prove invaluable and the cost will certainly be returned many times over through discovery of additional business deductions and tax-saving tips.

Home Business Taxation Basics

Small business taxation is complicated. You are always well advised to seek professional help in terms of business, incomes, and employee taxation issues.

Income/Business Earnings Tax

Paying tax on personal income or business earnings can be tied together if you operate a sole proprietorship or partnership that is not incorporated. As a sole proprietor the income that your business earns after expenses is your personal income, and you are taxed accordingly. If your business is incorporated, you are personally taxed on the income that you receive from the corporation, and the corporation is taxed on the profits that it earns after all expenses. Additionally, post-tax profits are taxed once again when distributed to corporation shareholders in the form of dividends. Additional information about the advantages and disadvantages associated with the various business legal structures can be found in Chapter 4, Legal Issues.

Employees

If you hire employees, you will need to obtain an employee identification number (EIN), prepare and submit employee income tax reporting forms, and withhold and remit the employees and employer's portions of Medicare, employment insurance, and Social Security. Additional information about hiring employees and employee issues can be found in Chapter 8, Building Your Business Team.

Sales Tax

Almost all states and provinces now have some sort of sales tax in place that businesses must charge on consumer purchases and then remit back to the appropriate government agency. Therefore, you will need to check with your local SBA or Business Service Center office to inquire about obtaining a sales tax number for your business. Likewise, in Canada all businesses that anticipate yearly sales to exceed $30,000 must obtain a federal Goods and Services Sales/Harmonized Sales Tax (GST/HST) number. A GST of 7 percent is charged on the sales of most products and services, collected by the business, and remitted to the federal government monthly, quarterly, or annually, depending on your bookkeeping preference. GST numbers can be obtained by contacting the Canada Customs and Revenue Agency, www.ccra-adrc.gc.ca.

Internal Revenue Service Small Business Tax Forms and Publications

The Internal Revenue Service provides small business owners with a number of free publications that explain small business taxation issues, and that can be used as a guide for completing small business and self-employed tax forms. You can order IRS small business information, tax forms, and publications in a number of ways, including:

- In person at your local IRS office
- Online at www.irs.gov/business/small
- Fax back service at (703) 368-9694
- Toll-free for mail delivery by calling (800) 829-3676

However, if you are going to download tax guides and forms online, you will need Adobe Acrobat Reader because the files are in PDF (Portable Document File) format. A free version of Acrobat Reader can be downloaded and installed in your computer at www.adobe.com. The following are the most popular and important publication guides for small business owners.

Sole Proprietorship
- Publication 334: *Tax Guide for Small Business*
- Publication 505: *Tax Withholding and Estimated Tax*
- Publication 533: *Self-Employment Tax*

Partnerships
- Publication 541: *Partnership Tax Guide*
- Publication 505: *Tax Withholding and Estimated Tax*
- Publication 533: *Self-Employment Tax*

Corporations
- Publication 542: *Corporation Tax Guide*
- S-Corporation: Form 1120S, *U.S. Income Tax Return for an S Corporation*

Limited Liability Corporations (LLC)
Limited Liability Corporations (LLC), are classified as partnerships if they have no more than two of the following corporate characteristics: Centralization of management, continuity of life, free transferability of interests, or limited liability.

- Partnership, Publication 541: *Partnership Tax Guide.*
- Corporation, Publication 542: *Corporation Tax Guide.*

Additional IRS Small Business and Taxation Publications
- Publication 583: *Starting a Business and Record Keeping*
- Publication 587: *Business Use of Your Home*
- Publication 538: *Accounting Periods and Methods*
- Publication 509: *Tax Calendar*
- Publication 1066: *Small Business Tax Workshops Workbooks*
- Publication 1635: *Understanding Your EIN (Employee Identification Number)*

- Publication 15: *Circular E, Employer's Tax Guide*
- Publication 15-A: *Supplemental Employer's Tax Guide*
- Publication 15- B: *Employer's Tax Guide to Fringe Benefits*
- Publication 946: *How to Depreciate Property*
- Publication 463: *Travel, Entertainment, Gift, and Car Expenses*
- Publication 560: *Retirement Plans for Small Business*

Canada Customs and Revenue Agency Small Business Tax Forms and Publications

Canada Customs and Revenue Agency also provides small business owners with a number of free publications that explain small business tax issues and can be used as a guide for completing small business tax and self-employed tax forms. You can order Canada Customs and Revenue Agency small business information, tax forms, and publications in a number of ways, including:

- In person at your provincial business service centers. Contact information for each business service center is available in the Resources section at the back of this book.
- Online at www.ccra-adrc.gc.ca/formspubs/request-e.html
- Or toll-free for mail delivery by calling (800) 959-2221

Additionally, in Canada all businesses that anticipate annual business revenues will exceed $30,000, are required to register for the Goods and Services Tax/Harmonized Sales Tax (GST/HST) and obtain a federal Business Number (BN), which is available through the Canada Customs and Revenue Agency Web site or provincial business service center offices. The following are the most popular and important publication guides for small business owners.

Major Guides
- *Sole Proprietorship.* Publication T4002: *Business and Professional Income*
- *Partnership.* Publication T4068: *Guide for the Partnership Information Return*
- *Corporation.* Publication T4012 T2: *Corporation Income Tax Guide*

- *Contractor.* Publication RC4110: *Employee or Contractor?*

Additional Canada Customs and Revenue Agency Small Business and Taxation Publications
- Publication RC4022: *General Information for GST/HST Registrants*
- Publication RC4027: *Doing Business in Canada GST/HST Information for Non-Residents*
- Publication RC4070: *Guide to Canadian Small Business*
- Publication T4001: *Employer's Guide—Payroll Deductions—Basic Information*
- Publication T4130: *Employer's Guide—Taxable Benefits*
- Publication 14-1: *Direct Sellers*
- Publication IT518R: *Food, Beverage, and Entertainment Expenses*
- Publication IT521R: *Motor Vehicle Expenses Claimed by Self-Employed Individuals*

Common Home Business Allowable Business Expenses

As previously mentioned, there are a number of tax advantages to operating a business from your home. They can ultimately trim your total tax bill, especially for the sole proprietor. The following are some of the most common allowable business deductions.

Communications
Communications used for business are allowable business expenses, including the cost of monthly telephone service, long distance calls, toll-free telephone lines, cellular telephones, answering services, pagers, and Internet connections. However, if you do not have a dedicated business telephone, then only a portion of the phone bill is an allowable business expense. For ease of record-keeping, as well as professionalism, it is best to have a dedicated telephone line for your home business if you can afford one.

Rent or Mortgage
A portion of your rent or mortgage will also be an allowable business expense. However, if you begin to depreciate your home, you can be subject to taxation if the home is sold or left to family in your estate.

Utilities

A portion of your total utilities equivalent to the percentage of your home that is used for business can also be written off against business earnings, including heat, electric, gas, water, and sewer.

Property Maintenance and Taxes

You can also reduce business earnings by claiming a portion of your property tax and maintenance costs.

Technology

Purchasing, renting, or leasing technology devices such as computers, printers, personal organizers, cellular telephones, software, and the costs associated with building and operating your business Web site are all business deductions. It should, however, be noted that equipment such as computers that are purchased instead of rented or leased are depreciated against business earnings overtime.

Transportation

The transportation costs directly related to operating your business are an allowable business expenses, including gas, maintenance, and a portion of lease payments.

Employee Wages and Benefits

All money paid to employees in the form of wages and benefits are an allowable business expense, regardless of whether they are employed full-time, part-time, temporarily, or seasonally.

Professional Services

The fees that you pay to lawyers, accountants, or consultants for professional advice and services relating to your business are allowable expenses and deducted from business earnings before calculating taxable income.

Marketing Costs

The money that you spend marketing and promoting your business is an allowable business expense, regardless of the type of marketing. Advertising, public relations, seminars, brochures, catalogs, simple fliers, trade shows, seminars, and more are legitimate expenses that reduce taxable business earnings.

Insurance Premiums

Business-related insurance premiums that you pay on coverage ranging from liability insurance to workers' compensation insurance are allowable business expenses.

Office Supplies

Supplies that your business consumes, such as paper, printer ink, pens, garbage bags, and paper clips are all allowable business expenses.

Interest on Loans

The interest portion that you pay on business loans is an allowable business expense. Tally up the amount of interest that you paid on all business loans during the year, and this amount comes directly off the total business revenues before calculating income.

Training and Educational Aids

Training classes, books, or audiotapes, if for business purposes, are allowable business expenses.

Additional Allowable Expenses

The above mentioned are only the tip of the allowable business expense iceberg, which is one reason why money spent for professional accounting and taxation advice is money wisely invested in your business success. Additional allowable business expenses, entirely or partly include:

- Postage and courier charges
- Business travel and entertainment
- Retirement plans
- Gifts, charity, and sponsorships
- Business and association membership dues
- Costs of business licenses, permits, and registrations
- Business cards, stationery, and letterhead

RESOURCES

📖 *Associations*

Canada Customs and Revenue Agency
333 Laurier Avenue West
Ottawa, ON K1A 0L9
(800) 959-2221
www.ccra-adrc.ga.ca

Canadian Venture Capital Association
234 Eglington Avenue East, Suite 200
Toronto, ON M4P 1K5
(416) 487-0519
www.cvca.ca

Internal Revenue Service (IRS)
Untied States Department of the Treasury
1111 Constitution Avenue, NW
Washington, DC 20224
(202) 622-5164
www.irs.gov

National Business Incubation Association (NBIA)
20 E. Circle Drive, Suite 190
Athens, OH 45701-3571
(704) 593-4331
www.nbia.org

National Venture Capital Association
1655 N. Fort Myer Drive, Suite 850
Arlington, VA 22209
(703) 524-2549
www.nvca.org

Suggested Reading

Alterowitz, Ralph, and Jon Zonderman. *Financing Your New or Growing Business: How to Find and Get Capital for Your Venture.* Irvine, CA: Entrepreneur Press, 2002.

Fishman, Stephen. *Working for Yourself: Law and Taxes for Independent Contractors, Freelancers, and Consultants.* Berkeley, CA: Nolo Press, 2002.

Pinson, Linda. *Keeping the Books: Basic Record Keeping and Accounting for the Successful Small Business.* Chicago: Dearborn Trade Publishing, 2004.

Stansell, Kimberly. *Bootstrapper's Success Secrets: 151 Tactics for Building Your Business on a Shoestring Budget.* Franklin Lakes, NJ: Career Press, 1997.

Stemmy, Thomas J. *Top Tax Ideas for Small Business: 6th Edition; How to Survive in Today's Tough Tax Environment.* Irvine, CA: Entrepreneur Press, 2004.

Web Sites

Barter News Magazine Online, www.barternews.com: Electronic publication dedicated to the barter and trade exchange industry.

CyberCash, www.cybercah.com: Online payment and financial processing options.

International Business Brokers Association, www.ibba.org: Links to more than 1,100 business brokers in North America, Asia, and Europe.

Internet e-Checks, www.internet-e-checks.com: Software enables you to accept electronic checks by mail, fax, telephone, and e-mail.

National Venture Capital Association, www.nvca.org: Association membership consists of venture capital firms and organizations who manage pools of risk equity capital designated to be invested in young, emerging companies.

Nolo, www.nolo.com: Online legal self-help information, products, services, resources, and links for consumers and business owners.

M.Y.O.B. (Mind Your Own Business) Software, www.myob.com: Small business bookkeeping and accounting software.

PayPal, www.paypal.com: Online payment processing options.

QuickBooks Software, www.quickbooks.com: Small business bookkeeping and accounting software.

Small Business Loans Online, www.smallbusinessloans.com: Online loan applications for financing new business start-ups and for financing existing businesses to help growth.

V Finance, www.vfinance.com: Directory of venture capital firms and angel investors.

CHAPTER 4

Legal Issues

F YOU'RE NOT THE TYPE OF PERSON THAT LIKES government red tape, you're going to run into some brick walls along the way to starting and operating your new home business. You will encounter red tape at every level of municipal, county, state or provincial, and federal government. The last thing that you want to do is to try to fight the system. It is much easier to conduct your research, find out what is required to start your business, and go out of your way to meet and exceed all the obligations. Go with the flow. Besides, the vast majority of laws and regulations governing businesses have been established to help, not hinder, business owners.

The following are a few of the legal issues that you will need to deal with when starting and operating your home business.

- You will have to comply with zoning bylaws and property use restrictions.
- You might have to deal with building and mechanical permits.
- You will have to select and register your business name.
- You will have to choose the legal structure that works best for your business and personal situation.
- You will need to apply for and obtain certain business licenses, permits, and certificates, depending on the type of business you operate.

- You will need to protect your intellectual property through the use of copyrights, trademarks, and patents.

As you can see, there are lots of legal issues to consider when starting a home business, and once your business is operational, there are just as many laws and regulations to satisfy. If you want to be in business, you have to become resigned to the fact that there will always be forms to complete, licenses to secure, and laws to comply with. You may as well take a proactive approach to legal issues pertaining to small business and educate yourself on the subject.

Information about selecting and working with experienced small business lawyers can be found in Chapter 8, Building Your Business Team. You can also contact the American Bar Association through its Web site at www.aba net.org or the Canadian Bar Association through its Web site at www.cba.org for information on finding a qualified small business lawyer.

HOME BUSINESS ZONING REGULATIONS

Can you legally operate a business from your current residence? Chances are you can, although probably with some restrictions. Unfortunately there are no standard, across-the-board rules set of rules on allowing businesses to operate from a residential location. Each and every community in the United States and Canada has their own home business zoning regulations and specific usage guidelines. With that said, the majority of municipalities do allow small home businesses to operate from a residence, providing the business activities do not negatively impact on neighbors and the neighborhood in general. From a zoning standpoint, the potential issues surrounding home businesses include:

- Exterior signage
- Parking
- Noise and airborne pollution
- Fire and hazardous substances
- Employees working from the home
- Client visits
- Deliveries and shipping

Long before you decide to open and operate a home business and certainly long before you start to spend money establishing one, you need to check out your local zoning rules, regulations, and restrictions. This is a very important first step. Even if you think nothing of operating your business from your home, there are zoning restrictions in every community that apply to homebased businesses. Some even require that your home be zoned and suitable for the type of business you intend to operate before a business permit or license will be issued.

With so much at stake, don't try to sidestep zoning requirements. There are ways local officials can find out. You could be caught and fined or even forced to close your business for noncompliance. If you think, "Hey, there is not way anyone will ever find out that I am running a business from my home," think again. All it takes is a few noise complaints from neighbors or a call to the zoning department from a business competitor, and it won't be long until the suits are knocking on your door, asking questions about the business that you are not running from home.

In some areas of both the United States and Canada because of the proliferation of new home business start-up and where "traditional" businesses have a strong voice and influence on local policymaking, setting up a home business can be much more difficult. This is mainly because traditional businesses operating from rented or owned commercial locations believe that the laws are inequitable and favor home business owners because they are not hindered by as much red tape in establishing and operating their businesses, and have relative tax advantages. In these areas, some business groups have successfully lobbied to make it more difficult to operate a business in a residential neighborhood, all together. In addition, even if home businesses are permitted in your neighborhood, you will usually find that certain types of business, such as automotive repair, manufacturing, and retail sales are not allowed.

Single-Family Residences

If you own or rent a single-family residence, in all likelihood you will have a much easier time of meeting zoning regulations for your home business than if you live in a multifamily complex. But even some single-family residential neighborhoods, especially affluent ones, have restrictive covenants in place limiting home business operations. Most often these restrictive covenants prohibiting home businesses are not enforced by the zoning department, but by the homeowners' association. If your home is not affected by neighborhood restrictive covenants, there are usually other restrictions in place, created and enforced by the zoning department. These typically include:

- A limit on the total amount of your home's square footage that can be used for the business purposes. It is generally indicated in percentage terms, such as 20 percent of the home's total area can be allocated for business activities.
- If exterior signage is permitted, it is almost always restricted to a certain size, style, and placement on the home or around the property.
- There are also generally restrictions on the number of employees or contractors that you can have working from your home. In some areas, only the legal owner(s) is allowed to work from the home; other areas do not even mention employee restrictions in the zoning ordinances.
- In addition to home business zoning regulations, you will also be forced to comply with building regulations and permits if you plan to

alter your home, build a secondary structure on the property, or expand the footprint of your current home. What you want to do may or may not be permitted, depending on your local building and zoning regulations.

- Environmental laws may also come into play, limiting what types of materials can be sold, stored, or disposed of by your business.
- Vehicles and equipment used in the business are items that are almost always restricted, by size, type, and number parked at the home or on the street. This also may extend to deliveries and traffic caused by clients coming to your home.

Multifamily Residences

Multifamily residential developments such as low-rise and high-rise condominiums, duplexes, town homes, mobile home parks, single-family strata communities, and cooperative buildings are much different from owned-land single-family residences in terms of a home business. The difference mainly lies in the fact that not only do you have to contend with local zoning ordnances, but also with your common property regulations, which are legally known as covenants, conditions, and restrictions (CC&Rs), that govern all aspects of individual unit use within the common development. Restrictive covenants are put into place to protect the interests of the majority of owners, rather than the interests of the individual unit owner.

In almost all situations, rules pertaining to establishing and operating a home businesses are considerably stricter than those found in your local ordinances. There are also more safety and security concerns in terms of operating a business within a multifamily residential development. Fire, crime, pollution, and noise are all valid concerns for residents of the development. If your development does allow home businesses to be operated, chances are the types of business permitted will be greatly restricted and will almost always exclude any type of manufacturing, retail sales, or businesses that necessitate clients visiting your home. Issues that will be more of a concern to you than to the strata or co-op board will be lack of storage, generally poor access, lack promotional signage, limited parking, and privacy concerns. However, there are many business ventures that are perfectly suited to a multifamily residential unit or apartment, including Internet ventures, consulting, freelance writing, bookkeeping, and photography.

Where Do You Find Out about Local Zoning Regulations?

There are two primary issues that you want to clarify in terms of starting a business from your home. First, are home businesses allowed? And second, if so what are the restrictions? The only way that you will find out for sure is to get a copy of your local zoning rules from city hall, the local public library, or from your lawyer and start investigating. Even if you discover that home businesses are permitted, you may find that some of the descriptions are vague and require further explanation. The zoning department or your lawyer should be able to clarify.

If you discover that you are not allowed to operate a business from your home, you can appeal and make a formal request to alter the zoning bylaws so that home businesses are permitted, or the type of business that you want to operate is permitted. This approach is generally successful, providing you can get the support of your immediate neighbors and are patient. It can take up to a year or more to work through all the proper channels and meetings. Do your homework in advance of any public meetings on the appeal and make sure to cover the important basics, such as parking, noise, and pollution so that you can assure city councilors and neighbors that your business will be a benefit and not a deterrent. Additional information about establishing a business at home and setting up your workspace can be found in Chapter 7, Establishing Your Home Workspace.

CHOOSING THE RIGHT BUSINESS NAME

There is much more than meets the eye when it comes time to choose and register a name for your business. You have to be forward thinking, you have to consider potential domain name matches, you have to think about the image you want to project, and you have to consider legally protecting your business name. You definitely want a business name that will describe with perfect clarity exactly what your business does or sells. In short, the business name game is an involved process that requires research and planning.

There are two basic options in terms of naming your new business. First, you can choose to name the business after your legal name, as in Joe Smith Marketing and Consulting. Second, you can choose to register and operate under a fictitious business name, such as Pacific Winds Marketing and Consulting. There is also a third option, which is to incorporate your business as a numbered company, but you will still need proper or fictitious name in conjunction with the numbered company. Most home business owners opt to create a fictitious name for their business. Once you have selected your business name, the next step is to register the business name to make sure that you can legally use the name and that no other business is operating under that name in the jurisdiction in which you register. Business name registration in the United States and Canada is covered later in this section.

Important Tips for Choosing a Good Business Name

More than anything else, your business name will promote your business and get used the most in print and verbally. So the importance of having the right business name cannot be understated. You will definitely want to test drive a few name variations by creating a short list of possible business names and then talking to family, friends, and other business people to see what they think works best relative to your business, image, products or services, and your target audience. Above all, don't rush the process. The name you choose is the name that you will have to work with for a long while. The following are some helpful tips to keep in mind when selecting a name for your new home business.

- Your business name should be descriptive so that it becomes an effective marketing tool. For instance, naming your mobile computer repair business On Call Mobile Computer Repair is far more descriptive and a much better

marketing tool than naming the business Zytech Computers.

- Your business name should be short, easy to spell, easy to pronounce, and very memorable. ABC Automotive Detailing may not be a very original business name, but it is easy to spell, pronounce, and remember, and it instantly tells people what your business does—automotive detailing. When naming your business, think visual impact and word-of-mouth referral, both rely on short, easy-to-spell and remember, descriptive names.

- Your business name should also project the appropriate image you want to project. For instance, Budget House Painting projects a low-cost image, while Opulence House Painting projects a more upscale image.

- Be forward thinking and do not limit growth opportunities because of your business name. For instance, Vancouver On Call Mobile Computer Repair greatly diminishes the effect of the business name in Dallas or New York. Keep your business name geographically universal.

- Don't order business cards, signs, and stationery until you have registered your business name. You do not want to risk making printed and marketing materials useless. It is a good idea to prepare a list of three or four alternate names when you go to file, in case your first choice is taken.

Registering a Business Name in the United States

It is important to remember that even if you want to use a specific business name you may be prohibited from doing so because someone else is already using that name for his business. Therefore, it is a good idea to have at least three names selected, your first choice and two runner-up business names. That way, if your first choice is already taken, you will have alternate options ready to go. And do not even think about operating your business without registering the business name. Otherwise, you could spend a small fortune on marketing the business and the name producing signs and stationery, produced only to discover later that another business has the legal right to the name and you must stop using it, or face legal action. Also, in some situations, you have to show proof of business name registration in order to establish bank accounts, and credit card merchant accounts. At the end of the day, there are no shortcuts. You have to select the best name for your business and register that name.

The next issue is where do you go to register your business name? It differs state by state, so check with your local SBA office or Chamber of Commerce. Generally, business name registrations are handled by the county clerk's office, but not always. However, what is uniform is the process of registering a business name. At the state level, you first conduct a business name search to make sure that no other business is using the name that you want to use. Name searches are usually included in the cost of the name registration and take a day or so or even less time if you are prepared to pay an extra fee to expedite the process. Many states also require that the business name registration be published in the local newspaper to inform consumers and other business owners of the intent to do business. This cost may or may not be included in the registration fee, so be sure to ask.

The final issue to consider when registering your business name is whether your business name also be trademarked. If you plan on expanding your business beyond your local area into other states and countries, then it is a good idea to trademark your business name at the federal level. By protecting your business name with a federal trademark, you are, in effect preventing any other business in the nation from using your exact business name. However, you should know that getting a federal trademark is a very costly process and best handled by an experienced trademark lawyer.

Registering a Business Name in Canada

Registering a business name in Canada is a very straightforward process and can be accomplished online, by mail, or in person at any provincial Canada Business Service Center location. The telephone number and Web site address for each province is shown below. Alternately, you can also register your business and business name at your local Chamber of Commerce. Consult your telephone book or log on

to www.chamber.ca to find the office closest to you. The current cost for a basic business registration is approximately $130 and must be renewed every five years. Once you have selected a business name, it can be trademarked through the Canadian Intellectual Property Office at (819) 997-1936 or www.strategis.ic.gc.ca at a cost of approximately $350, which includes filing and registration fees for a period of 15 years, at which time the trademark can be renewed.

CBSC Provincial Office Locations

Alberta
(800) 272-9675
www.cbsc.org/alberta

British Columbia
(604) 775-5525
www.smallbusinessbc.ca

Manitoba
(800) 665-2019
www.cbsc.org/manitoba

New Brunswick
(506) 444-6140
www.cbsc.org/nb

Newfoundland
and Labrador
(709) 772-6022
www.cbsc.org/nf

Northwest
Territories
(800) 661-0599
www.cbsc.org/nwt

Nova Scotia
(902) 426-8604
www.cbsc.org/ns

Nunavut
(877) 499-5199
www.cbsc.org/nunavut

Ontario
(800) 567-2345
www.cbsc.org/ontario

Prince Edward Island
(902) 368-0771
www.cbsc.org/pe

Quebec
(800) 322-4636
www.infoentrepreneurs.org

Saskatchewan
(800) 667-4374
www.cbsc.org/sask

Yukon
(800) 661-0543
www.cbsc.org/yukon

LEGAL STRUCTURE OPTIONS FOR THE HOME BUSINESS OWNER

After the decision has been made to start a home business, you have to choose the type of legal structure the business will operate under. The four most popular forms of legal structure are sole proprietorship, partnership, limited liability corporation, and corporation. The legal structure that you choose will be based on one or more of the following influences:

- Your budget and financing requirements
- The type of home business you start
- Personal liability issues
- The number of owners
- Your family situation
- Your goals and objectives for the future of your business

Ultimately, your decision will be based on what type of legal structure will best serve your specific needs, the needs of your new business, and the needs of your family. People will often choose a sole proprietorship if start-up funds are limited and if they are reasonably sure that liability issues are manageable. A partnership will be the right type of legal structure if you will be running your new business with a spouse, family member, or friend and if funds are still in short supply. A limited liability corporation or corporation will be the right choice if you have an eye towards growth and expansion, have concerns surrounding personal liability issues, or will be seeking financing or outside investors. At the end of the day, it is always a wise decision to talk to an accountant and lawyer familiar with small businesses for advice.

The Sole Proprietorship

The sole proprietorship is by far the most common type of home business legal structure for many reasons, but mainly because it is the simplest and least expensive to get started and maintain. In a nutshell, what a sole proprietorship business structure means is that your business entity and your personal affairs are merged together and become one—a single tax return, personal liability for all accrued business debts and actions, and control of all revenues and profits. However, as easy and straightforward as a sole proprietorship is to start and operate, it is still important for you to separate your business finances from your personal household and family finances as much as possible, mainly for record-keeping and income tax reasons. For instance, interest payments on business loans and credit cards used for business purchases are 100 percent tax deductible, while interest payments on personal loans and credit cards used for personal purchases are not tax deductible. Therefore, it is important for the sole proprietor to

establish separate bank accounts, one for the business and one for personal use, and to separate other financial matters as much as possible.

Sole Proprietorship Advantages

The advantages of a sole proprietorship are many, especially for cash-strapped entrepreneurs looking to get started quickly so that they can begin to earn revenues and income. They include:

- The process of establishing a sole proprietorship is so simple and inexpensive that you can decide to start a business today and be open for business tomorrow. A sole proprietorship can be started, altered, bought, sold, or closed at any time very quickly and very inexpensively.
- You have complete control over your business and any revenues and profits that the business generates.
- Outside of routine business registrations, permits, and licenses, there are few legal forms required or government regulations to comply with.

Sole Proprietorship Disadvantages

Like anything good in life, there are also some disadvantages. The biggest is unquestionably the issue of personal liability. The owner of the sole proprietorship (business) is 100 percent liable for any number of business activities gone wrong, including the risk of losing any and all personal assets—investments, real estate, and automobiles—as a direct result of successful litigation or debts accrued by the business. Unlike corporations that have built-in protection mechanisms that partly or entirely protect the principle of the business against personally liability, sole proprietorships have none. Additional disadvantages of the sole proprietorship include:

- It can be more difficult to secure business start-up and growth funds from banks, government sources, and private investors due to the lack of a formal organization and with a legal entity that is not a person.
- Often businesses that are not incorporated or limited liability corporations are not viewed as serious business contenders, which can play

against you when bidding for work against businesses that are incorporated.

- When it is time to sell the business, sole proprietorships almost always sell for equipment and inventory value, with little, if anything, paid for goodwill. In fact, in most cases when the proprietor decides to close shop, the business is shut down altogether.

The Partnership

A partnership is another popular type of low-cost legal business structure. It allows two or more people to start and own a business, and each partner can specialize in her area of expertise within the business. However, all—and I repeat all—partnerships should be based on a written partnership agreement, not simply a verbal agreement, even if the partners are friends, family, or spouses. The partnership agreement should address all of the usual hot buttons, such as:

- The amount of money each partner is to invest initially, as well as ongoing capital infusions as needed.
- Clearly defined responsibilities and duties for each partner.
- An exit strategy for each partner should the need arise.

Because many partnership agreements are informal, the lack a formal agreement can spell big trouble for one or all partners should disagreements that cannot be resolved arise or should one or more of the partners die or want out of the business. Also as in a sole proprietorship, business profits, split among partners proportionate to their ownership, are treated as taxable personal income.

Partnership Advantages

Perhaps the biggest advantage of the partnership legal structure is the fact that it enables like minded people with similar goals the ability to collectively assemble enough financial and physical resources to start or to purchase an existing home business quickly and easily. The start-up investment, financial risks, and work are shared by more than one person, which allows each partner to specialize within the business

for the benefit of the collective team. Additional advantages of the partnership include:

- The borrowing capacity of two or more people is generally greater than that of each individual separately, which in most cases means that it is easier for two or more partners in a business to borrow a greater amount of start-up or growth capital.
- The cost of establishing a partnership is minimal, financial risks are shared equally, and there are very few regulations governing who or how many people can legally form a partnership. And bookkeeping and record keeping requirements are basic and on par with a sole proprietorship.
- The partnership legal structure affords great opportunities for family members to work together building a business, with each equally responsible for the ultimate success or failure of the business.

Partnership Disadvantages

Unfortunately, partnerships have a number of disadvantages, with the biggest that each partner is legally responsible, i.e., personally liable, for the other partner's actions in the business, and even outside of the business in terms of some financial issues. Why? Because a partnership offers the owners of the business, regardless of the percentage of ownership, no legal protection. Each partner is equally responsible personally for the businesses debts, liabilities, and actions because the business is not a separate legal entity like a corporation. Liability issues can also extend to each partner's family members, especially spouses because of property and assets owned jointly in the marriage. What this means is that if you are in business with someone else and the business fails, creditors can take legal action to seize assets such as your home, to recoup their loans or debts, even if your home is co-owned by your spouse. If liability issues are a major concern, the business can be formed under a limited partnership, which is structured to limit liability and provides each partner some protection from personal liability issues. Additional disadvantages of a partnership include:

- Partners do not always agree on everything, and disagreements can cripple the decision-making process, resulting in loss of productivity, profitability, and even closure of the business.
- A general partnership ends upon the death, or withdrawal of one of the partners. So unless succession and continuity has been planned for and included in the written partnership agreement, the partnership and business are dissolved from a legal perspective.

The Corporation

The third type of business structure, and the most complicated for the home business owner is the corporation. When you form a corporation, you create a separate and distinct legal entity from the shareholders, the owners of the corporation. The shareholders of the corporation can include you, family members, business partners, and private investors. Because the corporation becomes its own entity, it pays taxes, assumes debt, can legally sue, can be legally sued, and, as a tax-paying entity, must pay taxes on its taxable income (profit) prior to paying any dividends to the shareholders. Also, unlike a general partnership or sole proprietorship, because the corporation is a legal entity, the company's finances and financial records are completely separate from your finances and the finances of the other shareholders. Because the corporation is a legal entity, people must be elected by the shareholders to conduct business and makes decisions on behalf of the corporation through a resolution process. Once authorized, the corporation officers then have the power to make all decisions for the company in terms of the day-to-day operations, borrowing money, making purchases, and so forth.

Corporation Advantages

Without question, the biggest advantage to incorporating your home business is the fact that you can greatly reduce your own personal liability. Because the corporation is its own entity, can legally borrow money, and be held accountable in a number of matters from a legal standpoint, in effect, this releases you from personal liability. For instance, if you are sued, chances are the corporation will be named in the lawsuit and not you. If the corporation borrows a substantial amount of money and cannot repay the debt, you will not be held responsible for the repayment of the debt personally unless you have personally guaranteed the loan.

It is worth noting, however, that even the seemingly impenetrable protection that a corporation offers to business owners in terms of personal liability for corporate debts and legal actions can be breached in a number of ways. First, lenders generally require home business owners, especially of businesses that are new and lack a track record of profitability, to personally guarantee any money that is loaned to the corporation. Second, if all corporate formalities and record-keeping responsibilities are not followed to the proverbial T, the directors of the corporation can be held legally, financially, and personally responsible for the actions of the corporation.

Other advantages of the corporation include:

- It is generally much easier to arrange financing and raise money for business expansion.
- Because a corporation is its own legal entity, it is very easy to sell the business or a portion of it, gift shares, and continue business should one or more shareholders die.
- Customers, business partners, and bankers generally see corporations as more stable than a sole proprietorship.

Corporation Disadvantages

The major disadvantage associated with a corporation is double taxation. Corporation profits are taxed, and then the same profits are taxed again in the form of personal income tax when distributed to the shareholders as a dividend. Still, double taxation can be significantly reduced if the shareholders are also employees in the corporation drawing a wage. These wages provide personal income and decrease the corporation's taxable profits. Unfortunately, the same does not hold true if the corporation loses money. Financial losses cannot be used as a personal income tax deduction for shareholders.

Additional disadvantages of the corporation include:

- Of the business structures discussed in this chapter, corporations are the most expensive to form and maintain.

Corporations require lots of paperwork to start and maintain. There are government regulations and rules that must be followed, at the state and federal level.

As with any group, conflicts or disagreements among the stockholders in a small corporation, such as a home business, can disrupt the decision-making process and result in reduced productivity, profitability, or even the demise of the business.

Online Corporation Filing Services in the United States

- Corp America, www.corpamerica.com
- CorpoMax, www.corpomax.com
- Biz Filings, www.bizfilings.com
- The Company Corporation, www.corporate.com
- Active Filings, www.activefilings.com

Online Corporation Filing Service in Canada

- Ontario Business Central, www.ontariobusinesscentral.com
- Canadian Corp, www.canadiancorp.com
- Corporation Center, www.corporationcenter.ca
- Corporation Creation, www.corporationcreation.com
- New Business Now, www.newbusinessnow.com

The Limited Liability Corporation

A limited liability corporation, a relatively new legal business structure, combines many of the characteristics of a corporation with those of a partnership. A limited liability corporation provides protection from personal liabilities like a corporation, but the tax advantages of a partnership. Limited liability corporations can be formed by one or more people, called LLC members, who organize a legal entity that is separate and distinct from their own personal affairs in most respects.

The advantages of a limited liability corporation over a corporation or partnership include:

- Protection from personal liability that partnerships do not provide
- Less expensive to form and maintain than a corporation
- Fewer rules and regulations than a corporation

- Simplified taxation rules in comparison to a corporation

Because of the advantages that limited liability corporations offer over partnerships and corporations, limited liability corporations have become the fastest growing form of business structure in the United States, and one that is embraced by home business owners who are seeking an affordable way to limit their personal liability and protect their assets.

Online Limited Liability Corporation Filing Services

- My Corporation, www.mycorporation.com
- Fast Corps, www.fastcorps.com
- Small Business Incorporator, www.smallbusinessincorporator.com
- USA Corporation Services, www.usa-corporate.com
- Executive Corporation, www.executivecorporation.com

BUSINESS LICENSES, PERMITS, AND PROFESSIONAL CERTIFICATIONS

Regardless of the fact that you will be operating from your home there are certain business licenses, permits, and certificates that you will need to legally operate your business. However, the types of licenses, permits, and certificates required will vary depending on the kind of business that you will be running and in the area where you establish the business. The best way to find out what is needed in your area and for the type of business that you intend to operate is to contact your local chapter of the Chamber of Commerce or city hall. You can log on to the United States Chamber of Commerce Web site at www.chamber.com and to the Canadian at www.chamber.ca to find the nearest chapter.

If you are thinking about skipping the required licenses and permits, you should reconsider. In some cases, you will be required to show various licenses, permits, or registrations to open a bank account, apply for loans, and purchase goods for resale. Also businesses operating without licenses can be subject to fines, and in extreme cases to closure if caught.

Business License

Almost all municipalities in the United States and Canada require home business owners to obtain a business license to operate their business legally. The cost of your business license can vary depending on three factors—your geographic location, your expected sales, and the type of business. Once again, city hall or your local Chamber of Commerce will be able to assist you in obtaining a business license.

Building Permits

If you plan on substantially renovating or altering the footprint of your home to accommodate your new business or altering your home's mechanical systems, you will probably need to apply for and obtain a building permit and possibly electrical and plumbing permits prior to carrying out the work.

Vendors Permits

Most U.S. states and Canadian provinces also require home business owners to obtain vendor permits for the resale of goods and certain services. To find out if you will need to obtain a vendor permit, contact your local SBA office or Chamber of Commerce.

Professional Certification

In addition to business licenses and permits, professionals such as dentists, veterinarians, and plumbers practicing or operating their businesses from home will also be required to obtain relevant certification in order to provide professional services. Professional and trade certificates information is available through applicable professional groups and trade associations and are generally issued at the state or provincial level.

Home Occupation Permit

In addition to a business license, many cities also now require home business operators to apply for and obtain a home occupation permit, which legally enables a business to be run from the residence specified in the permit. Your local zoning bylaws will indicate if you will require a home occupation permit and the requirements that must be satisfied to obtain one. Contact city hall or the city planning department to obtain a copy of your current zoning and land use bylaws.

Sales Tax Permits

Depending on the type of business you operate and the location of the business, you might also need to obtain a sales tax permit. And in Canada, you will be required to obtain a goods and services taxation number if your expected sales will exceed $30,000 per annum. Business taxation information is available in the United States through the Internal Revenue Service, www.irs.gov, and in Canada through the Canada Customs and Revenue Agency, www.ccra-adrc.gc.ca.

Additional Permits and Licenses

By now you're probably thinking the world has gone permit and regulation crazy, and you'd be right on the money. There may be other licenses, permits, certificates, and laws to comply with in terms of starting and operating your home business. These might include fire safety inspection permits, hazardous materials handling permits, import/export certificates, police clearance certificates, environmental laws, and laws pertaining to food and drug safety administered through the U.S. Food and Drug Administration (FDA). Keep in mind that the obligation is on the home business owner to find out the laws and regulations that must be followed and the relevant permits and registrations that will be required.

PROTECTING YOUR INTELLECTUAL PROPERTY

Intellectual properties can consist of a training manual that you have developed for your sales staff, a slogan that you use to help brand your business, or a product or process that you have invented. In short, intellectual properties are unique to your business and very valuable assets that are well worth legally protecting.

Depending on the type of intellectual property you want to protect, you can employ legally registered and documented copyrights, trademarks, or patents. Copyrights, though automatic each time a new piece of work has been created by the author, protect your written words, photographs, songs, and other original works. Trademarks are used to protect your brand and distinguish your products or services from a competitor's products or services. Patents are used by inventors to prevent other people from copying or benefiting from their inventions without permission.

Copyright Protection

The first, least expensive, and simplest form of intellectual property protection is the copyright. A copyright is a legal right given to creators of original works such as books, poems, lyrics, photographs, and paintings. The creators have exclusive right to publish, sell, or reproduce their works or to determine through agreement who gets the right to publish, sell, or reproduce their works. In the United States and Canada when you create an original work, it is automatically copyright protected, unless the work was created as an employee or as a work for hire, in which case the employer owns the copyright. Copyrights can be used to protect the following types of original works:

- Books, journals, and maps
- Song lyrics and musical scores
- Sculptures, paintings, and photographs
- Visual films and audio recordings.
- Computer programs, databases, and software code.

From the home business owner's perspective, copyrights would protect marketing brochures, reports, and the advertisements that you create to promote your goods or services. However, it is important to remember that if you have business, marketing, or promotional materials created for your business by others, you will want to make sure that it is clearly spelled out that you own the copyright to the work. If not, every time you use the material in your business the copyright holder could charge you a royalty or prohibit you from using it entirely. Copyrights protect only works that can be presented in a fixed format, not ideas you may have, or facts that you have researched and recorded for your business. In the United States for works created after 1977, the copyright lasts for the life of the author plus 70 years, and in Canada the copyright lasts for the life of the author plus 50 years. Copyrighted materials are generally accompanied by the following symbol ©. Use the following contact information to register a formal copyright.

United States
United States Copyright Office
Library of Congress
101 Independence Avenue SE
Washington, DC 20559-600
(202) 707-3000
www.copyright.gov

Canada
Canadian Intellectual Property Office
Place du Portage 1
50 Victoria Street, Room C-229
Gatineau, Quebec K1A 0C9
(819) 997-1936
www.strategis.is.ca/sc_mrksv/cipo/

Trademark Protection

A trademark can be a word, name, symbol, sound, or any combination of these that identifies your product or service and distinguishes it from your competitors' products or services. For instance, McDonald's trademarked golden arches are very distinguishable from Burger King's trademarked burger with a crown. Yet both companies sell fast food and market to a similar target customer. Trademarked materials are generally accompanied by a "TM" or "®" symbol. Trademarks can be applied for on a state or federal level. A federal trademark is more expensive, but it does provide national protection in all states and U.S. territories. A state trademark only provides protection in the state in which the trademark was registered and granted. If you plan on expanding your business beyond your current state, the extra cost to register a federal trademark is definitely worth it.

You have two options in terms of searching and registering a trademark. The first option is to do the job yourself, just be aware that this is a time consuming process that involves lots of paperwork and forms. The second option is to hire a trademark agent or lawyer to conduct the trademark search and complete the registration process. This too has a downside, which is that the process is very costly and can be more than $5,000 for a federal trademark.

In Canada you can contact the Canadian Intellectual Property Office to start the trademark search and registration process.

Untied States

United States Patent and Trademark Office
USPTO Contact Center
Crystal Plaza 3, Room 2C02
PO Box 1450
Alexandria, VA 22313-1450
(800) 786-9199
www.uspto.gov

Canada

Canadian Intellectual Property Office
Place du Portage 1
50 Victoria Street, Room C-229
Gatineau, Quebec K1A 0C9
(819) 997-1936
www.strategis.is.ca/sc_mrksv/cipo/

Patent Protection

A patent is a document protecting the rights of the inventor and offers the inventor exclusive rights to his creations. In the United States patents are granted and issued by the U.S. Patent and Trademark Office; in Canada patents are granted and issued by the Canadian Intellectual Property Office. The term *Patent Pending* means that a formal patent has not yet been awarded and is used by the inventor to let consumers know that a patent has been applied for. Applying for a patent is both time consuming and costly and best left to a patent agent or lawyer. In both, the United States and Canada the life of the patent is 20 years from the filing date. That gives the inventor the right to exclude others from making, using, selling, offering for sale, or importing the invention into the United States, Canada, or in any country where you have applied for and received a patent for that time. Patents are only effective within the country, and its territories, in which the patent was filed, granted, and issued. But patents can be filed individually in most countries, regardless of citizenship. Long before you decide to patent your product invention or process, you are well advised to conduct a market feasibility study to ensure that not only will there be a demand for your invention, but also that the process can be financially feasible, due to the extremely high costs associated with applying for and receiving a patent. The U.S. and Canadian

patent offices both provide a list of registered patent agents that can be contracted with for patent filings. For the very brave, you can choose to do it yourself.

Untied States

United States Patent and Trademark Office
USPTO Contact Center
Crystal Plaza 3, Room 2C02
PO Box 1450
Alexandria, VA 22313-1450
(800) 786-9199
www.uspto.gov

Canada

Canadian Intellectual Property Office
Place du Portage 1
50 Victoria Street, Room C-229
Gatineau, Quebec K1A 0C9
(819) 997-1936
www.strategis.is.ca/sc_mrksv/cipo/

RESOURCES

☞ *Associations*

American Bar Association
740 15th Street NW
Washington, DC 20005-1019
(202) 662-1000
www.abanet.org

American Intellectual Property Law Association
2001 Jefferson Davis Highway, Suite 203
Arlington, VA 22202
(703) 415-0780
www.aipla.org

Canadian Bar Association
500-865 Carling Avenue
Ottawa, ON K1S 5S8
(800) 267-8860
www.cba.org

International Bar Association
271 Regent Street
London, UK W1B 2AQ
44-020-7629-1206
www.ibanet.org

U.S. Small Business Administration (SBA)
409 Third Street SW

Washington, DC 20416
(800) 827-5722
www.sba.gov/indexbusplans.html.

📖 Suggested Reading

Fishman, Stephen. *Working for Yourself: Law and Taxes for Independent Contractors, Freelancers, and Consultants.* Berkeley, CA: Nolo Press, 2002.

Hupalo, Peter I. *How to Start and Run Your Own Corporation: S-Corporation for Small Business Owners.* Chicago: HCM Publishing, 2003.

Norman, Jan. *What No One Ever Tells You About Starting Your Own Business: Real Life Start-Up Advice from 101 Successful Entrepreneurs.* Chicago: Upstart Publishing Company, 1999.

Spadaccini, Michael. *Ultimate Great Big Book on Forming Corporations, LLCs & Partnerships.* Irvine, CA: Entrepreneur Press, 2004.

Steingold, Fred S. and Ilona M. Bray. *Legal Guide for Starting and Running a Small Business, 7th Edition.* Berkeley, CA: Nolo Press, 2003.

💻 Web Sites

Canada Legal, www.canadalegal.com: Thousands of Canadian laws organized by categories, including small business.

Entrepreneur Online, www.entrepreneur.com: Online small business resource center providing entrepreneurs with information, advice, products, services, and resources.

Licensing Industry Merchants' Association, www.licensing.org: Representing 1,000 member companies and individuals engaged in the marketing of licensed properties, both as agents and as property owners; manufacturers, consultants, publications, lawyers, accountants, and retailers in the licensing business.

Nolo, www.nolo.com: Online legal self-help information, products, services, resources, and links for consumers and business owners.

Ontario Business Central, www.ontariobusinesscentral.com: Canadian business registration and incorporation services.

SBA Business Law in the United States, www.businesslaw.gov: Legal and regulatory information for small business owners.

Training Registry, www.trainingregistry.com: National online directory listing professional business, management, and employee training consultants.

USA Corporation Services, www.usa-corporate.com: Online incorporation products and services.

CHAPTER 5

Home Business Insurance

WHAT TYPE OF INSURANCE DO YOU NEED to protect your home, assets, business, family, and clients? The answer will depend greatly on the type of business that you operate, the products that you sell, and the services you provide. But regardless of what you do and sell, one thing is for sure—if you operate a business from your home, you need the protection and peace of mind that home business insurance provides.

Many home business owners wrongly assume that the insurance they already have in place to protect their home and its contents will also cover business activities they engage in from home. This could not be further from the truth. In fact, otherwise normal, run-of-the-mill property damage or liability claims can be rejected by insurers if a business is operating from the home, but not included or fully disclosed in the insurance policy. From the insurance companys' perspective, they cannot take the risk of insuring what they do not know about, nor should they be required to. For instance, your existing homeowner's insurance policy probably provides insurance coverage that protects you in the event that a relative accidentally takes a nasty tumble on your icy driveway. But don't expect that the same insurance coverage will be extended to a client visiting your home on business who takes the same nasty tumble. What if your home burns to the ground because of faulty equipment used in your home business? Once again, do not expect your insurance policy to cover the damage unless you have specifically informed the insurance company that you operate a business from home and this is reflected in your policy, coverage, and premiums.

The vast majority of home businesses are registered as sole proprietorships. If there is a claim made against your business that is successfully litigated by the plaintiff, you could be held personally liable. In all likelihood the plaintiff would attempt to seize your and your immediate family's financial assets. So you can see the importance of being fully insured when operating a business from home. If you rent the home or apartment from which your business operates, do not think that this gets you off the hook. In fact, it places you in the position of not only having to obtain separate home business insurance, but also having to disclose fully any and all business activities to your landlord's insurance company to ensure your and its interests are protected.

Don't be afraid if you find that your lack of knowledge about home business insurance and insurance in general is causing frustration or be intimidated by the thought of having to figure out the ins and outs of insurance. This chapter of the *Ultimate Home Business Handbook* will help demystify home business and other insurance coverage by featuring the most common types of business insurance, why they are needed, and the resources to help you find additional information or suitable coverage for your individual needs.

WORKING WITH INSURANCE AGENTS AND BROKERS

You will quickly discover that tracking down the right insurance for your specific needs can be a very time intensive and frustrating endeavor because of the sheer number of insurance companies, coverage types, and programs available to home business owners both in the United States and Canada. For that reason, don't chance going it alone and getting the wrong insurance, paying too much, or spending too much time on it. Instead, enlist the services of a qualified and licensed insurance agent or broker to do the research and legwork for you. Not only will the agent be able to decipher insurance legalese into easily understandable, plain English for you, but she will also be able to find the best coverage for your individual needs and at the lowest cost. Keep in mind though that the agent you select should be knowledgeable about insurance needs specific to the home business owner because they are substantially different from that of the storefront retailer, manufacturer, distributor, franchisee, or general contractor.

To find a suitable insurance agent, you can check with business associations such as your local Chamber of Commerce or call other home business owners in your area to inquire about the type of insurance coverage they carry and their insurance agent. You might also want to check with specific industry associations; they often offer members insurance programs and packages that can be purchased at lower costs due to volume. You can also go online to find a qualified insurance agent or broker. In the United States, you can contact the Independent Insurance Agents and Brokers of America at www.iiaa.org. This non profit association offers a free online find-an-agent search service on its Web site, which is indexed geographically. In Canada, you can contact the Insurance Brokers Association of Canada at www.ibac.ca. This non profit association also offers visitors access to a free online directory that geographically lists more than 25,000 licensed and certified insurance agents and brokers across Canada.

HEALTH INSURANCE

Home business owners have lots to do—prospecting, selling, creating advertisements, bookkeeping, and attending meetings. The last thing you want to think about is your health. Unfortunately, it must be one of the first things that you consider when starting a home business. The ever-spiraling costs of health care means that without health insurance, paying for an unplanned trip to the hospital can easily put your business future in jeopardy. There are substantial differences in health care services and insurance for home business owners in the United States and Canada. The insurance concerns for each is highlighted below.

Health Insurance in the United States

Home business owners have access to two types of health insurance—fee-based health services plans or managed health care plans. Under fee for health services plans, you choose the medical professional and he submits his bill directly to the health insurer for payment, or you pay for the medical services and file a claim for reimbursement from the health insurer. Under the managed care health insurance system, you are treated by a medical practitioner that belongs to the health maintenance organization (HMO) that underwrites the health insurance plan.

Regardless of the health insurance plan you opt for, the major stumbling block for most would-be entrepreneurs is health insurance premiums, which can be staggering. One built-in safeguard for entrepreneurs that previously belonged to a health insurance plan provided by their employers is COBRA, an acronym for the Consolidated Omnibus Budget Reconciliation Act. Adopted in 1985, the act states that employers with 20 or more employees must let employees and their dependents keep their group health coverage for a minimum of 18 months, and in some situations up to 36 months, after they leave their employment. Sometimes employees that worked for employers with less than 20 employees also qualify. The act states that you have the right to pay the current cost of coverage, which is usually much less costly than purchasing individual health insurance. Another health insurance option is to join your spouse's health insurance plan if he is covered where he works and pay group rates instead of individual rates. If your health is considered very good, you might consider obtaining catastrophic health insurance coverage. Under this type of plan you pay for all visits to your doctor for minor treatments, but if you fell seriously ill, that is had a catastrophic illness, your health insurance would kick in and cover medial costs and the costs associated with recovery. You can also dramatically reduce health insurance premiums by increasing the deductible you pay. The higher your deductible, the lower your health insurance premiums will be. Of course, the risk of a higher deductible is unforeseen multiple visits to medical practitioners over a short period of time.

Regardless of the health insurance plan you select, the fact remains that your good health is your single largest asset and must be protected. Georgetown University Health Policy Institute publishes electronic and print consumer guides for getting and keeping health insurance for all 50 states and the District of Columbia. The guides are available free online at www.healthinsuranceinfo.net.

Health Insurance in Canada

The health care system and health insurance situation in Canada is much different from that in the United States. First, the cornerstone of the health care system in Canada is a legislated health act guaranteeing universal access. This means that all citizens of Canada have equal access to necessary medial services. Second, the health care system in Canada is publicly funded through the collection of federal and provincial taxes and provincial medical services premiums and is administered both federally and by provincial government agencies.

It should be noted that if you travel outside of your home province within Canada, there are limits on the medical services and benefits you can receive. If you travel to the United States or internationally on business or pleasure, you will need to obtain third-party health insurance to provide medical coverage in the event of accident, disease, or illness. Likewise, people traveling to Canada that are not Canadian citizens will also have to obtain third-party health care insurance if their current provider does not cover out-of-country medical services and expenses. Blue Cross and certain groups such as the Canadian Automobile Association provide Canadians that travel out of the country with third-party health insurance. More information about Canadian health care can also be found online at www.hc-sc.gc.ca, the Web site operated by Health Canada featuring health care information, resources, and links of interest.

WORKERS' COMPENSATION INSURANCE

Workers' compensation insurance serves two primary functions. First, it protects employees injured on the job by providing short- and in some cases long-term financial benefits as well as by covering medical costs and rehabilitation costs directly resulting from the on-the-job injury. Second, workers' compensation insurance protects employers from claims by employees injured while on the job. In the United States and Canada, workers' compensation insurance is mandatory for all the people your business employs regardless if they are full-time, part-time, or seasonal. If you have no employees and operate your business as a sole proprietorship or partnership entity with one or more owners, workers' compensation insurance is not mandatory; unless your business is incorporated, officers and any employees must be covered by workers' compensation insurance.

Workers' compensation rates are based on industry classification; generally, the more dangerous the work, the higher the workers' compensation premiums you pay on each employee's taxable earnings. The more claims for workers' compensation that your business files, the higher your rates will go. Workers' compensation classifications, forms, and guidelines can be especially confusing for first-time entrepreneurs to figure out. Fortunately information about workers' compensation coverage can be found by visiting the U.S. Department of Labor Office of Workers' Compensation Programs online at www.dol.gov/esa/owcp-org.htm. This Web page has links to all states and the District of Columbia explaining workers' compensation rules and regulations. In Canada, you can log on to www.awcbc.org. The Association of Workers' Compensation Boards of Canada, which provides links to all provincial and territorial worker compensation offices.

DISABILITY INSURANCE

If you were sick or hurt and could not work, would you have the ability to pay your business expenses, pay someone else to keep the business going, and pay yourself an income? Given that the majority of home business owners are sole operators of their businesses, chances are you would not. Disability insurance makes payments to you if a physical illness, mental illness, or bodily injury prevents you from working. Most people working are at an age when they are more likely to become disabled than die. Therefore, like life insurance, disability insurance is certainly something that every home business owner should consider carrying. Disability insurance will provide an income for you in the event that you are unable to work or conduct business because of an injury. There are basically two types of disability policies—short-term and long-term:

1. *Short-Term Disability.* This type of disability policy generally has a waiting period of 30 days after you have become disabled before you can collect benefits, and a maximum benefit period of up to 24 months before the full or partial benefits expire.
2. *Long-Term Disability.* This type of policy has a waiting period ranging from 30 to 180 days after becoming disabled before you can collect benefits and a maximum term that can range from 24 months to life. Of course, the longer the potential to collect benefits in the event of a disability, the higher the premiums you will be required to pay.

In addition to the length of disability policy that suits your needs best, the following are a few more important points to consider when purchasing disability insurance:

- Be sure to have a cost of living clause built into your disability policy, that is your disability benefits increase proportionally with the consumer price index. You will pay a higher premium for this feature, but should disaster strike, your disability benefits will keep in pace with the increases in the cost of living for the duration of the claim.
- Consider getting professional overhead expenses coverage added to your disability policy.

This coverage reimburses you for employee salaries, property tax, equipment and tool depreciation, and other fixed and non-fixed overheads.

- Tell your insurance agent that you want your disability coverage to include partial disabilities, which enables you to collect partial benefits while working part-time in your business if you cannot return to full-time active duty.
- Build in a clause that gives you the right to increase your disability insurance benefits as your business and income grows. This is known as an additional purchase option and can be extended to include key employee disability insurance as well.

Additional information regarding disability insurance can be found on the About Disability Insurance Web site at www.about-disability-insurance.com. Free online quotes for disability insurance for the United States can be found at www.disability-insurance-quotes-online.com and for Canada at www.getinsurance.ca.

LIFE INSURANCE

Life insurance pays out a benefit claim only if you or the insured policyholder dies. Whether you are self-employed or work for someone else, the basic function of life insurance remains the same: provide financial protection and stability to the beneficiaries named in the life insurance policy in the event that you die. Like most other forms of insurance, you have options. With life insurance these options come in two basic packages: term life and permanent, or sometimes called whole life insurance. Term insurance is life insurance with a fixed death benefit amount, while permanent insurance often includes a death benefit amount and a savings element or cash value to the policy as well. Of course, there are further sub-options available for both basic types— the amount of death benefit, the length of the policy, and the policy or savings benefit feature.

So what type of life insurance is best for you? The answer greatly depends. Most of you have probably had advice about each type of life insurance and why one is better than the other. At the end of the day, the best life insurance is the one that best suits your needs, your family needs, your business needs, and your financial situation.

Term Life Insurance

Term insurance is the most basic form of life insurance. It provides financial protection for a specific or set amount time, such as 10 or 15 years. Term life insurance is relatively cheap to buy and readily available, providing your current health is good. On the downside, on expiration of the term life policy, there is no cash or savings value built up in the account. The premiums that you paid over the term of the policy have no cashable value and were solely used to cover the costs of insuring the death benefit amount of the policy and nothing else. Entrepreneurs with limited financial resources right now should view purchasing term life insurance to protect your family as much better than no insurance at all. Additional benefits associated with purchasing term life insurance include:

- Simplicity—if the insured person dies, the policy pays out the stated death benefit to the beneficiary(s).
- Term life insurance is widely available and very straightforward, making getting comparative quotes very easy, especially if you compare prices and shop for term life insurance online.
- Term life insurance is very inexpensive. You can carry it for the times in your life when it is the most important and beneficial to do so, such as while you have children living at home and while you have a mortgage on your home.

Express Life Insurance Direct offers visitors to its Web site free information about life insurance and free online quotes. Its Web site is located at www.express-life-insurance.com.

Permanent or Whole Life Insurance

Permanent or whole life insurance provides long-term financial protection for policyholders in two ways, because it includes both a death benefit and some sort of cash savings or cashable benefit value that is built up over time. Due to the fact that money is built up in the policy or account, the monthly premiums tend to

be much higher than term life insurance. Benefits associated with purchasing permanent or whole life insurance include:

- Permanent life insurance coverage is guaranteed for your entire life, with fixed premiums that cannot increase if you pay the amount outlined in the plan.
- Depending on the plan, you can withdraw some or all of the premiums you have built from the policy.
- Permanent life insurance programs can be forced savings, protecting your family's long-range financial goals and future.

Call your local life insurance agent to find out more about permanent or whole life insurance options and rates. Free quotes for whole life insurance policies can be found online at Quote Smith, www.quotesmith.com.

KEY PERSON INSURANCE

Key person insurance is really just a catchall phrase that means one or more types of insurance policies, such as life or disability, that can be taken out on one or more people that are of critical, or of key importance to your business. These people can include the business owners or an employee(s). Think of it this way: If a person important to the operations, success, and profitability of your business was to become disabled or were to die, would your business continue to operate, grow, and be profitable in their absence? If the answer is no, there is a good chance that you need to take out life insurance or disability insurance on the person or people that your business could not substantially operate without.

Not all home business owners need to worry about insuring key people in the their business. In fact, if you are the sole owner of the business with few, if any, employees your insurance situation is very straightforward. Worry about insuring yourself to protect your family financially and your business in case of liability or disaster potential, and that's about it. However, if you jointly own a business with one or more partners, you should consider insuring each of the owners individually. The premise is that if one of the owners die or becomes disabled, the death or disability benefits can be used to purchase that person's share of the business from his beneficiaries. Or in the case of a key employee or spouse partnership, the money can be used to stabilize the business until other key people can be hired to get the business operating smoothly and profitably again.

Knowing what key people to insure and what types of key people insurance is best for your situation can be confusing. Talk to your insurance agent or a certified financial or estate planner to find out if key person insurance is a necessity for your particular business situation.

PROPERTY INSURANCE

Property insurance is the most common type of home insurance. It generally covers buildings and structures on the property as well as the contents of those buildings and structures. Depending on how extensive your property insurance is, often it will provide protection in the form of a cash settlement or paid repairs in the event of fire, theft, vandalism, flood, earthquake, wind damage, and other acts of God and malicious damages. Floods and earthquakes generally require a separate insurance rider.

Property insurance is the starting point from which home business owners should build, branching out to include specialized tools and equipment, home office improvements, inventory, and various liability riders depending on your business and what you sell.

Contacting your current insurance agent and asking questions specific to your business and equipment will quickly reveal what is or is not covered by your existing policy. In most all cases, you will want to increase the value of the contents portion of the policy if you use expensive computer and office equipment in your business. Below is a list of some items you will specifically want to be insured.

- Your house, apartment, or townhouse, owned or rented
- Other structures on the property, including garage, sheds, greenhouses, fences, and decks
- Improvements made to your home as a result of your home business

- Office equipment, furniture, and supplies, owned and leased
- Cash on hand and account receivable records
- Business specific items such as tools and specialized equipment
- Intellectual and intangible property such as customer lists and goodwill

Prudential Financial offers clients free property and home business insurance quotes on its Web site, located at www.prudential.com.

BUSINESS INTERRUPTION INSURANCE

Business interruption insurance is another coverage home business owners should carefully consider, especially once your business is generating profits and if it is your sole source of income. Business interruption insurance protects a home business owner against losses resulting from interruptions to the normal course of business. Owners can claim losses beyond damaged or destroyed equipment and inventory—the loss of income, business profits, and coverage of fixed operating overheads such as licenses, in-place advertising, and utilities for the period of time the business is shut down or for the time stated in the policy.

You must make sure the policy limits are sufficient to cover your expenses and loss of income for more than a few days. The price of the policy is directly related to the risk of a fire or other disaster damaging your premises. For example, all other things being equal, the price of interruption coverage would probably be higher for a home manufacturing business than a consulting service because of the greater risk of fire due to the business activity. Business interruption insurance is available in many different levels of coverage, with costs depending on the selected protection. The higher the insured amount, the higher your insurance premiums. Ask your insurance agent to conduct a business interruption analysis to determine the level of protection necessary to adequately cover your financial situation.

Do keep in mind that all business interruption insurance policies are extensions of other insured perils, such as fire, flood, and theft. Business interruption coverage is not sold separately. It is added to a property insurance policy for home business owners or included in a business insurance package policy if the business operates from another location. For example, if your business were shut down for two weeks because of flooding, you would have to be covered for floods in your property insurance if you wanted to claim loss of business profits and income for that period as a result of being closed because of the flood.

Multiple layers of insurance can become confusing when trying to figure out what will be best for your situation, which again, makes the case for having an insurance professional available to guide you through the maze. Call your current insurance agent to inquire about business interruption insurance and the added cost of coverage or go online to Quote Smith, located at www.quotesmith.com, to receive free property, liability, and business insurance quotes.

LIABILITY INSURANCE

The majority of homeowners have some sort of liability protection built into their home and property insurance policy. This is also true for people that rent their homes or apartments, as landlords are obligated by law in most places to carry property and liability insurance on buildings and lands they rent. But no matter how diligent you are in terms of taking all necessary precautions to protect your customers and yourself by removing potential perils from your business and the products and services you sell, you could still be held legally responsible for events beyond your control. Product misuse, third-party damages, and service misunderstandings have all been grounds for successful litigation in the United States and Canada.

Therefore, as the old adage goes, it's better to be safe than sorry. It should go without saying that the best way that home business owners can ensure safety is to get liability insurance that specifically provides protection for the type of business activities engaged in, and for the types of products and services sold. Often this type of extend liability insurance is referred to as general business liability or umbrella business liability. General business liability coverage insures a business against accidents and injury that

might occur at the home business location, at clients' locations, or other perils related to the products and services sold. General liability insurance provides protection for the costs associated with successful litigation or claims against your business or you depending on the legal entity of your business, and covers such things as medial expenses, recovery expenses, property damage, and other costs typically associated with liability situations.

There are also more specific types of liability insurance that some home business owners will need to protect their businesses and clients in the event of misadventure. The three most common are professional liability insurance, completed operations liability insurance, and product liability insurance.

Professional Liability Insurance

Professional liability insurance, also commonly known as errors and omissions insurance, is designed to protect you or your company from the financial losses that might arise if you are sued by a client(s) due to alleged negligence on your part while rendering professional services or advice. Professional liability insurance is one of the most common types of specialized liability insurance. Professional liability insurance is never included in a homeowner's insurance policy or a basic home business insurance policy. It is always sold separately as a specialized insurance specific to the nature of your profession or business. In fact, in many states and Canadian provinces such as Ontario, practicing professionals will find that professional liability insurance, or errors and omissions insurance, is mandatory. Without it you cannot legally practice.

What type of home businesses and business people need professional liability insurance? Until recently, professional liability insurance was generally only carried by practicing professionals such as lawyers, notary publics, certified accountants, and engineers. But it is now commonplace for just about every type of business professional and consultant to carry such insurance. This would include public relations specialist, advertising and marketing consultants, stockbrokers, home and building inspectors, software developers, webmasters, financial and estate planners, insurance agents, and real estate agents, just to mention a few. Anyone that charges a fee for advice or professional services should carefully consider carrying professional liability insurance to protect their business, personal finances, and their clients' interests.

Obtaining professional liability insurance is a relatively straightforward process. Begin by checking with your specific professional associations because many offer members various insurance programs. You can also ask you current insurance agent to recommend an agent that specializes in liability insurance coverage. American Professional Online provides visitors to its Web site with free professional liability quotes. The site is indexed by type of profession and then indexed geographically by state. It can be found at www.americanprofessional.com.

Completed Operations Insurance

Completed operations insurance is another specialized liability insurance, although less common than professional liability. This liability insurance is suited to home business owners that provide services at their clients' locations, and its basic function is similar to that of professional liability insurance. It protects you from a liability standpoint should a service that you provided a client cause harm to property or body after you have completed the service and left your client's premises. For example, plumbers that work from homebased locations might consider carrying completed operations insurance. This insurance protects them from financial losses from successful litigation or claims by a clients if a recently fixed pipe at the client's home bursts and causes bodily harm or damage to the home.

Obtaining completed operations insurance is very easy. You can contact your current insurance provider and ask for a quote or a referral to an agent that handles this insurance. You can also contact professional associations or unions to which you might belong and inquire about members' insurance options. Or you can go online to find completed operations liability information and quotes. One such online company is Stuckey & Company, which provides visitors to its Web site free, no-obligation insurance quotes, including completed operations coverage. It can be found at www.safetytek.com.

Product Liability Insurance

Many home businesses are involved in manufacturing a product, entirely or through a value added process and, therefore, should add product liability coverage to their insurance roster to protect their businesses and clients in the event their product malfunctions and causes property or bodily damage. Even if your business is not directly involved in the manufacturing process of the products you sell, you still must be proactive in terms of product liability insurance concerns. You can do this by first making sure that the manufacturers of the products you sell are reputable and fully insured. And you can also talk to your current insurance agent about the need for extended product liability insurance coverage even if you do not manufacture the product. In litigation situations, it is not uncommon for plaintiffs that have suffered some sort of damages as a result of product malfunctions to name numerous defendants in their claim. This possibility warrants extra precautions from the home business owner's perspective. No Cost Insurance Quotes provides visitors to its Web site with free insurance quotes online, including product liability quotations. It can be found at www.nocostinsurancequotes.com.

AUTOMOTIVE INSURANCE

There are myriad automobile insurance policies available to home business owners—commercial policies for people that use their vehicles exclusively for business, occasional business use policies, or special usage and driver restricted policies. The type of automobile insurance that you select for your car will be directly related to your business needs and situation. Many states and provinces in Canada have auto accident compensation laws permitting auto accident victims to collect directly from their own insurance companies for medical, hospital, recovery, and related expenses, regardless of who was at fault in the accident. This is commonly referred to as no fault insurance. Though the name of this insurance is a bit ambiguous, as most states and provinces still allow victims that were not at fault to sue the party that caused the accident. Many states and provinces also place restrictions on commercial use vehicles in terms of mandatory insurance coverage, specific maintenance schedules, and driver certifications, all of which must be researched in your area prior to using your vehicle for business purposes.

Basic Types of Automotive Insurance Coverage
Liability Insurance

The basic type of insurance for automobiles is liability insurance, and most U.S. states and provinces in Canada require that every vehicle licensed for the road be covered by basic liability insurance. Liability insurance protects you should you cause an accident and injure people or damage property. There is no set amount of liability insurance that must be carried, but because of our litigation crazed society, most insurance agents recommend a minimum of $1,000,000 in liability insurance. Of course, premiums increase as the amount of liability insurance protection increases.

Collision Insurance

In the event that your car is damaged in any type of accident and you are responsible for the damages, collision insurance will cover the costs associated with repairing or replacing the vehicle (market value) in the event that it is beyond repair. Generally, the rule of thumb is to carry collision insurance on vehicles that have a value of $5,000 or more. Collision insurance is a must if your vehicle is leased or financed.

Comprehensive Insurance

Comprehensive is another optional insurance that covers damage to your vehicle caused by an event other than a collision with another vehicle or object. Comprehensive insurance covers fire, vandalism, theft, and acts of God such as hailstorms, broken windshields and glass. Once again, depending on the value of your vehicle and your dependency on it for business use, comprehensive insurance should be carefully considered.

Tools and Equipment Riders

Do you transport tools, a laptop computer, inventory, expensive product samples, or other business-related equipment in your vehicle? If so, I strongly recommend that you get a tools and equipment rider placed on your automobile insurance. This rider protects you should these items be stolen from you vehicle or damaged in a collision or by an act of God. Tool and equipment insurance can also be extended to cover aftermarket items that you install in or on your vehicle and use for business purposes, such as signage, generators, ladder racks, and tool storage boxes.

Rental Insurance

Rental insurance or rental reimbursement insurance should be considered, especially for home business owners that rely on their vehicle daily for business use. In the event that your car is damaged or stolen and you must rent a car to conduct business, this insurance will cover the costs associated with the rental vehicle. But be aware that most policies have a set amount for car rentals that cannot be exceeded, unless you pay the difference. If you need a truck for business then make sure that your policy states that you can rent one as a replacement.

Leasing and Loans

If you lease your transportation for business use or if you have financed the purchase of a vehicle, in all likelihood the leasing company or company that holds the financing note may need to be listed as an additional insured entity in the event that the vehicle is a total loss, to protect their financial investment. This also protects the leasing company if it's named in a lawsuit as a result of an accident. If you are making lease or loan payments, you may also want to consider getting Gap Coverage. This coverage ensures that you receive the total amount of the loan or lease in the event the vehicle is a total loss. Gap coverage is especially important for new expensive vehicles because vehicles depreciate by 25 percent or more as soon as they are driven off the lot. Without gap insurance, you will receive only market value, not the loan value, in the event of a total loss.

Automotive Insurance Discounts

One way to increase bottom-line business profits is to reduce the costs you pay for goods and services you use in your business. The following are a few ways to reduce the amount you pay for automobile insurance.

Safe Diving Habits

Just about every insurance company rewards good drivers with lower insurance premiums. So the easiest way to reduce your automobile insurance premiums is to drive safely, don't speed, and keep your vehicle well maintained to reduce the chances for an accident resulting from mechanical failures. In many states and provinces, demerit points against your driver's license from traffic violations will increase your insurance rates.

Use Anti-Theft Devices

Most insurance companies give discounts ranging from 5 to 10 percent to customers that install and use anti-theft devices such as alarms, ignition immobilizes, and on-board GPS recovery devices. All are designed to eliminate or reduce the likelihood of your vehicle being stolen or to help in quick recovery, thus reducing financial risk to the insurer.

Defensive Driver Courses

In some states, defensive driver courses are offered through or sponsored by the department of motor vehicles to improve driving skills. Insurance companies generally reward graduates of defensive driver courses in the form of lower automobile insurance premiums. Check with your local department of motor vehicles to inquire about defensive driver courses. Ask your insurance agent if completion of these courses will lower your premiums.

Limit the Number of Drivers

Another way to reduce auto insurance premiums is to limit the number of people that can drive the vehicle. This works especially well in situations were one driver has a poor driving record, which dramatically increases the overall cost to insure the vehicle, even if all the other drivers have clean driving records.

Compare Prices

The final way to reduce your automobile insurance premiums is to compare prices to ensure that you are receiving the best value relative to the coverage you need. The simplest way to accomplish this is to go online and get free automobile insurance quotes.

Geico Direct can be found online at www.geico.com, and Quote Smith at www.quotesmith.com.

BUSINESS TRAVELERS INSURANCE

Home business owners that frequently travel in and outside of their home state, province, or country should also carry short-term business travelers insurance as needed or permanent coverage if frequent travel warrants. Business travelers insurance coverage can cover common problems such as trip cancellation protection and personal item replacement in the event of lost luggage to more extreme problems such as political abductions, extended hostage situations, false imprisonments, kidnapping negotiations and related costs, and political evacuation and repatriation expenses. A few of these are extreme situations, but in the wake of September 11, 2001, and the rise in global unrest, these extremes are becoming real threats for many business travelers.

The Association of Business Travelers offers members unique insurance options, including trip cancellation, political evacuation and repatriation insurance, and media evacuation. The association's Web site can be found online at www.abt-travel.com and includes information about member benefits as well as general information about business travel. Many credit card companies and other business and industry associations also offer members and customers travel insurance options at lower costs than can generally be obtained by individuals.

PROTECTING OFF-SITE ASSETS AND SUBCONTRACTORS

Never assume that just because people tell you they are fully insured they are. You might take all the required steps to ensure that you have all the necessary insurance in place to protect your business, customers, and family in the event of misadventure, disaster, or accident. But are your business alliances and subcontactors also fully insured? Before you hire subcontactors to carry out any work for your clients, make sure that they can provide you with proof of relevant insurance coverage, including workers' compensation, liability insurance, and such. Without it, if there is a problem on the job, you can be held liable as the contractor or the entity that was hired to conduct the work, even if another business or person conducts the work for you under a subcontract agreement

Also make sure that the other businesses and people you conduct business with are adequately insured. This includes your accountant or bookkeeper through to the self-storage business where you store inventory or equipment, the warehouse that fulfills your customer orders, the Webmaster that keeps your Web site files at his place of business. If any of these people are not fully insured and a catastrophic event occurs, you can be left holding a bag full of financial losses that cannot be recouped. The only sure way to know that others with whom you do business are insured for your protection, your family's protection, and your customer's protection is to ask for and receive proof of insurance. If they cannot provide proof of adequate insurance coverage, start shopping for a new business alliance that can.

TIPS FOR SAVING MONEY ON BUSINESS INSURANCE

Insurance companies base insurance premiums on statistical and specific evaluated risks. As the risks (financial exposure) associated with insuring a particular activity or item increase, so do the premiums charged. Of course, there are steps that you can take to reduce your odds of being charged or having to pay higher insurance premiums or that will make you eligible for reduced insurance premiums:

- Obtain at least three quotes for each type of insurance you need and analyze each for the comprehensiveness of coverage, cost-protection value, and reputation of the agent, broker, and insurance underwriter. But remember, the lowest cost certainly does not necessarily mean the best coverage. Regardless of cost, if the policy does not properly protect your assets, your family, and your clients, having insurance serves no purpose.
- Contact local business associations such as the Small Office Home Office (SOHO), www.soho.org, the Chamber of Commerce, www.uscham ber.com, or the American Association of Home Businesses, www.aah bb.org, to find out if they

offer members' group business and health insurance options. Most home business associations have business insurance programs in place for members at much lower cost because of volume purchasing. Often the savings will pay for the price of membership. Specific industry associations generally offer members these same packages and services.

- Contact your existing insurance broker and inquire about special home business riders. An insurance rider is an extension of your existing policy that protects or provides coverage for a specific item or activity, such as a home business. The popularity of home businesses has increased so much in the past decade that many insurance companies now offer existing policy holders numerous home business rider options, which can be tagged onto their existing homeowners policy for less than the cost of separate home business policies.
- Consider raising your claims deductible to a higher amount. The claims deductible is the portion of any insurance claim that you pay before the insurance coverage kicks in to pay the balance of the claim. As a rule of thumb, the higher your deductible goes, the lower your premiums become. But do not make your deductible so high that you would not be able to pay it in the event of a misadventure.
- Get creative and find out if there is a insurance agent or broker at one of the local business or barter clubs that would be willing to accept your product or service in exchange for decreasing or eliminating the cost of insuring your home business. Shoestring tactics such as these have been partially responsible for helping to build thousands of successful businesses.
- Take the logical approach to home business insurance, and make sure that you prioritize your true insurance needs. Insurance coverage can be added or increased as your business grows, and your ability to pay the premiums increases. Start with the basic plans that will deliver the best protection for your family and clients today and increase your insurance coverage as needed.

HOME BUSINESS INSURANCE WORKSHEET

You can use the following Insurance Coverage Worksheet (see Figure 5.1) to help determine if you need specific insurance coverage and the costs associated with each. In some cases, more than one insurance policy will be required to protect employees, partners, or family members. Simply check off the insurance needed, fill in the number of required policies and the unit cost per month of each, and multiply the unit cost by the number of policies required to arrive at the cost of per month for each specific insurance. Add the cost of each insurance cost to calculate the total combined insurance cost per month.

| FIGURE 5.1 | Insurance Coverage Worksheet |

Type of Insurance Coverage	Insurance Required		Number of Policies Needed	Unit Cost Per Month	Total Cost Per Month
Health Insurance	❏ Yes	❏ No	_____	$_____	$_____
Workers' Compensation	❏ Yes	❏ No	_____	$_____	$_____
Life Insurance	❏ Yes	❏ No	_____	$_____	$_____
Disability Insurance	❏ Yes	❏ No	_____	$_____	$_____
Property Insurance	❏ Yes	❏ No	_____	$_____	$_____
General Liability	❏ Yes	❏ No	_____	$_____	$_____
Business Interruption	❏ Yes	❏ No	_____	$_____	$_____
Errors and Omissions	❏ Yes	❏ No	_____	$_____	$_____
Professional Liability	❏ Yes	❏ No	_____	$_____	$_____
Product Liability Insurance	❏ Yes	❏ No	_____	$_____	$_____
Completed Operations	❏ Yes	❏ No	_____	$_____	$_____
Auto Insurance	❏ Yes	❏ No	_____	$_____	$_____
Travel Insurance	❏ Yes	❏ No	_____	$_____	$_____
Additional Insurance	❏ Yes	❏ No	_____	$_____	$_____
Additional Insurance	❏ Yes	❏ No	_____	$_____	$_____
Additional Insurance	❏ Yes	❏ No	_____	$_____	$_____
			Total insurance cost per month		$_____
			Total insurance cost per annum		$_____

Notes:

_____

_____

_____

_____

_____

THE FINAL WORD ON HOME BUSINESS INSURANCE

Though writing a check every month for intangibles like insurance can be very painful, especially for new home business start-up with limited working capital and cash flow, you must consider this expense as an absolute must. Purchasing business, life, disability, and liability insurance is the only way that you can be 100 percent sure that in the event of a catastrophic event, you and/or your family's well-being and financial security will be protected.

Keep in mind that you always want to be proactive and organized in terms of your business and personal records should the need to make an insurance claim ever arise. You want to be able to streamline the insurance claims process so that you can be paid your benefit or be reimbursed quickly and with as few obstacles as possible. Therefore, keep your account receivable and payable records up-to-date, keep inventory and equipment lists current, make duplicates of all records, and store them off-site at a relative's or friend's home, at your bookkeeper's or accountant's, or at a bank in a safety deposit box. For extra peace of mind, you might also want to consider filming or taking pictures of your home office, the improvements made, your inventory and supplies, and special tools and equipment that you use in business, and then store a duplicate tape or prints off-site. Losing business and equipment records to disasters is one of the main obstacles to quick and accurate insurance claims settlements.

RESOURCES

Associations

Health Insurance Association of America
1201 F Street NW, Suite 500
Washington, DC 20004-1204
(202) 824-1600
www.hiaa.org

Independent Insurance Agents and Brokers of America
127 S. Peyton Street
Alexandria, VA 22314
(800) 222-7917
www.iiaa.org

Insurance Brokers Association of Canada
1920-155 University Avenue
Toronto, ON M5H 3B7
(416) 367-1831
www.ibac.ca

Insurance Information Institute
110 William Street, 24th Floor
New York, NY 10038
(212) 346-5500
www.iii.org

National Association of Independent Insurers
2600 River Road
Des Plaines, IL 60018
(847) 297-7800
www.naii.org

Workers Compensation Research Institute
95 Massachusetts Avenue
Cambridge, MA 02139
(617) 661-9274
www.wcrinet.org

Suggested Reading

Baldwin, Ben G. *New Life Insurance Investment Advisor: Achieving Financial Security for You and Your Family Through Today's Insurance Products.* New York: McGraw-Hill, 2001.

Hungelmann, Jack. *Insurance for Dummies.* New York: Hungry Minds, 2001.

Mooney, Sean. *Insuring Your Business: What You Need to Know to Get the Best Insurance Coverage for Your Business.* New York: Insurance Information Institute Press, 1992.

Rubin, Harvey W. *Dictionary of Insurance Terms, 4th Ed.* New York: Barrons, 2000.

Insurance Information Institute Consumers Brochures

Insuring Your Business Against Catastrophe: Instructions on How to Develop a Catastrophe Plan Now to Avoid Losses Should Disaster Strike.

Insuring Your Home Business: A Guide to Help Home Business Owners Understand Their Insurance Needs.

Both business insurance consumer guides are available from the Insurance Information Institute by visiting their Web site at www.iii.org: or calling their office at ((212)-346-5500.

📠 *Web Sites*

The Association of Business Travelers, www.abt-travel. com: Insurance information and services aimed at frequent business travelers.

Chubb Insurance, www.chubb.com: Free quotes on all types of business and personal insurance, including its exclusive Find an Agent directory listing more than 8,000 independent insurance agents and brokers worldwide.

Digital Insurance, www.digitalinsurance.com: Employee benefit insurance programs and packages.

Express Life Insurance Direct, www.express-life-insurance.com: Free life and disability insurance quotes.

Geico Direct, www.geico.com: Online automotive insurance quotes for personal and commercial applications.

Health Insurance Resource Center, www.insurance values.com: Free quotes on all types of business, personal, health, and life insurance as well as general insurance information and useful links.

Health Plan Directory, www.healthplandirectory. com: Free directory service listing insurance health plan carriers indexed geographically by state.

InsWeb, www.insweb.com: Free quotes on all types of business, personal, health, and life insurance programs and packages.

Quote Smith, www.quotesmith.com: Free online home business insurance quotes.

CHAPTER 6

Preparing a Business Plan

FIRST AND FOREMOST, THE IMPORTANCE OF A business plan is not the document, but the process that went into creating the document. Anyone can write a business plan. There are hundreds, if not thousands, of sample business plans available on the Internet and in books, and most are free for the taking. All you have to do is copy them, change names, alter descriptions to fit your business, and, presto, you have a business plan. You can fill your business plan with all kinds of spectacular facts, figures, and statements. But unless these facts, figures, and statements are relevant to your business, revealed in the *process* of business planning, compiled from your own primary research and secondary data collection, and created as a road map that will take you from business start-up, to revenue generation, to profitability, and finally to meeting your stated business and marketing objectives, all you really have accomplished is a fancy document and nothing else.

I cannot emphasize enough that business planning has little to do with the actual business plan document and everything to do with the process of creating it. Far too many entrepreneurs get caught up in creating a great document instead of creating a great business plan. The document is of little value, whatever 10 or 20 pieces of paper are worth, it is the information

inside the business plan that is of value. You cannot cheat on the process of business planning and hope to win in today's highly competitive business environment.

GETTING STARTED

The first step in building a business plan is to determine the audience for your plan, you, or people outside of your proposed business. If the business plan is for your eyes only and created as an operational manual to guide your business through start-up, to management, and then to profitability, you need only to include the information that will enable you to identify each stage of business start-up and growth, how money will be raised and used in the business, what is needed to operate the business, who your customers are and where they are, your business and marketing objectives, and how these objectives will be reached.

If your business plan is going to be used as a tool to securing start-up or growth capital, you will need to cover all of the bases in creating the business plan. And a polished professional document will also be needed. If you are going to seek financing from a bank, venture capitalist, or private investor, it does not hurt to ask them up front what they like to see included in the business plan because there is no standard across-the-board set of rules. Because business plans vary by industry, type of business, funding requirements, location of the business, size of company, and stage of growth.

Keep in mind that you do not want your business plan falling into the hands of your competitors. Therefore, you must be careful to whom you show your plan, and to whom they show your plan. You may even want to consider having a lawyer write a confidential disclosure agreement, which basically states that you own the information contained within your business plan and that the recipients of the document cannot discuss the details of your business plan with others or use ideas and concepts from your plan for their own personal benefit. Before handing your business plan out ask people that will be reviewing your plan to kindly sign the confidential disclosure agreement. The majority of people that need to see your business plan will be familiar with confidential disclosure agreements and will not have any issues with signing it.

Do It Yourself or Hire a Pro?

The second decision that you make in terms of your business plan is will you prepare your business plan or will you hire a business consultant or freelance writer to prepare it? If the purpose of your business plan is to simply give you a road map detailing your objectives and the actions required to reach each objective, chances are you will want to save the fees that a business plan consultant charges and prepare your own business plan. Even if you do not have experience in business planning, fear not. If you need more specific information than is provided here, there are hundreds of books dedicated solely to business planning and writing business plans. A few of the more popular ones can be found at the end of this chapter in the Resources section.

There is also a plethora of business plan software and templates on the market that can assist you in terms of business plan contents and formatting, such as:

- Fundable Plans, www.fundableplans.com
- Plan Magic, www.planmagic.com
- Palo Alto, www.paloalto.com
- Planium, www.planium.com
- My Business Kit, www.mybusinesskit.com

Office and word processing programs such as MS Office and Corel Word Perfect also include basic business plan templates and tutorials that can help lead novice entrepreneurs through the business planning process step-by-step.

If you do not feel comfortable preparing your business plan because it will be used to secure funding you will need to hire a business consultant or freelance writer with business plan experience. Although a freelance writer will almost always be less expensive, the downside is that most do not have much business experience and rely more on form than process in the creation of the business plan. Business consultants with business plan experience are a far better choice because not only will they understand the format and form of a business plan, but they will also understand and have experience in the process of creating a business plan. They will be able to conduct research, collect data from secondary sources, create target customer profiles, conduct SWOT and PEST analysis, and do other activities required to prepare your business plan. The additional benefit of hiring a business consultant as opposed to a freelance business plan writer is the consultant will have the experience needed to critique your business concept and objectives, keeping you in touch with realities, and to measure the likelihood of your success from the facts revealed in the process of planning.

To find a business consultant to prepare your plan, you can ask other business owners who prepared their plans, and you can also ask your lawyer, accountant, or banker to refer you to qualified business consultants. Get three quotes, and base your final decision not on price, but more so on experience in relation to your type of business, reputation, and time frame. Talk to their current and past clients to get an idea of client satisfaction with the results. Hiring a business consultant is not cheap, nor should it be. Expect to pay from $2,000 to as much as $10,000, depending on the amount of research needed to compile, analyze, and catalog data and competitors, prepare financial budgets and forecasts, create draft plans for review, and write the final plan.

I must stress that the vast majority of people that start small businesses can easily prepare a proper business plan that will meet their specific needs and more. Do not feel intimidated by the business planning process. It is nothing more then collecting, analyzing, and recording the information that you need to know to be successful in business. Think of the business planning process as a family vacation: You need to know where you are going, what you need to take along, and how you will reach your destination to enjoy your vacation. The same principles can be applied to business planning.

Business Plan Outline

In terms of the business plan outline, there are no standard across-the-board set of rules, mainly because business plans vary by industry, type of business, location of the business, size of company, stage of growth, and plan audience (financing versus management). If you cover the basics, that is, you answer the who, what, why, when, and where, the end result will be a business plan that works for your particular business situation and meets your needs. The basic business plan is broken into five main sections: introduction, company, marketing, financial, and appendices. Each of these sections is broken down into subsections covering various topics under the main heading. The following is a basic business plan outline for a small homebased business.

Introduction
Cover
Title Page
Executive Summary
Table of Contents

Company
Mission Statement
Business Overview
Product Description
Management Team
Legal Issues
Operations
Risks and Contingencies
Key Objectives

Marketing
Executive Overview
Company Analysis
Market Analysis
Customer Analysis
Competitor Analysis
Marketing Objectives
Marketing Strategy
Marketing Budget
Action Plan
Support Documents

Financials
Funding Requirements
Funding Sources
Balance Sheet
Break-Even Analysis
Cash Flow Projections
Income Projections
Equipment and Inventory Lists

Appendices
Personal Documents
Legal Documents
Financial Documents
Marketing Documents

THE INTRODUCTION

The first section of the business plan is the introduction, which covers the basics such as a title page with full contact information, an executive overview that briefly summarizes key points within the plan, and a table of contents that lists the main sections and subtopics within each section. Business plans are generally printed on 8.5 x 11 standard white office paper, single-spaced, 12 point Times Roman or similar font, and spiral bound or placed in a soft cover binder. If you really want to make an positive impression on your audience, you can use a heavy stock paper, include color photographs of products, and use an upscale cover and binding. Basically you should match the look of your business plan to is purpose.

Cover

The cover is the first page, and if you choose to use a soft binder, make sure that you get one that has a business card pocket or window for easy identification of your business name. If you choose to go with a spiral binding, use a heavier stock of paper for the cover, perhaps even a dark color with your business name printed on the outside in silver or gold for visual impact. Personally, I like to keep the cover of the business plan very simple, with only the name of the business printed on the front cover and nothing else. Others prefer to include a contact person and address on the cover. It is really up to you to decide how you want the cover of your business plan to look and what information you want to include.

If you will be sending your business plan to a number of people, use a cover letter printed on your company letterhead and attach it to the front cover with a paper clip. The cover letter should include the name of the person to whom you are sending the business plan, along with the business name, title, and contact information. The opening paragraph should state why this person is being sent the business plan—they requested it, a third party referred them to you, and so forth. The second paragraph should briefly describe the business venture and product or service. The last paragraph should ask the recipient to call you so that you can further discuss the details of your exciting business and opportunity. Depending on the nature of your business, the purpose of your plan, and the person that will be reviewing the plan, you might want to get a confidential disclosure agreement signed before to sending it.

Title Page

The second page is the title page. This is where you will print your business name, contact person, and full mailing address, along with contact telephone numbers, fax numbers, e-mail address, and your Web site URL, if applicable. You may want to control the number of business plans in circulation to help ensure it does not fall into the wrong hands. One easy tracking system is to print a business plan number on the title page, handwritten, starting at one. Keep a log recording the name of the person that has the corresponding business plan. For an extra measure of protection, you can also include a copyright mark at the bottom of the title page indicating ownership. You can apply for a formal copyright through the U.S. copyright office if you like, although it certainly is not required, as any original work is automatically copyrighted by the author in the United States and Canada. Additional information about copyrights can be found in Chapter 4, Legal Issues.

Sample Title Page

Business Plan
ABC Consulting Ltd.

Joe Smith, President
555 Main Street
Any Town, CA 90210
Tel: (555) 555-5555
Fax: (555) 555-5555
E-mail: youremail@yoururl.com
Web site: www.yourwebsite.com

Business Plan Copy # _____
©2004, by ABC Consulting Ltd. All rights reserved.

Executive Overview

The executive overview section is a brief summary describing key points from every section of the plan, but short enough to fit on one page. Even though the executive overview is at the beginning of the business plan, for all intents and purposes it is usually the last section of the plan you create. You create the executive overview last because it is comprised of key points that are extracted from each section of the plan and you do not know what these key points will be until each section is substantially completed. The main purpose of the executive overview is to provide readers who do not have time or need a quick summary of the who, what, where, how, and why of the business plan. Depending on your business, industry, stage of growth, and purpose, the executive overview would briefly addresses the following information:

- Your business name and legal structure, sole proprietorship, partnership, limited liability corporation, or corporation.
- Your mission statement or philosophy.
- The purpose of the business plan—a tool for securing financing or an operational guide for the business. If the purpose is to secure financing, state the amount needed, how the money will be spent, the preferred source of financing, the security or collateral offered, and how the money will be repaid.
- If the business is currently operating or if you are purchasing an operating business, then briefly explain the current status of the business, including sales, competition, market positioning, strengths, weaknesses, opportunities, and threats.
- The principle(s) owners of the business, the portion of ownership, and the roles they will serve in the business, as well as relevant experience, training, and accreditations.
- The geographic area the business will serve including current size, potential, and competition in the marketplace.
- A description of the target customer, how many there are, and how they make purchasing decision.
- A brief description of the products and/or services that will be sold and the unique

advantages associated with these products and/or services.
- Company business and marketing objectives and the strategies that will be implemented to enable these objectives to be reached.
- The projected short-and long-term revenues.
- Finally, but equally important, describe why the business venture will be successful.

Table of Contents

As the name suggests, the table of contents is a single page that lists the major sections and subtopics of the business plan in order with the corresponding page numbers. If your business plan is only a few pages, a table of contents will not be required. But, if your business plan is broken into multiple sections with numerous support documents, a table of contents is required, especially if the purpose of the business plan is to secure funding.

THE COMPANY SECTION

The company section describes your business in detail with a mission statement, a detailed business overview, product descriptions, the management team, legal issues, operations, risks and contingencies, and your key business objectives and the strategies to be implemented to meet your goals and objectives. Developing the company section of your business plan is actually very easy, especially if you use the information provided below as a road map to create your own company description in step-by-step fashion.

Mission Statement

A mission statement or statement of purpose should begin the company section. Often overlooked by small business owners is the power that your mission statement can bring to your business, marketing activities, credibility, and vision for the future. After all, a mission statement is your declaration that clearly states who you are, what you do, what you stand for, and why you do it. But remember, the words chosen to create your mission statement should not be taken lightly. Your mission statement is an honest reflection of your core values and what you hold to be important or your purpose at the time you create the statement.

So who needs a mission statement? Basically any person, business, or organization that wants to publicly or privately state their purpose and what they stand for. Businesses both large and small should take the time to identify and create a mission statement. For example, "My purpose is to provide my customers with unsurpassed value, quality, and service and always conduct business in a fair and ethical manner."

There are no hard and fast rules in terms of creating a mission statement. Ask 100 experts how to write one and you will probably get 100 different answers. Most, however, agree that the following are key points to consider when developing a mission statement.

- Keep your mission statements brief, in the two- or three-sentence range and less than 40 words.
- A mission statement is not an advertisement, business plan, or promotional message activity, but it should be useable as a component of these and other marketing activities.
- Don't rush when creating your mission statement. Take your time, and edit it accordingly.
- Look at other mission statements to get ideas about how they were crafted. Check to see if the company or organization is living up to its purpose. Never copy someone else's mission statement.
- The best mission statements are simple, real, and honest. Never create a mission statement that you do not believe in. People will be quick to spot the difference between what you say in your mission statement and what you actually do.
- Your mission statement should be flexible. Don't be afraid to alter it to meet your customers' changing needs, or your new purpose.
- Skip puffery on how great you are and what a great job you do. Stick with what your audience will receive, the benefits to them through quality, value, and uncompromising service.

Business Overview

Once you have your mission statement, the next step is to provide a detailed overview of your business, such as the business name, legal structure, and starting date. If you are purchasing an operating business, the business overview will need to be much more detailed, documenting its entire history but in a capsulated format. You will need to discuss the history of the business, location, previous owners, why the business is being sold, challenges facing the business, and current customers, suppliers and vendors. Although much of this information will be included in other sections of your business and marketing plan, providing it here gives readers an overview of past business activities.

Business Name and Legal Structure

State your business name and legal structure of the company—sole proprietorship, partnership, limited liability corporation, or corporation. If your intention is to incorporate a sole proprietorship or partnership in the near future, also document this information.

Business Location

List the location of your business and the market area that it will serve, for example, "ABC Poll Cleaning is based in Port Moody and will serve the tri-city area of Port Moody, Coquitlam, and Port Coquitlam."

History or Stage of Development

Because the majority of entrepreneurs start their business before preparing a formal business plan, you will want to include the history of the business—when it started, success to date, and challenges to date. If the business is still in the developmental stages list what point your are at in terms of set up, what has been accomplished to date, and what is remaining to do to get the business fully operational.

Strengths

Strengths are the skills and resources you have that can be capitalized upon and used to your advantage to help you reach business and marketing objectives. Although strengths are featured in the competitive analysis section of the marketing plan, I also like to describe the company's strengths in the business overview.

Position

Describe how your company is, or will be, positioned in the marketplace, relative to competitors. Will you be known as the low price leader, provide quality and service above all, or cater to the high-end segment of the market?

Product Description

Your product or service description does not need to be long, but it should be detailed enough that it gives the reader a clear understanding of the product(s) or service(s) that you sell, segmented into three topics—product description, benefit description, and competitive advantage description. You might also mention product research and development issues and plans as well, especially those focused on improvement.

Product Description

Start off with a description of your product or service, such as what it does, what it looks like, how big it is, how long it takes to install, and what the average amount of time needed to provide the service is. Again, you must write visually so readers have a clear picture of your goods and services and understand their intended purpose.

Benefit Description

Briefly describe what benefits customers receive from purchasing and using your product or service. Do they save money, make money, get physically fit, become healthier, save time?

Competitive Advantage Description

Finally, describe your competitive advantages, what makes your product or service better than competitor's products or services. Is your warranty longer, is your price the lowest, or do you offer 24-hour service? Think of your competitive advantage as the one reason why consumers should buy your goods or services and not the competition's.

Management Team

When describing the management team keep two things in mind. First, briefly detail what type of people your business needs to hire or align with in order to operate the business and meet your key objectives. That is, what skills and experiences owners, managers, and key employees have that the business could capitalize upon for the benefit of the business

and customers. Second, you will want to list all owner(s), managers, key employees, contract agents, and professional service providers such as lawyers. Include their individual resumes, focusing on information relative to your business, products, or services, especially the special skills, experiences, training, and certificates that they hold. Additional information about business and management teams can be found in Chapter 8, Building Your Business Team.

Legal Issues

Here you want to describe key legal issues in terms of setting up and operating your business.

Licenses, Registrations, and Permits

Describe in detail any and all business licenses, registrations, and permits, needed to start and operate the business. Break this information down into what has been obtained to date and what must still be obtained. Depending on the type of business you will be operating from home, these licenses, registrations, and permits could include:

- Business license
- Employer Identification Number
- Vendors permit
- Sales tax permits
- Import/export certificates
- Professional certificates
- Police clearance
- Internet domain name registrations

Additional information about business licenses, registrations, and permits can be found in Chapter 4, Legal Issues.

Zoning

Because the business will be operated or managed from a homebased location, you will want to describe the zoning regulations that affect your business, how your business qualifies, or the steps that you must take to ensure that your business qualifies to be operated legally from your residence. Include information on home occupation permits, as may be necessary, as well as fire and safety regulations that also must be complied with. In the event you are ever challenged on the validity of your home business, you might also want to include a copy of your local zoning bylaws in the appendices section of the business plan under legal support documents. Additional information about zoning can be found in Chapter 4, Legal Issues.

Insurance

Describe in detail what the company's insurance requirements will be, such as business insurance, fire insurance, liability insurance, or business interruption insurance. Likewise, note the insurance company(s) that will be underwriting these policies, the insurance broker(s), and when the policies will come into effect. Additional information about insurance can be found in Chapter 5, Home Business Insurance.

Intellectual Properties

List any intellectual properties such as trademarks, patents, or copyrights that the business owns, has applied for, or that will be using under license from the property owner, the nature of these intellectual properties, and the advantages associated with ownership or right of use. Additional information about intellectual properties can be found in Chapter 4, Legal Issues.

Operations

Under operations you will want to describe your business location, which is obviously your home and include information such as what portion of the home will be utilized for business, what renovations are needed to make the space suitable for your business needs, how you will address visiting client issues, parking, storage, communication requirements, and shipping and receiving issues. You will also want to describe how the business will be managed on a day-to-day basis, and detail key policies such as customer service and human resources. If your business will involve the manufacturing or assembly of products at home, or if you will be providing professional services such as dentistry, your operations descriptions will obviously be much more detailed than if you were operating a freelance writing business from home.

Risks and Contingencies

It is important to discuss the risks associated with your business, products, services, marketing environment, and every other element of your business plan

(within reason) and the contingency plans that will be implemented should identified risks materialize. As the old saying goes, if plan A doesn't work, then we will go to plan B. Think of risks as plan A and contingencies as plan B. Examples of risks and contingencies would include the following:

A risk might be the loss of a key employee that brought specialized know-how to the business, as this loss could have a negative impact on your business. A contingency would be to identify two or three potential candidates in the area that might be hired should you lose this key employee.

A risk might be your supplier no longer supplying the goods or services used in your business. A contingency would be to identify additional supply sources that could be called upon if needed.

Key Objectives

In this section you list your company goals and objectives, the timeline in which these are to be reached, and the strategies and activities that will be implemented to ensure company goals and objectives are reached. You can break your key objectives into two categories: marketing objectives, which are discussed in detail in the marketing plan, and business objectives. An example of a marketing objective would be a sales target such as $250,000 for the forthcoming year or if you are already in business, to increase market share by 10 percent. An example of a business objective would be to have your new business open and fully operational within six months. When developing and setting key business and marketing objectives keep in mind the fact that they should be realistic, measurable, and always based on moving forward and improvement. I also like to end the company section of the business plan with a brief paragraph that states with perfect clarity why the business will succeed.

THE MARKETING SECTION

The marketing plan is a key component of your overall business plan. It is so important, in fact, Chapter 12 is entirely devoted to creating a marketing plan. Included in this chapter are worksheets for each section of the marketing plan that can be completed right in the book, giving you a head start on creating a marketing plan for your new business. You will also find numerous tips, ideas, and resources throughout the marketing plan chapter. Below is the marketing plan outline featured in the marketing plan chapter, along with a brief introduction to each section. My advice would be to complete the business plan and marketing plan as two separate documents, combining them when they are each completed. The main sections of the marketing plan are:

- Executive overview
- Company analysis
- Market analysis
- Customer analysis
- Competitor analysis
- Marketing objectives
- Marketing strategy
- Marketing budget
- Action plan
- Support documents

Executive Overview

Like the business plan, a marketing plan also begins with an executive overview or introduction, which briefly summarizes the key points from every section of your marketing plan in one page. Although the executive overview is at the beginning of your marketing plan, it is usually the last section of the plan that you create. The main purpose of the executive overview is to provide readers at a glance, the who, what, where, how, and why of the marketing plan.

Company Analysis

The company analysis is a full description of your company including in-depth information on the owner(s), key partnerships the business has entered into, and company's strengths and weaknesses. If your home business is currently operating, you will recount success, failures, growth, or decline in sales-to-date and describe where your company is now versus where it will be in the future should marketing goals and objectives be realized.

Market Analysis

The market analysis provides information about the marketplace your business currently operates in,

will operate in once started, or a market into which you want to expand. The market analysis section is divided into three main areas, which are the market size, the market segmentation, and marketing environment including a PEST analysis detailing current and emerging political, economic, social, and technology trends and issues that can have a potentially positive or negative affect on your business and marketing efforts.

Customer Analysis

The customer and prospect analysis section of the marketing plan is where you will answer the same important questions about your target customers and prospects. What is the decision-making process they use when buying? What are the critical benefits they look for when deciding which product or service to purchase? How do your target customers make choices between competitors? How sensitive are your potential customers to price, quality, service, and value issues? What promotional or marketing activities are they most likely to notice?

Competitor Analysis

The competitor analysis is an important section of your marketing plan because it gives information about your direct competition, that is, other businesses that sell the same or similar goods or services to the same target audience, within the same geographical area. Also included is a detailed SWOT (strengths, weaknesses, opportunities, and threats) analysis, which when completed will reveal your business's internal strengths and weaknesses and the external opportunities and threats in the marketplace. A SWOT analysis will also help you to identify your position within the marketplace, explaining how consumers view your business, products, or services in direct relationship to your competitors and their products or services.

Marketing Objectives

Every business needs to set concrete objectives so it will have a yardstick to measure progress. In the marketing objectives section, you will learn how to identify and set marketing objectives for your business, objectives that are realistic and attainable and not simply numbers pulled from a hat. Marketing objectives should include many individual goals such as increasing sales, increasing market share, decreasing customer complaints, and improving products, combined into a cohesive statement.

Marketing Strategy

The marketing strategy component of your marketing plan states your philosophy on how you can best reach your target audience and deliver the goods and service they need in the manner they would like these products or services to be delivered, such as quality over price or filling a well-defined niche in the marketplace. It should also indicate how your marketing strategy relates to the four marketing Ps—product, price, place (distribution), and promotion.

Marketing Budget

Your marketing budget answers the obvious question, how much will each marketing strategy and activity cost to implement, manage, and maintain? You have to know how much it will cost to implement marketing strategies to reach your marketing objectives, where the money will come from, and how much money you believe will be generated as a result of each marketing activity.

Action Plan

The action plan section is really nothing more than a big to-do list broken into marketing categories and timetables outlining when each promotional activity described in your marketing strategy section will be implemented in the calendar year. Also included in the action plan section are the systems that you will put into place to measure the results of your promotional and marketing activities and when these measurements will be taken and compared against the marketing plan.

Support Documents

The final section of your marketing plan is reserved for supporting documents such as resumes of the principles, research surveys, market studies, spreadsheets, supplier and vendor agreements, client testimonials, and press clippings. Basically, any document that can be helpful in supporting your research, forecasts, statements, and the information contained within your marketing plan is included. Support documents are especially helpful if your marketing plan will be used as an instrument to help secure business funding.

THE FINANCIAL DATA SECTION

A word of advice when you tackle the financial data section of your business plan: Do not be intimidated by having to create financial statements and projections, and do not let this prevent you from preparing a business plan for your new venture. Many new entrepreneurs feel intimidated by financial planning because of a lack of experience. But as I've said before, any section of your business plan only has to be as simple or as difficult as you want to make it. For a small home business venture, you have to cover the basics in financial planning and forecasting—funding requirements, sources of funding, a balance sheet, a break-even analysis, a cash flow projection, an income projection, and equipment and inventory lists, all of which are discussed in greater detail below. If you decide to purchase a business or a homebased franchise, the financial data section of your business plan will be more involved and cover current and past information including profit and loss statements, cash flow statements, and depreciation schedules.

The information featured here is more focused on the home business start-up rather than the purchase of an operating business or franchise. My intention is to explain what you need to include in the financial data section of your business plan and why in as simple and straightforward manner as possible. You will notice the absence of financial statement templates and charts. Almost all business plan software and most accounting software, such as the ones featured below, include customizable templates for financial forecasting such as break-even analysis, profit and loss statements, and cash flow projections.

- Fundable Plans, www.fundableplans.com
- Plan Magic, www.planmagic.com
- Palo Alto, www.paloalto.com

- QuickBooks, www.quickbooks.com
- Peach Tree, www.peachtree.com

Funding Requirements

The first financial information that you want to include is the funding requirements for your new business. In other words, how much money is needed to start the business and what will the money be used for? Funding requirements should be broken into three subcategories—current funding requirements, the use of the funds, and future funding requirements.

Current Funding Requirements

What are your current funding requirements? In Chapter 2, What Type of Home Business Should You Start?, there is a handy business start-up costs estimator that will help you pinpoint the amount of money needed to start your business.

Use of Funds

In the second section you simply explain what the money will be used for, such as purchasing equipment, marketing activities, buying inventory for resale, obtaining business permits, or renovating your home workspace.

Future Funding Requirements

You also need to describe any future funding requirements, including why the money is needed and when the money will be needed. Future funding requirements can include, for example, new equipment purchases, business expansion plans, or the addition of a company Web site.

Funding Sources

Now that you have identified your funding requirements, the next step is to identify and describe the sources of those funds. Keep in mind that if the purpose of your business plan is to obtain funding, this is the section where you describe the sources of the money you are seeking, that is, bank loan, private investors, or partnerships, how the money will be repaid (cash or equity), and where the money will come from to meet a repayment schedule, which is generally through the business revenues. If you will be seeking private investor funding, you must make the potential upside to the investment very attractive from a return on investment standpoint. If you are providing funding yourself, explain the source of the money, such as savings, borrowing against home equity, or sale of an asset as well as when the funds will be available. Chapter 3, Financial Issues, provides information about funding your home business start-up.

Balance Sheet

The balance sheet simply lists your assets and liabilities, allowing your to determine your net equity position. Assets are items that your business owns that have value, liabilities are debts that your business owes, and equity is the difference between the two. Balance sheets generally record short-term, or current, assets such as accounts receivable and fixed assets such as land and building owned by the business in one column. Short-term, or current, liabilities such as accounts payable and long-term liabilities such as business start-up loans with amortizations greater than 12 months, or debts are payable beyond the current fiscal year in a second column. Not included on the balance sheet are nontangible assets such as goodwill, and contingent liabilities such as future warranty claims. The purpose of the balance sheet is to paint a picture of what your business is worth.

Current and Fixed Assets

- *Cash.* The sum of all cash, including cash on hand and cash in business bank accounts.
- *Inventory.* The total value of in-stock inventory.
- *Accounts Receivable.* Completed and invoiced product/service sales owed to the business by the customer.
- *Loans Receivable.* The total outstanding value of loans from the business made to employees, managers, owners, shareholders, officers, suppliers, vendors, and other third parties.
- *Investments.* The sum of all investments, such as a guaranteed investment certificate owned by the business.
- *Fixed Assets.* The total value of physical assets owned by the business including land, buildings,

Balance Sheet

Current Assets	$ _____	Current Liabilities	$ _____
Fixed Assets	$ _____	Long-Term Liabilities	$ _____
Total Assets	$ _____	Total Liabilities	$ _____
		Total Assets ≠ Total Liabilities = Net Equity	$ _____

leasehold improvements, equipment, tools, transportation, furniture, and fixtures, less depreciation. This does not include your home unless the title is in the name of your business.

- *Miscellaneous Assets.* Miscellaneous assets include deposits prepaid and prepaid expenses.

Current and Long-Term Liabilities

- *Accounts Payable.* The total sum of money owed to your product and service suppliers for outstanding invoices, including items such as inventory and telephone bills.
- *Accrued Expenses.* The total sum of monies owed but not yet due, such as wages, taxes, benefits, and interest on loans.
- *Current/Short-Term Loans.* The total principle sum of short-term loans, or notes to 360 days, less interest, which is an accrued liability.
- *Long-Term Loans.* The total principal sum of long-term loans owed by the business to banks, investors, and shareholders.

Break-Even Analysis

The break-even analysis is used to determine how much product or service must be sold for the business to break even, for the total amount of incoming revenues to match the total amount of outgoing expenses. To calculate your break-even point, you will need to estimate your fixed expenses (overhead). (In Chapter 2, What Type of Business Should Your Start?, you will find an overhead estimator worksheet.) You will also need to know how much the variable costs are for purchasing products or delivering of services, as well as the gross margin for each sale, which can be found in Chapter 9, What Price Will You Charge? For example, if you sold bicycles from home, your fixed costs were $50,000 per annum, and you sold each bicycle for $1,000, which included variable costs and a gross margin of 25 percent, you have $250 gross profit per sale. You would need to sell 200 per year to break-even, $50,000 in fixed costs divided by $250 gross margin equals 200 sales per year or 17 sales per month.

Cash Flow Projections

The cash flow projection shows how money will flow into the business in the form of revenues and flow out of the business in the form of expenses (disbursements). For new business start-ups, the cash flow projection is important because it can tell you the times of the year when you can expect a cash surplus and the times of the year when you can expect a cash shortage. Knowing this information enables you to manage your money even before the money begins to come into the business, and it gives you the opportunity to secure working capital funding to avoid running out of cash to operate your business when you have projected a cash flow shortage. It should be noted that a cash flow projection is not a cash flow statement, which shows how cash has already flowed in and out of the business over a specific period, usually 12 months. The cash flow projection is the anticipated revenues and disbursements over the next 12 months. There are three parts to the cash flow projection—estimated monthly cash sales (products and service), estimated monthly cash disbursements (fixed and variable costs), and closing cash balance, which is the total cash sales less the total cash disbursements for each month. The cash balance can be a plus or minus and is then carried forward to the next month and the next, until you have projected your cash flow on a month-by-month basis for the entire year.

Income Projections

Income projections are the anticipated sales and expenses on a year-by-year basis moving forward. They should not be confused with income statements, also known as profit and loss statements, which are based on actual operating history. Ideally, as a new start-up, you will want to prepare income projections for at least three years in advance and then measure performance against actual income statements after each operating year. Doing so enables you to tweak your marketing strategies if actual revenues and expenses do not meet projected revenues and expenses. Income projections are prepared using a combination of elements, including your marketing objectives (sales target), estimated fixed overheads, variable costs, and gross margins or markups.

Equipment and Inventory Lists

Finally, the financial data section of your business plan includes equipment and inventory lists (see Figure 6.1). You can separate each list or combine them into one. Regardless of the form, equipment

---

FIGURE 6.1   Capital Equipment and Inventory List

Current Equipment

Equipment Description	# of Units	$Unit Cost	Total Cost
_____	_____	$ _____	$ _____
_____	_____	$ _____	$ _____
_____	_____	$ _____	$ _____
_____	_____	$ _____	$ _____

Needed Equipment

Equipment Description	# of Units	$Unit Cost	Total Cost	Date Required
_____	_____	$ _____	$ _____	_____
_____	_____	$ _____	$ _____	_____
_____	_____	$ _____	$ _____	_____
_____	_____	$ _____	$ _____	_____

Current Inventory

Inventory Description	# of Units	$Unit Cost	Total Cost
_____	_____	$ _____	$ _____
_____	_____	$ _____	$ _____
_____	_____	$ _____	$ _____
_____	_____	$ _____	$ _____

Needed Inventory

Inventory Description	# of Units	$Unit Cost	Total Cost	Date Required
_____	_____	$ _____	$ _____	_____
_____	_____	$ _____	$ _____	_____
_____	_____	$ _____	$ _____	_____
_____	_____	$ _____	$ _____	_____

---

and inventory lists should include what you currently have, what is needed in the short-term (less than 12 months), and what is needed on the long-term (more than 12 months). Additionally, you should include the number of units that are required, the cost of the items, and the date when the required items will be purchased. Equipment and inventory lists can be included in the financial data section of your business plan, or you can include the lists in the financial support documents in the appendices of your business plan.

THE APPENDICES SECTION

The appendices of your business plan are reserved for supporting documents such as resumes for the principles, research surveys, market studies, financial forecasts, supplier and vendor agreements, client testimonials, and press clippings. Basically, they include any documents that can be helpful in supporting your research, your forecasts, your statements, and the information contained in your business plan, as well as internal plans within your business plan such as a marketing plan, sales plan, advertising plan, and Internet plan. Supporting documents can be especially helpful if you are going to use your business plan as a tool to secure investment capital to start or grow your business. After reading the executive overview, bankers, accountants, and venture capitalists often go straight to the supporting documents section to make sure that you have done your homework, that you are committed to the project, and that there is verifiable documentation indicating a great potential to succeed. In short, they want to know that their money is going into the right venture and will be managed by capable individuals. Depending on the purpose of your business plan, you may or may not need to include copies of all or any of the supporting documents featured below.

Personal Documents

Personal support documents are generally focused on three areas—resumes, training, and financial statements. Resumes for all of the key players in the business, including owner(s), managers, key employees, sales agents, and subcontractors, should be included with the business plan, even if they are

only simple one-page resumes highlighting experiences in bullet-list format. Copies of training certificates or specialized licenses held by the owner(s), managers, or key employees relative to the business, products sold, or services supplied should also be included. Finally, if the purpose of the business plan is to secure funding, you will need to include a personal assets statement for each of the people that are applying for the loan. The asset statement should list all assets, such as real estate, automobiles, equities, and savings plans, and all personal liabilities, including property mortgages, personal loans, and credit cards. Subtract your total liabilities or debts from your total assets to arrive at a net worth.

Legal Documents

Copies of legal documents that should be included in the business plan are:

- Business registrations
- Domain name registrations
- Business and home occupation licenses
- Business insurance coverage documents
- If applicable, patents, trademarks, and copyright documents
- Product, workmanship, and third party warranties
- Vendor and supplier agreements already negotiated and in force

Financial Documents

Copies of financial documents that should be included are:

- Short-term and long-term sales projections
- Break-even analysis
- Audited financial statement if a business is being purchased or if a current business is applying for funds
- Marketing budgets and projections
- Start-up costs estimates
- Equipment and supplies projections, estimates, and lists
- Operating fixed costs projections

Marketing Documents

Documents supporting your marketing research, secondary data sources, and other marketing-related documents that support or prove your marketing statements within your business plan should also be included. Of all of the support documents that you include in your business plan, marketing documents probably carry the most weight with the majority of readers. It is through the process of researching the market, demand for the product, target customers, and competition that the true potential viability of the business is proven. Any or all of the following would qualify as marketing support documents:

- Primary research documents, including surveys, questionnaires, and focus group results
- Secondary data documents
- Target customer profile
- PEST and SWOT analysis
- Your marketing materials including brochures, product photographs, catalogs, price lists, and print advertisements
- Press clippings
- Client testimonials and company, individual, or organizational endorsements.
- Competitor brochures, price lists, warranties, and print advertisements, and Better Business Bureau report, if available

RESOURCES

Associations

Business Development Bank of Canada (BDC)
150 King Street West, Suite 100
Toronto, ON M5H 1J9
(416) 395-9014
www.bdc.ca

Canadian Chamber of Commerce
BCE Place, 181 Bay Street, Heritage Building
Toronto, ON M5J 2T3
(416) 868-6415
www.chamber.ca

Service Corps of Retired Executives (SCORE)
SCORE Association
409 Third Street SW
6th Floor
Washington, DC 20024
(800) 634-0245
www.score.org

U.S. Small Business Administration (SBA)
409 Third Street SW
Washington, DC 20416
(800) 827-5722
www.sba.gov/indexbusplans.html.

U.S. Chamber of Commerce
1615 H Street NW
Washington, DC 20062-2000
(202) 659-6000
www.uschamber.com

Suggested Reading

Bangs, David H. *The Business Planning Guide: Creating a Winning Plan for Success. 9th Edition.* Chicago: Dearborn Trade Publishing, 2002.

Covello, Joseph, and Brian Hazelgren. *Your First Business Plan: Learn the Critical Steps to Writing a Winning Business Plan.* Naperville, IL: Sourcebooks Inc., 1997.

Debelak, Don *Successful Business Models: Surefire Ways to Build a Profitable Business.* Irvine, CA: Entrepreneur Media, Inc., 2003.

Hargrave, Lee H. *Plans for Profitability: How to Write a Strategic Business Plan.* Titusville, FL: Four Seasons Publishers, 1999.

Hendricks, Mark. *Business Plans Made Easy: It's Not as Hard as You Think!* Irvine, CA: Entrepreneur Media, Inc., 1999.

Norman, Jan. *What No One Ever Tells You About Starting Your Own Business: Real Life Start-Up Advice from 101 Successful Entrepreneurs.* Chicago: Upstart Publishing Company, 1999.

Web Sites

American Demographics Magazine, www.demographics.com: Information and advice about marketing research and demographics.

Business Know-How, www.businessknowhow.com: Small business information, advice, tools, and services.

Center for Business Planning, www.businessplans.org: Visitors can access information about creating business plans, including free templates and samples as well as business planning products and services.

Market Research, www.marketresearch.com: Billed as the most comprehensive collection of published market research available on demand.

National Venture Capital Association, www.nvca.org: Association membership consists of venture capital firms and organizations that manage pools of risk equity capital designated to be invested in young, emerging companies.

Nolo, www.nolo.com: Online legal self-help information, products, services, resources, and links for consumers and business owners.

Palo Alto Software, www.paloalto.com: Business Plan Pro, software that enables the user to create business plans.

Small Business Loans Online, www.smallbusiness loans.com: Online loan applications for financing new business start-ups and for financing existing businesses to help growth.

Small Business Now, www.smallbusinessnow.com: Small business information, advice, tools, products, services, and links of interest.

U.S. Census Bureau, www.census.gov: Market demographics, information, and statistics.

V Finance, www.vfinance.com: Directory of venture capital firms and angel investors.

CHAPTER 7

Establishing Your Home Workspace

THIS CHAPTER IS CALLED ESTABLISHING YOUR home workspace, not establishing your home office, because every business that is operated or managed from home will require some sort of workspace or storage, but not all will require office space in the traditional sense. If you operate a freelance photography business, your main workspace in the home will be a darkroom. If you operate an office cleaning service, the majority of your in-home workspace will be storage space for equipment and supplies. If you operate an automotive paint shop, then chances are your workspace will be the garage or a freestanding shop out back. And, if you operate your dental practice from home, then your workspace will probably be a large portion of your home with a waiting room, workroom, and office space. In other words, no two home businesses will have the exact same workspace requirements.

While helping you determine you needs so that you can select the right home workspace for your particular business, this chapter is also broken into other distinct sections to help you establish your home workspace in a step-by-step fashion:

1. Selecting your workspace in the home based on your needs
2. Planning your in-home workspace
3. Renovating your in-home workspace
4. Equipping your workspace
5. Home business security and safety
6. Home business office furniture, equipment, and supplies checklist
7. Steps that you can take to build a positive image for your new business

The transition from working outside of your home to working full- or part-time in the home is a process that requires much thought in order to create a working environment that is suitable for your business and in balance with the needs of your family.

SELECTING YOUR WORKSPACE

The type of business that you will be operating or managing from a homebased location is key to determining the type, size, and location of the workspace you need. Careful consideration must also be given to the space needs of your family and how space in the home is currently being utilized for day-to-day living, as well as for special occasions, seasonal activities, and guests. Because selecting a home workspace requires balancing the needs of your business with the needs of your family, compromises will have to be made on both fronts.

If you will be operating your business primarily from within your home, you will want to incorporate as many of the following ideas as possible to help strike the required business-family balance:

- If available, choose a room with a door that shuts so that when required, you can keep business in, and family, friends, and pets out.
- If money is tight, select a room that will require the least amount of alterations. While having a big, new, fully functioning workspace is great, it means absolutely nothing if there is no money left to market and promote your goods and services.
- Pick a room or space that is as far away from routine household noise as possible, that is, the kitchen, laundry room, and main entertainment room.
- Select a workspace that is large enough to operate your business. Working out of two or three separate areas of the home is far less productive then working from one area; you are constantly searching for things rather than working.
- If possible, try to make your workspace a single-use area. The room should not double as the dining room at night, the children's playroom on weekends, or Aunt June's bedroom when she comes to visit every other week. If your home is small, single-use business space can be difficult to accommodate, but be creative and seek ways you can shift room uses around so that you can define a business-only workspace.
- If clients will be coming to your home, ideally you will want a workspace with a separate outside entrance or one very close to an existing entrance.
- If you will be operating a business that creates noise or generates byproducts (dust, mess, fumes) look to the garage or an outside structure as the workspace solution.

Your Workspace Options

Your workspace options range from any old corner of the home to a separate outside structure. I have used a converted garage, den, living room, basement, and a spare bedroom for various home business ventures over the years. Of course, each workspace option has advantages and disadvantages.

Spare Corner

Though by far the least expensive way to set up a home workspace, any old corner of the house where you have room also has the disadvantages of lack of privacy, noise, and storage issues. However, if all your budget allows is the purchase of a secondhand desk that will go in the corner of your living room and act as the head office location for you, new business enterprise, then go for it. Many successful businesspeople have started with far less. That said, if space allows, at least try to select a room with a door that closes so that you can separate business from your personal life a bit.

Dining Room

Believe it or not, the dining room is the most popular room of the house to convert into a home business workspace, mainly because it is cheap and quick to do, and busy lifestyles dictate that the dining room is an area that often is used only on occasion. The downside is that most dining rooms do not have doors that close, which is not very conducive to client visits. And, on those occasions when the dining room will be used, you'll find yourself packing up and moving your business out. Then you move back in later, which can be a real pain in the neck.

Extra Bedroom

A spare bedroom is the second most popular choice. Given the fact that the door probably shuts, it's a better choice for most people. At present, I use a second-story spare bedroom that I have converted into a home office, complete with all of the traditional office equipment and furnishings, which has served me well for my business and writing projects. However, I seldom have clients that visit, as nearly 100 percent of my consulting work takes me to the client's location.

Converted Garage

The garage can be a great place to operate your business, especially if it is attached to the home, has a separate entrance, requires few alterations, and is large enough to meet your needs. The downside is the large amount of money that will be needed to make the transformation from a typical garage to a fully functioning home workspace complete with electricity, heat, water, sewer, and communications. Depending on your needs and budgets, the advantages of a separate entrance, lots of space, and privacy, may make the cost of alterations a very worthwhile expense. Recently, an associate converted his double attached garage to home business use, leaving the one side for storage, shipping, and receiving, basically unchanged, while renovating the other into a very elaborate office that would rival any in a high-rise, high-rent downtown office district.

Attic Space

Attics can also work, providing they have been altered to suit your climate and have good access. The downside is that there is almost no chance of having a separate outside entrance for client visits, and if the attic space is the third floor, walking up and down two flights of steps with documents, mail, products, and client job files can be very tiring.

Basement

Basements provide yet another good option for home business space, if they have been altered for your climate and have good access, improved lighting, and adequate headroom. The additional concern with basement workspaces is dampness and water. Basements are notoriously damp and wet at certain times of the year. So careful thought will have to be given to this option, especially for storage of inventory and paper documents that can be easily ruined.

A New Addition

The most costly option is to design and build an addition onto your home to accommodate your new venture. Not only will you have to comply with building codes, zoning regulations, and other rules associated with adding square footage to your home, but there is also the cost to consider. On average, you can count on $80 to $100 per square foot in building costs alone, not including permits and equipment. Therefore, if you want to add on an additional 500 square feet for your new home business enterprise, you can count on spending $40,000 to $50,000 just on the addition and before you spend one dime on business equipment, inventory, marketing, or

any other aspect of setting up and getting your business rolling.

Outside Structures

Outbuildings on your property, such as tool sheds, enclosed cabanas, and freestanding workshops, are another option, if the structure is suitable and large enough to meet your needs. The downside to outbuildings is that most do not have water or sewer connections and only basic electrical services, lacking proper heat and light. By the time you renovate to suit and upgrade the mechanicals, you will be talking about a substantial amount of money that might be better spent renovating another space in your home, such as the attic or basement, that does not require as much alterations. Outbuildings are generally in the backyard, so you would have to address client parking and access, as well as access for deliveries and pickups. However, if you plan on operating a manufacturing or repair business, a renovated or new outbuilding on your property may be your only logical, or legal, option for your new venture.

Additional Workspace Issues

The type of home business that you will be starting also greatly influences your needs in terms of where in the house the workspace is established and, in many cases even if a business can be legally operated from home. Here are a few additional workspace issues to consider prior to starting up.

1. Will you have clients visiting your home office? If so:
   - Do you have the space required in your home office to accommodate client visits?
   - Do you have suitable parking for clients, and does your home have good access?
   - Will you be able to separate your home living space from your workspace in order to provide visiting clients with privacy, and privacy for your family?
   - Is the appearance of your home suitable for client visits? Peeling paint, threadbare carpets, and broken porch boards can send potential clients the wrong signals about your business.

- Can you provide clients easy and private access to washroom facilities in your home?
2. Will you have employees working from your home? If so:
   - Can employees or outside contractors legally work from your home?
   - Do you have the space required for one or more employees to work from your home office or workspace?
   - Can you provide employees working from your home with enough privacy to get their work done, and at the same time can you offer your family enough privacy from your employees?
   - Will employees have separate and easy access to your home workspace, and can you provide them with suitable parking?
   - Can you provide employees with the basic necessities, such as washroom facilities, space for breaks and lunch, and closet space for coats?
3. Will you be manufacturing or assembling products at home? If so:
   - Do local zoning regulations allow home-based manufacturing businesses?
   - Will you have to upgrade or install new mechanical services such as heat, cooling, electrical, and plumbing to accommodate your business?
   - Do you need to install ventilation systems, and if so, what about the air and odor pollution it expels? Will noise pollution bother your neighbors?
   - Do you have adequate access for parking, shipping, receiving, and storage?
   - Do you have to upgrade your home to meet fire safety standards because of the business or the product you manufacture?
4. Do you need storage space? If so:
   - Do you have enough room in your home to provide adequate storage space for inventory, equipment, business records, and client files?
   - Is your storage space easily accessed? Roomy attics are great, but if you risk life and limb every time you need to access equipment,

inventory, or information, alternate storage must be found.
   - Is your storage space suitable for the things that you need to store? Consider dampness, heat, critters, and cold.
   - Is your storage space secure so that valuable business equipment, inventory, and records are not at risk of being stolen?
   - If you do not have suitable storage space, is there suitable storage for rent close by with good access? And how much does it cost?

PLANNING YOUR WORKSPACE

You will greatly maximize your chances of putting together the most productive, functional, and visually appealing workspace at the lowest possible cost if you take the time necessary to plan your workspace well in advance of actually setting it up. Planning your workspace rather than charging in and slapping it together overnight enables you to carefully lay out your workspace, taking into account all of your needs, while avoiding costly mistakes that can happen when a job is rushed.

Assuming that no renovations are needed to alter the space, the first order of business is to completely clean the room and thoroughly clean the wall, ceiling, and floor surfaces. It may be a good time to give your new, and empty, workspace a fresh coat of paint. The next step is to take measurements of the room and make a scale drawing of the room on a large piece of paper or Bristol board, noting windows, doors, electrical outlets, telephone jacks, cable outlets, and lights on the floor plan drawing. Once you have an accurate, scaled floor plan, you can move on to purchasing equipment and furniture that fit your space and suit your needs. Install the furniture and equipment as per plan once everything is substantially purchased. This may seem like a time-consuming way of planning your office space, but you only want to do the job once, come in on budget, and get exactly what you need for your business right from the start. The extra time spent planning and designing your workspace now will ultimately save you time and money down the road by not having to interrupt business to redo your workspace or lose productivity because the space does not suit your business.

Hiring a Designer

Most home workspaces are basic enough so that they can be planned without the need of calling in help to professionally design and plan the space. However, if you intend to spend a substantial amount of money to create a workspace in your home, you might want to consider hiring an interior designer with home office experience to plan and design it. A key point to remember is that the ultimate goal of the designer is not to cost you money. The goal of the designer is to create the perfect workspace to suit your specific business needs while saving you at least their fee for designing and planning your workspace. That's right, in the end you will almost always find that a professional designer can ultimately save you enough money through their experience, contacts, and trade discounts to cover their fee, especially on contracts in excess of $25,000. Additionally, the finished product will probably be far superior to what you can plan and design yourself—contractors and designers excluded, of course. To find an interior designer with experience in home workspace design and planning, consult your local Yellow Pages directory, ask friends and associates if they know one, or you can log onto the Web site for the International Interior Design Association located at www.iida.org and use their free member finder service.

Creating an Environmentally Friendly Workspace

You will also want to get in tune with a go-green attitude and become an environmentally conscious home business owner. In addition to tying in your home business recycling with your existing household recycling program for convenience, find out how you can utilize a wide range of recycled products and use these products in the day-to-day operations of your business. And don't be afraid to let your customers know that you support recycling and environmentally conscious business practices. In fact, include this information in all of your advertising and business communications because you will never alienate a customer or prospect by being

an environmentally conscious business owner. You may even attract a few new customers simply because we all know that aiming for a healthier planet is not only right, but a must for this and future generations. Heidi Schimpl, Community Programs Coordinator at the North Shore Recycling Program in North Vancouver, British Columbia, advises putting simple and inexpensive practices into place in your home office will save money and contribute to a healthier environment:

- Place paper recycling bins in convenient locations such as beside your desk, areas where you pack and unpack shipments, and near file cabinets. The more convenient you make recycling, the more you will recycle.
- Hang on to paper that has been printed only on one side and use the other side for printing unimportant and draft documents and for use in your fax machine. You can also cut paper that has only been printed on one side and staple it together for use as note and memo pads.
- Purchase and use unbleached office paper with a high-recycled content; if available, 100 percent postconsumer waste is the best.
- Purchase and use ink and toner cartridge refill kits to cut down on waste and save money on printer cartridge costs. If your printer and toner cartridges are nonrefillable, contact the manufacturer because most have programs for cartridge recycling.
- Edit documents on screen rather than printing draft copies.
- Reduce fax-related paper waste by using a computer fax-modem.
- Turn off lights when not in use, and purchase energy-efficient office equipment with power saving sleep options.
- Use energy-efficient light bulbs and reusable items such as rechargeable batteries and mechanical pencils and pens.
- Purchase office supplies in bulk to cut down on packaging waste, and purchase only what you need regardless of what's on sale.

Additional helpful information and tips about recycling practices and your home business, as well as environmental information, can be found on the

North Shore Recycling Program's Web site, which is located at www.nsrp.bc.ca. Green Sites Online, located at www.greensites.com, also offers recycling information, resources, and links.

RENOVATING YOUR WORKSPACE

If you can use the space that you have selected with only minimal renovations, you are wise to do so. Sometimes, however, you will have to renovate your workspace or other areas of your home to accommodate your new business. This is especially true for practicing professionals setting up shop at home and for people engaged in manufacturing or assembling products at home.

Renovating your homebased workspace can be challenging for a number of reasons. There is the noise and disruption that is caused within the home, and if the renovations are extensive, the mess. There is the time factor. Once you have made the decision to start a home business, you want to be able to get moving as quickly as possible so that you can begin to recoup some of the money that will be going out at near lighting speed. Finally, there is the cost. Renovating is not cheap, especially when you consider that skilled trades charge upwards of $50 per hour plus the costs of materials. If you can get by with the workspace that you have without renovations, you should do so. And, if you must renovate your home to accommodate your new business, the information in this section should be very helpful.

Do It Yourself or Hire a Contractor?

Once you have action and design plans in place and know exactly what needs to be done, the next step is to decide if you can do the work, or if an experience contractor is necessary. Certainly, if the job is uncomplicated, and if you have the time, tools, and talents necessary to do the work, by all means do the work. It can save you a substantial amount of money on labor costs. If the job is small, but a bit outside of your comfort zone, hiring a local handyperson may suffice. If you choose the handyperson route, expect to pay about $25 to $35 per hour plus the costs of materials. If however, your new workspace is a major renovation that includes upgraded mechanicals, removing walls, installing new doors and such,

you will be well advised to call in a professional contractor to carry out the required work.

If you decide to hire a contractor, the following are a few tips to ensure the job goes smoothly:

- Explain the type of business that you will be starting and show the contractor your plans, equipment lists, and other necessary information. Doing so will help the contractor understand the true nature of the job, and he may have a few cost saving suggestions to pass along.
- Obtain three quotes, basing your decision not only on price, but also on value, quality, and reputation.
- Call the contractor's references to make sure past clients were satisfied with the finished job, and if possible, try to have a look at a home office that the contractor has built or substantially renovated.
- Make sure that the scope of work to be completed and the contracts are in writing, well-detailed, all-inclusive, and signed by both parties.
- Request proof of liability insurance and workers' compensation insurance from the contractor before the job begins.
- Set favorable payment terms in four installments, 25 percent deposit, 25 percent progress installment, 25 percent on substantial completion, and the balance 30 days after full competition of the renovation.
- Inspect materials delivered to the job site prior to installation to make sure they are the materials and products specified in the scope of work and contract.
- Find out which party is responsible for securing building permits and if the costs of these permits are include in the estimate. This is a very important point. If you decide to renovate without a permit and the required inspections from your local municipality, should there later be a structural, electrical, or other mechanical problems with the work that has been done, your insurance company may not compensate you if the work was completed illegally.

- Make sure that all warranty information is included in the written agreement. The workmanship portion of the warranty should be a minimum of five years from the date of competition.
- Don't be totally focused on cost. Remember, this is a job that you want to tackle only once. You may save $500 now by not installing that new outside entrance into your workspace, but if you elect to install it down the road, the cost can easily be as much as five times what it would have cost when the crew and tools were on the original job.
- Finally, before selecting any one contractor check with your local chapter of the Better Business Bureau to make sure that the contractor has no unresolved complaints outstanding.

I say unresolved because complaints that have been resolved in the past are generally not a sign of trouble, but unresolved complaints usually are.

Renovation Costs

Whether you plan on doing the required renovations yourself or hire an outside contractor, it is wise to have a general idea of the costs associated with the renovation, before getting started or asking for quotes and bids on the job. Below is a basic Renovation Costs Worksheet (see Figure 7.1) that you can use to estimate the approximate costs associated with renovating your workspace. You can, of course, make additions or deletions to the worksheet based on your specific needs. To arrive at the cost per unit or total cost of certain items or services, you will

---

| FIGURE 7.1 | **Renovation Costs Worksheet** |

	Quantity	$Unit Cost	$Total Cost
❑ Building and inspection permits	_____	$_____	$_____
❑ General construction	_____	$_____	$_____
❑ Finish carpentry	_____	$_____	$_____
❑ Plumbing and heating	_____	$_____	$_____
❑ New or upgraded electrical	_____	$_____	$_____
❑ Security alarms	_____	$_____	$_____
❑ Fire alarms and extinguishers	_____	$_____	$_____
❑ New or upgraded communications capabilities	_____	$_____	$_____
❑ Windows	_____	$_____	$_____
❑ Window coverings	_____	$_____	$_____
❑ Doors and locksets	_____	$_____	$_____
❑ Paint	_____	$_____	$_____
❑ Wall covering	_____	$_____	$_____
❑ Flooring	_____	$_____	$_____
❑ Build-ins	_____	$_____	$_____
❑ Decorations	_____	$_____	$_____
❑ Other _____	_____	$_____	$_____
❑ Other _____	_____	$_____	$_____
		Total	$_____

need to make a few calls, as well as visiting your local home improvement store to check product prices.

EQUIPPING YOUR WORKSPACE

You have selected, planned, and renovated your workspace, now it is time to equip it. Equipping your home workspace with the furniture, equipment, technology, communications, and supplies you need to operate your business requires you to consider three main points—needs, comfort, and budget. The need for office equipment, furniture, technology, and communications vary with the type of business planned. But every business will need at least a few items from each of the five main home workspace categories: furniture, equipment, technology, communications, and supplies. Each of these categories are discussed in greater detail later in the chapter.

The second issue will be comfort, which is of particular concern for home business operators that will be putting in long hours at their desks, in front of a computer, or on the telephone. In terms of comfort, there is no such thing as cutting corners. In order to be productive over the long term you have to be comfortable. In recent years, many new physical ailments such as carpal tunnel syndrome have been linked to long hours spent doing repetitive tasks, for example, typing at a keyboard. So even if you do not particularly care about being comfortable, think about the long-term physical effects of improper furniture and lighting. The study of the correct positioning of your body while at rest or work is called ergonomics, and it can play a major role in comfort and maintaining good physical health over the long term. When setting up and equipping your home workspace, you will want to ensure that it is ergonomically correct. To help you plan, you can purchase a book on ergonomics, or you can log on to Ergonomics Online, www.ergonomics.org, which provides in-depth information, links, and resources related to ergonomics.

The third determining factoring in terms of equipping your home workspace is your budget. The following are six ways a financially challenged entrepreneur can substantially reduce the cost of home office furniture, equipment, computers, and communication products or limit the amount of money needed up front:

1. *Barter.* You can barter and trade for needed office furniture and equipment. For instance, if you operate a painting service, ask local office suppliers if they would be interested in trading office furniture for a paint job. Alternately, you can join a local barter club and trade whatever products or services you sell with members that sell office furniture and equipment. Barter News, www.barternews.com, is an online magazine dedicated to the world of business barter clubs, organizations, and industry information.

2. *Borrow.* Create and copy a list of all needed office furniture, equipment, and supplies that you need and then distribute the copies to friends and family members. You will be amazed at how many of the things that you need to start and run your business are stored away in your friends' and families' basements, garages, and attics, just waiting to be borrowed. Most won't mind if you borrow these items. In fact, many will probably be happy just to get rid of them and free up some space for more clutter.

3. *Buy seconds or floor models.* Call around to your local office outfitters and inquire about factory seconds and the floor models they have available. Often you can save as much as 25 percent off the retail price by purchasing seconds with slight blemishes or floor models with nothing wrong other than a few fingerprints and smudges.

4. *Purchase secondhand.* Buy the office equipment and furniture that you need secondhand, and save as much as 75 percent or more off the retail price. Good places to begin your search for secondhand office equipment include auctions, business closeouts, newspaper classified ads, garage sales, and retailers that sell secondhand office furniture, equipment, and computers.

5. *Lease.* Take the no-money-down route and lease brand new office furniture, equipment, and computers for your business. You will have to pay for these items monthly, but you will not be tying up precious capital buying them, capital that can be used for marketing.

Lease payments can be written off taxes, and you will have the use of brand new equipment with full warranties.

6. *Rent.* You can also rent the furniture and equipment you need. Definitely rent specialized equipment for select jobs on an as-needed basis, so that you do not have to shell out all the cash up front to purchase it. Again, rent payments are a deductible business expense. If the equipment breaks down, in most cases you just return it and pick up a replacement with no repair charges. This also makes renting office furniture and business equipment a wise choice for cash-strapped start-ups.

Getting the Office Furniture and Equipment that You Need

Every business has different needs in terms of office furniture and equipment. If clients will be visiting your home office, your furniture and equipment will need to reflect this, both in appearance and function. If you do not have clients visiting your home office, you will have a little more leeway in your equipment and furniture choices. It won't really matter if the colors are mismatched, if you purchased your desk secondhand at your neighbor's garage sale, or even if you choose to build a few of the items yourself. All that really matters is that your furniture and equipment does what you need it to do, be reliable, and be comfortable. So what are the basics that every home workspace needs, regardless of business type?

Desk

You will need a desk large enough for a computer monitor with tower storage underneath, a printer, and a telephone and fax machine, or a telephone/fax combination. The idea behind having a desk large enough for the basics is that once you get working you can remain productive by not having to get up from the desk to answer the telephone or move to a separate computer workstation.

Comfortable Chair

If you can only splurge on one piece of office furniture, a comfortable and ergonomically correct chair should be that luxury item, especially if your business keeps you in front of the computer or on the telephone for long periods of time. I endured many uncomfortable chairs until I decided a few years ago to splurge on a comfortable and high-quality chair for my office. All I can say is that I should have done it ten years earlier. Sitting in an uncomfortable chair all day is like running a marathon in sneakers that are two sizes to small, both will leave you in physical agony. Key things to look for are distance from the seat to floor, adjustable armrests, and adjustable seating positions.

File Storage

You do not have to invest in a file cabinet for client files immediately if money is tight. Instead, for about five dollars you can purchase accordion-style file storage boxes that can hold up to about 100 documents. That is enough file storage space to get you going, especially if you purchase one for business records and a second for client files. Obviously, as your business grows, you will want to invest in quality cabinets with locking mechanisms.

Bookshelf

Bookshelves are another indispensable item for the home workspace. In addition to the obvious use of storing books, they can also be used to organize and store office supplies; in and out boxes; mail; radio, CDs and floppies; and just about anything else that needs to be organized and easily accessible. Ikea, www.ikea.com, is the king of bookshelves. If you don't mind assembling them yourself, for about $20 each you can get freestanding bookshelves that will store a ton of office stuff.

Lighting

If you are like me, as the years roll on things are just a little more out of focus then they used to be. Natural lighting from windows and skylights is best, but you will also need good quality electric lighting, which can make a huge difference in reducing eyestrain and increasing productivity. In addition to bright overhead lighting, also invest a few dollars in a good quality desk or clamp-on work lamp that can be positioned to help work on specific tasks.

FIGURE 7.2 Office Furniture and Equipment Costs Worksheet

	Quantity	$Unit Cost	$Total Cost
❑ Desk	_____	$_____	$_____
❑ Office chair	_____	$_____	$_____
❑ Client seating	_____	$_____	$_____
❑ File cabinets	_____	$_____	$_____
❑ Bookcases	_____	$_____	$_____
❑ Worktable(s)	_____	$_____	$_____
❑ Work lighting	_____	$_____	$_____
❑ Fireproof safe	_____	$_____	$_____
❑ Storage boxes	_____	$_____	$_____
❑ Photocopier	_____	$_____	$_____
❑ Postage meter	_____	$_____	$_____
❑ Radio	_____	$_____	$_____
❑ Paper shredder	_____	$_____	$_____
❑ Recycling bin	_____	$_____	$_____
❑ Labeling machine	_____	$_____	$_____
❑ Wastebasket	_____	$_____	$_____
❑ Other _____	_____	$_____	$_____
❑ Other _____	_____	$_____	$_____
		Total	$_____

Worktable

In addition to your desk, purchase or build a worktable separate from your desk if space allows. They can be used for working on lower priority jobs, opening and sorting mail, book and record keeping duties, packing and unpacking inventory, and much more.

Office Furniture and Equipment Costs

Figure 7.2, Office Furniture and Equipment Costs Worksheet will help you in calculating the costs of equipping your new home workspace with furniture and other related equipment. Once again, ignore items that are not relevant to your business and add items that are specific to it.

Getting the Technology You Need

There is basic technology that every business needs to operate: a computer, operating system, software, monitor, modem, printer, and a detail camera.

Computer

Assuming you know how to use a computer (if not, waste no time signing up for computer training at your local community college), the main considerations will be processing speed and data storage capabilities. Because both change on a daily basis, I won't talk about the specifics other than to say get as much file storage space and memory as you can afford. Desktop computers range in price from a low of $600 to as much as $3,000 for a top-of-the-line home office computer with more bells and whistles than you will ever need or use. Additionally, if your business takes you on the road a lot, you may want to consider purchasing a notebook computer; expect to pay in the range of $1,500 to $4,000.

Monitor

A computer monitor is another essential piece of office technology. You can purchase a standard monitor, a flat screen monitor or a flat panel LED monitor, which is great if you are limited in space. Monitors start at about $150 new, and are a third of that used. They can go as high as $1,500 for one that is suitable for professional desktop publishing.

Keyboard and Mouse

Studies have shown that ergonomics should play a major role in your decision about what keyboard and mouse to purchase for your computer. The reason is that hand, wrist, arm, and shoulder position are affected by your mouse and keyboard. Each has to be in balance to reduce the potential for injury. You may also want to consider purchasing a wireless keyboard and mouse set because it frees space on your desk and eliminates those pesky wires that seem to get wrapped around everything. Plan to spend about $100 to $150 for a decent keyboard and mouse set.

Modem

Most computers now come with a standard 56K modem, which is needed to connect to the Internet. You can also opt for a more expensive modem, giving you the ability to connect to high-speed cable Internet (if available in your area), which allows you to download files up to 20 times faster than a standard dial-up Internet connection.

Printer

Ink jet printers start at about $50. Home office laser printers are selling in the range of $200 to $1,000 depending on features, and print speed. Generally, because of ink cartridge prices, the cost to print each page with an ink jet printer is about four times as much as with a laser printer. So, if you are going to be doing a lot of printing, a laser printer will save you a substantial amount of money over the long term, even when you factor in the extra cost to purchase.

Digital Camera

Whoopee for the advent of digital cameras. They are indispensable to home business owners. You can take pictures of products, clients, completed jobs, or your trip to Florida, and because the images (photographs) use digital technology, they are easily transferred to your Web site, e-mails, or desktop publishing programs. You can easily create brochures, presentations, catalogs, and fliers using your own photographs. Good quality digital cameras cost in the range of $400 at the time of writing this book. However, like all technology, the costs are sure to drop as demand increases.

Computer Hardware, Accessories, and Software Costs

The following Computer Hardware, Accessories, and Software Costs Worksheet (see Figure 7.3) can help you calculate the costs of equipping your new home workspace with common technology. Ignore

FIGURE 7.3 Computer Hardware, Accessories, and Software Costs Worksheet

	Quantity	$Unit Cost	$Total Cost
❑ Desk	_____	$_____	$_____
❑ Desktop computer	_____	$_____	$_____
❑ Desktop monitor	_____	$_____	$_____
❑ Keyboard and mouse	_____	$_____	$_____
❑ Modem	_____	$_____	$_____
❑ Notebook computer	_____	$_____	$_____
❑ Printer	_____	$_____	$_____
❑ PowerPoint projector	_____	$_____	$_____

| FIGURE 7.3 | Computer Hardware, Accessories, and Software Costs Worksheet, continued |

	Quantity	$Unit Cost	$Total Cost
❏ Palm organizer	_____	$_____	$_____
❏ CD writer	_____	$_____	$_____
❏ Scanner	_____	$_____	$_____
❏ Digital camera	_____	$_____	$_____
❏ Surge protection	_____	$_____	$_____
❏ Word processing program	_____	$_____	$_____
❏ Accounting software	_____	$_____	$_____
❏ Contact management software	_____	$_____	$_____
❏ Database management software	_____	$_____	$_____
❏ Web site building software	_____	$_____	$_____
❏ Web site maintenance software	_____	$_____	$_____
❏ E-commerce software	_____	$_____	$_____
❏ Payment processing software	_____	$_____	$_____
❏ Inventory management software	_____	$_____	$_____
❏ Desktop publishing software	_____	$_____	$_____
❏ Multimedia software	_____	$_____	$_____
❏ Virus protection software	_____	$_____	$_____
❏ Other _____	_____	$_____	$_____
❏ Other _____	_____	$_____	$_____
	Total		$_____

items that are not relevant to your business, and add items that are specific to your business as required.

Getting the Communication Devices You Need

The proliferation of high-tech communication devices in the last few years makes it very easy to spend a whole lot of money in a very short time. But, once again, if you can get by with just the basic communication devices at first you have the potential to upgrade to new and better communication devices from the future profits of your business. For basic communication, you will need all or some of the following.

Telephone

If you are going to have a home business workspace, one of the first communication devices you should

purchase and install is the good old desktop telephone. Ideally this telephone will have business features and functions such as on-hold, conferencing, redial, speakerphone, broadcast, and message storage capabilities. Contact your telephone service provider; many offer customers multi-function business telephones on installments. The payments can be added to your telephone bill.

Fax Machine

Although fax transmissions have greatly declined in popularity in the last few years because of the increase e-mail use, a fax machine will still be needed to operate your business. Most contracts and agreements that need to be signed are legal when faxed if both parties agree and it is so stipulated in the contract. If you do not want to purchase a separate fax machine, you might consider purchasing an all-in-one office document center, which usually includes a telephone, fax, scanner, and copier built into one machine.

Cellular Telephone

A cellular telephone is now a must for business people. Not only do they enable you to take incoming calls from almost anywhere, but they also enable you to stay in constant contact with your best customers and hottest prospects, no matter where you go. Cellular telephone service plans are now very inexpensive, especially compared to ten years ago when the technology was new. (You paid as much as a dollar a minute plus other fees). Now for less than $50 per month you can have nearly unlimited access to as many minutes as you want. Consider purchasing a cell phone with Internet features as it is very convenient to have the ability to check e-mail when you are away from your computer. In fact, cell phones have become so popular and the services and features so varied that many home business owners are also choosing nothing more than a simple and inexpensive cellular telephone as their main piece of business communications equipment.

Telephone Headset

If your business keeps you working at a computer all day or in your car, a telephone headset will be a definite need. It leaves your hands free to work on the computer as you talk on the phone or to drive your car, walk down the street, or work in your garden when you are out of the office and on cellular. Headsets, both wired and wireless, are available for both your desktop phone and your cellular phone. Count on spending in the range of $100 for both types.

Internet Connection

You will also need an Internet connection that enables you to access the Internet, and send and receive e-mails. Unlimited dial-up access generally costs in the range of $15 per month; high-speed access generally runs in the range of $20 to $50 per month, but you will also need to upgrade your modem at an additional cost. Look under *Internet Service Providers* in the Yellow Pages and call a few to check prices and compare service features.

Tape Recorder

Tape recorders can be an especially handy communications device. Not only can they record your own thoughts and ideas throughout the day, but they can also be used to record client meetings and presentations (with the client's permission) so that no information is missed or for use as a training aid. For the high tech set there are even digital recorders available that transfer audio words into typed words when the recorder CD is downloaded onto your computer hard drive.

Communications Costs

The Communications Costs Worksheet (see Figure 7.4) will help you in calculate the costs of installing and equipping your new home workspace with common communication devices. Ignore items that are not relevant to your business, and add items that are specific to your business.

The Home Office Library

All successful entrepreneurs share a common trait—they never stop searching for ways to become better business people through education. And because time is always in high demand but short supply, the best way to educate themselves and find information that will make them better businesspeople is by purchasing and reading books, reports, magazines, directories, and journals. In fact, most successful businesspeople take pride in their business libraries.

For these reasons, you should start to purchase business-related publications so that you can begin to build your own valuable business library. Even with the Internet as a powerful research and educational tool, books are handy: Take them on the plane or read them in bed. They help you check facts quickly, without having to log onto the Net and conduct searches for the information. The Internet is an invaluable business tool, but the combination of a well-stocked and varied business library and the Internet gives businesspeople access to all the information that they need, without spending a bundle on multiple degrees. You will also want to subscribe to journals that are aimed at your specific business or industry. When you come across business and marketing ideas in print that will work for your

FIGURE 7.4 Communication Costs Worksheet

	Quantity	$Unit Cost	$Total Cost
❏ Specialty wiring and networking	____	$_____	$_____
❏ Telephone with business functions	____	$_____	$_____
❏ Install dedicated telephone line	____	$_____	$_____
❏ Install dedicated fax line	____	$_____	$_____
❏ Toll free line/number	____	$_____	$_____
❏ Internet connection	____	$_____	$_____
❏ Cordless telephone	____	$_____	$_____
❏ Cordless headset	____	$_____	$_____
❏ Cellular telephone with Internet features	____	$_____	$_____
❏ Answering machine or service	____	$_____	$_____
❏ Fax machine	____	$_____	$_____
❏ Pager	____	$_____	$_____
❏ Tape recorder	____	$_____	$_____
❏ Other _____	____	$_____	$_____
❏ Other _____	____	$_____	$_____
		Total	$_____

business, cut the article out and place it in an idea folder for later use. Prime topics that you should include in your business library include:

- Small business accounting, bookkeeping, and taxation
- Sales and marketing
- Business and marketing planning
- Administration and management
- Internet, Web site building, and e-commerce
- Advertising and public relations
- Personal and business goal setting
- Customer service
- Industry, product, service, and manufacturers' directories and source books

A good source for used books is Abebooks, www.abebooks.com, which boasts in excess of 45 million used books for sale in every imaginable category. Amazon is also a good source for new and used books, www.amazon.com. Pub List, www.pub list.com, is an online publications directory listing in excess of 150,000 domestic and international print and electronic publications including magazines, journals, e-journals, and newsletters. And remember to check with your local library about book sales; most sell titles for a fraction of what they cost new.

HOME BUSINESS SECURITY AND SAFETY

Protecting your family from criminal intrusion into your home and creating a safe working environment should be high on the list of priorities for all home business owners. Unfortunately, the most common crime in the United States and Canada is home burglary, bad news for home business owners. The potential loss is even greater for business owners with expensive computer equipment, cash, and specialized tools commonly on-site, making residences a tempting target, because seasoned burglars know which homes contain businesses.

As a rule of thumb, criminals look for items that are small, valuable, and can easily be sold for cash, such as notebook computers and digital cameras.

Even worse, with the increase in identity theft and e-fraud, your clients could also become crime victims if their financial and confidential information are stolen from your home business. For these reasons, all home business owners have to go out of their way to secure their homes and businesses for the protection of their families, businesses, clients, and neighbors.

Building Alliances with Neighbors

One of the simplest and least expensive ways to begin securing your home, family, and business is to forge close relationships with your neighbors so that you can keep an eye on each other's properties by watching out for suspicious activities. Knock on a few doors and introduce yourself to all your neighbors on the street, and suggest that you set up a simple neighborhood watch system. Establish a system so when people are away that other neighbors will pick up their mail and park cars in vacant driveways so that it appears as though the home is occupied. You will be amazed at how much crime can be reduced when there is a group effort to report suspicious activities to the local police. And most police departments have information available in booklet format about how to set up neighborhood watch programs; some even have existing neighborhood watch programs in which citizens can participate right away.

Home Security Alarms

The next logical step in protecting your family and business is to purchase and install a good-quality, monitored home alarm system complete with glass-break detectors, interior motion detectors, and window and door contact point detectors. Home security alarms offer three major deterrents to theft. The small alarm company sign that can be placed in front of the home in a visible area such as the corner of the driveway or in a flowerbed is a deterrent to thieves searching for homes to break into easily. Window and door stickers clearly spell out the house is alarmed, which is another deterrent. Lastly, the siren that blasts an ear-piercing screech after a contact point has been disrupted or a motion detector triggered is definitely a deterrent.

The majority of home alarm companies offer free, comprehensive written quotations. Be sure to get three so that you can compare features, benefits, and costs associated with having the alarm system installed and the monthly monitoring fee. Note, also that there are monitored alarm systems available that detect smoke and carbon monoxide as well as break-ins. Two major players in the home security industry are ADT Home Security, www.adt.com, and Brinks Home Security, www.brinkshomesecurity.com. Both companies offer clients numerous home alarm system and monitoring options that can be tailored to individual needs and financial budgets.

Securing Doors and Windows

Doors and windows are also a point of concern in terms of making your home more difficult to enter. Statistically, in over 70 percent of home thefts, entrance was gained through a door or window using no more than a simple screwdriver or pry bar. Consequently, you want to beef up locks, consider installing heavy-duty entrance doors, and follow a few other simple tricks that will make your home less of a target for theft and more secure for your family and business.

Entrance Doors

If your home or apartment does not currently have steel or solid wood entrance doors you should consider upgrading to heavy-duty steel doors. It is as a wise investment that cannot only help keep your home secure, but also be a business tax deduction if the improvements are made in conjunction with starting your home business. New passage sets and deadbolts that prevent entrance by means of twisting or prying on locks and jambs can be installed. These heavy-duty locks are not very expensive, easy to install, and available at your local hardware store.

Patio Doors

Sliding glass doors commonly known as patio doors are another easy entrance point for thieves, mainly because of inferior and defective locks. They are also easily lifted from their tracks. However, spending just a few dollars on an anti-lift device such as a pin that extends through both the sliding and fixed portion of the door track at the bottom can make it impossible for the door to be slid back or lifted from the track. Locking pins are cheap, quick to install with basic hand tools, and available at any hardware store.

Windows

Windows are another vulnerable area of the home that make easy entrance points for brazen thieves; windows are often left open for ventilation in the warmer months, making the thief's job that much easier. Ground floor windows, of course, are more susceptible to break-ins, and upper floor windows become attractive targets if they can be accessed from stairs, a tree, a fence, or that extension ladder most of us leave lying unlocked beside our homes. Most windows have basic latches instead of keyed locks but the addition of simple blocks and pin locks that prevent the window from being pried up, out, or over are easy to install, cheap, and available at your local hardware store. You can also install security bars on the windows. But be cautious here; the design of some window bars can prevent people inside the home getting out the window in case of emergency.

Security Lighting

Indoor and outdoor lighting also play a major role in home security, especially when darkness helps makes the burglar's work easier. You should purchase and install good quality exterior lighting that works on motion sensitive detectors to keep the outside of your home illuminated at night as needed. Lights will serve a duel purpose. First, when thieves approach your home, a light that suddenly turns on may surprise them into fleeing. Second, from a personal safety perspective, the motion sensitive light makes it safer for you to enter your home. Exterior motion detector lights are very inexpensive approximately $50 each, and can be installed in a few minutes by novices with nothing more than basic hand tools.

It also helps to keep shrubs and trees trimmed back from your exterior entrances and window areas to make your home more visible from the street and from your neighbor's homes so they can keep an eye

on your property and vice versa. Interior lighting is also important as it indicates activity inside your home. A home with no inside lights on, especially for extended periods of time, tips off burglars that you are probably away. To confuse burglars, you can purchase inexpensive light timers and connect them to key interior lighting at the front and back windows. A random pattern of interior lights coming on and shutting off indicates that people are home, and is the number-one deterrent to thieves.

Home Office Safes

Purchasing and installing a safe is another way home business owners can protect their valuables and important personal and business documents. There are various styles of home office safes available at many price points: flush wall-mounted safes, portable lockbox safes, floor-mounted safes, and safes that are disguised as pieces of office furniture and equipment. Ideally, you want a safe with a long burn rating and one that can be securely anchored to the floor or in a wall to prevent thieves from stealing the entire safe and its contents. In addition to cash, safes can also be used to store client files on disk, business documents such as incorporation papers and insurance policies, personal and family documentation, and copies of important documents such as your will or a copy of your drivers' license.

Because safes come in many styles, shapes, and price points, a little bit of research is needed to determine which one will best meet your specific needs. You can learn more about home business safes, features, and costs by visiting these Web sites:

- Liberty Safe, www.libertysafe.com
- Sentry, www.sentrysafe.com
- Gardall, www.gardall.com
- Hidden Safes, www.hiddensafes.com
- American Security Products, www.amsecusa.com

Fire Safety

Like property and personal security, fire safety is another high priority issue for home business owners. And while having sufficient fire insurance is certainly a must, it is not the sole answer to all fire safety concerns. The following are a few helpful tips that will help protect your family and your business:

- Carry sufficient fire insurance.
- Install hardwired smoke detectors with a battery backup system on each floor and in the home office.
- Install emergency battery-powered lighting in hallways and stair corridors.
- Purchase fire extinguishers and keep them in key areas of the home, such as the kitchen, home office, and upstairs hall closet.
- Install carbon monoxide detectors.
- Install second story fire safety ladders or ropes.
- Purchase fireproof lock boxes for important business and personal document storage.

Develop an emergency fire plan and make sure that the entire family knows it well. The emergency plan should include an exit strategy for each room of the house in case of fire, as well as contingency exit points in case of fire blocks. The plan should also include a central meeting place outside, at a safe distance from the home. To find out more about fire safety, log on to the U.S. Fire Administration's Web site at www.usfa.fema.gov. On the site you will find fire safety tips for your home and business.

Home Office Safety

In addition to security and fire concerns, you also want to ensure that your home office is a safe working environment for you, your family, and visiting clients. Believe it or not, the vast majority of preventable accidents and injuries happen at home, not on the highways, so extra precautions must be taken to make sure that you develop and maintain a safe working environment. Here are a few great tips to help you accomplish this objective:

- Keep emergency numbers for the police, ambulance, and fire department in a visible place by the telephone.
- Purchase a first aid kit and take basic first aid courses such as the low-cost CPR course offered by the Red Cross.
- The electrical panel should have the circuit breakers for your home office clearly labeled, including receptacle locations.

- All electrical outlets should be the grounded three-pronged type. Nongrounded outlets are easy and inexpensive to change to grounded outlets, which are readily available at hardware stores everywhere.
- Use surge protectors to protect expensive computer equipment against surges in your electricity service. Surges are common and rarely will your insurance company cover damage they cause to computers and other electronics.
- Lock your office or business space up tight when not in use to prevent children and pets from coming into contact with hazardous equipment such as paper cutters or automatic staplers.
- Keep your office, storage, and workspace free of clutter and obstructions, especially at doorways and aisles.
- Do not store any toxic materials, such as paints and cleaners, in the home office.
- Secure top-heavy or unstable furniture and equipment such as file cabinets firmly to the floor or walls.
- Secure lose telephone lines, extension cords, and computer and equipment wiring. Pin under desks, place under carpets, or tuck behind trim.
- In case of power outages, keep a flashlight in an easily accessible location.

HOME OFFICE FURNITURE, EQUIPMENT, AND SUPPLIES

Setting up a new home office is difficult because there are so many pieces of furniture, equipment, and basic supplies that must be purchased to create an efficient and organized office ready for maximum productivity. So it helps to have a handy checklist, such as the Home Office Furniture, Equipment, and Supplies Checklist (see Figure 7.5). You can use this as a yardstick to keep track of the office equipment, fixtures, and supplies you need. This checklist is very comprehensive, and chances are you will not need everything featured on it. Just ignore the items that you don't need and focus on the ones you do. If budget restriction is a concern, you can prioritize the list and purchase equipment and supplies that will assist in getting the business generating revenues and profits right

FIGURE 7.5 Home Office Furniture, Equipment, and Supplies Checklist

Office Furniture and Equipment

❏ Desk	❏ Comfortable chair	❏ File cabinets
❏ Overhead and work lighting	❏ Client seating	❏ Fireproof safe
❏ Desktop and pocket calculators	❏ Bookcases	❏ Postage meter
❏ Portable trade show booth and displays	❏ Worktable(s)	❏ Briefcase
❏ Wall whiteboard and markers	❏ Storage boxes	❏ Labeling machine
❏ Photocopier	❏ Radio	❏ Flip chart
❏ Paper shredder	❏ Air conditioner	❏ Wastebasket
❏ Recycling bin	❏ Desktop fan	❏ Space heater
❏ Outside courier delivery box	❏ Home alarm system	❏ Fire extinguisher
❏ Telephone Yellow Pages directory	❏ Smoke director	❏ First aid kit
❏ Telephone White Pages directory	❏ Rechargeable flashlight	❏ Office decorations
❏ Business and industry directory	❏ Reference books	❏ Product catalogs

Computer Hardware and Accessories

❏ Desktop computer	❏ Notebook computer	❏ CD writer
❏ Modem	❏ PowerPoint projector	❏ Palm organizers
❏ Keyboard and mouse	❏ Monitor	❏ Digital camera
❏ Computer and equipment manuals	❏ Dust covers	❏ Computer locks
❏ Printer	❏ Scanner	❏ Surge protector

Computer Software   **Specific Program or Brand**

❏ Word processing program   _____

❏ Accounting software   _____

❏ Contact management software   _____

❏ Database management software   _____

❏ Web site building software   _____

❏ Web site maintenance software   _____

❏ E-commerce software   _____

❏ Payment processing software   _____

❏ Inventory management software   _____

❏ Delivery tracking software   _____

❏ Desktop publishing software   _____

❏ Multimedia software   _____

❏ Virus protection software   _____

❏ Disk storage case   _____

❏ Fireproof lock box (disks)   _____

❏ Software reference guides   _____

| FIGURE 7.5 | Home Office Furniture, Equipment, and Supplies Checklist, continued |

Home Office Communications

❏ Dedicated telephone line	❏ Internet connection	❏ Dedicated fax line
❏ Toll-free line/number	❏ Cordless telephone	❏ Fax machine
❏ Answering machine/service	❏ Cordless headset	❏ Speakerphone
❏ Cellular telephone with Internet features	❏ Pager	❏ Tape recorder
❏ Desk telephone with business features and functions		

Home Office General Supplies

❏ Business cards (paper)	❏ Business cards (CD's)	❏ Envelopes
❏ Advertising specialties such as pens	❏ Mailing labels	❏ Letterhead
❏ Postage stamps	❏ CD and floppy disks	❏ Index cards
❏ Printer cartridges	❏ In box	❏ Out box
❏ Correction fluid	❏ Erasers	❏ Pencils
❏ Accordion files	❏ File folders	❏ Pens
❏ File labels and tabs	❏ Markers	❏ Hanging files
❏ Pencil holder	❏ Pencil sharpener	❏ Printer paper
❏ Note pads	❏ Fax paper	❏ Paper clips
❏ Paper cutter	❏ Paper punch	❏ Stapler/Staples
❏ Ruler	❏ Staple remover	❏ Packing tape
❏ Tape	❏ Rubber bands	❏ Glue
❏ Ring binders	❏ Scissors	❏ Cleaning supplies

away and purchase the other items from the profits that are earned as you go.

BUILDING A POSITIVE BUSINESS IMAGE

The majority of home business owners do not have the advantage of elaborate offices or elegant storefronts to wow prospects and impress customers. Instead, they must rely on imagination, creativity, and paying attention to the smallest detail when creating and maintaining a professional business image. We know there are disadvantages with operating a business from home in terms of projecting a positive and professional business image, but these disadvantages can easily be overcome and often turned into a competitive advantages. In most instances, your start-up costs will be lower than a similar business that chooses to operate from a commercial office or storefront.

Thus, you will have extra money to spend on materials that will go a long way towards projecting the best image possible for your new business venture—professional signage, uniforms, eloquent stationery, and descriptive advertising campaigns. Consider that you have no commute, thus extra time to prospect, build strong relationships with customers, and develop ironclad business and marketing plans. Consider that in most cases your overhead will be a fraction of what competitors are paying to maintain commercial office space or storefronts, thus creating an opportunity to funnel that money you saved into more productive activities aimed at attracting new clients—advertising, product demonstrations, and trade show marketing. You may also want to set aside some of the money you saved to incorporate your business or form a limited liability corporation business right from the start. Consumers, suppliers, and lenders generally view incorporated businesses as more stable, professional, and committed than unincorporated ones.

Building a positive business image also includes "keeping up appearances." Like it or not, many things in life really are measured at first glance. Therefore, you have to go out of your way to ensure that all business tools are kept in good repair and clean. In business these include:

- The outside of your home
- The inside of your home workspace
- Business signage
- Transportation
- Tools and equipment
- Uniforms
- Product samples
- Trade show and event marketing booths

In a nutshell, everything that is your business and that has the potential to come into contact with prospects, clients, and business alliances should be 100 percent maintained and clean.

Logos and Slogans

Once you have chosen and registered your business name, the next step towards building a positive business image is developing an eye-catching logo and a memorable slogan. Logos and slogans help to brand your business and build consumer awareness of your business, products, or services. Of course, the key here is consistency. Once you have decided on a logo design and a promotional or descriptive slogan, you must consistently incorporate these into every aspect of your business. Branding requires time. The more often consumers are exposed to your brand, the more they will remember it, giving you brand recognition.

Business logos and promotional slogans play a major role in branding, especially logos because of their instant visual recognition qualities. You see the swoosh and you instantly think Nike. You see the golden arches and McDonalds instantly comes to mind. You hear or read "like a good neighbor," and think State Farm Insurance. This is what logos and

slogans do: They act as a beacon in the competitive fog to tell consumers instantly that it is a brand they know, like, and trust.

Slogans are very straightforward to develop. Simply think about the biggest benefit that people receive from doing business with you, and build a slogan around that benefit. Then, keep editing until you have a few powerful words that perfectly sums up your big benefit. Presto, you have a slogan. Logos however, can be a little trickier to create unless you have design experience or a flair for the creative. Fortunately, there are many logo and business image design services that will be more than happy to help you create a professional logo for your business—a logo that makes sense and builds brand awareness. Logo design starts in the range of $50 and can go as high as a few hundred dollars depending on your needs. Listed below are a few online logo design services to get you on your way to creating a powerful business image through instant brand identification marks and slogans:

- Logo Design, www.logodesign.com
- Logo Bee, www.logobee.com
- The Logo Company, www.thelogocompany.com
- Online Logo, www.onlinelogo.com
- e-Logo Design, www.e-logodesign.com

Print Identity Package

Your print identity package is comprised of the various print elements that you use daily in the course of operating your business—business cards, letter stationery, receipts, envelopes, estimate forms, presentation folders, marketing brochures, catalogs, simple fliers, and account statements. High-quality printing is well worth the added expense, especially for home business owners. Even though high-quality printing on heavy stock paper may be more expensive than a standard print job, it is still relatively cheap when compared to other overheads, such as office rent, that home business owners do not have to contend with. Therefore, you can spend a little extra on items that will project a very positive business image.

Key to a great print identity package is consistency throughout the entire package, just as in your entire marketing program. You want to develop a standard color scheme, logo, slogan, and type of font, and use these consistently so that customers and prospects begin to visually link your business with your identity program. Consult your local telephone directory for printers near you. Remember to obtain three quotes for all of your printing needs, and do not necessarily go with price alone. Instead, base your purchasing decision on quality, value, reputation, and turnaround time. You can also log onto the Print USA Web site at www.printusa.com to find free online printing quotes for hundreds of business products, from mouse pads to business cards and everything in between.

Web Site

Once you have made the decision to take your business online, your Web site is an area where you do not want to go cheap by hiring your cousin to design your site just because she knows how to sell candles on eBay. It is true that with the use of Web building software it is very easy to build and publish a Web site to the World Wide Web in a matter of a couple hours. But that does not mean the site will meet your online marketing objectives, function in the way that it is meant to, or project the image that you want to project for your business.

Your online presence is a very important aspect of your overall business and marketing strategy and should be treated as such. Again, consistency is one of the key ingredients. You want to tie your offline business in with your online business image to project a uniform appearance. This is not to say that you, or someone you know, should not design and build your Web site; just take the time to plan carefully how you want the site to look, function, and meet your business and marketing objectives.

To locate a capable webmaster to build and maintain your Web site, ask local business people with Web sites you think represent their businesses well. Call them to find out who designed their sites, the cost of building and maintaining the sites, and other issues such as performance and order fulfillment. You can consult the Yellow Pages under Internet Services or a similar term, or check with local colleges and technology schools to find a

qualified student prepared to work for a little under going rate in exchange for job experience and a dandy resume reference. In Chapter 17, Internet and E-Commerce, you will find additional information, resources, and tips about Web site building, maintenance, and marketing.

Communications

Communications systems and devices can play a major role in projecting a positive and professional business image. You can use communications to project your business as much larger than it is, and communications will enable you to reach a broader audience, especially when you consider the following simple communications tips that every home entrepreneur can put in place:

- Install a dedicated business telephone line, and promote the number in all marketing activities and business correspondence. A business telephone number separate from your residential number really does say that you are in business.
- Purchase and carry a cellular telephone and pager so that important clients can keep in constant communication with you, and vice versa. Poor access is always one of the biggest complaints in any customer service survey.
- Provide customers with a toll-free calling option for inquiries and product orders. The toll-free calling option makes your business appear much larger, especially when the toll-free number is featured in all your advertising.
- Always return telephone messages and e-mails the same day when possible, especially to your best customers and your hottest prospects, and never wait longer than 48 hours.
- If you operate a service business, hire an answering service to take after-hours calls. Many people will not leave messages on voice mail systems and will keep calling competitors until they have a real person on the other end of the telephone line.
- Prerecord "promotional on-hold" messages featuring special offers or new product or service information enable you to take advantage of every selling opportunity when any prospects

or customers are placed on-hold. Impressions On Hold offers clients professionally produced and recorded telephone on-hold advertising message services. It can be found online at www.impressionsonhold.com.

- Expand geographically with telephone numbers in other cities. Calls to these numbers are then forwarded to your home office number. Imagine, for less than a few hundred dollars a month you can have offices in New York, Dallas, Los Angeles, and Chicago and have all the numbers call-forwarded to your home office in Toledo. Now that is projecting a positive and big business image.
- Use e-mail signatures with links to your e-mail and Web sites, as well as e-mail autoresponders when you are going on holidays.

Powerful, Image-Building Business Letters

People receive lots of letters daily, especially business people and professionals. If you want your business letters to stand out, get noticed, grab attention, and meet your objectives, you must get to the point quickly and have a clear and concise message. Start by letting your reader know right away what's in it for them. What will they get by continuing to read your letter? Write in short paragraphs, using subheadings, for each new section to ensure that skimmers get the message and stay engaged and interested. Perhaps most importantly, write from the reader's view point, anticipate questions, concerns, and objections the reader might have and try to answer them. Here are a few more tips for writing powerful business letters:

- Write a first draft and then wait a day before you go back to review. Often you will find points that you want to expand—or delete.
- Include a call to action. "Give me a call." "Visit my Web site." "Stop by our trade show booth."
- Replace technical words or explanations with basic and easy-to-understand language. Never make your reader work or think too hard to understand your points.
- Edit and proofread for errors at least twice before sending.

Finally, include a postscript (P.S.) at the bottom of all written communications, that restates the main theme of your message and the big benefit the reader will receive by taking action and responding to your communication.

Dress for Success and Uniforms

You may hate them, but stereotypes sell. Resist the urge to stand out or make a statement in terms of how you dress for work. Leave fashion trends to the Hollywood types. Society in general has expectations about the way businesspeople and professionals should dress. We expect doctors to be in a white lab coat, mechanics in coveralls, and bankers in business wear. It stands to reason that if you want one less obstacle between you and the sale, don't make your choice of business fashion an obstacle. Dress for success by wearing what the majority of your customers expect you to be wearing. If their expectation is a suit, wear a suit. If it is smart casual, wear smart casual, and if it is a uniform, wear a uniform.

Business people have long understood the marketing and professionalism benefits associated with uniforms emblazoned with your business name and corporate logo. Great looking uniforms do not have to be expensive; for as little as $20 each you can purchase smart casual golf shirts silk-screened or embroidered with your business name and logo. Uniforms Online is a national directory listing manufacturers and distributors of workplace and professional uniforms and can be found at www.uniforms.com.

Enter Business Competitions

Winning business, product, and customer service awards is a fantastic way to earn credibility, attract new business, and build a great business image and reputation. This is especially important for service providers who often build their entire sales and marketing campaign around trust, reliability, credibility, and the good reputation of their firm. Just about every community, city, and state has some sort of annual business competition classified by type, sector, or industry. Often these business excellence awards and competitions are sponsored and administered by local business groups such as the

Chamber of Commerce, the economic committee of local government, or even by local newspapers, radio and television stations. Many industry associations also hold annual best-of business award ceremonies. It is more than worthwhile to take the time and enter your business.

Get started in your quest to locate a suitable competition by checking with community business groups, your local newspaper, and industry associations for competitions and awards for your specific business. Study the details of each, and apply or get nominated for the ones that interest you and from which winning would have the most benefits for your business. The publicity and free advertising that winning can generate is priceless, and there are limitless marketing opportunities associated with being the best.

Custom Postcards

Another great way to project a positive business image is with custom-designed postcards emblazoned with your company name, logo, and promotional message. Not only do they scream professionalism, but also they are a terrific way to keep in touch with current customers and new prospects. In bulk, even custom-printed postcards can be designed and printed for less than ten cents each, making them less expensive than sending an ordinary run-of-the-mill sales letter. Use the postcards to promote a new product or service, or just to let customers know that you are thinking of them. Postcards also beat out business cards for networking purposes. You can say more on them, use bigger and bolder headlines for greater impact, and due, to their size, you are sure to be remembered as the person with the postcard. Furthermore, you can have the front of the postcard printed with pictures or graphics that best describes and promotes your business and leave the back blank so that you can personalize each one you send to customers. Use handwriting or run them through a desktop printer to add a promotional sales message. Postcard Printing Online provides free postcard printing quotes and can be found at www.postcardprinting.com.

High Tech Business Cards

Perhaps not a necessity for projecting a positive business image, CD business cards are the latest rage

in business cool, and they make a unique and memorable promotional tool. Take your business card into the world of high-tech presentation by putting it on a disk. These mini, CD-ROM format business cards are the latest high-tech business promotion tool. They can be die cut into virtually any shape and have your picture, logo, or business name and telephone number silk-screened on the outside of the disk. The disks can be played on any standard disk drive, have up to 50MB of space and can include graphics and sound and links directly to your Web site or e-mail. Imagine, with one simple business card-sized CD-ROM you can give a virtual presentation highlighting the benefits of your business, products, or services for as little as $1 per card. Media Supply designs and manufactures business card CDs and can be found online at www. mediasupply.com/bizcard.

RESOURCES

Associations

American Home Business Association
4505 Wasatah Boulevard S.
Salt Lake City, UT 84124
(800) 664-2422
www.homebusiness.com

Home Office Association of America
PO Box 51
Sagaponack, NY 11962-0051
(212) 588-9097
www.aahbb.org

National Association of Professional Organizers
PO Box 140647
Austin, TX 78714
(512) 454-8626
www.napo.net

National Association of Women Business Owners (NAWBO)
830-1100 Wayne Avenue
Silver Spring, MD 20910
(301) 608-2590
www.nawbo.org

Small Office Home Office Business Group (SOHO)
2255 B Queen Street East, Suite 3261
Toronto, ON M4E 1G3

(800) 290-7646
www.soho.ca

📖 *Suggested Reading*

Allen, David. *Ready for Anything: 52 Productivity Principles for Work and Life.* New York: Viking Press, 2003.

Carter, David. *American Corporate Identity.* New York: Hearst Books International, 2003.

Kanarek, Lisa. *Home Office Life: Marking a Space to Work at Home.* Gloucester, MA: Rockport Publishers, 2001.

York, David Allen. *Getting Things Done: The Art of Stress-Free Productivity.* New York: Penguin, 2001.

Zimmerman, Neal. *Home Office Design: Everything You Need to Know About Planning, Organizing, and Furnishing Your Work Space.* New York: John Wiley & Sons, 1996.

💻 *Web Sites*

Apple Computers, www.apple.com: Small business computer packages.

Dell Computers, www.dell.com: Small business computer packages.

Download Superstore, www.downlaodsuperstore.com: Free and paid business shareware downloads and software sales.

Ergonomics Online, www.ergonomics.org: Ergonomics information, articles, industry links, and resources.

IBM Computers, www.ibm.com: Small business computer packages.

Ikea, www.ikea.com: Retailer of home office furniture.

Office By Design, www.officebydesign.com: Retailer of home office furniture and design services.

Office Depot, www.officedepot.com: Office supplies, furniture, and equipment.

Office Furniture, www.officefurniture.com: Retailer of home office furniture.

Office Max, www.officemax.com: Office supplies, furniture, and equipment.

Organized Times, www.organizedtimes.com: Information, advice, tools, and services aimed at getting the home office organized and productive.

Power Home Biz, www.powerhomebiz.com: Home business information portal.

Staples, www.staples.com: Office supplies, furniture, and equipment.

Work-At-Home Parent, www.work-at-home-parent.com: Information and advice for parents working from a home office.

Work Spaces, www.workspaces.com: Information, advice, and links on setting up, organizing, and furnishing a home office.

CHAPTER 8

Building Your Business Team

BUILDING YOUR BUSINESS TEAM IS JUST AS important as any other piece of the home business puzzle, and is generally much more involved than new entrepreneurs even realize. Your business team has five divisions: the front-line business team, employees and agents, trade accounts, professional services, and business alliances. I have, of course, purposely left out the most important member of your business team—your customers. I have chosen to place customers issues in Chapter 10, Finding and Keeping Customers, and Chapter 12, Creating a Marketing Plan. That approach keeps the information together. Customer information can then be directly linked to research, customer service issues, and your marketing plan rather than splintered throughout the book.

Homebased Business Team Outline

Group 1. Front-Line Business Team
- Your family
- Your friends
- Your neighbors
- Your pets

Group 2. Employees
- Hired full-time and part-time employees
- Sales agents

Group 3. Trade Accounts
- Product and service suppliers
- Vendors

Group 4. Professional Services
- Lawyers
- Accountants
- Bankers
- Insurance agent/broker
- Consultants

Group 5. Alliances
- Business and industry associations
- Community business people
- Government agencies
- Media personnel
- Business and competitor partnerships

As you can see from the homebased business team outline, your team is very comprehensive and broad. Consequently, you have to develop a plan that addresses how you will build your business team, the players to be involved, and how you will maintain and grow it for your benefit, the benefit of your business, and for the benefit of your business team. In fact, all successful businesses share a common denominator—every person involved with the business benefits in their own fashion from that involvement. Conducting business is very much about creating and maintaining win-win situations for everyone.

BUILDING YOUR FRONT-LINE BUSINESS TEAM

I like to refer to your front-line business team as the people (and pets) your decision to start and operate a homebased business has the most immediate impact on—your family members, your pets, your friends, and your neighbors.

Working with Your Family at Home

At the very front your front-line business team are your family members, especially the ones living at home under that same roof from where your business will be operating. Without question, your business will have an affect on your family, and your family will have an affect on your business. It is inevitable with everyone being in such close proximity. Consequently, the goal of the business owners is two-fold. First, you have to have the support of the family for the venture. Not necessarily 100 percent support, but enough that they understand the reason why you want to start a business and are supportive.

Second, you have to create a workable set of ground rules for the benefit of both your family and your business. For example, the home workspace is off limits for anything but work, no bending or breaking this rule. If possible, set regular work hours so that your business does not also become your entire life. And if the kids are home during busy or important business days, hire a baby sitter or nanny to come in and look after them. At the end of the day, everyone will have to adjust to the new living/work situation and make compromises, and perhaps even a few sacrifices such as lost living space, no loud music, and no gang of friends over after school. But as long as there is an open discussion before starting the business so all family can voice concerns and make suggestions, none of these small challenges will be insurmountable.

I leave you with two final pieces of advice in terms of your home business and your family. Don't be upset if your family members do not share your level of enthusiasm for your new business. Remember that in most cases the new business will be your dream, not theirs. As in any new business venture, there are inherent financial risks, which may make some of your family members very nervous.

Perhaps more importantly, do not view your family members, especially the ones living at home, as a pool of temporary help when you get busy, or assume that they will want to work in the business now or in the future. The decision on whether or not to work in the family homebased business must be left up to each family member to decide free of pressure from you.

Friends and the Home Business

People that do not work from home, like most of your friends, have a widely held perception that if you are home during the day, you are really not working. You are definitely available for whatever reason: a quick chat, a game of golf, or to see a movie. You have to clearly spell out to your friends and family in no uncertain terms members that you will be operating a business, this is your livelihood, and that you are not simply parading around in your pajamas all day watching soaps and taking afternoon naps. You do not have to be mean spirited when you make this announcement, just firm and directly to the point. Even after more than a decade of working from home, on occasion I still have friends that will call or stop by during working hours to ask if I want to join them in whatever they are up to for the day. When I am swamped and this happens, it can be very frustrating to take the time out and once again explain that I am working. I tell you this because once you start to work from home, you will experience these same kind of interruptions. And, as I have, you will need to learn to be firm and say no. Do not fall into the trap of occasionally giving in and playing hooky. It can easily become habitual, especially when you are the boss and you do not have anyone to keep your nose pressed to the grindstone, but yourself.

Working with Pets at Home

Don't consider your pet a potential disadvantage to working from home. In fact, if you do not currently have a pet and are going to be working from home running a new business, consider this the opportune time to finally get one. Sure, working from home with a pet under foot or always under the desk does occasionally create a challenge, as does the odd awkward moment when clients visit and are greeting by a barking dog or a cat that likes to rub up against legs. But there are a whole host of advantages to having a pet at home while you work, including:

- If you have a dog, you have a reason not to become a workaholic. Schedule two or three walk times per day and get out and get some exercise and a much-needed break from work.
- Pets provide great companionship, especially for home business owners that are used to working in a busy office atmosphere. Don't feel silly if you catch yourself talking to Fido about business-related issues. If they answer you, however, you know it's probably time for human contact again.
- As mentioned in Chapter 7, Establishing Your Workspace, dogs also provide for a great sense of security. Home business owners have real concerns about security-related issues because of the expensive equipment and cash around the home, which provides a great temptation for thieves. However, a barking dog will scare off even the most brazen burglar.

As you can probably tell, I am a big fan of dogs. My 100-pound Rotti, Dana, spends most of her time under the desk in my home office, and I often take her with me when I go to see clients. In fact, many call and request that I bring her along so they can visit. There are some legitimate concerns in terms of working from home and with pets, but all are manageable:

- Keep your pets out of your office and the door closed when you're on the telephone.
- Keep your pet in the yard or in another area of your home when clients come to visit. Not everyone will share your enthusiasm for your pet, and lots of people have allergies to pet dander.
- Don't leave anything lying around in your workspace that your pet could take and destroy or that could potentially harm them.
- Pets like to be on a schedule. Try to feed them at the same time of the day, walk them at the same time, and set aside a little play time so

that they do not get bored and terrorize you while you work.

Keeping the Neighbors Happy

The neighbors living beside you, behind you, above you, below you, across the street, down the road, and even a few blocks away also have to be considered as part of your business team because your homebased business could have an impact on their lives. Most neighbors will immediately think of negatives as soon as you tell them you are starting a business that will be operating from home. If neighbors decide they want to make it tough on you because you are operating a home business, they can. And some will if you do not go out of your way from the start to appease all parties. To keep the peace with your neighbors, you must address certain issues, even if your property is zoned for a homebased business.

Exterior Signage

If you are going to install exterior signage, choose wisely and carefully consider how your signage impacts on your neighbors' homes. Will they be able to see it from their windows? If it is a lit sign, will it shine in their windows? Is the type of sign appropriate for the neighborhood? You certainly do not want immediate neighbors in on the ultimate decision of what type of signage you will use for your business, but at the same time you have to go out of your way to eliminate or minimize the impact that it will have on their property and lives.

Parking

Another issue that you will have to address with your neighbors is parking, especially if you expect lots of deliveries and client visits. Ideally, you want to contain parking for your business within your own property and not out onto the road. You will also have to address shipping and receiving issues because you do not want delivery vans with noisy diesel motors running for long periods of time while they drop off or pick up materials.

Visiting Clients

You will also need to set some ground rules for visiting clients in terms of working hours so that neighbors are not disturbed on Sundays or late into the evening. You will also have to clearly identify your business and the access to your home workspace so that clients and other visitors to your business are not left to wander around your neighborhood, upsetting or disturbing your neighbors.

Pollution

Without question, noise and airborne pollution will be the two biggest concerns your neighbors are likely to have about your business. Therefore, you have to make sure that you go out of your way to eliminate the potential for any type of pollutant. Do this by installing extra insulation to reduce noise transfer or build fences and install hedges. And, if airborne pollutants will be a problem because of a manufacturing or assembly process, install high-quality ventilation and air purification systems to eliminate that potential.

Safety Issues

You also want to assure your neighbors that there are no potential safety or environmental issues because of your home business. Do this by complying with local safety and fire regulations in terms of the storage and handling of toxic materials and with the installation of high-quality smoke detectors and extinguishing systems. On the upside, working from home does enable you to keep an eye on your neighbors' homes and the neighborhood in general for suspicious activity. Use this as a selling point when it comes time to talk with your neighbors about your new home business and safety-related issues.

In a nutshell, be respectful of your neighbors, and be the kind of neighbor that you want living around you. Understand that like you, their homes probably represent their largest, if not only, major investment.

GETTING STARTED WITH EMPLOYEES

To hire employees or not to hire employees, that is the question. You have to weigh your options carefully in terms of whether or not you should hire employees. Employing people adds lots of additional administrative work, on top of what most home-based business owners already consider to be far too much. When you employ people, there are laws and

regulations that govern employment practices, including, but not limited to, labor laws, minimum wages, health and safety workplace issues, work hours, and workers' compensation insurance coverage. As an employer, you are also required to withhold and remit employee income tax and Social Security insurance. Moreover, home business owners have additional concerns that traditional employers working from a commercial building or office do not face, which are:

- Can employees or outside contractors legally work from your home?
- Do you have the space required for one or more employees to work from your home office or workspace?
- Can you provide employees working from your home with enough privacy to get their work done, and can you at the same time offer your family enough privacy from your employees?
- Will employees have separate and easy access to your home workspace, and can you provide them with suitable parking?
- Can you provide employees with the basic necessities such as washroom facilities, space for breaks and lunch, and closet space for coats?

You do, however, have alternatives to employing people to fill needed roles within your business, hiring temporary workers on an as-needed basis, hiring agents or contractors, or building alliances with other home business owners and farming out overflow work to them.

Ultimately, if you decide that hiring employees is the best available option, you will need to familiarize yourself with labor laws and obtain an Employer Identification Number (EIN). Labor laws can be researched in the United States by contacting the Department of Labor or by logging on to DOL Web site. In Canada, you will have to contact Human Resources Development Canada or log on to the HRDC Web site for more information about labor laws. To obtain an Employer Identification Number in the United States, visit your local Internal Revenue Service office or log on to the IRS Web site and download the EIN form. In Canada, you can visit your local Canada Customs and Revenue Agency office or log on to the CCRA Web site and download the EIN form. Contact addresses and Web sites for these agencies are:

United States
Internal Revenue Service
500 N. Capitol Street NW
Washington, DC 20221
(202) 874-6748
www.irs.gov

United States Department of Labor
Frances Perkins Building
200 Constitution Avenue NW
Washington, DC 20210
(877) 889-5627
www.dol.gov

Canada
Canada Customs and Revenue Agency
333 Laurier Avenue West
Ottawa, ON K1A 0L9
(800) 959-5525
www.ccra-adrc.gc.ca

Human Resources Development Canada
140 Promenade du Portage
Hull, Quebec K1A 0J9
(800) 567-6866
www.hrdc-drhc.gc.ca

Hiring and Keeping Good Employees

At some point as your home business grows, you will probably need to hire employees. You will soon learn there is a great deal of truth to the old adage that a business is only as good as its employees. Poor customer service practices will alienate customers, and salespeople that prefer to talk when they should be listening can drive business to the competition faster than a speeding bullet. Unfortunately, discovering that you have hired the wrong person for the job generally comes too late, long after the damage has occurred.

One way that you can make sure that you hire the right person is to insist the candidate supply you with customer references. Don't rely solely on a

resume and character references supplied by the candidate; go directly to the source by asking job candidates to furnish customer references—people they have sold to, or serviced an account. No one is better qualified to give you the honest lowdown on a person's commitment to her job than the customer that has had dealings with the person. For home business owners new to the process of interviewing and hiring employees, you also need to know what the characteristics of a good employee are, what employees need, and what job benefits they prize most.

- What are the characteristics of a good employee?
  - ✓ Productive
  - ✓ Professional
  - ✓ Honest
  - ✓ Loyal
  - ✓ Pleasant
  - ✓ Respectful
  - ✓ Punctual
  - ✓ Confident

- What do employees need?
  - ✓ A fair salary so that they can pay their bills and maintain a lifestyle
  - ✓ Job security and an opportunity to advance
  - ✓ To be challenged so they do not get bored leading to less productivity
  - ✓ The ability to make some independent decisions
  - ✓ Recognition for a job well done, because we all need to feel as though we are positively contributing to a larger cause

- What are the benefits that employees rate as the most important?
  - ✓ Health care, insurance, and dental plans
  - ✓ Employer contributions to a retirement saving plan
  - ✓ Profit sharing
  - ✓ Rewards based on productivity
  - ✓ Flexible work schedules

How to Increase Employee Productivity

There are two very simple, proven ways to increase revenues and profits without finding new customers. You can sell more product or service or sell more frequently to your existing customers. You can increase employee and management productivity, without affecting fixed overhead costs or the costs associated with delivering goods or services to your customers. This chapter is focused on the latter. We'll talk about ways you can increase employee productivity, including your own. Here are a few surefire ways to motivate your employees to increase productivity:

- Give your valued employees the opportunity to earn more money through a salary plus performance-based commission pay structure. Once they discover how much more money they might earn, productivity will skyrocket.

- Give employees a job title befitting their loyalty and the respect they have earned. When people feel needed and respected, they work harder to fill those responsibilities.

- Implement a profit sharing program to increase productivity. The program can be based on all profits or alternately, and perhaps preferably, on profit increases based on productivity on a year-over-year basis.

- Recognition is also a very powerful motivator when it comes to increasing productivity. Set targets that are rewarded with trips, prizes, or even time off. Employees will work hard to meet these targets, thus increasing productivity. Recognizing employees for a job well done has the same effect—put their names on a plaque, throw a job-well-done party in their honor, or put their pictures in the local paper with a brief word on why they were honored.

- Believe it or not, adding responsibilities is also a very powerful way to motivate employees to increase productivity. If you hand over a job or task that you would normally do to an employee, they will feel they have earned your trust and will work extra hard to keep that trust. In the process, you will enjoy increased productivity based on nothing more than increasing your employee's normal duties or workload.

These are only a few ideas for increasing employee productivity; there are many more. Regardless of the method you choose, one of the fastest and least expensive ways to increase business revenues and profits is through increased employee and management productivity. Therefore, the goal of the home business owner with employees need not always to be looking for new customers. It should include developing programs that will increase productivity while keeping a lid on overheads. Ideally, a combination of finding new customers, while keeping a high level of productivity will garner the best and most profitable results. Motivation USA, located online at www.motivationusa.com, offers employee motivation products, services, and programs.

Hire Temporary Help as Needed

Instead of hiring full-time, part-time, or seasonal employees only to have to lay them off or let them go when things slow down, you might want to consider enlisting the services of a temporary help agency to supply experienced temporary workers to meet your short-term labor requirements. Though the cost of hiring temporary help through an temp agency is generally 25 percent more expensive per hour on average than you would have to pay if you hired an employee, when you factor in the advantages the cost difference is actually negligible. And that doesn't include the time saved by not having to run ads, interview, and check work references. The advantages include:

- The temporary help agency screens all workers, so that you can be assured of getting workers with the experience that you need.

- The temporary help agency does all bookkeeping and arranges to pay all payroll deductions, so that all you have to do is write out one check to cover it all.

- The temporary help agency in most cases arranges for workers' compensation and other specialized insurance coverage as needed. Once again, that saves you time.

- The service is fast and convenient. Most temporary help positions can be filled within 24 hours and often within hours of the call.

Perhaps the biggest advantage of using temporary help as opposed to hiring employees is the fact that once you no longer require their services, you are under no obligation to the worker and need pay no severance outside of that which is required under labor laws. Consult your Yellow Pages telephone directory to find a temporary help agency in your area, or you can log on to Web sites such as Labor Ready Temporary Help Agency at www.labor ready.com to find information about hiring temporary help.

Choosing Gray Power

The changing demographics in North America is toward an aging population. You as a business owner have to carefully consider hiring older workers as your home business grows. In some cases, you might have no choice as the competition heats up for the limited supply of younger workers entering the workforce. Don't despair. With age often comes wisdom and experience. Tapping into gray power can benefit a business immensely because of their business and sales know-how, which can be especially beneficial to small and new businesses. Never underestimate an older person's value to your organization when it comes time to hire new employees or fill contractor or consulting positions. Older people are generally more loyal, less focused on wages, and more reliable, but you can also tap into their business and marketing experience for new ideas to help your business grow. Not to mention the fact that people who have 30, 40, and even 50 years of business, marketing, or sales experience also have extensive customer and business contact lists that may be of value to you.

Working with Sales Agents

To expand revenues and market share, home business owners often hire seasoned sales professionals to prospect for new business and sell their goods or services. That can be a very wise and profitable decision. Not only can you tap into their sales and marketing knowledge, but many also have a large contact base that can be marketed to, creating instantaneous sales. The majority of sales agents (also known as sales consultants or freelance sales representatives) prefer to work on a contract basis for tax purposes and to maintain the ability to represent more than one business client at a time. This kind of arrangement is a bonus for the home business owner. You do not need to worry about extra paperwork, labor laws, and employee benefits, and they also come armed with the tools that they need to sell, including transportation, portable computers, and cellular telephones.

One of the best aspects about hiring or contracting with independent sales agents is the fact that they bring one skill to the table that the majority of home business owners lack—the ability to prospect effectively for new business. Prospecting is without a question one of the most difficult sales disciplines to master, especially if you are uncomfortable in unfamiliar surroundings or with rejection. The ability to read people and markets is what sales agents do best; they find people that need and are willing to purchase your goods and services.

Of course, these skills and experiences come at a cost, but don't worry. Outside of the cost of business cards, promotional literature, and products samples, most independent sales agents work on a performance-based fee system, retaining a portion of their total sales as a fee. The fee is typically in the range of 5 to 30 percent depending the product being sold, sales, value, and the costs associated with selling the product. You do have to take some precautions when hiring sales agents or any other subcontractor for your business. The agents' or contractors' work or performance is viewed as your work or performance in the eyes of your customers. Therefore, the agent or contractor you choose to work with will definitely have to be reading from the same page as you. You will also want to ensure the following:

- If applicable, make sure the agents or contractors are fully insured.
- Find out what types of warranties or guarantees they offer on their work.
- Ask for references, and make sure that their reputations are spotless. Once again, their reputation will become your reputation.
- Be sure they are reliable to a fault.
- Make sure they work only for you and not direct or indirect competitors in your same marketplace. It is also wise to insist that agents and contractors sign a confidentiality and noncompetition agreement, which can be drawn up by your lawyer.

- Always work from a written and binding contract that spells out all of the details, including payment, performance, and liability issues between the two parties.

To find independent sales agents, you can run classified ads under the Help Wanted section of your local newspaper or in newspapers that serve areas into which you want to expand your business. You can also conduct searches online, or visit The Manufactures' Agents National Association located on the Web at www.manaonline.org to view sales consultant listings.

BUILDING TRADE ACCOUNTS

The third group that makes up part of your business team is your product and service suppliers, as well as your vendors. For the sake of clarity, we will refer to your suppliers as the businesses from which you purchase goods and services, such as products for resale or the courier service that delivers your packages, and vendors as the businesses that sell your products or services to their customers, such as a distributor or retailer. Just like any other member of your business team, suppliers and vendors can play a major role in your ultimate success or failure. Therefore, these relationships need to be carefully developed and managed to ensure that business success and not failure is the ultimate outcome.

Building Strong Relationships with Your Suppliers

In order to sustain long-term stability, your working relationships with your product and service providers must be mutually beneficial and equitable. Decisions to select and work with one supplier over another cannot be based solely on who offers the lowest price; you also have to factor many other influences.

- *A Good Match.* The first rule of working with suppliers is that you are selecting people, as much as you are a business, product, or service. If you do not like, trust, or respect the people that operate the business, there is no hope for establishing a long-term, stable, equitable business relationship. Distrust and personality clashes only get worse over time and always work at undermining the relationship. Do business with people you like, trust, and respect.

- *Reliability and Performance.* If your suppliers cannot deliver what you need, when you need it, it will have a very negative effect on your business. Supplier reliability and performance are perhaps the two most important criteria that you should consider when establishing trade accounts. Your suppliers promises to you are your promises to your customers. If your suppliers let you down, you in turn let your customers down. Everybody loses when this happens.

- *Warranty Programs.* You also have to factor into your decision the supplier's warranty program. What kind of product warranty do they offer? What is their workmanship warranty? How do they handle warranty and claim issues? And what effect will any or all of this have on your business and customers?

- *Payment Terms.* Often more important than a lower cost is the payment terms you can negotiate with your suppliers. With the right terms, you can often sell what you have purchased before paying your supplier. That keeps your capital free and cash flow moving. Ideally, you want to secure 90-day payment terms on a revolving account basis. You will generally find most suppliers prefer 30-days and offer discounts for cash orders. A word of advice: treat all supplier accounts with respect and pay on time and in full when required to do so. Credit is a privilege for those that deserve it, not a right.

Also in written agreements with suppliers, try to build in as many of the following features as possible, because all are designed to protect your position and for the benefit of your business.

- If you will be handling a product line, you want an agreement in writing that gives you the exclusive to sell the product(s) in question, and any new or expanded models based on that product line, within a specific geographical area.

- You want the ability to transfer the agreement should you decide to sell your business. These types of exclusive product line agreements can dramatically increase the value of your business.
- You want the right to cancel the agreement on short notice, without having to give a reason and with no financial penalty.
- You do not want to have to purchase a certain amount of the product or meet sales quotas, although most suppliers will push hard for this. If you find that you must give in on this point, make sure the agreement stipulates that the more of the product you sell, the lower the unit cost will go.
- You do not want to have to commit to spending a certain amount of money each month, quarter, or year to promote and market the product line. Many suppliers or manufacturers will want this in the agreement, but avoid this one if possible. Try to turn it around so they have to spend a certain amount promoting the product in your exclusive sales area. At the very least, they should match your promotional expenditures dollar for dollar.
- You do not want to pay a premium for an exclusive product line. You want the product at the same unit cost or less. You should also never pay an up-front fee for the right to sell the product on an exclusive basis.

Tap Your Trade Accounts for the Works

What tools, equipment, or marketing materials that can be used in your business do your suppliers offer for free or at greatly reduced costs? Chances are there will be more than a few useful items. Home business owners must learn to tap their supplier's generosity. By this I mean, just like you, your suppliers are in business to make money. Therefore, many have programs in place in which they offer their trade accounts valuable equipment, marketing materials, and cooperative advertising opportunities that will enable their trade accounts (you) to be more efficient, productive, and profitable. The benefit to your supplier is, of course, as your business grows you will need to purchase more goods or services from them, increasing their revenues and profits, which is a win-win situation. Use the Trade Account Support Checklist (see Figure 8.1) to identify items that you need in your business and that your trade accounts can potentially supply to you for free, or at reduced costs.

FIGURE 8.1   Trade Account Support Checklist

Cooperative Advertising

- ❑ Newspaper and magazine display advertisements
- ❑ Newspaper and magazine classified advertisements
- ❑ Radio ads and program sponsorships
- ❑ Television ads and program sponsorships
- ❑ Internet and electronic publications advertising
- ❑ Print newsletters and specialty publication advertising
- ❑ Yellow Pages ads and business directory listings
- ❑ Direct mail, flier drops, telemarketing, and coupons
- ❑ Outdoor advertising, including billboards and transit ads
- ❑ Advertising specialties such as pens, notepads, and hats

Product

- ❑ Product samples
- ❑ Product displays

FIGURE 8.1 **Trade Account Support Checklist,** continued

Product

- ❏ Product deliveries
- ❏ Product packaging
- ❏ Product brochures and catalogs
- ❏ Exclusive product lines

- ❏ Product installations
- ❏ Product labels
- ❏ Extended product warranties
- ❏ Product training and upgrading

Promotional and Printed Materials

- ❏ Business cards
- ❏ Contest support and prize
- ❏ Stationery package
- ❏ E-mail and fax blasting

- ❏ Customer management software
- ❏ Gift certificates
- ❏ Estimate and presentation forms and folders
- ❏ Event posters, banners, and table tents

Signage

- ❏ Special event signs for trade shows and seminars
- ❏ Vehicle signs, fixed and magnetic
- ❏ Product display signs for point of purchase and countertop displays
- ❏ Exterior and site signs
- ❏ Window and bumper stickers

Additional Assistance and Items

- ❏ Education and training
- ❏ Technical assistance
- ❏ Customer service support
- ❏ Specialized equipment as required
- ❏ Public relations support

- ❏ Office furniture and fixtures, new and used
- ❏ Web site design and maintenance assistance
- ❏ Staff for special events and demonstrations
- ❏ Storage, meeting, and boardroom space
- ❏ Bookkeeping and general office support

Building Strong Relationships with Your Vendors

For home business owners that sell products or services through vendors such as retailers, wholesalers, distributors, and resellers, vendors are a very important part of your business team. After all, they are your customers. An often-overlooked aspect of working with vendors is the fact that no one knows your product's or service's benefits and features better than you. That is why it is of vital importance for you to take a hands-on approach to training each and every person that will be selling your product or service, even if it means training the retailers', manufacturers', or distributors' staffs and management teams. You have to educate them about your goods

or services, and also on why they should be pushing your products or services to their customers instead of the competition's. And, you may even want to develop a few creative incentives for people selling your products or services so they will be inclined to sell more and more often. Remember that your vendors' strengths and weaknesses are your strengths and weaknesses.

Here are a few training ideas that you should provide to your vendors:

- Provide your vendors with comprehensive product knowledge through initial and ongoing training, as well as support materials such as manuals, videos, and toll-free help lines.

- Ensure that all vendors have a clear understanding of your warranty program and your repair, return, and refund policies.
- Clearly explain and demonstrate your product's competitive advantages—durability, price, user-friendliness, reputation, and exclusivity—so that vendors can pass these advantages along to their customers with confidence and excitement.
- Make sure that your vendors know what the most common objections to the sale will be, and more importantly, give them the tools and knowledge to overcome these objections and close the sale.

GETTING STARTED WITH PROFESSIONAL SERVICES

The fourth group that defines your business team are high priority professional service providers such as bankers, lawyers, accountants, and consultants. When selecting professional service providers, it is important to keep the following criteria in mind:

- *Experience.* The first and perhaps most logical criteria to keep in mind is to work only with professionals that are highly experienced in their field. The last thing you want is to hire a professional that is learning on the job, while on your dime. Keep in mind that often it is the professional's experience, knowledge, and advice that you will be leveraging to keep you in business, to grow your business, to keep you out of trouble, and to help you with a whole host of other issues pertaining to the set up and management of your business.
- *Accessibility.* A second criteria to keep in mind when hiring professionals is accessibility. You want to be able to contact them and have their undivided attention (within reason) when you need their advice and guidance. Having to wait a few days to get an appointment is acceptable, having to wait a week, two weeks, or even longer to talk to your professional service providers is out of the question. Business decisions must sometimes be made quickly, and your professional service providers need to be accessible.

- *Affordability.* There is no doubt that good advice that can potentially make you a bundle, save you a bundle, or keep you out of hot water comes at a cost. At the same time, however, you have to select professional services in direct relationship to what your budget will afford.

Working with a Lawyer

Anyone who has ever been in business knows that operating a business and having access to good legal advice goes hand-in-hand. I can't imagine trying to take a business from start-up to operations to eventual sale without legal advice during each step, and many times in between. Competent lawyers with small business experience will be able to advise you on which legal business structure best meets your needs, insurance and liability issues, drafting of legal documents, money collection and small claims courts matters, estate planning and continuation of your business, supplier and vendor agreements, and many other legal issues. In short, lawyers will decipher the legalese for you and help make sense of complicated matters pertaining to business. Sound professional advice comes at a cost, and a lawyer's time is his product. Therefore, to keep legal costs in check, practice a few of the following timesaving tips:

- Always be fully prepared when meeting with your lawyer. Know what you want to talk about, give him a brief explanation of the situation, and have questions prepared in advance of the meeting.
- Stay focused on the task at hand and forget about social chitchat. Remember, lawyers sell their time and you are on the clock the minute you walk through their door or pick up the telephone to talk to them.
- Copy your own documents prior to meeting with your lawyer because all charge for copying and the time spent copying documents.

Additional information on the legal aspects of setting up and operating a homebased business can be found in Chapter 4, Legal Issues. To find a lawyer, you can contact the American or Canadian Bar Association at the addresses shown on the next page. They will help you locate a lawyer in your area that specializes in small business legal matters.

American Bar Association
740–15th Street NW
Washington, DC 20005-1019
(202) 662-1000
www.abanet.org

Canadian Bar Association
500–865 Carling Avenue
Ottawa, ON K1S 5S8
(800) 267-8860
www.cba.org

Working with a Banker

Establishing a relationship and working with a banker means working with all employees at the bank where you establish your business accounts, from the manager to the loan officers to the tellers to the guards that make sure no one takes off with your loot. Having a good working relationship with a bank or other financial institution such as a credit union is a critical factor in small business success— you never know when you will need to borrow working capital, growth capital, or just a quick loan to get you through the next 60 days until a client contract is completed, billed, and collected. Not only do you need a good working relationship with your bank so they will meet your special needs and requests, but you also must go out of your way not to blemish that relationship. Make all loan payments on time and in full to keep in good standing.

Working with a Accountant

Even with the proliferation of accounting and bookkeeping software, hiring an accountant to take care of more complicated money matters is a wise decision. Like many professionals, the vast majority of accountants pride themselves on the fact that they do not cost you money, but rather make you money by discovering items overlooked on tax returns, by identifying business deductions you never knew existed, and by creating financial plans that will enable you to enjoy the fruits of your labor later in life without having to worry about where the money will come from. Even if you decide to keep your own books, you will still want to make contact with an accountant familiar with small business money and tax issues. Should you decide to sell your business,

expand your business, or merge your business, you will have a competent accounting professional on your team to make sure that your financial best interests are being served. If you are unsure about your bookkeeping abilities even with the aid of accounting software you may want to hire a bookkeeper to do your books on a monthly basis and a CPA accountant to audit the books quarterly, and prepare year end business statements and tax returns. Additional information about homebased business financing, money management, and bookkeeping can be found in Chapter 3, Financial Issues.

To locate a qualified accountant or bookkeeper for your business, you can contact the following U.S. and Canadian associations.

Accountant and Bookkeeper Resources

United States
Association of Chartered Accountants in the United
    States
341 Lafayette Street, Suite 4246
New York, NY 10012-2417
(212) 334-2078
www.acaus.org

American Institute of Professional Bookkeepers
6001 Montrose Road, Suite 500
Rockville, MD 20852
(800) 622-0121
www.aipb.com

Canada
Chartered Accountants of Canada
277 Wellington Street West
Toronto, ON M5V 2H2
(416) 977-3222
www.cica.ca

Canadian Bookkeepers Association
2435 Mansfield Drive, Suite 201 D
Courtney, BC V9N 2M2
(250) 334-2427
www.c-b-a-c.ca

Working with an Insurance Agent

Having the right insurance to protect you, your family, your business, and your customers is imperative. But there are so many types of small business insurance programs out there that trying to find the right one could turn into a time-consuming and frustrating task. For these reasons, don't chance going it alone and ending up with the wrong insurance, paying too much, or spending too much time figuring it all out. Instead, enlist the services of a qualified and licensed insurance agent or broker to advise you on small business insurance matters. Not only will the agent be able to decipher insurance legalese into easily understandable English for you, but he will also be able to find the best coverage to fill your individual needs and at the lowest cost.

In the United States you can contact the Independent Insurance Agents and Brokers of America at www.iiaa.org. This nonprofit association offers a free online Find an Agent search service on its Web site, which is indexed geographically. In Canada you can contact the Insurance Brokers Association of Canada at www.ibac.ca. This nonprofit association also offers visitors access to a free online directory that geographically lists in excess of 25,000 licensed and certified insurance agents and brokers across Canada. You will find more information and resources for finding and working with insurance agents and brokers is listed in Chapter 5, Home Business Insurance.

Working with Business Consultants and Trainers

Professional consultants have long played a role in helping small business owners to meet and exceed their business and marketing objectives through coaching, planning, new business development, and training strategies. There are consulting experts available in just about every business discipline imaginable, including:

- Small business consultant
- Logistic consultant
- Marketing consultant
- Sales and sales training consultants
- Financial planning consultant
- Computer, Internet, and Web site consultants
- Advertising and public relations consultant
- Direct marketing consultant
- Franchise and licensing consultants

Quite literally the list goes on and on. The sheer number of consultants certainly does not diminish the positive impact they can have on your small business should you elect to contract with one or more to take on specific business challenges. The first step in hiring a business consultant is to define your objective. What do you want to fix, improve, or venture into? Once you know your objective(s), then you can select and interview a few potential candidates for the job. Key to selecting the right consultant is to make sure that she has experience in the topic. Ask for and check references. Ask her to provide a brief written proposal outlining how she believes she can assist you with your task.

As always, don't base your final decision on costs. Make sure the fit feels right and that the consultant has a firm grasp on your specific situation and the result that you want. Once you select the consultant you will be working with, ask for a detailed proposal that includes payment terms, a scope of work, and applicable guarantees. The Training Registry located online at www.trainingregistry.com is a directory service listing thousands of experienced, professional consultants covering every imaginable business topic. The Web site is indexed both by topic and geography.

COMPLETING YOUR TEAM WITH ALLIANCES

The final component of your business team is the alliances you establish within your industry and the community in which your business operates. These alliances include business and industry associations, other community business owners, competitors, government agencies, schools, and the media. Not as crucial as the other members of your business team, business alliances nonetheless can play a major role in helping you achieve your business and marketing objectives and your success and profitability.

Business and Industry Associations

The first group that you want to align your home business with is business and industry associations, such as your local Chamber of Commerce and industry associations relevant to your business or profession. Many home business owners neglect to join business and industry associations because of the cost and the time commitment. The cost of membership dues can range from a few hundred to a few thousand dollars per year, depending on the association. Once you join there are various functions and events that will require a time commitment on your part.

However, it is important not to view joining business or industry associations in such cut and dried terms. Instead, you should base your decision on whether or not joining will help you reach your goals and objectives through the various events and the education and advocacy opportunities.

If you do join, the key is to mine the value of membership, which can include member discounts on products and service, networking opportunities, new business alliances, advertising opportunities, and learning and education opportunities through seminars and workshops. It is important to remember that business and industry associations must provide value and benefits to their members in order to secure new members and retain current ones. Most associations provide great opportunities, but the rest is up to you. Profiting through membership requires a plan and participation to realize the value and benefits to the fullest extent.

Member Services

The services that associations often provide can be very beneficial to home business owners. Start by asking if this association has the resources and specialized services that would be helpful to your business and if you can easily tap into and take advantage of these resources and services. Resources and services could include a print and electronic library of industry-related information, meeting space and boardroom rentals, equipment lending such as tradeshow displays and PowerPoint projection systems. Are there experts on staff to answer questions and provide assistance when needed? Many small business and industry associations have economists, business planners, and marketing specialists to assist members with their specific business challenges.

Member Discounts

Discounts on products and services that small business people routinely need are yet another potential benefit of joining small business or industry associations. The second question to ask before joining is whether this association offers member discounts on products and services that you need to purchase for use in your business. Common member discounts include reduced credit card merchant rates with major credit card providers, discounted courier

fees, savings that can be as much as 10 percent on office products and supplies, and fleet rate fuel cards through major gas companies rebating up to 10 cents per gallon of gas. There may also be weekly and monthly specials on business travel, and small business insurance, and reduced fees for seminars, trade shows, and other marketing events.

Business Building Opportunities

Depending on your marketing objectives, business building opportunities may be more important than member services or discounts. Consequently, you will want to find out if the current members of the association match your target audience. If so, are there opportunities to market your products or services directly to association members? Business building opportunities include trade shows, networking meetings, advertising opportunities in the association's publication and on its Web site, and direct promotional mail-outs to members. For instance, if you operate a home travel business, in all likelihood just about any small business association such as the Chamber of Commerce will have a membership base that matches your target audience criteria: People that travel for business and pleasure.

Education Opportunities

The potential to learn can also be an important reason for joining a business association. Prior to signing up, you will want to know if the association provides educational opportunities. These learning opportunities could include workshops, training classes, and seminars featuring keynote speakers. Also, does the association provide members with valuable and up-to-date industry research, news, and emerging trends? Generally you will find that most business association host educational events on a monthly basis on a wide variety of topics, including sales, advertising, public relations, logistics, management, bookkeeping, and networking.

Advocacy

For many home business owners, having a voice in the business community is important, but nearly impossible as a small operation. Therefore, if advocacy is important to you, it is important to know if the association has a strong voice within the industry and is respected enough that it can influence the decision-making process at the regional and federal levels of government. Like labor unions, business associations take a strength-in-numbers approach to making their voices heard on issues important to members and the business community.

To locate business and industry associations specific to your needs, contact Marketing Source atwww.marketingsource.com/associations/. Marketing Source publishes a print and electronic business association directory containing information on more than 35,000 associations. Additionally, the Chamber of Commerce also offers home business owners good value for specific products and services, and useful business information and networking opportunities. There are Chamber of Commerce chapters throughout North America. To find one close to you in the United States log on to www.uschamber.com, and in Canada, www.chamber.ca. More information about creating new business and selling opportunities through business and industry associations can be found in Chapter 14, Public Relations and Networking.

Cross Promotional Partners

You want to establish relationships with other businesses in your community so that you can create and benefit from cross promotional opportunities and referrals. The business world is abuzz with terminology such as strategic alliances, relationship marketing, and joint ventures as we enter into a global marketplace with fierce competition around every corner. Given this new business environment, one of the best ways to grow your home business is by joining forces with other small business owners to create powerful cross promotional activities. These cross-promotional activities should be developed so they increase brand awareness, have the ability reach a broader audience, and drive new business to you while driving down the cost for each partner to market and promote their respective businesses. In a nutshell, cross-promotional activities enable entrepreneurs that share similar goals and objectives to band together and reduce financial risk and share financial rewards.

Lifestyle Packages

Creating lifestyle packages is one of the best ways to build your business through cross promotional opportunities because they enable you to be extremely creative and clearly separate your business from your competitors. For instance, if you designed and installed custom sundecks, logical matches to create a lifestyle package are a retailer of custom patio furniture and accessories and one of hot tub spas. Together you could create a Family Outdoor Living Package that includes a custom sundeck, matching custom patio furniture, and hot tub, sold at a discount when compared to purchasing each separately.

Sponsorships

Band a business team together to share the expense of community sponsorships, but still receive the full impact of beneficial exposure. The sponsorships could be in the form of a youth baseball team, a Clean Up the Park Day, or a local charitable cause.

Advertising

An obvious but effective cross promotional activity is to form an advertising club with other noncompeting small businesses. In doing so, you will generally find that you can negotiate lower costs for print and broadcast media as well as for printed promotional literature such as brochures, coupons, and product catalogs because of your greater buying power based on volume.

Web Site

A great e-commerce Web site can be very expensive to create, not to mention very costly to maintain both in terms of money and time commitment, especially for home business owners that are short of the aforementioned resources. Consequently, banding together with other noncompeting but like-minded home and small business owners to create and maintain a community Web site that features all of the participating businesses' products and services is a great way to create an award winning and highly useable Web presence without breaking the bank. I suggest that if you go this route, you hire an outside contractor to build and maintain the site for all of the businesses that participate in the program and split the cost.

Government Officials

Building your business team also means opening lines of communications between your home business and elected or appointed public officials at all levels of government, especially local government. By including local officials such as politicians, planners, police, and fire services in your business team and keeping lines of communication open, you can help local government understand what effects its decisions have on your business by making your business voice and opinions known. You will also gain a clearer understanding of the issues and challenges facing the community and how this relates to policy making. When you take an active role in your community, you help to shape the kind of community in which you want to live and conduct business.

The Media

The media can also be an important member of your business team if you take the time and steps necessary to include it. Of course, the benefits of doing so can include very valuable media exposure for your business, products, or services. Through continued media exposure you can also position yourself as an expert in your field, which can have a very positive impact on your business. Get to know the local media by sending out a letter introducing your business and the products or services that you sell, and let it be known that you welcome any questions they have about your business, industry, products, or services. Also get in the habit of regularly sending out press releases to announce company news, and letters to the editor to voice opinions. You may even want to hold a press conference occasionally if you have big news to release about your business and how the community will benefit. Additional ideas about how to target and work with the media can be found in Chapter 14, Public Relations and Networking.

Schools

Home business owners are also wise to establish working relationships with local schools and educational institutions because many have co-op work programs in place that are designed to bring community businesses and young people together so that students can receive much needed, hands-on work experience and business can benefit from the students' fresh ideas and creativeness. Students can also be great teachers, helping home business owners with

- computer hardware and software training.
- marketing research and planning.
- access to a pool of eager part-time, seasonal, or temporary, help as needed.

And many of these same students may very well be your customers in the not too distant future.

Competitors

Yes even your competitors can make up part of your business team, especially if you join those competitors that operate outside of your geographical trading area to build strong business coalitions. Companies that share similar goals and objectives can band together to share risk and rewards. In doing so, you may find that as a group you are able to negotiate lower supply costs based on increased purchasing power. And as part of a larger coalition you may find that you are able to bid on and secure goods and services supply contracts that would normally be too large for just your business to handle alone. By building and being involved in a coalition, you will be able to identify and overcome marketing and business challenges facing the industry through collective brainstorming and the planning process. You can also build working relationships with local competitors, offering to assist each other with overflow work during busy times.

RESOURCES

📋 Associations

American Home Business Association
4505 Wasatah Boulevard South
Salt Lake City, UT 84124
(800) 664-2422
www.homebusiness.com

Human Resources Development Canada
140 Promenade du Portage
Hull, Quebec K1A 0J9
(800) 567-6866
www.hrdc-drhc.gc.ca

Service Corps of Retired Executives (SCORE)
409 Third Street SW 6th Floor
Washington, DC 20024
(800) 634-0245
www.score.org

SOHO Canada
Small Office Home Office Business Group
2255 B Queen Street East, Suite 3261
Toronto, ON M4E 1G3
(800) 290-7646
www.soho.ca

United States Department of Labor
Frances Perkins Building
200 Constitution Avenue NW
Washington, DC 20210
(877) 889-5627
www.dol.gov

📖 Suggested Reading

Blanchard, Kenneth H., and Spencer Johnson. *The One Minute Manager.* Berkley, CA: Berkley Publishing Group, 1983.

Bly, Robert W. *Become a Recognized Authority in Your Field in 60 Days or Less.* Dulles, VA: Alpha Books, 2001.

Carnegie, Dale. *How to Win Friends and Influence People, Reissue.* New York: Pocket Books, 1994.

Collins, Jim. *Good to Great: Why Some Companies Make the Leap…And Others Don't.* New York: Harper Collins, 2001.

Hiam, Alexander. *Making Horses Drink: How to Lead and Succeed in Business.* Irvine, CA: Entrepreneur Press, Inc., 2002.

Nelson, Bob. *1001 Ways to Energize Employees.* New York: Workman Publishing Company, 2004.

Parlapiano, Ellen H., and Patricia Cobe. *Momprenuers: A Practical Step-by-Step Guide to Work-at-Home Success.* Berkley, CA: Berkley Publishing Group, 2001.

💻 Web Sites

Better Business Bureau, www.bbb.org: Consumer and business protection group.

Entrepreneur, www.entrepreneur.com: Online small business resource center.

Entrepreneurial Parent, www.en-parent.com: Web site dedicated to the work at home parent, providing information, support, and links of interest.

Expert Click, www.expertclick.com: Online directory listing expert services for media members and contacts.

Family Business Magazine Online, www.familybusinessmagazine.com: Information, tips, articles, and advice about starting and operating a family business.

Marketing Source, www.marketingsource.com/associations: Online directory listing more than 35,000 business association indexed by industry.

Monster, www.monster.com: Monster brings employers and job seekers together online.

Motivation USA, www.motivationusa.com: Employee motivation products, programs, and awards.

Small Office Home Office of America, (SOHO) www.soho.org: Homebased business association providing support and information to members.

Team Building Adventures, www.teambuilding.com: Corporate and team-building adventure programs.

Training Registry, www.trainingregistry.com: National online directory listing professional business, management, and employee training consultants.

Welcome Wagon, www.welcomewagon.com: Newcomer programs bringing people and community businesses together.

CHAPTER 9

What Price Will You Charge?

PRICING IS A VERY IMPORTANT ELEMENT OF THE marketing mix and your marketing strategy. If your prices are too high, you will meet with great resistance trying to sell your goods or services. If your prices are too low, you may meet with great resistance selling your goods or services because of perceived quality issues. Clearly, a balanced approach must be taken when establishing your prices and developing your pricing polices and strategies moving forward. Factors influencing pricing formulas and strategies include:

- Product costs
- Costs of delivering services
- Fixed operating overheads
- Market supply and demand
- Economic conditions
- Competition for market share
- Desired return on investment
- Method of distribution
- Seasonal pressures
- Political pressures
- Psychological factors (consumer perceptions)
- How you want to position your business, products, or services within the marketplace and in comparison to competitors

As you can see, there are a great many factors influencing the formula used to set your prices initially and how you deal with changes in the marketplace and product lifecycles (growth, decline, static) moving forward. A key pricing concept to keep in mind when devising pricing strategies is that consumers see prices in very clearly defined terms—the price that you charge for your product or service versus how the product or service will fill their needs and give value.

When was the last time that you purchased a loaf of bread and thought about all the costs associated with getting the seeds planted, the wheat from the farm to the mill, the flower from the mill to the bakery, and the loaf of bread from the bakery to the supermarket? If you are like most consumers, you don't give it a second thought. All you see is loaves of bread on the shelf. One is 10 cents cheaper than the next, and the one next to that is 50 cents more, but claims it is better for you. Once again, you have to price versus needs and value.

When your pricing is correct for what you sell, consumers don't think twice because they feel the price is fair in comparison to the value and what the product or service will do for them. However, as soon as your price goes below or above the threshold of what consumers feel is in the fair range for your goods or services, you will meet resistance to the purchase. At this point, consumers must begin to justify why they will make the purchase, and you never want your target audience to have to convince themselves to buy your products or services. That is always your job and is achieved through proper pricing, promotion, and positioning strategies.

THE BASICS

Covering the basics in terms of setting your prices means that you first have to determine the costs associated with the sale and delivery of goods and services from an internal perspective, excluding any outside influences such as competition or economic conditions. The internal factors to consider when setting your prices include fixed costs, direct costs, incomes and wages, and profit. It is combinations of the aforementioned that will help you determine what prices you have to charge for your goods and services to satisfy your internal financial requirements.

Covering Fixed Costs

The first area of your internal operation to analyze is your fixed operating costs, that is, your overhead. Overhead is the cost of doing business. Even though these fixed costs cannot directly generate a profit, they nonetheless must be present in order to operate the business. Costs such as the telephone bill are business expenses that must be paid regardless of how many sales you make or how

---

FIGURE 9.1 **Monthly Overhead Estimator (Home Business Portion Only)**

Rent or mortgage	$_____	Transportation parking	$_____
Utilities	$_____	Advertising	$_____
Property taxes	$_____	Public relations	$_____
Business taxes	$_____	Direct marketing	$_____
Alarm monitoring	$_____	Event marketing	$_____
Workspace cleaning and maintenance	$_____	Web site hosting	$_____
Business loan and interest repayments	$_____	Web site content and software	$_____
Bank charges	$_____	Web site maintenance	$_____
Accounting or bookkeeping fees	$_____	Equipment loans and leases	$_____
Business licenses and permits	$_____	Equipment repairs and maintenance	$_____
Business insurance	$_____	Off-site storage	$_____
Workers compensation	$_____	General office supplies	$_____
Dedicated telephone line	$_____	Business or industry association dues	$_____
Toll-free line	$_____	Uniforms and dry cleaning	$_____
Cellular telephone	$_____	Subscriptions	$_____
Answering service	$_____	Other _____	$_____
Pager	$_____	Other _____	$_____
Two-way radio	$_____	Other _____	$_____
Transportation lease or loan payment	$_____	Other _____	$_____
Transportation fuel and oil	$_____	Other _____	$_____
Transportation insurance and license	$_____	Total overhead per month	$_____
Transportation repairs and maintenance	$_____	Total overheads per year	$_____

much revenue is generated. Some overhead costs do, however, increase as sales volumes increase, necessitating good record-keeping and bookkeeping habits so that you can stay on top of changes. Use the worksheet Monthly Overhead Estimator (see Figure 9.1) to determine how much your fixed monthly expenses will be for each month and for the year. Complete only the sections that are relevant to your business, and remember to separate out what is specific to your business from your personal expenses.

Covering Direct Costs and Consumables

Direct costs and consumables refer to the costs specifically associated with the sale and delivery of products or services. In other words, if you are not selling products or services, then you do not have any direct costs. Examples of direct costs include the postage to send your client an invoice, the wholesale cost of the tennis racket (inventory) that you resell to a client, or equipment or tools that have been purchased or rented and used on a specific job for a client. Estimating direct costs in association to selling and delivering products is very straightforward. You know how much your wholesale costs are for the product (inventory), and you have a good idea about what will be needed to get the product from your supplier to your business and then to your customer. Therefore, if the tennis racket costs you $20 and the cost to get the tennis racket delivered to your business is $5, then the tennis racket has directly cost you $25 to date.

Determining direct costs in the delivery of services is more involved, especially for consulting or services in which the final outcome cannot be predicted. For instance, if you provide window washing services, you can easily estimate your direct costs associated with each job on an averaged basis. But if you provide highly specialized services, you will need to probably invoice clients on an hourly basis plus materials and expenses. Later in the chapter, under additional pricing information for service providers, you will find a Client Job Logbook for Time (see Figure 9.3), which is a handy record-keeping tool for service providers. Through trial and error and experience, most service providers develop a system to estimate

direct costs on an averaged basis and use this formula when estimating contracts. In time, you will also find that in time you will be able to adjust your prices more accurately based on previous experience.

Covering Your Income and Wages

In the prices that you charge for your goods and services, you have to be able to cover the costs of your income and any employee wages, as well as related benefits and employee contributions. Calculating employee wages, benefits, and employer contributions is pretty straightforward. In terms of employee wages and benefits, you have a few options. You can pay employees what competitors pay the going market rate. You can pay employees market rate plus, based on special skills and training. Or you can pay employees on a performance-based system such as commission on sales. You can also combine these options. In terms of employer contribution you must simply pay what is legally required. If you do not want to hire employees, hire only independent contractors that pay their own taxes.

The wage that you pay yourself for running and working in the business is where is gets a little more tricky. In the first place, seldom can business owners immediately draw a wage from a new business. The business must generate sufficient revenues to cover an owner's salary. This means that if you need to draw a weekly or monthly wage but the business is generating insufficient revenues, you have to calculate this amount into your business start-up costs. Nonetheless, even if you are not drawing a wage, what normally would be your wage must still be built into pricing so that when the business is generating sufficient revenues, your wages will be available to you.

Second, you have to calculate how much income you plan on drawing from the business and the incremental stages when your income will increase. So perhaps the first year you will draw a wage of $500 per week, than to $700 per week the second year, and $1,000 per week the third year. You may be able to survive on a few hundred dollars income right now, but in the future, to justify the business

FIGURE 9.2   Family Monthly Expenses Worksheet

Housing Expenses

Mortgage or rent $ _____

Common property fees $ _____

Utilities $ _____

Telephone, cable, and Internet $ _____

Property insurance $ _____

Property taxes $ _____

Property maintenance $ _____

Other _____ $ _____

Other _____ $ _____

Other _____ $ _____

Other _____ $ _____

Other _____ $ _____

Transportation Expenses

Auto loans or leases $ _____

Fuel and oil $ _____

Licensing $ _____

Maintenance $ _____

Insurance $ _____

Other _____ $ _____

Other _____ $ _____

Other _____ $ _____

Other _____ $ _____

Other _____ $ _____

Personal Expenses

Food $ _____

Clothing $ _____

Pets $ _____

Health care $ _____

Dental $ _____

Insurances $ _____

School $ _____

Retirement plans $ _____

Entertainment $ _____

Recreation and hobbies $ _____

Memberships and subscriptions $ _____

Church $ _____

Credit card payments $ _____

Other _____ $ _____

Other _____ $ _____

Other _____ $ _____

Other _____ $ _____

Other _____ $ _____

Total expenses per month $ _____

Less other income $ _____

(Spouse, Investment Income, or Pensions)

After-tax income needed per month X 12 months $ _____

After-tax income needed per year $ _____

and the amount of work that you put in, you will have to pay yourself what you feel is a fair or comfortable income. If you do not, you will quickly lose interest in your new business venture. It is hard to stay motivated when earning only subsistence wages for long periods of time. Use the Family Monthly Expenses Worksheet (see Figure 9.2) to determine how much income you need to make each month to pay your personal expenses. The amount that you need can be used as the starting point for the income that you will draw from the business and build into your pricing formulas.

Including a Profit

Profit is the money left over after you deduct all business expenses from the total revenues that the business brings in. For example, if your business generates $100,000 in total revenues and the total cost of doing business, including product, wages, overheads, and consumables, totaled $88,000 during the same period, your business would be left with a pretax profit of $12,000. Alternatively, if your total costs of doing business were $113,000 in that period, you would have an operating loss of $13,000. Generating a profit is great, breaking even is good, but operating at a loss is not so good. You expect to operate a loss for a few months or even for the first year with a new business start-up, but the longer the business fails to break even or profit, the higher the operating losses climb. Eventually, the business fails.

The main point here is to include a profit when setting your prices. There is no standard formula. Most business owners use a cost-plus formula when setting prices, with the plus in the equation being profit. There are, however, other influences that may not allow you to use this approach. These influences include competition pricing, supply, demand, and market conditions—all covered in greater detail later in this chapter.

Tying It All Together

Finally, you have to be able to tie all of the internal factors together to create a pricing formula for your goods or services. New entrepreneurs often use a cost-plus formula to establish a retail selling price for their products or services. For example, my cost is $10. I will mark up my costs by 30 percent and sell my gizmos for $13 each. The danger in a cost-plus approach is that you do not know how many products that you have to sell to break even or profit, or how many hours that you have to work to break even or generate a profit. Therefore, a more logical approach is to use a cost-plus pricing formula but also create a break-even analysis, which will tell you how many products you must sell at your cost-plus pricing to break even or how many hours you must work to break even. The break-even analysis enables you to know that your pricing is accurate in terms of expected sales volume, as the following example indicates:

Unit cost price	$10
50% markup	$5
Retail selling price	$15 (33.333% gross margin)
Estimated business expenses per year	$15,000
Number of units to sell to break even	3,000 per year
	250 per month
Break-even revenues	$45,000 per year
	$3,750 per month

Once you have determined how much of a product or service that you need to sell to break even it can help you to establish your pricing formula based on your projected sales. Of course, at this point external factors can begin to play a role in your pricing formulas. Economic conditions or competitor pricing that may hinder you from charging what you need to charge. Additional information about break-even analysis and sales projections can be found in Chapter 6, Preparing a Business Plan, and in Chapter 12, Creating a Marketing Plan.

DETERMINING YOUR PRICING STRATEGY

Setting your prices or determining your pricing strategy has much to do with positioning your business and the goods or services you sell in the marketplace and with external factors that can potentially influence the prices you charge. You can position yourself and become known for low prices, moderate prices, or prestige prices. However, once you have determined your pricing strategy you are advised to stick with your strategy. Do not change back and forth, because doing so will leave customers confused, not knowing what to expect. The only exception to this would be circumstances that require you to be flexible or promotional pricing tied in with a special event. Your pricing positioning strategy must also match the rest of your business and marketing positioning strategy in order to deliver a consistent promotional message and project a consistent business image, both of which are critical to successful branding.

Your positioning strategy answers two vital questions:

1. Where do your business and products or services fit into the market?
2. How does your target audience view your business and products or services in relationship to your competitors?

Obviously price makes up a large part of the answers. You might position your business as the low-price leader in the marketplace, or perhaps you will choose a quality-first philosophy and opt to charge a premium for your goods or services. Much of your positioning is affected by your competitors and where they are positioned in the market, by perceptions consumers already have or expect for the type of goods or services you sell, and by the beneficial advantages you can create for consumers purchasing from your business. You can try to alter consumer perceptions and buying habits, but this is a costly and long-term process that most home business owners with limited capital cannot attempt. A more logical approach to defining your pricing strategy is to analyze the current marketplace, identifying what competitors are charging and how consumers respond to those prices.

Factors Influencing Pricing

There are internal factors that influence your pricing strategy as well as external factors that can potentially influence it. You will not always have absolute power in terms of the prices that you charge. Sometimes external factors will be positive and in the favor of your business, and at other times these factors will be negative and have a detrimental affect on your business. A few of the more common external influences on pricing include:

- *Demand factor.* If your products are in high demand, you can charge a premium, or at least not have to discount. Alternately, if supply is high and demand low, you might have to lower your prices to increase sales and capture market share.
- *Economic factors.* The state of the local economy will also play a role in your pricing strategies. If the economy is robust, then consumers have discretionary income to spend, which generally keeps prices stable to high. If the economy stumbles, usually see this result in lower prices.
- *Competitive factors.* You also have no control over what your competition charges for the same goods and services, unless you operate in a regulated industry where a commission or agency sets all market pricing. Your competitors can choose to sell for less than you, more than you, or at the same price. Of course, competitor pricing affects what you will charge for your products and services. The most common competitor-pricing issue is a price war.

- *Phantom factors.* Political unrest in the Middle East drives up the price of crude oil, affecting what we pay for a gallon of gas at the pumps. Pine beetles devour thousands of trees in the Pacific Northwest of the United States and Canada, driving up the price of softwood lumber and affecting what we pay for lumber to build a deck. Early frost wipes out half of the Florida citrus crops, affecting what we pay for an orange at the market. All of these are examples of phantom factors, factors that are difficult if not impossible to predict, but can dramatically affect the prices you charge.

Five Basic Pricing Strategies

There are a great number of pricing strategies, some which are aimed at market entry, others at specific promotional activities, and still others at competitors. Five pricing strategies are worth looking at in greater detail—low pricing, moderate pricing, prestige pricing, discount pricing, and performance pricing.

Low Pricing

Selecting a low-price strategy simply means that you will strive to sell your goods or services at the lowest or near lowest price in the marketplace, a bargain basement approach to pricing, if you will. A low-pricing strategy means you will have to sell a greater volume of goods or services than you would at higher prices to produce an equivalent profit margin. It should be noted that the majority of home business owners wisely choose not to compete on or position their business in the marketplace based on low prices. Many chain retailers and national franchise services providers have already adopted a low-price strategy, making it very difficult for the small independent business to compete on this level.

Moderate Pricing

A good-quality product or service delivered to consumers at a fair price best sums up moderate pricing. This is the pricing strategy that the majority of home business owners choose. It leaves enough financial leeway for competitive advantages to be developed and introduced to separate their offerings from competitors. The moderate pricing strategy gives home business owners the most flexibility in terms of combining value and good service at a fair price, which is difficult to achieve if you adopt a low price strategy.

Prestige Pricing

Generally, a high-quality product or service is delivered in an upscale or exclusive environment. Although the quality or delivery of the goods or service is not necessarily always superior. Prestige pricing can be a deliberate pricing tactic in which you set your prices higher to separate your goods or services from competitors, and project an image of quality and exclusivity. Consumers pay a substantial premium for the quality and the prestige generally associated with purchasing the product or service.

Discount Pricing

Discounting is a pricing strategy that can be utilized to achieve a number of business and marketing objectives, such as entering into a new market, celebrating a company milestone, or rewarding your most loyal customers. The downside of discounting is that you are selling your products or services for less than the full price that you had previously established. There are a number of discounting methods you can use.

- You can offer a straight *cash discount*, represented in monetary terms, such as $25 off, or as a percentage, such as 25% off the retail price.
- You can offer a *quantity discount*. The more product or service that a customer buys, the lower the unit price goes.
- You can offer a *rebate discount* in which the consumer must first pay full price and apply or redeem a form for the stated rebate, or the rebate can be instant at the point of purchase.
- You can offer a *trade discount* to commercial clients, which is standard practice.
- You can offer a *seasonal discount* to liquidate off-season inventory, such as selling swimwear in the winter, or to boost off-season service sales, such as a discount if you replace your roof in the winter months when few people think of roofing.

- You can offer any number of *promotional discounts* such as save the tax. Most promotional discounts, however, are tied to specific events or holidays, such as your company's anniversary or Christmas.

Performance Pricing

Another pricing strategy that can be utilized by service providers is performance pricing, which means that you are paid for your service based on your performance. For instance, an expense reduction consultant might work on a performance pricing structure, retaining 50 percent of the total amount of money that she saves a client by reducing overall operational expenditures. The risk in a performance-based pricing strategy is that you will be working for free unless you perform as promised. The upside of a performance-based pricing strategy is the fact that it is very easy to close new sales because all the client has at stake is a little time.

Why You May Have to Change Your Prices

Price changes are yet another pricing issue with which home business owners must plan for and deal with, generally on an annual basis to keep up with inflation or other issues affecting pricing. Depending on the situation, your prices may have to move upward or downward. In both cases you will need to determine the best way to control fluctuating prices while retaining customers.

Why Prices Increase and How You Can Deal with It

The prices you charge for your goods and services may have to be increased for any number of reasons, including:

- Increased costs that you pay for products, supplies, and labor
- A shortage of supply and heavy consumer demand
- Need for a higher gross profit margin

Price increases have to be dealt with in a sensitive manner when being passed on to consumers. You do not want to lose a loyal customer because you have to charge them more; at the same time you do not want to eat higher costs and earn less per sale. Ultimately, you have two options. You can explain to your customers why prices have increased, or secondly, you can work with your customers to find ways to hold the line on prices, which generally means a reduced level of service or lower quality or quantity of product.

Why Prices Decrease and How You Can Deal with It

Your prices may also decrease, which is much easier to deal with in terms of breaking the news to your best customers. Reasons for price decreases include:

- You find a new and less expensive supplier and pass the savings on to your customers.
- There is an abundance of supply in the marketplace and little demand, forcing prices lower.
- You want to increase sales volumes and attract new business with lower prices.

ADDITIONAL PRICING INFORMATION FOR SERVICE PROVIDERS

Although the fundamentals of price setting are similar for product sellers and service providers, there are other issues that service providers should consider when setting their prices, especially if they provide a specialty or niche service. One common thread that ties most service providers together is that more often than not the service they provide is worth far more than they are currently or will be charging clients. This is generally due to a "trading skills for an hourly rate mind set." To assist in the process of price setting all service providers should first clearly identify and list what the service does for their customers. For instance, do customers save money as a direct result of using your service, and if so, how much and can you clearly demonstrate to prospects and customers how much money they will save? If you can, should you set your price for your service as a percentage of the savings? Saving a client $10,000 and asking for only 50 percent of the savings as a fee is realistic and fair, especially if you could prove it with the assistance of client testimonials, tangible documentation, or a savings guarantee in writing. But, in order for that to happen, you would probably have to guarantee clients that they will save money and if they did not, you would not be paid.

Do customers substantially profit from using your service, and if so, can you clearly demonstrate this to new prospects? Once again, what value can you place on earning someone money, and what is that worth—10 percent of the earnings, 20 percent, or more? Does your service positively benefit your prospects health or prolong their lives?

As you can see, the list goes on and on. But at the core is the simple concept that you have to clearly identify what your customers get from buying and using your service to get past price objections. You have to be able to justify the price you charge in exchange for the value you provide. When developing service pricing, you have to stop thinking of the value of your service in terms of an hourly or daily fee. Value your service based on what it will do for your customers. There are limits, of course, especially in very competitive service industries such as cleaning and home services. If the going rate for carpet cleaning averages out at $40 per hour, you might have a difficult time justifying and convincing customers that they should pay $80.

Working with Budgets

Another factor that should be considered is your client's budget for the service or services that they wanted. This is an area in which service providers should remain flexible to the possibilities. Flexible to the possibilities means that if your client's budget is $1,000 for a project and you have quoted $2,000, don't view this situation as a lost cause. Instead, determine what services you can provide to meet your client's budget by prioritizing the job and eliminating those with the lowest priority. You will be amazed at how many more jobs you can close by remaining flexible. Also, once your foot is in the door, budgets have a way of increasing as the benefits of the service become apparent to the client.

Index Your Contracts

Before you sign any long-term contracts to provide services, make sure that you have included a provision for indexing the contract. Inflationary and deflationary pressures on the economy can affect labor, materials, transportation, and all other direct costs associated with providing a service. These costs can rise dramatically or drop dramatically, with effects on your business and your ability to generate a profit. To protect yourself, you should consider having an indexing clause written into all of your service supply contracts. Depending on the value of the contract, the clause does not have to be a legal document, just one that serves to protect both party's best interests. For instance, you could tie the indexing clause to a specific indicator such as the cost of living inflation index. The contract would then be automatically adjusted annually to match this selected indicator for example, if the previous year's annual rate of inflation was 3 percent, then your service contract for the following year would increase by 3 percent to keep pace with inflation. Alternately, you and your client could create your own indexing system, basing the index on key components of the contract, such as labor, materials, and transportation. Select a median number, such as 100, based on today's prices, and should the index increase or decrease beyond a certain point, perhaps ten points in either direction, the indexing clause would automatically change the contract pricing to reflect economic conditions.

You want to try and minimize the potential effects that external factors can have on your ability to generate a profit, especially the external factors you cannot control. Consequently, it is wise to develop a indexing formula that can be used to automatically adjust long-term service contracts, keeping in mind the major external influences that can have the biggest impact on your ability to generate a profit:

- Inflation
- Currency fluctuation
- Interest rates
- Supply and demand factors
- Political influences

Choosing Your Contracts Carefully

Choosing your contracts carefully is not a service provider's pricing strategy or formula, but it is nonetheless very valuable information. More than any other industry, service providers have long been plagued by not being paid or paid on time for work completed. This is especially prevalent for service providers that subcontract for other contractors in the construction and home improvement industry. Before eagerly signing that new contract to provide services, you really must stand back, study the situation, and ask yourself if the proposed contract or new job is work that you really want. Before saying yes to a job, always question your customer's motives for wanting to contract with your service. For instance, if you run a house painting service and a general contractor or home builder asks you to paint five houses, a red flag should go up. Assuming the contractor is established, why is the usual house painter not painting these houses? Is the contractor a slow payer or nonpayer, or is it a legitimate case of the contractor seeking new subcontractors?

Secondary service providers are often the last in line to get paid and the first not to get paid when money runs short for whatever reason. Before jumping at that great opportunity to expand your business, make sure that you protect yourself and know who you are dealing with and how and when you will be paid. In Chapter 11, Managing Your Home Business, you will find additional information about extending credit, establishing payment terms, and collecting on completed contracts.

Be Detail Oriented

It is in the service provider's best interest to keep a detailed log of each client's job, noting the exact amount of time spent on the job and the time related to the job, such as estimating, picking up supplies, and administrative work. You must also keep very accurate records in terms of the consumables used in the delivery of the service, including small items such as postage and easily forgotten items such as paying the parking meter out in front of your client's location. The reason that each job needs to be well documented in terms of time and direct costs is twofold. If your client challenges the invoice, you will have documentation to support your billing. And, by keeping an accurate log of each contract, you will not overlook small items and time spent on the job, which can cost you money by not being invoiced. A basic Client Job Logbook for Time template is presented here (see Figure 9.3) that you can create on your computer and customize to meet your specific needs. Also, presented here is a basic Client Job Logbook for Direct Costs (see Figure 9.4). Once again, you can create this on your computer and customize to meet your specific needs

---

FIGURE 9.3   **Client Job Logbook for Time**

Client Name: _____

Client Address: _____

Telephone Number: _____

Job Number: _____

Start Date: _____   Completion Date: _____

Time Log

Date	Time Started	Time Finished	Hours/Minutes	Total Time To-Date
_____	_____	_____	____/____	_____
_____	_____	_____	____/____	_____
_____	_____	_____	____/____	_____
_____	_____	_____	____/____	_____
_____	_____	_____	____/____	_____
_____	_____	_____	____/____	_____
_____	_____	_____	____/____	_____
_____	_____	_____	____/____	_____
_____	_____	_____	____/____	_____
_____	_____	_____	____/____	_____
_____	_____	_____	____/____	_____
_____	_____	_____	____/____	_____
_____	_____	_____	____/____	_____
_____	_____	_____	____/____	_____
_____	_____	_____	____/____	_____
_____	_____	_____	____/____	_____
_____	_____	_____	____/____	_____
_____	_____	_____	____/____	_____
_____	_____	_____	____/____	_____

Total billing hours   _____

Rate per hour $ _____

Total labor costs $ _____ A

| FIGURE 9.4 | Basic Client Job Logbook for Direct Costs |

Client Name: _____

Client Address: _____

Telephone Number: _____

Job Number: _____

Start Date: _____ Completion Date: _____

Direct Costs Log

Date	Description	# of Units	$Cost Per Unit	$Total Cost
_____	_____	_____	_____	_____
_____	_____	_____	_____	_____
_____	_____	_____	_____	_____
_____	_____	_____	_____	_____
_____	_____	_____	_____	_____
_____	_____	_____	_____	_____
_____	_____	_____	_____	_____
_____	_____	_____	_____	_____
_____	_____	_____	_____	_____
_____	_____	_____	_____	_____
_____	_____	_____	_____	_____
_____	_____	_____	_____	_____
_____	_____	_____	_____	_____
_____	_____	_____	_____	_____
_____	_____	_____	_____	_____
_____	_____	_____	_____	_____
_____	_____	_____	_____	_____
_____	_____	_____	_____	_____
			Total direct costs	$_____ B

Invoicing

Total labor A $_____

Direct costs B $_____

Markup $_____

Total invoice $_____

(Plus Applicable Taxes)

RESOURCES

Associations

American Marketing Association (AMA)
311 South Wacker Drive, Suite 5800
Chicago, IL 60606
(312) 542-9000
www.marketingpower.com

Business Marketing Association (BMA)
400 N. Michigan Avenue, 15th Floor
Chicago, IL 60611
(800) 664-4262
www.marketing.org

Canadian Marketing Association (CMA)
1 Concorde Gate, Suite 607
Don Mills, Ontario M3C 3N6
(416) 391-2362
www.the-cma.org

Marketing Education Association (MEA)
PO Box 27473
Tempe, AZ 85285-7473
(602) 750-6735
www.nationalmea.org

Marketing Research Association (MRA)
PO Box 230
1344 Silas Deane Highway, Suite 306
Rocky Hill, CT 06067-0230
(806) 257-4008
www.mra-net.org

Suggested Reading

Daly, John L. *Pricing for Profitability: Activity-Based Pricing for Competitive Advantage.* New York: John Wiley & Sons, 2001.

Dolan, Robert J., and Herman Simon. *Power Pricing: How Managing Price Transforms the Bottom Line.* New York: Simon & Schuster, 1997.

Nagle Thomas T., and Reed K. Holden. *The Strategy and Tactics of Pricing: A Guide to Profitable Decision Making, 3rd Edition.* New York: Prentice Hall, 2002.

Reilly, Tom. *Value-Added Selling: How to Sell More Profitably, Confidently, and Professionally by*

Competing on Value, Not Price. New York: McGraw-Hill, 2002.

Shenson, Howard L. *The Contract and Fee-Setting Guide for Consultants and Professionals.* New York: John Wiley & Sons, 1990.

Weiss, Alan. *Value-Based Fees: How to Charge—and Get—What You're Worth.* New York: Jossey-Bass/Pfeiffer, 2002.

Web Sites

Entrepreneur Online, www.entrepreneur.com: Small business information products and services portal featuring marketing planning advice and custom Marketing Calculator software.

More Business, www.morebusiness.com: Marketing and business information, advice, and free templates.

SBA, www.sba.gov: United States Small Business Administration.

Society for Marketing Professional Services, www.smps.org: Nonprofit association representing professional marketing organizations and consultants. Web site visitors can find information about the services provided by marketing professionals.

CHAPTER 10

Finding and Keeping Customers

THIS CHAPTER COVERS THREE MAIN TOPICS— conducting research and collecting data to identify your target customer, understanding competition and building competitive advantages, and learning how you can provide incredible customer service to make sure you keep the customers you get. These important topics are grouped because you need to identify your business's target customers so you will know who to sell your products to. And you need to know who your business's competition is that wants to market to the same customers as you, and you need to know how to keep your customers once your have them. In short, every business needs customers and cannot survive without them.

Therefore, an entire chapter devoted to finding and keeping customers is warranted. However, keep in mind that this chapter is also closely tied to Chapter 12, Creating a Marketing Plan, which details the steps needed to identify markets and market potential, as well as developing marketing strategies that will enable you to meet your marketing objectives. There is also information featured about the research and data collection methods needed to create various sections of your marketing plan. I have identified and noted the crossover areas in both chapters for your convenience.

STARTING YOUR RESEARCH

All areas of business and marketing planning are only as strong as the research foundation on which they are built. Plans are simply a road map of information about how and when you will reach certain objectives and goals, while the research that goes into the planning process is what makes all of the planning, goals, and objectives feasible and attainable. Through research you gain insights into your business, industry, competition, customers, product or services, and marketplace enabling you to make fact-based forecasts and statements, which are required in all your planning activities. Without research to back up your statements and forecasts, your plans are nothing more than pure fiction, based on not what you know but what you hope will happen.

Research will reveal:

- If there is a market for your invention before you spend $150,000 to have prototypes designed and apply for a patent.
- If the marketplace can support a tenth office cleaning company.
- Who your target customers are and where they live.
- Where you should position your business and products in the market.
- What types of user benefits consumers need and want.

- What motivates people to buy.

In short, research will reveal if there is the potential for your business or product, and what marketing strategies you need to employ to succeed.

Types of Data

Before you begin your research you first have to identify the types of data that are needed to completely research and analyze specific business and marketing activities—primary data, secondary data, quantitative data, qualitative data, geographic data, demographic data, and psychographics data.

Primary Data

Primary data is the information and facts that you get by conducting your own research. If you are already in business you can collect primary data for free by talking to your customers, suppliers, competitors, other business people, and business alliances about your business, products, services, and marketplace. If you are not currently in business, other methods of collecting free primary data are making general observations about your target customers, the goods or services that you will be selling, competitors, and the marketplace in general. There are additional methods of collecting primary data, such as conducting formal surveys, hosting focus groups, giving product or service demonstrations, and mystery or comparison shopping, but most of these will cost money to develop and manage. Some are discussed later in this chapter.

Secondary Data

Secondary data is information and facts that you did not personally generate, but comes from secondary or outside sources. Obtaining secondary data for business research and planning purposes is very easy because it is everywhere, and much like primary data, most secondary data can be acquired for free. Secondary data is available from schools, the media, business and industry associations, books and journals at your local library, the Internet, private and publicly held corporations, and government agencies.

You must, however, be careful and not get too far ahead of yourself. You must first identify your research objectives, that is, what you want to do with the data that you collect. Identify the current size of the market? Find a solution to a marketing dilemma? Or start your home business? Data, information, and statistics are available on just about every product, person, thing, or place that you can think of.

- Patent, copyright, and trademark data from the copyright office and trademark and patent offices both in the United States and Canada
- Manufactured product specifications, available through manufacturers' associations, and print and electronic manufacturers' product directories
- Demographic statistics and psychographics data reports, available through government agencies, the media, almanacs, and research organizations
- Public opinion polls and media surveys, available through research organizations, government agencies, schools, and private companies
- Transportation data, available through transportation-related associations, almanacs, and government agencies
- Legal and crime data, available at a federal level or on a local level though court and police services
- Business statistics, available through business and industry associations, as well as government agencies
- International statistics, available through business and industry associations, as well as government agencies
- Political statistics and data, available through various government agencies
- Weather statistics, available through government agencies, the media, and almanacs
- Personal finance and monetary markets data, available from banks, government agencies, business and industry associations, and consumer groups

Endless volumes could easily be filled about the types of data, statistics, and information available from secondary sources. So identify what you want to learn, and then contact the sources that have compiled the type of data you are seeking.

Quantitative Data

Quantitative data is always expressed in numbers, quantities, and percentages and represents most data analyzed and used by small business owners to create business and marketing plans. Because quantitative data is expressed numerically, it is very tangible, easily measured, and therefore easy to understand and transfer into charts, lists, and graphs for planning purposes. Quantitative data is valuable to small business owners because it enables them to look at and understand the marketplace in broad terms at a glance. For instance, if you circulated a questionnaire that asks yes or no questions, the results can be easily represented as quantitative data. The results are tabulated into numbers, either as a fixed quantity such as 53 said yes, and 47 said no or in percentage terms such as 53 percent said yes and 47 percent said no. Another example is comment cards that ask customers to rank your service on a scale of 1 to 5. Once again, the results are quantitative data such as 15 people of the 30 that ranked our service gave us 5 out of 5. This could also be given in percentages, such as 50 percent of our customers are 100 percent satisfied with the level of service we provide.

Qualitative Data

Qualitative data is not expressed in tangible numbers, but rather in specific answers and statements. It is what people say about your business, products, services, prices, quality, or anything else they reveal in responses that cannot be presented numerically. Examples of qualitative data include:

- Surveys, questionnaires, or polls that are designed to let people freely answer questions in their own words without suggestions.
- Discussion groups comprised of your target audience, who are encouraged to speak or comment on how they feel about or perceive a product, service, price, value, or quality in regards to the topic of the discussion.
- Informal discussions held with customers, suppliers, or employees in which you ask questions and record their comments, such as "I think the price of your proposed service is too low."

Qualitative data is valuable to small business owners because it has the ability to reveal more precise details and information about what your customers or target audience thinks about specific issues relevant to your business or to the goods or services that you sell.

Geographic Data

Geographic data is segmenting your target customers geographically, by country, state, county, city, neighborhood, and even street, if you are so inclined. There are five basic questions in terms of collecting geographic data about your target audience:

1. Where are your target customers located?
2. Is the target audience in the geographic area large enough to be profitable?
3. What is required to access the geographic area where your target audience resides?
4. What means of promotion will enable you to tap the target market in that specific geographical area?
5. Will the target audience respond to your promotional activities?

Even on a basic level, geographical segmentation information about your target audience is extremely valuable. For example, if you operate a pool cleaning service, you would want to know where in the city most people who own swimming pools live. Having this basic information enables you to target your advertising and promotion activities to that area.

Demographic Data

Demographic data is statistical information about the population. It can be used for segmenting your target audience by gender, age, race, religion, education, income, and profession. Demographic data can be further expanded to include information such as the type of car that your target audience drives, or how many people reside in their household. It can tell you

- if the majority of your target audience is male or female.
- into what age range the majority of your target audience falls.

- if the majority of your target audience is married, single, or divorced.

If you are already in business then you can collect demographic information from your current customers to help create a demographic profile of your target audience. If you are at the business research or start-up phase, you can contact local government agencies, libraries, and business associations and inquire what type of demographic data they have on file for your trading area.

Psychographics Data

Psychographics is segmenting your customers by their common characteristics, such as lifestyle, values, behavior, and opinions. Psychographics is used as a continuation of geographic and demographic data. Once you know where your target audience is located (geographic) and who your target audience is (demographic), you can begin to find out what they think and care about (psychographics) in terms of your business, industry, competitors, pricing issues, and goods and services. It can answer a variety of questions.

- What does the majority of my target audience have in common? Do they go to church or belong to a certain social club?
- What does the majority of my target audience care about most—price, quality, fast service, value, or a wide selection of goods and services?
- What publications does my target audience read, what television shows do they watch, what radio stations do they listen to, and what recreational activities do they pursue?

Basic assumptions can be made in terms of psychographical profiling of your target market, providing they are logical assumptions. For instance, it is a safe assumption that the target market for custom designed and manufactured golf clubs are not university students.

Research Methods

Next, you need to consider the research methods that are available. But before you do, you will have to decide if you will conduct your own primary research, hire a research firm or consultant, or perhaps

combine the two options. If you decide to conduct your own research, start by not overlooking one of the easiest and least expensive ways of conducting research—looking out your window to see what is going on in your own community.

- Is the economy hot?
- In what *lifecycle* stage is the product and market—growth, decline, or static?
- How many other businesses are selling the same products and services?
- Is unemployment high, low, or static?
- Are there any current issues or emerging trends that will affect the market?

This type of research is more than looking out your window in the literal sense. It is keeping your finger on the pulse of the community at all times to stay in step with local trends. Then, you will have the knowledge and information needed to make business and planning decisions for the future.

One way to keep in touch with what is going on in your own community is to conduct informal research. You have to make an effort to get out and talk to people such as your potential suppliers, target customers, community leaders, business associations, and other small and homebased business owners. Informal research can happen over a coffee, at the point of purchase, during a business or social function, or just about any other place or time. There are also many other ways of collecting primary data, including hosting formal focus groups, looking through your local Yellow Pages business directory, and going online.

Focus Groups

One of the best ways to research the viability of a new product or service is to conduct a focus group to see if the people in the group like the product or service, features, benefits, competitive advantage, durability, reliability, performance, and price point. Unfortunately, focus groups can be very costly for budding entrepreneurs with little money left in the kitty for research. To save some money, consider creating your own homemade focus group to test, make suggestions, and report on your product or service. Choose people that are from your intended primary target audience. Providing you get the OK from everyone in the group, you may also want to consider either video or audio taping the discussion to ensure that no information is overlooked when analyzing the data.

Ideally, the focus group should have six to eight participants to ensure accurate results. Create a general outline of the topics, points, and ideas that you would like the focus group to consider, but remain open to the process and allow for deviations from the outline if warranted and useful. Everyone in the group should be made aware of the fact that their input, ideas, suggestions, and complaints are important and will be heard. After all, that is the whole idea behind the process. Each person in the group should have the opportunity to speak to voice individual opinions. If you feel the individual opinions could sway, influence, or alter group opinions, let each individual describe experiences with or thoughts about the product or service in private. Once this has been completed then have them discuss and debate the merits and faults openly as a group.

Yellow Pages Research

Flipping through your local Yellow Pages business directory is a fast, cheap, and a very effective way to conduct market research. In the Yellow Pages you will find a nearly unlimited amount of information about your competitors and often even key information about your target audience as well. Study your competition's Yellow Pages advertisements to discover information about what products and services they sell, including their specialty, competitive advantage, and unique selling proposition. You will find out about their hours of operation, how many stores or office locations they have, and where these offices or stores are located. You will also find complete contact information, including mailing address; telephone, toll-free, and fax numbers; e-mail address; and Web site URLs. Many ads also feature warranty information, customer satisfaction guarantees, length of time in business, main geographic area serviced, as well as their primary target audience. Some advertisements even include payment option information about credit cards, checks, and debit cards, financing and leasing plans, and in-house installment plans. Special discounts they provide,

such as senior's discounts, association discounts, and trade-in discounts, may be supplied. You'll learn if competitors offer free delivery, free installation or setup, free estimates, free consultations or if their service vehicles are radio dispatched. And, if you are really lucky, you may also discover information about insurance coverage, licenses, training certificates, and any affiliations they may have with professional or business associations. Without question, the Yellow Pages can provide a nearly unlimited amount of information about competitors, the marketplace, and even consumer buying habits and preferences.

Research Online

Just a short decade ago finding a foreign distribution source for your widget or even learning about out-of-state laws and regulations pertaining to business expansion were extremely time consuming and often frustrating. Countless hours could be spent on the telephone, writing letters, or purchasing expensive books and directories just to get the business information you needed to start your business, find products and services, and learn more about potential customers. Fortunately, all of that has changed thanks to the advent of the Internet. Facts, information, leads, and just about anything you ever wanted to know or needed to know about business domestically and internationally is now just a painless mouse click away. If you're not hooked up to the Internet already, then do it so that you can take advantage of the vast resources available there for business research and planning purposes.

Using Surveys for Research Purposes

Surveys have long been used by small business owners and marketers as a highly effective business and marketing research tool. Like most research activities, there are numerous options for conducting consumer surveys for business research and planning purposes, including by mail, by telephone, in person, or online.

Mail Surveys

Mail surveys are a popular way to find out what consumers think, but they can also be a very costly research option when you factor in time, postage, advertising, and renting mailing lists. The first mail survey option is to rent consumer mailing lists comprised of people that match your primary target audience and mail a survey to them along with a postage paid return envelope. The second method is to create your survey in a tear-away response card format and have it inserted in a newspaper, magazine, newsletter, or trade journal read by your primary target audience and ask readers to complete the survey and mail it back. In both cases you will likely have to provide some sort of incentive to motivate people to take the time to complete and mail in the survey. The incentive could be automatic entry into a contest, a discount coupon, a gift certificate, or any number of rewards that would entice people to complete and send in the survey.

Telephone Surveys

Calling your target audience at their home or office is also a survey method, but one that requires skill, time, and patience. In fact, you might even want to leave this surveying method to the professionals that have the communications skills, equipment, and expertise to ensure accurate and usable results. However, if you do tackle telephone surveying yourself, then make sure that you call consumers in the early evenings and business consumers during the day. Evening calls are best placed between the six and eight, and daytime office calls are best place between ten in the morning and four in the afternoon Tuesdays through Thursdays. Be aware that at the time of writing, telephone surveying was still permitted in the United States and not included in the Do Not Call legislation. Still, you might want to make sure that random telephone surveys are still allowed. Log on to the Do Not Call regulations Web site at www.donotcall.com for additional information.

In-Person Surveys

In-person surveys are another way that you can find out what your customers and target audience think about your proposed or current products and services. In-person surveys can be conducted at malls on weekends with permission, at trade shows and seminars, or out on the street. The benefits of personally surveying consumers is that it enables you ask questions of a more qualitative nature, as respondents will often answer these kinds of questions verbally but not take the time to answer them if they have to write their answers down.

Online Surveys

A quick and cheap way to survey your target audience is to use the Internet. This can be done through your Web site, if you have one. Alternately, there are literally hundreds of survey services that for a fee will develop a survey for you and place it in Web sites on the Internet that are frequented by your target audience. An online survey is a great option for small business owners that are on tight budgets and need results quickly.

Regardless of the survey method that you choose, there are some general guidelines to follow in terms of creating a survey that is unbiased and that will get the results that you want.

- The first rule to creating an effective survey that will deliver the type of information that you want is to identify the objective of the survey and what you want to learn from responses.
- If you want quantitative results, then ask closed-ended questions that require a yes or no response, or that require only one response from multiple choices. For example, a carpet cleaning service might ask:
  How many times a year do you have your carpets cleaned? ❏ 1 ❏ 2 ❏3
- If you want qualitative results, then ask open-ended questions that require people to reveal what they think or how they feel. Once again, a carpet cleaning service might ask open-ended qualitative questions to reveal something unique about how their target audience feels about a certain aspect of their service—What is the biggest benefit you receive from having your carpets cleaned?
- Try not to word your questions in such a way that it will lead people to respond the way you hope they will. The surveying exercise must be focused on real results, free of bias, leading, or

manipulative questioning techniques if it is to be of any value to you. Otherwise, it will be a waste of time, money, and energy.

- Words and phrases that you select to create questions should be easy to read and understand, free of technical expertise, double meanings, or abbreviations. Questions should also be very easy to answer. The harder you make it for people to have to answer the questions, the less likely they are to complete the survey accurately and truthfully, if at all.

- Finally, prior to surveying a large number of people, create and test a sample survey on a smaller segment of your intended audience to make sure that your survey has questions that follow a logical sequence, is error free in terms of grammar and spelling, can be completed in a reasonable amount of time, and has questions that return responses that will help you achieve your survey objectives.

Creating a Target Customer Profile

Once you have compiled and analyzed your research data, you should have a very good idea of who your target customers are and their special characteristics. At this point, you should create a simple profile of your target customer so that you can use the profile as a handy reference tool when planning advertising and promotional activities. You will know where to allocate your marketing budget so that it will have the best chance of reaching your target audience and minimize the potential to waste money on promotional activities that will not reach your target audience. The target customer profile presented here (see Figure 10.1) is for consumer use and is very comprehensive. You may elect to delete some of the items to suit your specific needs. Likewise, you may choose to add items to the profiling worksheet, perhaps including, the type of television programs your target audience watches, the types of sports they participate in, or the types of music they listen to.

FIGURE 10.1 Primary Target Customer Profile Worksheet

Where do my target customers live?

Country: _____ State: _____

County: _____ City: _____

Neighborhood: _____

How many people match my target customer profile in the geographical area in which that I will be doing business? _____

What is most important to my target customer when making purchasing decisions?

❑ Price _____ %   ❑ Value _____ %   ❑ Quality _____ %   ❑ Service _____ %

What percentage of my target customers are male and what is their age range?

❑ 0–17 _____ %   ❑ 18–29 _____ %   ❑ 30–39 _____ %   ❑ 40–49 _____ %
❑ 50–64 _____ %   ❑ 65 + _____ %

What percentage of my target customers are female _____ % and what is their age range?

❑ 0–17 _____ %   ❑ 18–29 _____ %   ❑ 30–39 _____ %   ❑ 40–49 _____ %
❑ 50–64 _____ %   ❑ 65 + _____ %

What is the marital status of my target customers?

❑ Single _____ %   ❑ Married _____ %   ❑ Divorced _____ %   ❑ Widowed _____ %

FIGURE 10.1   **Primary Target Customer Profile Worksheet,** continued

What level of education do my target customers have?

❏ Grade School _____ %   ❏ High School _____ %   ❏ Post Secondary _____ %

What do my target customer do to earn a living?

❏ Labor _____ %   ❏ Office Work _____ %   ❏ Retail _____ %   ❏ Management _____ %

❏ Sales _____ %   ❏ Professionals _____ %   ❏ Executives _____ %   ❏ Self Employed _____ %   ❏ Retired _____ %

How much do my target customers earn per year?

❏ $0–$15,000 _____ %   ❏ $15,000–$25,000 _____ %   ❏ $25,000–$40,000 _____ %

❏ $40,000–$55,000 _____ %   ❏ $55,000–$70,000 _____ %   ❏ $70,000 + _____ %

How much is my target customer's average household income per year?

❏ $0–$20,000 _____ %   ❏ $20,000–$35,000 _____ %   ❏ $35,000–$50,000 _____ %

❏ $50,000–$75,000 _____ %   ❏ $75,000–$100,000 _____ %   ❏ $100,000 + _____ %

Do the majority of my target customers own or rent their homes? Own _____ % Rent _____ %

What types of home do my target audience live in?

❏ Apartment _____ %   ❏ Condo _____ %   ❏ Single Family _____ %   ❏ Town House _____ %

❏ Duplex _____ %   ❏ Cooperative _____ %

How many people live at home?

❏ 1 _____ %   ❏ 2 _____ %   ❏ 3 _____ %   ❏ 4 _____ %   ❏ 5 _____ %   ❏ 6+ _____ %

Which types of pets do my target customers have?

❏ Dog _____ %   ❏ Cat _____ %   ❏ Fish _____ %   ❏ Bird _____ %

What type of automobile do my target customers like to drive?

❏ Sports Car _____ %   ❏ Family Car _____ %   ❏ Truck _____ %   ❏ Van _____ %   ❏ SUV _____ %

How many vacations do my target customers take each year?

❏ 1 _____ %   ❏ 2 _____ %   ❏ 3 _____ %   ❏ 4+ _____ %

GETTING STARTED WITH IDENTIFYING THE COMPETITION

Evaluating competition is tricky business to say the least. You do not want to overestimate, and certainly not underestimate, your competitor's ability to effectively compete in the marketplace and their resolve not to lose market share to new competitors. Competing businesses have to realize that they are engaged in war with each other and that to the victor will go the spoils of war, which in business means customers. Regardless of the type of business you are in or the kinds products or services you sell, you will always have competition for customers and their money. You have two options, or you can combine these two options. The first is to go *toe to toe* with your competitors and beat them by developing competitive advantages and by providing more user benefits to the consumer. The second option is to carefully research and analyze all areas of your industry, marketplace, business, and competitor's businesses to identify niche markets that are presently being ignored or underserviced and "specialize" your business so that you can cater to that niche market. The later is probably the easier path for home business owners because their competition is almost always better financed and longer established and has more resources to draw upon in competition wars. But before you decide if you will specialize within the industry or market, you should be able to identify the various types of competition and learn how to develop a competitive advantage. Both topics are covered later. A very comprehensive Competition Comparison Worksheet (see Figure 10.2) is also provided to enable you to better understand your competitors, their products and services versus yours, and their position in the marketplace versus your position.

The Four Kinds of Competition

Like all businesses, homebased businesses face four different types of competition—direct, indirect, phantom, and future.

Direct Competition

Direct competition is by far the easiest to identify because direct it is the most obvious. It is the competitors operating in the same geographic area as you, selling a similar product or service, and targeting the same primary audience. An example of direct competitors is two lawn care services that offer clients very similar services in the same geographical area.

Indirect Competition

The second type of competition your home business will face is indirect—businesses that sell numerous products or services, some of which are the same or similar to your core product or service line. For instance, if you exclusively sell and install rain gutters, indirect competitors would include home improvement centers that sell rain gutter products and contractors who occasionally offer the service in the course of completing a larger contract.

Phantom Competition

As the name suggests, phantom competition is tough to nail down with any great accuracy because it can be in the form of anything from self-help books, to consumers that simply choose not to buy

for whatever reason, to unusual weather patterns, or to media influences that sway or change consumer opinion. For instance, a self-help book about financial planning for retirement might cost a financial advisor work if someone interested in retirement planning chooses to purchase the book rather than hire him.

Future Competition

The final type of competition that business owners face are competitors that have not yet opened for business, that is, future competition. Future competitors come in two forms, businesses that are yet to open, and businesses that expand their product or service line to include the products or services you sell. For instance, if you operate the only pet taxi in town and are swamped with business, expect that in the near future someone will open a pet tax service to cash in on the obvious demand for the service. Alternately, a people taxi service might decide that because your pet taxi service is so successful, they to will expand the services they offer to include driving pets as well as people. When there is demand, supply will always follow.

Building a Competitive Advantage

Every business, product, and service needs a competitive advantage. In fact, in today's extremely competitive business environment, a competitive advantage is crucial if you ever hope to compete, survive, and grow your business. Think of your competitive advantage as the main reason people choose to buy your product or service instead of your competitor's. For that reason, the competitive advantage you create should be used in all business and marketing activities to describe what your business excels at and what specialized advantage people can expect when they do business with you. Thus, you will need to develop a central message to describe your competitive advantage. It should be brief, to the point, easy to understand, and, above all, clearly state why people should do business with you, not the competition. Your competitive advantage must be beneficial. People want to know *upfront* what they will get out of doing business with you. Simply put, if there is no benefit to doing business with you then why do business with you at all? Do you offer the lowest price? Can people make money by purchasing your goods or services? Do the products or services that you sell help people to fix a problem, make people feel better, or fill a special need? If you want to beat the competition, you must have or create an advantage that your competition does not have, and that advantage must be beneficial to your target audience to pull them into your camp.

In addition to beneficial, your competitive advantage must also be exclusive to your business. This does not necessarily mean exclusive in the sense that nobody else sells the same products or services, but more so in the way that your products are sold or in the way you provide your service. Creating a beneficial competitive advantage that is exclusive to your business does not have to be difficult or costly to achieve. In fact, it can be something as simple as a plumber offering a ten-year workmanship warranty instead of a five-year workmanship warranty, which is the typical industry standard. The exclusive competitive advantage is that the plumber guarantees workmanship longer than the competition, an exclusive competitive advantage that will definitely appeal to a large percentage of people needing the services of a plumber. An exclusive competitive advantage does not have to reinvent your business or the industry, it just has to be something that you do or sell that is different and not available from competitors in your area.

Your competitive advantage must also be easy to remember, simplistic in nature, and one that people can easily identify and link to your business. For example, a wedding planner's competitive advantage might be, "We guarantee a stress-free wedding day, or "We'll pay for the cake." That is easy to remember, beneficial to the customer, and exclusive to the business. You must be able to explain your competitive advantage in one sentence or in less than ten seconds in such a way that people say, "Yeah I get it, now let me buy it." Keep working on it until you can.

Competition Comparison

Even with the assistance of a SWOT (Strengths, Weaknesses, Opportunities, and Threats) analysis, which is featured in Chapter 12, Creating a Marketing Plan, it can prove difficult to get a firm grasp on the competition and how your business, products, and services compare to theirs. Below is a Competition Comparison Worksheet (see Figure 10.2) that I first created for *The Ultimate Small Business Marketing Guide* (Entrepreneur Press, 2003) and revised for this book. You can copy it and use it to rate each of your competitors. Once completed, use this information to help you identify and build upon your strengths and opportunities in the marketplace, while correcting internal weaknesses and eliminating external threats. Complete only the items that are relevant to your specific business or industry. You may also discover a few items that you want to add that are specific to your business, industry, market, or target audience.

FIGURE 10.2 **Competition Comparison Worksheet**

Competitor Information _____

Competitor Company Name _____

Years in Business _____   Estimated Annual Sales $ _____

Number of Employees _____   Estimated Market Share _____%

Is their market share   ❏ increasing or   ❏ decreasing?

What is this competitor's number one specialty? _____

Business Location   ❏ Homebased   ❏ Storefront   ❏ Office   ❏ Other

---

FIGURE 10.2 Competition Comparison Worksheet, continued

Rate the Competition's Reputation	Poor	Fair	Good	Great
Company Reputation	❑	❑	❑	❑
Product(s) Reputation	❑	❑	❑	❑
Service(s) Reputation	❑	❑	❑	❑
Customer Service Reputation	❑	❑	❑	❑
Pricing Reputation	❑	❑	❑	❑
Product(s) Benefits	❑	❑	❑	❑
Product(s) Positioning	❑	❑	❑	❑
Product(s) Quality	❑	❑	❑	❑
Product(s) Value	❑	❑	❑	❑
Product(s) Reliability	❑	❑	❑	❑
Product(s) Performance	❑	❑	❑	❑
Product(s) Ability to Meet Market Trends	❑	❑	❑	❑
Product(s) Ability to Meet Market Needs	❑	❑	❑	❑
Product(s) Availability	❑	❑	❑	❑
Product(s) Packaging	❑	❑	❑	❑
Product(s) Labeling	❑	❑	❑	❑
Private Label/Exclusive Product(s)	❑	❑	❑	❑
Product(s) Warranties	❑	❑	❑	❑

Rate the Competition's Services	Poor	Fair	Good	Great
Service(s) Benefits	❑	❑	❑	❑
Service(s) Positioning	❑	❑	❑	❑
Service(s) Quality	❑	❑	❑	❑
Service(s) Value	❑	❑	❑	❑
Service(s) Reliability	❑	❑	❑	❑
Service(s) Performance	❑	❑	❑	❑
Service(s) Ability to Meet Market Trends	❑	❑	❑	❑
Service(s) Ability to Meet Market Needs	❑	❑	❑	❑
Service(s) Availability	❑	❑	❑	❑
Exclusive/Proprietary Service(s)	❑	❑	❑	❑
Service(s) Warranties	❑	❑	❑	❑
Workmanship Warranties	❑	❑	❑	❑

Rank the Competition's Marketing	Poor	Fair	Good	Great
Advertising	❑	❑	❑	❑
Yellow Pages	❑	❑	❑	❑
Radio	❑	❑	❑	❑

FIGURE 10.2	Competition Comparison Worksheet, continued

Rank the Competition's Marketing	Poor	Fair	Good	Great
Television	❏	❏	❏	❏
Direct Mail	❏	❏	❏	❏
Magazines	❏	❏	❏	❏
Trade Shows	❏	❏	❏	❏
Seminars	❏	❏	❏	❏
Publicity	❏	❏	❏	❏
Contests	❏	❏	❏	❏
Coupons	❏	❏	❏	❏
Catalogs	❏	❏	❏	❏
Signage	❏	❏	❏	❏
Newsletters	❏	❏	❏	❏
Networking	❏	❏	❏	❏
Seasonal Promotional Events	❏	❏	❏	❏
Telemarketing	❏	❏	❏	❏
Event Sponsorships	❏	❏	❏	❏
Cross Marketing/Promotional Activity	❏	❏	❏	❏
Customer Clubs/Loyalty Programs	❏	❏	❏	❏

Rate the Competition's Operations	Poor	Fair	Good	Great
Customer Policies	❏	❏	❏	❏
Reliable	❏	❏	❏	❏
Consistent Message	❏	❏	❏	❏
Leadership	❏	❏	❏	❏
Proactive Thinking/Planning	❏	❏	❏	❏
Customer Service	❏	❏	❏	❏
Communications	❏	❏	❏	❏
Technologically Advanced	❏	❏	❏	❏
Community Involvement	❏	❏	❏	❏
Charity Involvement	❏	❏	❏	❏
Corporate Citizenship	❏	❏	❏	❏
Business Associations	❏	❏	❏	❏
Better Business Bureau Report	❏	❏	❏	❏
Vendor(s) Support	❏	❏	❏	❏
Manufacturing Capabilities	❏	❏	❏	❏
Research/Development	❏	❏	❏	❏
Distribution Channels	❏	❏	❏	❏

FIGURE 10.2 Competition Comparison Worksheet, continued

Rate the Competition's Operations	Poor	Fair	Good	Great
Equipment	❏	❏	❏	❏
Transportation	❏	❏	❏	❏
Overall Financial Stability	❏	❏	❏	❏
Accept Credit Cards	❏	❏	❏	❏
Accept Paper/E-Checks	❏	❏	❏	❏
Offer Financing Options	❏	❏	❏	❏
Pay Suppliers on Time	❏	❏	❏	❏
Pay Employees on Time	❏	❏	❏	❏
Business Hours	❏	❏	❏	❏
Computerized	❏	❏	❏	❏

Rate the Competition's Employees	Poor	Fair	Good	Great
Loyal	❏	❏	❏	❏
Training	❏	❏	❏	❏
Remuneration	❏	❏	❏	❏
Benefits	❏	❏	❏	❏
Work Conditions	❏	❏	❏	❏
Education	❏	❏	❏	❏
Specialized	❏	❏	❏	❏
Subcontractors	❏	❏	❏	❏
Professional Appearance	❏	❏	❏	❏
Energized/Motivated	❏	❏	❏	❏

Rate the Competition's Web Site	Poor	Fair	Good	Great
Regularly Updated	❏	❏	❏	❏
Relevant Content	❏	❏	❏	❏
Efficient Shopping Model	❏	❏	❏	❏
Customer Service Support	❏	❏	❏	❏
Visitor Interactive (community)	❏	❏	❏	❏
Fast/Efficient	❏	❏	❏	❏
Relevant to Audience	❏	❏	❏	❏
Links	❏	❏	❏	❏
Navigation	❏	❏	❏	❏
Helpful User Tools	❏	❏	❏	❏
Keyword Search	❏	❏	❏	❏
Opt-In/E-zine/E-Newsletter	❏	❏	❏	❏
Online Advertising	❏	❏	❏	❏

FIGURE 10.2 Competition Comparison Worksheet, continued

Result Analysis

Based on how you have rated this competitor, what do you think its biggest competitive advantage within the marketplace is, and why?

_____

_____

What do you think this company's greatest strength is, and why? _____

_____

_____

What do you think this company's greatest weakness is, and why? _____

_____

_____

What opportunities do you see in terms of competing against this company or filling a niche within the market that they do not, and why?

_____

_____

What is the greatest threat that this company poses to your business, and why? _____

_____

_____

What is the greatest threat that your business poses to this company, and why? _____

_____

_____

What is your greatest advantage in terms of competing against this company? _____

_____

_____

What does this company do well enough that you should also be doing? _____

_____

_____

Now that you know this company better, what products or service can you provide to its customers to lure them onto your team? Or, what marketing activities can you implement to reach this company's core target audience? _____

_____

_____

_____

_____

GETTING STARTED WITH CUSTOMER SERVICE

Your ability to survive in business and be financially viable will be based on many factors, but perhaps the biggest contributing factor will be your ability to retain customers and foster long-term and profitable selling relationships with them. Just how important is customer service in terms of the very survival of your home business? Well, a recent survey conducted by the U.S. Small Business Administration revealed that the number one reason customers stop doing business with a particular business and choose to start doing business with a competitor was poor customer service. In fact, in excess of 60 percent of respondents to the survey stated poor customers service was the number one reason that they no longer did business with certain companies. This is an eye opening revelation when you consider that the poor customer service response exceeds all other reasons people stop doing business with a particular company—moving away, death, or changing priorities—combined. Specifically, the SBA survey found

- 1 percent of customers died or become physically immobile and unable to continue shopping at a particular business.

- 4 percent of customers moved out of the geographic trading area.
- 15 percent of customers go to competitors because of lower prices.
- 15 percent of customers stop shopping because they are dissatisfied with what they buy.
- 65 percent of customers stop shopping because of the poor service they receive.

The results of the SBA survey provide business owners a picture of what will eventually happen to their customer base if providing great customer service is not one of their highest priorities. Providing great customer service is much easier and cheaper than trying to find and satisfy new customers constantly. As the saying goes, "It is ten times easier and less expensive to keep the customers that you have than it is to find new ones."

At the end of the day, the best way to provide great customer service is to treat your customers the way that you like to be treated when you trade your hard-earned money for goods and services at other businesses. In fact, creating a How I Like to Be Treated as a Customer Worksheet (see Figure 10.3) listing both how you like to be treated as a customer,

---

FIGURE 10.3 **How I Like to Be Treated as a Customer Worksheet**

As a customer I like:

1. _____
2. _____
3. _____
4. _____
5. _____

As a customer I dislike:

1. _____
2. _____
3. _____
4. _____
5. _____

and how you very much dislike being treated is one of the best ways of developing customer service policies for your own business.

Key Customer Service Components

One of the easiest customer service concepts to grasp is the simple fact that people like to do business with people that they like. Let's face it, when was the last time that you returned to a business run by someone that you disliked, just for the privilege of giving them your hard-earned money? I hope never. Therefore, it stands to reason that you should go out of your way to be likeable. It is not tough to do. Smile, be presentable, take an interest in your customers, treat them fairly, and thank them for their continued support of your business; that's about all it takes to make your customers like you. In addition to being someone that people like to do business with, there are three other important components to providing great customer service—reliability, flexibility, and contact.

Reliability

All home business owners, especially service providers should promote and practice reliability. If you say you'll be there at ten, arrive five minutes early. If you guarantee your work, then fix it, no questions asked, if something goes wrong. And if you promise to get a customer or prospect more information about a specific topic, make it a priority and get it done. Once again, reliability is one of the common denominators that all successful businesses share, especially businesses that provide services, because your track record of happy clients is often your main marketing tool needed in most cases your only marketing tool that carries any weight. Make a pledge to all customers that they can trust you to do what you say you will do when you say you will do it. And stick to this reliability pledge like glue. No one wants to be left waiting, and worse no one wants products or services they have paid for not to live up to promises in terms of the reliability. We all want to know that when we purchase a product or service, the company that sells it to us is reliable and will be there for us in the future should something go haywire.

Flexibility

A huge advantage that home business owners have over large competitors with highly developed chains of commands and customer service policies set in stone is the ability to be very flexible in terms of looking after your customers. Recognize that customers are not all the same, they want and need different things. Each person must be viewed as an individual, not merely as part of a group. Be flexible and willing to bend the rules once in a while when your customers need you to, even if it is an inconvenience to you and your business. Ask customers what they truly want, and develop solutions to meet each individual's needs. Let them know that customer satisfaction really is your primary concern, and let them know you will go that extra mile when called upon to do so. Being flexible and going the extra mile for customers can greatly benefit your business. Price will be less of a factor in buying decisions. Instead, service and how you deliver upon your promises or on customer's special requests will be the determining factor. When you are flexible and go out of your way to treat people special, you no longer have to work as hard to persuade them to your way of thinking. When was the last time that you stopped shopping at a particular business because you received exceptional treatment? Once again, I hope never. Remember, too, everyone knows someone else, so going that extra mile will give you access to your customer's circle of prospects. A warm prospect is ten times easier to sell to than a cold prospect, and such referral costs a mere fraction of what it costs to market to and find a new customer.

Customer Contact

The third important component to great customer service is contact. In business it is very easy to become complacent in terms of our good long-standing customers. There are two reasons for this complacency. Because they are good customers, you just expect that they will always be there. And we become engrossed in looking for new customers, we forget about the customers we already have. Unfortunately, if over time customers do not feel that they are appreciated or that you value their business, they will take their business elsewhere. Don't let this happen to you. Stay in constant contact with all of your customers, large and small. Do this by sending them e-mails, or letters, making occasional telephone calls, or by making personal visits. Let them know that you appreciate their business, and ask if they have any special requests, such as new products or services. Send out greetings to your clients on their birthdays, anniversaries, during the holidays, and on other special occasions. The more you stay in contact with your customers, the better you will be able to serve them, which greatly diminishes the potential for them to take their business elsewhere.

Customer Service Surveys

Customer surveys have long been one of the best methods for finding out what consumers think about the level of customer service your business provides. There are a number of ways you can conduct customer service surveys: by mail, in person, by telephone, and through your Web site. Your budget will probably determine which is the best method for your business. Regardless of the method you use, once you have identified a surveying method that gets the results you want, continue to use this method quarterly to ensure that your business keeps up with ever changing customer needs and wants. Even a basic please-rate-our-service customer comment card distributed to and completed by customers can provide you with valuable information about the level of service you provide and overall customer satisfaction.

Developing a customer service survey is very straightforward. Simply ask specific questions about each area of your business, from initial contact right through to completion of the sale or job, and overall satisfaction of doing business with you. If you mail your customer service survey, and include a self-addressed stamped envelope, which makes it easy for people to respond, ensuring a higher response rate. Use the results of your ongoing customer surveys to identify problems or weaknesses within your business so they can be corrected and to identify strengths within your business so that they can be built upon and expanded into other areas of your business. Here is a basic Sample Customer Service Survey Form (see Figure 10.4) that you can use as an outline to create one suitable for your business and needs.

FIGURE 10.4 Sample Customer Service Survey Form

Your business name and contact information here

We greatly value our customers! So please help us serve you better by rating our service.

Your personal information and responses will not be shared with anyone outside of our business. Ignore personal information spaces if you do not want to identify yourself. Thank you for your help.

❏ Mr. ❏ Mrs. ❏ Ms. Name _____

Address _____ Apartment _____

City _____ State _____ Zip/Postal Code _____

Home Telephone _____ Work _____ Fax _____ E-mail _____

	Great	Good	Poor
How was your initial inquiry to our business handled?	❏	❏	❏
Did you find us knowledgeable about our products and services?	❏	❏	❏
How would you rate the value of our service?	❏	❏	❏
How would you rate the price of our products and services?	❏	❏	❏

FIGURE 10.4	Sample Customer Service Survey Form, continued

	Great	Good	Poor
How would you rate your overall experience with our service?	❏	❏	❏
How would you rate the quality of our service?	❏	❏	❏
How would you rate the performance and reliability of our service?	❏	❏	❏
Would you like to receive free and valuable information occasionally?	❏ Yes	❏ No	
Would you refer other people to our business?	❏ Yes	❏ No	
Would you be prepared to provide a written testimonial?	❏ Yes	❏ No	

We welcome additional comments, questions, or concerns you may have.

_____

_____

_____

Thank you, we appreciate your comments and business!

Cultivating Customers

No businesses, regardless of size, are actually in the business of selling products or services; they are, in fact, in the business of finding and keeping customers that want to trade their cash for products and services that are distributed through businesses. For that reason, being in business is as much about knowing your customers as well, as it is about what you are selling. At the end of the day, if you have customers that are loyal to you, believe in you, and want to give you their money, you will sell whatever they need and want to buy. That is what business is all about, catering to the wants and needs of people that have money to spend on products and services they want and need. So it makes sense that to truly know and understand customers, you have to identify them, know what they are buying, know how often they buy, and figure out ways to sell them more of what they want and need. There are some steps that you can take to track your customers, rank your customers, identify your most profitable customers, sell your customers more, and build lifetime selling relationships with your customers. It is a five-step process to set up, manage, and maintain on a regular basis.

Step 1. Develop a Customer Management Database

The first step is to set up a customer database so that you can compile and store information about who your customers are, what they are buying, how often they buy, complete contact information, and other useful data such as birthdays. Every business owner should take the time and invest the money required to build a customer database. It is an essential business and marketing tool that is necessary to survive in today's hyper-competitive business environment. You will have the information you need to make special offers based on each individual client's needs or wants. Get started by asking every new customer to take a few minutes to complete a new customer form. Ask questions that can be used to determine what your customers really want or problems they need addressed, along with their contact information, especially an e-mail address. Your database should be built using sales or customer management software, such as Maximizer, www.maximizer.com.

Step 2. Rank Your Customers

Next, based on the information you capture in your customer management database, develop a simple customer ranking system so that you can identify who your best customers are and any similarities they might share. Assign each customer an alphabetical or numerical ranking, from weakest to strongest, based on factors such as buying frequency, types of products or services bought, profitability associated with these purchases, special requests, or complaints, and if they pay on time or are slow.

Step 3. Concentrate on Your Most Profitable Customers

Ranking your customers will enable you to pinpoint who your best and most profitable customers are. By knowing this, you will be able to direct more of your marketing efforts at your core target group to increase sales, introduce new products, and ask for referrals. Additionally, through customer ranking and analysis you will generally discover that 20 percent of customers are responsible for 80 percent of sales and profits. This is commonly referred to as the 80/20 rule, a widely accepted measure of customer loyalty. It is the top 20 percent of your best and most profitable customers on which you should focus the majority of your marketing efforts and activities on. Once again, it is ten times easier and less expensive to sell more and more frequently to existing customers than it is to find new customers. Ultimately, the goal is to turn every existing customer and new customer into a lifetime customer. But start with your core group of best customers who give you the largest profits with the least amount of trouble.

Step 4. Look for Ways to Increase Buying Frequency

Now that you know who your best customers are, start to look for ways to sell them more products or services on a more frequent basis. This can be accomplished in many ways, including introducing a product- or service-of-the-month club, gift registry service, automatic replenishment service, reminder or alert service, or whichever you feel is relevant to your business, customers, and the goods and services you sell. Regardless, a key to success is knowing who your best customers are and then using promotions specifically focused on ways to entice them to buy more and more often.

Step 5. Cement Relationships with Customers for Life

The final step in cultivating great customers is to go out of your way to secure every customer for life. Do this by catering to each customer's individual needs and by paying close attention to the small details of each of your best customer accounts. Institute customer loyalty programs, rewards, and appreciation gifts. Work with customers to keep prices low, value high, and service a top priority. Doing so will go a long way to cement lifelong business relationships with your best customers and ensure that your business remains strong and profitable.

Overcoming Customer Complaints and Challenges

The first rule of overcoming customer complaints and challenges is to make it a policy to try and clear each one by the end of the working day. This is especially important advice for home business owners with few, if any, support staff or external resources. Let's face it, the vast majority of customer complaints are nothing more than a simple miscommunication between buyer and seller. However, even the smallest of complaints has a way of quickly turning into a full-blown problem unless it is dealt with in a timely and decisive fashion. Never let yourself get caught in the "I'll look after it tomorrow" procrastination trap. Instead, make a conscious effort to clear all customer challenges by the end of each business day, and carry over only those that require input from a source that is temporarily unavailable, such as a sales rep, manufacturer, or distributor. If you are unable to fix the problem, let your customer know why and when the problem will be corrected. Give them a firm call-back time, and tell them that their concern is priority number one. Clearing all challenges by the end of each day will save time, headaches, money, and, most importantly, you'll keep your customer.

Log Complaints

Get customer service savvy by recording all customer complaints, questions, and concerns you receive, and use the information you collect to find weak areas within your business, products, services, staff, or customer service policies. Basically, look for repetitious problems that need to be corrected. Once you have identified your weaknesses, you will be able to look for solutions and ways to fix the problems. Even homebased businesses can benefit by recording all customer complaints; simply write them in a daily journal notepad or on customer management software. By recording complaints, you will also have the information needed to measure the performance of your suppliers' products and services as well. Once again, if you find that patterns start to develop with a particular supplier, you'll be armed with the information that you need to confront the supplier and look for mutually beneficial way to fix the deficiencies, or find a better supply source.

Eliminate Mismatched Expectations

The vast majority of customer service complaints arise from mismatched expectations, usually caused by a breakdown in communications or in the way a product or service was described and understood. The cost resulting from mismatched expectations is enormous, especially when you factor in the potential for lost customers and the amount of time that it takes to find solutions and fix any problems. So it makes sense to reduce the chances for mismatched expectations between you and customers, by developing a "predelivery customer expectation survey." The survey should review all details of the sale, such as delivery, installation, color, quantity, warranty, price, and financing or payment terms, and ask specific questions about what the customer expects the product or service to do for them or their business. The number of incorrect details, mismatched expectations, and potential problems that such a simple yet effective survey uncovers will amaze you.

Fix the Customer First

Regardless of the source of the customer service complaint or problem, always look for ways to fix your customer first, quickly, and without hesitation. Once this has been achieved, turn your attention to the source of the problem or complaint. "I'll get back to you" or "That is a manufacture's problem" excuse just does not cut it in today's highly competitive business environment. If you have an angry customer on the telephone or standing in front of you, you have the ability to fix the customer. In all likelihood, you cannot do anything about the problem itself at that moment; what caused the problem is probably out of your immediate control. But it is in your immediate control to fix your customer, the person who most deserves your immediate and undivided attention.

Make Friends

Remember the old adage that an unhappy customer will tell ten times as many people about their experience with your business then a happy customer will. It is still true today. You need to make unhappy customers happy. You can make friends and allies from even your angriest customers by trying a few of the following actions when you receive customer complaints.

- Don't interrupt. Let people get what's on their minds off first. Interruptions only further infuriate a person that is already angry, frustrated, and upset. By interrupting, you are telling customers that you do not care about them or their problem.
- Once customers are through venting, empathize with them and show them that you're on their side by telling them that you understand their situation. Continually use their name so they feel valued and important.
- Ask your customer to restate the chain of events that led to the complaint. Ask for details such as other people in the company they might have spoken to or that were involved, product or service problems, and resulting problems caused by the deficiency.
- Don't start finger pointing. First make sure that there have been no miscommunications on either side, and then seek solutions by asking the customer how they would like the problem resolved.
- Fix what you can immediately. For the problems that cannot be fixed during the first contact, make promises about when the customer will be called back and restate the solution that both sides feel will correct the situation.

Post Resolution Follow Up

Sometimes problems that appear to have been resolved are not. It is wise to implement a post-customer complaint and resolution follow-up program. Wait a few days after the complaint has been resolved, and then call your customer to find out if they are truly satisfied with the way the problem was handled. Develop a checklist of questions that you ask: "Are you satisfied with the way we responded to your complaint?" "Are you happy with the way the problem was resolved?" "Would you purchase from our business in the future?" "Would you refer our business to other people?" You can also develop more specific questions that are suited to your business and the problem. But keep in mind that it is important to find out if a customer is truly satisfied with the solution.

Show Your Customers You Appreciate Them

Business is going well. Now you want to thank the people that made it happen—your customers. But how will you go about showing your customers that you appreciate their continued support? Here are a few ideas

Customer Appreciation Events

Host a customer appreciation party and invite your best customers and hottest prospects. The party can be held at local restaurant or, if your budget is tight, host the party right at your home, perhaps a backyard barbecue if weather permits. Customer appreciation parties are a way to say thank you for your business and reinforce your business relationships. Make it an annual event, and you'll soon discover that customers start to look forward to it.

Subscriptions

Find out what newspapers or magazines your customers like to read and give them a monthly subscription. Every time they receive and read the magazine or newspaper, they will automatically think of you and your business.

Hobby Gifts

Get to know your clients by asking them questions about their hobbies and the activities they like to do when they are not working. Armed with this information, you can purchase gifts for them that are relevant to their hobbies and interests, anything and everything from concert tickets to continuing education classes or a custom kite.

Referrals

Make an effort to send quality and qualified referrals to customers who own small businesses or professional practices. After all, what better gift is there than helping someone build a business, practice, or career?

Imprinted Items

Have your business name, logo, and marketing message boldly emblazoned on items such as key chains, pens, notepads, calendars, coffee mugs, travel mugs, clocks, or mouse pads; and give these to prospects and customers as gifts. These items make good customer appreciation gifts because they are things that most people use daily, keeping your name in front of them and fresh in their memory. Promo Mart offers a huge selection of imprinted promotional and advertising specialties. They can be found at www.promomart.com.

RESOURCES

Associations

American Marketing Association (AMA)
311 S. Wacker Drive, Suite 5800
Chicago, IL 60606
(312) 542-9000
www.marketingpower.com

Business Marketing Association (BMA)
400 N. Michigan Avenue, 15th Floor
Chicago, IL 60611
(800) 664-4262
www.marketing.org

Canadian Marketing Association (CMA)
1 Concorde Gate, Suite 607
Don Mills, Ontario M3C 3N6
(416) 391-2362
www.the-cma.org

International Customer Service Association
401 N. Michigan Avenue
Chicago, IL 60611
www.icsa.com

Marketing Research Association (MRA)
PO Box 230
1344 Silas Deane Highway, Suite 306

Rocky Hill, CT 06067-0230

(806) 257-4008

www.mra-net.org

📖 *Suggested Reading*

Abraham, Jay. *Getting Everything You Can Out of All You've Got: 21 Ways You Can Out-Think, Out-Perform, and Out-Earn the Competition.* New York: St. Martin's Press, 2000.

Blanchard, Ken, and Sheldon Bowles. *Raving Fans: A Revolutionary Approach to Customer Service.* New York: William Morrow & Company, 1993.

Colombo, George W. *Killer Customer Care: Five Star Service That Will Double and Triple Profits.* Irvine, CA: Entrepreneur Press Inc., 2003.

Porter, Michael E. *Competitive Strategy: Techniques for Analyzing Industries and Competitors.* New York: Free Press, 1998.

Raskin, Oliver, and Joshua Grossnickle. *Handbook of Online Marketing Research: Knowing Your Customers Using the Net.* New York: McGraw-Hill, 2000.

Sclein, Alan M., JJ. Newby, and Peter Weber. *Find it Online: The Complete Guide to Online Research.* Tempe, AZ: Facts On Demand Press, 2002.

Stephenson, James. *The Ultimate Small Business Marketing Guide: Over 1500 Great Marketing Tricks That Will Drive Your Business Through the Roof!* Irvine, CA: Entrepreneur Press Inc., 2003.

💻 *Web Sites*

American Demographics Magazine, www.demographics.com: Information and advice about marketing research and demographics.

Better Business Bureau, www.bbb.com: Nonprofit consumer protection organization that encourages reputable business practices. To register your business with the BBB, log onto its Web site to find a chapter new you.

The Canadian Chamber of Commerce, www.chamber.ca: Business association offering members information, advice, and business building opportunities. Visit the Chamber's Web site to find a chapter near you.

Marketing Masters Inc., www.surveydsaid.com: Survey Said-Survey Software, including custom applications for phone, Internet, paper, laptop, and kiosk surveys.

Maximizer, www.maximizer.com: Contact and customer relationship management software.

Sales Force, www.salesforce.com: Contact and customer relationship management software.

SRDS Media Solutions Inc., www.srds.com: Standard Rate and Data Service, publishers of print and online lifestyle and demographics sourcebooks.

U.S. Census Bureau, www.census.gov: Market demographics information and statistics.

The United States Chamber of Commerce, www.uschamber.com: Business association offering members information, advice, and business building opportunities. Visit the Chamber's Web site to find a chapter near you.

CHAPTER 11

Managing Your Home Business

YOU HAVE RESEARCHED, PLANNED, FINANCED, set up your home workspace, opened your business, and have a few customers. Now it is time to manage your business on a day-to-day basis for success and long-term growth. As easy as managing your business sounds, this is exactly the point where lots of new entrepreneurs become unglued because every aspect of your home business must be managed and maintained. Not one single element can be ignored. This can be very overwhelming day in and day out. Just think, on any one day you might have to manage any or all of the following:

- Your time
- Customer complaints
- Banking and record keeping
- Employees, sales agents, and contractors
- Supplier and vendor accounts
- Shipping and receiving
- Account receivables and payables
- Client jobs and contracts
- Web site maintenance
- Communications, including the telephone, fax, mail, and e-mail
- Sales and networking
- Advertising and public relations
- Family and friends' distractions
- Equipment malfunctions

- Warranty questions, problems, and claims
- Permit and insurance renewals
- And on, and on, and on, and…

There is lots to manage when you are in business, regardless of the size or type of business that you run. Operating a business is nonstop managing, you will always be managing or maintaining something every day. It is a never ending task. Of course, the savvy business operator develops systems and schedules for every activity imaginable so that he can stay on top of management tasks, maximize his time, and become more productive. Much of this chapter revolves around time management because of the importance it plays in business, especially homebased businesses which are often run by one person with little if any support structure. Additional issues covered in this chapter include handling the pressure of operating your own business, how to make wise decisions, money and debt management, how to grow your business, and when the time is right, how to sell your home business.

HANDLING THE PRESSURES OF OPERATING A HOME BUSINESS

Business owners face all kinds of pressures each and every day ranging from irate clients to collection problems or product deficiencies, and everything in between. Being under continual pressure to deliver, correct, and explain can really take a toll on home business owners, because they rarely have any support staff or resources available to help deal with these pressures. Unfortunately, being under continuous pressure can negatively affect your decision making abilities, leading to poor decisions that hurt your business. The real objective is not to sidestep pressure, but rather learning how to meet it head-on so that you can handle it and remain levelheaded. Below is a five-step process that will help you handle the pressures associated with operating your home business:

1. *Evaluation.* The first step is to identify the source of the pressure: customer complaints, supplier problems, issues within the family, or financial or legal troubles. Knowing that you are under pressure gets you no closer to fixing the problem. Instead, you must identify the source of the pressure so that you can develop a plan to overcome or eliminate it.

2. *Remain flexible.* The second step is to keep an open mind and remain flexible so that you can seek a compromise to solve the situation causing the pressure. For instance, if it is money problems, work with the other parties and be flexible to their needs to create mutually beneficial solutions. It has to be a win-win situation in order to work effectively. This can only happen by remaining flexible and keeping the lines of communication open so solutions can be found.

3. *Seek advice.* Step three is to look to people around you that you admire and trust and ask them for advice when the pressure gets to be too much. Simply talking to other people is often enough inspiration and venting to get thinking clearly again. However, if the source of the problem is very complicated, always seek the advice of a professional or expert on that subject.

4. *Employee separation techniques.* The fourth step is to understand that sometimes a combination of unavoidable business pressures is the problem. At this point you have to be able to separate your business life from your personal life and take a break, even if it is just a day or two.

5. *Take affirmative action.* Finally, once you have identified the source of the pressure, you must take immediate and affirmative action to reduce or eliminate it entirely. Left unchecked, pressure will only become worse and continue to grow. It could even become a major issue and lead to health problems.

Making Wise Decisions

Much like learning to handle the pressures associated with operating a home business, many new home-based entrepreneurs also struggle with the decision-making process. This is mainly because a bad decision tends to have a much more negative result when you're the boss and your own money is at stake than it does when you are an employee with someone's else money on the line. On top of that, you must also add into the equation that you are making decisions that affect you and your business—and also your family. This adds further pressure on you to make the right decision.

In truth, the ability to make fast, concise, and wise decisions is needed to operate a home business, or any business. You can no longer rely on others to make decisions affecting your business when you are the boss, you have to become self-reliant and take full responsibility for your actions and decisions. Learning how to make wise decisions takes practice, and certainly not all of the decisions you make will be the right ones. Many will probably have a negative impact on your business. However, what separates the winners from the losers is the fact that winners do not use bad decisions as an excuse to throw in the towel. Instead, they learn from their errors so that they are not repeated and become wiser businesspeople in the process. Here are a few more tips that can help you make wise decisions.

- Next to persistence, the second rule of decision making is to carefully consider all of the consequences that might arise as a result of a decision. You have to weigh each, while of course not losing sight of your objectives. Know that the advantages outweigh the disadvantages before starting.

- Never make snap decisions when it comes to spending money. Instead set a monetary limit in terms of making business purchases. For instance, any purchasing decision that requires you to spend more than $1,000 must be held off for at least 24 hours. Doing so affords you extra time to make sure that you are making a carefully thought out purchasing decision and not an impulsive or emotional one.

- Once you have made a decision to take action, don't procrastinate. Take the required action right away. If not, as time passes, you will begin to second-guess yourself and this can quickly become habitual. Entrepreneurs that continually procrastinate or cannot be decisive decision makers, generally find themselves out of business in short order.

- A common trait of all successful entrepreneurs is that they are not afraid to make the occasional, but well thought-out, risky business decision. By nature entrepreneurs are calculated risk takers, and this plays a large role in what separates them from the working masses. You must learn to control fear in decision making, because if you do not, through indecision fear will always control you.

- When in serious doubt, seek second opinions from trusted sources. Never let your pride get in the way of asking for help, but make sure that the person dispensing the advice is an expert on the topic.

TIME MANAGEMENT

Managing your time is just about as important as any business discipline. At the top of the list of most common complaints shared by business owners is the fact that there is never enough time to complete the seemingly endless number of tasks they face daily. Managing your time well enables you to be more productive and get more done in less time. Time management also affords you the option of spending your time where it can best be put to use and it also allows you time off to recharge your batteries.

Most time management gurus agree that the first rule of productivity is having the right tools to do the job at hand. That means that in order to squeeze the most productivity from the time you have available, you must invest in business tools that enable you to be 100 percent efficient. Business tools include training, education, equipment, technology, and supplies, to mention a few. Basically any item, information, or piece of equipment that can be used in your business to save time will make you more efficient and allow the best use of time, one of the most precious business commodities. Having to run down to the local Internet café to send or receive e-mail is not the best use of your time. Having to dart out to purchase a new ink cartridge in the middle of preparing an important and time-sensitive presentation is not the best use of your time. Having to tear down your home office and set it up again day after day because you use the kitchen table as your workspace is not the best use of your time. And responding to every low-level or junk e-mail that you receive is certainly not the best use of your time.

Heather Cartwright, noted integrated logistics and supply chain management systems expert and owner of Logixsource Consulting Ltd.,www.logixsource.com, (905) 877–2134, offers entrepreneurs the following valuable advice. In order to be successful as an entrepreneur in a small, homebased business, it is critical to manage the business effectively and efficiently and yet be flexible enough to change when market conditions or key customers require you to do so. There is a plethora of information available about business planning and financing. However, this information is focused on providing critical success factors from a business success management perspective. As an entrepreneur, time is a critical success factor, and entrepreneurs are faced with an overwhelming number of decisions to make because typically there are a limited number of people who are responsible for, and ultimately able to make, business decisions. Effective and timely decision making is in itself key to success, and both timing and importance can be guided by the well-known Time Management Decision Matrix in Figure 11.1.

The decisions that need to be made can be guided by these three important questions:

1. Is what I am doing now leading me closer to my short-term and long-term goals? If not,

FIGURE 11.1 Time Management Decision Matrix

Urgent and Important Activities	Not Urgent But Important Activities
∂• Crises	• Prevention
∂• Pressing problems	• Learning
∂	• Recreation outside of the business
∂	• Client and alliance relationship building
∂	• Business and marketing planning
∂	• Business building opportunities
Urgent But Not Important Activities	**Not Urgent, Not Important Activities**
∂• Interruptions	• Trivia
∂• Some telephone calls	• Procrastination
∂• Mail	• Junk mail
∂• Reports	• Nonbusiness calls during business hours
∂• Some meetings	• "Escape," such as reading and television

what should I be doing to get back on track, focused on goals and objectives?

2. What would happen if I didn't do this task? Can I learn to say no to some requests? Learning to say no is one of the biggest challenges faced by small business owners. We all feel the need to accommodate every client request, but sometimes saying no is in our best interest from a business and time management perspective.

3. By working on this task, am I putting my time to the best possible use? If not, what could I be doing that would be the best, most productive, and potentially most profitable use of my time?

At an operational level, major business, management, and marketing decisions can be categorized in four key areas—skills and experience, business processes, technology infrastructure, and business organization.

1. *Skills and experience.*
   - Experience or access to knowledge and best practices
   - Support networks, including accountant, lawyer, banker, and business advisor
   - Core and noncore suppliers of products and services
   - Tools and techniques to design, develop, and deliver your products and services

2. *Business processes.*
   - Marketing and sales management
   - Quality and risk management processes
   - Financial analysis and management
   - Continuous improvement procedures

3. *Technology infrastructure.*
   - Facilities and equipment
   - Computer hardware and software
   - Telecommunications
   - Managing historical records

4. *Business organization.*
   - The organization of the business, including how work gets performed and how decisions are made
   - The business governance structure, and how decisions will be made
   - The key business processes performed internally and outsourced to suppliers
   - Who is responsible for what decisions and how they will be implemented

• Communications process to employees, customers, alliances, and suppliers. For the home business owners, this list also includes family members

Daily To-Do List

Before calling an end to your workday, try to get in the habit of creating a to-do list for the following day's important activities. You can combine business and personal tasks into the list so that you do not inadvertently overlap tasks and times. I would also suggest that you include important telephone calls and e-mails that have to be made or returned. You

can create your to-do list in print or on an electronic medium such as time management software on your PC or a handheld organizer. Or you can purchase time planner books and calendars at your local office supplier. Below is a sample Daily To-Do List Worksheet (see Figure 11.2) that you can use as a guideline to create your own using any word processing program. Photocopy it for each new day. Regardless of how you create or record a daily to-do list, the importance of this simple management tool should not be overlooked. It is guaranteed to save you time and frustration because there is always potential for missed tasks or overlapping activities.

FIGURE 11.2 Sample Daily To-Do List Worksheet

Date _____   Day _____

Specific Tasks and Projects

Task	Comments	Completed

Telephone Calls to Make

Time	Person	Comments	Completed

FIGURE 11.2	**Sample Daily To-Do List Worksheet,** continued

E-Mails to Send

Person	Purpose	Completed
_____	_____	❑
_____	_____	❑
_____	_____	❑
_____	_____	❑
_____	_____	❑
_____	_____	❑
_____	_____	❑
_____	_____	❑
_____	_____	❑

Daily and Weekly Planner

Like a daily to-do list, most home business owners also find daily and weekly work planners very helpful in keeping appointments and key tasks recorded and prioritized. Once again, you can purchase preprinted daily and weekly planners at any office supply shop. Or you can opt to use an electronic organizer and planner. Below is a sample Daily and Weekly Planner Worksheet (see Figure 11.3); simply circle the appropriate day and fill in your appointments and projects as needed. You can use this form as is or create a customized one on your PC. Keep in mind that the key to success in using planners to save time and be more productive. You have to use them day in and day out in order to realize their benefits.

FIGURE 11.3	**Sample Daily and Weekly Planner Worksheet**

Date _____   Day * S * M * T * W * T * F * S * (circle)

Time	Activity	Comments	Completed
7:00	_____	_____	❑
7:30	_____	_____	❑
8:00	_____	_____	❑
8:30	_____	_____	❑
9:00	_____	_____	❑
9:30	_____	_____	❑
10:00	_____	_____	❑
10:30	_____	_____	❑
11:00	_____	_____	❑
11:30	_____	_____	❑
12:00	_____	_____	❑

FIGURE 11.3 **Sample Daily and Weekly Planner Worksheet,** continued

Time	Activity	Comments	Completed
12:30	_____	_____	❏
1:00	_____	_____	❏
1:30	_____	_____	❏
2:00	_____	_____	❏
2:30	_____	_____	❏
3:00	_____	_____	❏
3:30	_____	_____	❏
4:00	_____	_____	❏
4:30	_____	_____	❏
5:00	_____	_____	❏
5:30	_____	_____	❏
6:00	_____	_____	❏
6:30	_____	_____	❏
7:00	_____	_____	❏
7:30	_____	_____	❏
8:00	_____	_____	❏
8:30	_____	_____	❏
9:00	_____	_____	❏

Monthly and Yearly Planners

In addition to daily and weekly planners, monthly and yearly planners are great for keeping track of long-term appointments and projects. However, you have to get in the habit of using these regularly so you remember to transfer important meetings and activities into your daily and weekly planners. Erasable yearly planners and markers can be pur-

chased for less than $25 from most office supply stores and generally include a monthly and yearly calendar space on which you can record key information on. Here is a Sample Monthly Planner Worksheet (see Figure 11.4) that you can use as is or as a template to create your own using any word-processing program and your computer.

FIGURE 11.4 **Sample Monthly Planner Worksheet**

Month * J * F * M * A * M * J * J * A * S * O * N * D * (circle)

Date	Key Appointments and Projects	Comments	Logged
1	_____	_____	❏
2	_____	_____	❏

FIGURE 11.4 **Sample Monthly Planner Worksheet,** continued

Date	Key Appointments and Projects	Comments	Logged
3			❏
4			❏
5			❏
6			❏
7			❏
8			❏
9			❏
10			❏
11			❏
12			❏
13			❏
14			❏
15			❏
16			❏
17			❏
18			❏
19			❏
20			❏
21			❏
22			❏
23			❏
24			❏
25			❏
26			❏
27			❏
28			❏
29			❏
30			❏
31			❏

Great Time Management Tips

The greatest time management tip is, and always will remain, that you must be healthy. If you are not feeling physically or emotionally well because of burnout, it will always be difficult to be productive and manage your business and time efficiently.

Small business burnout is the result of a combination of factors—trying to do too much, lack of a support structure, long working hours, and often the inability to say no when asked to do work outside of their field, commanding considerable time while producing few results. You must get in the habit of scheduling time off and time away from your business on a regular basis. Make it a personal goal to stay fit and healthy by taking time off, maintaining a balanced diet, staying physically active, and getting lots of rest. As clichéd as this advice may sound, it is still good advice. Other great time management tips and ideas to help you get more accomplished in less time include:

- The second greatest time management tip for home business operators is to purchase a simple do-not-disturb sign for your office door. Let family members know in no uncertain terms that when the sign says do-not disturb that you do not want to be disturbed, period. Even seemingly harmless and basic interruptions to a work routine can cause mayhem to the daily schedule and drastically reduce productivity.

- Establish a primary workstation in your home office for working on client projects and other key money making projects and a secondary workstation for lower priority tasks such as mail sorting, filing, and general administrative recording. Doing so will help you stay organized and focused on the areas of your business that make you money while still keeping other required business activities organized but clearly secondary.

- Try to set aside specific times when you open mail, pay bills, and complete administrative paperwork. This simple trick will save you an incredible amount of time when calculated over the year. And best of all, the time saved can be utilized in more productive and money-making activities such as prospecting, closing sales, and staying in contact with key clients.

- Plan out-of-the-office appointments and errands in blocks of time such as an entire morning or day so that you can minimize wasting time in traffic or duplicating commuting efforts. Confirm all appointments twice, the first time a few days prior to the meeting, and again before you leave the office for the appointment. A telephone call takes only a moment, but hours can be wasted if the person you are to meet is not available.

- Purchase and use color-coded files to indicate high priority projects, perhaps red for the most important, green for medium priority, and blue for low priority. Invest in a good filing systems so you can spend more time working on a client's file and less time looking for it. Be sure to purge your paper file and electronic files of outdated or nonrelevant information on a monthly basis to keep your moneymaking files lean and easy to find and work with. However, be sure that the purged files are moved to an archived filing system so that you can occasionally revisit them to mine for further business.

- Install an erasable board on the office wall so that you can keep an ongoing list of office supplies that are running low, so they can be picked up once per month instead of weekly or even daily. Dashing down to the office supply store in the middle of the day to pick up a printer cartridge can easily chew up an hour or more in traffic.

- Keep your workspace free of clutter, banish most personal items, turn the television off, and work only with the radio on if you find that it does not distract you. For most home business operators, staying focused on work and not being distracted by their working environment is difficult. Throwing in temptations such as television will sink productivity. Remember that you have to be the hardnosed manager who keeps squawking to get to work. So increase the potential for being more productive by getting rid of any temptations that can distract you and make you less productive.

- Create a plan for telephone calls based on priority and the probability of accomplishing your objective. Set time aside each day to make prospecting calls when you know that you can reach the intended parties. Also, set aside blocks of time to follow up with prospects and make administrative calls. Bouncing back and forth with no focus can chew up time and make you unproductive.

- Plan telephone calls prior to dialing: Know to whom you want to talk, know what you want to say, and know what you want to accomplish as a result of the call. Such planning will greatly reduce the amount of time you spend on the phone and the number of calls you make back to the party to get additional information you missed. Also, when leaving a voice messages, include a specific time range and day that you can be reached, such as "I'll be in the office Tuesday morning between nine and eleven. Can you please call me then?" You can reduce or eliminate time-wasting telephone tag this way.

- Keep all e-mails in your in basket until you have had the opportunity to read, respond, or delete. Try to set aside a block of time each day to deal with e-mail communications. If you receive hundreds of e-mails each day, use e-mail autoresponders as a way to reduce the amount of time you spend answering low priority e-mails.

MONEY MANAGEMENT

Money comes in, and money goes out. Of course, at the end of the year you want more money to have come into your business than went out. Managing your small business cash flow is tricky because it is needed to keep the business machine oiled and operating. Cash flow, after all, is what will ultimately keep you in business or send you bust. Consequently, understanding money management must then become a priority for all home business owners. Even if you elect to hire an accountant or bookkeeper to manage your money, you will still need to familiarize yourself with basic bookkeeping and money management principles and activities such as understanding credit, reading bank statements and tax forms, and making sense of account receivable and payables. The key aspects of money management are:

- Establishing a business bank account
- Developing a bookkeeping system
- Establishing payment terms
- Extending credit
- Getting paid
- Debt collection

Information pertaining to small business taxation, establishing merchant accounts, and accepting various

payment methods such as credit cards, e-checks, and debit cards is featured in Chapter 3, Financial Issues.

Establishing a Bank Account

Once your business is registered and ready to roll, you will need to establish one or more business bank accounts. You should establish a business bank account that is separate from your personal savings or checking account for a couple reasons. First, you will be able to separate your business finances from your personal finances, which will make completing business sales and expense reports and tax forms at the end of the year much easier. Second, having a business bank account will enable you to have checks printed with your business name as well establish a credit card merchant account with deposits made after processing directly into your business account. Banks and payment processing companies will not directly deposit into personal bank accounts, only business bank account. Setting up a business bank account is very straightforward. Get started by selecting the bank that you want to work with (think small business friendly) and setting up an appointment to open an account. When you go, make sure that you take personal identity as well as your business name registration papers and business license because these are usually required to open a business bank account. The next step will be to deposit funds into your new account (even $100 is okay). Then you are ready to go.

Keeping the Books

The next aspect of money management is keeping the financial books. You have two options—keep the books yourself or hire an accountant or professional bookkeeper to look after the books. Some business owners also choose to combine both, keeping their own books but hiring an accountant to prepare year-end financial statements and tax forms. Personally I prefer to use the combined approach to bookkeeping. If you opt to keep your own books, you have lots of help available via accounting software such as QuickBooks. The nice aspect of using accounting software to manage your money and books is the fact that you can create client accounts, invoices, and mail merge options, as well as track bank account balances, merchant account information, and accounts payable. Most of the accounting software available is very easy to use; the learning curve for even the more complex functions is only a few weeks of trial and error.

- *QuickBooks,* www.quickbooks.com
- *M.Y.O.B.,* (Mind Your Own Business) www.myob.com
- *Peach Tree,* www.peachtree.com
- *Quicken,* www.quicken.com
- *Find Accounting Software,* www.findaccountingsoftware.com

Accountant and Bookkeeper Resources

United States

Association of Chartered Accountants in the United States
341 Lafayette Street, Suite 4246
New York, NY 10012-2417
(212) 334-2078
www.acaus.org

American Institute of Professional Bookkeepers
6001 Montrose Road, Suite 500
Rockville, MD 20852
(800) 622-0121
www.aipb.com

Canada

Chartered Accountants of Canada
277 Wellington Street West
Toronto, ON M5V 2H2
(416) 977-3222
www.cica.ca

Canadian Bookkeepers Association
2435 Mansfield Drive, Suite 201 D
Courtney, BC V9N 2M2
(250) 334-2427
www.canadianbookkeepersassociation.ca

Establishing Payment Terms

Once you have established a bookkeeping and invoicing system, the next step is to establish your payment terms policy. While you certainly want to standardize the way you get paid for products or services, you also have to be flexible enough to meet an individual client's needs. Setting payment terms covers deposits, progress payments, and extending credit. Providing customers with institutional or retail financing and leasing payment options is covered in Chapter 3, Financial Issues. It is important to remember that you want to establish clear, written payment terms with clients prior to providing services or delivering product. Your payment terms should be printed on your estimate forms, included in formal contracts and work orders, and be on your final invoices. It is also best if you provide signature space so that clients can sign off on the agreed payment terms in writing. Should you need to go to court to get paid, you will be glad that you have taken the time to establish your payment terms in advance, in writing, with the client's signature.

Securing Deposits

All home business owners should get in the habit of asking clients for a deposit prior to ordering materials. The deposit should be for at least the value of the materials plus delivery costs. Any job or product orders over a certain dollar value also will require a deposit, usually based on a percentage of the total value, such as 25 percent. Most consumers expect to pay a deposit when ordering products, especially from small business owners. If you are supplying labor only, try to secure a deposit of at least one-third to one-half of the total value of the contract. Your order form or contract should have the deposit information clearly stated. Information on canceled orders or contracts and the amount of the deposit that will be refunded should also be on your forms. Securing a deposit is the home business owners' best way of ensuring that at least basic out-of-pocket costs are covered should the customer cancel the job or contract.

Progress Payments

Progress payments are also a way to ensure that you do not leave yourself open to great financial risk when working on larger jobs. In the home renovation industry, it is standard practice to invoice clients at various stages of completion, and this practice could easily carry over into many industries and businesses, such as consulting, software programming, and Web site design. The key to successfully securing progress payments is to prearrange your contact and payment terms. Agree on the amount that will be due at various stages of the project. You can use percentages to calculate the progress payments, such as 25 percent deposit, 25 percent upon delivery of the product, 25 percent upon substantial completion, and the balance at completion or within 30 days of substantial completion. Or you may state more concrete progress payments based on indicators that are relevant to the specific scope of work, the job, the products being sold, or the services provided. Regardless of the system you use, progress payments on larger jobs can dramatically lessen your exposure to financial risk.

Extending Credit

Should you extend credit? In most cases, home business owners do not extend credit to consumers unless they deliver a service such as pest control that is billed on a monthly schedule or a major renovation. However, in the case of commercial clients (business to business) home business owners will generally be required to extend some type of credit on revolving account basis, 30, 60, 90, or sometimes 120 days after delivery of the product or service. Ideally, you want to be paid as quickly as possible, so you might want to offer clients a 2 percent discount if invoices are paid within one week. The steps involved in extending credit should cover the following:

1. Create a standard credit policy, which includes acceptance and denial guidelines.
2. Develop a standard business credit application and a consumer credit application if you plan on extending credit to nonbusiness customers.
3. Conduct credit and reference checks from information supplied by customers on their credit applications.
4. Approve or decline based on credit and reference checks, and any extenuating circumstances.
5. If approved, establish an initial credit limit, along with an increase schedule should customer's credit worthiness remain in good standing.
6. If declined, work with customer to help find other ways to secure credit from a third party.
7. Bill customers on time as scheduled, keeping a watch for telltale signs of trouble.
8. Reward customers that continue to pay on time and in full with gifts, special discounts, or value-added rewards.
9. Develop a collection policy, schedule, and action plan for delinquent and nonpayment accounts.

Business Credit Application

The following is a basic Business Credit Application (see Figure 11.5) that you can copy and use in your own business as is or modify to suit your particular needs.

FIGURE 11.5 **Business Credit Application**

Date _____

Legal Business Name _____

Doing Business As _____

❏ Sole Proprietorship   ❏ Partnership   ❏ Limited Liability Company   ❏ Corporation

Address _____ Apartment _____

City _____ State _____ Zip/Postal Code _____

Telephone _____ Fax _____ E-mail _____

Owner Name 1 _____

Owner Name 2 _____

FIGURE 11.5 **Business Credit Application,** continued

Manager Name _____

How long in business? _____ Credit line requested $ _____

Bank Reference _____

Name _____

Address _____

Telephone _____ Fax _____ E-mail _____

Contact Person _____ Title _____

Account Number _____

Trade Reference _____

Business Name _____

Address _____

Telephone _____ Fax _____ E-mail _____

Contact Person _____ Title _____

How long have you had an account with this business? _____ How much is your credit line with this business? $ _____

Trade Reference _____

Business Name _____

Address _____

Telephone _____ Fax _____ E-mail _____

Contact Person _____ Title _____

How long have you had an account with this business? _____ How much is your credit line with this business? $ _____

Trade Reference _____

Business Name _____

Address _____

Telephone _____ Fax _____ E-mail _____

Contact Person _____ Title _____

How long have you had an account with this business? _____ How much is your credit line with this business? $ _____

The undersigned authorizes _____ (your business name) to conduct credit inquiries and checks as required and further acknowledges that credit may or may not be granted, and if credit privileges are granted, they may be withdrawn at any time.

Applicant's Signature	Business Name	Date
Co-Applicant's Signature	Business Name	Date

Office Use

❏ Bank Reference Checked/Date _____

Comments _____

❏ Trade References Checked/Date _____

Comments _____

❏ Credit Rating Checked/Date _____

Comments _____

❏ Credit Approved/Date _____ Credit Limit $ _____

Comments _____

❏ Credit Declined/Date _____

Comments _____

Credit Checks

Make sure to conduct credit checks when new clients ask you to establish revolving credit accounts for their business. Checking an individual's or business's credit is a very straightforward process. There are three major credit reporting agencies serving the United States and Canada—Trans Union, www.tuc.com; Equifax, www.equifax.com; and Experian, www.experian.com. All three credit bureaus compile and maintain credit files on just about every person, business, and organization that has ever applied for credit. All are given a credit rating ranging from poor to excellent based on their credit history. Credit card companies, banks, and trust companies, supply information to these credit-reporting agencies, as do other businesses that lend money or extend credit to people and businesses. From this information the credit bureaus assign a credit rating based on the individual's or business's credit history. Nonpayment of loans, bankruptcies, slow repayment of loans, and litigation to collect funds can all have a negative impact and greatly reduces a credit rating.

Financial institutions, credit card companies, mortgage brokers, retail stores, leasing companies, and other businesses have credit checks conducted to determine if the person or business that is applying for credit is a good credit risk; that is, are they likely to repay the debt and interest on time and in full as set forth in the agreement. Home business owners can subscribe to these credit reporting agencies, and for a fee they can have a credit report compiled on a person or business that wants to purchase products and services on credit. You must first, however, have the applicant's permission to conduct the credit check and a signed credit check and application form.

Returns, Refunds, and Contract Cancellations

Inevitably, all home business owners will be faced with a customer that wants to return a product, requests a refund, or wants out of a contract that both parties have executed. Consequently, it is best to establish your return, refund, and contract cancellation policies before being caught off guard. In formulating your policies, consider:

- Will you allow customers to return products?
- What is acceptable return condition?
- What will be an acceptable return time frame?
- What will be the return options: A new product or equal value, a product credit, a cash refund, or something else?
- Can customers return product that was purchased at less than your normal retail price?
- Will all sales be final?

Contract Cancellations

Most U.S. states and Canadian provinces have consumer protection mechanisms in place that enable consumers to cancel contracts within a prescribed time that is generally referred to as a *cooling off period*. However, there is not a single standard time limit to this law. You will need to contact the SBA or your lawyer to inquire about your specific area and how the law is applied.

DEBT COLLECTION

You will discover that no matter how careful you are in terms of extending credit privileges to customers, once in a while you will be paid late or not at all. What can you do to get paid? You have a number of options. First, you can keep the lines of communication open with your delinquent client and keep the pressure on to get paid. In most cases, the use of letters, telephone calls, and personal visits will generally result in your getting paid in full or in part. Keep in mind, however, that you cannot legally intimidate someone into paying you. All you can do is to keep on top of the situation and explain why it is in their best interests to pay you, that you can hurt their credit rating or sue them in court. Most often you will find that clients have not paid because of a financial problem, which can be short-term and only require you to carry the debt until they are in a position to pony up. If this can be accomplished, it may well be worth the effort so that you can keep an otherwise good customer. Your second option is to hire a collection agency, that in exchange for a fixed fee or a portion (usually 50 percent) of the outstanding unpaid debt they will attempt to collect the account for you, under an assignment agreement. The Association of Credit and Collection

Professionals, www.acainternational.org, is a good starting point in terms of finding a collection agency to work with. Your third option is to take the delinquent account to small claims court. This option is discussed in detail later in this section. Your fourth and final option is not to collect the debt at all. Depending on the amount owed, the time involved in trying to collect the debt, and other factors, you may decide that writing off the account against taxes as bad debt might be your best option. Before you choose this route, however, make sure you talk with your bookkeeper or accountant, because the total debt may not be an allowable deduction.

Small Claims Court

If you choose not to enlist the services of a collection agency and you have exhausted all means of trying to collect the debt, without success, you may want to consider taking the debtor to small claims court. Just remember that small claims courts have limits to how much you can sue for in your state or province. In some cases the maximum amount that you can sue for varies because of special circumstances or a higher limit exists for a specific county. Filing fees vary by state and province. You must pay these fees upfront, but should you win, the fees can be added to your award amount. As a rule of thumb, small business owners that take people to court for nonpayment of accounts or nonperformance of services and contracts generally represent themselves, as the amount of the potential award is usually small and does not justify lawyers' fees and expenses. Keep in mind that even if you win, you will not necessarily be paid the amount that you are awarded. You may win a judgment, but still have to chase the defendant through garnishment of income or seizure of assets to get paid.

You can learn more about the small claims court process and filing fees by contacting your local courthouse. A table outlining maximum small claims court dollar amount limits for each state and province at the time of writing is presented here (see Figure 11.6).

| FIGURE 11.6 | **Small Claims Court Limits** |

United States Small Claims Court Limits		Maine	$4,500
Alabama	$3,000	Maryland	$5,000
Alaska	$7,500	Massachusetts	$2,000
Arizona	$2,500		
Arkansas	$5,000	Michigan	$3,000
California	$2,500–5,000	Minnesota	$7,500
Colorado	$7,500	Mississippi	$2,500
Connecticut	$3,500	Missouri	$3,000
Delaware	$15,000	Montana	$3,000
District of Columbia	$5,000	Nebraska	$2,400
Florida	$5,000	Nevada	$5,000
Georgia	$15,000	New Hampshire	$5,000
Hawaii	$3,500	New Jersey	$3,000
Idaho	$4,000	New Mexico	$10,000
Illinois	$1,500–5,000	New York	$3,000
Indiana	$3,000–6,000	North Carolina	$4,000
Iowa	$5,000	North Dakota	$5,000
Kansas	$1,800	Ohio	$3,000
Kentucky	$1,500	Oklahoma	$4,500
Louisiana	$3,000	Oregon	$5,000

FIGURE 11.6 **Small Claims Court Limits**, continued

United States Small Claims Court Limits		Canadian Small Claims Court Limits	
Pennsylvania	$8,000–10,000	Alberta	$7,500
Rhode Island	$1,500	British Columbia	$10,000
South Carolina	$7,500	Manitoba	$7,500
South Dakota	$8,000	New Brunswick	$6,000
Tennessee	$15,000–25,000	Newfoundland	$3,000
Texas	$5,000	Northwest Territories	$5,000
Utah	$5,000	Nova Scotia	$10,000
Vermont	$3,500	Nunavut	No limit set yet
Virginia	$2,000	Ontario	$10,000
Washington	$4,000	Prince Edward Island	$8,000
West Virginia	$5,000	Quebec	$3,000
Wisconsin	$5,000	Saskatchewan	$5,000
Wyoming	$3,000	Yukon Territories	$5,000

OPTIONS FOR GROWING YOUR HOME BUSINESS

At some point, most home business owners must make a decision on whether or not to grow their home business. Of course, like any business decision, you have to weigh the advantages and disadvantages the decision will have on your business, you personally, and your family. There are obvious benefits to business growth:

- The potential for increased revenues and profits
- Accelerating equity accumulation and a more secure future for your family
- The ability to bring family members or friends into the business
- Personal satisfaction that comes from success

On the other hand, there are also disadvantages in growing a home business. Many entrepreneurs that have chosen to grow their business have not succeeded because the business model that made the business successful originally does not work on a larger scale. Still, this should certainly not dissuade you in any way if you have an eye and ambition to grow your home business into a large and profitable concern. Your objective and goals must be weighed to determine if business growth is in your best interests.

Additional disadvantages of growing a home business include:

- Increased overhead and greater financial risk
- A loss of some control if additional people are brought into the business to assist with the workload and growth
- Increased management responsibilities that can leave you less time to do what made the business successful in the first place

If you do decide that growing your home business is the best option for you, your business, and your family, that it will help you achieve your personal and business goals, you have numerous growth options that you can pursue—geographic growth, people growth, expanded product lines, franchising, and mergers and acquisitions.

Grow Geographically

There are basically two ways to grow geographically: physically or electronically. The first is to build satellite locations in the same city, county, state, country, or even internationally. The second way is by harnessing the power of the Internet to make your goods and services available electronically to a global audience of consumers connected to the Internet. Of course, savvy home business owners with an eye on substantial growth will usually elect to combine both methods to grow their small businesses.

To grow your home business geographically in the real world there are many choices, including agents, licensees, new offices with managers, new business partners, franchising, or mergers and acquisitions. All are discussed in further detail in this chapter. Growing your business geographically via the Internet is somewhat easier and definitely less expensive then growing your business in the real world. There is no need to rent costly office space and pay employees and management wages. Once the decision has been made to expand via the Internet, you can move into foreign markets relatively quickly, efficiently, and with virtually no red tape to worry about. Still, no less attention must be paid to planning and executing growth strategies utilizing the Internet. More information about growing your business electronically via the Net can be found in Chapter 17 Internet and E-commerce.

Grow by People Power

You can also substantially grow your home business by getting more people involved in the business. This can be accomplished by hiring more employees so that you can increase productivity and afford to take on new clients. Or you can hire sales agents and contractors to sell your goods and services to a broader customer base to increase sales, revenues, and profits. If you choose to grow your home business by bringing in new people, you must be prepared to invest the time necessary to find people that share your enthusiasm for the business and its long-term grow prospects. You must also be prepared to invest the money required to train, equip, and support employees until they can become productive team players who can add revenues and profits to the bottom line.

Before growing your business by bringing new people into the operation, consider the following questions:

- What type of training is required to bring new people up to speed in terms of your business operations, products or services, and your customers?
- Who will perform the training? Will you do it yourself, or will you bring in outside trainers?

If the latter, what is the cost and where will the training take place?
- Will your new employees, agents, or subcontractors work from their own homes, or will they be working from your home? If at your home, do you have the space required to accommodate additional people, and does zoning allow outside employees to work from your home?
- What type of new equipment must you acquire for your expanded work force, where will the equipment come from, and how will you pay for it?
- How much do you have to pay your expanded work force, and how will they be compensated? Will they be paid a salary, a performance based structure, or a combination? Do you have to supply employee insurance and benefits? If so, how much will this cost, and where will you get the money from?

These questions only scratch the tip of the iceberg in terms of bringing new people into your business to fuel growth. There are labor laws to consider. There are health and safety regulations to consider. There are management issues to consider. There are most definitely financial issues to consider. At the end of the day, growing your small business into a larger business takes people; it simply cannot be accomplished without help. You need to develop a strategy for bringing in new people so that you can maximize the potential for success, much as you would for expanding into new markets. Additional information about employee and contractor issues can be found in Chapter 8, Building Your Business Team.

Grow by an Expanded Product or Service Line

Another way to grow your home business is to expand your product lines or offer customers new services in addition to the services that you currently provide. Growing by expanding the number of products and services you sell is highly advisable. You already have valuable customer relationships in place. You do not immediately have to go searching for new customers for your new product or service line; you can just tap into your existing customer base. Keep in mind, however, that your current customers must want and need your new products or services. Before expanding your line talk to customers and ask: What additional products or services do you want or need? Would they be willing to purchase these from me? How much are you prepared to spend? It is a safe bet that your customers are purchasing products and services elsewhere that you could easily supply to them, probably at the same or a competitive cost. You will never know for sure unless you ask. As a word of caution, if you do decide to expand your product or service line, make sure that they are complementary to your current lines and that the expansion is logical. For instance, if you operate an office cleaning service, then offer your client's employees mobile dry cleaning pick-up and drop off services as a logical add-on service. That would be easily managed, cheap to get rolling, and in all likelihood earn additional profits.

Grow by Franchising and Licensing

Many home businesses have also expanded to become national and international corporations by successfully franchising their business model or by licensing their products or intellectual and proprietary properties. The potential for growth through franchising and licensing is nearly limitless, but these are very tricky waters to navigate nonetheless. Home business owners that choose this route for growth are well advised to seek the services of a lawyer and accountant well-versed in franchising laws and financial issues. You will also want to talk with a franchise consultant who, through analysis of your business, products, and services, can advise you on the viability of franchising your business. The most successful franchises are ones that follow the KISS formula, which means *keep it simple stupid.* The franchise must be easy to operate, sell something that consumers want, and have the potential to cover expenses and the operator's income. The best franchises do not try to reinvent the wheel, but rather improve upon a current product or service and its distribution through their own unique selling proposition. If your home business meets these criteria it may very well be an ideal candidate to expand into new geographic areas by securing qualified people to own and operate the business under

a franchise agreement. Additional information about franchising can be found in Chapter 2, What Type of Business Should You Start, or you can contact or visit the Web site of the International Franchise Association for more information about franchising and licensing opportunities. The IFA members include franchisors, franchisees, and product and service providers to the franchise industry.

International Franchise Association (IFA)
1350 New York Avenue NW, Suite 900
Washington, DC 20005-4709
(202) 628-8000
www.franchise.org

Grow by Mergers or Acquisitions

Mergers and acquisitions are also a growth option for home business owners, although certainly not as popular as the growth options already discussed. It is, however, possible to merge your business with a competing or noncompeting business. If you do your options would include retaining a portion of ownership of the new operation or selling out completely not retaining any ownership but remaining involved as an employee or consultant. Growing a business by merging it with another business can be a wise growth strategy. When the two businesses become one, they benefit by being able to take advantages of each other's resources and strengths while offsetting weaknesses through specialization. It may also afford you the opportunity to own a piece of a larger pie with further growth potential, instead of a larger piece of a small pie with little, if any, opportunity for growth. Business growth through acquisition can also prove a wise move. Purchasing direct or indirect competitors, or businesses that sell complimentary goods and service enables you to expand your current line. There are advantages and disadvantages associated with growing your business through mergers and acquisitions. But provided enough research is conducted and the new organization appears viable, there is no reason why you cannot use these types of growth instruments to help you reach your business goals.

SELLING YOUR HOME BUSINESS AND OTHER WAYS OUT

Eventually, you will also face a decision about selling your business, passing it to a family member, or closing out. At some point this decision will be inevitable. Nothing lasts forever, or at least we humans don't. There can be a plethora of reasons why you may want or need to get out of your business:

- The time is right to retire.
- You want to slow down to a part-time or seasonal home business operation.
- You want to move on to new business challenges and opportunities.
- A family member is biting at your heels to push you out of the way so he can take over.
- You want to cash out your equity and enjoy the fruits of your labor.
- You want to return to the corporate world as an employee or manager.
- Health-related issues make operating a business no longer possible.
- Family-related issues such as marriage, divorce, or starting a family develop.
- You want to move to a new city, state, or country.
- You have lost interest in your business because it did not live up to your expectations.

There are many valid reasons that you might want to sell or close your home business, but before you do, consult with your accountant before making change. There will probably be tax implications to consider, regardless if the business is sold or closed. Of course, you also have options in terms of how your objective will be reached. You can sell your business outright, you can close the business down, you can pass it on to a family member or employee, or you can reduce the business to a seasonal or part-time effort.

Selling Your Home Business

Home business operations can be sold, provided you have something of value that is attractive to a new owners—inventory, a good customer base, protected intellectual properties, or exclusive product lines. That said, it is not always easy to sell a home business. Many are successful because of the specialized skills of the business owner, not the business. This is not to say that your business cannot be sold. It just takes time to find the right buyer. The next logical question is how much is your home business worth. There are various approaches that you can use to place a value on your business. If you feel that you can sell your business for a substantial amount of money, it may be wise to hire a business broker or consultant to use standard valuation techniques to establish a value for your business. You may, however, choose one of the following easy and less costly routes:

- *Asset value.* The most basic way to value your business is to calculate the value of your physical assets, such as inventory, equipment, and transportation, and sell the business for the accumulated total of these physical assets. Selling your business based on its asset generally makes it very easy to find buyers. You can first contact competitors to find out if they are interested in any or all of your business assets, including inventory, equipment, customer lists, telephone number, and office fixtures. Failing the competitor approach, you can run classified advertisements or hold an auction to liquidate your business assets. Keep in mind that the assets can be sold individually to many people as well as to a single buyer.

- *Comparative value.* What have similar home business operations sold for in your area, or what is the going rate for a similar homebased franchise? Comparative value is also an easy way to place a basic value on your business. For instance, if you operate a lawn mowing service and lawn mowing distributorships or franchises are selling for $25,000 in your area, then chances are you can place a value on your business that is close to $25,000, if not slightly more depending on your equipment list, steady clientele, and net profits. Comparative values can be researched by scanning local newspapers under the Classified headings Business for Sale and Business Opportunities, as well as by visiting business-for-sale Web sites to find out what other entrepreneurs are selling their business for.

- *Income value.* You can also base the value of your business on the income that is generated, that is, the amount of money that is left over after total expenses have been deducted from total sales. If your business had few, if any, physical assets, but generates a pretax income of $35,000 annually, you could use a factor such as two times the earnings to place a value on your business for sale purposes. In this example 2 x $35,000 would equal a $70,000 value. After all, to most people the enticement to buy a non-franchise, operating business is that the business already generates an income and the new owner can immediately draw a wage. Therefore, if your business is generating an income, regardless of the amount, it has value and is a saleable asset.

Of course, you can also use a combination of all three simple valuation techniques to arrive at a selling price. Regardless of the way you arrive at the selling price, you do not want to underprice your business and sell it for a song. Nor do you want to overvalue your business and generate no interest.

If you decide to hire a professional to sell your business, you have two options. You can list your business for sale with a real estate firm in your area. If you choose this route, you will want to list with an agent that specializes in selling businesses and commercial properties. You can also enlist the services of a certified business broker that specializes solely in the marketing of businesses and franchises. The International Business Brokers Association, located online at www.ibba.org, has listings of more than 1,100 independent business brokers in North America, Asia, and Europe. In both cases you will be required to pay a commission generally in the range of 5 to 10 percent based on the total sale price of your business.

You might decide that you are best qualified to sell your business. In that case, you can advertise your business for sale locally, but be discreet. Do not include your business name in the advertisements; you do not want your current customers to find out that your business is for sale, because it might make them nervous and cause them to take their business elsewhere. There are also many business-for-sale print and electronic publications and Web sites that will list your business in exchange for a fee. Generally, these publications and online services are broken into business sections or industries such as home businesses, distributorships, retail, services, and manufacturing. Biz Buy Sell, located online at www.bizbuysell.com, is one of the largest business-for-sale Web sites with over 20,000 current listings.

Giving Your Home Business Away

Another option is to give your home business away, although not necessarily for free. You could give your business to one of your kids, an employee, a relative, or friend with an interest in operating the business. Even though you are giving the business to someone, you could still receive consulting payments over a set period in exchange for fully training the new operator and providing occasional consulting services as needed. Or you could agree to be paid a percentage of the sales for a specific time. In some cases, giving your business away, as opposed to selling it, makes a lot of sense, especially if the recipient is a family member. There are also tax benefits that may be derived from this kind of arrangement that might be worth consideration. And, of course, if you can give the business away and still generate income through consulting fees, royalty payments, or part-time employment as needed then there is also a benefit in terms of financial security that also might be worth careful consideration.

Taking Your Home Business to Part Time

You can always decide not to sell, close down, or give your business away at all. Instead you may choose to scale back your business operation to a part-time or seasonal platform. If you decide on this route, keep your best and most profitable clients and hang on to a minimum amount of equipment, only what is needed to operate the business part time or seasonally. The rest of your business assets such as excess inventory, equipment, fixtures, and customer lists that you will no longer need can be sold to competitors or other entrepreneurs seeking a fast start-up.

There are two main benefits to taking your business part time instead of selling or closing it all together. First, you can continue to generate a part-time or seasonal income that is derived from your best customers, which should also be your most profitable ones. Shed unprofitable and time-consuming business relationships. If 80 percent of your business comes from 20 percent of your customers why not cut out that 80 percent and keep the most profitable 20 percent? Second, there are also great tax benefits associated with keeping your business operating part time or seasonally, even if you decide to take an outside job. Deductible expenses derived from a part-time business are little different from those of a full-time business and can include a portion of your household expenses, transportation costs, insurance premiums, health care premiums, and travel expenses. Of course, not all expenses will be 100 percent tax deductible. But any time you can reduce your taxable earnings through allowable business expenses, it is certainly wise to take advantage of the opportunity.

Closing Your Home Business

Many home business operations are unique in the sense that the value of the business really lies in the experience and special skills of the operator, and not so much the business. For that reason, it is not uncommon for home businesses to close instead of being sold or passed on to family members or others. This is especially true of professional practices and businesses that provide highly specialized services. If you choose to close your home business know that you are not alone. Many home business people simply decide to close their businesses when it comes time to retire or move on to new adventures and challenges.

There are still issues that must be dealt with before you can unplug the phone and turn the sign over to Closed—primarily your customers. You do not want your loyal clients left in a lurch, and forced to find new product or service providers without notice or assistance. Instead, plan your exit strategy carefully, and give clients as much notice as possible. Offer to help them find new providers to fill their needs. Ideally, if you do decide to shut your business, you want to go out on very good terms with all of your customers, suppliers, and business associates. Should you decide to reopen the business or another

business these are valuable business relationships that can be re-ignited for your benefit if the need arises.

RESOURCES

Associations

American Home Business Association
4505 Wasatah Boulevard S.
Salt Lake City, UT 84124
(800) 664-2422
www.homebusiness.com

American Management Association
1601 Broadway
New York, NY 10019
(212) 586-8100
www.amanet.org

Association of Credit and Collection Professionals
P.O. Box 390106
Minneapolis, MN 55439
(952) 926-6547
www.acainternational.org

National Association of Professional Organizers
35 Technology Parkway S. Suite 150
Norcross, Georgia 30092
(770) 325-3440
www.napo.net

U.S. Small Business Administration (SBA)
409 3rd Street SW
Washington, DC 20416
(800) 827-5722
www.sba.org

Suggested Reading

Allen, David. *Getting Things Done: The Art of Stress Free Productivity.* New York: Penguin Books, 2003.

Eisenberg, Ronnie. *Organize Your Office: Revised Routines for Managing Your Workspace.* New York: Hyperion, 1999.

Hugos, Michael. *Essentials of Supply Chain Management.* New York: John Wiley & Sons, 2002.

McCormick, Blane. *Ben Franklin's 12 Rules of Management.* Irvine, CA: Entrepreneur Press Inc., 2000.

Pinson, Linda. *Keeping the Books: Basic Record Keeping and Accounting for the Successful Small Business.* Chicago, IL: Dearborn Trade Publishing, 2004.

Stemmy, Thomas J. *Top Tax Ideas for Your Small Business: How to Survive in Today's Tough Tax Environment.* Irvine, CA: Entrepreneur Press Inc., 2004.

Web Sites

Canadian Business Service Center, www.cbsc.org: Canadian equivalent of the SBA.

Entrepreneur Online, www.entrepreneur.com: Online small business resource center providing entrepreneurs with information, advice, products, services, and resources.

Home Business Magazine, www.homebusinessmag.com: Online magazine with information, advice, tools, and links for home business owners.

Logixsource Consulting, www.logixsource.com: Integrated logistics, technology, and supply chain management.

M.Y.O.B., (Mind Your Own Business) Software www.myob.com: Small business bookkeeping and accounting software.

Office By Design, www.officebydesign.com: Retailer of home office furniture and design services.

Organize Your World, www.organizeyourworld.com: Home business organization tips, products, and resources.

Power Home Biz, www.powerhomebiz.com: Online information, advice, and tools for home business owners.

QuickBooks Software, www.quickbooks.com: Small business bookkeeping and accounting software.

Time Management Guide, www.time-management-guide.com: Tips and information on time management topics.

Work At Home Parent, www.work-at-home-parent.com: Information and advice for parents working from a home office.

CHAPTER 12

Creating a Marketing Plan

WHAT WILL A MARKETING PLAN DO FOR your business? The answer is simple: You will be able to prove, based on your research and data, that there is sufficient consumer demand for your product or service, that you can compete based on user benefits and competitive advantages, and that the market is large enough to support your business. Many small business owners take a "fly by the seat of their pants" approach to business and market planning, choosing to forego any type of formal or even informal planning. They opt to make important marketing decisions on a day-by-day basis. In spite of this practice, some are very successful. Some are not and go broke because of lack of planning.

Like most entrepreneurs, I can chalk up more than one bad marketing experience, due to a lack of planning. When I say bad marketing experience what I am really saying is, "Ouch, that dumb idea just cost me a bundle, what was I thinking?" This may be what qualifies me to advise you that creating a marketing plan for your business should be one of your top priorities. You can then maximize your positive marketing experiences, minimize your bad marketing experiences, and reach your marketing goals in a clearly defined and measurable step-by-step way. These are what a marketing plan affords.

Keep in mind, of course, that the small business marketing plan does not have to be a sophisticated and highly detailed volume like those multinational corporations need to satisfy nervous bankers and investors. In fact, even just a few detailed and well-documented pages covering the basics are often sufficient to reveal the information you need to identify your customers, your product's beneficial advantages, your marketing goals, your marketing strategies, and your action plan. The extent of your marketing plan is a function of its purpose. If your marketing plan is going to be used to secure start-up or growth financing it will need to be comprehensive and satisfy the needs of those from who you are seeking funding. If the purpose is to merely act as a road map that eventually helps you reach your marketing goals, the fit and finish only must satisfy your personal objectives and needs.

A final word of advice before you start your marketing plan or any business-related plan for that matter: Don't be intimidated by the planning process, and especially do not let business gurus or academic terminology prevent you from developing plans that are perhaps outside of *business school models*. Just make sure that the information you research, record, analyze, and document is valuable and specific to your business situation.

The process of business and marketing planning only needs to be as difficult or as easy as you want to make it.

In Chapter 10, Finding and Keeping Customers, you will find a plethora of information about conducting market research, collecting secondary data, and creating a target customer profile. All will be required to fully develop your marketing plan. Like a business plan, a marketing plan is grounded in as much fact as is possible, with perhaps a few safe assumptions. Simply stating in your marketing plan what you hope will happen or what you believe will happen is utterly useless. Therefore, take the time that is required to fully research, record, and analyze each section of your marketing plan before you put all of your findings into a formal marketing plan document. The result should be a step-by-step guide that acts as a road map to transport your business from where you are currently to where you want to be.

MARKETING PLAN OUTLINE

The format of a marketing plan has no rules set in stone because plans vary by industry, type of business, location of business, size of company, stage of growth, and plan function (financing versus management). The marketing plan you need to help guide your homebased lawn care service to success is much different than the marketing plan that Coca Cola Inc., needs to guide their multi-billion dollar international business though the competitive waters of the soft drink industry. Remember, for the small business operator the marketing plan format is really a nonissue. Format your marketing plan in such a way that it makes sense to you in terms of how the information is recorded and how the information contained within the plan can be applied to your particular business situation. The true value of the plan is the information that is revealed about your business, products, customers, market, competitors, and strategies in the process of creating it. Provided that you cover the basics, the result will be a marketing plan that works for your particular situation. The following is a basic marketing plan outline for a small business:

- Executive Overview

- Company Analysis
- Market Analysis
- Customer Analysis
- Competitor Analysis
- Marketing Objectives
- Marketing Strategy
- Marketing Budget
- Action Plan
- Support Documents

Worksheets are included for most sections of marketing planning so that you can begin the process of creating a marketing plan as you read, gather, and record the basic information that can create your marketing plan.

EXECUTIVE OVERVIEW

Just like a business plan, a marketing plan also begins with an executive overview or introduction. This section is a brief summary describing key points from every section of your marketing plan, short enough to fit onto one page. Even though the executive overview is at the beginning, it usually the last section you create. The executive overview is comprised of the key points extracted from each section of your plan, and these key points are not known until each section is substantially completed. The main purpose of the executive overview is to provide readers the who, what, where, how, and why of the marketing plan.

Depending on your business, industry, stage of growth, and purpose, the executive overview would include any or all of the following information:

- Your business name and legal structure
- Mission statement or philosophy
- A brief mention of the owner, management team, and relevant experience and training
- How long you have been in business, or when your business will start
- The geographic area served
- The type of product or service that you offer or will offer
- Your product's or service's unique benefits and competitive advantage
- Target customer
- Market size and potential

- Position in the marketplace
- Company objectives
- How objectives will be reached
- Projected revenues
- Short-term and long-terms goals

Once you have substantially completed your marketing plan, you will be ready to create your executive overview. Answering the following ques-

tions on the executive overview worksheet (see Figure 12.1) with information extracted from the appropriate section of your marketing plan will enable you to create an executive overview. Of course not, all the questions are relevant to your business. Answer those that are and ignore the rest. Also, keep in mind that the executive overview is brief, limit answers to a few sentences.

FIGURE 12.1 **Executive Overview Worksheet**

What is your business name and legal structure? _____

_____

What is your mission statement, or purpose for being in business? _____

_____

Who will manage the business, and what special skills, experience, or training do they have? _____

_____

When did the business start? _____

_____

Where is the business located? (City) _____

_____

What geographic area does your business service? (City, county, state, or other) _____

_____

What type of products or services do you sell? _____

_____

What is your product's or service's unique user benefit(s)? _____

_____

What is your main competitive advantage? _____

_____

Who is your target customer? _____

_____

How big is your current market? _____

_____

How big is the potential market? _____

FIGURE 12.1 **Executive Overview Worksheet,** continued

What is your position in the marketplace, or what is your positioning strategy? _____
_____

What is your company's key marketing objective(s)? _____
_____

How will your objective(s) be reached? _____
_____

What is your first year revenue projection? $ _____

What is your long-term revenue projection? (Five years) $ _____

What is your short-term goal(s)? _____
_____

What is your long-term goal(s)? _____
_____

COMPANY ANALYSIS

The company analysis is a full description of your company, including in-depth information on the owner(s), key partnerships the business has entered into or will enter into, as well as the company's strengths and weaknesses. If your home business is currently operating, recount successes, failures, and growth or decline in sales to date and describe where your company is now versus where it will be in the future should marketing goals and objectives as set out in the marketing plan be reached. The company analysis will include as much of the following information as possible, or as is applicable to your type of business and situation.

- Business name and legal structure
- Business location (city), and the area that the business serves (city, county, state, or other).
- Owner(s) and/or partner(s) biography, including relevant experience, skills, and training
- If applicable, a list of key managers and employees including relevant experience, skills, and training
- If applicable the history of the company: when it was formed and growth or decline in recent years. If the business is new, give a starting date, mission statement, and full description of why the business will succeed
- Key joint venture or cross-promotional partners
- Relationships with key suppliers
- Relationships with key vendors
- Company strengths, such as highly trained service personal. (See SWOT analysis later under competitor analysis.)
- Company weaknesses, such as lack of capital that could be used to fuel growth. (See SWOT analysis later under competitor analysis.)
- Obstacles or challenges that stand in the way of reaching key marketing goals and objectives
- Special licenses and intellectual property ownerships, such as exclusive sales agreements, product representations, product or service licenses, patents, trademarks, and copyrights
- Associations the business belongs to—professional, industry, or business
- Any accreditations or endorsements that the business has received from schools, private industry, government agencies, or nonprofit agencies

Answering the following questions on the Company Analysis Worksheet (see Figure 12.2), and completing any descriptions or lists required will help you create a company analysis. Ignore questions that are not relevant, and add any you believe will paint a more accurate picture of your company. Now you want to go into great detail in terms of

information, statistics, and facts when developing these other sections of your marketing plan. The goal of the marketing plan is to leave no unanswered questions in terms of the company and its marketing intentions, especially if the marketing plan will be used as a tool to secure business funding.

FIGURE 12.2 Company Analysis Worksheet

What is your business name and legal structure? _____

What is your mission statement or purpose for being in business? (See Chapter 6, Preparing a Business Plan, for an explanation of how to create a mission statement for your business.) _____

Where is your business located? (City) _____

In detail, describe the trading area that your business serves. (City, county, state, or other) _____

Describe the owner(s) of the business, including relevant experience, skills, and training. _____

List key employees, sales agents, or contractors associated with the business and their specific experience, skills, and training. _____

If your business is currently operating, give a brief history of the company, including when it was formed, successes to date, failures to date, current market share, and growth or decline to date. Include yearly sales figures. _____

If your business is new, describe why you think it will be successful in terms of marketing. _____

List any joint venture or cross-promotional partners, and the nature of the partnerships. _____

List key suppliers, and what they supply, and describe their importance to your business. _____

List key vendors selling your goods or services, and describe their importance to your business. _____

Describe what you believe are your company's strengths. _____

Describe what you believe are your company's weaknesses. _____

FIGURE 12.2   Company Analysis Worksheet, continued

Describe the obstacle(s) that stand in the way of your company reaching marketing goals and objectives. _____
_____

List any product or service licenses or exclusive sales/supply agreements your company has. _____
_____

List any intellectual property your company owns, and describe the property protected. _____
_____

List any professional, industry, or business associations to which your company belongs. _____
_____

List any accreditations or endorsements that your business has from schools, private industry, government agencies, or nonprofit agencies.
_____
_____

MARKET ANALYSIS

A market analysis is information about the marketplace that your business currently operates in, will operate in once the business is started, or might expand into. The biggest benefit of conducting and recording a market analysis is that the information you discover enables you to greatly reduce your exposure to financial risk, while at the same time increasing your chances of capitalizing on marketplace opportunities. It also proves that there is a big enough marketplace to support your business. Use Figure 12.3 to help you.

Information included in your marketing plan will be based on your primary research, as well as data from secondary sources, such as schools, government agencies, and private companies. Chapter 10, Finding and Keeping Customers, describes the various methods that you can use to conduct primary research, methods such as focus groups and surveys. It also tells where you can find secondary sources of data and statistics to compile the information that will eventually be used in to support your statements, forecasts, and objectives. The market analysis section of your marketing plan should include research based on in-depth information in three main areas: market size, market segmentation, and marketing environment.

Market Size

The starting point is to define your market. Most home business owners will elect to use geographical boundaries because most home businesses serve a specific market, selling goods and services directly to consumers within that market. So what is the current size of the market? A pool cleaning service might describe the current size of the market as 1,000 single-family homes of which 200, or 20 percent currently have a swimming pool. Therefore, the current market is the 200 people that have swimming pools. How big is the potential market? The city planning department estimates that 5,000 new single-family homes will be built over the next ten years, giving us a potential market of 1,200 single-family homes (people) with swimming pools. How many other companies are currently competing for this market? There is currently one pool-cleaning service operating in this area, but it is based 50 miles away. Additionally, you would go on to describe the current stage of the market lifecycle, growing, declining, or static (no growth or no decline). As you can see, the market size needs only to be detailed in broad, statistical terms. You will supply this information by your own primary research as well as from secondary sources you have used as a yardstick to determine the current market situation and estimate the future market trends.

Market Segmentation

Market segmentation is breaking your target audience down into groups for easy identification and targeting. The three market segments that are researched, analyzed, and recorded are geographics, demographics, and psychographics. Market segmenting is very important to your business because segmenting the market is really narrowing focus on potential customers: where they live, who they are, and what common characteristics they share. Knowing this crucial information enables you to focus your marketing and promotional efforts on these groups and in these areas to minimize wasting money by targeting the wrong people in the wrong areas. In Chapter 10, Finding and Keeping Customers, you will find geographic, demographic, and psychographic information, how each can be researched, and how this information can be applied to your business and marketing planning activities.

Geographics

The first step is to isolate where the majority of your target audience lives. Be specific as to the country, state, county, city, and even neighborhood. Also, if you intend on servicing more than one geographic market, you will have to create a geographics profile for each. Even on a basic level, geographical segmentation information about your target audience is extremely valuable. For example, if you operate a pool cleaning service, you would want to know in which part of the city the majority of people who own swimming pools live. Having this information enables you to target your advertising and promotion activities to the area of the city where the majority of your target audience resides.

Demographics

The second step is to segment your target audience demographically by gender, age, race, religion, education, income, and profession. Demographic data can be further expanded to include information such as how many people reside in the household, and marital status. In Chapter 10, Finding and Keeping Customers, you will find a customer profiling worksheet, which can assist you in demographically segmenting your target audience.

Psychographics Data

Psychographics is segmenting your customers by their common characteristics, such as lifestyle, values, behavior, and opinions. This data is used as a continuation of geographic and demographic profiling. Once you know where your target audience is located (geographic) and who your target audience is (demographic), then you can begin to find out what they have in common—the type of music they like, the type of social clubs they belong to, or the type of cars they drive.

Marketing Environment

Marketing environment is the third area in the market analysis and answers the question, "What are the current issues or emerging trends that can positively or negatively affect my business and the marketing of my products or services?" The best way to research the marketing environment is to conduct a PEST (Political, Economic, Social, and Technology) analysis, which divides the marketing environment into four key areas that can potentially affect your business and marketing efforts: political and legal issues, economic issues, social and cultural issues, and technology issues. Keep in mind that a PEST analysis should be completed for all of the geographic regions in which you plan on conducting business because while the economy may be strong in one area, it may not be so good in a different one.

Political/Legal

When you research and analyze political and legal issues, you are looking for current issues or emerging trends that can influence the way you do business. These issues and trends can have either a positive or negative impact. Is the political situation in the area where you want to conduct business stable? Are there impending tax regulations that will affect your business? Are the zoning laws regulating home businesses in your area about to change? Are there any current or emerging environmental issues or laws that will affect your business? Basically, you want to take an in-depth look at the political and legal environment to determine if there are current issues or emerging trends that can affect your business.

Economic

Researching and analyzing economic issues and trends is very straightforward. You can start by conducting good old "look out your window research." Take a walk around your local community to see what's going on. Is the economy hot, flat, or declining? Is unemployment high, low, or static? Current and emerging economic factors can also include issues such as fluctuating interest rates, fluctuating currency values, or forthcoming mass layoffs or hiring campaigns by major employers. Consider economic factors that can affect the purchasing power of your target customers, impacting on your business because they will have more or less money to spend on your products.

Social/Cultural

Social and cultural factors revolve around demographics, social activities, and cultural attitudes of people. For example, if you operate a fitness consulting business and the shift is toward health consciousness, this could have a positive impact on your business. It would certainly alter how you promote your fitness service. Research and analyze the changes taking place or trends emerging in demographics and social attitudes and activities. Look at population growth, age distribution, views on environmental issues, sports and recreational activities, personal safety, and the actions people take as a result. These are all examples of social or cultural changes, which can have an influence on your business.

Technology

You do not have to look hard or far to see how much technology affects business and the way business is conducted, especially over the past decade with the proliferation of Internet users and with the introduction and wide consumer acceptance of digital technologies. When researching technology in relationship to your business, market, and marketing plan, you want to look at current and emerging technologies and how these technological changes, improvements, or forthcoming technologies will impact on your business and customers, and how you promote and deliver products and services.

FIGURE 12.3 Market Analysis Worksheet

Summarize the research methods and the sources of data used in the creation of the market analysis, noting specific market size, market segmentation, and marketing environment. _____

Market Size

Define your market. _____

How big is the current market? _____

How big is the potential market? _____

Is the market large enough to be profitable? _____

How many other competitors are operating in the market? _____

FIGURE 12.3 **Market Analysis Worksheet,** continued

In what lifecycle stage is the market—growth, decline, or static? _____
_____

Market Segmentation

Where are your target customers geographically located? (Be specific.) _____
_____

What means of promotion are available that will enable you to reach your target audience within the specific geographical market(s)?
_____
_____

Demographically speaking, define your target audience by gender, age, race, religion, income, education, number of dependants, and marital status. (Target customer profile.) _____
_____

What are the common characteristics that your primary target audience shares? _____
_____

What publications do your target audience like to read, what television shows do they watch, what radio stations do they listen to, and what recreational activities do they pursue in their free time? _____
_____
_____

Marketing Environment

Is the geographical area in which you will be conducting business politically stable? _____
_____

Are there new or forthcoming changes in any laws or regulations that will affect your business, products, or services, and if so, what will these affects be? _____
_____

Are there any current or emerging social or cultural issues that will affect your business, and why? _____
_____

What is your biggest concern in terms of the economy, and how may this affect your business? _____
_____

Will an increase or decrease in interest rates affect your business, and why? _____
_____

Will an increase or decrease in employment rates affect your business, and why? _____
_____

Are there any current or emerging technologies that will affect your business? If so, what is the technology, and how will it affect your business?
_____

Will the rate of technological change affect your business, and how? _____
_____

CUSTOMER ANALYSIS

The customer analysis section of your marketing plan is really a fine-tuning of your target customer profile that digs deeper to help you better understand what is important to your target customers. I believe that the only way to accurately collect this information is through conducting your own primary research, using methods such as surveys, focus groups, and personal interviews. You have to get out, talk to your potential customers, and ask specific questions that will reveal how they choose between competitors. How sensitive are price, quality, service, and value issues? And what type of promotional or marketing activities do they typically respond to? These are commonly referred to as consumer drivers. What drives your target customers to make the purchasing decisions that they do? In terms of marketing, you have two choices. You can try to change consumer perceptions and buying habits so that they will buy what you are selling. Or, you can follow the path of least resistance and simply ask your target customers on what they base decisions when purchasing products and services that they need and want. You can attempt the first, but you better have really deep pockets because altering consumer buying habits is a long and very costly process.

COMPETITOR ANALYSIS

The competitor analysis is an important section of your marketing plan because it tells you who your direct competition is, that is, the other businesses that sell the same or similar goods or services to the same target audience within the same geographical area. It sheds light on indirect competitors, such as the supermarket that rents carpet cleaning machines and competes with a carpet cleaning service. It also uncovers the phantom and future competitors discussed in Chapter 10, Finding and Keeping Customers.

Keep in mind that the purpose of conducting and recording a competitor analysis in the marketing plan is not to knock the competition. It is to take an objective and realistic look at their business practices, products, and services versus your own, so that internal strengths can be identified, internal weaknesses can be corrected, external opportunities capitalized upon, and external threats reduced or eliminated. This method of competitor analysis is commonly referred to as a SWOT (strengths, weaknesses, opportunities, and threats) analysis and is featured further along in this section. An additional benefit of completing a competitor analysis includes the fact that you'll be able to pinpoint why customers will choose

---

FIGURE 12.4 **Customer Analysis Worksheet**

Summarize the research methods and the data sources used in the creation of your customer analysis. _____
_____
_____

What are the critical benefits that your target customers look for in terms of your product or service? _____
_____

How and on what criteria are choices made between competitors? _____
_____

What does the majority of your target audience care about most—price, quality, fast service, value, or a wide selection of goods and services?
_____
_____
_____

to do business with you instead of a competitor. Or, if you discover that certain markets for specific products and services have reached saturation you will be able to avoid those markets and concentrate on growth markets. Objectively analyzing the competition will enable you to:

- identify direct competition
- identify indirect competition
- identify competitors' strengths and weaknesses
- identify niche markets for products or services that are not being serviced by competitors
- identify the advantages and benefits of a competitor's products and services, as well as the benefits and advantages of your own products and services
- see how each competitor is positioned in the marketplace compared to you, or where you need to be positioned in the marketplace to take advantage of available opportunities
- identify who the competition's target audience is, and what promotional methods they use to reach their audience
- determine what share of the market they control and their estimated sales
- understand how competitors change depending on the influences affecting the marketplace

In the Competition section in Chapter 10, Finding and Keeping Customers, you will discover all the vital need-to-know information for identifying competition and for competition against other businesses in the markets that your business serves.

SWOT Analysis

Business owners and managers will often conduct a SWOT (Strengths, Weaknesses, Opportunities, and Threats) analysis to help determine their ability to compete against other businesses that sell similar products or services in the same marketplace and to the same target audience. A SWOT analysis will also help you to identify your position within the marketplace, that is, how consumers view your business, products, or services in direct relationship to your competitors and their products or services. When creating your marketing strategies, try to think about how your competitors will react to these marketing strategies. Remember Newton's third law, "for

every action there is an equal and opposite reaction." You have to remain cognizant of the fact that your competitors will react to or counteract your marketing efforts. The trick is to know beforehand what action they will take, so that you can stay two steps ahead, even when they think you are one step behind.

Strengths

Get started by identifying your internal strengths—those skills and resources you currently have that can be capitalized upon and used to your advantage in reaching business and marketing objectives. For instance, your strength might be that you have 25 years experience in your particular field. Answering questions such as, "What are your current competitive advantages in the marketplace?" and "What is the biggest benefit that people receive by buying your products or services?" will assist you in identifying your internal strengths. Compile a list of at least five points that you consider to be your business's greatest internal strengths. Once you have identified your greatest internal strengths these can then be leveraged into other areas of your business.

Your businesses internal strengths are. . .

_____

_____

_____

_____

_____

Weaknesses

Weakness is a critical factor that diminishes your competitiveness, or obstructs your ability to reach specific business and marketing objectives. For example, if you lack specialized equipment that precludes you from bidding on certain jobs, this would be considered an internal weakness within your business. Remember, a business weakness is anything that diminishes your ability to compete—everything from cash flow problems to lack of credibility to limited product selection are all examples of internal weaknesses. Make a list of your internal weaknesses, basically anything that you believe diminishes your ability to effectively compete within the marketplace. Answering basic questions like, "What could we be doing better?" will help you to identify your internal weaknesses so that corrective measures can be implemented to overcome them.

Your businesses internal weaknesses are. . .

_____

_____

_____

_____

_____

Opportunities

An opportunity is best characterized as a positive situation that arises and that can be capitalized upon. It can improve your position within the marketplace and increase your profitability. What external opportunities are currently available or will be coming available that could be capitalized upon for the benefit of your business? Changes in technologies that would enable you to increase productivity or market share? Forthcoming changes in government regulations that would have a positive impact on your business? Or your main competitor going out of business? These are all external opportunities that your business can capitalize upon to improve your position in the marketplace. Compile a list of all the external opportunities currently or soon to be available that you feel could be capitalized upon for the benefit of your business.

What external opportunities can your business capitalize upon?

_____

_____

_____

_____

_____

Threats

Threats are negative situations that exist or arise and have the ability to damage your position in the marketplace or your profitability. Has a new competitor opened for business in your area? Is your industry in a maturing or declining phase? Are there changes coming in government regulations or technology that could have a negative impact on your business? Answering questions such as these will help you to identify the threats that your business currently

faces or will soon be facing. Write these down, starting with the biggest external threat first.

What are the main external issues threatening your business?

_____

_____

_____

_____

_____

Analyzing the Data and Creating a SWOT Action Plan

The next step is to carefully analyze and prioritize the data collected by identifying your internal strengths and weaknesses, as well as the external opportunities and threats. Often you will see patterns start to form, perhaps competitor strengths built upon one of your internal weaknesses. Once you have analyzed and prioritized all of your data you will be able to create a SWOT action plan listing the following information.

Maximize Strengths. Knowing what your greatest internal strengths are will allow you to build upon these strengths and maximize their positive impact on your business. For instance, if your greatest strength is that you posses 20 years of experience in your field, this should become your main competitive advantage and the message that anchors all advertising and marketing activities.

Minimize Weaknesses. Knowing your internal weaknesses will force you to resolve them or work out ways to minimize the impact that they have on your business. This is one of the greatest benefits of conducting a SWOT analysis. When you see your weaknesses in print, it is very difficult to ignore the problem and hope it goes away.

Capitalize on Opportunities. Identifying external opportunities enables you to properly plan for the future and take action to capitalize on the opportunities that can have an immediate impact.

Eliminate Threats. Now that you have identified external threats and how they can affect your business, you can create a course of action that will reduce or eliminate them. You may even choose to find a way to avoid the threats if that is possible without damaging your business.

In Chapter 10, Finding and Keeping Customers, there is a very comprehensive Competition Comparison Worksheet (see Figure 10.2) which can be copied and used to analyze all of your competitors in the marketplace. Answering the questions below (see Figure 12.5) will also give you a good starting point in terms of identifying and analyzing competitors. It is worthwhile to complete both worksheets.

FIGURE 12.5 **Competition Comparison Worksheet**

Summarize the research methods and the data sources used in the creation of the competitor analysis. _____
_____

Based on your research, who are your biggest competitors?

Direct competition: 1. _____
2. _____
3. _____

Indirect competition: 1. _____
2. _____
3. _____

What is the estimated market share of each of your direct competitors?   1. _____ % 2. _____ % 3. _____ %

What is each direct competitor's biggest competitive advantage?
1. _____
2. _____
3. _____

What do you think each direct competitor's greatest strengths and weaknesses are, and why?

Strength: 1. _____
2. _____
3. _____

Weakness: 1. _____
2. _____
3. _____

What opportunities do you see in terms of competing against each direct competitor or filling a niche within the market that they do not, and why?
1. _____
2. _____
3. _____

What is the greatest threat that each direct competitor poses to your business, and why?
1. _____
2. _____
3. _____

FIGURE 12.5 **Competition Comparison Worksheet,** continued

What is the greatest threat that your business poses to each direct competitor, and why?

1. _____

2. _____

3. _____

What is your greatest advantage in terms of competing against each direct competitor, and why?

1. _____

2. _____

3. _____

What does each direct competitor do well enough that you should also be doing?

1. _____

2. _____

3. _____

Now that you know each direct competitor better, what products or service can you provide to their customers to lure them to your business?

1. _____

2. _____

3. _____

What marketing activities can you implement to reach direct competitor's core target audience?

1. _____

2. _____

3. _____

MARKETING OBJECTIVES

The next section of the marketing plan states your marketing objectives, although if your business is a new start-up, you should stay focused on first-year goals. Your marketing objectives should be given in easily measured, quantifiable financial terms and/or units, be realistic and financially defendable, and be combined with a firm date when the objectives will be reached. For example, our objective is to increase sales revenues by 10 percent, to $200,000, within 12 months. This will give us a 20 percent share of the current market. To reach our marketing objective, we will be updating our installation equipment at a cost of $11,000, commencing January 15th and being completed by February 10th. Additionally, to help reach our marketing objective, we will be hiring one additional part-time

sales representative in March who will solely focus on new business generation.

Three key concepts to keep in mind when developing your marketing objectives are:

1. If your marketing objectives include expansion into a new geographic territory or an expanded product or service line, do not lose sight of your current products, services, or marketplace. It is very easy to get an extreme case of tunnel vision when working hard to reach new goals and objectives. Unfortunately, a side effect of tunnel vision can be losing sight of the rest of your business, and the moment you let your guard down expect competitors to rush in and scoop up your customers.

2. Marketing objectives that do not have the potential to provide a return on the money

---

FIGURE 12.6   Marketing Objectives Worksheet

Summarize the research methods and the data sources used in the creation of your marketing objective(s) if your business is new. If your marketing objective(s) are based on a previous year(s) in business, mention if past objectives were reached, and why or why not?

_____

_____

What is your first-year sales objective, and what strategies will you put into place to reach your sales objective? _____

_____

_____

What is your five-year sales objective? _____

_____

_____

List what actions you will take to protect your existing business. _____

_____

_____

List any improvements that you have planned in terms of your business, equipment, technologies, products, services, training, or customer service which will help you reach your marketing objective(s). _____

_____

_____

_____

invested to reach them are not marketing objectives. A marketing objective is not to give away the most helium-filled balloons at October Fest celebrations this year. It would, however, be a marketing objective if you wanted to sell more helium-filled balloons than any other balloon vendor at October Fest celebrations.

3. Marketing objectives should always revolve around some kind of improvement in your business, be it in training, products, or customer service. For instance, if your objective is to increase your sales team's closing rate from 30 percent to 50 percent, a subsequent strategy would be to retrain your sales force in their closing skills so that you can meet your objective. In this example, the objective is increasing sales closing rates, which revolves around improving the skills of the sales team. The strategy that will be implemented to reach the marketing goals is sales training.

MARKETING STRATEGY

The marketing strategy section of the marketing plan is where things start to get exciting, not to mention creative. You have identified your company's strengths, weaknesses, the competition, your market size and potential, your primary target customers, and the reasons why they buy, and you have set your marketing objectives. Now it is time to develop marketing and promotional strategies that will enable you to reach your stated objectives. In other words, now it's time to build your marketing game plan. The marketing strategy component of your plan really consists of two parts. Part one is your positioning strategy while part two covers the four marketing Ps: product, price, place (distribution), and promotion.

Your positioning strategy is a very important element of your overall marketing strategy. After all, your positioning strategy answers two vital questions: "Where do your business and products or services fit into the market?" and "How does your target audience view your business and products or services in relationship to your competitors?" You might position your business as the low-price leader in the marketplace, or perhaps you choose a "quality first" philosophy. The positioning of your business and the products or services you sell has much to do with competitors and where they are positioned in the market, what perceptions consumers already have for the type of goods or services you sell, and the beneficial advantages you can create in terms of consumers purchasing from your business and involving your products or services.

You can try to alter consumer perceptions and buying habits but that is a costly, long-term process that is beyond most home business owners with limited capital. A more logical approach to defining your positioning strategy or philosophy is to analyze the current marketplace (which you already have done) identifying what competitors are doing, how consumers respond, and then make beneficial improvements to products or services or in the delivery. In other words, look for a niche market that is being ignored by competitors, or make subtle improvements to your goods or services in terms of user benefits to define your positioning strategy. Developing the right positioning strategy for your business is critical, and warrants additional research and a more in-depth understanding. An excellent book to read on positioning, by the men who developed the concept is *Positioning: The Battle for Your Mind* (McGraw-Hill) by Al Ries and Jack Trout, which is available at most libraries and booksellers nationwide.

The second component in developing your marketing strategy is the four marketing Ps —product, price, place (distribution), and promotion. It is the combination of the four Ps that creates your marketing mix, which is in effect the entire marketing process. In the perfect marketing world, you would have an in-demand product with incredible user benefits, priced in such as way that it is irresistible to your target market and profitable for your business, distributed in a fashion that enables you to have access to your entire target audience, and promoted in a such a way that it forces your target audience to take action and buy. Essentially that is what the four Ps are all about: Finding the right portions of each, enabling you to create the perfect marketing mix comprised of your marketing strategies that will allow you to meet and exceed your marketing objectives. The following are a few points that should be discussed in the marketing plan in terms of product, price, place (distribution), and promotion.

Product

The first P is your product (keeping in mind that this also means a service), which you want to describe in great detail. There are numerous aspects of your product to consider in relationship to your marketing strategy, including:

- What is the main benefit that consumers receive from purchasing and using your goods or services? Do they save money? Do they make money? Will it make them more fit or healthy? Will they save time? You have to go into detail about what benefits consumers receive by purchasing and using your product(s).
- You will also want to describe the scope and range of your entire product line, including the benefits and features of secondary or support lines.
- Talk about how your product will be packaged to separate it from competitors' packaging.
- What warranties and guarantees will you provide—product, workmanship, and third party? How do these compare to competitor's warranties, expected claim percentages, expected cost of warranty program, possibility of turning the warranty program into a profit center as well as the policy in terms of honoring warranties.

Price

Next you want to tackle price-related issues, which are very important elements of the marketing mix and your marketing strategy. If your prices are too high, you will meet great resistance trying to sell your goods or services; if your prices are too low, the same could happen because of perceived quality issues. Clearly, a balanced approach must be taken when establishing your prices and your pricing polices. Contributing factors when establishing pricing formulas include product costs and overhead, desired profit margin and return on investment, market supply and demand, local economic conditions, competition, consumer perceptions, and your positioning strategy. You also have to include information in the plan such as specialty pricing reflecting volume discounts, bulk purchasing, vendor programs, and payment options you will provide to consumers—credit cards, in-house financing, and consumer financing. Additional helpful information about product and service pricing issues can be found in Chapter 9, What Price Will You Charge?

Place (Distribution)

Place or distribution means where can your customers purchase your products, and how do your products get to your customers? The majority of home businesses sell their products directly to consumers through their Web sites, at trade shows, in person at the client's location, through the mail, or directly to consumers by providing services. Even so, you will still have to describe your methods of distribution in the marketing strategy section of the marketing plan. If by chance you will be utilizing other means of distribution for your goods and services such as vendors, independent sales agents, wholesalers, or licenses, you will have to go into greater detail, revealing the nature of those relationships, the agreements in place, storage and transportation methods, and the logistics chain from inquiry to fulfillment to receiving payment. Additionally, you will need to discuss how the image of your business and products matches that of your distributor or vendor. For example, if you design and create one-of-a-kind wedding dresses at home, then logically the dresses should be sold through bridal boutiques and not discount women's fashion chain stores.

Promotion

The promotion section of your marketing strategy is where you describe the various promotional activities you will undertake in the promotion of your

goods and services. Depending on how extensive your promotional activities will be, you might have to create individual plans to cover the major promotional categories such as an advertising or media plan, a sales plan, a public relations plan, an Internet marketing plan, and a direct marketing plan. These individual plans are formatted much like your marketing plan, but on a smaller scale. They describe the promotional activity, the cost, the frequency, contingency plans, and the like. However, for the majority of home business owners these individual promotional activity plans will not be needed.

The following is the type of promotional activities information that you might need to cover in your marketing plan:

- The types of advertising mediums that you will use to promote your goods and services, the costs of each, the frequency of each, and a description of the advertisers' medium and their target market.
- You will also have to cover your personal contact selling strategies, including the number of people in your sales force, how inquiries and presentations are handled, preferred closing techniques, and how leads and referrals will be generated.
- If you intend on engaging in direct marketing promotional activities such as telemarketing, fax or e-mail blasts, or a direct mail campaign, you will need to describe this fully in your plan, with costs and expected response rates.
- Promotional activities will also include public relations and sponsorships and how these will be utilized for promoting your goods and services. Include relationships with the media, the preferred choice of information release (press release, press conference, or expert positioning), charity and activity sponsorships, and public speaking opportunities. You will also want to include affiliations or memberships in business clubs and associations and how these relationships can be advantageous in the promotion of your goods and services.
- Describe if you will construct and publish a Web site, the costs associated with such, how

the Web site will be utilized in the promotion of your goods and services, and the online marketing methods that will be employed.

- List and describe any events such as trade shows, expos, and seminars that will be used in the promotion of your goods and services, where they will be held, the type of event, and the demographics of who and how many people attend the event.

- You will want to discuss your plans for utilizing advertising specialties or premiums such as pens, hats, and mouse pads that are emblazoned with your business name and promotional message.

Additional information about various promotional methods can be found in the next five chapters—Advertising and Promotions, Public Relations and Networking, Sales, Event Marketing, and The Internet and E-Commerce.

FIGURE 12.7 **Marketing Strategy Worksheet**

Positioning

Describe your positioning strategy in detail, and why you believe it will work. _____

_____

Describe your main competitor's positioning strategy in detail. _____

_____

Describe how consumers respond to your competitor's positioning strategy. _____

_____

Product

Describe your product in detail. _____

_____

What is the unique user benefit(s) associated with your product? _____

_____

What special features does your products have? _____

_____

What is the competitive advantage(s) associated with your product? _____

_____

Describe how you product will be packaged. _____

_____

Describe the product warranties and guarantees that you will provide customers, including product warranties, workmanship warranties, third-party warranties, and customer service guarantees. _____

_____

Price

Describe your pricing strategy in detail. _____

_____

FIGURE 12.7 **Marketing Strategy Worksheet,** continued

How much will you charge for your product, and how did you arrive at your selling price? _____
_____

How sensitive are your target customers to pricing issues, and why? _____
_____

How much do competitors charge for their products? _____
_____

List the payment options that you will provide to your customers, including any initial and ongoing fees that your business must pay for offering these payment options. _____
_____

Place (Distribution)

Describe how you sell your products. _____

Describe how consumers receive your products. _____

Describe the management of the distribution system you intend on using. _____
_____

Describe your logistics system, including order fulfillment, warehousing, and transportation needs. _____
_____

Promotion

Describe the company marketing materials that you will use in the promotion of your business, including brochures, CD business cards, and corporate videos. _____
_____

Describe what advertising mediums you will utilize in the promotion of your products or services, including print, broadcast, outdoor, and indoor advertising.
_____
_____

Describe what tactics you will employ in the direct sales of your goods and services, including personal selling, mail, telephone, and electronic.
_____

Describe how you will utilize public relations in the promoting of your goods and services. _____
_____

Describe if you will utilize the Internet in the promoting of your goods and services, including your Web site and online marketing strategies.
_____
_____

FIGURE 12.7 **Marketing Strategy Worksheet**, continued

Describe what type of events you will use to promote your goods and services, including trade shows, seminars, expos, and sponsorships.

_____

_____

Describe what advertising premiums and specialties that you will use in the promotion of your goods and services, such as hats, bags, bumper stickers, and pens emblazoned with your business name and promotional message. _____

_____

_____

MARKETING BUDGET

List and discuss how much it will cost to implement, manage, and maintain each of the marketing activities described in your marketing plan. The obvious question is, "How much should your marketing budget be?" There is only one answer, "How much will it cost to reach your marketing objectives?" Every home business owner will have different marketing objectives, different marketing strategies planned to meet these objectives, and different timetables to reach them.

If you are already in business, you have a bit of an advantage in terms of setting your marketing budgets because you can use previous sales figures as the basis to calculate your marketing budget. For instance, as a simple approach, if your sales last year were $40,000 and your sales objective for this year was $50,000, then you could simply increase your marketing budget by 25 percent over last year's marketing expenditures, which would correspond with the increased sales objective. If your business is new, then you will have to use a ground-up approach; you will have to break down each marketing activity as defined in your marketing strategies by individual cost and add them together to estimate your overall marketing budget. You also may want to consider

FIGURE 12.8 **Marketing Budget Worksheet**

List your main marketing activities and the cost of each, including the source of data used to calculate marketing and promotional costs.

1. _____

2. _____

3. _____

4. _____

5. _____

Describe where the money will come from to cover the costs associated with implementing, managing, and maintaining your marketing activities as described in your marketing strategies.

_____

_____

_____

_____

the use of a break-even analysis. Once you know how much the marketing activity will cost, you can then calculate how many product units or billable service hours will have to be sold to cover, or break even with, the cost of the planned activity. Break-even analysis has a way of bringing orbiting marketing ideas down to earth. Once you see how much you have to sell to break even, the marketing activity may no longer seem like such a great idea after all.

ACTION PLAN

The action plan component of your marketing plan is really nothing more than a big do-to list broken into marketing categories and timetables outlining when each promotional activity will be implemented throughout the calendar year, who will manage the activity, and how results will be measured. If you are already in business, your action plan might also include existing promotional efforts and when these may be expanded, improved, or possibly deleted throughout the year in addition to new promotional activities. Once again, depending on the promotional activities you intend to use to reach you objectives, you may decide for reasons of clarity to develop

individual plans and implementation timetables for each promotional category such as the advertising or media plan, sales plan, direct marketing plan, public relations plan, event marketing plan, and Internet marketing plan. The majority of home business owners will not have to go to such lengths and instead can develop a simple marketing calendar which indicates key dates when promotional activities will be implemented measured for success, and concluded. The marketing calendar should be included in your marketing plan under the action plan section. You may also want to purchase a large wall-mounted calendar that can be written on in erasable marker and outline promotional activities and relevant dates. This type of calendar is especially handy because it enables you to look at the entire year, and not just each week or month.

Measuring Results

Your action plan must also include a measurement section that details how and when you will measure the progress, success, or failure of each promotional activity implemented. By measuring results incrementally, you can make sure that the promotional activity is working and that you are on track to meet

FIGURE 12.9 **Action Plan Worksheet**

Describe how each marketing strategy will be implemented. _____

Outline the timetable for when each marketing strategy will be implemented. _____

Who will implement and manage each marketing strategy as identified in your marketing plan? _____

Describe the measurement systems you will put in place to track the effectiveness of each marketing strategy. _____

Outline the timetable that will be used to measure progress and performance of each marketing strategy. _____

Describe who will implement and manage the measurement system. _____

your marketing and sales objectives. Should you discover that one or more activities are not working, you can make adjustments to improve the performance or eliminate the activity altogether. As to the question, "How long should you wait to measure results?" the answer is not so clear. Some promotional activities may take longer than others to root and produce results, and you do not want to pull the plug too quickly. Your budget will also be a major factor. If marketing money is tight, you certainly cannot afford to waste it on unproductive marketing and promotional activities. At the end of the day, you will have to determine what best suits your needs in terms of measuring results during and after the run of a marketing or promotional activity, but at minimum results should be measured at least quarterly, though monthly is preferred.

SUPPORT DOCUMENTS

The final section of your marketing plan is reserved for supporting documents, such as resumes of the principles, research surveys, market studies, spreadsheets, supplier and vendor agreements, client testimonials, and press clippings. Basically, any documents that can be helpful in supporting the research, forecasts, statements, and information contained within your marketing plan should be included. Supporting documents can be especially helpful if you are going to use your marketing plan as a tool to help secure investment capital to start or grow your business. After reading the executive overview, bankers, accountants, and venture capitalist often go straight to the supporting documents section of the marketing plan to make sure that you have done your homework, that you are committed to the

| FIGURE 12.10 | Support Document Checklist |

Personal Documents

❏ Owners resume   ❏ Partner's resume(s)

❏ Sales agent and contractor resume(s)   ❏ Key personnel resume(s)

Financial Documents

❏ Personal assets statement   ❏ Sales forecasts

❏ Audited financial statement   ❏ Marketing budgets

❏ Break-even analysis   ❏ Commission estimates

Legal Documents

❏ Business registration   ❏ Training or course certificates

❏ Business license   ❏ Insurance coverage

❏ Patents, trademark, or copyright papers ❏ Product and workmanship warranties

Research Documents

❏ Survey results   ❏ Target customer profile

❏ PEST analysis   ❏ SWOT analysis

Miscellaneous Documents

❏ Supplier agreements   ❏ Vendor agreements

❏ Press clippings   ❏ Competitor price lists, etc.

❏ Client testimonials   ❏ Better Business Bureau report project, and that there is real verifiable documentation indicating a great potential to succeed. In short, they want to know that their money is going into the right venture and will be managed by capable individuals.

Depending on the purpose of your marketing plan, you may or may not need to include *copies* of supporting documents in your marketing plan. If you do, use this helpful Support Document Checklist (see Figure 12.10) as a reminder of the documents to be included to support your plan. Don't be afraid to include other supporting documents that are not in this list, but that you feel support your marketing plan. For example, a letter from an experienced and successful businessperson stating that they feel the venture has great potential carries much weight, especially if financing is sought.

RESOURCES

Associations

American Marketing Association (AMA)
311 S. Wacker Drive, Suite 5800
Chicago, IL 60606
(312) 542-9000
www.marketingpower.com

Business Marketing Association (BMA)
400 N. Michigan Avenue, 15th Floor
Chicago, IL 60611
(800) 664-4262
www.marketing.org

Canadian Marketing Association (CMA)
1 Concorde Gate, Suite 607
Don Mills, Ontario M3C 3N6
(416) 391-2362
www.the-cma.org

Marketing Education Association (MEA)
PO Box 27473
Tempe, AZ 85285-7473
(602) 750-6735
www.nationalmea.org

Marketing Research Association (MRA)
PO Box 230
1344 Silas Deane Highway, Suite 306
Rocky Hill, CT 06067-0230

(806) 257-4008
www.mra-net.org

Suggested Reading

Bangs, David H., Jr. *The Market Planning Guide: Creating a Plan to Successfully Market Your Business, Products, or Services, 6th Edition.* Chicago: Dearborn Trade Publishing, 2002.

Beckwith, Harry. *Selling the Invisible: A Field Guide to Modern Marketing.* New York: Warner Books, 1997.

Copper, Scott W., and Roman G. Hiebing Jr. *The Successful Marketing Plan: A Disciplined and Comprehensive Approach.* New York: McGraw-Hill, 2003.

Kennedy, Dan S. *The Ultimate Marketing Plan: Find Your Most Promotable Competitive Edge, Turn It into a Powerful Marketing Message, and Deliver It to the Right Prospect.* Avon, MA: Adams Media Corporation, 2000.

Kotler, Philip. *Marketing Management.* Upper Saddle River, NJ: Prentice Hall, 2002.

Stephenson, James. *The Ultimate Small Business Marketing Guide: 1500 Great Marketing Tricks That Will Drive Your Business Through the Roof!* Irvine, CA: Entrepreneur Press Inc., 2003.

Treacy, Michael, and Fred Wiersema. *The Discipline of Market Leaders: Choose Your Customers, Narrow Your Focus, Dominate Your Market.* Boulder, CO: Perseus Publishing, 1997.

Web Sites

American Demographics Magazine, www.demographics.com: Information and advice about marketing research and demographics.

Entrepreneur Online, www.entrepreneur.com: Small business information products and services portal featuring marketing planning advice and custom Marketing Calculator software.

More Business, www.morebusiness.com: Marketing plan information, advice, and free templates.

MPlans, www.mplans.com: Marketing plan information, advice, templates, and custom software.

Palo Alto Software, www.paloalto.com: Marketing Plan Pro software enables users to create their own marketing plans and strategies.

SBA, www.sba.gov/starting_business/marketing/plan .html: The United States Small Business Administration offers marketing plan information, advice, and samples.

Society for Marketing Professional Services, www.smps.org: Nonprofit association representing professional marketing organizations and consultants. Web site visitors can find information about the services provided by marketing professionals.

U.S. Census Bureau, www.census.gov: Market demographics information and statistics.

CHAPTER 13

Advertising and Promotions

ADVERTISING IS A MEANS OF DELIVERING YOUR sales message to your target audience through various mediums—newspapers, magazines, Yellow Pages, radio, television, promotional fliers, and the Internet. For the majority of home business owners, advertising is necessary to achieve your marketing and business objectives. But at the same time, advertising costs should be viewed as a valuable investment into your business and not merely as a business expense. Of course, the real challenge is to make sure the money that you invest in advertising is money wisely spent, that more times than not your advertising will reach your target audience and they take action. If not, your investment in advertising could end up being a waste of precious business capital.

There are three key points in terms of home business advertising—creating advertising buzz, selling the advertising buzz, and getting the most mileage possible from it. Creating the buzz means that it is your opportunity to be creative and make your advertising sizzle so that it will entice people to purchase. Advertising is one way to separate your business from your competition. You might sell the same or similar goods and services, but often the business that can create the most buzz through advertising and promotional efforts is the business that captures the largest share of the marketplace. Advertising can make your telephone ring but seldom will it sell. That job is left up to you. Being prepared to sell your advertising buzz means that you are armed and ready with the tools, knowledge, and drive needed to turn advertising inquiries into profitable sales. Long before you create and run advertisements, you must have a system and the ambition in place to maximize every single dollar you spend on advertising by turning each new inquiry into a new sale.

Home business owners are almost always strapped for cash in terms of advertising and promoting their businesses. You have to get the most mileage you can every time that you create advertising buzz, and this must carry through your entire advertising campaign. For instance, your Yellow Pages advertisement must feature your Web site address, your radio spots should mention special events such as trade shows and seminars that you participate in, and your glossy magazine ad should be reprinted and used as a promotional brochure. And if you have artwork or copy professionally created, make sure that it is suitable for a wide variety of promotional uses throughout your entire marketing campaign. Doing so greatly increases the value of each advertising and promotional activity, while dramatically reducing advertising and promotional costs over the long term.

ESTABLISHING YOUR ADVERTISING BUDGET

How much do you spend on advertising? The answer will depend on the type of business that you operate, your growth ambitions, and how much money you can afford to spend. However, one thing is certain: You can sell the best products or services available, but if you cannot afford to get your name out there in front of people through advertising and promotional efforts, then chances are you will have to rethink your business strategy or go bust. Some home business operations, such as a yard maintenance service, can be easily marketed through low-cost and no-cost promotions such as flier drops, knocking on doors, or word-of-mouth referrals. Other home businesses specializing in custom or niche products and services may need to spend a considerable amount of money on advertising to reach and grab the attention of their target audience.

Some advertising specialists suggest that 5 percent of your gross sales be used for advertising. But in practical terms, this strategy is far too broad. Much will depend on your business, marketing objectives, and future growth plans. Competition also plays a larger role in determining your advertising budget than you might think. Going head-to-head with competitors trying to capture the lion's share of the marketplace is not cheap and generally requires pouring all profits and often the better part of your own wages back into advertising and promotional actives. Developing an advertising budget requires balancing your business and marketing objectives, deciding what advertising medium is needed to reach your target audience, and determining the amount of money that you can afford to invest in advertising. If you only have $1,000 as an advertising budget to get rolling, in most situations you would be wise to test advertising methods such as low-cost fliers instead of throwing your entire ad budget at one newspaper display ad and hoping (or praying) for the best. Until your business is established and you can begin to test advertising and promotional mediums and activities, you will have to rely on three basic formulas to develop your budget—percentage of estimated sales, keeping pace with competitors, or identifying your objective and creating a budget that ensures you reach it.

TRACKING YOUR ADVERTISING TO GAUGE EFFECTIVENESS

Key to developing a successful advertising program for your home business is tracking your advertising activities so that you can determine the effectiveness

FIGURE 13.1 How Did You Hear about Us? Form

Advertising or Promotional Source	Additional Information
❏ Newspaper or magazine advertisement	_____
❏ Yellow pages of telephone directory	_____
❏ Specialty publications	_____
❏ Television or radio advertising	_____
❏ The Internet or our Web site	_____
❏ Publicity or public speaking engagement	_____
❏ Flier, insert, or door hanger	_____
❏ Contest or special promotional event	_____
❏ Telemarketing or direct mail	_____
❏ Trade show, conference, expo, or seminar	_____
❏ Referred by a customer, friend, or family	_____
❏ Seen a job in progress or service vehicle	_____
❏ Seen promotional or event signage	_____

of each. This is important information because it allows you to allocate your advertising dollars where they have the greatest impact in terms of reaching your target audience and generating the most revenue. Of course, some types of advertising and marketing activities are easier to track than others. For instance, tracking the effectiveness of a coupon drop is much easier than tracking the effectives of television commercials, designed to build brand awareness over a longer period through repetitive exposure. You can use various telephone extensions, have customers ask for a specific person, or give away different special offers or gifts in different advertisements. But perhaps the easiest way to track your advertising and marketing efforts is to simply ask the people that contact you how they heard about your business. You can create a simple How Did You Hear About Us? Form, like the one featured (see Figure 13.1), include only advertising and marketing activities that your business engages in, and complete it every time people call. Over time, you will be able to identify patterns, which enables you to focus your efforts on advertising and marketing activities that are working, while ditching the ones that show poor results.

COOPERATIVE ADVERTISING PROGRAMS

Many corporations, manufacturers, and distributors have in place advertising assistance programs, generally called advertising or marketing cooperatives. These advertising cooperative programs allow the larger corporations to assist their vendors in their advertising endeavors. This is, of course, a mutually beneficial arrangement for both parties. Often all that is required of the small business owners is to ask for help, apply to their suppliers' cooperative advertising program, or to demonstrate by way of a written proposal how both parties will benefit and ultimately realize a return on investment. You will want to appeal to your suppliers and business alliances to assist with the following types of advertising through cooperative programs:

- Newspaper display and classifieds advertising
- Magazine advertising
- Spokesperson programs
- Radio commercials and program sponsorships
- Television commercials and program sponsorships

- Transit advertising campaigns
- Outdoor and indoor specialty advertising
- Yellow Pages and business directories
- Internet and e-advertising activities

But don't stop there. Also tap suppliers for additional business and marketing materials, including:

- Special event signs and displays
- Printed marketing and sales materials, including business cards, brochures, and catalogs
- Advertising specialties like calendars, pens, hats, and notepads
- Contest assistance, including printing and prizes
- Product samples and giveaways
- Educational help, including training and books
- Marketing and business help, advice, and guidance

The National Register Publishing Company publishes an annual Co-Op Advertising Program Source Directory listing hundreds of co-op advertising programs. They can be found online at www.national registerpub.com.

CREATING A MEDIA QUESTIONNIAIRE

If you know what your customers and target audience like to read, which programs they like to watch on television or listen to on the radio, which search engines they use, and which Web sites they visit most often, you can purchase advertising where you know your customers are most likely to be reading, watching, listening, or surfing. This, greatly increases your odds of reaching your intended audience through targeted advertising and spending less in the process. But how do you find this sort of information? There are a few ways, but perhaps the easiest and least costly is to create a simple media questionnaire and ask your current customers, prospects, and people that fit your target customer profile to kindly complete it. Asking existing customers to complete the questionnaire is very straightforward. You can give it to them in person, fax it to them, mail it to them, take advantage of your opt-in list and e-mail to them, or post the questionnaire on your Web site. Getting the questionnaire into the hands of those with whom you have no contact requires a little more innovation. Set up a survey booth in a mall or other high traffic area, and give away a small gift to people who take the time to complete the questionnaire. Or you can hand deliver the questionnaire with a stamped return envelope to homes in your community. A discount coupon redeemable toward the purchase of your products or services is an incentive to get people to respond. Whatever method you use to distribute your questionnaire, if you know what your customers are reading, watching, or listening to, you can create effective target advertising campaigns that stand a greater chance of securing the results you want.

| FIGURE 13.2 | Sample Media Questionnaire |

The following is a detailed sample media questionnaire that you can use as a guideline to create one suitable for your business and advertising objectives. Keep the stuff that you want and delete the rest until you are satisfied that you have created one best suited for your specific needs.

(Print your business name and contact information here.)

We ask that you take a moment to complete the following questionnaire. Your responses
will be used to help us better serve our customers. Thank you.

Optional Information

❏ Mr. ❏ Mrs. ❏ Ms. Name _____

Street Address _____

City _____ State _____ Zip/Postal Code _____

Home Telephone _____ Work _____ Fax _____ E-mail _____

Can we contact you periodically with information and special offers? ❏ Yes ❏ No

Newspapers

Please list any newspapers that you typically read, along with your favorite section. Indicate if you have a subscription.

Newspaper Name _____

	Subscription		Favorite Section
1. _____	❏ Yes ❏ No		_____
2. _____	❏ Yes ❏ No		_____
3. _____	❏ Yes ❏ No		_____
4. _____	❏ Yes ❏ No		_____

Magazines

Please list any magazines that you typically read, and indicate if you have a subscription.

	Magazine Name	Subscription
1.	_____	❏ Yes ❏ No
2.	_____	❏ Yes ❏ No
3.	_____	❏ Yes ❏ No
4.	_____	❏ Yes ❏ No

FIGURE 13.2 **Sample Media Questionnaire,** continued

Special Interest Publications

Please list any special interest publications such as trade journals, newsletters, or reports that you frequently read, and indicate if you have a subscription.

	Publication Name	Subscription
1.	_____	❏ Yes ❏ No
2.	_____	❏ Yes ❏ No
3.	_____	❏ Yes ❏ No
4.	_____	❏ Yes ❏ No

Radio

Please list any radio station that you typically listen to and any favorite programs.

Radio Station Name
Favorite Program

	Radio Station Name	Favorite Program
1.	_____	_____
2.	_____	_____
3.	_____	_____
4.	_____	_____

Where do you typically listen to the radio? (Check all that apply.)

❏ Home   ❏ Car   ❏ Office

What time of the day would you typically be listening to the radio? (Check all that apply.)

❏ 6:00 A.M.–9:00 A.M.   ❏ 9:00 A.M.–12:00 Noon   ❏ 12:00 Noon–3:00 P.M.

❏ 3:00 P.M.–6:00 P.M.   ❏ 6:00 P.M.–9:00 P.M.   ❏ After 9:00 P.M.

Television

Please list any television stations that you typically watch and any specific programs that you try not to miss.

	Television Station Name	Favorite Program
1.	_____	_____
2.	_____	_____
3.	_____	_____
4.	_____	_____

What time of day do you typically watch television? (Check all that apply)

❏ 6:00 A.M.–9:00 A.M.   ❏ 9:00 A.M.–12:00 Noon   ❏ 12:00 Noon–3:00 P.M.

❏ 3:00 P.M.–6:00 P.M.   ❏ 6:00 P.M.–9:00 P.M.   ❏ After 9:00 P.M.

FIGURE 13.2   Sample Media Questionnaire, continued

Which local news programs do you watch and at which times?

	Program	Station	Time
1.	_____	_____	❏ A.M. ❏ Noon ❏ P.M. ❏ Late Night
2.	_____	_____	❏ A.M. ❏ Noon ❏ P.M. ❏ Late Night
3.	_____	_____	❏ A.M. ❏ Noon ❏ P.M. ❏ Late Night
4.	_____	_____	❏ A.M. ❏ Noon ❏ P.M. ❏ Late Night

Please list any specialty news programs that you watch.

1. _____

2. _____

3. _____

4. _____

Internet

Are you currently connected to the Internet?   @ Work ❏ Yes ❏ No   @ Home ❏ Yes ❏ No

Which search engine do you most commonly use to find information, products, and services?

❏ AOL   ❏ Google   ❏ Yahoo!   ❏ MSN   ❏ AltaVista

❏ Other _____

Do you receive or subscribe to any online or electronic publications? If so, please list.

E-Publication Name

Web Site URL

	E-Publication Name	Web Site URL
1.	_____	_____
2.	_____	_____
3.	_____	_____
4.	_____	_____

What is the most common type of Web site you visit?

❏ General News   ❏ Financial News   ❏ Sports

❏ Shopping   ❏ Entertainment   ❏ Travel

❏ Other _____

Which Web sites do you visit the most? Please list their name and URL.

	Web Site Name	Web Site URL
1.	_____	_____
2.	_____	_____
3.	_____	_____
4.	_____	_____

FIGURE 13.2   Sample Media Questionnaire, continued

General Questions

What types of advertising medium have the most influence on your buying decisions or habits?

❑ Newspaper   ❑ Magazine   ❑ Radio   ❑ Internet

❑ Television   ❑ Direct Mail   ❑ Live Demonstration

❑ Other _____

Have you ever purchased a product through a mail or e-mail offer?   ❑ Yes   ❑ No

Do you belong to any shopping clubs, such as a music club or book club? (Please specify.)

_____

_____

_____

_____

Do you receive any product catalogs, and if so, which ones?

_____

_____

_____

Do you clip and redeem coupons and special offers from newspapers and magazines?

❑ Always   ❑ Sometimes   ❑ Rarely   ❑ Never

What do you do with the advertisements that you receive in the mail?

❑ Read and save   ❑ Read and trash   ❑ Straight to the recycling without reading

❑ Other _____

Thank you for your cooperation. We appreciate your help.

CREATING GREAT ADVERTISING COPY

Having the ability to create clever and convincing advertising copy extends beyond print, broadcast, and electronic advertising and into all areas of your home business operation. Great copy that is informative and sells your goods or services is also needed in your business communications, printed fliers, proposals and presentations, catalogs, newsletters, and Web site content. At the core of creating great copy is the time-tested AIDA advertising formula—attention, interest, desire, and action. Your copy must grab the attention of your target audience, create interest in what you have to say, build desire for what

you have to sell, and compel people to take action and buy or contact you for further information.

Creating great copy takes practice. Few have the ability naturally so don't fret if you find yourself with writer's block when it comes time to produce that great advertisement or convincing sales letter. Instead, buy books on the subject of writing copy for advertising and business communications and continue to hone your skills over time and through trial and error until you will find the right combination of words and phrases that get the results you want. Later in this section you will find some helpful information and ideas about how to create copy that gets results. Whenever you create advertisements, sales and marketing materials, presentations, simple fliers, or any other type of promotional material for your business, make sure to examine carefully what you are saying and how the message is being delivered so that you do not inadvertently offend some people. Skip stereotypes like the pennywise Scotsman cartoon used to depict a big sale, and instead of gender-specific terms like *he* or *she* use generic terms like *people* or *person* unless the product is specifically aimed at one gender. Also avoid any references to religious and political views and opinions. Great copy is more difficult to write than most people think. You have to take into account many people in terms of perception, feelings, and values. If you feel that your advertising or promotional copy might offend just one person, don't bother using it. Find a word, phrase, picture, or illustration that you know won't offend anybody.

Powerful Headlines Styles

In terms of writing good advertising copy, the headline is king because you only have a brief moment to grab the readers' attention and pull them into your message. This is also true of other printed marketing materials such as newsletters, sales presentations, sales letters, and promotional fliers. There are a few powerful headline styles that when used correctly can explode responses to ads and promotional materials.

How-To Headlines

One of the best headlines to use in advertising is a How-to, which can deliver a powerful, beneficial, and clear message in few words when crafted correctly. For instance, a financial planner might create a headline that reads, "New Seminar Reveals How to Retire a Millionaire!" How-to headlines deliver the message efficiently, have dream appeal or solve a problem, and speak directly to the intended audience.

Promise Headlines

Stating a promise in your headline such as "Nobody beats our low prices, guaranteed" is another powerful way of grabbing the readers' attention and pulling them into your materials. Of course, the promise that you make will be directly related to what you sell and to your advertising and marketing objectives. The best headline promises are ones that specifically solve a problem or meet the needs of your target audience.

Question Headlines

Headlines that ask readers a question are also a popular method of capturing attention and drawing them into your message. "Would you like to lose ten pounds before summer?" This question headline would grab the attention of anyone wishing to shed a few pounds and compel them to read further to find out more.

News Headlines

Creating headlines to look and read like news also works well in speaking directly to readers. For instance, a house painting service might create a headline for a newspaper ad that reads "Local Painting Contractor Helps to Lower the Unemployment Rate," followed by an advertisement informing readers that because of their quality painting at reasonable costs they have hired more painters to keep up with referral business from satisfied customers. What makes news headlines so effective is that they stand out from the mass of advertisements. Many people are immune to advertisements, skipping right past to the real news stories. By disguising an advertisement as news, you often stand a better chance of getting a reader's attention.

Photographs and Illustrations

Second to a powerful attention-grabbing headline is a visually descriptive photograph or illustration in your advertisements and printed business communications. In terms of advertising effectiveness, the old adage that a photograph is worth a thousand words is true. Photographs have the unique ability to showcase the best qualities of your product or service without saying a word. Include photographs of the products you sell or the services that you provide in your advertisements and marketing materials, as well as photographs of you. Both will go a long way to help brand your business and build consumer awareness within your target audience. Photographs and illustrations need not be expensive. If you or a friend is good with a camera, there is no reason not to create your own photograph for your copy. You can also go online to find free or inexpensive stock photographs and illustrations. There are numerous stock photography services on the Internet offering a wide variety of photographic images at low user fees or in some cases free of charge. Index Stock is one such service. It can be found online at www.indexstock.com. Another is 1 Stop Stock, found online at www.1stopstock.com.

Developing a Single Clear Message

A common denominator that all great advertising and marketing copy share is a clear and singular message that is presented in a simplistic and straightforward manner. Keep your copy short, to the point, and focused on your headline and main selling message. If your main selling message is quality, this theme should be continued throughout. This message is referred to as your unique selling proposition (USP), your statement about why people should buy what you are selling instead of what the competition is selling.

The image or brand you create needs to be consistent, through design, look, tone, consumer benefit, and, once again, message. The reason that brands must be consistent is that they take a long time to build, maintain, and evolve. This combined consistency is what builds consumer awareness of your brand. This is what makes consumers think of your particular business, service, or product when they have a specific need that is relevant to what you do or sell.

Listing prices in advertisements is not always the best course of action unless you have major pricing information or discounts to reveal. Pricing issues can become very complex, thus destroying the first rule of great copy—keep it simple stupid. In general, a 10, 20, or even a 30 percent discount no longer wows consumers when 50-percent-off sales are commonplace. This is especially true for home business owners who cannot afford to get into pricing wars or contests with larger competitors. Instead, keep focused on reaching your primary audience

with your message on what makes your business unique in the marketplace and how people benefit by doing business with you.

Appealing to Your Target Audience

Clever advertising copy also appeals to people on an emotional level. It uses emotional triggers, basic human feelings such as the need for friendship, the need for security, and the need to achieve. The goal is to combine one or more emotional triggers with copy that is relevant and supports what you sell. For instance, a financial planner might use a photograph of two youthful, healthy, happy baby boomers standing beside their dream beach home to depict the benefits of professional financial planning services. Figure out what emotional trigger is best suited for your goods or services and then build a unique selling message around that need.

Also keep in mind the reasons that your target audience buys. These reasons are called consumer drivers and include shopping based on convenience, buying image, purchasing on low price, buying quality, or seeking out the best service, regardless of the rest. Your copy must single out and talk directly to your target audience in the same way that they would think and act. That is what great copy does. While reaching the masses, it makes everyone in your target audience feel as though you are talking to them directly as an individual.

Asking for the Sale

The final, and arguably most important aspect of creating great copy is to always ask for the sale. You can have the best attention-grabbing headline, super visually descriptive photographs, a wow sales pitch, and an unbeatable offer, and all of it will be for nothing unless you ask your audience to buy, give compelling reasons to do so, and provide the tools for them to take action. To motivate people to take the desired course of action, you can build a sense of urgency into your copy and special offers with the use of an ordering deadline, limited supply, or a special promotion discount. Or, you can boost the appeal of your offer with tactics such as extended warranty offers, free delivery or some other freebie, a price discount, or value-added techniques such as two-for-ones and upgrades-at-no-cost. Remember, regardless of medium, all great copy asks for the sale. Never assume that your reader will know what to do next. Tell them what you want them to do next and give them the tools and motivation they need to take action.

NEWSPAPER ADVERTISING

Most business owners feel compelled to purchased advertising in newspapers because that is what other business owners do. Don't play follow the leader. Instead, purchase newspaper advertising based on your marketing plan, advertising budget, and the publication's ability to reach your target audience. Never let yourself be lured in by advertising sales reps that talk huge circulation numbers, critical placement promises, and frequency discounts to entice you to advertise. Only advertise because you have done your research and the potential benefits outweigh the potential disadvantages of not advertising. More information about display and classified advertising is featured under those heading in this section.

To locate newspapers, magazines, and specialty publications for advertising purposes, you can visit News Link, on line at www.newslink.org. News Link publishes an online directory listing publications from the Untied States, Canada, Mexico, and Central and South America, which are indexed geographically and by type of newspaper. News Directory offers a similar online publication listing service, and it can be found on line at www.newsdirectory.com. Both services can be used free of charge.

Display Advertising

For the majority of home business owners, display advertising in national and regional newspapers is not effective. In the first place, large display ads tend to be very expensive and placing ads occasionally because of a limited budget does not work. Generally, outside of special sales or promotional events, you need repetition in order to build long-term beneficial awareness of your business, products,

or service. Also, most newspapers, regardless of size, are crammed with display advertisements. That leaves the advertiser fighting with hundreds of other ads to capture the readers' attention. And because of the vast number of ads, many readers have become numb to them and take no notice. Another important reason most display ads do not work is that they are poorly created lacking a powerful headline, competitive advantage, main selling benefit, and call to action. Finally, advertising in the wrong publication and thus not reaching the target audience is perhaps the number-one reason why most newspaper display advertising is highly ineffective.

Display advertising can work, but there are certain steps to follow, starting with getting the media kit or card for newspapers you are considering. The media kit will tell you all about the newspaper' readership base, who they are, where they come from, what they do for a living, their level of education, and how much money they make. That information can then be used to determine if the newspaper's target audience is your target audience. If not, move on until you find a match. There is no sense advertising in a newspaper if the majority of readers have no need or desire for what you have to sell.

Home business owners that sell products can greatly increase the effectiveness of their display ads by using powerful attention-grabbing headlines and by giving people a reason to take action and contact you. Use the words *free*, *sales*, and *special offer* to entice people to pay attention and take action. Likewise, service providers can use the same tactics, mentioning *free quotes* or *free estimates*, and running their advertisements in the Services section much like the Yellow Pages people go to the Services section specifically looking for a service provider.

Of course, once you find one or more newspapers you feel meets your advertising needs, you do not want to pay full price for the ad space. Negotiate every time. Start off by offering 30 percent less than the ad card rate, and never settle for anything less than a 10 percent discount. Here are a few other ways to reduce the cost of display advertising.

- *Frequency discounts.* Once you have tested a few publications and find one that is getting the desired results, tell the sales rep that you'll sign up for a year's worth of advertising if you can have a frequency discount. Depending on the publication and the length of advertising term to which you are prepared to commit, frequency discounts can cut your display advertising costs by as much as 75 percent.

- *Soft periods.* Just about every publication, including national and regional newspapers, have soft periods when their advertising sales are the lowest for the year. This is the time of year when publishers tell their sales reps to make deals, which can save you a substantial amount of money on your advertising. Soft periods vary from publication to publication, depending on their target audience or the market they serve. However, be careful when buying advertising in soft periods, even at deeply discounted rates, because there is generally a smaller readership then.

- *Free flag advertisement.* Insist that you receive a free flag advertisement every time that you purchase and run a display ad because that can greatly increase the odds of your display advertisements being seen and read. A flag advertisement is nothing more than a small two-or three-line advertisement, generally located in the Classifieds section of the publication. The purpose of the flag ad is to grab the readers' attention and direct them to your larger display advertisement for further details and information. For instance your free flag ad might state, "Get free carpet cleaning from Jim's Carpet Cleaning. See our big ad in today's Real Estate section."

Classified Advertising

Classified advertising is unquestionably home business owner friendly because it is easy to create and cheap to run. And they also almost always have a higher response rate than display advertisements per dollar spent because people generally read the Classifieds looking for a specific product or service and they are ready to buy. This is good news. It enables you to sell your goods aggressively because readers expect these types of ads. Write short, powerful copy that sells, create urgency by stating a

deadline or limited availability, appeal to a basic human emotion like need, love, family, or friendship, and most importantly list the main benefit that a person receives by buying your products. And write an attention-grabbing headline that jumps off the page and pay a few extra dollars to have it placed in bold type, flagged with an icon, or surrounded by a border. Also, give some thought to the type of publication and the Classified heading or section under which your advertisement will appear. Pick publications that are read by your target audience, and choose a section that your target audience is most likely to read. Because classified advertisements are cheap and quick to post, continually look for ways to improve your results by testing new ads in various publications read by your target audience. Test your headline, your main sales message, and your special offers on a regular basis. However, once you find an advertisement and publication that is pulling the desired response and sales, repeat it over and over. Repetition is one of the main ingredients of successful advertising.

MAGAZINE ADVERTISING

Magazines ads have a definite edge over many other types of advertising: They have a tendency to be around for a while—on a desk, in the waiting room, in the lunchroom, or on the coffee table. Because magazines have a longer user shelf life than newspapers, newsletters, coupons, and fliers, the advertisements also tend to be seen by the same reader more than once. In fact, most advertising gurus will tell you that next to radio, magazine advertising offers small business owners the best opportunity to reach a very select target audience in a relativity cost efficient manner. However, unlike classified advertisements and direct coupons, you cannot expect immediate results from magazine advertisements. It takes continuous and consistent exposure to your target audience before results will begin to surface. Therefore, you must be patient and not too quick to pull the *advertising plug* if the telephone doesn't start ringing the day after the magazine hits newsstands.

Otherwise, magazine advertising is like any other form of advertising. There are insider secrets that you should be aware of to help you get the most advertising bang for your money. One such insider secret is to call magazines you are considering and ask that they mail or e-mail you their editorial calendar. An editorial calendar is a schedule of forthcoming special issues that will be featured in the magazine. The value of having the magazine's editorial calendar is that it enables you to better target your advertising related to these special issues, as well as potentially having a story related to your business featured.

For instance, if you operate a ocean kayak tour business and an outdoor recreational magazine is featuring a special feature on kayak touring in a forthcoming issue, you can contact the magazine and offer to submit an article about ocean kayak touring and your business. Or you can offer to be interviewed about ocean kayak tours or for your expertise on the subject and tell the magazine that you will purchase a full-page advertisement in the same issue as an incentive for accepting your feature article or interview. In this example, the benefit of having the editorial calendar for this particular magazine is twofold. First, you can place your advertisement when the magazine will be covering information specific to your business, thereby reaching your target audience—in this case people that are interested in ocean kayaking. Second, there is the potential for the magazine to interview you because of your expertise relative to the topic, or for it to accept and publish your feature article in exchange for an advertising commitment. These types of mutually beneficial arrangements are not uncommon because the magazine needs both information of interest to the intended audience and advertising revenues in order to create and deliver the product to its audience.

Reaching Your Target Audience

Magazines are unquestionably one of the best advertising mediums for reaching a specific audience because magazines have a tendency to cater to one specific portion of the population, based on geographic, demographic, and psychographic profiling, or a combination of market segmenting. The first place to find out more about a magazine's particular target audience is through the publisher's media kit or fact sheet. In the kit you will find information about who reads the magazine, how many subscribers, the subscriber's average income, their hobbies, education, and income levels. Magazine publishers go to great lengths to compile information about their readers because this is the crucial data that sells advertising space. Not features or articles, not editorials, not glossy photographs, and certainly not the joke of the month, just facts and figures about their readers. Therefore, before jumping in and signing up for a year's worth of full-page magazine ads, carefully research the publication's readership to determine if these people meet your target or primary audience requirements. To locate magazines and other publications that cater to a specific audience, you can check out Pub List online at www.publist.com. Pub List is a directory that lists in excess of 150,000 domestic and international print and electronic publications, including magazines, journals, e-journals, and newsletters.

Designing the Right Magazine Advertisement

If you have professionally designed artwork that you use in other areas of your business, this can easily be incorporated into your magazine advertisement. But if you do not it is best to have a professional design your ad due to the relatively high cost of the advertising. The first place to start looking for a design pro is through the magazine sales representative. Most magazine publishers have in-house design and copy editors that have a great deal of experience in crafting some very elaborate and clever ads for clients. Small publishers that do not offer this service certainly will be able to refer you to a trusted local source. But, regardless of who designs your advertisement, insist that you own the copyright and get this in writing. You do not want to pay a royalty every time you use the artwork for other advertising or promotional reasons.

Unlike newspaper or even radio, magazine advertising requires planning well in advance of the publication date. Actually, have your advertisements ready to go at all times and keep a list of cut-off advertisement commitment dates for magazines that you would like to advertise in close by. On the day of the cut-off date, call a sales rep or the publisher and ask about availability of ad space. Often you can negotiate as much as a 50 percent discount for last minute ad insertions. I stress that you have to have everything in terms of your advertisement ready to go in a package that can be couriered or e-mailed to the publisher as soon as you hang up the telephone.

Whenever you run a key or important full-page and full-color advertisement in a magazine or specialty publication, make sure to order a lot of reprints of the advertisement from the publisher. Reprints are like a full-color brochure, but available at a fraction of the cost of designing and printing a full-color brochure. The ad reprints can be used for in wide variety of marketing activities. Include a reprint in all of your mailings, invoices, sales letters, newsletters, letters to the editor, and any other type of mail or business correspondence you send out. You can also use reprints of full-page ads in sales presentations or as promotional handouts at seminars, trade shows, and networking meetings. Once again, the idea at work here is that if you have created a great looking advertisement and have paid for it, why let it stop producing results for you just because the publication is no longer current? Right, you shouldn't. Instead, stock up on reprints and get the most promotional mileage you can from great looking advertisements.

Advertisement Size, Position, and Frequency

There is much debate about which size advertisement is the best: full-page, half-page, third-page, quarter-page, and so forth. All have their pros and cons. Full-page advertisements can be costly, on the flip side you get great exposure. While quarter page ads are much cheaper, but they are often featured near the back of the magazine with one or more other advertisements on the same page.

If full-page ads are not in your budget, you can try two different tactics to increase the exposure of your smaller advertisement. The first tactic is to negotiate for a second ad of the same size to run in the same magazine and issue. Often a second ad discount can be substantial, in the range of 40 percent or greater. The benefit of this tactic is that it doubles the odds of your advertisement being seen and read by readers, while still costing much less than a full-page

advertisement. The second tactic is to try to negotiate a specific position within the magazine, preferably beside a regular column or feature. Readers will be exposed to your ad for a longer time while they read the feature or column.

Frequency refers to the number of times that your target audience is exposed to your advertisement, that is, how many times you advertise in the same magazine. Most advertising experts agree there should be a minimum of three times, but preferably six to twelve times concurrently, for an ad to have real impact for your business.

Card Decks

The vast majority of card deck advertising opportunities are provided by magazine and report publishers that mail advertising card decks to their subscribers, generally three times per year, though some offer these services more or less frequently. The typical card deck will feature 10 to 100 advertising cards, which are mailed to prospects wrapped in plastic. Because card decks are small, approximately 3- x 5-inch, there is not a lot of space for copy, product descriptions, or photographs and illustrations. Clever copy skills and a bold attention-grabbing headline will be required. A few card deck services offer different sizes and styles, such as folding cards, but most are standard sizes and printed in black and white or limited colors.

The key to success with card deck advertising lies in your ability to reach your target market. So great importance must be paid to who is receiving the card decks. A good source of information about market segmentation by lifestyle, geographic locations, demographics, and psychographics is the *Standard Rate and Data Service Sourcebook*. A print and electronic version of this book, published by SRDS Media Solutions Inc., is available online at www.srds.com.

The costs associated with card deck advertising programs vary greatly from a low of about $15 per thousand mailed to a high of $75 per thousand mailed plus the cost of return postage and ad design. Response rates also greatly vary. Studies have shown that card deck advertisements that offer money back guarantees, free trial periods, and special incentives receive a much higher response rate than those that do not.

You will want to concentrate your ad copy on selling the offer or the incentive to respond and not on the product that you are trying to sell. The objective is to get readers to respond so that you can increase your selling opportunities, and the best way to accomplish this is with a powerful incentive or offer to motivate readers to respond. Make it clear on the card that you want people to respond with step-by-step instructions. "To receive your free gift and our valuable report, check this box and drop it in the mail. It's just that easy." Never ask people to work or spend money in order to respond. Always use postage paid business reply cards, and do not rely on prospects sending your card back. Include other ways that prospects can contact you, a toll free telephone number, e-mail address, and Web site URL and make sure these are printed on the card. Finally, if you are currently running display or classified ads in a particular magazine, call to find out if they have a card deck program in place. If they do, it may be well worth getting involved because readers have already been exposed to your ads, business, products, or services in print, which can add credibility when it comes time to respond to your card deck offer.

YELLOW PAGES ADVERTISING

Not every home business needs to advertise in the Yellow Pages, especially when you consider that full-page ads can cost $1,000 per month, or more depending on the market. But, if you're in the business of providing services, you may find that advertising in the Yellow Pages is the only source of advertising and new business generation you need. Without question, some service providers need to advertise in the Yellow Pages in a big way, especially service providers that fix emergency problems such as a leaky roof, a burst plumbing pipe, or a serious pest problem. In fact, depending on your situation you might need to take out full-page advertisements in numerous Yellow Page editions in your market area.

The next level of service providers such as house painters, cleaning services, landscapers and yard maintenance, Web site designers, and theft prevention consultants can benefit from being in the Yellow

Pages, yet they all have other advertising options available that can generate equally good results. Some home businesses, such as art consulting are so highly specialized that Yellow Pages advertising will be of little benefit, and their monies should be spent on advertising and promotional activities guaranteed to deliver better results. Most home business owners will have to weigh factors such as budget, priorities, and ability to reach the target market when determining if Yellow Pages advertising is right for their specific advertising needs.

Due to the high cost of Yellow Pages advertising and inability to alter your advertisement for one year after it is published, consider hiring an independent Yellow Pages advertising consultant to help to design and coordinate your advertising campaign. Yellow Pages Blues, which can be found online at www.yellowpagesblues.com, is one. A second is Yellow Pages Profits, which can be found online at www.yellowpagesprofits.com.

Tips for Creating a Great Yellow Pages Advertisement

The Yellow Pages advertisement that you create and run is the image that you want your business to project. Therefore your ad must represent the best qualities and most superior advantages that your business has to offer customers. Design your advertisement from your customers' perspective: Why do they do business with you, and what do they like best about your business, products, or services? Your answers should be incorporated into your Yellow Pages advertisement so that it will speak directly to and appeal to the majority of your target audience. The following are more great tips for creating high-impact and effective Yellow Pages advertisements.

- Statistically speaking, size matters. The larger your ad is, the more people that you can expect to call. So if you have decided to make the Yellow Pages one of your main advertising mediums, buy the biggest, boldest advertisement you can afford. Of course, a larger ad means you can fit more information in the ad, generally implies your business is successful, and positions you closer to the beginning of each new alphabetical heading, ahead of competitors with smaller advertisements.

- Motivate people to contact you by using phrases like, "Call now for a free estimate." And give them lots of ways to contact you with a boldly displayed main telephone number, toll-free calling option, fax number, cellular telephone number, e-mail and Web site addresses, and after-hours contact information. The purpose of Yellow Pages advertising is to motivate people to call you, not to build brand awareness through long-term repeated exposure to your ad. People do not read the Yellow Pages for entertainment, they read it to find specific products and services that they need and want to buy. But keep in mind that even though Yellow Pages advertising will make your telephone ring, it is still up to you to make the sale. Therefore, always be ready to make a great first impression and sell your advertising by providing the best products and services delivered with exceptional customer service and follow-up.

- Yellow Pages display advertising is one of the rare advertising occasions when you want to list as much information as possible. List what you sell including specific brands; all of the services you provide, including specialized services or authorized services; all the ways that people can pay including credit cards and financing options; credentials and special training that you have; and special information such as liability insurance coverage, bonding, special certificates or permits, and professional association memberships. The more compelling reasons you can give people to call you instead of the competition, the more people will choose to do so.

- Focus on your company's greatest strengths, emphasizing the benefits of your products and services. What need does your product or service fulfill for customers? Spell out your biggest benefits in no uncertain terms. What is your competitive advantage? Is it best quality? Is it convenient 24-hour service? Is it lowest prices, guaranteed? Or are you the most qualified to handle the job in the area? Regardless of what

your competitive advantage is, it must be included in your ad and stand out like a beacon leading people to your ad in the fog of competitor's ads.

- Keep your advertisement consistent with your business image and the rest of your advertising and marketing activities. Use your logo, consistent fonts and colors, sales message, and, if you are known for a specialty, make sure your specialty is a main feature. Research has also shown that ads with photographs or illustrations greatly out perform ads without. A picture really works in describing what products and services that you sell.

RADIO ADVERTISING

One of the key advantages of radio advertising over other types of advertising is that radio has the ability to speak to your target audience on a more intimate basis, usually one-on-one, in their cars, at the office, or at home. For that reason, radio has long been a favorite advertising medium for small business owners and marketers. Still, that said the key to successful radio advertising is repetition. In radio advertising terms, repetition is referred to as *frequency*, the number of times the audience is exposed to your broadcasted message. If you choose to use radio to advertise your business, you must commit to the program for a minimum of three months to realize any benefits. Radio ads do not have the ability to create a need for a product or service, unlike live or televised demonstrations or infomercials, thus the importance of repetition. Through repeated exposure to your message, when a need for a particular product or service arises, your business will be on the prospect's mind.

Another big consideration is placement. Ideally, you will want to have the same time slot day in, day out. Most marketers find the morning 6 A.M. to 10 A.M., or afternoon 3 P.M. to 7 P.M. drive slots are the best. You should be consistent in the delivery of your message and stay focused on a central theme, like the video store that counts down the top five movie rentals or the restaurant that reads the daily lunch special.

If you are considering creating your own radio advertisement, make sure that you check with the stations first because some will include the cost of producing a simple radio spot if you sign up for a minimum 13-week contract. Also, negotiate to get one of their more popular disk jockeys, program hosts, or on-air personalities to record the ad or read it live.

If you sell products globally, don't overlook Internet radio stations as a potential vehicle for advertising your goods. Internet radio advertising costs only a fraction of traditional radio, and stations are popping up all over the Web as the popularity of listening to online radio continues to increase, especially for people working in offices who keep their computers tuned to Web casts from around the country. Radio Tower, www.radiotower. com, and Virtual Tuner, www.virtualtuner.com, are two online directories listing more than 10,000 Internet radio and television stations.

Even if you decide that traditional radio commercials and Internet radio is too costly and not right for you there are still other advertising opportunities available beyond standard radio commercials—segment sponsorships and live or call-in guest opportunities.

Making Radio Work for You

Two important things should be kept in mind in radio advertising. You are always buying the audience, never the station, regardless of what sales reps might have you believe. You need to make sure to match the image you want to project for your business to the appropriate radio station.

Once again, keep in mind your target audience. If your target audience is mature folks, try talk radio and easy listening formats. If your target audience is teens, urban and pop stations will be a wise choice. If you are not effectively reaching your target audience, your ads will simply not be productive, regardless of how frequently they are broadcast. Wise entrepreneurs have also discovered that using radio advertisements to support other advertising and marketing activities greatly increases the effectiveness of each. Cross promotions would be "Drop by our booth at the auto show. Visit our Web site today. See our full-page advertisement in this Friday's newspaper."

When writing copy for your radio ads you have to think and create visually. You must paint an exact visual portrait of what your product looks like, how it works, and how people will benefit, so listeners can fully understand and appreciate what you have to sell. Purchase 30-second commercial spots over 15. The latter seldom allows enough time to create a lasting and memorable message. Thirty seconds will enable you to get across about 50 to 75 words comfortably, along with a simple jingle or memorable audio hook.

Radio jingles work extremely well in making your business memorable to the listening audience. In fact, great jingles can transcend time. Many of us still remember advertising jingles we heard 10, 20, and even 30 years ago. Radio jingles do not have to be expensive to write, produce, and record, especially if you enlist the services of local talent seeking to build a resume or body of work references.

Finally, radio audiences are extremely loyal to their favorite stations, on-air personalities, and on-air programs. Therefore, once you have identified you're target audience and the station and programs they listen to, stick with that station, time slot, and program like glue. You want these listeners to feel the same loyalty to your brand, and through repeated exposure to your marketing message, this will begin to happen.

FINDING YOUR PLACE ON TELEVISION

It will come as no surprise to readers that television viewing has the highest participation numbers of any entertainment and information medium, including listening to the radio, surfing the Web, or reading the newspaper. On average, North Americans now spend more than 30 hours per week glued to the tube, which is only slightly less than the average amount of time people spend working each week. As a result, television has a very broad reach, crossing all demographics and greatly influencing consumer buying habits and trends.

Before you rush out and get a second mortgage on the house to finance the production of a lavish television commercial, you should also be made aware of the fact that television advertising is certainly not a suitable marketing vehicle for the majority of home business owners. It is far too costly for the average home business owner to have a television commercial produced and regularly aired in a way that reaches mass audiences. This is certainly not to say that home business owners are precluded from television advertising, especially those that want to reach a smaller audience within specific regional markets.

The introduction of specialty cable channels has increased competition on the airways, which in turn has forced broadcasters to be inventive and create new low-cost, yet effective, advertising opportunities that will appeal to business people and marketers with small advertising budgets. These new advertising opportunities include news ticker and full program or segment sponsorships, which generally means the sponsoring business's logo and name will be seen on screen in static billboard fashion or that an on-air personality will read a sponsor's message, ideally both. Another opportunity includes the airing of 15- or 30-second active spots on programs that are produced locally by the broadcaster or by cable distributors. The cost to air commercials on locally produced television is generally a fraction of what the networks charge. Home business owners also have the potential to get their names and products on television through cooperative television advertising.

Ask suppliers if they have any pre-produced television commercials that can be broadcast in your local area with the addition of your business name and sales message tagged on or overlaid onto the commercial. The majority of these television commercials will fall under manufacturer's or supplier's cooperative advertising programs, and generally you must pay for a portion of the associated costs to air the commercial in your local markets. While the reduced costs of pre-produced cooperative advertisements are attractive, the downside is that these commercials usually are not best suited for branding your business, one of the key objectives of any good television advertising campaign. Of course, if you feel that television commercials are the best venue for showcasing your product's or service's unique benefits and will be the most effective and cost-efficient way to reach your target audience, make sure you create powerful television commercials.

Grab the Attention of Your Target Audience

Television is like any other form of advertising: You have but a precious moment to grab the viewers' attention and pull them into your story. There are various ways to grab attention, and much depends on your marketing objectives and the image that you want to project. However, as a rule of thumb, the best way to grab the attention of your target audience is to deliver a combined visual and audio message that makes your target audience feel as though they are being singled out and spoken to directly as individuals. You must identify what your target audience needs and then deliver solutions or benefits directly related to their specific needs. Scream out that you have the right, and perhaps the only solution available to fill their specific needs. Give them the tools to contact you and a compelling reason why they should contact you right away and not next week, next month, or a year from now. The true power of an active visual medium like television is that it allows you to fully demonstrate the benefits associated with your products, an advantage that other forms of advertising do not have.

Branding Is Vital for Long-Term Positive Impact

Mercedes automobiles are synonymous with quality and prestige, while Ford automobiles are known for providing families with reliable and safe transportation at a reasonable cost. Both companies manufacture automobiles, but are dramatically different in consumer perceptions and the image they project. Branding is the foundation of all marketing and should be consistently delivered in all promotional and advertising activities, including television commercials. If you are known for low prices, your commercial should deliver that message. If you are known for fast service, once again that should be the focus of your television advertisement. Branding also means that the look of your business and products remains constant in all advertising—the same corporate colors, the same logo, the same sales and benefits message. You want to project this consistent brand image in your television ad and make sure that your brand always remains on the screen via signage, logo overlay, uniforms, banners, music, and props. This does not mean you cannot change the look of your television commercial; you can. But your commercials must remain consistent with your overall business image. Unique advertising hooks and ideas work, but avoid creating commercials around current fads. Production costs are steep, and you do not want to have to create new commercials as fads fizzle, which they do.

Appeal to Emotional Triggers

Key to the success of many well-known television commercials is their ability to appeal to the emotional triggers of their target audience. Emotional triggers are numerous and include feelings such as the need for physical and financial security, the need to achieve and lead, the need to learn, and the need for friendship and love. Long distance telephone carriers produce and air television commercials that show loving parents talking to kids away at college or relatives far away at Christmas. Home security companies show the unsuccessful burglar running away as the home alarm blares. Financial planners show young looking and active retired people frolicking on the beach without a worry, financial or otherwise. In these examples, the television commercial is appealing to emotional triggers of their intended target audience, the need for family, the need for physical security, and the need for financial security in our golden years. Analyze your product or service to determine which emotional triggers that will appeal to your target audience and develop your commercial around these emotional triggers.

DIRECT MAIL

Direct mail is most commonly associated with mail order sales. However, direct mail is really a catchall phrase covering numerous advertising and promotional materials, such as sales letters, postcards, catalogs, newsletters, simple fliers and brochures, and product sample packs. The purpose of sending these items to a targeted audience via the mail is generally to sell a product or service, but direct mail campaigns can also be used to fill other business and marketing objectives, such as research surveys, satisfaction polls, special company announcements, or holiday greetings. Still, the vast majority of small business owners use direct mail for advertising and promoting products, services, and special offers. One of the main benefits of a direct mail campaign is that unlike other advertising methods such as radio or television results are often swift, within weeks, if not days. Not every home business owner will benefit from developing, implementing, and maintaining a direct mail advertising and promotion program. It can be very costly on a per contact basis, and not all products and services are suitable candidates for marketing via direct mail. But for marketers of products or services that fill a specific niche in the marketplace direct mail can be an extremely effective method. Often products that sell best when direct mail marketed share a few of the following characteristics:

- They are unique, interesting, and not readily available in the marketplace.
- They are easy and inexpensive to pack and ship, and have a extended self life.
- They have mass appeal or fill a highly specific niche.
- They have large markup and profit potential.
- They unlock the secrets to a mystery or provide the user with a formula.
- They are consumable, requiring consumers to regularly reorder.

Developing Your Direct Mail Package

Developing your direct mail package will largely depend on the products and services that you intend to sell and your marketing objectives. Some products or services can easily be sold with one mailing, while others require numerous mailings and follow-ups with prospects to build a relationship and complete the sales cycle. To get started, create a plan listing your objective(s), such as to sell, to generate leads, or to introduce new products or services. Next you will want to estimate a budget to create and implement the campaign, taking into account all expenses such as printing, postage, advertising, and delivery. Once you have a cost estimate, you can conduct a cost/benefit analysis to ensure that direct mail is the right marketing method to meet your objectives.

If you determine that you want to proceed, the next step is to storyboard your mailing package. Storyboarding enables you to carefully analyze each element of your mailer and to make adjustments prior to having your material printed. Knowing exactly what you want printed is often overlooked in the excitement and rush to marketing. Many small business owners quickly realize the value of storyboarding, proofreading, and creating a complete sample mail package after they have picked up completed print runs. Spelling errors, poor grammar, missed components, and last minute changes are common, leaving you on the hook financially because printers do not assume responsibility for errors from proofs that you have signed off before printing.

Stick to printing industry standard sizes and weights for your paper, envelopes, catalogs, response cards, and all other components of your direct mailing package. Straying from industry standard sizes or having lots specially die cut and printed can be very costly, easily doubling or tripling your costs.

Unless absolutely necessary, avoid dating key components of your direct mail package like catalogs, brochures, response cards, and order forms. Be especially careful when expensive and colorful photographs, pictures, and graphics are used in your package. The benefits of not dating these printed materials are that you can reuse the same inserts in future offers and mailings and you will not be bound to meet specific mailing or offer dates. There is no question that setting deadlines is the backbone marketing strategy of direct mail and is often required to motive people to take action and respond or buy. However, use stickers, small individually dated deadline insert or response cards, and bold printing on cover letters to indicate when a special offer ends instead of dating key printed materials that can be used over and over in new campaigns.

One of the keys to a successful direct mail campaign lies in your ability to know which offer and mail package gets the best responses and maximizes your return on investment. There is only one way to know this information for sure, and that is to test everything. You want to test your mailing list(s), test your product, test your price point, and test your special offers. Direct mail marketing is an ever-evolving process that requires constant testing and management in order to succeed and generate revenues and profits.

A good source of additional information about direct mail marketing is the Direct Marketing Association, which provides members with helpful information and advice about direct mail and direct marketing. It can be found online at www.the-dma.org. The National Register Publishing Company publishes an annual directory called *Direct Marketing Market Place*, which is packed with information, resources, and product and service listings for direct marketers. It can be found online at www.dirmktgplace.com.

Selecting the Right Mailing List

The lifeblood of any direct mail marketing campaign rests solely on your ability to compile or rent the best mailing list available, the one that will enable you to reach your target audience and achieve your marketing objectives. Yet this is easier said than done because the variables affecting mailing lists are numerous, including list size, list source, cost, compilation criteria, and profile information. And many types of direct mail marketing lists are available.

In-House Mailing Lists

In-house lists are mailing lists that you create, compiled from the names of your current and past customers and prospects. In-house lists are without question the best mailing lists, because the majority of people on the list have purchased from you in the past, are currently purchasing, or are familiar with your products or services. The downside to in-house mailing lists is that you must manage and maintain the list in order for it to remain current and effective. Managing your list will require computer hardware and client management software so that you can customize your list into categories, such as geography, demographics, and buying habits, for specific mailing and marketing purposes.

Opt-in Mailing Lists

Electronic mailing opt-in lists are compiled from e-mail addresses of people that have given a business, organization, or individual permission to send them information via e-mail, and to share their address with "friends," a polite way of saying that the lists will be rented, sold, and traded with other online marketers. Most cybermarketers rely exclusively on opt-in lists to generate new business because of the ease of contact and the low cost of reaching each person, business, or organization on the list. There are a number of services that will help you to build your own opt-in list, rent you opt-in lists, supply you with electronic message blasting, or do all of this.

Subscription Mailing Lists

Subscription lists are composed of individuals and businesses that subscribe to print or electronic publications. These subscriber publications can be magazines, newsletters, trade journals, industry reports, newspapers, and electronic magazines. Subscriber lists are generally a good choice for small business marketers because the names and addresses are usually valid and the people or businesses on the list have an interest in specific topics related to the publication that compiled the list.

Attendee Mailing lists

These are lists of people that have attended a specific event, everything from seminars, trade shows, sports events, concerts, and workshops, to timeshare pitch sessions. Attendee lists are available in various configurations based on geography, special interests, and even demographics, depending on the event that gathered the names. Attendee lists are generally accepted as a good alternative to response lists or an in-house list.

Assembled Mailing Lists

These lists are compiled from various published information sources such as telephone directories or industry association directories. Assembled lists are generally mailing lists of business people and companies and are usually categorized by industry or profession, such as lawyers, engineers, or chiropractors. Assembled lists provide a great opportunity for business-to-business marketing to reach specific target industries, but they are not very valuable to marketers of consumer goods. You will also want to keep in mind that when you rent assembled mailing lists, the only prequalification of the names is that the business or individuals on the list belong to a specific industry or profession.

Response Mailing Lists

Response lists are compiled from names of people that have purchased through a direct mail or marketing offer in the past. Response lists are usually broken into groups representing various special interests, such as people that play golf, or own a boat. For direct marketing purposes, a good response list is second only to a good in-house list in terms of the potential to pull a high response rate to your offer. The downside of response lists is that they can be very expensive to rent, up to twice as much as other types of lists because the quality is generally very good and the names are very specific, categorized, and targeted.

What You Need to Know about Mailing Lists

Now that you know which types of mailing lists are available, the next step is to understand what you need to know specifically about mailing lists so that you can use them as a powerful marketing tool. The first issue is that mailing lists are generally rented from the list owner or manager; seldom does anyone want to sell their mailing list. It is possible to get free or publicly accessible mailing lists, such as the lists found online at www.paml.net, which has information about 6,900 free public mailing lists. But publicly accessible e-mail or opt-in lists are generally not well maintained and include dead links and lots of spam addresses. So unless your budget for mailing lists is nonexistent, I would strongly advise you to stay clear of free print or electronic mailing lists. They are generally a waste of precious marketing time.

There are only three reliable sources for mailing lists. The first source is to build your own in-house list, once again derived by compiling information from directories, current customers, and prospects, holding a draw and capturing information from entry ballots, or retrieving information from warranty cards.

The second option is to rent mailing lists directly from list owners, which come from marketers and business owners who have spent considerable time, money, and energy to build lists. They often rent these lists to earn extra revenues. The third option is to rent lists from mailing list brokers, which may manage the list for the owner, own the list outright, or represent numerous mailing lists of every type. Finding a source for mailing lists is as easy as a "Mailing List" keyword search on any search engine or directory. You can also visit Info USA at www.infousa.com. This organization is billed as the world's largest suppler of mailing lists, which are indexed by consumer, business, industry, hobby, geographic location, and demographics.

Regardless of where your mailing list comes from, before renting the list you will want analyze the data card, which features information about the mailing list to determine if the list is right for your specific target audience and marketing objectives. On the data card you will find information about the following:

- *Cost.* The cost shown on the data card is per one thousand names and can range from a low of about $10 per thousand names up to $250 per thousand names for highly specialized and targeted lists.
- *Size and minimum order.* The total number of names on the list will also be shown on the data card, as well as the minimum number of names that can be pulled from the list and rented, such as 5,000 from 100,000.
- *Profile information.* A profile description outlines details such as the source of the list, history of the list, average value of orders, and hotline information like the kinds of products or services that people on the list recently purchased.
- *Restrictions.* There will also be information covering list usage restrictions. List owners reserve the right to review and approve or decline your mailing, based on their own criteria, but few get declined unless competitive, legal, or moral issues are involved.
- *Selections.* The selections area of the data card is important because it tells you if the list can be segmented and to what degree. Only a certain portion of the list may appeal to you and meet your target audience. This is common, especially for lists that are business-related and

for marketers who want to target specific businesses, industries, or job titles within a specific industry. Selections information will generally be shown as a percentage indicating the portion of the list that can be selected, such as 25 percent, along with the additional fee for segmenting the list.

Dramatically Increasing Your Response Rate

One of the keys to a successful direct mail campaign is to ensure that you receive a high response rate to your product or service offers. A person that responds to your mail offers affords you the opportunity to sell and build a profitable ongoing sales relationship. Without responses, the ability to sell is obviously not present. With that goal in mind, here are a few time-tested ways that you can use to dramatically increase your direct mail response rates.

- *Reach your target audience.* The best way to dramatically increase your response rate and sell more through direct mail is to reach the right audience. This may seem obvious, but identifying and reaching your target audience is the foundation of all marketing. If people do not need what you have to sell, more often than not they will not buy, regardless of how fantastic your offer may be. Take the time required to identify, locate, and reach your target audience, and your response rate will skyrocket.
- *Fill a niche.* Finding a niche is a two-part process. First, the product or service you sell should be something that is not readily available. If it is not, why would people choose to buy from you through the mail when they can buy it locally at a store? Second, what makes your product or service different from competitors' products or services? Perhaps you have the longest warranty, the lowest cost, or the best quality. All of these would be considered a competitive advantage, and every business needs a competitive advantage in order to succeed in today's global marketplace.
- *Buying motivation.* You want people to buy immediately, not next week, month, or year. In direct mail marketing, time is critical. You have to create a sense of urgency in order to motivate

people to take action and buy right away. You can do this by limiting the number of products for sale, having a firm order deadline date, offering a limited time financial discount, offering an upgraded model for free, or sending a free, special bonus gift to the first 50 people that respond to the offer, or a similar kind of promotion.

- *Make it simple for people to respond and buy.* Key to the success of direct mail marketing is to make it as easy as possible for people to respond to your offer and to buy what you are selling. You can make it easy for people to respond by including postage-paid response cards, a 24-hour toll free hotline, and online information and ordering through your Web site. You can also make it easy for people to buy by accepting credit cards, money orders, electronic personal checks, COD, installment plans, and bill-me-later options.

- *Reduce buying risk.* People often do not buy via direct mail because of the potential risks associated with making the purchase. How do they know it's what they want? How do they know your company is legit? How do they know the product will be delivered? Therefore, you have to go out of your way to eliminate the fear of buying and the risks associated with buying. This can be accomplished by offering a strong unconditional-satisfaction guarantee, by aligning your business with credible organizations such as the Better Business Bureau, and by offering bill-me-later payment options, or no-risk product trial periods.

TELEMARKETING

Telemarketing dramatically changed in the United States on October 1, 2003, with the introduction of the National Do Not Call Registry, which is managed by the Federal Trade Commission. The National Do Not Call Registry was put into place to protect consumers against fraudulent telemarketing organizations and telemarketing scams. At present only consumers, not businesses, can register for the list, which means that business owners and telemarketers can still randomly telephone businesses and consumers not on the list to market goods and services. The following are a few highlights of the National Do Not Call Registry:

- Only people that sign up for the National Do Not Call Registry will be placed on the list; consumers are not automatically registered.
- Only citizens of the United States can register. Canada does not have a Do Not Call Registry, but overseas business owners and telemarketers cannot call U.S. consumers on the Do Not Call list. If they do they face the same fines as U.S. companies that violate the law.
- Businesses or telemarketers that violate the Do Not Call rules face fines of up to $11,000 for each violation.
- Consumers can register personal telephone numbers and mobile cellular telephone numbers, but the telephone numbers must be in their own name.
- Business owners can continue to call customers that have made purchases within the last 18 months, even if they are on the Do Not Call list.
- Business-to-business telemarketing is exempt from the Do Not Call rules, as well as telephone surveys and charity fundraising.
- Business owners and telemarketers can download the entire Do Not Call list or any segment of the list, which is indexed by area code.

More information about the National Do Not Call Registry can be found online at www.donotcal.gov. Home business owners and telemarketers that would like to download part or all of the Do Not Call list can do so by visiting www.telemarketing.donotcall.gov.

Reinforcing Other Marketing Activities

Although telemarketing has greatly changed with the introduction of the National Do Not Call Registry it is still a great way to reinforce other marketing activities such as direct mail, seminars, trade shows, print ads, mobile sales force, and radio and television advertising campaigns. The reinforcement telemarketing strategy should be two-part. First, calls should be made before the launch informing prospects and customers about the reason for the marketing activity, for example, a special offer, an invitation to your booth at a trade show, or the introduction of a new product or service. The call is to alert prospects and customers about the forthcoming activity and build excitement. It should be made about three days before the marketing activity begins. The follow-up call is made three days after the marketing activity has taken place. Its focus should be on turning prospects into paying customers, set further appointments, and to answer questions.

Reinforcement telemarketing is a hands-on action that makes prospects and customers feel you care about their welfare and interests. And nothing, can replace the effectiveness of personal selling because a prospect cannot ask an advertisement or television ad for additional information. But remember; take the time to download the Do Not Call list if you are planning on telemarketing on a random basis.

A Low-Cost Sales Visit Strategy

Identify your best customers in relation to the impact they have on your total business revenues and profits. In most situations, you will find that 20 percent of your total customer base will account for 80 percent of your total sales. For this reason, make the best use of your time and develop a system to identify your best customers. Visit these people in person. The other 80 percent of your customers can be contacted via telemarketing. Not only will this simple system save time, but it also enables you to stay in close personal contact with your best customers while not leaving out the others, who may over time become better customers.

High-Impact Telemarketing Techniques

Telemarketing is nerve-racking work, even for the thick-skinned telemarketing professional. You want results, not rejection. The following high-impact telemarketing tips and techniques will help you get the results you want.

- *Define your objective.* Before you make calls, clearly define your objective(s). Do you want to set appointments, follow up with prospects or customers, inform people about a special event or promotion, or sell? Know why you're calling, and what action you want your prospect or customer to take as a result of the call. Get comfortable before you start making calls, especially if your calling list is large. Have a glass of water handy to cure dry-throat, park yourself in your most comfortable chair, have your script, notes, presentations, and fact sheets ready so you can answer specific questions. Remember, if you do not know why you're calling or if you're not prepared, don't expect that the person on the other end of the phone line will help you to figure it out or wait.

- *The right audience and person.* Make sure that you are calling your target audience, the people most likely to need what you have to sell. Also make sure that you are talking to the right person, the one who can make the buying decision and pay for the purchase. If you're not talking to this person, ask to speak to him or her.

- *Get to the point.* Get right to the point by clearly stating your business, your name, and the purpose of your call. Engage in conversation that it requires your prospect's immediate involvement. Few people will sit back and listen to another ramble on without quickly becoming irritated and tuning them out. Respect your prospect and customer's time and never take it for granted or waste it. Instead, move on to someone that needs and wants to buy what you have to sell.

- *Be polite and use plain English.* Be polite, use *please, thank-you, may I,* and *you're very welcome.* Avoid using technical terms. Speak in plain English that your customers and prospects will understand and appreciate. Never talk down to people or use terminology that you know they will not understand, because it will make prospects feel uneasy, or stupid. Go out of your way to make the person feel special, important, and the center of the universe at that precise moment.

CREATING YOUR OWN NEWSLETTER

Newsletters can serve many useful purposes for the home business owner. They can build a positive image, brand your business, promote products and services, position your expertise, introduce new product lines or services, or announce important company news. Creating and distributing your own newsletter can also be a powerful tool to enhance, complement, and support other advertising and marketing activities. Newsletters are a great way to keep your business name and products or services in front of prospects and clients in a consistent and cost effective manner.

Designing, Publishing, and Distributing Your Newsletter

Print or electronic format newsletters, which are best? There are pros and cons with each. While printing and distribution costs are nearly negligible with electronic newsletters, pushing "Delete" is very easy. Your newsletter might be zapped before it is ever read. Print newsletters stand a better chance of being read, but this comes at a higher cost for printing and distribution. Ultimately, you will have to size up your target audience, marketing objectives, and budget to determine which newsletter format will be best for your specific needs.

Who will create your newsletter? It depends on your budget, marketing objectives, publishing plans, and the number of people on your mailing list. With practice and the appropriate software, print or electronic newsletters can be designed, produced, and distributed in-house; alternately, you can hire a desktop publishing service to handle the job. A relatively small production and distribution run of a few hundred print newsletters can easily be looked after in-house, and with suitable computer hardware and software, the number is nearly unlimited for electronic newsletters. Larger print runs or more complicated e-newsletters with audio/visual features should be left to professionals to design. If you tackle the job yourself, most word processing programs such as Microsoft Office and Corel WordPerfect have newsletter templates that can be used for basic design. There is also advanced software available,

such as Newsletter Toolkit, which gives you the ability to produce and publish a professional newsletter right on your own computer. Newsletter Toolkit software can be found online at www.howto writeanewsletter.com.

Next on the agenda is the distribution of you newsletter. Again, there are many options available.

- *Mail.* Mail is the preferred way to distribute printed newsletters. Just, keep in mind that if your mailing list is large, you will want to use a postage meter and possibly a lower class of mail delivery to reduce postage costs. Also make sure to include your newsletter in your regular out going business mail, account statements, sales letters, catalogs, and presentations.
- *Handout.* Another method is personal delivery during sales visits, meetings, seminars, trade shows, and networking functions.
- *Fax.* Though inexpensive, the least preferred method of distributing printed newsletters is by fax. If you can afford other methods, use it. The low distribution costs of faxing is more than offset by the reduced print quality on the recipient's end. Remember, image and presentation are an important aspect of the marketing mix.
- *E-mail.* E-mailing your electronic newsletter is the final option in terms of distribution. While this is certainly the least expensive way to distribute your newsletter, it does require the set up and constant maintenance of an opt-in subscriber database.

Your Target Audience

As a sales and marketing tool, newsletters serve no purpose unless you can get them into the hands of people that are likely to buy your products or services or that can influence the buying habits and decisions of other people that are your target market. In part, who receives your newsletter depends on your budget and how you distribute your newsletter. The following are a few people that should be if possible, on your newsletter mailing list.

- Current and past customers and clients
- Current and past prospects

- Suppliers, vendors, and subcontractors
- Editors, journalists, producers, and reporters
- Business allies
- Employee and their families
- Influential leaders in your community, business associations, and industry

Depending on your marketing objectives, you may also want to distribute your newsletter to locations were it could be read by many people, thereby increasing your audience. You could distribute your newsletter to restaurants, waiting rooms, public libraries, schools, and community centers. Basically, anywhere in the community people gather and read what is in close proximity to them while they wait for appointments, eat lunch, or have a quiet coffee break. Call it your idle-hands target audience.

Content

The main purposes of your newsletter should be marketing and then communications. Like any good advertisement, you want your newsletter to be a vehicle for information that motivates your customers and prospects to buy. But you also must maintain a balance approach so that your newsletter does not become four pages of aggressive advertisements or irrelevant information of little interest to your target audience. In short, you have to give your audience information that they would find interesting and beneficial and pepper this information with promotional messages and advertisements for your products and services.

Interview customers and include their stories in your newsletter, especially customers that have benefited from doing business with you. Include their photographs and if they are in business, thank them by giving them a plug that describes their products and how they can be contacted. Also feature news about your industry, joint ventures, mergers, impending government legislation, statistics, and special events. Include stories on local, national, and international industry news. Readers like this type of highly specialized information, especially when it revolves around their business, hobbies, or interests. Newsletter content can also be created around business milestones,

such as number of years you have been in business, number of customers served, or complaint-free or employee injury-free days on the job. Feature monthly product and service spotlights along with a special discount to entice customers to buy. Provide real information that will benefit your readers, such as question-and-answer interviews with experts in the industry, tips of the month, and how-to articles. Also keep in mind that the content does not have to be all business. You can and should include some fun stuff—business- or industry-related trivia, crosswords, word games, and quizzes. Reward readers with small prizes for the first person to correctly answer skill-testing questions. You can also add a small section that regularly features local, industry, and community news, special events, and volunteer opportunities.

CREATING YOUR OWN CATALOG

Like newsletters, product catalogs can be created in print or electronic format. The decision about what format is right greatly depends on factors such as the price of the product you are selling, your budget, and your target audience. The benefits of an e-catalog are obvious. It's cheap, fast, and the orders can pour in almost immediately. However, there is a downside. Because people are deluged with e-mail pushing the "Delete" button immediately is commonplace.

There is custom software available that enables you to create your own in-house electronic catalogs. One such program is Catalogue Creator, which can be found online at www.cataloguecreator.com. Or, for the technology-challenged home business owner, print or electronic product catalogs can be designed professionally. Catalog Printer provides visitors to its Web site free catalog design and printing quotes. It can be found online at www.catalog printer.biz.

Regardless of the catalog format you chose, there are the questions of who will receive it, current customers and prospects or only new prospects, and how you will reach these people. Will you use your in-house mailing list or rent mailing lists? Will you have the catalog delivered by the postal service or electronically through an e-distribution service?

One great aspect of catalogs is that they allow you to fill a very specific niche in the marketplace. You can organize your catalog and feature products very specifically—specialty replacement parts, used or collectable items, by function such as specialized software, or by price. The most successful small catalogs serve a niche market because that is who catalog marketing appeals to—people that cannot find a specific product in their area or people that like the convenience that catalog shopping provides. Catalog shoppers are seldom impulse buyers unless there is a very compelling reason or offer on the table. Therefore, if you are trying to hawk products that consumers can easily get elsewhere, catalog marketing is not the best promotional vehicle. Here are a few more helpful tips that can improve your catalog:

- Include two order forms with your catalog, a loose insert and a tear-away or cut-out order form.
- Make it easy for people to order and pay for their purchases. Use toll-free order hot lines, include a complete mailing address, and let people pay with credit cards, e-checks, money orders, COD, and by way of installment plans.
- Feature your best selling and most profitable products near the front of the catalog because the first few pages are almost always read or at least glanced at by customers and prospects.
- Send out your catalog accompanied by a sales letter with a special offer, even if the offer you are making means selling at below cost. One critical aspect of mail order is to get new people buying. Once they have and once they have discovered how easy the process is, they are much more likely to continue to buy. So view the initial loss as a business cost that can be recouped over lifetime selling to the customer.
- Use photographs and illustrations in your catalog to help explain and sell your products.

PRINTED FLIERS: THE HOME BUSINESS OWNER'S BEST FRIEND

The majority of home business owners will find printed fliers represent one of the best advertising vehicles and values available, particularly for new start-ups and entrepreneurs working with restricted advertising budgets. Fliers are a fast and frugal, yet highly effective, way to promote a wide range of products and services, especially if you take the time needed to learn basic design skills so that you can create high-impact, printed promotional fliers in-house. Beginner desktop publishing courses encompassing flier, brochure, report, and presentation design and layout are available in just about every community through colleges, continuing education programs, or private tutors and generally at very reasonable costs. If you already possess basic computer skills, you can purchase desktop publishing software applications that include flier templates, which can be customized to suit your specific needs, or you can create promotional fliers from scratch using the design tools provided in the software. Adobe Software, www.adobe.com, and Corel Software, www.corel.com, are widely known for very user-friendly desktop publishing programs. Some of the benefits associated with creating fliers and other promotional materials in-house include the ability to:

Save Money and Time
Artwork and layout design is very costly. Most commercial printers charge $60 to $80 per hour for graphic design services for marketing materials like fliers, product brochures, newsletters, and other printed items commonly used for promotions. In addition to saving money you will also be able to save precious marketing time. You have the ability to create in-house printed promotional materials within a day, perhaps even within a few hours, instead of waiting days or weeks working around the printer's schedule and making numerous trips to proofread and sign off on artwork and copy.

Experiment and Test
Having the equipment and skills needed to produce your own promotional materials gives you the ability to experiment, at little cost, with various print marketing tools, messages, and special promotions until you find the right mix. On day one design, print, and test two-for-one coupons. On day two designs, print, and experiment with a newsletter. On day three, design, print, and experiment with a customer service survey. The list goes on. Create,

test, and implement marketing messages and activities that will work for your specific business.

Project a Professional Image

Imagine being able to print the name of your customers on gift certificates and other special promotional materials with the click of a mouse. You can if you have the skills and equipment to do so, and you will be able to personalize every correspondence with your best customers: thank-you notes, greeting cards, and letters that have been individually created with one customer in mind. That is powerful marketing and customer appreciation.

Flier Distribution and Community Bulletin Boards

Once you have created and printed your fliers, they can be copied in bulk for as little as two cents each at your local copy center, or you can invest in a high-speed laser printer for about $350 and keep the printing in-house too. The great benefit of printed promotional fliers is that they can be used everywhere and for everything. They can even replace business cards. Why not? You can get 10 times as much information on them as on business cards, 20 times as much if you print on both sides of the paper.

You can hand out fliers everywhere: at seminars, trade shows, networking meetings, to the attendant. You can canvas busy parking lots tucking fliers underneath windshield wipers, hand out fliers outside of community gathering places such as movie theaters, sports complexes, and conventions centers. Visit local retailers and institutions, and ask if you can leave the fliers describing your products and services for their patrons. This works well, especially if you purchase and use "please take one" plastic brochure boxes at the location. Stock with your advertising fliers, and return weekly to refill. You can leave your advertising fliers in public transit areas like buses and subway cars for riders to read and take home, as well as in bus stations, train stations, airports, and bus shelters.

Entrepreneurs on a tight advertising budget should also regard community notice boards as a super valuable source for advertising your business, products, and services for free. Stock a supply of promotional fliers and thumbtacks in your car so

you can make a weekly run posting the fliers on every community notice board in your area. Community notice or bulletin boards are typically found in the following locations:

- Supermarkets and public markets
- Convenience stores
- Public libraries
- Community colleges, universities, and high schools
- Self-service laundry and dry cleaners
- Automotive service stations
- Community and recreational centers
- Fitness centers and sports complexes
- Churches and club or association buildings

Of course, you can also hire cash-starved students to distribute your fliers and contract with the postal service to have your fliers included in home delivery. Additionally, check with your local newspaper; most offer flier insert programs with home delivery at reasonable rates.

Coupons

Promotional coupons offer home business owners another cost-efficient way to promote their products and services. Once again, with basic skills, a personal computer, desktop publishing software, and a printer, you can design, print, and distribute your own promotional coupons. Alternately, take part in a community coupon marketing campaign where retailers and service providers join together to create a coupon book that is distributed throughout the community. Coupons can feature a discount in the form of money off such as, "Present this coupon and save $25 when you get your carpets cleaned." Or the discount can be shown in the form of a percentage such as, "Get your carpets cleaned before the end of this month and save 25%." Other uses for coupons include two-for-one specials, free product or service trial periods, and free upgrades when you purchase the standard product and service. The Association of Coupon Professionals provides visitors to its Web site with information about coupon design and distribution services, as well as general coupon information. It can be found online at www.couponpros.org.

Door Hangers

Door hangers are another kind of printed promotional flier, one designed so that it fits over and hangs from any standard doorknob or handle. The advantage of door hanger fliers is obvious. People can enter their homes without seeing and touching the flier, but not door hangers, which generally results in their having a much higher readership rate. Door hangers can be multipurpose. Print information about your products or services on the front, and print a coupon or special offer on the back. Door hangers are cheap, they get noticed, and they don't get lost in a mailbox full of junk mail. They are a great marketing tool for home business owners that need to stand out in the crowd. Print USA provides free online quotes for door hanger design and printing. It can be found at www.print usa.com/quotes/door-hangers.html.

SIGNAGE NEEDS FOR YOUR HOME BUSINESS

Without question signs are one of the lowest-cost, yet highest-impact forms of advertising for home business owners. Signs work to promote your business, products, or services, 24 hours a day, 365 days a year virtually for free once the signs have been purchased. Your signs tell people at a glance your business name, what you sell, why they should contact you, and the information needed to contact you. That makes signs the ultimate salesperson for your business. Your signage must be professional, in keeping with the image that you want to project, informative, yet free of too much secondary information. You do not want to clutter your sign with information you use to close sales. Once signs were hand-painted and expensive, but most signs today are designed on a computer, printed, and cut on large sheets of vinyl, easily installed, long lasting, and very inexpensive. You want to always make a positive first impression, so keep all of your signage in tip-top condition. Faded signs, peeling paint, torn banners, or signs that require maintenance in general send out negative messages about your business. Use graphics and pictures of what you do in your signs to lend visual description, and keep your signs consistent with your corporate image. Use a unified color scheme, the same font and style, and a consistent logo and marketing message. More helpful information about business signage can be found online at Sign Web, located at www.signweb.com.

Signs at Your Home

Installing signs at home is tricky business because there are many people and issues that must be taken into account. There are local bylaws that will stipulate if signage is allowed at your home. These bylaws generally stipulate the size of the sign, as well as placement, style, and more. There is no one set of regulations in terms of home business signage. Each municipality has its own regulations. Generally, a call to the planning department at city or town hall is all that is required to find out the local laws and regulations on home business signage.

Neighbors are also an issue. Even if signage is allowed, you want to consult your immediate neighbors to find out their feelings on the issue and get their input on the signs. The last thing that you want to do is alienate neighbors over business signs. If you do, expect a backlash in terms of customer parking, noise, or any other reason that they can find to complain, justified or not.

The final sign issue is multisegmented and includes your budget, the style to match your home and business image, and maintenance issues. Keep in mind that unless you are going to have clients come to your home, chances are you will be better off not having signs at all. If you will be having prospects and customers coming to your home, keep your signs in open view, make them tasteful to match your home and streetscape, perhaps carved wood or brass on stone, and keep lighting to a minimum unless you can incorporate your sign into your exterior house light or motion lighting. In addition to calling your local planning department about home business sign regulations, Sign Wave Designs offers some good advice about home business signage and has viewable product samples on its Web site, which can be found online at www.sign wavedesigns.com/Home_Based_Business_Signs.htm

Vehicle Signs

Some home business owners struggle with the decision about whether to sign their vehicles, especially if it also doubles as the family transportation. My advice is to sign your vehicle, and if need be, get magnetic signs that can be quickly installed or removed and stored in the trunk when using your car for family activities. However, if you are going to sign your vehicle with semi-permanent stick-on vinyl or magnetic signs, make sure to have the signs professionally designed. The look of your vehicle signs should be consistent with your overall business image in style, color, tone, logo, and unified marketing message. With today's high-tech computers even very elaborate signs can be inexpensively designed and printed, making that a very worthwhile marketing expenditure. I would not only sign the vehicle, I would also be sure to park in highly visible and high-traffic locations when not in use, even if this means feeding parking meters. Always think about maximizing the marketing value of these rolling billboards.

Props can also be used in combination with signs to better describe your business and make a more memorable impression. The plumber replacing the door handles on the service van with faucets is an example. Regardless of the signage or props that you use all signs should include your business name, a brief promotional message that best describes what you do, and contact information, including telephone numbers and Web site. Magnetic Signs manufactures and distributes custom made-to-order magnetic signs for cars and truck. It can be found online atwww.magnetic signs.com. Car Signs online sells custom car signs. It can be found at www.carsigns.com

Job Site Signs

Owners of home businesses that install products or provide services at their customer's homes and offices should consider investing in professional attention-grabbing job site signage, especially if jobs last more than a few days. Job site signs come in all sizes and are priced to fit all budgets. Some are metal with metal stands, while others are Coroplast® or even simple plastic sleeves, similar to political yard signs, but emblazoned with your business name, logo, and promotional message. The plastic sleeve style fits over preformed wire stands, which push easily into the ground, making for very fast installation and pick up at a later date. Purchased in bulk, the plastic sleeve style signs are very inexpensive, less than $5 each, and can be reused many times. The metal and coroplast signs tend to be more expensive and much more bulky to move around and install.

Many home businesses such as landscape services, house painters, interior and exterior designers, renovation firms, and window cleaners can benefit by actively using job site signs. Job site signs are without question a very simple and economical way to market your business during work in progress. Business Signs Online sells metal and Coroplast made-to-order site signs in various sizes. It can be found at www.businesssigns.com. Political Lawn Signs manufactures lightweight plastic site and lawn signs. It can be found at www.politicallawnsigns.com.

PLACES WHERE YOU CAN ADVERTISE

The following Advertising Checklist (see Figure 13.3) has been created to help you identify places where you can advertise your business, products, or services, and to provide a few additional advertising ideas that might work for you. The checklist is broken into three categories: print advertising, electronic and

---

FIGURE 13.3 **Advertising Checklist**

Print Advertising

- ❑ Display advertisements in national and regional newspapers
- ❑ Classified advertisements in national and regional newspapers
- ❑ School newspapers: high school, college, university, alumni, and trade schools
- ❑ National and regional magazines, card decks, and postcards
- ❑ Trade and industry newspapers, journals, and reports
- ❑ Special interest and club publications
- ❑ Newsletters: In-house, corporate, organization, union, and community
- ❑ Business, consumer, and industry directories

FIGURE 13.3   **Advertising Checklist,** continued

Print Advertising

❏ White Pages and Yellow Pages telephone directories

❏ Direct mail promotions and catalogs

❏ Coupon books, clip outs, and inserts

❏ Seasonal greeting cards and calendars

Electronic and Broadcast Advertising

❏ Your own Web site

❏ Active and static banner advertisements

❏ Search engines and search directories

❏ Google and Overture adwords

❏ Internet directories

❏ Reciprocal Web site links

❏ Newsgroups and chat forums

❏ Web malls and auction sites

❏ Electronic publications: e-zines, e-newsletters, and e-reports

❏ E-mail blasting and signature files

❏ Radio commercials

❏ Radio program and segment sponsorships

❏ Live event radio broadcasting

❏ Internet radio

❏ Drive-by FM broadcasting (talking signs)

❏ Television commercials

❏ Television program sponsorship

❏ Infomercials and cable shopping channels

❏ Internet television

❏ Community and nonprofit television

❏ Guest appearances on radio and television

❏ Telemarketing and facsimile blasts

❏ Telephone on-hold messages

Community and Specialty Advertising

❏ Supplier, manufacturer, association, and industry cooperative advertising programs

❏ Exterior and interior billboards

❏ Transit advertising: bus, light rail, train, subway, taxicab, and ferry

❏ Community bulletin boards

❏ Flier and door hanger distribution

❏ Restaurant placemats, napkin dispensers, and menus

❏ Community event, sports, and charity sponsorships

❏ Community take-one brochure boxes

❏ Tourist and information bureaus

❏ Window, point of purchase, and counter displays

❏ Arial banners, blimps, and inflatable advertising

❏ Signage: car signs, job site signs, portable electronic signs, and special event signs

❏ Trade and consumer shows, conventions, seminars, and expos

❏ Amateur sports: team sponsorships, complex signs, and playing field signage

❏ Promotional specialties: hats, t-Shirts, bags, buttons, pens, magnets, and mouse pads

❏ Bumper and specialty stickers

❏ Cash register receipts, shopping bags, and shopping carts

❏ Exterior park benches and garbage receptacles

❏ Human billboards and mascots

❏ Outbound business communications

❏ Movie theater screen shots and play event programs

❏ Newcomer programs such as Welcome Wagon

❏ Parade floats

❏ Score sheets: golf and bowling

broadcast advertising, and community and specialty advertising.

RESORCES

Associations

Advertising Photographers of America
PO Box 361309
Los Angeles, CA 90036
(800) 272-6264
www.apanational.com

American Association of Advertising Agencies
405 Lexington Avenue, 18th Floor
New York, NY 10174-1801
(212) 682-2500
www.aaaa.org

Association of Canadian Advertisers
175 Bloor Street East
South Tower, Suite 307
Toronto, ON M4W 3R8
(416) 964-3805
www.aca-online.com

Direct Marketing Association
1120 Avenue of the Americas
New York, NY 10036-6700
(212) 302-6714
www.the-dma.org

International Advertising Association
521 Fifth Avenue, Suite 1807
New York, NY 10175
(212) 557-1133
www.iaaglobal.org

The Outdoor Advertising Association of America
1850 M Street NW Suite 1040
Washington, DC 20036
(202) 833-5566
www.oaaa.org

Suggested Reading

Bly, Robert. *The Copywriter's Handbook: A Step-by-Step Guide to Writing Copy that Sells.* New York: Henry Holt, 1990.

Corbett, Michael. *The 33 Ruthless Rules of Local Advertising.* New York: Pinnacle Books, 1999.

Fowler, David. *Newspaper Ads that Make Sales Jump: A How-To Guide.* New York: Marketing Clarity, 1998.

Koval, Robin. *Bang!: Getting Your Message Heard in a Noisy World.* New York: Doubleday, 2003.

Krause, Jim. *Layout Index: Brochure, Web Design, Poster, Flyer, Advertising, Page Layout, Newsletter, Stationery, Index.* Cincinnati, OH: North Light Books, 2001.

Scissors, Jack, and Roger B. Baron. *Advertising Media Planning.* New York: McGraw-Hill, 2002.

Stephenson, James. *The Ultimate Small Business Marketing Guide: Over 1500 Great Marketing Tricks That Will Drive Your Business Through the Roof!* Irvine, CA: Entrepreneur Press Inc., 2003.

Ogilvy, David. *Ogilvy on Advertising.* New York: Vintage Books, 1987.

Web Sites

Adobe Software Corporation, www.adobe.com: Adobe is a leading software development company with numerous desktop publishing products for a wide variety of user applications. Great for creating newsletters, brochures, fliers, reports, presentations, table cards, and much more, on your desktop.

Advertising Age Magazine Online, www.adage.com

American Copy Editors Society, www.copydesk.org

Brand Week Magazine Online, www.brandweek.com

Catalogue Software, www.cataloguecreator.com: Online distributor of custom software that enables you to design your own print or electronic product catalogs.

Cheap T.V. Spots, www.cheap-tv-spots.com: A full-service television commercial production company providing scripts, directing, filming, editing, music, and narration services and packages starting at $499 for the budget-minded home business advertiser.

Corel Software Corporation, www.corel.com: Corel is a leading software development company with numerous desktop publishing products for a wide variety of user applications. Great for creating newsletters, brochures, fliers, reports, presentations, table cards, and much more, on your desktop PC.

Freelance Online, www.freelanceonline.com: Online directory listing hundreds of freelance copywriters and editors, indexed by specialty and geographically.

Index Stock, www.indexstock.com: An online stock photography service offering thousands of royalty-free and royalty-paid stock photography images that can be used in your advertising, all available for instant download.

Indoor Billboard Advertising Association, www.indoor advertising.org

National Register Publishing, www.nationalregister pub.com: National Register Publishing produces an annual co-op advertising program source directory listing hundreds of co-op advertising opportunities and programs.

News Directory, www.newsdirectory.com: An online magazine and newspaper directory featuring worldwide listings indexed by geographical region and publication topic.

News Link, www.newslink.org: An online newspaper directory serving the Untied States, Canada, Mexico, and South America, indexed geographically and by type of newspaper.

Political Lawn Signs, www.politicallawnsigns.com: Manufacturers and distributors of reusable and inexpensive advertising lawn signs.

Print USA Inc., www.printusa.com: A full-service printer with fast delivery throughout the United States and Canada and offering free online quotes for all of your printing needs.

Pub List, www.publist.com: An online publications, directory listing in excess of 150,000 domestic and international print and electronic publications including magazines, journals, e-journals, and newsletters.

Radio Advertising Bureau, www.rab.com

Radio Locator, www.radio-locator.com: An online directory linked to more than 10,000 radio stations indexed by format and geographic location in the United States and Canada.

Sign Web, www.signweb.com: Free online helpful information and links covering everything to do with commercial signage and the sign industry.

SRDS Media Solutions, www.srds.com: SRDS Media Solutions publishes print and online advertising rate card sourcebooks covering print and broadcast media advertising rates.

Target Marketing Magazine Online, www.targetmar ketingmag.com

Virtual Tuner, www.virtualtuner.com: An online directory listing more than 10,000 Internet radio and television stations, broadcasting from over 100 countries in 75 languages directly to your computer.

CHAPTER 14

Public Relations and Networking

SMALL BUSINESS OWNERS IN GENERAL TEND TO shy away from publicity. Few take the time to create and send out press releases, and even fewer actually develop and implement a public relations strategy for their business. Why, when the potential to reach thousands or perhaps even millions of people at little or no cost is a real possibility?

- Do any of these sound familiar?
- I do not have any contacts in the media.
- I don't have time to write and send out a press release.
- I don't have any publicity ideas.
- I do not know anything about public relations.
- Only big corporations can benefit from publicity.
- No one wants to hear about my business.
- Where would I even get started?

What most home business owners fail to realize is that every business owner could easily create some sort of news or publicity buzz out of what they sell or the services they provide. All that is required is taking the time to understand how public relations works and using a little bit of imagination to develop ways of sharing your specialized knowledge and expertise.

More than 50 percent of news is generated by non-news sources. That means half the news we read in publications or on the Web, hear on radio, or see on television was submitted or initiated by people who are not reporters, journalist, producers, editors, or media personnel. Who are the people creating the other 50 percent of the news we get? Professional publicists, small business owners and managers, politicians, sales people, marketing consultants, community leaders, and basically anyone else who has learned that becoming a junior reporter is one of the best ways to get their message out to a news-hungry public via the media. Every day journalists, editors, reporters, and producers have the daunting task of filling the news pipeline. It's a job that never ends because we have come to expect news and accept news as part of our everyday lives.

The need for news has also created a vacuum in the media industry and a problem for media workers. There are not enough people working in the media or enough hours in the day to research, write, film, or record all the stories and get them to the public. This problem creates an excellent opportunity for you to benefit by becoming a junior reporter, developing news and life stories and angles that relate to your home business and submitting these stories to the media. Everyday people just like you are benefiting by having their message (news) displayed in the media, and so can you by understanding how these people learned to become junior reporters. Getting in the habit of automatically creating news around everyday business activities will grab the attention of the media and generate publicity. These activities include:

- Opening for business, new management, or joint ventures
- Launching new or improved products and services
- Community information, such as events, sponsorships, and charity drives
- Winning business awards or receiving special recognition for your business
- Health and safety news and information
- Contests, promotions, and special events
- Specialized information such as poll results or new regulations
- Business milestones, such as five years in business or one thousandth customer served
- Customer success stories as a result of doing business with you
- General information, such as hiring employees

Another overlooked benefit of developing and implementing a public relations campaign is that a successful campaign enables small businesses to level the playing field and compete against larger and, more often than not, better financed competitors. Public relations costs little outside of time. Yes, it is true that advertisements in the Yellow Pages can be in front of your target audience longer than a feature newspaper article about your business, product, or service. But the newspaper article can be just the tip of the publicity iceberg if you learn to master and apply the art of seeking and securing free or low-cost publicity for your business. Whether media outlets pick up your "news" is completely up to you and your ability to make your "news" irresistible to the media. A well-received and publicized press release can easily have the same pull or awareness benefit that an advertisement costing five figures has, but with the advantage that it costs little.

PUBLIC RELATIONS BASICS

Home business owners need to plan and implement an ongoing public relations campaign as an active component of their overall marketing plan. Few forms of advertising or other marketing activities can match the effectiveness and credibility of the media; our daily lives revolve around media and the news. We read newspapers, watch television, surf the Internet, and listen to the radio, and we do so because we want to be entertained, informed, and learn. A great movie review in your local newspaper is more likely to peak your interest and pull you into a movie theater than the advertisement for that movie in the newspaper. That is publicity at work. It grabs your attention, spells out the basic details, creates interest and desire, and compels you to take action.

At the core, public relations is much more than just clever ways to secure free media attention and exposure for your business. Public relations is really an umbrella that covers many positive image-building techniques aimed at five key audiences: your target market, the media, your community, government agencies and personnel, and your business team.

Relations with the Target Market

Your first public relations audience is your target market, people that are the most likely to buy your products or services. In terms of relations with your target consumer audience, you must focus on the message that you want to send, the image that you want to build, and the level of awareness that you want this audience to have about your business, product, or service. Remember, reaching your target audience is not limited to channeling a message through the media. Relations with your target audience are all encompassing and include how you present yourself and your business in public and the words and images you choose to describe and depict your business in marketing materials.

Relations with the Media

Media is the second key audience under the public relations umbrella and the one that the vast majority of us are aware of the most, simply because it is the most publicized use of public relations. It is through print and broadcast media exposure that you gain access to your target audience from within the media's broader audience or highly specific or niche audiences. Relations with the media can be ongoing or a one-shot deal, depending on your PR objectives and strategy.

Relations with the Community

The third key audience is the community(s) in which your business operates. Community-related public relations activities include joining business and nonbusiness associations, volunteering to pitch in with various community activities and events, and often throwing your small business weight behind one or more local charitable causes. Of course, any time you are out in the community, you are a goodwill ambassador for your business. These community public relations and goodwill activities are generally referred to as being a good corporate citizen, a common characteristic that every successful small business owner shares.

Relations with the Government

Public relations is also building open lines of communications between your business and elected or appointed public officials at all levels of government, but especially local government—its politicians, city and community planners, police, and fire services. The goal is twofold: One is to help local governments understand what effects their decisions and actions have on your business by making your business voice and opinions known. Also, you need to understand what challenges local officials face in terms of community issues and how these relate to decision and policy making. Again, being heard and listening to local officials is accomplished by being an active member of your community and taking a leadership role when necessary.

Relations with the Business Team

Communications between you and your business team is important. Your business team includes both internal team players such as employees, managers, investors, and family members and external team players such as your banker, accountant, business and industry associations, and product and service suppliers. Relating to your business team is accomplished by attending industry and association events and trade shows, and creating special meeting opportunities to discuss the challenges that face your business, industry, product, or service. Other means of contact and interaction, such as print and electronic newsletters, speeches, seminars, personal visits, and telephone calls also helps communications here.

DEVELOPING YOUR PUBLIC RELATIONS STRATEGY

Developing a public relations strategy is a relatively straightforward process, if you follow a logical sequence. The starting point is to determine who will develop and implement your PR program, what are your PR objectives, what is your PR message now and in the future, who is your target audience, and what do you want people to do as a result of your PR message? These are only a few of the components of an overall public relations strategy.

Who Will Develop Your PR Program?

Home business owners have three options in terms of developing a PR program. You can do it yourself, hire a freelance public relations specialist on an as-needed basis, or you can contract with or retain a full service public relations agency.

Do-It-Yourself Option

The vast majority of home business owners will create and maintain their own public relations program and key campaigns within the program because of the costs associated with hiring a freelance PR specialist or contracting with a full-service PR agency. The do-it-yourself option requires you to educate yourself in the finer arts of public relations. But over time and with practice, you will start to get the results that will help your business grow.

Freelance Option

The second option is to hire a freelance public relations consultant or a marketing/advertising consultant with a strong public relations background. Often freelancers break away from larger firms to build their own agency and you will generally find that their fees are about 60 percent of those a charged by a full-service public relations agency. To find freelance PR consultants, contact your local chamber of commerce for referrals or do a telephone book search.

Agency Option

The third option is to hire an agency that specializes in creating, maintaining, and growing public relations programs based on each client's individual needs and budget. The downside of hiring a PR firm is that most will not take on small jobs or one-time jobs. They prefer to sign longer term contracts with monthly payment guarantees and extra billing for services provided over the basic agreement. If you are going to hire a professional PR firm, be prepared to shell out $2,000 per month—and that is only to get going.

Defining Your PR Objectives

Next you want to define your public relation objectives, which are usually, but not always, tied to your marketing objectives. Your objective(s) can cover wanting to increase sales, introduce a new product or service, generate sales leads, repair damage from negative press, or simple build awareness of your business and what you sell. Keep in mind that your public relations objectives will never remain static, they will change throughout the year to reflect current and forthcoming business and marketing objectives, strategies, and campaigns. So before you actively seek any type of publicity, write down what you want to achieve as a result of the publicity that you are seeking. Common objectives include:

- Increasing awareness of your business, product, or service
- Promoting a special business, community, or charity event, or a sponsorship
- Driving people to your Web site or toll-free hotline
- Becoming known as an expert within your specific industry or field
- Introducing a new or greatly revamped product or service
- Generating new sales leads
- Changing public perceptions and consumer buying habits

- Announcing information that benefits the local community, such as business expansion or hiring new employees
- Seeking the public's help to solve an internal problem, such as naming a new product

Creating Your PR Message

Every time that you seek publicity or share information with one or more of your key audiences you will need to devise a central PR message. Your PR message will change depending on your objective, but each time you seek publicity or share information with a key audience, there must be a main message that you want to get across. You cannot have mixed or multiple messages. If your objective is to secure media exposure for a new product launch, your PR message must exclusively revolve around that theme and nothing else. It should include facts, statistics, benefits, how-to info, and other details related to the new product. Or if your objective is to release information about a community event sponsorship, your message should focus on the event, your participation in the event, and how your business supports the local community.

Identifying Your PR Audience

Prior to launching a public relations program or any segment of the program, you have to identify who you want your message to reach, your target audience. Your target audience might change with every new release or advisory you send to the media, but to effectively reach an audience, you must first identify it. Identifying the target audience can be accomplished quite simply. Break it down into three categories—demographics, location, and benefits, and ask yourself questions relevant to the categories. What is the age, sex, education level and income level, of the audience you want to reach? Where is your target audience located geographically? Who will benefit the most from coming into contact with your news by way of media exposure? If you know the answers you can properly target the media that reaches the audience that you want your message to reach.

Identifying the Media

Knowing which audience you want to reach helps you identify which media works best for you. For instance, if your target audience is business managers, you will want to target your efforts to securing exposure in media that reaches business managers, perhaps industry publications or specific broadcast programs. If your target audience is high school students, you want to target your PR efforts at school publications and other forms of media that regularly cater to this demographic.

A Call for Action

Once the media has picked up on your story and your target audience has seen, read, or heard your message, you have to have made two decisions. What action do you want your target audience to take? And, what tools will you give them to take the desired action? This is commonly referred to as a call to action. In the information you release or share with the media, there must be a compelling reason why people should contact you, and there must also be tools for them to do it. For instance, if your message is that you want people to come out and support a community clean-up that your business is sponsoring, you must include the details in your release. Compelling reasons why people should attend the event and details such as time, place, things they should bring, people they can contact before and during the event, and registration information.

Setting a Budget

Though publicity is often referred to as free advertising, there is still a cost associated with creating, maintaining, and growing a PR program. You have to set a PR budget and know where the money will come from to support the program. Like many forms of advertising, it is difficult to track the success of publicity. So once you have committed to the program, follow through and do not let early disappointments dissuade you from further PR endeavors. The budget you set will be in direct relationship to what you can afford. After all, you are operating a small business, probably with limited financial resources so budget will be a concern.

Creating a Time Table

Sending out a press release in June to inform the media about an ice castle sculpture contest you are hosting in January to raise money for charity will garner little if any reaction or attention from the media. It is simply too far in advance to motivate them to take action. You must identify your time line in advance for each segment of your PR program. Your own schedule will have to also be considered. If you are a one-person business, planning a media event or release during your busiest time of the year will be counterproductive.

CREATING A PRESS RELEASE

Home business owners should consider the press release as their most important tool in securing media attention and exposure. Fortunately, with practice it is one that can be used by everyone. Practice, however, is the key word. Before you sit down and struggle to put your thoughts into words on paper, make sure to research press releases first to get a feel and understanding of the style, tone, format, voice, and structure commonly used. Simply read other press releases, especially ones that have been picked up and covered by the media. Would you sit down and write a book without having read at least a few first? Not likely. So why would you attempt to write a press release without having read a few first? There are numerous Web sites where you can read current and archived press releases. One of the best is PR Web, which can be found online at www.prweb.com. On PR Web, not only can you browse and read through thousands of press releases for free, they are also conveniently indexed by industry. Remember, you don't want to reinvent the wheel, you just want to write an effective release that gets picked up. Use what's available, and modify it to meet your own PR objectives.

Formatting

Press release formatting is very basic. The following overview will give you a guideline that can be used when preparing your press releases.

- *Paper.* Use company letterhead to print your press release on if you have it, and if not, standard 20 lbs 8.5- x 11-inch white office paper is totally acceptable. Forget using fancy, colored, or extra heavy paper stock. You're best just to stick with your letterhead or standard office paper. The same applies to envelopes; use a standard white office envelope with no window.

- *Font.* Standard 12 point fonts such as Times New Roman or Arial are fine. Avoid fancy fonts, italics, or bolding too many words and sentences. Always use black ink on white paper. The only color should be in your business name or logo if you are printing the release on company letterhead.
- *Spacing.* Double spacing makes the release easy to read at a glance. Use 1 inch to 1.5 inch margins all around.
- *Length.* Generally press releases are between one and three pages long. As a rule of thumb, expect to fit 200 to 250 words on each page so it won't be hard to read.
- *Templates.* Most of the popular word processing software programs such as Microsoft Office and Corel Word Perfect have press release templates that you can customize to suit your particular needs. Or you can easily create your own press release template using Notepad, Word, or a similar word processing program and saving it as a document.
- *Proofread.* Always proofread your press release for grammar and spelling errors before sending it out, and do not solely rely on your word processor spell-check program. Use exclamation marks sparingly and other punctuation only as required. When you are done proofreading your release, give it to an employee, friend, or family member to proofread again.

Contact Information

Your contact information should be repeated a few times in your press release. It should be on the top of the press release. If you print the release on company letterhead you will have your full contact information there. If you do not use letterhead, you can print your business name and address at the top of the page, followed by a contact name and the direct telephone number and e-mail address of the contact

person. The contact information should then be repeated at the end of the news on the last page.

Release Information

Near the top, on the right hand side of your press release, indicate a release date for the news. If the news can be released any time, simply print in all upper case letters and underscored —FOR IMMEDIATE RELEASE. Alternately, if you have a specific date you would like the news or information to be released on, write that specific date in all upper case letters and underscore such as TO BE RELEASED SEPTEMBER 1, 2005. Have a good reason for releasing the news on a specific date. When you narrow the date the information can be used or released, you greatly reduce the odds of securing media exposure. You are telling media personnel to work around your timetable and not to do what is convenient for them.

Headline

The headline is one of the more important aspects of the press release if not the most important. It grabs the attention of the reader and separates your press release from the other releases sent to media personnel. Your headline should be bold, in larger type, and printed directly across the top of the press release. The headline could be in the form of a question, a statement that reveals part of the news, or a statistical fact. Use whatever you feel is relevant to your main message and will grab the attention of readers and draw them into the body of the release. Under the headline, a few lines down, or under an opening paragraph should be a subheadline that reveals just a little more information about your main marketing message or answers the question your headline has posed. The subheadline should be used to generate additional interest from the readers.

Dateline and Lead Paragraph

Start your first paragraph with a dateline followed by your lead into the story that you want to release. Make this powerful, interesting, and unique. This is as far as many readers will get before they lose interest in what seems like another advertising message, not information that would benefit their readers, viewers, or listeners.

Text Information

Follow the lead paragraph with the text information, that is, the body of the press release. This should be a few paragraphs in length and tell the rest of your story. It basically answers the who, what, why, when, where, and how questions. Think of this as the area where you state your compelling case or argument about why this information should be made available to the public.

Boilerplate Information

The boilerplate information is a single paragraph that gives some brief information and details about your company or organization, how long in business, current ownership, numbers of employees, and whatever else you feel is relevant or will help to support your news story. After the boilerplate paragraph, use three pound (# # #) or triple x signs (x x x) or simply print *END* to indicate the press release is completed. You can also repeat your contact information on the bottom of the last page in your press release.

Press Release Content

Start by being creative. Write about an event, news, information, or story is that unique and that does not happen everyday. Editors, producers, reporters, and journalists receive tons of press releases. You have to make sure that yours stands out in the crowd if you want to grab their attention and get the exposure. What you decide is news does not have to necessarily be groundbreaking stuff, just look for a new way to get the information across or put a new twist on an old story. Also, try to be objective about the information that you include in the press release, looking at it from the perspective of the media's target audiences. How will being exposed to this information benefit them? And, think in terms of mass appeal. The more people that would be interested in knowing the information in your press release, the higher the odds go of securing media exposure. Include support information or documents with

your press release if you feel that it is relevant. These documents can include a fact sheet in bullet format that lists the highlights of your news, photographs, or illustrations that will help to paint a complete picture.

Media Contacts

A key to the success of securing media exposure is to make sure that you target the right media and the right media personnel. Research the media's target audience before you send the press release or media advisory. You must benefit the majority of the media's target audience. It is also important to know specifically to whom your release should be sent to. If you are unsure what department or person should be receiving your press release for review and consideration, call first and ask. Try to get a full name and title, and address the release directly to her. Departments are diverse, including real estate, lifestyles, business, and book reviews.

Sourcing out-of-area or national media contacts requires more research. You can purchase media directories like Oxbridge Communication's *Annual Media Directory* or subscribe to its online media database at www.mediafinder.com, but these are costly options. A free alternative media directory is News Link, which can be found online at www.newslink.org. Ultimately, you will want to combine different ways of collecting media contact information using a contact management software program such as Maximizer, which can be found online at www.maximizer.com. Additionally, you can use a simple Media Contact Form (see Figure 14.1) to keep track of key media contact people.

Press Release Distribution

Some editors, journalists, and producers still like to receive press releases the old fashioned way, by snail mail or fax. But they are quickly finding themselves in the minority as more and more join the technology revolution, preferring to receive and review press releases via e-mail. The Internet has transformed the way publicists, marketers, and small business owners can release information to the media. Most print and electronic media directories include e-mail contact information for key media people and companies. Of course, when in doubt,

| FIGURE 14.1 | Media Contact Form |

Contact 1

Company _____ Person ❏ Mr. ❏ Mrs. ❏ Ms. _____

Telephone _____ Fax _____ E-mail _____

Comments _____

Contact 2

Company _____ Person ❏ Mr. ❏ Mrs. ❏ Ms. _____

Telephone _____ Fax _____ E-mail _____

Comments _____

Contact 3

Company _____ Person ❏ Mr. ❏ Mrs. ❏ Ms. _____

Telephone _____ Fax _____ E-mail _____

Comments _____

Contact 4

Company _____ Person ❏ Mr. ❏ Mrs. ❏ Ms. _____

Telephone _____ Fax _____ E-mail _____

Comments _____

Contact 5

Company _____ Person ❏ Mr. ❏ Mrs. ❏ Ms. _____

Telephone _____ Fax _____ E-mail _____

Comments _____

simply call and ask how they prefer to receive a press release or media advisory.

CREATING A MEDIA KIT

A media kit is generally in the form of a decorative folder with an interior pocket which holds various loose information sheets (8.5-x-11-inch) inside. The information sheets are intended to give the reader insights into your business, what you sell or what you do, who is involved, and other information that is considered newsworthy or relevant to your business, industry, products, or services. The media folder can be basic, but the outside should be visibly imprinted with your business name, logo, and contact information, including telephone and fax numbers, Web site and e-mail address, and your complete

mailing address. These heavy paper presentation folders can be purchased at most office supply stores and in bulk cost about 50 cents each. Most include an indentation outside so that you can insert a business card there, a good alternative to printed folders for those on a tight budget. A variety of information can be included in your media kit. There are no set rules, and you can add or delete items as required to meet your own specific needs and objectives.

Summary Sheet

A summary sheet is much like a table of contents. It allows the reader at a glance to quickly decipher what is in the media kit and what may be of particular interest to him. The summary sheet should include the name, address, and other contact information of

FIGURE 14.2 Sample Press Release

Complete contact information here, including:

Business name, full address, and Web site URL

<u>FOR IMMEDIATE RELEASE</u>

CONTACT: John Doe
(555) 555-5555
john@doe.com

ENTREPRENEUR MAGAZINE'S ULTIMATE HOMEBASED BUSINESS HANDBOOK
By James Stephenson

Irvine, CA, August 1, 2004–Finally, a one-stop source of valuable need-to-know business information that has been specifically developed for the thousands of entrepreneurial-minded people in North America that will start their own home business this year.

New Book Unlocks Home Business Success Mystery!

To many the concept of starting a home business is often overwhelming, frustrating, and bewildering. Where do they begin? How do they set up a home office? Where should they invest their precious start-up dollars? How do they avoid costly mistakes and dead ends? And most important, when will they see needed results? All of that has changed thanks to *Entrepreneur Magazine's Ultimate Homebased Business Handbook* (Entrepreneur Press, 2004), the most authoritative and comprehensive home business book available today. In fact, this book is packed with thousands of useful home office and business ideas that are guaranteed to take new entrepreneurs from start-up to success, painlessly, quickly, and for life.

Author of *Entrepreneur's Ultimate Start Up Directory* and *Entrepreneur Magazine's Ultimate Small Business Guide*, James Stephenson invests his 15 years of small business and sales experience into this book. Stephenson advises, "You will discover everything you need to know to get your home business started and, more importantly, how to generate profits in no time."

Entrepreneur magazine, now in it's third successful decade of providing small business owners with all the vital business and information know-how that they need to start and grow their businesses, is committed to helping all business owners and managers succeed through timely and expert information in book, magazine, and software formats.

# # #

If you would like more information about this book, a review copy, or to schedule an interview with the author, call John Doe at (555) 555-5555, or, john@doe.com the person that the media kit is intended for, be it a journalist, editor, or CEO, and your contact information or the contact information of the person handling your public relations program. It is always a good idea to print your summary sheet on company letterhead.

Press Release

Include a current and up-to-date press release in the kit and try to have more than one press release ready to go at any one time. The theme or angle of each should be different so you can appeal to a broader audience in terms of your two target audiences—the media and their audience.

Review Sheet

A review sheet is generally a one-page sheet that lists the compelling reasons why a reporter, editor, or any member of the media should give you coverage. One paragraph can be devoted to describing the product or service. A second paragraph can be devoted to the benefits that using the product or service will deliver. A third paragraph can be used to describe how the product or service can be used to solve a problem and any competitive advantages associated with it. The review sheet is the place for fascinating facts and figures about your product or service.

Company Fact Sheet

A company fact sheet can be included with the media kit. It briefly describes the history of your company and the vision you have for the future. You can also use this sheet to describe any awards your company has won and to point readers to a company Web site if you have one. If you are going to include a fact sheet in your media kit, make sure you print your company mission statement on this sheet. Your mission statement will instantly provide the readers with a clear understanding of what your company does, why you do it, and what people get out of doing business with your firm. Don't be afraid to use a highlighter pen to draw attention to key information on the company fact sheet and other information sheets in the kit, but at the same time, don't go overboard. You can also include biographical information about yourself, key employees, and important business allies. Include more specific facts on the sheet in terms of your business industry and marketplace.

Testimonials

Include glowing testimonials that you have received from clients in your media kit. Just, make sure that the testimonials are complete in terms of information about the people who wrote them. This information should include their company and title, how they can be contacted, and what solutions your products or services provided them and how they benefited as a result. Beware, if you include testimonials, there is a better than average chance that the reader (media personnel) will contact this person to back up or support claims.

Support Materials

Support materials can include everything from relevant photographs, condensed charts, maps, and graphs to specialized illustrations, public opinion polls, research testing results, and step-by-step product instructions. A picture is invaluable, so if you can incorporate a picture that leaves no doubt as to what your product or service is and how people benefit by using it, then make sure to include one. You might also want to include past press or media clippings that have featured your business, products, or services.

PUBLIC RELATIONS TIPS, TECHNIQUES, AND GREAT IDEAS

Home business owners can never have enough public relations tools, tips, strategies, or ideas in their toolbox. After all, for the most part publicity is free, valuable, and yours for the taking, especially when you know how to get it.

Start a Great Public Relations Ideas Folder

One of the main reasons that most home business owners do not actively seek free publicity and media exposure for their businesses is a lack of great publicity ideas. What makes information, news, and not merely a promotional plug for your business that sounds like an advertisement? One of the easiest ways to figure this out is to profit from other people's great publicity and news-making ideas. Do this by starting your own public relations ideas folder or box. Every time you see, hear, or read a great publicity idea, write it down in detail or clip it out it of the paper and put it in your PR ideas box. Set aside a few moments each week to mine the box for ideas you think would work to secure media exposure for your business. Encourage staff and friends to do the same. They collect great ideas and you file them in your publicity idea box for future review and, with any luck, use.

Media Advisory

A media advisory is a bit different from other forms of contacting the media discussed in this chapter. Media advisories or alerts are prepared and sent to the media outlining an event that will be taking place. In other words, a media advisory is very much like an invitation that spells out the details of the event you believe should be covered by the media in print, on air, or as a good photo opportunity. The details in the media advisory should include:

- *What.* The advisory should clearly detail what the event is all about—a special promotion, a charity event, or a publicity stunt.
- *Where.* The event location and detailed directions about how to get to the location, including parking facilities and an attached a map for difficult-to-find locations.
- *When.* The complete day, month, year, and time of the day the event will be taking place. Additionally, if the event will be broken into various segments such as a ribbon cutting at 10 and celebrity appearance at 11 be sure to include a schedule or itinerary with the advisory.
- *Who.* Include a breakdown of the people you expect to be in attendance, including customers, politicians, celebrities, company executives, contest winners, or children getting their picture taken with Santa. Basically, who is the event being staged for? Ultimately, that is what will spark the interest of the media.
- *Why.* Why is the event taking place—to raise money for charity, draw a contest winner, or present an award? The reason will be relevant

to the event. More importantly, why do you think the media should attend? The reason could be a great opportunity for a human-interest story, a photo opportunity, or general information that benefits their audience and the community.
- *How.* Include how the media can contact you for further information about the event—telephone, appointment, Web site, press conference before the event, e-mail, or a combination.

Media advisories can be mailed, faxed, e-mailed, or hand delivered to the media you want to target and can be printed on company letterhead or standard office paper. Send out your media advisory at least a week prior to the event, and there is no reason why you cannot follow up with members of the media to check on whether they will be attending.

Speeches

Another great way to share your expertise with others is through giving speeches and hosting workshops. There are numerous business associations, agencies, and clubs in every community across the nation. All of these business clubs and associations have one thing in common: They all have experts speak to members on various business and business-related topics throughout the year. For instance, if you're a marketing consultant, contact one or more of these business clubs and offer to host a free marketing speech or workshop information event. If you operate a copyediting service, offer to speak about the importance of great copy and the positive effects it can have on business sales letters and brochures. Free is a relative term, however; while you may speak for free at these meetings or host a free workshop, the potential for getting business from people in attendance or referral business is real.

Talk Radio

Talk radio represents a potential publicity windfall for savvy home business owners that take the time to develop a strategy for being featured on talk radio programs locally and nationally. Start by researching the radio show and its audience; nothing will scare off a producer faster than pitching a story or talk idea that is not even close to being relevant to the station or individual program's format, style, and target audience. Next, develop a story idea, something that would be interesting to the producer and the audience. If you can tie it in with current or local events, then all the better. Once you have developed your idea, put it on paper in the form of a pitch letter, which is basically a professional business letter that tells about your story and why you should be invited to discuss the topic on air. Along with your pitch letter, include a background sheet that clearly spells out your qualifications and expertise on the topic. Back this up with facts or statistics, and perhaps even a customer testimonial, or talk about special work you have done for a recognized person or business. Of course, if you have written books, or articles, taught classes or courses, or anything else in terms of the topic, let the producer know about it in your bio sheet. List anything to build and capitalize on credibility. Send your pitch letter or set up an appointment to meet with the producer in person. If you are an experienced public speaker and carry yourself well I strongly suggest a personal appointment approach to pitching. Producers like to know that they will be booking an exciting, knowledgeable, and engaging guest. Additionally, try to develop an overall angle or concept that will secure a regular spot on one or more programs. You can visit www.radio-locator.com, an online directory with links to more than 10,000 radio stations, indexed by format and geographic location in the United States and Canada, to track down information about talk radio stations and specific programs.

Press Conference

A press conference is simply asking reporters, journalists, editors, and broadcasters to come to a central location so that you can release special news, make an important announcement, answer questions, and hand out related print materials to a group of media personnel, rather than contacting each individually. Few home business owners will ever have the type of groundbreaking news required to draw major media players to a press conference.

But almost all home business owners can create or generate news that is interesting enough to draw secondary media sources. These secondary media sources can include school newspapers, business associations, local cable TV, small radio broadcasters, special interest groups that regularly publish a magazine or journal in print or electronically, and local politicians. Sometimes media coverage can go beyond being featured in traditional big media and include word-of-mouth coverage or print coverage in smaller publications. If you plan on calling or hosting a press conference, a few of the following ideas will go a long way to ensuring that your press conference is successful:

- Forget hosting the press conference at your home office. Find a suitable location like a small banquet room, the Chamber of Commerce, or a supplier office or warehouse. You will also need chairs, a PA system, and basic refreshments like water, coffee, and a snack tray.
- Plan your conference for a convenient time when the majority of media people that you invite will be able to attend. Ten at night will draw few, if any, but 10 A.M. will definitely grab the interest of more than a few.
- Always think photo opportunity from the media's perspective when arranging the room where the conference will be conducted. Make sure that products, logo, business name, and anything else that can identify your business or products will be included in photographs or film footage.
- Don't give long-winded speeches. If appropriate, use live demonstrations instead of or in association with speeches. Try to have on hand an expert who is credible and able to answer questions and who can back up any claims that you may make about a product, service, or featured information.
- Create a media kit that can be handed out at the conference, and consider handing out sample products, photographs, and promotional materials. Basically, do anything you believe will help to explain your message and product or service in the best light possible.

What Do You Have to Offer?

Even if you don't think so, every home business owner business owner has expertise or valuable information that can be offered to the media in exchange for free publicity. For example, consider these careers:

- *Homebased travel agent.* Contact the local television station and go on air once a week or even daily. Talk about travel information, tips, destinations, and the best travel deals of the day.
- *Financial planner.* A financial planner could write a weekly column for the local newspaper featuring information about investing, planning for retirement, and college education fund advice in exchange for a signature at the end of the column featuring her business name and contact information.
- *Handyperson service.* Create a strategy to be featured on local talk radio to answer home repair questions from call-in listeners.

The key to successfully securing media exposure is to develop a news or story angle that will appeal to a large segment of the media's target audience. The media loves this stuff because it's cheap to produce and feature, it appeals to and benefits their target audiences, and it needs good news, information, and activities to fill the airways and publications.

Expert Postcards

Creating expert postcards is a very clever way for media savvy business owners and professionals to become known as an expert in their field or industry among members of the local and even national media. As the name suggests, expert postcards are king-sized versions of business cards and state all of your qualifications, training, special permits, and anything else that can be used to substantiate your expert claim or build credibility in the minds of media personnel. Expert postcards should be professionally printed in high-gloss color like regular postcards. You may even want to include your photograph or a photograph relevant to your business, industry, product, or service on the front and the detailed expert information on the back. Expert postcards can be sent to members of the media along with a brief introduction letter asking that they file your expert postcard for future reference and when they need information related to your field of expertise, you welcome any and all questions, interviews, and inquiries. Update your expert postcard annually, and send the new version to all of your media contacts.

Photo Opportunities

Often when thinking about how to secure publicity, it is very easy to be so focused on trying to create a news story or angle that the obvious is overlooked—creating a photo opportunity instead. Print and television media love a good photo opportunity, and often it is much easier to create a great photo opportunity, than it is to create a good news story. There are two ways to contact the media about your photo opportunity. You can send a press release or media advisory. Give them a telephone call, or pitch them in person about the photo opportunity and why you believe it should be featured. You also can take the photograph yourself and send it to newspapers and magazines along with a paragraph or two explaining the details. The photo opportunity and accompanying story must be something that will appeal to a large segment of the media's target audience, of course. Great photo opportunities can be created around:

- Contests and prize awards
- Community and charity events
- Business grand opening ceremonies
- Company milestones like how long in business
- Winning industry, business, or community awards
- Team sponsorships, especially sports teams that win a game or a major tournament
- Holiday events such as Christmas decorations, Santa visits, and Easter egg hunts

E-Public Relations Page

Design a public relations page and include it in your Web site. Your PR Web page should be listed in your navigation bar, linked from the home page, include current and past press releases, and a downloadable full media kit in PDF format. Also include the latest breaking news about your business, key personnel, and detailed information about the products and services you provide to customers. Be sure to provide information that spells out the unique benefits and competitive advantages associated with these products and services. Make sure you regularly update your PR Web page, and include the fact that you have a PR page in your Web site when you send out press releases and media kits.

Letters to the Editor

Writing letters to the editor is another simple method for home business owners to secure exposure. Keep in mind that your letter cannot be an outright advertisement for your business, so perhaps you can tie your letter into a local hot topic or position yourself as an expert on a particular subject. A home alarm installer might write a letter to the editor on the topic of break-ins and how not to become a victim. The letter should be signed followed by a business name and telephone number. Published letters can provide you with all sorts of free advertising. Often the letter will be talked about for many days or weeks in the same publication via letters written by readers with supportive or opposing views. In fact, your letter will stand the best chance of being published if it is related to a recent article or letter featured in the publication.

Editorial Calendars

Media players like daily newspapers, magazines, and online news portals use editorial calendars for planning key media features, usually a year in advance. For instance, a newspaper's editorial calendar might have a ten-page feature section to run in October on pre-winter car maintenance information. Perhaps on the same editorial calendar will be a feature sections in April on camping and recreational pursuits, to prepare for the approaching summer season. Media calendars give you the opportunity to fashion your news and publicity efforts around upcoming media events and features. For instance, if you operate a homebased career consulting service, you could create a news angle around finding the right career to match your personality type and submit it to media outlets that have upcoming features on career planning and

searches. Editorial calendars are a must for business people that want to use public relations as a serious means of marketing. By going online and visiting www.edcals.com, you can find annual editorial calendars for more than 4,000 media companies throughout the country.

Invent an Event

One of the best ways small business owners can secure positive publicity for their business year after year is to create a special community event that is held on an annual basis. The event could be tied into charity, such as a 10 K run held every August to support the American Cancer Society, or a just-for-fun event, such as a restaurant that hosts an annual hot dog eating contest. The key idea behind inventing an event is, of course, to name it after your business or a product or service that you provide, such as "Joe's Restaurant Annual Hotdog Eating Contest."

Public Opinion Polls

Public relations specialists have long relied on public opinion polls and surveys to secure their clients exposure in print and broadcast media, and now that you know this closely held PR secret, so can you. If there is one thing that media loves to deliver to their readers, listeners, and viewers, it's the results of public opinion polls and surveys. The media and the news-hungry public have a love affair with statistics and numbers, mainstream or way out there. It doesn't matter just as long as there are numbers that the media can sink its teeth into. This fact creates a fantastic opportunity for home business owners to develop and conduct their own public opinion poll or survey. And once complete, release the results to the media so that it can pass this information along to its audience. For example, a homebased income tax accountant could poll 500 taxpayers to find out what their biggest pet tax peeve was, tabulate the results, and release the results to the media a few weeks before the beginning of income tax return season.

Breaking Records

Attempting to break a world record is an interesting and fun way to promote your business and perhaps get a ton of valuable media exposure in the process. Go through the *Guinness Book of Records* to determine if there is a record that is suitable to try to break. Guinness records can be found online at www.guinnessrecords.com. If there is not a record that you feel comfortable trying to break, start making inquires locally to find out if any residents in the community are attempting to set a world record in the near future. If so, offer to sponsor that person or group of people in exchange for being known as the "official sponsor." World record attempts attract lots of media attention and exposure, which is why this is a very worthwhile promotional activity to pursue, no matter how far fetched it may seem on the surface. Even if the attempt fails, the media exposure, lingering goodwill, and word-of-mouth advertising can have a very beneficial impact on business. Make sure before you sponsor any type of record-breaking attempt that your liability insurance will cover you in case of unfortunate circumstances.

GETTING STARTED WITH NETWORKING

Personal contact networking is still one of the best and easiest ways to form long-term and profitable business relationships with like-minded business people and new prospects that can be turned into paying customers. Networking gives you the power of one-to-one relationship building that few other methods of marketing or advertising can match. Through proper networking activities, you are able to build your own powerful sales force of alliances that work tirelessly at selling your business, products, and services to others by way of referral and word-of-mouth advertising. Even better, this eager sales force is not even on the payroll!

Successful small business people have long understood the power of networking and make an effort to include networking activities into their weekly schedules. In fact, they create a networking plan so that they know who can have the biggest and most positive impact on their business. Because they take the time to identify these individuals, they know whom they have to seek out and build business relationships with. There is no question that networking works and will go a long way to help you reach marketing and business objectives. But it

works only if you make a conscious effort to master the art of networking, develop a networking plan, actively seek networking opportunities, and maintain and manage a networking schedule. It all starts by setting your networking objectives.

Start by Setting Objectives

Like any business or marketing activity that you implement, you will get the most out of networking if you know why you are doing it and what you want to accomplish. Set networking goals and objectives so that you know what you want to accomplish and have a yardstick to measure your performance. Your networking objectives will vary depending on your needs, but common networking objectives and goals include:

- To generate new sales leads
- To sell products and services
- To make new business contacts and form new business alliances
- To introduce new products or services
- To find new suppliers, vendors, or employees
- To conduct business and marketing research
- To brand your business and build a positive image within the community
- To become known as an expert in your industry or field
- To seek new business and joint venture opportunities
- To keep informed about current issues facing your business, industry, and community

Simply stating that you want to increase sales through networking means little unless you have a measurable plan in place that you can use as a map to reach your goals and objectives.

Business Card Networking

Business cards are an inexpensive and a very powerful networking tool when used correctly. Get in the habit of handing out at least ten business cards a day. Give one to the mailperson, store clerks, and gas station attendant because you never know where your next sale or referral may come from. Take a moment to personalize every card you hand out; this could be writing a promotional offer on the back, a quote for the day, or simply jotting down "give me a call." Always introduce yourself when handing out your business card, and give recipients a moment to review your card before initiating conversation. To really increase the power of business card networking, consider including a business card with all outgoing mail and correspondence. When someone asks for your business card, give them three, one for them and two extras so they can share them with friends, family members, and co-workers. Tack a few business cards onto every community bulletin board in your community, and arrange with other businesses to leave a plastic cardholder and a supply of your business cards in their reception areas. Of course, don't forget to leave a business card behind every time you go to restaurants, gas stations, dry cleaners, grocery markets, or movie theaters. And most importantly, every time you hand out a business card, let the person know that you are always seeking and appreciate new business. And, when you receive business cards from others take a moment after you finish the conversation to jot a few notes on the back of the card about key points that came out of the conversation. Just practicing a few of these business card networking techniques can have a dramatically positive effect on your business and the number of referrals you receive.

Become a Great Conversationalist

The ability to converse effectively with others is one of the main ingredients in successfully mastering the art of networking. Lousy conversationalist tend to interrupt or argue when they disagree, talk when they should be listening, and, more often than not, offer lots of opinions without being asked. On the other hand, great conversationalist take a greater interest in what other people have to say, frequently address others by name, and, most importantly, enter into conversations knowing what they would like to say and learn, but without preconceived ideas or judgments about the other person. Great conversationalists have learned that you control the conversation by asking questions and carefully listening to what people are really saying. Talking is not controlling. Listening is remaining in control so that you can guide others into revealing the information

that you would like to know. A police detective takes control by asking questions and taking notes. You should be taking mental notes and writing them on paper, the back of their business card, or in your networking notepad after they leave.

Community Networking

It's a proven fact that people like to do business with people that they know and like. They also like to refer other people to businesses run by people they know and like. Your church attendance, local charity activities, or even a run for a seat in municipal government, can have an enormous, beneficial long-term effect on your home business. Get out and shake hands, smile, pitch in and help out for a good cause. Make the decision that you will get in the game instead of watching from the sidelines. In terms of building a positive business image and loyal customer base, no marketing effort can match getting involved with and giving back to the community that supports your business and success. Be genuine in your efforts, and get involved because you want to help out your community, not because you want to promote your business. Don't worry about the upside because over time the business promotion aspect of getting involved will take root, flourish, and show positive and beneficial results. Best of all, it will be the people in the community that benefit from your involvement that will take up the cause and promote your business for you.

Expand Your Networking Reach

Expand your networking reach by networking with people and at places that you normally would not traditionally network. Build friendships and alliances with people from outside of your ethnic, social, economic, and cultural background. Develop a wide net of valuable people alliances to broaden your networking circle and increase your referral and word-of-mouth marketing opportunities. At some point, staying within your current networking circle will become counterproductive. You will be able to make better use of networking time by enlarging your networking circle to include new people and places. One of the best ways to enlarge your networking circle is to join a new club or association—business, social, sports, hobbies, or just about anything. Perhaps a skiing club, a book club, or getting involved with a local charity is an option. Basically look for ways to make new contacts in new places so that you can broaden your marketing reach through new networking activities. You could start your own networking club, or be the first to welcome new people to your community through supporting a newcomers program like Welcome Wagon or by developing your own newcomers program. Regardless of your approach, try to expand your networking circle to have new business contacts that can be used to fuel the growth of your home business.

Create a Mini Sales Pitch

Ditch long-winded explanations about what your business does or sells; replace them with a high impact mini sales pitch. Keep your pitch short, simple, and directly to the point—the biggest benefit your customers receive from doing business with you. For example, a fast, fun, and highly effective mini sales pitch for a financial planner might be, "Hi, my name is Fred, and I help people retire young and very rich." Bingo, who doesn't want to retire young and rich, and who wouldn't want to hear more about this? Very few people would not want to find out more, especially when young and rich are used in the same sentence. Keep your pitch short, to the point, easy to understand, and free of technical jargon. Use it religiously every day—on the street, in restaurants, on the bus, or in line at the grocery store, and watch your sales go through the roof.

Network Online

Take advantage of technology and the Internet to go online and network for new customers and business contacts. Join online discussion groups, post messages in chat rooms, and join online communities with people that share similar interests or fit into your target audience for the products or service you sell. In recent years, many online networking clubs have started to spring up, offering members traditional networking opportunities, but online without an actual bricks and mortar meeting location. Networking via the Internet can be a great way to find new prospects and customers and to build valuable business relationships. But, be aware that it will take time to establish a base of people you can network with, and of those, many will also be networking. So expect to hand out referrals and advice to others when called upon to do so. The following are a few popular online business networking associations and their Web sites.

- Online Business Networking, www.onlinebusiness networking.com
- Net Party, www.netparty.com
- Networking for Professionals, www.networking forprofessionals.com
- Its Not What You Know, www.itsnotwhatyou know.com

Create a Contact List and Follow-Up System

Fully capitalize on business cards and personal information you collect while networking by developing a contact list so that you can stay in touch with your new prospects by sending them your newsletter, a special offer through the mail, or your monthly e-zine if you publish one. Build your contact list using customer and prospect management software, such as Maximizer, which can be found online at www.maximizer.com. One of the most valuable mailing and contact lists that you can use for marketing purposes is the one you have personally created, a compilation of the names of people with whom you have personally been in contact. This is called a house list and must be considered as one of your most valuable business assets. The first time you mail to a new prospect, be sure to remind them where you met. Say it was a pleasure to meet them and you enjoyed the conversation you shared. Remember that effective networking is not meeting someone today and then giving them a call ten years later to see how things are going. Effective networking is a three-part strategy that begins with making the contact, following up with your new contact almost immediately, and staying in contact with your new business alliance or customer for the long term.

RESOURCES

Associations

Canadian Public Relations Society
4195 Dundas Street West, Suite 346
Toronto, Ontario M8X 1X4
(416) 239-7034
www.cprs.ca

Public Relations Society of America
33 Irving Place
New York, NY 10003-2370
(212) 460-1490
www.prsa.org

SOHO America
(Small Office Home Office)
PO Box 941
Hurst, Texas 76053-0941
(800) 495-SOHO
www.soho.org

SOHO Canada
(Small Office Home Office)
PO Box 49266
Four Bentall Center, Suite 908
1055 Dunsmuir Street
Vancouver, BC. V7X 1L2
(800) 290-SOHO
www.soho.ca

Suggested Reading

Barber, Anne, and Lynne Waymon. *Make Your Contacts Count: Networking Know How for Cash, Clients and Career Success.* New York: AMACOM, 2001.

Levinson, Jay Conrad, Rick Frishman, and Jill Lublin. *Guerrilla Publicity: Hundreds of Sure-Fire Tactics to Maximize Sales for Minimum Dollars.* Avon, MA: Adams Media, 2002.

MacKay, Harvey. *Dig Your Well Before You're Thirsty: The Only Networking Book You'll Ever Need.* New York: Doubleday, 1999.

Pinskey, Raleigh. *101 Ways to Promote Yourself: Tricks of the Trade for Taking Charge of Your Own Success.* New York: Avon Books, 1997.

Stephenson, James. *The Ultimate Small Business Marketing Guide: Over 1,500 Great Marketing Tricks That Will Drive Your Business Through the Roof!* Irvine, CA: Entrepreneur Press Inc., 2003.

Yudkin, Marcis. *6 Steps to Free Publicity, Rev Ed.* Franklin Lakes, NJ: Career Press, 2003.

Web Sites

Ali Lassen's Lead Club, www.leadsclub.com: An online lead referral and exchange club with 400 chapters representing more than 5,000 people nationwide.

Business Network International, www.bni.com: Billed as the world's largest referral organization, with more than 2,600 chapters worldwide and thousands of members.

Canadian Welcome Wagon Association, www.welcomewagon.ca: Community newcomer programs.

Council of Public Relations Firms, www.prfirms.org: A free online directory service listing public relations firms and consultants.

Internet News Bureau, www.internetnewsbureau.com: A subscription-based online press release distribution service.

News Link, www.newslink.org: A free online media directory service providing valuable contact information for print and broadcast media companies, indexed geographically.

Online Press Releases, www.onlinepressreleases.com: Custom software that enables you to build a media database and create and distribute press releases via e-mail.

Oxbridge Communications Inc., www.mediafinder.com: Publishers of print and electronic CD ROM media directories covering magazines, newsletters, journals, and newspapers; it also provides a subscription-based online media directory service.

PR Web, www.prweb.com: A free online press release distribution service.

United States Welcome Wagon Association, www.welcomewagon.com: Community newcomer programs.

CHAPTER 15

Sales

I N *THE ULTIMATE HOMEBASED BUSINESS HAND-book*, heavy emphasis has been purposely placed on selling. In this chapter you will discover many super-advanced selling techniques that top business and sales professionals use daily to find more prospects, sell more goods and services, and win more customers for life. These are essential selling skills for home business owners and include:

- Preparation
- Sales communications
- Prospecting
- Qualifying
- Presentations
- Trial closing
- Overcoming objections
- Identifying buying signals
- Closing
- Negotiations
- Referrals
- Following-up

Don't feel overwhelmed or intimidated by these essential selling skills. After all, the vast majority of those who start home businesses are not professional sales people nor do they have to be to succeed in business. But you must understand that it is sales that drive the growth of your business and generate your income. New computers with the latest and greatest features and functions don't sell. A toll-free hotline doesn't sell. And an exclusive distribution agreement for the best and most innovative products doesn't sell. These are all merely aids to help *you* sell. It is not the end of the world if you are not a master of the essential selling skills. What is important is that you are aware of these skills and you recognize the importance of discovering your own sales strengths and weaknesses. Through education and practice, you can work to improve your selling skills.

PREPARED TO SELL

Preparation is the starting point for all selling, much like a family vacation. Before you leave home on a trip, you need to know where you are going, how you will get there, why you are going, and what will see you to your destination safely, on time, and as planned. In sales there is knowledge you need to acquire to get you from prospecting to closing to building lifetime business relationships with customers. Pre-selling knowledge is necessary—what you are selling, who you are selling to, who else is selling it, and what will assist you in the selling and closing process. Preparation can be divided into four main categories: products or services, customers, competitors, and sales tools.

1. *Products or services.* You have to know what you are selling inside out and upside down. Knowledge about your product or service can be acquired from research, specialized training, suppliers, information in books and other published formats, feedback from customers, and hands-on experience. The better you know your product or service, the more you will be able to identify potential customers and sell them what they need. Product and service knowledge must also extend to your business and how products and services are delivered and guaranteed.

2. *Customers.* The second aspect of sales preparation is customer knowledge. You must know who needs what you are selling, where these people are located, how much they buy, and how often they buy. You must also know things such as what clubs your customers belong to, what newspapers they read, and the types of cars they typically drive. Customer knowledge also includes how prospects and customers view or rate your goods and services and the level of service your business provides in delivery and follow-up. Perhaps more importantly sales preparation means you know the answers to the questions your prospects and customers have in advance of their asking. More information about customer profiling and customer service can be found in the research, planning, and customer service sections of this book.

3. *Competition.* Sales preparation means that you know your competition thoroughly—how long they have been in business, their managers and key employees, what people like and dislike about their businesses, their prices, guarantees, and level of customer service as compared to yours, and how they promote their business, secure paying customers, and build long-term relationships with their clients. Basically, you need to know how your business stacks up against direct and indirect competition, today, tomorrow, and in the future. More information about identifying and conquering competitors can be found in the competition section of this book.

4. *Sales tools.* The final aspect of sales preparation is to have a sales toolbox packed with great sales tools. These sales tools are the instruments you will use to grab your prospects' attention, create interest and desire, and motivate them to buy. Sales tools include product or service literature, product samples, customer testimonials, training, and knowledge about your products, services, customers, and competition. Promotional aids, support documents, credentials, payment systems, and delivery and presentation systems are all important to the sales process. Your sales tools and aids must be in good condition, plentiful, and unique to your particular business.

SALES COMMUNICATIONS

Sales communications are any and all contact you have with prospects and clients, regardless of the method—telephone, letter, personal visit, e-mail, or fax. The importance of communications as an essential selling skill cannot be overstated. It is the communication between you and prospects that ultimately determines your success. If you cannot effectively communicate with prospects and customers, regardless of contact method, you will not close sales. It is that simple. Below you will find helpful advice to enable you to become a more effective communicator in your selling endeavors.

Mastering the Art of Listening

The importance of effective listening skills in selling cannot be overstated. In fact, it is one of the most important skills to learn, master, and apply. Being able to understand what prospects and customers are telling you so that you can meet expectations and needs is the cornerstone to all selling. It is the starting point, where you learn the most and gain the ability to close more sales because of what you have learned. You can ask the greatest qualifying questions in the world, but unless you carefully listen to what prospects and customers are telling you, your qualifying questions will be of no value. To be an effective listener, you must be prepared, and willing, to shut up. Stop talking and start listening. Do this by getting rid of any distractions; try to create an environment with as few interruptions as possible. Give people your full and undivided attention and politely ask that they do the same. Ask, Can we speak uninterrupted? when you set sales meetings and presentation. Here are a few more helpful hints:

- Never finish someone else's thoughts or sentences during a conversation. Be patient and allow them to fully articulate.
- Avoid being argumentative, even if you disagree. If you must show exaggerated emotions, make them positive ones—excitement, appreciation, or happiness. As the wise old saying goes, "It is impossible to win an argument with a prospect or customer, even when you know you are right and they are wrong."
- Remember to be empathetic to what other people are telling you. Look at the situation from their point of view and never assume that any concern they have is a small one. People don't mention concerns or objections unless they are important.
- Ask lots of questions to completely flush out all of their needs, motivations, and objections. The clearer you can get your prospect or customer to paint the picture of what they want, the better position you will be in to help.

Creating Effective Sales Letters

How do you get prospects to buy, customers to buy more frequently, and close a whole lot more sales? One way is to create powerful sales letters aimed at grabbing attention, demanding action, and bolstering sales.

- Develop a central sales theme that is focused on your prospects' needs, desires, benefits, hopes, and dreams. Focus on emotional appeal when targeting consumers, and on logistical appeal when targeting business owners and managers. Before you send the letter, know and include the answer to the question that every prospect asks before making a purchase: What is in it for me? The answer should be the central theme of the letter.
- Address the letter to a person by name. Single out the reader as an individual, make her important, special, and your second highest priority. The first is the main benefit she will receive by taking the desired action. Of course, the two should go hand in hand, as in "Helen, I guarantee that you will save $2,349 annually by using recycled ink!"
- Grab attention right away with a bold headline at the top of your letter that solves a problem, creates a fantastic opportunity, states a special limited offer, creates controversial or provocative ideas, or highlights an important and informative statistic about the prospect's business, industry, or target market. Increase the impact of your headline by including the reader's name whenever possible, and use subheads throughout the letter to introduce other interesting information you know will benefit the reader. Subheads work incredibly well at keeping the skimmers interested and involved in your letter.
- Keep the content of the sales letter relevant to the topic or purpose, particularly when you discuss the action that you want your to reader to take. Be brief, to the point, and perfectly clear. If content is not 100 percent relevant to your objective, audience, and main message, get rid of it. It is a waste of valuable selling space.
- Always write to sell, even if the message or theme is not selling. The sub context should be leading the reader on a path to the close. Every contact you make with your prospect, be it a letter, telephone call, or personal appointment, should take you and your audience one step closer to making the sale. Handing out information is useless unless it helps you reach your ultimate marketing objective, which is always to sell.
- Based on the letter you have drafted ask, Would I buy? If yes, list the reasons. What is the appeal, what is the advantage, and what is the motivation and urgency to buy? If your answer is no, list the reasons why not. What's missing? Be honest. If you or someone close to you is not excited by what you are offering or how you are offering, get back to work until you are satisfied you would buy.

- Use action-oriented power words and powerful sales phrases, such as *free samples, call now, set an appointment*, and *delivery on time, guaranteed*. Action words and phrases get the reader instantly involved in the message of the letter and make them want to learn more.

- If your letter is more than one page long, do not end a sentence on the bottom of the page or in the last paragraph. Instead, force the reader to continue reading by starting an incentive or special offer at the bottom of the first page and completing it on the next. Use an additional benefit that your product or service provides readers as a way to keep them involved in the letter. Basically, be it an incentive, guarantee, or second big benefit, use something that is powerful and important to readers to turn the page and stay involved.

- Make sales letters visually appealing with bright color, graphics, and bold paragraph headings on great looking, professionally printed letterhead emblazoned with your business logo and unified marketing message. And, make sure that your color selection, font, and logo are all consistent with the rest of your printed materials. People visually link consistent styles with a business when they are continually exposed to a unified corporate image. Your prospects and customers will begin to instantly identify your business just by the envelope, letterhead, or color scheme that you use in your marketing and promotional activities.

- Make the letter easy to read and understand. Skip the technical jargon, and never make the readers feel stupid by using language or terms that they could not possibly understand. Nothing will turn readers off faster. Check spelling, grammar, and structure. If time allows, let the letter sit for a few days, then return to complete the editing. You will almost always find information you want to include and some that you want to delete.

- Always tell the reader what you want them to do next: Call me, stop by our trade show booth, order now, or log onto our Web site for more exciting information. Always make sure

you give them the tools required for them to take the desired action. These tools can include full contact information, an incentive coupon, a customer testimonial if you want them to contact happy customers, a self-addressed stamped envelop if you want them to respond by mail, your Web site address, or your toll-free order hotline. The easier you make if for people to do what you want them to do, the more people that will do it.

- Include a postscript that reinforces the benefits and values of your main offer or the key elements and message of the letter. For example, "P.S. We have the best widgets in the industry. If you call now, I'll prove it by sending you ten free samples by overnight courier and give you $100 credit toward your first order. But only if you call before the end of the week!"

Staying in Constant Contact with E-Mail

Keep in front of customers and prospects by creating an e-tip, e-advisory, e-opportunity, or e-insight, and e-mailing it to customers and prospects daily. Your daily e-mail should be relevant to what you sell and be valuable to people that receive it, read it, and share it with others. You decide what will be valuable in terms of information you share with prospects and clients. Send it out to everyone on your database list, and politely ask them to share it with their friends, family, and co-workers. Your original e-mail should include a signature file at the end that identifies your business and that is linked back to your e-mail and/or Web site. This is new age word-of-mouse advertising, often called virtual marketing. It works great to get information out to the people that can benefit from it and, in turn can help build your business.

Productive Cold Calling

Telephone cold calling can be a tough grind, but there are a few cold calling techniques that are productive and secure more sales appointments and meetings. Start by knowing what your objective is: to set up a fact-finding or presentation appointment, send promotional literature or samples, introduce your company, products or services, or find out who the decision makers are within the organization? Plan what you are going to say in advance, and write it down in brief script format. Anticipate objections to your objective, and be ready to answer and overcome those objections during the conversation.

Once on the telephone, start by identifying who you are, your company, and why you are calling. Make sure to state the main benefit of your product or service and how this relates to your prospect as quickly as possible. Be very clear about this. The person you call must benefit directly; if not, you will soon lose their interest. But only give enough information to get your prospect interested and involved in the conversation. There is power in mystery, so use mystery to reach your objective. Ask for an appointment in a way that it is assumed the prospect will agree, such as, Which is best for you, Thursday at ten or Friday at eleven? Based on this type of assumptive question, the choice becomes when to meet; not meeting is no longer an option. And finally, don't give up if they say no. Ask for a personal appointment at least three times. If you get nowhere, ask if you can place them on your newsletter and e-mail list.

Leaving Messages that Get Returned

Leaving a voice mail message is easy; getting people to return the message is an entirely different story. One of the best ways of leaving a voice mail message that will get returned is to anticipate that you will have to leave a voice mail message. Knowing exactly what to say, why you are calling and why they should call you back, is one of the keys to getting your calls returned. Being caught off guard and leaving behind a broken string of mumbo jumbo is a surefire way of not getting your call returned. Here are a few more helpful tips:

- Speak clearly and slowly so that the person will understand exactly what you are saying without having to guess. Spell out any words that are difficult to pronounce.
- Use your voice effectively and with energy and enthusiasm, as if you have some ground moving information that they need to know.

Excitement and mystery combined will almost always get your call returned.

- Leave your main contact telephone number at least twice, near the beginning, and repeated at the end of your message.
- State a best call back time or blocked window of time such as, "I will be in the office Tuesday afternoon between noon and four in the afternoon and would appreciate if you would call me back then."
- State the main reason why you are calling. Your reason should be something that will benefit the person you are calling so that they will be motivated to call you back right away. The benefit should be your biggest gun, mind boggling, something they could not possible resist. Tell them you'll make them rich, save them money, make them more productive, make them feel and look 20 years younger, or that you have information that will be shared with no one other than them, providing they call you back right away. Tie the biggest benefit of what you do or sell into your prospects' biggest need, desire, want, or problem, and I guarantee that your call back response rate will skyrocket.

HIGH-IMPACT PROSPECTING

Typically, three things define a good prospect:

1. They need your product or service.
2. They have the ability to pay for it.
3. They have the authority to purchase it.

Identifying and initially qualifying a prospect is outlined in the next section of this chapter. This section is aimed at prospecting techniques and skills, which can help overcome the common home business owner's complaint, "Business is always feast or famine. I have no business, or I have more business than I can handle." Feast or famine can be eliminated entirely or at least regulated through constant and consistent prospecting so that your sales pipeline remains at a stable level. Prospecting for new customers serves two main needs, depending on your situation.

1. *New business start-ups.* For new business start-ups, prospecting for customers in all likelihood

will dominate your initial marketing efforts. You lack an existing customer base to expand on, and because your marketing budget is probably tight, making telephone, e-mail, and personal visits to drum up new business are very attractive.

2. *Existing business operations.* There are a multitude of reasons why you should continue to prospect for new business, regardless of how busy your sales schedule is presently, or how rosy your sales future looks. One of the most important reasons to continually and systematically prospect is to ensure that your business pipeline remains full, with prospects you are currently working with to turn their interest into sales. Where have my customers gone? is one of the biggest complaints of business owners after years in business profits begin to slide and their once-loyal customer base slowly vanishes. Hence, there is always the need to prospect for new business.

Regardless of your business stage, prospecting remains the foundation for all selling because it takes people (prospects) to buy what you are selling. You must keep your pipeline of potential customers full at all times. Of course, once your business is established, you will begin to know who your best customers are. They are the people that frequently buy products or services from you, always pay on time and in full, refer others to your business, and rarely complain. Leading businesspeople take the time to identify their best customers, and then set out to clone them. They identify common characteristics of their best customers and use this information to develop marketing and action plans aimed at people that are similar. They find out information such as the publications they read, radio and television programs they like to listen to and watch, and other key facts on education, income, family, and career. You can use this information to identify patterns, things your best customers have in common. Perhaps a high percentage of them subscribe to the same newspaper. Then it would be wise to advertise your business in that newspaper to appeal to people like your best customers. Or maybe a high percentage of them belong to particular community

associations. Logically, you would want to join these associations and network with their members. There is much wisdom to the old adage "Birds of a feather flock together." Identify the feathers your best customers have in common, and you won't be far from discovering where the entire flock is located. More information about target customer demographics and profiling can be found in the research section of this book.

PROSPECT AND CUSTOMER MANAGEMENT DATABASE

There are numerous database management software programs available, such as Maximizer 7, which can be found online at www.maximizer.com. These programs enable you to build and manage your contact and customer lists, and they are a highly effective sales tool for small business owners. However, your database is only as good as the information you enter and manage, so here are a few ideas for maintaining a good prospect and customer relationship management database.

- Create two ranking systems: one for customers and one for prospects. Both should use a ranking system such as A,B,C, listing your best customers and hottest prospects as A to your least frequent customers and coldest sales prospects as C. This saves time and money when it comes to sending out direct mail marketing materials, telemarketing to present new offers, or following up.
- Update your database on a regular basis, focusing on new client and prospect information input. Update files and delete outdated information as needed.
- Include only information that is helpful in terms of meeting your database objectives. Include information that assists in recognizing your clients and prospects as individuals, including birth dates, hobbies, and family members. This information is especially important when developing presentations and proposals that will appeal to each individual based on needs and wants.
- Develop and maintain a system about how information will be entered and recalled—by company name, personal name, alphabetically,

or order of importance. And although the type of information that you choose to capture and record about your customers will change depending on your marketing objectives, you should also capture the bare minimum, which includes individual or company name, full address and contact information, buying history, job title or occupation, demographic information, including age, sex, and level of education, and special requests.

Eight Prospecting Laws

The following eight prospecting laws have been developed to help you get up to speed quickly and efficiently, so you can get the most benefit from the you spend prospecting.

1. *Set prospecting goals.* The first law of prospecting is to set prospecting goals. How many new contacts do you want to make each day, week, and month? Having a set number is the only logical way to ensure that you are constantly making new prospect and business contacts.

2. *Fact finding.* The second law of prospecting is to treat initial contact with new prospects strictly as a fact-finding mission. Most business owners spend far too much time trying to sell their products or services during first contact, instead of carefully listening to prospects and asking well-crafted questions to truly identify what the prospect's needs.

3. *No preconceived ideas.* The third law of prospecting is to never prejudge a person's ability to buy and pay for a purchase until careful questions and answers have established what they need, when they need it, if they can make the buying decision, and if they have the financial ability to pay for it. Until these questions have been asked and answers given, everyone must be equally considered a prospect regardless of how they look, act, dress, or speak.

4. *Keep it simple.* The fourth law is that your product or service and how you market it must be clear and easy to understand and grasp in moments, not hours or days. Consequently, you must develop your sales message around

clarity in order to appeal to the largest segment of your target audience. Make it plain English, easy to understand, and free of boring technical jargon that only works to confuse the vast majority of people. Never make what you sell or do difficult for people to understand.

5. *Beneficial.* The fifth law of prospecting is that what you sell has to benefit the person you are trying to sell it to. Living in balmy Vancouver, I have little use for a snowmobile, no matter how many features and how much horsepower is stashed under the hood. But a rain jacket would be very beneficial here on the "wet coast" of Canada. Appeal to your target audience by giving them what they need—help them fix a problem, make them rich, save them money, or make them feel better. Selling is about matching what you have to sell to what people need. After all, if I need a rain jacket and you're selling them, your job of persuading me to buy one becomes rather easy, wouldn't you agree?

6. *Value.* The sixth law of prospecting is that what you sell has to represent value to your prospect. Regardless of the price, prospects must be able to see, and therefore justify a direct correlation between your offering and the price that goes with it, and what your product or service will do for them. Products and services are only worth what people will pay for them. But the more value (benefits) a person can derive from buying a product or service, then the more likely they are to pay a premium or not object to the price.

7. *Never sell only what you like.* The seventh law of prospecting is that no one cares what products or services you like. You're not the one who will be using, and paying for, them with your hard-earned money. If you sell based only on your likes, then you are telling prospects what you like, you not listening to what the prospect wants. So you break the golden rule of selling, which is to listen to what your prospects and customers are telling you at all times. Sell what your prospects' need and like, even if you don't happen to agree with their choice. If they're happy with their choices and are prepared to

pay for it, get the contract signed, thank them for their support, ask for referrals and tell them that you look forward to doing more business with them in the near future.

8. *Manage your prospecting time.* The eighth law of prospecting is to manage your prospecting time well to ensure maximum productivity. It stands to reason that the better you manage your time, the more time you will be able to devote to prospecting for new business. Therefore, employ time management tactics such as:

- Set aside a block of time each day strictly for the purposes of prospecting, creating new ways to promote your products or services, and finding unique ways to position what you sell in the marketplace.

- Prepare your daily to-do list the evening before, and make an effort to check every item off before you call it quits the following day.

- Develop a scheduling system and stick to it. Prospect the same time each day when you are most likely to reach your target audience on the phone or in person. Group sales presentations and meetings together to save time and stay in the same focused mindset.

- Carry a hot-prospects folder with you so you can benefit from any unexpected down time by calling them or working on solutions to fix their product or service problems. Inspirational ideas are lost if they are not written down in an easily retrievable format. Keep your prospecting goals and objectives written down and in front of you as a daily motivator.

Simple Lead Generation Ideas and Techniques

One way to secure fresh sales leads is to develop a customer list and lead swap program with business owners and sales professionals in your area that represent noncompeting but compatible products and services. For example, if you sell home renovation products and installation services, swap your customer and prospect list with an appliance store-owner. They are noncompeting businesses, but share common characteristics that could benefit each party. In this example, it's likely that customers and prospects for both businesses own a home, and the lifecycle of many building products, such as bathroom fixtures, is approximately 20 years, the same as major appliances. Therefore, it's a safe assumption that someone having a washroom renovated would also need or soon need new appliances. Customer list and lead exchange programs are a very efficient way to prospect for new business because they greatly reduce the time you spend finding and qualifying new prospects. Here are seven more great lead generation ideas.

1. *Staging contests.* Stage contests as a way to generate sales leads from the information you capture on the entry ballots. Strike a deal with a local retailer to host the contest, and install the ballot box at that location. Alternately, send out entry form in the mail or as an advertisement in the newspaper, and let people mail the completed ballots back. Use trade shows and other marketing events to host contests, and collect sales leads from the ballots.

2. *Apply for a job.* Calling all consultants. It is time to tap into the thousands of employment advertisements that appear in print newspapers and online employment Web sites daily. Get started by creating a specialized resume and introduction letter that explains the benefits of your service, including a few client success stories. Send your consulting service package to companies that are seeking to fill specialized positions in your area of consulting expertise. Attend job and career expos to make introductions and network with business owners and managers that could also benefit from hiring your service as opposed to hiring an employee. Just because a corporation, organization, or small business thinks that they are looking for an employee, doesn't mean that they aren't in fact really seeking the services of a highly skilled consultant to help fuel their growth or solve specific challenges that face their businesses. The very fact that they run an employment advertisement means that they are to a certain degree qualified and definitely have a need to fill. Maybe all that is required is an in-depth explanation about how hiring your consulting

service will be more beneficial and productive than hiring an employee. Certainly, it is an option that consultants should carefully consider.

3. *Give your service away for free.* Try giving your service away for free to make more money. For instance, a friend that operates a carpet cleaning service routinely gives away his carpet cleaning services for free. However, there is a catch. He carefully selects an apartment building and takes a name off the front door registry. Using the White Pages he calls that person to offer carpet cleaning services for free. Seldom does he get turned down, especially when he honestly tells them that he needs access to the building a few days prior to cleaning the carpets so that he can place a simple door hanger on each door in the building stating,

> We are going to be cleaning the carpets in apartment #_____ on _____. We can offer you a special discount of 20 percent to clean your carpets too. However to take advantage of this special offer you must call within the next 24 hours and reserve your appointment.

Without fail, he always secures more carpet cleaning work to do at the same time and gets back the free work through volume.

4. *Target yourself.* Another way to generate sales leads is not to overlook people like you who work from a home office. In most cases, you will find other home business owners are far more open to cold calls and proposals, simply because they share a common bond with you. They understand, relate to, and appreciate the challenges that others home business operators face as they struggle to build their business and take on larger competitors daily. Start by going online to find mailing lists that specifically include home business owners, and join home business associations such as SOHO (Small Office Home Office), www.soho.org in the United States and www.soho.ca in Canada. Many home business associations like SOHO operate only in the cyber world, so you'll be able to network and prospect with other small business owners right online from home via e-mail and discussion boards.

5. *Life cycle prospecting.* Life cycle prospecting opportunities are abundant, but only if you take the time required to identify them. Every product has a definable life span, both in terms of usefulness and time. In the postwar era, residential housing subdivisions became a popular way to develop large tracts of land to provide affordable housing for returning military personnel starting families. This was the start of the baby boom generation and the suburbs. From that time to this, building houses in subdivisions has remained popular. About 90 percent of all new homes built in the last 60 years have been constructed in subdivision developments. This is an example of hidden life cycle prospecting opportunities. A residential housing subdivision that is now 15 years old represents a wealth of life cycle prospecting opportunities because almost all building products and fixtures have a definable lifespan of 15 to 20 years. Consider the vast numbers of products used in the construction of these homes that are reaching the end of their useful life span. There are roofing, kitchen and bathroom fixtures, appliances, windows, fencing, and the list goes on.

The greatest benefit of life cycle prospecting is that most contacts you make in this way are already qualified to a certain degree. Because every product and even most services have a definable life cycle, the key to successful life cycle prospecting is knowing exactly what the life span of your product or service is, and then planning strategies to capitalize. Life cycle prospecting simple means you are seeking prospects with products or services that are nearing the end of their useful life span before these people contact you and your competition for bids.

6. *Demonstration prospecting.* For centuries street performers have been using demonstrations as a successful way to prospect for new business. A juggling street performer sets up in a busy park and begins to juggle bowling balls (demonstration). Soon people start to take notice and crowd around to watch (prospects). Some people leave, while others stay to watch (qualifying). The performer continues to

demonstrate juggling skills to an amazed audience (presentation). The juggler completes the presentation and takes a bow as people drop lose change into a box (closing). By doing no more than demonstrating a service (entertainment the juggler has attracted prospects, qualified some, presented to a crowd, and closed a few sales. Its a complete sales cycle, all in the matter of minutes. The larger point is that most products and services can be demonstrated in public for prospecting purposes—in more than the usual demonstration forums of trade shows and seminars. For instance, if you sold fishing poles and went to a crowded beach on the weekend and cast a line, it would not be long before people approached you and asked if the fish were biting. Or if you operated martial arts training facility and took the class to a local park for a training session, it would not be long until a crowd gathered and been asking questions about your school.

7. *Expert prospecting.* Prospecting does not always mean searching for new customers. It can also mean developing prospecting strategies that have people seeking you out for your expertise. Society in general accepts the notion that published authors or speakers on specific topics and issues are mostly experts within their field. And people seek expert advice to help solve problems or challenges. Therefore, it makes sense to capitalize on your expertise to persuade people to come to you. Get started by writing a book, newspaper column, or magazine feature, or actively look for places where you can speak on topics related to your specialty. Becoming known as an expert not only distinguishes you from the competition, it also means that, in all likelihood, people will seek your advice when they are trying to solve a problem, need advice, or help in a decision, all of which can be turned into selling opportunities.

QUALIFYING PROSPECTS

Qualifying prospects in the sales cycle is the process of asking carefully crafted questions and using the responses to determine if they need, want, and can afford what you are selling. The importance of qualifying cannot be overstated. The better qualified a prospect is, the greater the chance of closing the sale. Business owners often feel uncomfortable asking qualifying questions because they wrongly think they are being pushy, nosy, or aggressive. But realize that every person must ask questions in order to help others or to determine what the others need. Doctors ask questions about symptoms so they can make informed diagnoses. A fitness trainer will ask about specific goals so they can develop an exercise program that will help achieve those goals. So, you have to get comfortable asking questions, even when your prospect is not forthcoming with answers. It is the only way you will be able to determine if you can help them, and if they want and are in a position to buy what you are selling. Another, yet often overlooked, aspect of qualifying is the fact that you can make one generalized assumption—seldom do people stray too far from what they already have, are comfortable with, or understand. For instance, most people currently driving a family vehicle such as a mini van or stationwagon will purchase a similar vehicle when it comes time to do so. People in general are creatures of habit, making consumers extremely transparent in terms of the products and services they purchase and use. Knowing this can help in the qualifying process because much of your work is already done for you if you take the time to ask people what they are currently using.

Are You Asking Open-Ended Questions?

Key to the success of effective prospecting is asking open-ended qualifying questions. A common example of a closed-ended question is a sales clerk asking a shopper "Is there anything I can help you find?" This is a closed-ended question that will result in a yes or no response. Even a small improvement such as "What brought you into our store today?" is a vast improvement because the shopper must then reveal information the clerk can use to determine if they can help the shopper find what they need. By asking open-ended questions, you get your prospect involved in the conversation and sales process. Try experimenting with various open-ended questions related to what you do or sell, and keep a log detailing the success or failure rates of each question. This will enable you to build an arsenal of open-ended questions you know will be effective more times than not. Here are a few examples of open-ended sales questions: "What challenges does your business face?" "How did you hear about our company?" "When do you need to take delivery?" "Who are the other people that will be involved in this decision?" "What financial budget has been established for this purchase?"

Who Makes the Buying Decisions?

Always make sure that you are dealing with the person or people that can ultimately make the decision to buy your products or services. If the person or people you are dealing with are not the decision makers, then find out who is and deal with them. Nothing is more frustrating then having a hot prospect on the line, only to discover after spending much time and energy with them that they cannot make the decision about buying. Or you find out there are more people involved in the decision-making process than just the person you are dealing with. The best way to find out the identity of the decision maker is to simply ask your prospect questions such as: "Who will be making the purchasing decision?" "Will you be making the decision on your own, or will there be other people involved in the purchasing decision?" "If you find my _____ suitable, are you authorized to make the purchase?"

Do They Need It?

Determine up front during initial contact if your prospect needs what you are selling. If not, you are wasting your time and theirs by continuing the conversation. If you have in-depth knowledge of what you sell and how people benefit by owning or using it, qualifying a prospect with a few simple questions should be easy: "What problems need solving?" "What are their requirements?" "What needs to be improved?" "What is wrong with what they currently have, or alternately what would make their job or life easier?" There is one exception to the qualifying needs rule, which is appealing to emotions in such a

way that it overrides and sometimes defies logic. Few people need a sports car that will reach 200-miles per hour, yet many people sure want one. But unless you are selling a product or service that can be sold strictly on an emotional level with logic thrown out the window, stick with pursuing prospects that truly need what you are selling. Always ask yourself what is the best use of your time at that very moment. I will guarantee it is not trying to sell something to someone that doesn't need it.

Can They Afford It?

Many small business owners feel extremely uncomfortable asking people questions about their personal or business financial situation. And, of course, even if you do ask the right qualifying questions, the answers you receive might be somewhat embellished. Most people want to be perceived as being better off than they are. So where does that leave you? It leaves you knowing two things for sure. The first is that you must get comfortable and in the habit of asking prospects about their ability to pay for what you are selling or their ability to secure credit. Ask your prospect if they have the money put aside to pay for the purchase, if they will be using credit cards or arranging financing, or if you can take the liberty of arranging financing for them. Second, you have to be realistic about your prospect's purchasing power and always be prepared with a less expensive option should financial matters become an obstacle to closing the sale. If you spend all your time focused on one product or service and suddenly money becomes an issue, you have little latitude to move. However, if you keep in mind that money could become an obstacle and have a plan in place, you are armed to save the sale and still do business with your prospect.

When Do They Want It?

When is your prospect in the market to buy what you are selling, and how committed is your prospect to this buying schedule—very committed, somewhat committed, or just tentative based on other factors that could influence the final buying decision? You can learn more in terms of timing by asking easy open-ended questions such as: "How soon do you need the _____?" "When will you be ready to have the product installed?" "What is your time frame for completing this project?" "When would you like to take delivery?" These are nonthreatening questions, and the beauty of asking time line questions early is that the answers give you a good indication of their openness to an early close in the sales cycle. If your prospect answers positively to your qualifying time line question then echo with a trial close question "Can I get this before the end of the week?" To which you would reply "If I can arrange delivery before the end of the week are you prepared to make the purchase?"

What Other Obstacles Stand in the Way?

Effective qualifying means that you are carefully listening and watching for other obstacles that can stand between you and making the sale. Other obstacles are usually the quiet deal killers, the stuff that was overlooked during the initial qualifying process because you did not think to look for them or the prospect was not forthcoming with information about potential obstacles. These other obstacles could include things such as your prospect's health, his level of training or education to use your product or service, or personal priorities. While a person might be genuinely interested in purchasing a new car, is the leaky roof at home that needs to be replaced the true priority instead of the shiny new car? Regardless of the obstacle, the trick is to listen carefully to what your prospect is telling you so that you will be able to identify potential obstacles. Sometimes they will be subtle, while other times the obstacles will be glaring. Of course, if you think there might be a hidden obstacle in the way of the sale, it is always best just to come out and ask.

Who Else Is Trying to Sell It to Them?

Knowing who the competition is can often be as important as knowing what your prospects' needs are, especially in highly competitive industries where thin profit margins are the norm. Identifying the competition will help you to prepare your presentation, develop special benefits and advantages for individual prospects, and enable you to know where

your product or service is positioned in terms of the competition and how this will relate to the prospects' needs and wants. The easiest way to find out who the competition will be is to simply ask, "Who else will be bidding on the job?" Knowing who you are up against for the sale is not important in terms of competitors' price, because if you are selling only based on price, you won't be in business long anyway. The importance of knowing who you are competing with is that you will then be able to design the best package for your prospect, stuff the competition does not do or sell or perhaps special permits or training that you know they do not have. The more information you have about your prospects, their wants and needs, and who the competition for their sale will be, the better you can position your own offering to meet and exceed your prospects' expectations.

WINNING PRESENTATIONS

Generally the objective of the sales presentation is to close the sale, but not always. Other objectives can include booking a second meeting, introducing a new or improved product or service, or conducting research to get valuable feedback. The reason I mention this is that all presentations must be built on a clear objective. You have to know what you want to accomplish and what your prospect is expecting to happen at the presentation. Nine times out of ten, of course, your objective is to sell, sell more, sell more frequently, or a combination. It is during the presentation stage of the sales cycle that the full impact of your product or service and the benefits associated with owning them is delivered to your prospect. Call it delivery of the total package, including samples, colorful brochures, testimonials, and live demonstrations. Home business owners have one disadvantage to overcome that businesspeople with an office or storefront do not, which is lack of personal contact presentation space. As a general rule, clients, prospects, and sales representatives feel extremely uncomfortable traipsing through your home for a meeting unless they know you really well. And even then key meetings and presentations should always be conducted outside of your home office at a suitable location. Meeting location can include local business associations such as the Chamber of Commerce, where meeting boardrooms or office facilities can often be rented by members. Or you can strike a deal with a key business alliance or supplier so that you can use their office space and meeting facilities when conducting meetings and presentations. Also check to see if any restaurants in your local area are suitable meeting places. Many have small banquet and meeting rooms that can be rented by the hour very inexpensively. Or for the truly innovative entrepreneur, you can even take clients to unusual places for meetings—to the park or on a boat ride, or even a drive through the country.

Key Presentation Points

While much goes into developing great sales presentations, at the core there are four key presentation fundamentals. These fundamentals are keeping your prospect's attention, focusing on your prospect's needs and wants, making your presentations memorable, and leading your prospect to the action you want them to take.

Attention

Seldom will a piece of paper such as a brochure, estimate, or proposal close the sale. Closing is left up to you and the interaction you establish and maintain with your prospects. For that reason, it is important that you keep your prospect's attention at all times during presentations. A good way to accomplish this is not to distribute sales materials or a typed presentation at the beginning of the meeting. Hold printed sales materials back until the end of the presentation; distribute them to prospects after you have presented your information and conducted demonstrations. The focus of the sales presentation should be on persuading the prospect to buy through questions, answers, and demonstrations. None of this can be achieved if your prospects are busy flipping through and concentrating on printed sales material. Your words and actions are lost. And worse, prospects form opinions and make decisions based on what is in print, and unfortunately, all these printed words cannot show the best and biggest benefits of your product or service.

Focus

During the presentation stay focused on your prospects' needs and on the results that you want. Your entire presentation should be needs based—how what you sell fills their needs, solves a problems, or, for business clients, creates new opportunities that they need to compete or increases productivity that they need to be profitable. Common needs include the need to make more money, save more money, increase productivity, expand market share, and improve one's health. Also focus on results. Never assume your prospects saw, heard, read, or understood what you wanted them to during the presentation. Instead, restate the benefits of your product or service in terms of fulfilling their needs.

Memorable

Strive to make your presentation unique, interesting, and memorable by utilizing every available media and presentation aid—live product or service demonstrations, colorful statistical charts and graphs, audio and visual clips, static pictures and illustrations, customer testimonials, and online technologies. The objective is to make the presentation more memorable so that your prospects will want to be involved and invested in every aspect of the presentation.

Action

Your presentation must end with some sort of action taking place, preferable the action you want your prospect to take, such as buying. Therefore, always end your presentation by asking that your prospect take action. The action might be to buy, buy more, buy more frequently, set up a follow-up meeting, or whatever you determine. The desired action should be directly related to the initial objective of the presentation. Remember, people are not mind readers, and unless you specifically tell them what you want them to do next, do not expect that they will automatically take action.

Powerful Presentation Sales Tools

Perhaps the most powerful presentation tool you have at your immediate disposal is you. Making a positive impression on people is the first use of this powerful presentation tool. Seldom do we get the opportunity to reinvent ourselves to people that we have already met. The old saying that you only get one chance and a few brief moments to make a favorable lasting first impression is very true. In fact, most public speaking gurus contend that you are limited to only a few minutes to make a favorable first impression. Therefore, careful attention must be paid to appropriate attire, body language, verbal skills, and interaction with other people. Like it or not, a book is judged by its cover. Sales is not selling, it is persuasion and perceptions. We assume that a doctor must be wearing a white overcoat while working and a banker a suit, and that a boxer with a black eye must not be very good, though his opponent may very well have two black eyes. Consequently, the importance of making a positive impression through personal packaging and people skills is vital to success in selling. Here are a few additional powerful presentation sales tools.

Customer Testimonials

Few consumers want to sail into uncharted waters alone. We all want to know that someone has gone before us and that everything worked out just fine. That's the benefit of customer testimonials; they prove that others have purchased your product or service and that everything worked out just fine. Share customer success stories with your prospects to clearly demonstrate to them that they are not alone. Use customer testimonials to remove buying anxiety, doubt, and fear. Without question, client testimonials are one of the best sales and marketing tools available to home business owners. And there are ways to maximize the positive impact that a testimonial can have on prospects.

- Customer testimonials should include the full name of the author, printed and signed. This carries much more clout then just a first name, or an initial and a last name. Whenever possible include a photograph of the person(s) giving the testimonial, because this will help appeal to emotions. People love to hear and read about good things that happen to people that don't look so different from them, or their family members, and their friends.
- If you have a celebrity client that is well known in your local area, ask that person to write a shining testimonial about your business. Celebrity testimonials can be used as a wonderful icebreaker, as most people feel especially at ease if the others who have gone before include a person they know and trust. The community celebrity could be the police or fire captain, school principal, city councilor, bank manager, minister, or the head of a local charity.
- Business client testimonials should include the business name and mailing address, title of the author, and contact telephone number and if possible, be printed on their company letterhead. This makes the testimonial much more tangible and credible than a testimonial with a few words followed by an illegible signature.
- Ask the author to use a bullet list or short quotes featuring what she likes about your product or service and the benefits she received from doing business with you. Make sure that you get permission to copy the testimonial and use it in other forms of marketing and advertising.

Support Documents

Much like client testimonials, there are also various support documents and certificates that can also be used to build confidence, credibility, and trust with your prospects:

- Business and vendor licenses and permits
- Liability and special insurance coverage
- Training certificates and/or professional accreditation certificates
- Workers' compensation coverage
- Industry, association, and Better Business Bureau memberships
- Business and customer service awards
- Publicity or media spotlights
- Product patents or intellectual property trademarks and copyrights
- Customer security and privacy policies

Support documents should be included in the presentation phase of the sales cycle and copies of appropriate documents should be given to your prospects and customers. Not only will you be building confidence and credibility with your prospects, but you also demonstrate your commitment to your business. It is also a great icebreaker and a great way to separate your presentation from a competitor.

Physical and Visual Aids

Great presentations should not be spectator sports for your prospects. They should be involved players, perhaps even the MVP, in the presentation. Always use props and physical devices during presentations, ones that will appeal to your prospect's emotions or logic. A financial planner can tell a prospect that they have devised a plan so the prospect will be able to retire at age 55, using only black and white facts and figures on a page. Or in addition to the facts and figures, the financial planner can use colorful charts, graphs, and pictures of retired, young-looking 55-year-olds frolicking on the beach and having a lot of fun. A travel agent selling vacations packages can use a multitude of clever props to aid sales. For tropical destinations, devise ways to incorporate flowers, sand, and surf into your sales presentations. For European destinations, develop a strategy for incorporating art and other items of cultural significance. Your presentation objective should always be to take advantage of every emotional and logical appeal that you can, including the five human senses—taste, sight, touch, hearing, and smell—to get your prospects physically and mentally involved in the sales process.

TRIAL CLOSING THE SALE

What is trial closing and when should you use it? Trial closing is nothing more than asking prospects for the sale early in the sales cycle or presentation. There are two reasons for asking a trial close question early the sales process. One, your prospect might be just as eager as you to move forward and close the deal, but you will never know unless you ask. Two, few people will take it upon themselves to offer you the sale unless they are asked to do so. Whether you are meeting prospects face to face, talking over the telephone, or communicating through sales letters, you should always attempt at least one trial close early in the sales process. The following are a few trial closing techniques that you might find useful.

Trial Close by Assuming the Sale

The first rule of trial closing is to simply assume that every prospect you present to or you come into contact with will buy what you are selling. Do this by making statements like "I will have this shipped to you buy the end of the week." "I just need your signature on this agreement so we can start processing your order." If the response or action is favorable, then complete the paperwork, restate the benefits and value of your goods or service, thank him for his business, and move on to your next appointment. If your prospect raises objections, you will know exactly what obstacles stand in the way of closing the sale and can commence overcoming them with the appropriate response and information.

Trial Close by Being Quiet

Always ask for the sale early, but be quiet after you do. Even if you feel you have more to say, resist the urge to speak. The goal of the quiet trial close is to place your prospect in the position of having to make a decision or at least respond to the trial close question with an answer, objection, or question. If you choose to talk after you ask for the sale, you negate the trial closing question. Your prospect is no longer bound to answer or respond to the trial closing question. The vast majority of people do not like to be placed on the hot seat, especially if all around them is uncomfortably silent. This can lead to a "Yes, let's proceed" just to get the spotlight off them. This technique should be used any time you ask a closing question.

Trial Close by Offering an Alternate Choice

As the name suggests, this trial: closing technique is nothing more than giving your prospect more than one option in terms of the product or service you sell. By doing so and by asking a question similar to "So which choice would you prefer, the desk in maple finish, or the desk in oak finish?" you pull the prospect into making a buying decision and selecting one of the options. Not buying is no longer an available option, based on the alternate choice trial closing question. The alternate choice questions can also be used effectively to increase the quantity of a particular product that you want your customer to buy. For instance, "Would you like one bookcase to go with your new maple desk, or two matching maple bookcases so you can balance the look of your office?" Once again, this pulls your customer into a buying decision. The question is no longer will you buy, but rather how many are you going to buy.

Trial Close with Incentives

Offering incentives is also an excellent way to approach a trial close situation: "Mr. Jones, I just wanted to let you know that for a limited time we are offering a 15 percent discount to any new customer that signs up for our monthly pool maintenance service. Would you like to take advantage of this valuable time-sensitive offer?" A percentage discount, free delivery, a two-for-one offer, or a trip to Spain if you buy—incentives work well at speeding up the sales cycle, at creating buying excitement and urgency, and more importantly for attempting a trial close early in the sales process.

OVERCOMING OBJECTIONS

When your prospects start raising objections or reasons why they shouldn't buy from you, don't turn tail and run for the hills. Instead, welcome and even encourage these objections. People raise objections simply as a way of telling you they are interested in what you are selling. If they were not, they would tell you they are not interested, a flat refusal. When prospects raise objections, they are asking you to do two things. First, they have one or more points (objections) that they do not fully understand about your product or service or the buying process. They need these points explained by you in greater detail before they can commit to buying. Second, they are giving you a signal for you to do your job and persuade them that buying is the right decision. However, if you are not prepared to answer and overcome objections, you will lose sales. Consequently, prior to sales meetings and presentations, you must anticipate objections and develop a four-step strategy to overcome these objections.

1. *Step one.* Never sidestep an objection. If you do, you will sidestep closing the sale. Every single objection that prospects raise during presentations must be listened to, confirmed, and

answered. Often due to lack of confidence or experience, many home business owners sidestep objections during sales presentations by pretending the objection was not raised, by ignoring it, or by quickly changing the topic or rushing to the next point in the presentation to take the prospect's mind off of the objection. Generally, this happens because you had not planned for objections and therefore cannot overcome them when raised. Or you did not give weight to the objection. Both are deadly, because prospects seldom forget about the objections they raise; they are always there like a beacon in the fog, flashing, as a constant reminder of why they should not buy.

2. *Step two.* Listen to the objection, and never assume that you know exactly what objections your prospect will raise. While it is true that you must anticipate objections, it is still more than possible that a prospect will raise a new objection, one that you have never heard before. You must give your prospects the opportunity to voice their objections and be prepared to listen to what they have to say with an open mind. You must consider the validity of the objection to determine if it is a major or minor obstacle in the way of the sale, and know how you will respond to the objection.

3. *Step three.* Confirm every objection your prospect raises so that you fully understand what they are saying and how it relates to your what you are selling. Ask them to restate the objection and any other details they think relevant, or why they feel the objection is valid. Doing this gives you the opportunity to understand the objection from their perspective. Additionally, you have extra time to consider how you will respond to and overcome the objection. And sometimes as the prospect restates the objection, they will see things in a new light and realize that they have misunderstood something. They will answer their own objection before you even have to respond, clarify, or explain.

4. *Step four.* And finally the last step in the objection process is to answer and hopefully overcome the objection by revealing additional

information about your offering that will satisfy your prospects that their objection has been overcome. Once you have answered their objections, make sure that they are happy with your response by asking if they understand and agree with your explanation.

Overcoming Price Objections

It should come as no surprise that most people will automatically respond to your offer or closing question with "the price is too high" or "the price is too much." More often than not, most people have not even considered if the price is too much. They just say it because it comes naturally for many of us. Perhaps the best way to debunk this all too common response is to put it back in your prospects' court by simply asking, "The price is too much in comparison to what?" This throws the majority of people off balance, especially if they have not actually considered why the price is too high. Another strategy for overcoming price objections is to simply agree with your prospect that indeed your price is more than competitors', and then explain why your price is higher. Perhaps it is higher quality, a longer warranty, specialized training, or some other competitive advantage that justifies charging more for your goods and services. By justifying your price through valid reasons and explanations, you can actually increase your prospects' desire to buy. They better understand the value of your offering in relation to the price that you are charging. Explain to your prospects that they are not buying price, or even a product or service; they are buying a solution, something that will benefit them immensely and help solve a problem, make them money, save them money, or better their health. When you can clearly demonstrate that the benefits or results far outweigh the price, price will become less of an obstacle that stands in the way of the sale. Also try and ask your prospects "Is price the only objection you have, or are there also other objections that would stop you from proceeding with the sale?" Doing this makes it clear that there are no other objections and that they honestly feel the price is too steep for their budget or comfort zone. If so, then perhaps you could give them the option of cutting something out of the

deal that would reduce the cost. Or propose a second option or alternate choice that is less costly. Both are great ways to get beyond the price objection because when you give people a choice between A a more costly buying option, and B a less costly buying option, not buying is no longer a choice. The choice now is do we spend more for something better or less for something almost as good?

Overcoming No Money Objections

When prospects tell you that they cannot afford to buy, ask them why. You cannot overcome the no-money objection unless you know all the details and the reasons for their decisions so that you can develop workable solutions that might otherwise go unnoticed. Clearly demonstrate that the benefits of buying are so important to their particular situation that a no-money objection would not be wise. In other words, the cost of not buying far outweighs the cost of buying. In a business-to-business selling environment, the first way to overcome a no-money objection is to make sure that you are calling on business prospects and making proposals when they are planning their budgets for the forthcoming year, not in the process of spending their budgets for the current year. Of course, the danger is that you educate your prospects and open the door for them to secure competing bids. Hence, you have to be clever in how you approach this method of overcoming the no-money objection. When you receive a no-money objection, the first thing that you should do is suggest that you try to arrange suitable financing. When you can show people that they can purchase by using financing means they had not thought of, often the no-money objection fades, and they warm up to the idea of buying because now they can. Finally, when you are positive that your prospect is sincere about not having the resources available, and you have exhausted all means of finding money, try to get him to commit to the purchase in the future when money does become available.

Overcoming Let-Me-Think-about-It Objections

When a prospect says he wants to think about whether or not to buy, suggest that you go over things again while the details are fresh in everyone's minds. This works because going over the details of the product or service and the overall offer gives you another opportunity to open the lines of communication and persuade him to buy. Another way to overcome the let-me-think-about-it objection, especially if you feel you are at the end of the line with your prospect, is to offer an incentive for closing on the spot. Justify the incentive to your prospect as a way to save time for both parties by not having to meet at a later time. However, be firm. Say in no uncertain terms that your incentive, whether it is a discount, a better model at the same price, extended warranty, or whatever the incentive might be that the offer is only valid right then and now they must make a decision to buy if they want to take advantage of it. You can also try to overcome let-me-think-about-it by trying the Benjamin Franklin closing technique. List the advantages of a decision to buy in one column, while listing the disadvantages in a second column. When people can see in black and white that the pros of buying far outweigh the cons, often that is all the persuasion they need to make a buying decision. If, however, you are going to use this closing technique to overcome the let-me-think-about-it objection, just make sure that the advantages of ownership really do outweigh the disadvantages. If not, you will lose any chance of closing the sale. Another way to overcome and close in this situation is to ask your prospects why they need more time to think about it. The answer will help determine if they are still truly interested in your product or service. By forcing them to give reasons, you are also opening the lines of communication once more and gaining the opportunity to overcome these objections. Finally, simply ask your prospects what the chances are that they will go ahead and buy tomorrow, next week, or next month. If the response is positive, suggest that you save time by completing the paperwork now and that you will tear up the contract should they decide not to buy. This is a logical enough approach for many people; you are placing them in a position of having to buy.

IDENTIFYING BUYING SIGNALS

Let's face it, knowing when to ask your prospects for the sale is one of the most important skills needed to succeed in small business. If you can pinpoint the exact moment that a prospect is apt to respond positively to a closing question, that leaves little doubt as to the outcome of the sales process. One surefire way to know when to ask prospects for the sale is when they start sending out buying signals. These signals are generally verbal, though they can be shown through emotion such as excitement or body language such as smiling. But generally they are verbal statements and questions. The following are a few of the more common buying signals.

Can-I Questions?

When prospects begin to ask can-I questions, they are really sending you a clear signal that they are ready to buy. For instance, a prospect might ask, "Can I have this home theater system installed by the end of the month?" To which you would reply, "If I can arrange to have the home theater system installed by the end of the month, are you prepared to go ahead with the purchase?" With such a reply, you accomplish two things. First, you have identified your prospect's buying signal. And second, you have echoed his can-I buying signal question with a closing question. Now the prospect is placed in a position of having to make a decision or raise an objection(s), which you can answer and once again attempt to close. Basically this works, unless the buying signal is misidentified or the response is "I'm not sure if we can install the home theater system before the end of the month, I have to get back to you." There is a vast difference in these two responses. The first clearly picks up on the buying signal and responds with a closing question. The second response misses the target completely and leaves the prospect and the salesperson no closer to a confirmed sale or the installation of a new home theater system, which is what both parties want to take place.

Comprehensive Questions

Another buying signal is when prospects begin to ask comprehensive questions about your product or service. For instance, a prospect may ask about a product warranty and follow your response with further product warranty questions that go deeper, trying to flush out more detail. Often sales professionals will refer to comprehensive questioning as the prospects talking themselves into purchasing, or justifying the purchase. As the comprehensive questions go deeper and deeper, prospects will eventually start to answer their own questions before you have an opportunity to respond. The deeper the questions go in terms of one particular point, or number of points, the stronger the buying signal becomes. And, keep in mind that comprehensive questions are not objections; as your prospect is not objecting to anything that you are saying or anything about your product or service.

Talking about Ownership

Talking about ownership is one of the strongest buying signals. Once a prospect begins to talk about ownership of your product of service, he has generally satisfied himself that the product or service has met his needs, represents value, and ownership would be beneficial. For instance, during a presentation your prospect might say, "Your software is great. It will save me thousands of dollars a month." This is a clear example of a buying signal because the prospect is talking about the benefits of taking ownership before actually purchasing the software. The next time your prospects start talking about taking ownership and its benefits. You know that they are sending you a clear signal that they are ready to buy.

Raising Objections

Objections are another buying signal, but this is also the precise moment that ultimately separates successful small business owners from the not-so-successful small business owners. Successful small business owners love objections and view them as a clear buying signal from their prospect. Struggling business owners hate objections and regard them as obstacles they cannot overcome, a sign of a lost sale. It is an objection when a prospect says, "I am not interested in what you have to sell; for the last time leave me alone." The signal is clear: they do not want to do business with you. However, when a prospect says, "I am not going to buy because the price is just

way too high," that is a buying signal loud and clear. He just told you that he wants to buy, and the only thing stopping him is a concern about the price. Now all you have to do is help him understand the true value of what you are selling to justify your price and satisfy them it is fair. Welcome objections, and take them as a buying signal. Your prospects are really telling you that they are still in the game and just want you to do what you are being paid to do—persuade them to see things your way and make the right buying decision.

Offering Referrals

The best buying signal is when prospects give you a referral before they have even purchased what you are selling. It clearly illustrates that you have done your job properly. Your prospects are so impressed with the entire buying process that they are prepared to reward you by helping you to find new sources of business before they have committed to purchasing themselves. The offering-a-referral buying signal is quite common, and usually a prospect will say something along the lines of "I know that this gizmo would work perfect for Sally. It sure would save her a lot of money." When this occurs, your prospect is so impressed with the advantages and benefits of your product or service that she is thinking about others that would also benefit. When your prospects start offering referrals, you know that it is time to ask for and close the sale.

CLOSING THE SALE

Only 1percent of your time spent selling is devoted to closing, yet success is 100 percent dependent on closing the sale.

This fact perfectly illustrates the importance of closing; it is an essential selling skill. But bear in mind that no matter how much closing intimidates you in reality it is nothing more than the natural progression in the sales cycle. You prospect, you qualify, you present, and you close. Therefore, if you have followed the logical steps in the sales cycle, asking for the sale should be nothing more than a formality. With that said, the following are a few time-tested and proven closing techniques.

Summary Closing

The summary close is perhaps the most common and easiest closing technique to master. Carefully note the benefits and features that your prospect found the most valuable and useful during your initial contact and sales presentation. Then use these hot buttons to close the sale by summarizing them to your prospect at the end of the presentation. In doing so, you place positive emphasis on all the things that your prospect finds beneficial about your product or service while conveniently leaving out any disadvantages. Constantly remind your prospect about these hot button benefits throughout the presentation, and get your prospect to reconfirm that these are the most important and beneficial aspects.

Fear Closing

Fear is an extremely powerful closing tool—the fear of missed opportunity, fear of poor health, or fear of what other people think about us. Fear can represent many different things to many different people, yet fear is an emotion that is an influential component of the decision-making process for us all at one point or another. The fear close is obviously more productive for some than for others. It is difficult to make someone fear not buying a new lawnmower. But place this same closing technique in the hands of a seasoned stockbroker, and watch the success rate soar. The fear of not having money or not making money is by far the most compelling way to motivate people to do what you want them to do. And there are other ways to introduce and use fear to close a sale. A property developer, for example, may use the fear associated with a violent society to sell houses in a gated and security patrolled community.

Chip-Away Closing

You can gently lead prospects to make a buying decision by getting them to agree to small or minor points about your product or service during the course of the sales presentation. This is referred to as the chip-away close. What makes this a powerful closing technique is the fact that you are subconsciously reducing buying risk. You are not placing your prospect in the situation of having to say yes to the entire deal all at the end, or at any time during the presentation, but only to small pieces along the way. These small nonthreatening pieces of the deal could include the color of the item, delivery schedules, product features, or warranty information. Try to get your prospect to agree to at least four or five minor points during the sales presentation, and restate the benefits of these minor points prior to asking for the sale. Often you will find the prospect becomes used to saying yes and along the way a trust relationship begins to form as you eliminate risk and doubt and show the prospect that saying yes does not have to be difficult or have dire consequences.

In Hindsight Closing

This closing technique is aptly named because we all have times in our lives that in hindsight we would have made a different decision then we did. Bought a bigger house, invested in a certain stock, or, alternately, liquidated a stock. When prospects are indecisive about going ahead with a purchase or about upgrading to a better and more expensive model, try the in hindsight close as a way to persuade them to make the right buying decision. The true power of this closing technique is being able to make what you sell relevant to an hindsight decision. For instance, if you sell camping trailers and your prospect is having a difficult time deciding between the smaller cheaper model or the larger more expensive model, you might say something along the lines of, "Mr. Jones, I know that this is a difficult decision for you. But I don't want you to look back two years from now and say, 'In hindsight I wish I had purchased the bigger camping trailer.' Saving a few bucks now will look like money foolishly wasted if you are stuck with something you aren't happy with or that does not completely fill your needs for the long term."

Convenience Closing

People will often buy based on no more than the overall convenience of the buying process. How many times have you chosen to buy at one shop instead of another because there was free parking, convenient shopping hours, free delivery and set up? If you are like most, the answer is probably often because you based your buying decisions on convenience of the overall buying process. Consequently, from a home business owner's perspective, it is a wise move to make it as easy as possible for all prospects to say yes by making it convenient. For instance, if permits or licenses are required to buy what you are selling, secure or assist in securing them for your prospects. Meet with prospects at times and locations that are convenient for them, regardless if it is for you. Complete warranty cards and registrations for customers, or arrange financing if they need it. Go the extra mile to make it as easy as you can for people to buy, and a certain percentage will buy simply because of that convenience.

Suggestion Closing

Not all people are comfortable with making decisions. Often in a sales presentation this discomfort can cause your prospects to come across as uninterested, when they just may be unsure and uncomfortable with the process and with making buying decisions. When you see that your prospect is uncomfortable in sales situations, ask, "Do you mind if I make a suggestion?" More times than not, you will see instant relief wash over your prospect's face. Suggesting that your prospect buys and giving reasons why is not a bad thing is your job. We have all made bad decisions and wished that at the time someone had helped us see the way to the right decision by making a suggestion. Based on my own experiences, once I have made suggestions to my prospects about what I think they should buy and why, they are for the most part very grateful that I helped them understand better and interpreted what they themselves were thinking.

Maximum Benefits Close

For those not familiar with this closing technique, it simply means that you go to great lengths to ensure that your prospect will get the maximum benefit by owing and using your product or service. Think of the maximum benefit as the ace that you remove from your sleeve precisely at the right time to wow

the prospect and close the deal. For instance, a recreational vehicle dealer might include a driver training program with every new or used motor home sold and use this maximum benefit to close more sales. The driving training course would be a maximum benefit to the buyer because this specialized training could save their lives in hazardous driving conditions. The driver safety course also ensures that the buyer gets the maximum benefit from the RV because by knowing how to operate and maintain the RV properly means it will provide many years of safe travel enjoyment for the entire family. Creating your own maximum benefit can also be a great way to separate your business, products, and services from your competitors', making the effort more than worthwhile.

Last-One-In Close

This is a very uncomplicated closing strategy. In fact, the last-one-in close is nothing more than getting a commitment from your prospects that they will not make a buying decision until they have spoken to you last. And believe it or not, when you ask your prospects not to go ahead and buy until they have spoken to you, it works. In the first place, they don't know what you have up your sleeve. Why do you want to speak to them last, a special offer, or what? Mystery and suspense are great for keeping prospects involved and invested in the sales process. In the second place, if you have done all your homework and have established a trust relationship with your prospect, then to a certain degree they will feel obligated to meet with you and hear you out one last time. Being the last one in enables you to play the devil's advocate in terms of competitors' bids and also enables you one last opportunity to persuade your prospects on your way of thinking. Once I realized the power of this closing technique, my closing ratio increased from 40 percent to in excess of 60 percent. It might just work for you.

NEGOTIATE LIKE A PRO

The ability to negotiate effectively is unquestionably a skill that every home business owner should strive to master. In business, negotiation skills are used daily. You negotiate with prospects and clients to sell your goods and service for a higher price. You negotiate with suppliers to receive a lower cost per unit or better payment terms. Or you negotiate with your bank to secure lines of operating capital or lower credit card merchant rates. Keep in mind, however, every negotiation has to have two winners, you and the person with whom you are negotiating. Never go into negotiations expecting to get everything you want while the other side gets nothing. If you do, expect to close fewer sales, be constantly searching for new suppliers, and face a revolving door in terms of business alliances. In every successful negotiation, both sides must win in order for the relationship to be mutually beneficial. Generally this requires some compromise; without it, one side will feel cheated, which again is no way to start any long-term customer or business relationship. Win-win negotiations mean that both sides benefit, that long-term relationships are established, and that multiple issues on each side are appeased at the table through fair and honest negotiations. Never try to negotiate with someone that is unwilling to find a win-win solution. If you do, the negotiating effort will be for nothing; every time that person wants something in the future he will expect to get it on his terms.

Be Prepared to Negotiate

The more information you have, the stronger your position becomes for getting what you want and at the terms and conditions you want. Information is the cornerstone of preparation. Find out as much as you can about your prospect's wants and needs, and how these wants and needs are prioritized—by budget, by benefits, by ability to solve a problem, or by schedule. Make sure you have a good understanding of what your prospect is trying to achieve through negotiations, a better price, faster delivery, more features for free, or a longer warranty. Arm yourself with all the relevant documents and data; nothing will kill a negotiation faster than having to come back with one missing element at a later date. The act of negotiation serves no purpose unless you can take advantage of the exact moment you have successfully negotiated to close. Otherwise, never be drawn into negotiating. Being prepared also means

that you are prepared mentally to negotiate—your mood is good, your confidence is high, and your rapport with your prospect is excellent.

Set Your Objectives

Know exactly what you want before you negotiate by setting negotiation objectives prior to any meeting. Your objective might be to get the sale at any price because of the potential for repeat or referral business. Or your objective might be to get your current customer to order more products or order on a more frequent basis. The key is to write down what you want the outcome to be before meeting with the other side. By setting objectives before the negotiation process begins, you know exactly what you want to accomplish and have a plan in place to help you stay the course and achieve the objective.

Position Your Value

Price is a relative term. If you really need a product or service, then price becomes a secondary issue. If you do not, then the price of the product or service will always be too much. Before you ever reach the negotiations stage with any prospect, you must first position the value of your product or service. It is a critical step in the negotiation process. If your product or service is properly positioned in terms of value, it gives you increased leverage and power to get what you want out of the negotiations process, without having to concede on a major point or give away money. But you do not want to place value on the wrong things, such as the price or specific features. You want to value the benefit your prospects will receive as a resulting of buying—what your product or service will do for them, how they will benefit by using and owning it, or what problem it will fix. If you do not clearly position the value of your product or service in terms of the benefit to the potential customer, you lose the ability to justify your price as compared to the relative value of what the product or service does for the prospect. For example, I am selling a car with a five-star safety rating and my prospect has a family. I want to position the value of this five-star safety rating and why it should be first priority with my prospect (protect the family) before negotiating the sale. In doing so, I would place myself in a strong negotiating position because you cannot put a price on safety, thus justifying a higher price.

Develop a Yes Strategy

Early in negotiations, get your prospect to say yes to a few small nonthreatening issues. Perhaps there is a time issue regarding delivery of the product; use this to your advantage early in the negotiations and ask, "If I can assure early delivery do you still want it?" Your prospect will say yes because he has already indicated that he wants early delivery. Therefore you have asked a question that is guaranteed to get a yes. Continue to ask small issue questions that you know your prospect will say yes to, such as product colors, features, and warranty information, and in the end try to narrow the negotiations down to a single point. Doing this will make it much easier for you to make one small compromise, if any at all, and for your prospect to accept that compromise and feel he has won. Additionally use questions that begin with *what*: "What would you suggest?" "What are the alternatives?" "What would you think about if. . . ?" By asking *what* questions you force your prospect to reveal what he wants and therefore, weaken his position in the process. You are now armed with the valuable information of knowing exactly what he wants.

Do Not Accept First Offers

Never accept your prospect's first offer. If you do, I can almost guarantee that you will be leaving money on the table or, alternately, paying too much for a product or service yourself. Few people will walk away from negotiations when you decline a first offer and say you need more money in order to go ahead or you need to pay less money in order to go ahead. If you automatically accept first offers, most people will begin to doubt the entire negotiation process: "I could have paid less, or I could have sold it for more." This is because you have made it too easy for them to get a discount on what you sell and cheapened its value, or you have paid a premium for what they sell, driving up your cost of doing business.

Always avoid accepting prospects or supplier's first offers. Counter the offer even if you are satisfied with the deal. Paying a mere 3 percent less for products and services that you use in business, and/or selling your goods and services for a mere 3 percent more, can add thousands to your annual bottom line profits.

Keep Emotions in Check

Always strive to keep your emotions in check during negotiations, and never react in an argumentative way with a prospect or client over a price objection or any other aspect of the negotiation or sales process. You must learn to keep emotions in check and rely strictly on logic to guide you past the rough spots that will invariably arise during some negotiations. Emotions can come in many forms—fear that you won't get the sale, excitement that you will, anger because of something your prospect said, or frustration because negotiations are not going as planned. Regardless of the particular emotion, any emotion can take over and greatly reduce your ability to think clearly; stick with your plan, don't weaken your overall negotiating abilities.

Use Incentives as a Powerful Negotiating Tool

Incentives are a great way to help motivate a prospect to buy or entice existing customers to buy more frequently. But the incentive you offer must provide real value and be relative to your main offering in order to be an effective negotiating tool. What this means is that if you were not giving away or including the incentive in the deal, would this incentive be valuable enough that it could actually be sold as an individual product or service? Ideally the incentive offered to increase the value of your main offer and motivate your prospect to buy should be something that you sell. A good example is including an extended warranty in the deal for free. You can actually indicate the value of the incentive in terms of dollars, and the benefit to your prospect, which is the extra security and peace of mind that extended warranties provide. Other examples of valuable incentives that could be sold individually include more product or service for the same price, free upgraded features, free delivery or installation, or a free $50 gift certificate that can be applied toward future purchases on other products and services you sell. Strong incentives that add real value to your main offering should also create buying motivation and urgency, benefit the buyer, and enhance your offer. Incentives should avoid straight cash discounts or percentage discounts because they reduce the perceived value of your product or service. Giving cash discounts can become a habitual negotiating and closing technique and quickly devour bottom line profits.

Confirm and Reconfirm the Details

I cannot overstate the importance of confirming all the details once negotiations are complete and an agreement has been successfully reached. These details have to be recorded, and it is best if they are also mutually signed off on or at least initialed beside each major point in the deal. Handshakes and verbal agreements are fine on small jobs or orders if you have an established working relationship with a client. If not, you must get all the details on paper; and when you're done, reconfirm these details step by step with your customer. Equally important is to reconfirm to your clients that they have made a wise purchasing decision and that you appreciate their business. Confirming the details works to strengthen the business relationship and close negotiations and the meeting in a very professional manner. All of these actions can increase repeat and referral business.

Learn When to Walk Away

When required, be prepared to walk away from negotiations if you are positive that you have nothing to gain by continuing. When your prospects' only concern is price and nothing else matters, they shop solely on price, and they will never become a long-term, loyal, and repeat customer. They will always be searching for the lowest price. If you take their business, you will always be looking for ways to reduce your price and ultimately quality to satisfy them. This type of person is loyal to a low price, grinding you out of a buck, and nothing or any body

else. Therefore, when the result of the negotiations is no longer beneficial to you or your business, then you must walk away. If not, be prepared to sacrifice profits, quality, reputation, or a combination.

GETTING MORE REFERRALS

Which type of sales lead would you prefer? Cold leads that requires knocking on doors talking to people in person or picking up the telephone and speaking to people to drum up business? Warm leads, which are prospects that contact you directly as a result of your advertising, a special promotional activity, or publicity your business has received? Or hot leads, people that seek you out because they have been referred to your business by one of your customers or a business alliance? Obviously, you want the hot leads, people that seek you out because they have been referred to your business by other people. Let's face it, one surefire way to increase sales and profits, while reducing sales cycle time and costs associated with finding new prospects and developing profitable business and selling relationships, is to secure more referrals. In fact, for home business owners, referral business is often the instrument that will define business success versus business failure. Therefore, the importance of securing referrals and ensuring your business gets referred cannot be understated.

The first step toward securing more sales referrals is simply to set a target amount of referrals you want to secure and create a recording system so that you know how many times your business is being referred and who is referring your business. Most home business owners do neither. Thus there is no system in place to measure how referrals are secured and how these referrals affect your closing rate, revenues, and profits. By setting referral targets, the act of securing sales referrals is an ongoing, conscious effort, as it should be at all times. Once you have set a goal for referrals, you can implement strategies to reach these goals and secure more referrals. Likewise, you will receive more referrals by providing excellent service, quality products, value, and benefits, and by keeping your word and delivering as promised to all customers. Never let an opportunity pass to ask people for referrals—prospects, customers, suppliers, alliances, friends, and family members. Basically, anytime you come into contact with people, you have to get comfortable with asking them for the names and contact information of people that would benefit from what you have to sell. At the end of this section, there is a Sample Referral Form (see Figure 15.1).

Thank the Ones that Got Away

Another way to secure more referrals is to thank prospects that did not buy by sending them a *sorry letter*. A sorry letter is simply one sent to prospects

that did not buy. It should be sent within two days of the proposal rejection, thanking prospects for the opportunity to fulfill their product or service needs. Restate the value and benefits of your product, service, and proposal. And, closing by stating that if they should have a change of mind you would like the opportunity to earn their business. You might be surprised to learn how useful this practice is. Recipients will keep you in mind for future proposals. Should the winning bidder of the current job not live up to expectations, you may very well be called back to save the day. They may very well refer your company, product, or service to

FIGURE 15.1   Sample Referral Form

Below is an outline of a simple referral form. Use this form as a template to develop your own referral form and hand it out to customers, suppliers, alliances, and friends and family members.

(Your Business Name Here)

❏ Mr. ❏ Mrs. ❏ Ms.

Name: _____   Occupation: _____

Address: _____   City: _____

State: _____   Zip Code: _____

Telephone: (home) _____ (work) _____   Fax: _____

E-mail: _____   Web Site: _____

How do you know this person? ❏ Personal Friend ❏ Family Member ❏ Co-Worker
                             ❏ Current / Past Customer   ❏ Business Associate

Can we let this person know that you referred them to us?   ❏ Yes   ❏ No

Additional Comments: _____

Referred By: ❏ Mr. ❏ Mrs. ❏ Ms.

Name: _____   Occupation: _____

Address: _____   City: _____

State: _____   Zip Code: _____

Telephone: (home) _____ (work) _____   Fax: _____

E-mail: _____   Web Site: _____

Can we contact you with special offers and information?   ❏ Yes   ❏ No

If so, which contact method do you prefer?   ❏ E-mail   ❏ Fax   ❏ Ground Mail   ❏ Telephone

"Thank you, we appreciate your help."

others even though they did not purchase from you—especially, if you ask for referrals in your letter and offer an incentive for giving you these referrals. Think of it this way, you would not invest time and money into the restoration of a house, just to walk away from it (and your investment) if the roof leaked. Building profitable selling relationships is an ongoing effort that does not happen overnight. You invest time and money to bid on and attract new business. Do not simply throw in the towel if you are at first unsuccessful with a sale you want to land. Stay in contact with your prospects and give them many reasons to say yes, even after they have initially said no.

Offer Referral Rewards

Offering incentives for referrals is truly a win-win situation. Your incentives could range from a gift certificate, to product or service discounts, to cash payments. Much depends on the circumstances and the value of the goods or services you sell. I use to send all customers a simple referral form along with a self-addressed return envelope asking that they kindly complete the referral form and return. Enclosed with the referral form was a discount coupon related to what I sold that they could give to a friend, along with a letter stating that if any referrals lead new work that I would send them a gift certificate for dinner at a nice restaurant. The incentive was basic, but month after month the referral forms would pour in by mail and I would make new contacts and close new sales as a direct result of the referral forms I sent out. This worked because of the honesty. I wanted more sales. We offered an excellent product and service. And because of that customers were happy to refer other people they knew that would benefit from what I sold. The small incentive I gave was just a way of saying thank you, and the dinner was always welcomed and appreciated.

PROFITING FROM FOLLOW-UP

There are two types of follow-up. First, follow-up with prospects that have not yet bought and turn them into paying customers. Second, following up with current customers to strengthen the relationship so that they will buy more and more frequently. Briefly, follow-up enables you to:

- turn prospects into customers, thus expanding your customer base.
- increase the value of each sale, which generates more revenues and profits.
- boost customer buying frequency, once again generating more profits.

With so much at stake, it should be obvious that you can never procrastinate. Follow-up is as important as any other part of the sales cycle or continuing customer relationship.

Prospects

Following up with prospects after a sales meeting or presentation can be done in various ways: e-mail, fax, telephone, or by writing a letter. The benefits of immediate follow-up are many. Number one, it is an opportunity to compile all the information that was discussed at the meeting and to reconfirm the information, right down to the smallest detail. Second, it illustrates to your prospects that you are interested in their needs, you want to solve their problems, and you conduct business in a very professional manner. And third, practicing immediate follow-up provides you with a great opportunity to reconfirm all of the details with your prospect so that there will be no missed communications when you get back together for the sales presentation.

Customers

The real work begins after the sale. It is easy to sell a prospect, but it takes effort and hard work to retain a customer for life. According to the U.S. Small Business Administration (SBA), in excess of 60 percent of consumers stop doing business with a company because they feel they are being ignored and forgotten after the original sale. Couple that startling statistic with the fact that it costs ten times as much to find and sell to a new customer as it does to serve and keep existing customers, and I am sure you see why the real work begins after the sale. Never be deluded into thinking that once you have made a sale, it's over; it isn't. In fact, the real work begins after you make a sale—with regular follow-up, great customer service, and maintaining a close working relationship with your customer for life. It is what you do once you make a sale that will determine its true value.

Survey Lost Sales

Even lost sales should be followed up by creating a survey form. Ask prospects that did not buy from you to complete the survey and send it back. Ask questions on the survey form that will help you better understand why your prospects did not buy. The questions you ask will be relevant to your business, industry, and what you sell. Consider the type of information that would be helpful to know and the questions that would get it. Obviously you would have preferred to close the sale. But, at least by surveying prospects to find out why they did not buy, you can get insights so that you can make changes in the way you sell and/or your products and services.

The 30-Minute Follow-Up Close

Another closely guarded follow-up secret that professionals use is to practice the 30-minute, follow-up closing technique. More often than not, people will have made a decision about whether or not to buy within 30 minutes after the sales meeting or presentation, especially with consumer goods. Therefore, it is wise to follow up with all prospects within 30 minutes after a sales presentation. Call your prospect, and let them know it is your policy to place a courtesy call to ensure 100 percent customer service and complete understanding of the products or services presented. Not only will this follow-up call open the lines of communication with the prospect once more, but it also provides an incredible opportunity for you to take advantage of the situation and close.

Revisit Your Bid Archives

Also make sure that you keep and file unsuccessful bids and estimates for a few years. You just might be sitting on a goldmine of potential new sales and not even realize it. Prospects do not go ahead with a purchase for a number of reasons: lack of money, poor timing, a change in circumstances, or just about anything else. But revisiting or contacting prospects

that have previously said no can always secure new sales. Start by creating a standard form letter that thanks your prospect for their time during the original presentation. The letter should also restate the benefits of your product or service and include a special incentive offer as a way to motivate them to take action and reopen the lines of communication. Personally, any proposal I gave that did not result in a sale I would follow-up with in this manner every six months for a two-year period, even if the prospect initially said no or said that they were going to do business with a competitor. As a result of this simple follow-up system, I would always secure at least a few new sales and, at the bare minimum, get a few great referrals that were turned into new sales.

RESOURCES

🗏 Associations

American Marketing Association (AMA)
311 S Wacker Drive, Suite 5800
Chicago, IL 60606
(312) 542-9000
www.marketingpower.com

Canadian Marketing Association (CMA)
1 Concorde Gate, Suite 607
Don Mills, Ontario M3C 3N6
(416) 391-2362
www.the-cma.org

Direct Marketing Association (DMA)
1120 Avenue of the Americas
New York, NY 10036-6700
(212) 768-7277
www.the-dma.org

Sales and Marketing Executives International (SMEI)
PO Box 1390
Sumas, WA 98295-1390
(312) 893-0751
www.smei.org

📖 Suggested Reading

Berg, Bob. *Endless Referrals: Network Your Everyday Contacts into Sales.* New York: McGraw-Hill, 1998.

Blackman, Jeff. *Stop Whining! Start Selling!: Profit-Producing Strategies for Explosive Sales Results.* New York: John Wiley & Sons, 2003.

Carnegie, Dale. *How to Win Friends and Influence People.* Reissue, New York: Pocket Books, 1994.

DeSena, James. *The 10 Immutable Laws of Power Selling: The Key to Winning Sales, Wowing Customers, and Driving Profits Through the Roof.* New York: McGraw-Hill, 2003.

Dyche, Jill. *The CRM Handbook: A Business Guide to Customer Relationship Management.* Boston, MA: Addison-Wesley, 2001.

Fisher, Roger, and William Ury. *Getting to Yes: Negotiating Agreement Without Giving In.* New York: Penguin, 1991.

Fox, Jeffery. *How to Become a Rainmaker: The Rules for Getting and Keeping Customers and Clients.* New York: Hyperion Books, 2000.

Gregory, Kip. *Winning Clients in a Wired World: How to Leverage Technology to Grow Your Business.* New York: John Wiley & Sons, 2003.

Groth, Robert. *Data Mining: Building Competitive Advantage.* New York: Prentice Hall, 2000.

Hopkins, Tom. *How to Master the Art of Selling.* New York: Warner Books, 1994.

Parinello, Anthony. *Secrets of Vito: Think and Sell Like a CEO.* Irvine, CA: Entrepreneur Press Inc., 2002.

Porter-Roth, Bud. *Developing Winning Proposals: How to Get the Bid and Clinch the Deal.* Irvine, CA: Entrepreneur Press Inc., 2004.

Rackham, Neil. *The S.P.I.N. Selling Fieldguide: Practical Tools, Methods, Exercises and Resources.* New York: McGraw-Hill, 1996.

Stephenson, James. *Ultimate Small Business Marketing Guide: Over 1500 Marketing Tips and Tricks that Will Drive Your Business through The Roof!* Irvine, CA: Entrepreneur Press Inc., 2003.

Ziglar, Zig. *Zig Ziglar's Secrets of Closing the Sale.* New York: Berkley Books, 1984.

Web Sites

Brian Tracy International, www.briantracy.com: Sales and motivational expert, coaching, information, products, programs, and services.

Business Network International, www.bni.com: Billed as the world's largest referral organization, with more than 2,600 chapters worldwide and thousands of members.

Guerilla Marketing Online, www.gmarketing.com: Weekly online magazine for small businesses, entrepreneurs, sales people, and marketers.

Maximizer Software, www.maximizer.com: Sales and contact management software.

Presentations Magazine Online, www.presentations.com

Sales & Marketing Management Magazine, www.salesandmarketing.com

SBA Pro-Net, www.pro-net.sba.gov: United States Small Business Administration, Pro-Net: Procurement, Marketing, and Access Network.

Secure Tenders, www.securetenders.com: Online service connecting buyers and sellers worldwide.

Selling Power Magazine Online, www.sellingpower.com: Information, products, and services aimed at improving your sales abilities.

CHAPTER 16

Event Marketing

I N ADDITION TO TRADITIONAL SALES AND MARKET-ing activities home business owners can harness the power of event marketing to help drive revenues and profits. Covered in detail are:

- Trade and Consumer Shows
- Seminars
- Public Speaking
- Contest
- Sponsorships

TRADE AND CONSUMER SHOWS

For the home business owner, few marketing activities can match the effectiveness of trade and consumer shows as a way to showcase your products, services, and expertise to a large and captive audience at one time and in one place, in a relatively cost-effective manner. Over the course of one day to a few weeks, depending on the show, you can make personal contact with hundreds, if not thousands, of qualified prospects, affording you hundreds if not thousands of opportunities to sell your products or services. Imagine how long it would take to see that same amount of prospects by way of traditional one-to-one personal sales visits? Trade and consumer shows are one of the best ways to generate well-qualified sales leads. In fact,

depending on how you generate and qualify leads at the show, it is possible to collect thousands of leads at a single event, which can easily be turned into profit-generating sales through post-show follow-up and presentations. The trade and consumer show environment is also a great forum to introduce new or improved products and services to a wide and qualified audience in one shot and at one time. This is especially true at the more specialized industry shows, exhibits, conferences, and expos, which can substantially drive down your marketing and personal presentation costs.

You can also take advantage of the many contacts you make exhibiting at trade and consumer shows to build a valuable database or expand your current database to include new contacts. Best of all, these new contacts will be qualified and unique to your business. Home business owners with tight research budgets should also consider trade and consumer shows as a fantastic forum to collect research data and information about the competition, the industry, customers, new trends, and your business, products, and services. Trade shows are almost always covered by one or more media outlets, giving you the opportunity to potentially secure valuable free media exposure for your business, which can be turned into new sales.

Well-conceived exhibits, displays, in-show seminars, and live demonstrations also enable you to showcase your expertise in the industry to many people in one place over a short period of time. Of course, showcasing your expertise in this fashion will help build a brand image so you can position your business, products, and services within your industry and in your customers' and prospects' minds. Trade and consumer shows are a wonderful way to find new suppliers, vendors, and employees. Many entrepreneurs also use trade shows to support their current field reps, agents, and vendors by generating leads for them, holding training and education workshops, or by introducing and demonstrating new or improved products and services that they plan on making available to their business team in the near future. And you can do the same. In a nutshell, trade and consumer shows provide home business owners with so many opportunities to expand their business that it is nearly impossible to list all of the potential benefits.

How to Locate the Right Show

Once you have made the decision that exhibiting at trade and consumer shows, expos, and other types of special marketing events will become part of your overall marketing strategy, the next step is to locate shows that will meet your marketing and exhibiting objectives. When you consider that there are in excess of ten thousand trade and consumer shows hosted annually in North America alone, this task could be overwhelming if it wasn't for the Internet. Fortunately, the Internet makes finding trade shows and expos a relatively easy and painless task, especially when compared to the old days when you would have to pour through print trade show directories and make endless telephone calls to industry associations. Now you can click through hundreds of trade-show listings online in no time, gain valuable insights into each show, and, more importantly, learn more about the audience that attends to make sure they match your primary target market. One such online directory is Trade Shows Online, which can be found at www.tradeshows.com. This site includes trade and consumer shows, conferences, and expos listing all geographically and by industry.

To help you keep track of basic trade shows and events, you can use the trade show contact form (see Figure 16.1).

Follow the KISS Formula When Designing Your Exhibit

When designing your trade show booth and displays, follow two time-tested and proven marketing concepts—the KISS and AIDA formulas. Both are acronyms. KISS stands for *Keep It Simple Stupid*, or for the politically correct, *Keep It Simple Silly*, and AIDA stands for *Attention, Interest, Desire, and Action*. You want to keep your booth and displays very simple and straightforward, to grab the attention of passing prospects, stimulate their interest in your products or services, instantly create desire for what you sell, and make them take action and inquire about more information or buying. The purpose of your exhibition booth and displays is to attract the attention of people passing by and to project the appropriate image for your company, products, and services. At a glance people should be able to know instantly what your company does or sells. You should not, however, display every single product or service that you sell because your booth will appear cluttered and disorganized. Keep your booth lean and move displays and tables back and to the sides of your booth so that you have lots of space to greet prospects and engage in sales conversation. Far too many exhibitors try to arrange their booths and product displays like a retail store or office and restrict the flow of people, creating a funnel effect that makes people uncomfortable and skip your booth altogether.

There are no one set of standard rules when it comes to designing trade show booths and displays. Exhibitors have their own sales and marketing objectives, specific budgets, and reasons for exhibiting their goods and services. But here are a few ideas that you can employ to help grab attention and maximize the interest of your target audience:

- Use attention-grabbing devices such as a strobe lamp, a loudspeaker playing a prerecorded promotional message or a live message, a computer monitor or television running a corporate advertisement or product or service video, or a

| FIGURE 16.1 | Trade Show Contact Form |

Event 1

Event Name _____ Date _____

Location _____

Contact Person ❑ Mr. ❑ Mrs. ❑ Ms. _____

Telephone _____ Fax _____

E-mail _____ Web site _____

Duration of event _____ Booth size _____ Booth cost _____

Number of exhibitors _____ Expected gate attendance _____

Event 2

Event Name _____ Date _____

Location _____

Contact Person ❑ Mr. ❑ Mrs. ❑ Ms. _____

Telephone _____ Fax _____

E-mail _____ Web site _____

Duration of event _____ Booth size _____ Booth cost _____

Number of exhibitors _____ Expected gate attendance _____

Event 3

Event Name _____ Date _____

Location _____

Contact Person ❑ Mr. ❑ Mrs. ❑ Ms. _____

Telephone _____ Fax _____

E-mail _____ Web site _____

Duration of event _____ Booth size _____ Booth cost _____

Number of exhibitors _____ Expected gate attendance _____

Event 4

Event Name _____ Date _____

Location _____

Contact Person ❑ Mr. ❑ Mrs. ❑ Ms. _____

Telephone _____ Fax _____

E-mail _____ Web site _____

Duration of event _____ Booth size _____ Booth cost _____

Number of exhibitors _____ Expected gate attendance _____

FIGURE 16.2   Media Invitation Form

	Media Company	Contact Person	Date Invitation Sent	Date Followed-Up
1.	_____	_____	_____	_____
2.	_____	_____	_____	_____
3.	_____	_____	_____	_____
4.	_____	_____	_____	_____
5.	_____	_____	_____	_____

lively, ongoing, hands-on in booth product or service demonstration.

- Create a freestanding durable product display, preferably a working model of what you sell that can be used for interactive demonstrations. Interactive computer terminals on swivel bases also work well for presentations and demonstrations purposes.
- Keep a whiteboard and markers handy in case you have to construct diagrams to respond to unique visitor questions.
- Display products, scale models, and photographs and graphics at eye level, about five feet from the floor to the key focal point or feature(s) of the product or display that you want to spotlight.

Also keep in mind that booths alive with exciting product or service demonstrations draw considerably more interest and larger crowds then static booths without demonstrations. Therefore, consider ways you can demonstrate your products or services in the booth to grab attention and build interest.

Invite the Media to the Event

Trade shows and expos are favorite places for members of the media to get news and information about new or improved products and services for their target audiences. Take advantage of this fact. Sing your praises in a dynamic media invitation outlining the special features and benefits of your products or services, along with exhibition details. Send the invitation to media outlets two to three weeks prior to your trade show. Let reporters know in advance the why, when, where, who, and how of the event and your products and services. Remember that the media need news to relay to its audience. That's its business and the job never ends. Good reasons to invite the media to your booth include the following:

- New or improved product or service launches
- Specialized demonstrations or in-show information seminars
- Celebrity or expert guest appearances in your booth
- Company milestones, such as number of years in business
- Publicity stunts at the show, such as record setting, events, contests, or product trade-in exchange

Additional information about working with the media and securing free publicity can be found in the public relations and networking chapter. Use the Media Invitation Form (see Figure 16.2) to list the media outlets that you will be inviting to your next trade show, seminar, or expo, and remember to follow-up with them before the event.

Presenting and Selling in the Booth

The trade show pace can be fast and furious, and time is a commodity that is always in short supply. Therefore, it is important to have an effective and well-rehearsed sales plan ready to put into action. Your sales plan should revolve around five key elements—

engage, qualify, generate leads, present, and close. Four of these sales elements are discussed here and lead generation is discussed in greater depth in a following section. Remember, rarely will your booth, exhibits, or displays do the selling in the trade show environment. The job of selling is left up to you and your staff through the personal contact you make with prospective customers in the booth and through follow-up after the event. In a matter of moments, you must be able to engage prospects, listen, question and qualify, generate a lead, present, or close.

Engage

There are three main types of exhibitors. There are exhibitors that stand back in their booth and do or say nothing as prospects look over their products and displays. There are those who approach prospects with irrelevant questions or opening statements. Then there are exhibitors that are proactive and approach prospects as they enter the booth with well prepared opening questions. The questions are designed to provoke meaningful conversation and qualify the prospect's level of interest. I cannot stress the importance of decisive in-booth engagement. You have to be direct and engage in conversation that is focused on what you sell and how it fills their need. Conversation about the weather, other displays, or anything else is irrelevant.

Qualify

You know what you sell, who your target audience is, and what your target audience needs. Combine your knowledge of your goods and services with your knowledge of your target audience and their needs to develop a series of qualifying questions that you can ask prospects to determine if they are hot prospects or cold fish. In addition to qualifying questions that are specific to the products or services that you sell, remember to cover the basic, but important, qualifying information. That information includes prospects' need for your goods or services, their ability to make the buying decision, their ability to pay for the purchase, what other companies are bidding on the job, and the time frame when they would like to buy.

Present

Presenting in the booth is much different from presenting outside of the trade show environment, where you typically might spend 30 minutes to a few hours with your prospect in a sales presentation. In the trade show booth you are often limited to five minutes or less to deliver your sales presentation. Any longer and you will run the risk of qualified people wandering away because they are not being taken care of. Prior to the show, you must have your standard sales presentation and shrink it down considerable to only a few moments, while still delivering the same high-impact message. You do this by focusing on the benefits of what you sell and with sales aids such as samples, printed literature, computer presentations, and live demonstrations. And above all, you must constantly refine your sales pitch until you have it down to a few moments long and can recite it backwards.

Close

Closing in the booth is very straightforward; simply ask for the sale. The majority of people that attend trade and consumer shows do so with the intention of making a purchase at the show or within a few weeks of attending the show. If you spend time qualifying and presenting in the booth only to let prospects get away without attempting to close by asking for the sale, all you have accomplished is to educate your prospect. Your competition at the show can close them with nothing more than a little persuasion and asking for the sale. You must also give people a very strong reason for buying at the show, and this is best achieved by creating buying urgency. Buying urgency can be created by offering an exclusive show discount, limiting the number of items sold, or by adding value to the sale through free delivery or installation.

Lead Generation in the Booth

Next to selling in the booth, the second most common trade show objective is collecting leads that can be turned into sales after the show. Like any marketing activity, there are a few key points to consider—lead forms, generating leads, and lead follow-up—prior to collecting leads

The Lead Form

Lead generation in the booth starts with a system to capture prospect information, either a paper lead form or an electronic one via an in-booth computer terminal. Regardless of the format, the information that you want to capture remains the same.

- Complete name and contact information, including address, telephone, and e-mail address. You might want to also capture business or occupation.
- A checklist of qualifying questions relative to what you sell.
- A best time to contact—morning, afternoon, or night—as well as day of the week and best contact telephone numbers for those times.
- Rank each lead so that when the event is over you'll be able instantly to identify the hottest prospects and contact them immediately. Ranking leads is as easy as assigning a number, such as one for the hottest leads, two for good, and three for cool or poor quality. If you do not want people to catch you ranking leads, develop an alternate ranking system, such as placing hot leads in a red file folder, good leads in a green file folder, and cool or poor quality leads in a blue folder.
- An additional information section that will assist you in understanding each prospect's unique situation and needs during follow-up.

Figure 16.3 is an example of a simple lead form you can use to collect names, qualify, and rank prospects. The sample lead form would be suitable for a window replacement company. You can use this sample form to create your own lead form relevant to your business and the products or services you sell.

Generating Leads

Depending on your marketing objectives, you can talk to every prospect personally and generate leads based on the conversations. Or alternately, you can assemble a lead generation station wherein prospects complete their own lead forms, either on paper or electronically. Both methods have specific pros and cons. While personally talking to each prospect and completing the lead form yourself generally tends to

result in better qualified leads, the downside is the process can be very time consuming and you will generate less leads overall during the event. On the other side, having people complete the lead form by way of a contest entry ballot or similar promotion without talking to you generally means having to spend much more time after the show personally qualifying each lead, or spending a bundle on direct marketing to reach and qualify every lead.

Contests and special promotions, such as the old favorite "Trade Show Special Discount," are great ways to lure people into your booth. These gimmicks are only productive when they are self-explanatory. If you have to take time out to explain contest details or how your special promotion works, simply don't bother with the promotion or create one that is less involved. The time, energy, and money you spend on exhibiting is not to promote a contest; it is the result of the contest that will meet your marketing objective. Generally in the case of contests, this means collecting leads via entry forms to follow up with after the show. The main objective of trade show marketing should always be to sell or collect leads. If you are taking time to explain contest details or other promotions to prospects, you are reducing the amount of time you have to sell, to make contact, and qualify other prospects.

If you do stage a contest or similar promotion to generate leads, remember that the leads will not be qualified unless you put a qualifying measure in place. The qualifying measures should include asking questions on the entry form that the contestant must answer in order to be eligible to win the prize. Likewise, the prize can be more specific, thus qualifying people to a certain degree before they enter the contest. A security company might give away a free alarm system to winners, hoping to secure monthly monitoring contracts, because winning a free alarm still requires alarm monitoring. Only people in the market for home alarms and a monitoring service are likely to take the time to enter the contest, thereby qualifying themselves.

Lead Follow-Up

Generating leads at trade shows is often the easy part because you can generate hundreds of leads at just one single event. But what do you do with them

FIGURE 16.3   Lead Form

Prospect Information

❏ Mr. ❏ Mrs. ❏ Ms. Name _____

Business Name (Business Customer) _____

Street Address _____

City _____ State _____ Zip code _____

Telephone _____ Fax _____

E-mail _____ Web site _____

What is the best day and time to contact you? _____ Day _____

Time _____ Contact Number _____

Questions

Do your current windows need to be replaced?   ❏ Yes ❏ No

Do you own the home where the windows are to be replaced?   ❏ Yes ❏ No

What is wrong with your current windows?   ❏ Steaming/condensation   ❏ Poor condition   ❏ Not energy efficient

How old are your current windows?   ❏ Less than 10 years   ❏ 10–20 years   ❏ 20+ years

What type of windows do you currently have?   ❏ Wood   ❏ Aluminum   ❏ Vinyl   ❏ Other

When do you want to have the windows replaced?   ❏ 1–3 months   ❏ 3–6 months   ❏ 6–12 months   ❏ 12 + months

Have you established a budget for your window replacement project?   ❏ Yes ❏ No

Do you want one of our qualified window replacement experts to give you a no-obligation free quote to replace your window?   ❏ Yes ❏ No

Have you received or will you be getting other quotes to replace your windows?   ❏ Yes ❏ No

If yes, from which window replacement company or contractor: _____

Have you heard of our company before today?   ❏ Yes ❏ No

How did you hear about our company?

❏ Print advertising   ❏ Yellow Pages   ❏ Radio/Television advertisement

❏ Referral   ❏ Job in progress/Site sign   ❏ Other: _____

Can we include you on our mailing list and send you valuable information periodically?

❏ Yes   ❏ No   By: ❏ Mail   ❏ Fax   ❏ E-mail

Rank: ❏ Hot   ❏ Warm   ❏ Cold

Additional Comments: _____

_____

_____

_____

once you've got them? Obviously, you follow up and attempt to turn as many of the leads into sales as quickly as possible to maximize the value of the leads and to get the highest rate of return on the money you invested into exhibiting at the show.

Develop a lead follow-up package before the show so that when it ends, you're ready to start following up on the hottest leads with no down time. The follow-up package should include sales letters, telemarketing scripts, presentation templates, and just about any other item or service required to maximize the value of the leads by contacting and re-qualifying prospects right away. Remember that competitors at the show are probably chasing the same leads as you. You'll want to carefully gauge the progress you make with each prospect, too fast or slow and the competition could scoop them out from under you. The key to beating the competition is to position your follow-up with your prospect so that you can maximize your chances of closing the sale.

SEMINARS

Much like trade shows, seminars are another great forum for home business owners to market their goods and services, showcase their specific expertise, and present the main benefits of their products or services to a select and captive audience. Best of all, seminars need not be formal or conducted in fancy, high-rent rooms. On the contrary, seminars and workshops can be informal and hosted in just about any location imaginable—a banquet room, a living room, a supplier's warehouse, or at a local restaurant. The specific place will depend on the audience, the objective of the event, and the topic or subject mater. Regardless of the location, seminars provide home business owners with many marketing and business building opportunities, as the following information reveals.

- *Sell, sell more, and sell more frequently.* When you consider that every marketing activity that you engage in should be developed with selling in mind then seminars should be near the top of the list in terms of creating great forums for selling. Organize, host, or participate in seminars, and use the event to sell products or services.

The seminar selling environment is especially productive for the sales of products and services that can be easily demonstrated, revealing all of the benefits to a live audience. Seminars can also greatly reduce the length of the sales cycle and motivate prospects to purchase through building excitement, sharing vital information, and creating a sense of buying urgency at the event.

- *Prospect and build a powerful database.* Through seminar events, it is possible to generate a wealth of well-qualified leads by utilizing the attendee list or by staging a contest and using information captured on the entry ballot for direct marketing purposes. Using the information you collect at the seminar, you also have the ability to build your database, even if all in attendance are not currently qualified prospects, simply because over time and through continual direct-marketing contact, many can become qualified or refer other people that are qualified to your business. To that end you want to collect as much information as possible, including full names, job titles and descriptions, complete addresses, and any information specific to your goods or services and their needs.

- *Seek publicity and showcase your expertise.* Use seminars to position or to reconfirm yourself as an expert in your industry or specific field. Becoming an expert is relatively easy. It is maintaining your status as an expert that can prove difficult, which is what makes seminars such a great forum for maintaining your expert status. You can reach a large audience very effectively, giving more substantial amounts of information or advice than you can through other formats such as print advertisements. Seminars also present a fantastic opportunity to get the media involved and secure publicity. Send out a press release to the media outlining the seminar details about three weeks prior to the event, and follow up the first mailing with a telephone call or a second mailing a week prior to the event as a reminder. In addition to the seminar details, include in your news release why you think each individual media outlet should be there, and how the information you provide will benefit their target audience. The more beneficial the information is to their target audience the greater the chance they will attend and provide coverage.

- *Support, recruit, and educate.* Seminars can also be the perfect vehicle to recruit employees, sales agents, suppliers, vendors, and, more importantly, customers. It is a highly effective and cost-efficient way to recruit people for every role you in your business. You can also employ the seminar format to train or educate a room full of people. It is a cost-effective way to ensure that customers or your business team members are trained in the details of your product or service. One-on-one, this type of training would be far too costly for most home business owners, but in a seminar the cost of training or educating each person is dramatically reduced.

Promoting Your Seminar on a Shoestring Budget

Fortunately for small business owners with tight marketing budget, seminars can be promoted effectively and with success for little cost. Of course, this is providing that you are prepared to roll up your sleeves, dig in and do the hard work yourself rather than hiring out the job of promoting your seminar. However, keep in mind the ideas listed below are best suited for promoting a free seminar, one that creates revenues and profits by way of sales at the time of the seminar or through follow-up of sales leads collected during the seminar.

Handouts

Design a basic, yet colorful, promotional flier on your personal computer. List the details of your seminar or workshop event, print a few dozen copies, and post the fliers on free notice and bulletin boards throughout your community. These free notice boards are usually located in community centers, churches, gas stations, schools, libraries, grocery stores, and laundromats. You can also enlist students to hand deliver the fliers door to door or tuck them under windshield wipers on parked cars.

Telemarketing

Devote a few hours each day before the seminar to calling past and current clients and hot prospects to inform them about your seminar and invite them to attend. Maximize the impact of this shoestring budget marketing method by also asking them to bring a friend or two to the seminar, even go as far as offering special incentives to people that bring others to the event.

Word of Mouth

Let everyone you come into contact with know about the event and ask that they also help to spread the word by telling others. This is an especially effective technique for informal seminars were people are not asked to preregister, just to show up on the day of the seminar with a friend, co-worker, or family member. Word-of-mouth marketing is the home business owner's best and by far most effective marketing weapon.

Media

Create a news release about your seminar event, and send it off to local media outlets. Also take the time to invite key members of the media to the seminar, as the coverage they might provide afterwards can be just as valuable as the exposure before the event.

Outbound Communications

Include details about the seminar in all of your current outbound business communications and correspondences, including telephone voice messages, company newsletters, invoices and sales receipts, faxes, and e-mails, and by promoting the seminar on your Web site and through your business alliances' Web sites and outgoing communications.

Securing Speakers and Sponsors

Before organizing and hosting a seminar you will also need to decide who will speak at the event, and if you will endeavor to find event sponsors or co-producers of the event.

Speakers

One thing that every seminar requires is a presenter—one person or a number of people who will speak at the event and have expertise or qualifications for doing so. There are basically two types of presenters that speak at seminars, paid speakers and non-paid speakers. Paid professional speakers are available to speak at any occasion across the country. Their fees vary from a low of about $250 per day to as much as six-figures per day, plus expenses. Obviously, the majority of small business owners cannot afford to pay professional speakers and will have to rely on non-paid ones. So non-paid speakers make up the bulk of presenters at seminars hosted by small business owners. It is very easy to secure non-paid speakers for an event. However, there must be a benefit for them if you want to secure high-quality speakers. The benefit more times than not will be an opportunity to sell their own products or services, either directly at the event, or by generating leads that can be followed up and turned into sales later.

Sponsors

Planning and hosting seminars can be costly and time-consuming. Because of this, many small business owners forego using seminars to market their goods or services. However, before you eliminate seminars from your potential marketing toolbox, consider securing an event sponsor to share in the time, energy, and financial investment required to plan and host the event. Sponsors can be active or non-active. As the name suggests, active sponsors are ones that take an active role in planning and presenting at the seminar. An example of an active sponsorship match would be a real estate broker that hosts a first-time homebuyer's seminar, which is co-sponsored by a home inspector and a mortgage broker. All have similar target audiences, and each can benefit from being in contact with people at the seminar. Non-active sponsors refer more to sponsors that can benefit from the exposure associated with the event, but do not necessarily want to play an active role in the event beyond financial sponsorship. These types of non-active sponsors typically include financial institutions, manufacturers, and insurance brokers that want to be associated with the event and recognized through signage, advertisements, and article features in the printed

seminar guide. Securing non-active sponsors requires time, planning, and a formal presentation. You must be able to demonstrate successfully to the sponsor that the financial investment will generate a return based on the exposure they receive at the event.

Three Key Considerations for Success

In addition to the topic of your seminar, how will you promote the event, meet your key objectives, and secure a return on investment? And there are a few other critical considerations to keep in mind and plan for while creating your seminar action plan.

1. *Competition.* The first issue that can affect the success of your seminar event is competition for your audience's time and attention—not literally by way of competing seminars on the same day, same topic, with the same target audience, but more by distractions that can lure your target audience away. These distractions can include special live or televised sporting events, political elections, community parades or fairs, seasonal holidays, and major local entertainment events.

2. *Timing.* The timing of your seminar is another consideration. Most seminar and professional meeting consultants agree that the best time to plan and host a seminar is in the spring between late March to very early June or in the fall from early September to mid-November. Of course, the timing of your event will be greatly dependent on your seminar topic and marketing objective. Other timing considerations include holidays and target audience availability. If you want to reach business people, a mid-week daytime seminar works best. If you want to reach consumers, plan your event for when your target audience is not at work, generally weeknights and weekends. Though Tuesday through Thursday evenings are generally considered the best time.

3. *Accessibility.* The third consideration is accessibility of the seminar location. Accessibility encompasses everything from uncontrollable

situations, such as poor weather conditions and unexpected traffic congestion, to controllable issues such as parking and transit availability. Ideally, you want the seminar location to be central to the majority of the people attending. You also want on-site or nearby secure parking and access to public transit. If guests will be attending from out of town, the location should also be central to hotels and the airport.

PUBLIC SPEAKING

Public speaking is another highly effective way for small business owners to showcase their expertise, brand their business, and market their goods or services. Yet, public speaking is also one of the most underutilized marketing activities, mainly because the vast majority of people are scared to death at the prospect of having to speak in front of a live audience. Fortunately, there are techniques that can be employed to eliminate fear of public speaking and that can vastly improve your public speaking skills. Many home business owners will find themselves in the position of being asked to speak publicly—at the local chamber of commerce, industry or trade meetings, business schools, or community clubs and organizations. It is a common practice for these groups and organizations to bring in experts on various subjects to speak to their members, guests, and students. But, before committing time and resources to free public speaking, there are a few requests that you should make for the benefit of your business:

- The guest list, including names and full contact information for both people in attendance, and those who signed up but did not attend. Use this list as a lead source for prospecting and selling opportunities.
- If appropriate, ask if you can sell or demonstrate your products or services during and after the event.
- Permission to take printed promotional literature about your business to hand out or place on all seats before the event.
- Ask for a display advertisement promoting your business, product, or service in the function

schedule and other printed literature that is handed out to guests at the seminar or mailed to guests before and after the event.
- Ask to be included in any pre-event press releases and post-event mailings to guest.

Overcoming the Fear of Public Speaking

The fear of speaking in public is real. In fact, it is the number-one fear shared by more American adults than any other fear or phobia. Not the fear of heights, claustrophobia, or even the fear of dying! Fear of public speaking is number one. Fortunately there are proven methods that can help you overcome the fear of public speaking, which is especially important for small business owners that want to capitalize on public speaking as a highly effective method of marketing their products or services. Simple ways to overcome the fear of public speaking included arriving early to the speaking location so that you can familiarize yourself with the room. Walk around the stage or dais area to get comfortable in your surroundings, and test all audio and visual equipment before guests arrive. Introduce yourself to the organizers of the event and their staff. Try to get to know everyone by name and what their responsibilities are so that if you have any problems you'll be able to go directly to the person that can fix it. Try to get to know the audience before you speak by greeting people as they arrive. You'll find it much easier and more relaxing to speak if you can look at the audience and see a few familiar and friendly faces smiling back.

You should also understand that everyone in the audience will be sympathetic to your task. Public speaking can be difficult and nerve-racking even for the most experienced professional speakers. Therefore, remember that the audience is behind you, they support you and want you to be informative and entertaining, and most of all they want to see and hear you succeed.

Finally, before you begin, use breathing and light physical exercises as a way to relax and ease nervous jitters. The Advanced Public Speaking Institute offers visitors to its Web site additional information and advice about overcoming the fear of public speaking and public speaking advice in general. It can be found online atwww.public-speaking.org.

Tips for Professional Public Speaking

As mentioned above, public speaking is no Sunday walk in the park; it is hard work and requires much practice in order to master. But where do you begin? One good starting point is with the length of your speech, which will depend on the situation and the information you want or need to share. As a rule of thumb, however, after 30 continuous minutes of listening, the majority of the audience will start to lose interest unless there are preplanned breaks or intermissions. Likewise, you will want to talk at the educational level of the room or slightly below, never above. Skip technical jargon that might be lost on the audience, and use plain easy-to-understand English. Here are a few more helpful public speaking tips that can assist you in your public speaking efforts.

- Master speakers get their audience involved and invested in the speech within the first minute and keep the audience involved until the end. The best way to learn how to get your audience interested, invested, and involved in what you have to say is through practice and by continually seeking out places to speak.
- Make eye contact with members of the audience, try to get them acknowledge you, and nod in agreement to what you are saying.
- Freely use visual aids such as charts, props, printed handouts, and audio/video aids when appropriate.
- Know the central message and theme of your speech inside out and upside down, but don't try to memorize your speech word for word. If you do, you will come off as manufactured, rigid, and boring.
- Avoid rocking back and forth as you stand at the podium and speak, and try to use normal hand gestures and voice fluctuations in your tone and pacing. Be slightly animated and move as you would naturally.
- Avoid talking too fast, rambling on beyond the point made, and speaking in a high pitch or monotone voice. A comfortable pace for yourself and the audience is about 160 words per minute, which gives you a reference point in writing and practicing your speech prior to the event.
- Avoid talking so quietly that people cannot hear or so loudly the audience feels as though they are being scolded. Using slang, profanity, poor grammar, and politically incorrect humor is also inappropriate for any audience, regardless of the topic or situation.

CREATING AND STAGING PROFITABLE CONTESTS

Contests have long been a favorite promotional tool for small business owners as a way to generate sales leads, increase exposure, and to help build awareness about their business, products, or services. But, long before you decide what type of contest to hold, you first should identify what the objective) is for holding the contest. What do you want to achieve as a result of staging the contest? Keeping in mind that increasing sales is not an objective, but a potential result of an objective. Do you want to capture and qualify leads from the completed entry ballots? Generate publicity and media coverage as a result of the contest? Build or update your database for direct marketing purposes from the information you collect? Use the contest to introduce a new product or service, or celebrate a company milestone such as an anniversary? Support a local charity or organization? Or perhaps you want to build goodwill within the community or cross-promote your business with other businesses or organizations by becoming an official sponsor of a contest? There are lots of reasons to create and host a contest. Once you have determined your contest objective, you will be in a better position to decide which type of contest is best suited to achieve it. There are, of course, many other points to consider before creating and holding a contest, as the following information illustrates.

What Type of Contests?

The type of contest that you stage must be relevant to your business and marketing objectives. And it must be able to be successfully executed within your established event budget and support structure. There is no point staging a labor-intensive contest when you are a one-person operation. One simple contest for small business owners is an entry ballot contest, which requires contestants to complete a ballot and deposit it into an on-site box or mail it in for the drawing. Entry ballot contests are a wise choice for small business owners because you can use the information you collect on the entry form to build a prospect database, which can be exploited for direct marketing purposes. You can also ask additional questions on the entry ballot as survey or polling questions that can assist in marketing research and planning.

Other contests include scratch cards that revel prizes, counting games, and customer interactive contest such as celebrity look-a-like costumes, or essay contests. You can purchase insurance if you decide that you want to stage in high-stakes contests, such as million-dollar hole-in-one, or million-dollar basketball free throw competitions. In the event a participant wins, the insurance company covers the prize value. National Indemnity offers insurance packages to cover up to one million dollars in prize money for hole-in-one contests, football field goal contests, and half court basketball shots, as well as insurance programs to cover other types of unique contests and promotional risks. It can be found online at www.nationalindemnity.com and offers visitors a free and instant online quote service.

What Is the Prize?

What will you award as the grand prize and will there be secondary or participation prizes also awarded? Or if you partner with other businesses, will the prize consist of numerous prizes donated by each partner to create a grand prize package? Regardless, the prize(s) should be relative to your business and complement the products or services that you sell. For instance, if you operate a landscaping service, a "backyard landscaping makeover" would be a suitable grand prize. Or, if you operate a maid service then "win a free maid for a year" makes

a great prize. Above all the prize should enhance and complement your core product line and be valuable enough that it compels people who are not otherwise customers to want to enter for a chance to win. The reason the prize should be complementary of your core business, products, or services, is that the people that enter but do not win will to a certain degree be qualified prospects. You can follow up with after the drawing and persuade them to buy your goods or services. Few people that live in an apartment will bother to enter a landscaping makeover for their yard. Therefore, it is a safe assumption that the people who enter will have backyards and that need attention in terms of landscaping.

Consider All of the Legal Issues

Once you have determined the type of contest you will be holding and the prize that will be awarded, the next step is to seek legal advice to make sure that you will not be placing yourself, your business, your family, contestants, or contest promotional partners in a position of liability as a direct result of the contest or prize. In most cases, the lawyer that you deal with for business matters qualified to advise you on the contest and potential liabilities associated with hosting the contest. However, if the contest is just a small one-time or ongoing weekly draw or a similar small promotional event with low-value prizes, the need for legal advice is probably not warranted. In addition to seeking legal advice on larger contests, be sure to call your insurance broker and inquire about liability insurance to cover the event and matters relating to the contest. Once again, you do not want to be left holding the bag in terms of liability should something go wrong. Be proactive and make sure you are protected. It should also be noted that not every state is created equal when it comes to the rules and regulations surrounding promotional contests and you will need to check with local government agencies before conducting any contests to make sure you comply with state rules. Arent Fox Attorneys offers visitors to its Web site information and articles about the legalities of staging promotional contests. It can be found online at www.arentfox.com.

Establish a Contest Budget

The contest budget is also a major consideration for the majority of small business owners. Not only will you have to cover the cost for the contest prize(s), but also for the cost of promotion, the drawing, publicity, time and labor to cover the event, interruption to current business, organizing the event, potential legal and liability insurance costs, and collecting and recording the information you receive through the entry forms. Much in terms of the budget will depend on your marketing objectives, the prize, and how the contest is promoted. There is no one standard financial formula that can be used when establishing a contest budget. Its budget will be directly reflected by what you can afford to spend and what you plan to get in return. Of course, one method for reducing costs is to ask suppliers to furnish the prize free or at a reduced cost. You can also build cross-promotional partnerships with one or more noncompeting businesses in the community and split the cost of the prize and the expenses associated with promoting the contest. And you can purchase insurance to cover specialty contests with large cash prizes.

As a cautionary note, understand that if you cannot afford to properly create, implement, and manage a contest, you will be better off not staging it at all. Reaching your objective is the goal of the event. If financial restrictions hamper that effort, the result will not be what you planned for and expected.

Promoting the Contest

How will you promote the contest to ensure maximum benefit to your business and secure a return on investment through your stated objective? How you promote the contest will be mainly reflective of your marketing objective, the prize awarded, and your financial budget. If the budget is tight, consider creating simple promotional fliers revealing contest details and pinning the fliers to notice boards throughout the community. Or initiate a direct mail campaign aimed at current customers and alliances and ask that they spread the word about the contest. But if budget allows, create and run elaborate advertisements on radio, television, and in print publications promoting the contest and details. Do this because contests are becoming commonplace for small business, people become immune to them unless they are promoted consistently and uniquely. Regardless of the budget level be sure to seek free publicity and media exposure for the contest by contacting local media through a press release, media advisory, telephone call, or personal visit. Let local media know that your contest will be a great photo opportunity for a human-interest story and will benefit their audience.

Awarding the Prize

Awarding the prize is the final important consideration. You want the maximum promotional bang possible. Contact local media and get them interested in covering the official prize awarding ceremony. Don't forget your camera. Take pictures of the winner and the event, and use these pictures in your printed promotional materials throughout the year. Ask the prizewinner to submit a testimonial about how happy she was to win, why she entered, and a few nice comments about your business. Basically, seek ways to make awarding the prize a grand event. The more people, media, and interest that you can create, the more exposure your contest, and subsequently business, will receive. Always make a big deal out of every contest that you hold, regardless of the size of the prize. The more fanfare the better.

SPONSORSHIP OPPORTUNITIES

Sponsorship of various community associations, organizations, and events is yet another method small business owners can use to promote and market their goods and services. The added benefit is assisting these same community associations, organizations, and events through the donation of monies, products, or services. It should be noted that marketing via sponsorships requires a long-term commitment in order to realize a return on investments of time, money, and energy. There are three main categories of sponsorships—charity, sports, and community events. Often it is not uncommon for the three types of sponsorships to become entwined. For instance, you might sponsor a community pancake breakfast wherein proceeds are donated to a charity or number of charities and the event is hosted by a local youth sports association. In this example, all three main types of sponsorships are connected through the single event.

Charity Sponsorships

Great wisdom can be found in the old saying "charity begins at home," and this should especially ring true to small business owners. Support the community that supports your business by picking a worthwhile local charity or charitable event and help out any way you can—financially or with other resources at your disposal. Much goodwill can be secured by contributing to charity within your community, and over the long run that will benefit your business through the contacts that you make and the relationships that you forge. One of the best ways to support a charity is to create your own charitable event that is hosted annually under your banner, but includes others from the business community. A ten-mile run for cancer, bathtub races to raise money for AIDS research, or an annual food drive to collect nonperishable foods for the local food bank. The charity sponsorship options are nearly unlimited. Advertise the fact that you support or sponsor one or more local charities, and watch customer loyalty and repeat business grow exponentially because of your acts of kindness. Even home business owners on tight financial budgets can get involved by donating products or services to a charity or charitable event, or by providing assistance in organizing the event, finding transportation, or even providing a location to host the event.

Community Sports Sponsorships

The majority of amateur sports teams and leagues have various business sponsorship packages available to small business owners based on the team budget and sponsorship needs. Your sponsorship may only partially cover a teams' requirements such as uniforms or, if your sponsorship is more extensive, it could cover the teams' entire needs, everything required for the team to compete. If you can afford to get involved with sports sponsorship, do

it. It helps to build a good corporate image and shows that you support the community that supports your business. But don't forget it is not enough just to have your business name emblazoned across the backs of the team jerseys, you also have to get out to the games and cheer your team on. I think that is the most gratifying aspect of sponsoring a local sports team. Consider the following advice to ensure the maximum bang for your sports' sponsorship bucks:

- Try to have the team you sponsor named after your business, which can usually be arranged with full sponsorships. Check with league officials. The team uniforms should boldly display your business name as the sponsor of the team.

- Have a sign banner made promoting your team and business and fly the banner at home and away games. Also consider setting up product or service displays and demonstrations at games, especially during tournaments. Attend games and network by handing out business cards, product samples or coupons, and your monthly newsletter.

- If you sell products, arrange to have a door or seat prize drawn at every home game. Make sure the announcer names your business at least twice during the drawing and subsequent awarding of the prize.

- Have team pictures taken and display the pictures in your office, newsletter, and printed promotional materials. Let your customers and prospects know that your business is a proud sponsor of community sports.

- Pay to have game rosters and schedules printed for distribution, but make sure that your business name, logo, and marketing message is boldly printed across the header of all pages. Printed promotional opportunities can extend to ticket stubs and player cards. Also be sure to give away tickets for special tournaments to your best customers as an appreciation gift or to your hottest prospects.

- Create team and individual player awards, with trophies and certificates. Ensure your business name and sponsorship is engraved or printed on them. Likewise, consider sponsoring an end-of-season celebration for players, parents, fans, and coaches, and invite the local media for coverage and photo opportunities.

- Inquire about advertising opportunities around the playing field, in the bleachers, or in the arena. These opportunities can include signs, banners, and displays in the bleachers, around the field, or on the scoreboard, helping to brand your business, products, or services with those in attendance.
- Look for ways to turn sponsorship into media or publicity events. Send out press releases about the team, write a weekly community sports column for the local newspaper, or get the scores out to radio disc jockeys to read on air, along with your business name, of course.

Community Event Sponsorships

Community event sponsorship is much like charity sponsorship; ultimately you want the event to assist people and organizations in your local community through raising money, awareness, products, or services depending on the event and the goals of the event. And you want your business name to be associated with the event. Once again, if you have the financial resources and the time necessary, try to create an annual event and take ownership of that event. For example, even something as simple and inexpensive as a community clean-up day in which you supply school-age kids with garbage bags to stash trash from school yards and playing fields can have an extremely positive benefit on your business. Other forms of community sponsorships and events include raising money for community buildings such as renovations to the library or expansion of the community center, tree planting events at local parks, or raising money to send a local choir to various competitions. Community sponsorships can be small things such as the donation of a park bench with an engraved plaque naming your business as the donating sponsor. Whichever sponsorship avenue you choose, make sure you support the community that supports you and your business.

RESOURCES

🗒 Associations

American Seminar Leaders Association
2405 E. Washington Blvd.
Pasadena, CA 91104
(800) 735-0511
www.asla.com

American Training and Seminar Association
365 S Ocoee Street
Cleveland, TN 37311
(866) 572-0142
www.americantsa.com

Canadian Association of Exposition Management
6900 Airport Road, Suite 239 A
Mississauga, ON L4V 1E8
(905) 678-9377
www.caem.ca

National Speakers Association
1500 S. Priest Drive
Tempe, AZ 85281
(480) 968-2552
www.nsaspeakers.org

Trade Show Exhibitors Association
McCormick Place
2301 S Lake Shore Drive, Suite 1005
Chicago, IL 60616
(312) 842-8732
www.tsea.org

📖 Suggested Reading

Carnegie, Dale. *The Quick and Easy Way to Effective Speaking.* New York: Pocket Books, 1990.

Esposito, Janet E. *In the Spotlight: Overcome Your Fear of Public Speaking and Performing.* New York: Strong Books, 2000.

Gleek, Fred. *Marketing and Promoting Your Own Seminars and Workshops.* New York: Fast Forward Press, 2001.

Jolles, Robert. *How to Run Seminars and Workshops: Presentation Skills for Consultants, Trainers, and Teachers.* New York: John Wiley & Sons, 2000.

Levinson, Jay Conrad, and Mark Smith. *Guerrilla Trade Show Selling: New Unconventional Weapons and Tactics to Meet More People, Get More Leads, and Close More Sales.* New York: John Wiley & Sons, 1997.

Miller, Steve. *How to Get the Most Out of Trade Shows.* New York: McGraw-Hill, 2000.

Miller, Steve, and Robert Sjoquist. *How to Design a WOW Trade Show Booth without Spending a Fortune.* Federal Way, WA: Hikelly Productions, 2002.

Shenson, Howard. *How to Develop and Promote Successful Seminars and Workshops: The Definitive Guide to Creating and Marketing Seminars, Workshops, Classes, and Conferences.* New York: John Wiley & Sons, 1990.

Stephenson, James. *The Ultimate Small Business Marketing Guide: 1500 Great Marketing Tricks That will Drive Your Business Through the Roof!* Irvine, CA: Entrepreneur Press Inc., 2003.

Web Sites

Advanced Public Speaking Institute, www.public-speaking.org: Public speaking portal providing visitors with products, services, information, resources, and public speaking links of interest.

Contests and Sweepstakes Directory, www.sweepstakes-contests.com: List your contest in the site's directory and get ideas about the various types of contests that can be held.

National Seminar Group, www.natsem.com: Seminar industry information, resources, and links, as well as products and services to aid in planning and hosting seminars and workshops.

SCA Promotions, www.promotionalcontests.com: SCA offers prize coverage services and creative solutions to eliminate risk in marketing and contest programs. This includes guaranteed payment of prizes from $5,000 to $1 billion, which allows you to add or upgrade a prize for a fraction of the cost.

Toastmasters International, www.toastmasters.org: Toastmaster members learn by speaking to groups and working with others in a supportive environment to improve their public speaking and presentation skills. Go to its Web site to locate a club near you.

Trade Show Exhibits Sales & Rentals, www.trade-shows.org: Free online quotes for exhibit sales and rentals, and a nationwide trade show directory and resources page.

Trade Show Week Online, www.tradeshowweek.com: Print and electronic magazine serving the trade show, consumer show, and convention industry with information, product and service listings, resources, and helpful links.

Trade Shows Online, www.tradeshows.com: Directory service listing trade show, conventions, and expos worldwide, indexed by country. The site also provides visitors with helpful information and resources to improve trade show performance.

CHAPTER 17

Internet and E-Commerce

W ELCOME TO THE WONDERFUL WORLD OF Internet marketing and e-commerce sales. If you want to develop a Web site to complement your home business that operates in the real world, there is information here to get you up and on your way. But if your intention is to start a homebased business that operates solely as a stand-alone Internet business, you will need to obtain more information than is featured in this book. Space simply does not afford the opportunity to include all the information needed to develop, build, and maintain a truly outstanding Web site and e-commerce business model. In the resources section you will find book and Web resources that provide much more detail on commercial Web sites.

DO YOU NEED A WEB SITE?
The first and most obvious question for any homebased business person is, Do you need a Web site? Much depends on the type of business you operate, the goods and services you sell, your business and marketing objectives, and your future plans.

The Internet does afford home business owners and marketers from all walks of life, geographic regions, and financial budgets, a level playing field with larger and often better-financed competitors. The Internet enables home business owners to reach a wider and broader audience, sell to more people, share more information with more people, keep their current customers better informed and serviced, and test new products, services, and markets inexpensively, quickly, and effectively, all with the click of a mouse. The Internet has forever changed the way the world does business and shares information, and it will only continue to expand and prosper with more new online technology.

If this appeals to you or if you feel it could have a beneficial impact on your business, it is safe to assume that you do need a Web site so that you can promote your business, sell, share information, conduct research, train business alliances, or do all of them. To truly benefit from operating a Web site, you must first determine what you want your Web site to do for your business. There are several objectives for starting and maintaining a Web site, either as a stand-alone business or as a natural extension of your existing business.

- *Sell.* The most common objective of a Web site is to sell your goods or services to global consumers. The advantages of Internet marketing includes the fact that your store is open 24-hours a day, you can send information to customers in minutes, not hours, days, or weeks, and you can update or alter your marketing message and strategy quickly, conveniently, and very inexpensively.

- *Brand.* Another common objective is to use the Internet to help brand your company and products and help build awareness of your company and products—for a fraction of the cost it would take to attain the same exposure in the bricks-and-mortar world. The steps that are taken today to e-brand a business, products, and services will separate the online business winners and losers ten years from now.
- *Share information.* Using your Web site to share information with customers, business associates, suppliers, and sales agents is yet another common online objective and one that can be achieved for a fraction of the cost of using conventional methods such as telephone, fax, mail, and courier delivery.
- *Support.* Through your Web site you can support contractors, sales agents, and your customers by hosting virtual workshops, and training seminars, and by posting specialized product and service information and customer service support features.
- *Research.* You can use the Internet, and more specifically your own company Web site, to conduct research on a wide variety of important issues affecting your business via online polls, surveys, questionnaires, and research forums. Discover how your customers view your products or services in comparison to competitors' products or services, what other types of products or services would your customers be willing to purchase from you, and what customers think about the level of customer service you provide.
- *Expand.* The Internet presents incredible opportunities to expand your business in a number of ways—by selling your goods or services to people outside your geographical trading area, by finding new employees or distributors to market your goods and services, or by finding new joint venture opportunities that can help expand your business.

BUILDING YOUR PLACE ON THE WEB

Once you have made the decision that you will build a Web site and make Internet marketing an active part of your overall marketing strategy, there are many decisions that must be made, including:

- How much is your budget to build your Web site?
- Who will build the Web site?
- Who will maintain your Web site, and how much will it cost?
- Who will host your Web site, and how much will it cost?
- What type of content and interactive Web tools do you need, where will they come from, and how much will they cost?

Ultimately, you will need to develop a plan for your new Web site that tells how your site will look, function, and be marketed; how much all of this will cost; where the money will come from to cover these costs; what the Internet marketing strategy is; and what projections indicate how you will secure a return on investment.

Who Will Build, Host, and Maintain Your Site?

Your first option is to design, build, and maintain your own Web site. There is a plethora of Web site building programs available to enable novice webmasters to build and maintain their own Web sites. You will still, of course, need to be familiar with computers and the Internet if you choose this option, regardless of the "no experience required" advertisements. The cost to maintain your site will vary by the content you feature, how often the site needs to be updated, and the objectives of the site. In terms of hosting, costs will also vary depending on the services you select—e-commerce shopping carts, payments systems, order tracking, Web site statistics, and database storage option. There are even services that will host your Web site for free, but in exchange you have to allow them to place banner advertisements, and often other types of advertising, on your site, and to attach ads on outgoing e-mails initiated from your site. For paid services, expect to pay a minimum of $50 per month for basic business Web site hosting and about $250 per month for hosting that includes premium services, features, and functions.

The second option is to hire a professional to design and build your Web site. Fortunately through advances in Web building software and tools, the cost to hire a professional Web designer has dramatically decreased in the past few years. In fact, for less than $1,000 you can have a complete, fully functional Web site built with e-commerce, visitor interaction, and database marketing options. Entrepreneurs that do not have the gumption, time, or skills required to build and maintain a Web site would be well advised to hire a professional to do it.

Choosing the Right Domain Name

Choosing your domain name or URL (Uniform Resource Locator) is more difficult then you might think. In the first place, short, high-impact .com designations are becoming increasingly difficult to acquire. Second, the domain name you select must suitably match the image that you want your business to project. Ideally, you will want your business name and domain name to match. For instance, if you operate Jim's Pool Cleaning, you would try to acquire the right to use the URL www.jimspool cleaning.com or another designation such as jims poolcleaning.biz, .tv, .org, or .net. The dot com designation, however, is by far the best for commercial enterprises, especially in North America. If you are planning on doing business internationally, you might also want to register your domain name under individual country designations, such as .ca for Canada, .au for Australia, to protect your business identity in those countries and to enable you to use the same domain with alternate designations should you choose to expand your online or even geographic, presence.

The domain name that you select should also be short, preferably 15 letters or less, easy to remember and spell, and something that best describes the type of business that you operate, the products you sell, or the services that you provide. As the example above indicates, there is no mistaking that Jim provides pool cleaning services. Additionally, make sure that you register your own domain in your business name, instead of using any one of the numerous extension services offered on the Web. You want the security in knowing that your domain name is yours and under your control. Once you have decided to create a Web site as an extension of your existing business or as a stand-alone enterprise, start the process of choosing a domain name right away and register a few variations as soon as you have compiled a short list. Good names are hard to come by. Ones that do come available or have not already been selected go fast. Don't worry if your site is not ready. Once you have paid your domain registration fee, you can park the domain until your site is built and ready to be published to the World Wide Web. Domain name registration fees vary greatly from a low of $10 per year to as much as $75 per year depending on the designation and the registration service you choose. The majority of domain registration services also provide customers with various additional Internet and e-commerce services and packages, ranging from Web site design to shopping carts, hosting and maintenance services, and Web site promotional services. The following are a few of the most popular domain registration services, and where you can find them online:

- Network Solutions, www.networksolutions.com
- Register, www.register.com
- Domain Direct, www.domaindirect.com
- Dotster, www.dotster.com
- Unclaimed Domains, www.unclaimeddomains. com

You can use the Domain Name Tracker form (see Figure 17.1) to record your preferred domain name choices. Simply log on to any domain name registration service and check availability of specific domain names for free. Once again, the most common and perhaps most prestigious designation is .com. However, .net, .biz, .us (United States), and .ca (Canada) are also popular choices for online commercial enterprises.

Elements of a Web Site

All successful Web sites share qualities that make them tops in their industry and with their customers and visitors. Many elements go into building a great Web site that appeals to your target audience, creates a sense of online community, is easy to navigate and

FIGURE 17.1 — Domain Name Tracker

Possible Domain Names	Available Designation	None Available
www. _____	❏ .com ❏ .net ❏ .biz ❏ .us ❏ .ca	❏
www. _____	❏ .com ❏ .net ❏ .biz ❏ .us ❏ .ca	❏
www. _____	❏ .com ❏ .net ❏ .biz ❏ .us ❏ .ca	❏
www. _____	❏ .com ❏ .net ❏ .biz ❏ .us ❏ .ca	❏
www. _____	❏ .com ❏ .net ❏ .biz ❏ .us ❏ .ca	❏
www. _____	❏ .com ❏ .net ❏ .biz ❏ .us ❏ .ca	❏
www. _____	❏ .com ❏ .net ❏ .biz ❏ .us ❏ .ca	❏
www. _____	❏ .com ❏ .net ❏ .biz ❏ .us ❏ .ca	❏
www. _____	❏ .com ❏ .net ❏ .biz ❏ .us ❏ .ca	❏
www. _____	❏ .com ❏ .net ❏ .biz ❏ .us ❏ .ca	❏

use, and is consistent in the delivery of beneficial content, products, and services to fill the needs of your target audience.

A Sense of Community

All successful Web sites have managed to create and maintain a sense of community for their customers and visitors. People enjoy visiting and participating in these Web sites because they feel they are part of an online community of other like-minded site visitors. Community building is not as easy as it sounds; it requires research, finding the right mix of content and tools through trial and error, and hands-on management to perfect. Creating community is not a single entity; it is a combination of elements, such as beneficial content, products, or services that fill specific needs, and interactive Web tools, such as discussion boards and online workshops, to unite visitors, convert them to customers, and keep them returning not only as repeat customers but also as active members of your Web site community.

Keep Your Content Fresh

Successful Web sites also have content that is beneficial to their visitors, original, and regularly updated.

OK, so not all home business owners with Web sites need to update their content on a regular basis, especially if you sell a service that doesn't change. But for businesses that focus on information as the cornerstone of their online marketing strategy, it is critical to remember that content is king. Use bold attention-grabbing headlines and sub-headlines that spell out in perfect clarity how your visitors benefit from the information or products or services you are promoting. Try to keep articles and explanations brief, powerful, and to the point by using bullet lists and photographs and illustrations as descriptive aids. Edit your content for spelling, and grammar, and avoid using all capital letters and too many exclamation points. Above all, provide visitors and customers with information that they cannot get anywhere else. If people can get the same information elsewhere it greatly reduces the chances of their returning to your site, which equals fewer selling opportunities.

For home business owners that absolutely do not have the time to constantly write, edit, and update their own Web site content, content providers will supply and automatically update your content for a fee, or in some cases for free. The following content providers perform these services:

- ISyndicate, www.isyndicate.com
- Hot Plug-Ins, www.hotplugins.com
- Free Sticky, www.freesticky.com
- Bravenet, www.bravenet.com
- Sticky Server, www.stickyserver.com

Appeal to Your Target Audience

Everything you feature in your Web site, including content, products, services, interactive Web tools, links, and resources, must appeal to your primary target audience. Keep this in mind, especially when building your site. There are so many cool and easy to plug-in Web tools and features available that it is very easy to get sidetracked and lose sight of your target audience, and your online marketing objectives. Perhaps the best way to design a site packed with information and tools that appeal to your target audience is to use a competitors' Web site as a yardstick. To locate competitors' Web sites read industry magazines and publications, conduct keyword search engine submissions, and visit your suppliers' Web sites. Once you have identified your online competition, visit their Web sites and make extensive notes about the content they feature, site design and function, interactive Web tools used, and payment, cart, and delivery systems available. Combine the best features of these sites to make sure your site appeals to your target audience.

Consistency

Consistency is critical in two areas. Your Web site should be consistent throughout—the look of its pages, the delivery of content and tools, the sales message, and entire site functions. Your Web site should also be consistent with your offline business image—the central sales message, the use of identifying marks such as a logo and central color scheme, and the business philosophy such as lowest priced or highest quality. Building an online and offline image and branding your business is a long process that requires hands-on management. Therefore, it makes sense to develop and stick with a consistent image so that people will begin to recognize your business instantly and favorably.

Keep Your Site User Friendly

As a rule of thumb, people will stay longer and return more often to Web sites that are user friendly and lightening fast, so make sure to build your site to meet these important criteria. Start by using a white background with dark letters, preferably black, in a font that is easy to read. Create a site map and include it in the navigation bar on each page because with keyword searches you never know what page visitors will enter first. Even small issues such as a frequently-asked-questions (FAQ page) and automatic formatting for printing text only, with a printer friendly button, make a big difference in terms of visitor usability. You also want to keep your site lightning fast; so skip large, slow-loading graphics, scrolling messages, and other features that serve only to slow down your site and the delivery of pages to visitors. Remember, the majority of people are still connected to the Internet with a 56K or slower modem.

Registering with Search Engines and Directories

The number one way people find the information, products, and services on the Internet is by keyword and phrase search submissions on search engine and search directories. In fact, some studies suggest that as many as 90 percent of Internet users search for the information, products, and services this way. Because you never know which search engine or directory people will use, your Web site and Web pages need to be listed or registered with many of them. But, before you start registering with every search engine and directory out there, you should know the basics. Search engines such as Google are indexed by bots or spiders, which extract specific information from Web sites and Web pages, and use that information for indexing. Search directories such as Yahoo have people called directory editors who compile the information by hand, generally indexed and grouped based on relevancy to the submitted search. These days, however, the line between search engine and search directory is increasingly blurred. Most major search engines and directories use both mechanical and human power to build and index information or supplement each other's services. You will want to submit your Web site and pages to be listed in both for search rankings purposes.

Many entrepreneurs new to Internet marketing find registering their Web site and pages with search engines and directories somewhat frustrating because there is no one set of rules, regulations, or guidelines for registering. Most search engines and directories have their own individual submission policies. Of course, you can always choose not to register with the major search engines because the ones that send out bots and spiders will eventually find you and automatically list your site, but your search rankings will be poor and buried behind hundreds of your competitors' search results. Because 90 percent of Web surfers use search engines and directories, you would be well advised to learn how to submit to each engine and directory for registration purposes. Or use one of the search engine and directory submission services. These companies automatically submit or register your Web site to all major search engines and directories. Often you only have to complete one relativity basic form. Some submission services are free, but the majority charge fees if you want quick listings, regular maintenance, and other premium listing services. For small business owners with limited time to optimize their Web sites and keywords for the best search rank results, these online multiple search engine submission services offer great value for a relatively small fee. Listed below are a few of the more popular search engine submission services:

- Add Me, www.addme.com
- Submit Today, www.submittoday.com
- Add Pro, www.addpro.com
- Submit It, www.submit-it.com
- Submit Express, www.submitexpress.com

If you plan on using your Web site to generate revenues and profits through the sales of goods and services, take the time required to select the right submission and maintenance service. Remember, your goal is to secure a top search ranking or result on all of the major search engines and directories, preferably on the first page, and ideally in the top ten search results. Listed below are a few popular search engines and search directories:

- Google, www.google.com
- Yahoo, www.yahoo.com
- WiseNut, www.wisenut.com
- Excite, www.excite.com
- All The Web, www.alltheweb.com
- Teoma, www.teoma.com
- Lycos, www.lycos.com
- ix Quick, www.ixquick.com
- dmoz Open Directory Project, www.dmoz.org
- Microsoft Network, (MSN) www.msn.com
- All Search Engines,www.allsearchengines.com (International search engine directory)
- Big Search, www.big-search.com (Domestic and international search engine directory)

Use the Search Engine and Directory Tracking Form (see Figure 17.2) to list search engines and directories that you want to register your Web site with, with the cost of registration.

FIGURE 17.2 Search Engine and Directory Tracking Form

Search Engine/Directory	Fees	Comments	Registered
_____	$_____	_____	❑
_____	$_____	_____	❑
_____	$_____	_____	❑
_____	$_____	_____	❑
_____	$_____	_____	❑
_____	$_____	_____	❑
_____	$_____	_____	❑
_____	$_____	_____	❑

Choosing Your Keywords

Because 90 percent of Internet users search via keywords and keyword phrases, you need to optimize your Web site for keyword searches. Most online marketing specialists suggest that you aim for a keyword density of about 5 percent, meaning that keywords will comprise 5 out of every 100 words of your content. You will also want to include keywords in your page titles, headers, Meta tags, and hyperlinks. Each page is unique in terms of the information featured and its marketing objective; be sure to select different keywords for each subsequent page in your site. Be very descriptive when selecting your keywords and phrases. Keep in mind that few people type in single search words, so combining keywords into short descriptive phrases is wise. A good starting point is to list what you sell and begin to conduct your own searches using variations made up of the descriptive words you use to describe your goods or services. There are also keyword generators and even keyword creation services that will optimize your keyword selection on your Web site for a fee. A few of the more popular ones are:

- Word Tracker, www.wordtracker.com
- Keyword Creator, www.keyword-creator.com
- Meta Builder, www.vancouver-webpages.com/meta/mk-metas.html
- Keyword Handbook, www.keywordhandbook.com
- 1st Position, www.1stposition.net/keyword-generator.html

You can also develop your own keyword list by writing down words you feel best describe your business, products, or services and then conducting your own search engine and directory submission using your keywords and phrases. When you begin to see businesses that sell similar products or services appearing in the first page of the search rankings, you know you are choosing the right keywords. Narrow the field until you have found suitable matches, and then repeat this exercise for each page in your site. Always include the maximum number of keywords the search engines allow. Just keep in mind that directories base ranking more on the quality of the content and not just on keywords, so concentrate on quality content. Use the 52 spaces

below to begin to build, search, and perfect your keywords and phrases.

Creating a Linking Strategy

Much like developing a keyword strategy, developing a linking strategy for your Web site is also very beneficial. Many popular search engines use links found within your site as part of the formula to establish search result rankings; the greater the number of relevant links related to the keyword words or search phrases found within your site, the higher the search ranking. In addition, providing customers and visitors access to additional sources of information, products, and services via links is a great way to help build your online community. Once again, the more needs and wants people can fulfill at one site, the greater the odds that they will return to your site. And, having your Web site featured in other sites on their Resources or Links pages is also a great way to market your site. Ideally,

FIGURE 17.3	Web Site Linking Worksheet

URL	Comments	Completed
www._____	_____	❏
www._____	_____	❏
www._____	_____	❏
www._____	_____	❏
www._____	_____	❏
www._____	_____	❏
www._____	_____	❏
www._____	_____	❏
www._____	_____	❏
www._____	_____	❏

you want your Web site and link featured on sites visited by people that match your target audience. To do this create a list of Web sites that you would like your site linked to like the Web Site Linking Worksheet (see Figure 17.3), contact each site's Webmaster, and ask to be linked. You can use this handy form for compiling the sites that you want to be linked to and check off the compiled box each time you are successful in your linking quest.

You might also want to consider adding a free-for-all links service to your site, which will enable any business or organization to automatically sign up to be featured on your links page within your site. Of course, like any online marketing activities, there are pros and cons associated with free-for-all linking. One pro is the fact that you can keep the linked site within your site, keeping your own visitors within your site longer. One con is that unless you check your free links page daily or use a customizable program that enables you to approve links prior to posting, you risk having an unsuitable site linked to yours. Still, keep in mind that you do not want to be too quick to send your visitors off to another site. Keep links off your home page. And you may even want visitors to link to another site through an exit page so you can ask them to bookmark your Web site or subscribe to your electronic publication before leaving. And, finally for webpreneurs short on time, there are services such as the ones featured

below that for a fee will automatically link your Web site to other Web sites that use their service:

- Star Linker, www.starlinker.com
- Links Manager, www.linksmanager.com
- Reciprocal Link, www.reciprocallink.com
- Cyber Robotics, www.cyber-robotics.com
- Link Strategy, www.linkstrategy.com

Test Before You Go Live

In terms of building a new Web site or revamping an existing one make sure that you have totally *debugged* the site and that everything is working properly before you publish your site to the World Wide Web so that your visitors and paying customers aren't guinea pigs. You can enlist the help of friends, workers, and family members to test every aspects of your Web site. Ask them to proofread content, order products, test links, submit keyword searches to search engines and directories to determine search result rankings, and aggressively test all the other functions and features of your Web site prior to going live. Testing goes beyond just new Web sites; it should also include sites that are undergoing minor or major renovations. Post a clone of the reworked site with a variation to your URL, and once again ask friends, workers, and family members to rigorously put the site through its testing paces to get the bugs out. Not only will this help to identify problems with your Web site, but it will also go a long way to ensure that when you do go live, you have a Web site that is 100 percent effective and efficient for visitors and customers alike.

MARKETING YOUR WEB BUSINESS

Before marketing your new Web site, products, or services online, identify your online and Web site marketing objectives, such as drive more people to your site, increase sales, or use it for research purposes. You also have to create an online marketing strategy that outlines the promotional methods and activities you will employ to reach each of your online marketing objectives. And, finally you have to develop a budget that shows how much each marketing strategy will cost, where the money will come from, and the projections estimating your return on investment. Ideally, you will tie your Internet marketing plan in with your overall business and marketing plans as discussed in Chapters 6 and 12, respectively. Once you have identified your objectives, mapped out a strategy, and developed a budget, your options in terms of how you will market and promote your Web site, products, or services are almost unlimited, especially if you combine online and off-line promotional activities. Online marketing activities featured in this section include online grand openings, banner advertising, electronic publications, pay-for-performance keywords, opt-in lists, securing repeat visits, and permission-based marketing.

Start with Your E-Grand Opening

Once your Web site is built and you have tested it to make sure that it is working properly, the next logical step is to host an online e-grand opening. You will want to create special incentives and offers to lure visitors to your site and get them to purchase or inquire for additional information, much like you would if you where opening a retail shop or showroom in the bricks and mortar world. However, unlike the real world were you can rely on signs, banners, and balloons to grab attention and promote your grand opening, you must rely on other ways to promote your grand e-opening. The following ideas should help:

- *E-mail blasts.* Rent opt-in electronic mailing lists and send out a grand opening message and special offer to promote the opening of your new Web site. Maximize the effectiveness of this promotional effort by repeating the blast two to three times before launching.
- *Contact the media.* Send out electronic and print news releases, media advisories, and letters to the editor to announce the opening of your new site. Keep in mind that you will want to follow standard news release format guidelines and make your release read like news, not like an advertisement for your site.
- *Newsgroups.* Post messages in Usenet newsgroups, discussion groups, and message boards related to your business, products, services, and industry to announce the launch of your new Web site. You might even want to post messages about your new site in competitors' discussion forums, message boards, and chat rooms.
- *Advertise in various mediums.* Purchase advertising space on Web sites that are frequented by your target audience and in electronic publication that are read by your target. Include a link back to your site in the advertisements. Also consider purchasing advertising space in print publications that are read by your target audience to promote your grand opening.
- *Direct mail campaign.* Create a direct mail campaign aimed at your target audience by sending out information about your new Web site along with an exciting offer or incentive to drive traffic to it. Rent high-quality mailing lists of people that meet your target audience and marketing objectives.

Banner Advertising

Though once thought to be on the way out, advertising banners are making a huge comeback as more and more online marketers fight to grab the attention of consumers shopping online. But, before you blindly throw money at a banner advertising campaign, you should first understand the most common banner advertising terms, which will assist you in planning your entrance strategy.

- *CPM.* It means the cost per impression and is used to describe the fee charged for a fixed number of banner advertising impressions, that is, the number of times the banner was displayed on a Web site or within a network of sites. M represents 1,000 impressions. If the CPM of banner advertising on a particular Web site was $30 and the number of impressions the advertisement had was 5,000, the cost to the advertiser would be $150 (5x$30 per thousand impressions). Banner impression costs are largely based on the audience that will be exposed to the message, and costs range from a few dollars per thousand impressions to a few hundred dollars per thousand impressions.

- *CT/CTR. Click through* is a term used to describe the action when a person clicks on a banner ad or text message and the link takes them to the advertiser's Web site. Click through rate is the number of times that a specific banner is clicked-through on a given number of impressions. For instance, if 100 people click on a banner advertisement that has been displayed 10,000 times, then the click through rate of the banner would be 1 percent. Click through rates vary greatly from almost nil on untargeted or mistargeted sites, to as high as 10 percent when displayed on perfectly targeted Web sites. The cost per lead can be determined from your click through rate by dividing the number of clicks by the number of impressions that were purchased, then multiplying that number by the CPM rate. For instance, if the CPM rate were $25 and you purchased 10,000 impressions, your total cost would be $250. ($25 per 1,000 x 10,000 impressions = $250) If you received 100 clicks in total, the cost of each lead (click through) would be $2.50 (100 click through divided by the total cost of the impressions, $250/100 = $2.50 per lead).

- *CPC.* The cost per click, which means that instead of paying for CPM, you might agree upon a click through rate prior to advertising and pay each time people click through to your site or link via your banner advertisement or text link advertisement.

- *ROS/RON.* Run of site and run of network, which describes how your banner will be displayed, on one or more of the pages within a specific Web site or on a network of Web sites. Few banner advertising services and programs guarantee placement on any one certain page or site, unless guaranteed banner placements are specifically arranged for in the contract.

- *Static banners.* This refers to banners that remain on one particular Web page within a site without moving to another page within the same site until the advertising contract is over or the agreed upon advertising period or number of impressions has been reached.

- *Rotating banners.* Refers to banners that move throughout the Web site or network of Web sites that you are advertising within. The rotation can operate on a specific time loop or rotate each time there is a new visitor to the page.

- *Animated banners.* As the name suggests these banners have movement, which can mean anything from a changing promotional, message, or graphic, to a banner with flashing colors, lights, and icons. Basically, it is some change in appearance or motion to grab visitors' attention. Animated banners can be static on one specific page or number of pages, or rotate through the site or network of Web sites depending on your advertising contract.

With a better understanding of the more common banner advertising terms, you can begin to map out your strategy. Get started by keeping your target audience in mind when renting banner advertising space. While the lure of cheap run of site or run of network deals might be alluring from a financial budget perspective, your results can suffer dramatically by not presenting your advertising message to your primary target audience. Also, bigger is not always better. While brand name Web sites and search engines sites attract untold numbers of visitors, that does not necessarily make them the right sites for your message. Once again, it's all about reaching your target audience and meeting your online marketing objectives. Studies have shown that banners created to resemble Web forms and polls pull a higher click though rate, and you can also dramatically increase your click through rate by telling people what you want them to do next, by using words and phrases such as *Click Here* or *Start Here* or *Win Here* in your banner. And don't forget to give some thought to the page that you want click through visitors to land on.

There are a number of online advertising banner creation services that for a fee will create your banner advertisements; some services also offer clients banner advertising posting and placement packages. You can also create your own banner advertisements online using any one of the number of free services such as Animation Online located at www.animation online.com and Banner Dudes, which can be found at www.bannerdudes.com. Both services offer step-by-step advertising banner creation instruction as well as many banner templates that can be customized to meet your specific needs and marketing objectives.

Banner Advertising Exchange Programs

Over the past few years, banner exchange programs have become an extremely popular marketing method for webprenuers with tight advertising budgets, mainly because the programs are cheap and yet highly effective. Most banner exchange programs are similar. In exchange for providing banner advertising space on your Web site, you receive banner advertising space in other members' Web sites. Each banner exchange program has its own specific criteria ranging from a points and credits placement system to exchange ratios ranging from 1:2 to 1:5, and other individual nuances that define the service and program. Few programs swap one for one because to earn revenue the services sell the excess advertising space to advertising marketers, brokers, corporations, and small business owners. Before you commit to a banner exchange program, check with the operator to make sure that there are restrictions limiting the banners displayed on sites to tasteful ads from reputable businesses. Likewise, make sure that there are also size restrictions in place so that you do not end up with gigantic banners that take forever to download on your site. You can log onto the following Web sites to find out more about the banner exchange programs they provide:

- Banner X Network, www.bannerxnetwork.com
- Banner Exchange Program, www.bannerexchange program.com
- E Banner Exchange, www.e-bannerx.com
- Banner Advantage, www.banneradvantage.com
- Free Banners, www.free-banners.com

E-Zine Advertising

Home business owners in particular have found advertising in e-zines to be a highly effective way to reach their target audience for a very modest cost. I say a highly effective way because even though there are an estimated 100,000 e-publications distributed monthly to a worldwide audience, these e-publications are broken into specific categories of interest, such as small business, travel, or entertainment. There are even small subcategories that allow for even better targeting in terms of reaching a very select audience.

Before committing to advertising in any one or number of e-zines or e-publications, you will want to know the basics, the relevant statistics in terms of audience size and demographics. This information will be featured on the publisher's data or media card. You also want to know its policies in terms of competing advertisers. A larger subscriber base is not necessarily better because e-zines with large subscriber bases often contain more advertisements.

One of the best ways to determine if a particular e-zine is right for you is to subscribe to it and track the ads that are featured. Ads running continuously generally mean that they are getting the desired response for the advertiser. You might even want to contact a few and inquire about their success rate with that particular e-zine. Always make sure to track the results of your ads, especially if you are advertising in more then one e-zine at a time. Knowing which ads in which e-zines are pulling the best response rates will help you to spend your advertising dollars where you will get the best results. Because there are some many e-zines published, the best starting point in terms of narrowing the field for advertising purposes is to visit a few e-zine directories to track down those e-zines used by your target audience:

- Ezine Listings, www.ezinelistings.com
- Ezine Universe, www.ezine-universe.com

- The Ezine Directory, www.ezine-dir.com
- The Book of Zines, www.zinebook.com
- Ezine Directory, www.newsletter-directory. com

Pay-per-Click Advertising Programs

Another form of advertising on the Internet is through pay-per-click programs. Google's AdWord program located at www.adwords.google.com/select/overview.html and Overture's Pay-For-Performance program located at www.overture.com are unquestionably the biggest and arguably by far the most effective. Pay-per-click programs involve bidding on choice keywords that you believe your target audience uses when they search for the products or services you sell. For instance, if you sell movie DVDs, you would want to bid on prime keywords such as DVDs, movies, and celebrities. Both programs have different requirements and rules in terms of how you select your words and how they make sure your site is relevant or optimized for the keywords that you select or bid on. However, both programs are similar in the way you bid for the keywords you want. For instance, you can bid one dollar for a specific keyword, and if yours is the highest bid, you win and would get top search results rankings. On the other hand, if you bid 20 cents and other Web marketers bid more for the same keywords, your ranking will be greatly diminished. Google and Overture only charge you when someone actually clicks on your listing, that is, you get a click through. Targeted pay-per-click advertising can greatly increase your search result rankings and dramatically increase your click-through rate. Still you will want to research these programs, carefully reading information provided to make sure that participation will help meet your online marketing objectives and fit your advertising budget.

Surefire Ways to Keep Customers and Visitors Coming Back

Online marketing is really comprised of three separate but equally important elements: attracting visitors to your site, turning visitors into paying customers, and making sure that customers and visitors alike return to your site frequently. Studies have shown beyond a doubt that the more often people visit a Web site, the more likely they are to make a purchase. Therefore, to increase your selling opportunities, you have to provide reasons for customers and visitors to return to your Web site frequently. Online marketing gurus refer to this as developing your Web site's stickiness, which is accomplished through the use of content, features, and Web tools, all of which benefit customers and visitors.

Ask Visitors to Bookmark Your Site

One way to lure back customers and visitors is to simply to ask them to bookmark your Web site and specific pages within your site. Do this by boldly displaying a "Bookmark Us" icon on all of your Web pages. Adding a bookmark-us button is one of the easiest ways to increase the number of repeat visits. How many times have you visited a Web site and later wanted to return, but couldn't remember the URL or even how you found your way to the site in the first place? Plenty, I am sure. A bookmark icon prominently featured on all of your Web pages is no guarantee that visitors will take the time to bookmark your site, but it's no guarantee they won't either.

Providing Useful Tools

Another effective way to ensure that visitors and customers keep coming back is to provide useful interactive tools on your Web site. Is there a calculator or customizable template that you can provide to visitors that they would find beneficial, make their job or life easier, or solve a specific challenge? You can find out by asking your visitors to supply suggestions for interactive tools and also by checking out your competitor's Web sites. There is a good chance that if it works for the competition, it will work for you. Once you have selected the tools, you can add them to your site or if they are too costly to install or develop, provide visitors with a link to them. Bravenet is home to lots of free and user-paid interactive tools, sticky content, and community building plug-ins, it can be found online at www.bravenet.com.

What's New?

It's no mystery that the more often you can get a visitor back to your site, the greater the chances they will make a purchase. Adding a "What's New" page is a great way to draw visitors back on a regular basis so they can get updated on the latest news and information related to your business, products, or services. Ideally, an icon should be placed on your home page so that visitors can quickly navigate to the What's New page. Ask visitors if they would like to sign up for e-mail reminders that alert them electronically every time your What's New page is updated with fresh information and features.

Expert Advice

Providing visitors with an online ask-an-expert-advice service is a very powerful community-building tool that can be extremely effective in terms of securing repeat visits. Securing experts to answer questions and provide advice about topics that relate to your business and target audience should not prove difficult, providing, of course, that there is a benefit, such as a link back to their Web site or free advertising for their products or services. For instance, if you sell antique car parts online, enlist an expert in the classic car restoration field to answer questions in chat forums, message boards, or in an e-mail letter of the week. One of the key ingredients to securing repeat hits is to create a sense of community on your Web site. A place where a person can interact with like-minded people and get expert advice creates community.

Contests

Another way to increase repeat visits is to hold regular contests—daily, weekly, or monthly depending on your marketing objectives and financial budget. Prizes need not be expensive, just something that is valuable to your target audience, perhaps extended warranties, one-hour free consultations, or special reports. There are also pooled contest services available where many online marketers sponsor a contest together so that they can offer bigger prizes and more frequent drawings. These types of pooled contest are very inexpensive when compared to the value of the goods awarded to winners. One such service is ePrize, which is located at www.eprize.net. If contests are going to be part of your online marketing strategy, be sure to get listed in contest directories such as Contest Hound, found at www.contesthound.com. Most contest services and directories

also offer free legal advice about online contests and sweepstakes, which is great if you are going to use these services or get listed in the directories. If not, you might want to consider obtaining your own legal advice before doing anything so that you can better understand the rules and regulations.

News, Weather, and Sports

You can also increase your Web site's sticky content and secure more repeat hits by providing up-to-date news headlines, sports scores and information, international and local weather forecasts, and stock market information. There are literally hundreds of online suppliers that provide this type of content, and many will customize content packages to suite your specific business and marketing needs. You can even get free content. The selection, however, is often limited, and if the same content is featured on too many sites, it greatly dilutes the value and potential pull to get visitors back to your site. News Clicker provides automatically updated news, weather, sports, and financial information content. It can be found at www.newsclicker.com.

Entertainment

Providing visitors with some fun stuff to read and do on your site can be a big draw in luring visitors back often. Entertainment information and activities can include music and video clips, trivia, interactive games, columns and lists, and skill testing quizzes. Regardless of the type of entertainment that you provide, fun stuff can be a great way to build a loyal visitor base for your Web site. Free Sticky is an online provider of free and fee based content, plug-ins, and live feeds, which include games and entertainment features. It can be found at www.free sticky.com.

Interactive Forums

Installing interactive forums on your site is one of the best ways to keep customers and visitors returning to participate in your online community. These interactive forums can include discussion boards, message boards, chat rooms, workshops and private offices, free classified advertising, letters of the day submitted by visitors, and other visitor submissions.

Marketing through Usenet Newsgroups

Usenet newsgroups are discussion groups on the Internet that focus on a specific subject or topic such as business, sports, computers, or entertainment. At present it is estimated that there are in excess of 100,000 newsgroups on the Web, each comprised of members that share a common interest in the newsgroup topic. The most common newsgroup categories, include:

alt	Any conceivable topic
humanities	Fine art, literature, and philosophy
biz	Business products, services, and opportunities
news	Information about Usenet newsgroups and administration
rec	Games, hobbies, and sports
talk	Current news issues, general conversation, and debates
comp	Computer hardware and software

In terms of marketing and promoting your business, Usenet newsgroups can be very powerful because they are free and many consist of thousands of members. That gives a broad reach for your promotional message. You should, however, be aware that some newsgroups are monitored. Before your message gets posted, it will be reviewed to make sure that it fits the theme of the group. If it does not, it will be rejected. Unmonitored newsgroups generally post any message in the forum unchecked for content. There are newsgroups that allow and encourage commercial or marketing postings while others do not. This type of information can only be learned by tracking groups that meet your target audience or are relevant to your products and service. Research is required to make sure you devote time to the right newsgroup. It is very time consuming to post and track discussions in the group, so read other posts carefully so that you can better understand what the people in the group are truly seeking in terms of information, products, and services. To promote your business, you can also sign off of each message using a signature that includes a link to your Web site. The following are a few popular newsgroup directories and services:

- Open Directory Project, www.dmoz.org
- Google Groups, www.groups.google.com
- Usenet, www.usenet.org
- Message Board Blaster, www.messageboard blaster.com
- All The News Groups, www.allthenewsgroups. com

Permission-Based Marketing

Permission-based marketing is a term used to describe asking and securing permission from your Web site customers and visitors to send them information via e-mail. Providing they agree and give you permission, the information you send can be just about anything ranging from simple e-special offers to elaborate e-newsletters and e-catalogs, depending on your marketing objectives. Regardless of the information and special content that you send, gaining permission serves three main benefits. First, if people ask to be included in your electronic mailings, in all likelihood they have an interest in the products you sell or the services you provide. Second, by securing permission, you won't be spamming, sending e-mail messages without the recipient giving the permission. Third, you will be building a very valuable in-house mailing list that can be used for any number of research and marketing purposes. There are many ways to ask and secure your Web site visitors' permission to send them electronic information and special offers. One way is to create a weekly e-publication and ask visitors to your site to subscribe for free. Or you can offer special incentives to people that sign up for your e-information mail outs. Much will depend on your marketing objectives and the type of e-information that you are planning to send. One of your main online goals should always be to get as many visitors as possible to agree to receive information via e-mail from your business. The value of building an in-house permission-based mailing list cannot be overstated from a marketing and customer relationship perspective.

You will need to compile, store, and manage your subscriber base. Fortunately there are numerous contact and customer management software programs available that will enable you to build your permission-based opt-in list. Alternately, you might want to have your contact list managed by an online contact list management service from a remote server location. The cost for this type of service generally starts at about $10 per month and increases based on size and usage. The benefits of a list management service is that they supply the subscription form link from your Web pages and automatically sign up visitors that want to join. If you decide to build and manage your own in-house subscriber database, Maximizer offers contact management software solutions. It can be found online at www.maximizer.com.

Renting Opt-In Lists for E-Mail Blasting

Electronic opt-in lists are name lists of people that have requested to receive by e-mail specific information or offers on one or more subjects or topics of interest. The list could be specific to people with an interest in cars, sports, entertainment, or just about any conceivable topic. The words *opt-in* refer to people who have requested or given their permission to receive information by way of e-mail, as opposed to spam, a term to describe an e-mail promotional message that was sent to people that did not request it. You should know that although not routinely enforced, spamming is illegal. At the time of writing, there is even talk of legislation to create a Do Not E-Mail List similar to the Do Not Call telemarketing list. You have to be careful because not all opt-in lists for rent are spam free, but you can increase your odds of renting good lists by going through reputable sources, which include:

- *List owners.* Many online marketers and business owners that have spent time, money, and energy to build optimal opt-in lists often rent these lists out to recoup some of the expenditures and generate profits.
- *List managers.* Often list owners do not have the time to manage their own mailing list and will hire the services of a list manager. The list owner and management service divide the rental proceeds. List managers generally provide list marketing and rental services for numerous list owners, covering a wide range of lists.
- *List brokers.* As the title suggests, the third option for renting opt-in lists are business people that represent many opt-in lists, bringing

list renter and owner together in exchange for a commission.

Renting well-targeted opt-in lists is a challenge faced by most online marketers. You might even want to ask other home business owners and online marketers about their opt-in list sources and their success rate with these lists. The next challenge is trying to decipher a great opt-in list from a mediocre one. The difference can be between reaching your target audience successfully and meeting your marketing objectives or not.

Data Card

The first item you want to review is the data card associated with the opt-in list that you are considering renting. The data card features information such as list size, cost per thousand names, a brief background about the type of people on the list, selection—meaning that you can segment out certain names that you want to reach—the frequency with which the list is updated or cleaned, and the list use report that tells who else used the list (although this information is not always included with opt-in list data cards). You will want to ask the list supplier more specific questions, such as "Does the rental cost include formatting your message and delivery of the message?" Some list brokers will advertise cheap lists as a lost leader to reel you in, but the advertised list rental does not always include everything that you need to get your message from point A to point B, so be sure to clarify that the cost to rent the list includes all services. You will also want to ask if you pay for e-mails sent or e-mails received. There can be a vast difference in the two, especially with lists that are not frequently updated, so you want to make sure that you are only paying for people that actually received your message and not for hard or soft bounce backs, that is, messages that have been return unopened. Ultimately, renting an opt-in mailing list is very much a caveat emptor (let the buyer beware) situation, so it is in your best interests to research the list source, terms, and audience before making a financial commitment. Type in "opt-in list rentals" into any search engine or directory and literally thousands of matches will be returned. Below are a few suppliers to get you started on your quest for the best opt-in mailing list for your online marketing objectives:

- Topica, www.topica.com
- HT Mail, www.htmail.com
- Email Universe, www.emailuniverse.com
- Web Traffic Marketing, www.webtrafficmarketing.com
- Trident, www.tridentlist.com

Try Word-of-Mouse Marketing

Through the decades, small business owners have relied heavily on word-of-mouth advertising and referrals as one of their main sales and marketing tools to promote and grow their businesses. Today, in the cyberworld, top Internet marketers also have learned to rely heavily on this powerful marketing weapon, but in the electronic commerce world this is called word-of-mouse marketing.

You can greatly increase your odds of online e-commerce success by making it as easy as you can for your visitors and customers to help promote your business and spread the word about your Web site by adding a simple, yet highly effective "tell a friend" button onto the end of feature articles and special interest content that appears on your Web site. When visitors click on the "tell a friend" button,

a simple Web form appears that instructs them to fill in one or more names and e-mail addresses of people to whom they want to send the information. Once completed, a click of the mouse sends off the information to the intended recipient. At the same time to really increase the effectiveness of this simple marketing trick, you can also ask if they would like to subscribe to your e-newsletter or special offers. In fact, you can add "tell a friend" tags onto as much content as you like—contests, columns, newsletters, games, special offers, coupons, workshops, and tips of the day.

An added benefit of this powerful marketing technique is the fact that there is software available that enables you to customize the e-mail that customers and visitors send to friends. So, in addition to the information that is sent you can also include a promotional message or special offer in the e-mail as a headline over the information that was sent. You can use this space to promote a sale, introduce a new product, ask people to sign up for your newsletter or e-zine, or even just to say, "hello and thank you for the interest in our Web site." Regardless of how you use this powerful tool, you can greatly increase your odds of success when you have an army that is promoting your e-business through word-of-mouse marketing.

FIGURE 17.4   Driving Traffic to Your Web Site Checklist

Below is a checklist of ideas that will help you drive traffic to your Web site and ultimately improve sales and profits.

❑ Start driving more traffic to your site by asking everyone that you know to refer your Web site to everyone they know.

❑ Register your Web site and Web pages with major search engines and search directories and smaller search engines that serve a niche market relative to your business, products, or services.

❑ Link your Web site and pages to numerous Web sites, and use linking services to increase the number of sites to which your site is linked.

❑ Purchase targeted keyword advertising at the major search engines and use keyword generating services and software to optimize your keyword selections to increase your search rankings and results on all of the major search engines.

❑ Publish a monthly e-zine or e-newsletter peppered throughout with numerous links back to your Web site.

❑ Ask your site visitors to subscribe to your electronic publications and offer an incentive to motivate them to do so, with additional incentives if they help recruit additional subscribers.

FIGURE 17.4 **Driving Traffic to Your Web Site Checklist**, continued

❏ Write articles for online and offline publications and include a tagline text link featuring your Web site URL.

❏ Create an e-mail signature for all outgoing e-mail that includes an active link to your site.

❏ Start an affiliate program enlisting other Web marketers to promote and sell your goods on their sites and in their e-publications.

❏ Use direct marketing techniques such as mail, telemarketing, public speaking engagements, and personal visits to promote your Web site.

❏ Ask all visitors to bookmark your Web site for their convenience.

❏ Purchase online and offline display and classified advertising in print newspapers and magazines, as well as in electronic publications, promoting your Web site, products, and services.

❏ Include your Web site address in all online and offline business communications, such as letters, faxes, voice-mail messages, business cards, sales presentations, receipts, and product brochures.

❏ Join professional, business, and industry associations and have your Web site URL listed in their print and online member directories and newsletters.

❏ Create press releases around a news event or information that is posted on your Web site and send the news releases to the media.

❏ Add a "tell a friend tag" onto content and information featured in your Web site.

❏ Through the use of pop-up windows, ask visitors to sign up for newsletters, reminder services, and special e-offers.

❏ Create e-coupons discount offers and e-gift certificates, and get listed in the numerous online coupon sites and gift certificate portals and sites.

❏ Use paid banner advertisements and banner exchange programs to increase click through traffic to your Web site.

❏ Build your own in-house opt-in list, and e-mail valuable offers to everyone on your list routinely. Also ask recipients to share the information and offers with others by forwarding the e-mails to friends and family members.

❏ Create and host online contests and list your event in any one or all of the numerous contest directories on the Web with links back to your site.

❏ Rent opt-in lists and send out valuable offers on a regular basis via e-mail blasts or message board blasts.

❏ Participate in online discussion groups and chat rooms using your Web site URL as your user name and identification.

❏ Give away free stuff and get listed in numerous online free stuff and giveaway Web sites and portals.

❏ List your products and services in cybermalls, storefronts, and auction sites with "additional information" links back to your Web site.

SELLING ONLINE

Marketing online and selling online are two entirely different things. Marketing means getting people to your Web site, utilizing any number of the promotional methods discussed in this chapter. Selling is getting people to buy what you have for sale once they get to your Web site. There are various steps that have to be taken beyond offering a great product or service in order to maximize the odds of turning your Web site visitors into paying customers and

hopefully forging long-term selling relationships. You have to create credibility. You have to reduce or eliminate buying doubt and fear. You have to provide strong guarantees. You have to provide an efficient and easy-to-use shopping cart. You have to provide multiple ways that people can pay for purchases. And all the while, you have to provide great customer service.

Retailing online is in many aspects more difficult then retailing in the bricks-and-mortar world. In that world retailers have the benefit of a tangible product on the shelf that shoppers can pick up, analyze, and decide if it meets their wants and needs or a service that can be demonstrated live, revealing user benefits. And, in the electronic world, you also have to decide if you will take advantage of other online options, such as online auctions, Web malls, and affiliate programs to promote and sell your goods and services. And, of course, there are also decisions to be made involving order fulfillment, shopping cart options, online payment options, customer service, guarantees, and return policies. Selling online is very complicated and requires as much research and planning as offline selling. Indeed, in many aspects more research and planning is required if you want to succeed in today's highly competitive, global e-tailing environment.

Creating Online Credibility

Before you can even consider shopping carts, or online payment systems, the first order of business is creating online credibility. How do you gain the trust of consumers in the faceless world of cyberspace? One way is to create a Web page within your site that chronicles the history of your business: when you started, employee information, customer profiles, and photographs. That helps provide reassurance. Remember, online you are appealing to a global audience. While your business might be known in Los Angeles, chances are someone from Toronto or Glasgow will never have heard of you before.

Instill a sense of confidence in your visitors by being an open online book. Include contact information within your Web site that enables visitors and customers alike to reach you offline. Let your visitors know who you and key people within your organization are, what they do, and how they can be contacted directly by e-mail, and by snail mail, fax, and telephone. If you are not confident enough to let people know who they are doing business with, how they can contact you, and what steps you take to ensure their security and privacy, you may as well pack up your cyber venture and hit the road. No one wants to do business with a computer. People do business with people, and they want to know who is connected to the other end of the power cord.

Privacy

Create a privacy policy that clearly spells out the steps you take to ensure privacy and protect security for all visitors and customers alike. Every page in your Web site should be linked to your privacy and security policy page. Include what you do to protect your visitors and clients. If you do not share customer information with others, clearly spell out that fact. If you employ the latest encryption technologies to ensure secure online financial transactions, let customers know.

Alliances

Establish alliances with larger, more well-known companies, organizations, and associations by offering them free advertising on your Web site and by joining their affiliate vendor program. When your visitors see that your business is aligned with these well-known and trusted companies and organizations, they will link your business with theirs, lending instant credibility and professionalism. Also join professional business associations that are relevant to your business and industry, as well as consumer protection organizations such as the Better Business Bureau. Not only will this assist in building trust with visitors, but many of these organizations and associations also have well-known logos and graphics that can be displayed on your site, once again, lending credibility.

Testimonials

Create a client testimonial page within your site and try to feature at least three or four from your happiest and best customers. To get the maximum benefit from the testimonial, include the author's full name, business and title, if applicable, contact information such as an e-mail link, and his photograph. Update the testimonial page twice per year with your newest and greatest customer testimonials. Client testimonials are without question one of the best ways that online marketers can establish credibility for their business, products, and services.

Expertise

Go the extra mile to make your Web site a one-stop source for expert information that is relevant to your business, products, services, and industry.

Write articles and columns in your area(s) of expertise for other online news and general information Web sites and link your articles that are featured on these other sites, back to your Web site so that your visitors and customers become aware of your expertise. A ton of credibility comes with being known as an expert in your field or industry.

Charities

Include a page in your Web site that lists and describes in detail any and all charities that your business supports, including fundraising activities and ongoing charity causes that your business is partnered with so that visitors can also become involved. To really increase the creditability impact, show a dollar amount. If your business has raised $10,000 through fundraising and donation activities for various causes, let your visitors know it.

Awards

Enter your business and Web site in competitions that hand out awards to businesses that provide the best customer service, have the most user friendly Web sites, or have the best products or services. Proudly display all awards that your business, products, services, or site has won. Winning awards goes a long way to boost your credibility and help earn the trust of customers.

Getting Paid Online

Unlike the real world where customers can personally hand you a check, cash, or a credit card to pay for their purchases, in the faceless world of the Internet you have to provide customers with online payment options that are safe and secure. To cover all the bases in terms of consumer payment preferences, your online payment options should include electronic money transfers, credit cards, electronic checks, and offline payment options.

Money Transfers

Money transfers, like the one pioneered and perfected by Pay Pal, have become a very popular way for consumers to pay online, and one online retailers also like because of the low cost to participate, easy bookkeeping, and relatively quick processing time

that enables them to have access to their money very quickly. The basic premise of online money transfers works like this: People deposit money into an electronic bank account, which they can then use like cash to pay for purchases they make online, providing, of course, that the retailer accepts this payment option. Some of the companies that provide this service are:

- Pay Pal, www.paypal.com
- Yahoo Pay Direct, www.paydirect.yahoo.com
- Veri Sign, www.verisign.com
- World Pay, www.worldpay.com
- Pay Systems, www.paysystems.com

Credit Cards

Credit cards are still the most popular way that people pay for online purchases. They simply provide their credit card information during the checkout phase of the purchase. For online retailers, providing customers with a credit card payment option is absolutely essential. Without it, there is a good chance that your online retailing venture will not succeed simply because consumers will choose to buy from competitors that do accept credit cards. Online Credit Card Merchant Account Services, include:

- Charge Cardservices, www.charge.com
- USA Merchant Account, www.usa-merchant account.com
- Merchant Account Express, www.merchantex press.com
- Monster Merchant Account, www.monstermer chantaccount.com
- Merchant Systems, www.merchant-systems.com

E-Checks

A third option is to provide customers with e-check payment options, which work much like cash or a debit card in the real world. If the customer has adequate funds in a checking account to pay for purchase from your site, and the purchase and payment amount have been verified, the funds are directly deposited into your bank account electronically.

- Advanced Payment Solutions, www.eadvanced paymentsolutions.com
- Internet E Checks, www.internet-e-checks.com

- Pay By Check, www.paybycheck.com
- E-Check Processing, www.e-checkprocessing. com
- Alpha Check Express, www.alphacheckexpress. com

Offline Options

Finally, even if you incorporate the latest and greatest encryption technology into your Web site to ensure safe and secure online shopping options for all customers, you will still find that many people are reluctant to give out credit card or other financial information online. For that reason, don't take a chance on limiting potential sales and profits; make it easy for all of your Web site visitors to give you money by providing them with offline product ordering and payment options. Offline payment options should include a 24-hour toll-free telephone order hotline and/or mail-in payments. Post the details on your Web site. In both cases you can enlist fulfillment services to answer the telephones, check postboxes for orders and checks, and warehouse and ship products to your customers for a fee, which is generally based on a per customer order transaction basis. These companies can often do this for much less than it would cost an individual business to set up and operate these services. Fulfillment services work on a volume basis, serving many business clients at one time. In today's super competitive online marketplace, often all that separates the winners from the losers is who empowers consumers to make choices that fill their individual needs. This can only be accomplished by providing people with numerous options so they can decide which suits them best.

Choosing a Shopping Cart

One of the greatest challenges facing online e-tailers today is shopping cart abandonment. A recent survey suggested that as many as 50 percent of online purchases are abandoned before checkout, and the number one reason for this is simple frustration with the shopping cart. The shopping cart was difficult to use, slow, and unreliable, and because of this, shoppers gave up on the process and abandoned their cart before checking out and paying up. So it

stands to reason that the shopping cart program you select for your Web site is very important to your online business, perhaps one of the more important e-decisions you will have to make. Submit a "shopping cart software" search to any of the major search engines or directories. You will be overwhelmed by the response: Thousands of choices, but which shopping cart program is the best for your specific e-business?

The shopping cart decision will largely be based on your needs and your budget. There are free shopping cart programs and services available, but most are highly unreliable and ultimately will cost you sales. (Remember shopping cart abandonment because of poor reliability is the number one reason online consumers do not complete the sale.) Thus they are not a very good value. There are shopping carts that you can rent and that operate from a remote server location. Some of these are very good quality, have a good reputation and a terrific performance record, and can be subscribed to for less than $100 per month. But like most good things, there is also a downside. Many programs require that your customers link over to the shopping cart provider's Web site to complete the purchase. You lose the opportunity to up-sell and sell more because you lose control of your customers when they are not within your Web site at the time of checkout. Additionally, some remote shopping cart programs are very limited in terms of space for product description and photographs. Another option is to purchase your own shopping cart program and server, and operate the program in-house. If you choose this route, be prepared to shell out a substantial amount of money for quality hardware and software.

Ultimately, the best way to find out which shopping cart program or service is best suited for your particular needs and budget is to ask other online e-tailers. And check with your Internet service provider. Many have expanded their operations and now include reliable shopping cart programs and services, or they can refer you to a reliable source. Whichever you choose, make sure that your shopping cart is safe, secure, fast, easy to use, reliable, and cost effective for your needs. If a cart does not meet every one of these criteria, keep shopping for another. Keep asking other online marketers for advice and guidance until you find a cart that won't be abandoned and left as road kill before checkout. The following are a few popular shopping cart programs and services:

- eCart Software, www.ecartsoft.com
- Monster Commerce, www.monstercommerce.com
- Shop Factory, www.shopfactory.com
- Quick Store, www.quickstore.com
- Cool Cart, www.coolcart.com

How to Turn Visitors into Paying Customers

Another problem plaguing online retailers and marketers is trying to turn Web site visitors into paying customers. Let's face it, if you are selling goods and services online, and you have ten million hits a year on your site, you must turn a portion of these visitors into paying customers or you will not remain in business long. Therefore, you have to develop ways to turn visitors into paying customers. There are many reasons why people will choose not to buy, such as doubt or lingering questions about the goods or services being offered. There are an equal number of ways to entice people to purchase, such as value-adding and special incentives. The goal of online retailers is to find a balance that will enable them to entice people to purchase while still generating a profit.

Removing Fear

One of the best ways to motivate your online visitors to buy and become customers is to remove the fear or doubt associated with making a purchase. This is especially important for online sellers. In the bricks-and-mortar world, consumers can pick up and examine the goods; they cannot do the same in cyberspace. Even if the product you are selling is relatively well known and accepted, there will always be a degree of intangibility to your offering. There may be doubt or fear that it might not work as advertised, might not fit, might not be delivered, might not be exactly what is wanted, or might be too expensive. Doubt and fear are the two biggest obstacles that all online sellers face—period. You can,

however, remove or substantially reduce consumer doubt by:

- offering a 100 percent satisfaction and risk-free money-back guarantee.
- offering free no-obligation product or service trial periods.
- letting the customer buy now and pay later by offering a "bill me later payment option."
- dividing the total cost into installments over a fixed period of time; $20 per month for 12 months appears much less risky than a flat-out, one-time payment of $240.
- offering financing options or convenient payment options such as e-checks and credit cards.

Regardless of the method that you choose, the fact remains that fear and doubt are major stumbling blocks to online sales. By reducing or eliminating them, you will have the potential to dramatically increase your online sales revenues.

Value-Adding

Adding value to your online offers is another way to entice people to buy. For instance, instead of offering a one-year product warranty, increase the value of the product and your offer by upping the warranty to two years. If you sell widgets for $10 each, increase the value by offering three widgets for $20. You can also greatly increase the value of the goods you sell by offering free delivery or free installation to entice people to buy. The most powerful way to make your value-added incentives irresistible to your site visitors is to give away something for free that enhances the value of the product or service being sold and that you would normally charge for as a stand-alone item. For example, if you sell computers online, offer a free extended warranty that protects the customer's purchase for two years instead of one. You are offering an incentive that is not only a product that could be sold on its own, but its also an incentive that is relevant to your main offer and that greatly increases the value of your offer.

Affiliate Programs

Affiliate programs are simply establishing alliances with other online businesspeople to sell their products or services via your Web site and receiving a commission in the range of 5 to 25 percent depending on the program and profitability of what is being sold. Alternately, you can pay other online marketers a commission on the your products and services they sell through their Web sites. Online bookseller Amazon was one of the first major players to embrace the affiliate system. The program has proven to be so successful that it has grown its number of affiliate sellers to more than 900,000 strong at the time of this writing.

There are basically two ways to profit from affiliate programs. You can sign up affiliates to sell your products and services through their Web sites and electronic publications. Or, you can sign up to any one of the number affiliate programs to sell other retailers' and service providers' products and services through your Web site and electronic publications. Selling is not really the best description of the activity. You do not actually warehouse and ship goods or even collect payment in exchange for goods and services. The affiliate's main role is to promote the goods or services on their Web sites via an advertisement, banner, or text message that takes your visitor to the retailers' Web site so they can purchase the item featured. You are assigned a code so that the retailer knows where the purchase originated, allowing you to receive your commission. In most cases there are no or low fees to join affiliate seller programs, but the potential to earn extra revenues from your Web site is quite substantial. More information on affiliate programs as well as affiliate programs directories can be found at the following Web sites:

- Associate Programs, www.associateprograms.com
- Affiliate Match, www.affiliatematch.com
- Affiliates Directory, www.affiliatesdirectory.com
- Associate Search, www.associatesearch.com
- Clicks Link Affiliate Program Directory, www.clickslink.com

Cyber Storefronts and Auctions

Cybermalls are much like bricks-and-mortar shopping malls in that numerous businesses and marketers are grouped together to sell products and services from one central e-location so they can take advantage of increased promotional efforts and the potential to reach a large global audience of consumers. The Internet is home to thousands of cybermalls selling every product or service imaginable and serving every industry and niche market. But don't think that the market is saturated or has reached critical mass, because it hasn't. In fact, online sales of goods and services continue to experience double-digit growth yearly, far outpacing growth of bricks-and-mortar retailers and service providers.

Fees to join or participate in cybermall retailing are based on your needs and level of participation. Some malls charge a commission on all items sold while others charge only a monthly flat fee ranging from $25 to $1,000 depending on the services and marketing options you sign up for. Still others charge both a flat monthly fee and a commission on every sale processed through the mall. Ultimately, what is best for you will be based largely on expected sales, your initial and ongoing budget, and the services that you require. A word of caution though before you jump in and join any cybermall or auction site; make sure that you confirm the following with the cybermall operator that:

- The number of visitors and purchasers in any given day, week, and month meet your needs.
- The entire Web site is maintained and updated on a regular basis.
- There is a powerful and wide-reaching promotional campaign in place to market the mall and mall tenants.
- There are security features in place for the consumer's protection and privacy.
- Shopping cart options, credit card processing, and fulfillment services, are offered.

For many home business owners, cybermalls and auction sites have much they could not otherwise afford to develop and maintain. The advantages of joining one or more cybermalls or marketing your goods and services through auction Web sites include the potential to drive more traffic to your Web site, access to a larger online shopping audience, reduced costs associated with purchasing the hardware and software required for operating your own online secure shopping cart, a low initial investment to get online and sell your products to a global audience, the opportunity to join the cyber-mall's credit card merchant account if you do not currently have your own merchant account established or are having difficulty establishing your own, and cost-effective group promotional and marketing activities. All of the following companies provider online marketers with various Internet mall, auction, and e-storefront retailer services:

- Amazon, www.amazon.com
- eBay, www.ebay.com
- Mall Park, www.mallpark.com
- Web Square, www.websquare.com
- Active Plaza, www.activeplaza.com

Great Online Customer Service Tips

First, resolve all customer challenges as quickly as possible. Complaints move much more swiftly on the Internet than in the real world. An unhappy cyber customer can tell thousands of other people about a negative experience with your business in a matter of moments with a click of their mouse. If possible, interact with your customers and visitors through your online discussion boards and chat rooms in your site. This will go a long way to making customers and visitors feel as though they are part of your online community. A few other online customer service tips that will go a long way in helping you to build long-term and profitable selling relationships with all of your customers are:

- Give customer and visitors lots of choices, a wide product and service selection, multiple payment options, and specialized Web tools and information on your site.
- Give customers and visitors options beyond e-mail to get in contact with you, including telephone, fax, and standard ground mail. Add an online FAQ page outlining answers to the most frequently asked questions.
- Get in the habit of e-mailing customer satisfaction questionnaires a few days after people have purchased and their order has been delivered. Ask questions that are relevant to your business, Web site, industry, and products. Use responses to identify weak areas of

your business so that they can be eliminated or improved.

- Stay in contact with customers on a regular basis by creating an e-publication and sending it out weekly or monthly, along with the occasional greeting card to let them know that you are thinking about them on holidays and special occasions.
- Tell your customers and visitors how much you appreciate their business and their continued support. Show your appreciation by delivering great service and access to products, services, and information that is beneficial and meets their needs.

ELECTRONIC COMMUNICATIONS

There is no question that the Internet is an amazing sales and marketing tool, but it is also an incredible communications system that empowers business owners and marketers with the ability to speak with hundreds, thousands, or even millions of prospects and customers daily and at little cost. No other medium has the ability to reach so many people in so many places. So how can home business owners use the Internet to communicate with customers, prospects, alliances, suppliers, and vendors cheaply and effectively? In lots of ways, such as building and publishing your own Web site that features information about your business and what you do. You can develop your own electronic publication to keep your business team and customers up-to-date on your latest business news. You can send out daily e-mail blasts featuring company information and special offers, or you can even start and operate your own online radio or television station that broadcasts nothing but information about your business, products, or services 24 hours a day, 365 days a year. In short, the Internet provides every home business owner with an incredibly cheap, yet highly effective means of communicating with customers, employees, alliances, and everyone else associated with your business. Volumes could be written on the numerous electronic communications options as well as the benefits associated with each. However, only a few electronic communication options and the benefits associated with each are included—e-mail signatures, electronic publications, and automatic e-mail responders.

E-Mail Signature

For anyone not familiar with e-mail signatures, they are a text message, link, or image that is automatically attached at the bottom of your outgoing e-mails. The majority of e-mail programs give you the option of setting up your own e-mail signature. Look under "Tools" or "Toolbar," for "new signature" or "set up new mail signature options," which you simply click, complete as instructed, and use as your default outgoing e-mail option. If you have problems setting up an e-mail signature file, consult the tutorial section of your e-mail program for a detailed explanation. In the e-mail signature, include your business name, title, and contact information such as telephone and fax numbers and mailing address. You can also include a text link in your signature that links directly to your Web site or an alternate site where you would like to send your reader. But perhaps one of the biggest benefits of an e-mail signature is that you can develop a new marketing message every day and attach it to all out-going e-mails automatically. Announce a sale or a special offer, introduce a new product, promote a forthcoming event, include company or industry news, or provide any type of information or announcements that you think your customers and prospects need and want.

Creating Your Own E-Publication

Home business owners that operate e-commerce sites or sell products and services online and offline should consider creating and maintaining some sort of e-publication such as an electronic newsletter, an e-zine, or even a simple weekly e-alert that can be sent to customers and prospects on a regular basis. Not only can your e-publication be a useful tool to market your Web site and the goods or services that you sell, but it also can help you effortlessly stay in touch with all your customers and prospects on a regular basis, building stronger customer relationships and substantially increasing selling opportunities.

Of course, like any publication, it needs content. Fortunately, there are numerous options available in terms of the content you include and the source of the content. The first option is to write the content yourself, which means you can create content that is beneficial to your customers and target audience. The downside is that writing the content can become very time consuming. The second option is to subscribe to a content service and pay for content. This option will be out of reach for Web marketers with restricted budgets. But the quality of the content tends to be good, and you can choose articles and information directly related to your business and the goods and services that you sell. Another option is to get content directly from the source, which means directly from the author's computer to your e-publication. Probably the best way to find direct content is to post messages in writers' Web sites and forums stating exactly what type of content or articles that you are requesting. If you choose this option, be ready for a flood of takers even if you are offering only a "written by" tagline and promotional blurb about the author instead of payment. You can also get free content from services such as E-zine Articles located at www.ezinearticles.com, or you could even ask your own customers and Web site visitors to submit articles and information for publication.

In the end, regardless of how you secure content for your electronic publication, the information must be beneficial to your target audience and relevant to the business you are in and the goods and services you sell. E-publications can be a very powerful marketing and customer service tool, but they require subscribers to flourish. In addition to asking current customers and prospects to subscribe, you can also try a few of the following ideas to motivate visitors to your Web site to subscribe to your e-publication:

- Offer people that subscribe to your e-publication special offers and discounts.
- Hold an exclusive new-subscriber contest and only people that subscribe to your e-publication can enter to win.
- Give away free gifts, such as T-shirt emblazoned with your logo, or a free upgrade on a product order to people that subscribe to your e-publication.

Automatic E-Mail Responders

Autoresponders are a must for all entrepreneurs that are serious about building a powerful and efficient online presence and electronic communications network. They give you the ability to respond automatically to hundreds of e-mail inquiries painlessly, with the simple installation of a autoresponder program or by using a remote e-mail autorespond system integrated with your Web site, e-mail, and/or electronic publication, or a combination of any or all. There are even tools available with some autorespond programs that integrate voice messages and digital video clips into your HTML e-mail responses.

Perhaps one of the most beneficial aspects of autoresponders from a marketing and customer service perspective is the fact that the program will automatically send follow up e-mail offers to customers after they have made purchases or inquired about products and service. You can also personalize your messages with mail-merge features so that you can single out and talk directly to a person by using their first name in all electronic correspondence that you send or that are automatically responded to through the system. Many autorespond systems also have built in tracking mechanisms so that you will know exactly which recipients are opening your messages and clicking through on Web links that are included.

Even webpreneurs with limited experience will find most autorespond programs very simple to use. In no time you will be changing or updating your communications or marketing message within moments, and as often as you like. Autoresponders can help you stay in touch with thousands of customers, prospects, and visitors in the matter of moments rather than the days that it would take to respond personally to each individual message. Just, beware of free autorespond systems and programs because some feature advertisements from other companies that show up on the e-mails that are automatically responded to through your e-mail. Auto Responders Online, located at www.autoresponders.com, provides visitors with information, products, and links of interest about e-mail autoresponder marketing and communications. E-mail and e-business automation software and services can be found online at www.mailloop.com.

RESOURCES

Associations

Better Internet Bureau Association
318-19567 Fraser Highway
Surrey, BC V3S 9A4
(646) 383-1595
www.better-internet-bureau.org

E-Marketing Association
5600 Post Road, Suite 114-312
East Greenwich, RI 02818
(401) 884-0614
www.emarketingassociation.com

International Internet Affiliate Marketing Association
World Trade Center
PO Box 691, Aeroport
Geneva, CH 1215
Switzerland
www.iafma.org

International Internet Marketing Association
PO Box 4018
349 W. Georgia Street
Vancouver, BC V6B 3Z4
www.iimaonline.org

International Webmasters Association
119 E. Union Street, Suite F
Pasadena, CA 91103
(626) 449-3709
www.iwanet.org

Web Design Developers Association
8515 Brower
Houston, TX 77017
(435) 518-9784
www.wdda.org

Suggested Reading

Brelsford, Herry. *Connecting to Customers.* Redmond, WA: Microsoft Press, 2002.

Davidson, Jeffery P. *101 Internet Marketing Tips for Your Business: Increase Your Profits and Stay Within Your Budget.* Irvine, CA: Entrepreneur Press Inc., 2002.

Eglash, Joanne. *How to Write a .Com Business Plan: The Internet Entrepreneur's Guide to Everything You Need to Know about Business Plans and*

Financing Options. New York: McGraw-Hill, 2000.

Gregory, Kip. *Winning Clients in a Wired World: How to Leverage Technology and the Web to Grow Your Business.* New York: John Wiley & Sons, 2003.

Kim, Amy Jo. *Community Building on the Web: Secret Strategies for Successful Online Communities.* Berkley, CA: Peachpit Press, 2000.

Krug, Steve, and Roger Black. *Don't Make Me Think: A Common Sense Approach to Web Usability.* Indianapolis, IN: Que Publishing, 2000.

Lewis, William J. *Data Warehousing and E-Commerce.* Upper Saddle River, NJ: Prentice Hall, 2001.

Macpherson, Kim. *Permission-Based E-Mail Marketing that Works.* Chicago, IL: Dearborn Trade Publishing, 2001.

Reynolds, Janice, and Roya Mofazali. *The Complete E-Commerce Book: Design, Build, and Maintain a Successful Web-Based Business.* Gilroy, CA: CMP Books, 2000.

Stephenson, James. *The Ultimate Small Business Marketing Guide: Over 1500 Great Marketing Tricks That Will Drive Your Business Through the Roof!* Irvine, CA: Entrepreneur Press Inc., 2003.

Sweeny, Susan. *101 Ways to Promote Your Web Site: Filled with Proven Internet Marketing Tips, Tools, Techniques and Resources to Increase Your Web Description.* Gulf Breeze, FL: Maximum Press, 2002.

Usborne, Nick. Net Words: *Creating High-Impact Online Copy.* New York: McGraw-Hill, 2001.

Wilson, Ralph. *Planning Your Internet Marketing Strategy: A Doctor Ebiz Guide.* New York: John Wiley & Sons, 2001.

Web Sites

American E-Commerce Association, www.aeaus.com: Non-profit association representing American electronic merchants and marketers.

Animation Online, www.animationonline.com: Online banner generation service with free and paid services available.

Associate Programs, www.associateprograms.com: Directory service listing numerous associate and affiliate reseller programs.

Banner Dudes, www.bannerdudes.com: Banner generation service with free and paid banner creation options.

Banner Swap, www.bannerswap.com: Banner exchange services and program options.

Bravenet, www.bravenet.com: A gigantic source of interactive Web site tools and content.

ClickZ, www.clickz.com: Daily electronic newsletter providing information on e-commerce and Internet marketing.

Cyber Atlas, www.cyberatlas.internet.com: Billed as the world's leading online resource center for Internet trends and Internet statistics.

eBiz Chronicle, www.ebizchronicle.com: E-commerce and Internet marketing portal providing daily news, features, advice, links, and special reports.

eCommerce Times, www.ecommercetimes.com: E-commerce and Internet marketing portal providing daily news, features, advice, links, and special reports.

E-Marketer, www.e-marketer.com: Billed as the world's largest source for online marketing research and data.

E-Merchants Association, www.emerchantsassociation.com: Non-profit association representing electronic merchants and marketers.

Ezine Directory, www.ezine-dir.com: Ezine directory service index by topic.

Ezine Universe, www.ezine-universe.com: Ezine directory service index by topic.

Free Sticky, www.freesticky.com: Providers of free and paid content and other useful online tools.

Institute of Certified E-Commerce Consultants, www.ceccertified.com: E-commerce training programs, products, and services, and directory listing certified independent e-commerce consultants.

Internet Mall, www.internet-mall.com: Online shopping mall providing home business marketers with various tenant packages and programs.

Link Leads www.linkleads.com: Web site linking, link management, and advertising service.

Message Board Blaster www.messageboardblaster.com: Software that automatically submits your message to more than 1,300 online message boards and Usenet newsgroups.

News Clicker, www.newsclicker.com: Providers of automatically updated free and low cost news, weather, sports, and business content.

Publicly Accessible Mailing Lists, www.paml.net: Directory service listing information about 6,900 publicly accessible mailing lists.

Register, www.register.com: Domain name registration and renewal services.

Systran Software, www.systransoft.com: Web site and e-communications language translation software.

Unclaimed Domains, www.unclaimeddomains.com: Online directory listing once registered but dropped domain names that are available to be registered.

USPN Technology, www.uspntech.com: Providers of automatically updated free and low cost news, weather, sports, and business content.

*Webopedia,*www.webopedia.com: Online dictionary and search engine for computer and Internet technology.

CHAPTER 18

Home Business Start-Up Ideas and Home Franchise Opportunities

THIS CHAPTER OF *THE ULTIMATE HOMEBASED Business Handbook* features 99 great home business start-up ideas. The information included about these opportunities is brief in nature because it is meant to give you a snapshot, or short synopsis, of the venture. It's a collection of 99 great home business start-up ideas that can be used as a catalyst to get you thinking about these and other various home business enterprises that can be started, and ultimately one that is right for you.

Of course, all new home business ventures require that you apply for and receive a business license or permit, as well as register or incorporate your business at the local, state, or federal level. A major component of starting a home business is to research all the legal aspects of the business venture, including, but not limited to, licenses and permits, liability insurance, zoning and building-use codes, fire and health regulations, employee regulations, and certificates of training. A successful entrepreneur is one who carefully researches and plans every aspect of a new business venture, including the financial investment needed to start a business and the working capital required to achieve positive cash flow. That said, the following 99 great home business start-up ideas should get you going.

99 GREAT HOME BUSINESS START-UP IDEAS

1. Mystery Shopping Service

Go undercover and mystery shop at clients' businesses to assess aspects such as employees and management, operational procedures, and customer service policies. In the past decade more companies, organizations, and retailers have introduced mystery shopper programs into their business, and for good reason. Mystery shopper programs work extremely well at uncovering customer service, employee, or product problems. Generally, the mystery shopper prepares a document detailing their findings, relaying their experiences, and making recommendations to clients upon completion of their visit(s). Expanding the business is as easy as hiring additional mystery shoppers to work on a subcontract-as-needed basis. The industry is competitive, so the more relevant experiences and training you can bring to the table, the better. These experiences could include managerial training, prior customer service postings, human resources experience, and operations specialist. There are even mystery shopper training courses available that can put you on the path to starting and operating your own homebased mystery shopper service.

Mystery Shopping Providers Association, www. mysteryshop.org: Members receive industry information, advice, and support.

2. Inflatable Advertising Rentals

Twenty-foot high inflatable gorillas, holiday reindeer, and cartoon caricatures get noticed by traffic, especially when these large inflatables are sitting on a retailer's rooftop with a "sale in progress" sign emblazoned across them. Renting inflatable advertising objects is a fantastic new home business venture to get up and going. You can operate the business on a full or part time basis, and a potential client list can include retailers, sports teams, community organizations, or just about anyone else who wants to draw attention to a sale or special occasion. Currently, new inflatables are retailing in the range of $5,000. But as a method to reduce start-up investment, you can purchase secondhand inflatables in good condition for half the cost of new. Rental rates are in the range of $75 to $200 per day, including delivery and set up.

Wind Ship Manufacturing, www.windship.com: Manufacturers of hot and cold air advertising inflatables.

3. Public Relations Specialist

Public relations firms and consultants are often selected by clients based on whom they know and not what they know. An outstanding PR person representing an individual, business, politician, product, or service can be the equivalent of having someone in your corner that can pick the winning lottery numbers long before the draw. The main duty of a public relations specialist is to promote in a positive and informative manner, regardless of what is being promoted. Promotion techniques and services include creating press releases, press kits, organizing media conferences and special events, performing damage control services, and, networking around the clock on the client's behalf. Getting started in the business can be difficult, given that public relations industry is fiercely competitive. However, as an entry point, consider starting small and representing one or two clients on a local basis until you have mastered the art.

Public Relations Society of America, www.prsa.org: Members receive industry information, advice, and support.

PR Web, www.prweb.com: Free online press release distribution, industry information, resources, and links.

4. Manufacturer's Representative

Utilizing print and online manufacturers' directories can help you identify products that are not being offered for sale in your local community, better quality products for businesses and consumers at lower costs. Using this information you can establish a home business as a manufacturer's representative and have the potential to earn in excess of six figures annually. Once you have identified the right products and conducted your own market analysis into their visibility in your area, you will be able to contact the manufacturers of these products using the directory. Working as a manufacturer's representative means that you promote and market the products on a local, city, state, or entire country basis. In a nutshell, you sell the manufacturer's products to the target audience, be it businesses or consumers. Always try to negotiate exclusive service contracts with the manufacturers so that you represent them within certain geographic boundaries as set out in the agreement. Remuneration can be by way of a commission charged on total sales, or you can mark up your wholesale costs on the goods and resell at a higher price.

National Association of Manufacturers, www.nam.org: Association representing American manufacturers.

5. Energy Management Consultant

Corporations and homeowners combined spend billions of dollars annually on energy to light, heat, and air-condition their homes and buildings. Imagine how much healthier the environment would be, as well how much money each of us could save every year, if we all could reduce our energy consumption by a mere 10 percent? Working as an energy management consultant from a home office, you can teach home and business owners practical and useful energy management tips about reducing energy consumption and eliminating energy waste. Getting this enterprise off the ground will require a great deal of research, planning, and perhaps training, depending on your background and experience in this area. However, with energy costs continuing to soar, the need to take care of the environment and save money at the same time is becoming more of a concern for everyone. Given this, the future for energy management consulting looks very bright.

United States Department of Energy, www.energy. gov: Government Web site featuring energy management and conservation programs, information, resources, and links.

6. Personal Chef Service

Take your pots and pans, cooking skills, and love of food mobile, and hit the road as a personal chef for hire. Prepare gourmet meals for people hosting house parties, special occasion events such as birthdays or anniversaries, and for corporate luncheons—basically anywhere there is a kitchen on-site that you can use. Personal chefs are becoming a very popular alternative for people that do not have the budget for a full-scale catered event or for people that are hosting small events that do not require complete catering services. The advantages for start-up are apparent: low overhead and initial investment, full-time or part-time operating hours, and easy management from home. Promote the service by joining business associations and community social clubs to network and spread the news about your service. The business can easily be supported by word-of-mouth advertising and repeat business once established, providing the food is great and the service is second to none. Typically rates are quoted on each job and vary according to factors such as the supply of food and the type of menu requested. However, on average earning are in the range of $35 to $50 per hour.

United Stated Personal Chef Association, www. uspca.com: Members receive industry information, advice, and support.

7. E-Zine Publisher

Electronic e-zine publishing and distribution has exploded over the past few years with no less than 100,000 individual e-zine publications being distributed to millions of readers monthly. And best of all, there is room for lots of new up-starts in the e-zine publishing world. Develop your e-zine based on what you know and like; it could be a monthly e-zine covering model trains or a weekly e-zine featuring career advice and information. E-zines are generally free to subscribers and supported by advertisers that want to reach your subscribers because they match their target audience. For instance, if you publish and distribute a monthly camping e-zine featuring lots of great camping tips and information, logical advertisers would include camping equipment retailers, travel agents, and tour operators. The key to success is to serve a well-defined niche market, provide interesting and informative content that readers cannot get anywhere else, and build a large and solid subscription base that will appeal to advertisers seeking to reach them.

Ezine Universe, www.ezine-universe.com: Online e-zine directory listing hundreds of electronic publications index by topic.

Ezine Directory, www.ezine-dir.com: Online e-zine directory listing hundreds of electronic publications index by topic.

8. Graffiti Removal Service

Graffiti is everywhere—walls, sidewalks, and fences—making a graffiti removal service a very timely and in-demand start-up. This business does not require a deal of work experience, and the market is unlimited, largely untapped, and is constantly being renewed. The equipment required is a portable water pressure washer and portable sandblaster, both which can be conveniently mounted on a trailer for easy transportation to job sites. One marketing option is to visit businesses that are often the victims of graffiti vandalism and offer them a low-cost graffiti removal solution. Provide clients with a monthly graffiti removal option in which for a fixed monthly fee, you will check in once a week to see if there is any new graffiti to be removed. If new graffiti is present, you simply remove it. If no graffiti is present, you move on to your next client's location. Additionally, graffiti removal services can also be marketed to schools, libraries, homeowners, and just about any other location with graffiti problems.

Graffiti Gone Inc., www.graffitigone.com: Graffiti removal equipment, supplies, and business opportunities.

9. Pedicab Service

Peddle your way to profits by starting your own bicycle or pedicab taxi service. A romantic ride through a park or a sightseeing visit around town, tourists love to take in the sights, sounds, and local color on their vacations with a relaxing ride in a pedicab. There are many styles of pedicabs available ranging from two occupant models all the way to models that will accommodate six people. The cost to purchase a new pedicab is in the range of $3,500. Ride or rental rates are currently about $12 per 15 minutes, with a minimum charge of $5. Expand the business by purchasing more pedicabs and hiring subcontract drivers to operate them on a revenue-split basis. The business will need to be established in an area that is frequented by tourists and with a climate that will enable a year-round or extended operating season to maximize revenues and profits. Be sure to build alliances with hotels, tourist associations, event planners, and travel agencies so they can refer your pedicab service to their customers.

Hi Wheel Manufacturing, www.hiwheel.com/pedicab.asp: Manufacturers of bicycle pedicabs and accessories.

10. Wedding Planner

The cost of a typical wedding can easily exceed $20,000. It's easy to see why many couples now realize spending $1,000 to hire a professional wedding planner is not only money wisely spent, but also a cheap insurance policy on their substantial wedding investment. It is the duty of the wedding planner to plan the wedding, hire caterers and musicians, book a reception hall, find a florist, and make one heck of a lot of suggestions and fix even more last minute crises. In other words, the planner does everything required to plan and carry out a unforgettable, perfect wedding. Be forewarned, the wedding consulting industry is competitive, with more than 8,000 professional wedding planners in the Untied States. However, more than 2.5 million people tied the knot in 2003. Thus a very lucrative opportunity exists for the entrepreneur with great planning and marketing skills.

The National Association of Wedding Professionals, www.nawp.com: Members receive industry information, advice, and support.

11. Garage and Estate Sale Promoter

Weekend profits await entrepreneurs with good marketing and organizational skills who become garage and estate sales promoters. Garage, lawn, and estate sales are hugely popular events in every community across North America. As a promoter, you can provide clients who do not have the time or gumption to hold their own sale with the service of organizing and conducting the sale for them. Duties include promoting, organizing, selling items, and cleaning up after everyone has gone home. In exchange for providing this valuable service you retain a percentage of the total revenues generated, 25 percent for larger sales and up to 50 percent for smaller ones. Once you have secured a client, be sure to canvas the immediate neighborhood and solicit for additional items. Why hold a small sale if you can increase revenues and profits by enlisting neighbors to provide items, too? Promote the sales with professional site signage and in community newspapers that do not charge for small classified ads or for garage sale postings.

Best Yard Sales, www.bestyardsales.com: A national yard sale directory, and information and resources pertaining to garage sales.

12. Local Tour Guide

Do you live in a tourist area, and do you know that area well? If you do, why not consider starting a business as a personal tour guide? It can be managed from home, started for literally peanuts, and has the potential to generate an income that can easily top $50,000 per year. The first key to success is to promote your service aggressively by building contacts with businesses and individuals that can refer your tour guide services to their clients such as coach and taxi drivers, event planners, hotels, and travel agents. Currently, tour guides are charging $150 to $200 for half-day tours, and up to $350 for full-day tours plus the cost of transportation, and tickets to events and attractions. The second key to success is to provide clients with incredible service and an unforgettably fun local tour experience.

World Federation of Tourist Guide Associations, www.wftga.org: Members receive industry information and support as well as a listing in the association's directory, which features tourist guide associations worldwide, indexed geographically.

13. Desktop Publishing Service

Combine your design and computer skills and offer clients a wide range of desktop publishing services. With the aid of desktop publishing software such as Adobe PageMaker or Corel Printhouse software, you can easily create promotional fliers, brochures, product catalogs, custom reports, coupons, and company newsletters. The desktop publishing industry is and has been experiencing double-digit growth for more than a decade and will continue to flourish and keep pace with software and technological innovations for years to come. Create samples of your work and set up appointments with business owners and professionals to present your talents and explain the benefits associated with your service. Also attend business and association meetings to network and spread the word about your new desktop publishing business.

Desktop Publishing Online, www.desktoppublish ing.com: Billed as the ultimate source of information, products, and links for the desktop publishing industry.

14. Mobile Art Gallery

Take a traditional art gallery, place wheels on it, and you have this home business opportunity in a nutshell. You will want to work with artists that work in all sorts of mediums: paint, photograph, prints, and sculpture. Once you have selected the artists, begin to establish locations where the artwork will be displayed for sale. These locations should include doctor's office waiting rooms, office lobbies and reception areas, restaurants, hospitals, and all other high-traffic places. The art can be displayed along with a small place card that reads, "This art is for sale. For further information call (your business name and toll-free 1-800 number)." I would suggest giving the artist 50 percent of the selling price, the host location 10 percent, and you the balance (40 percent). On a volume basis, there is enormous potential to profit. However, key to the success of the business will be your ability to work with artists that produce great art and your ability to find high traffic locations in which the art can be displayed.

World Artists Directory, www.worldartistdirectory. com: Directory service listing 1,000s of artists in all mediums indexed geographically.

15. Disaster Preparation Service

Earthquakes, floods, hurricanes, tornadoes, blizzards, and wildfires reap havoc and destruction of enormous magnitude annually. We cannot control these forces of nature, but with careful planning we can be prepared when disaster strikes. Being prepared for a natural disaster can literally mean the difference of life or death. There are two aspects to the business: products and services. Products can include the sale of first-aid kits, backup generators, emergency lighting, and nonperishable food and water products. Services can include one-on-one consulting with clients to identify potential threats in disaster situations, to teach how to react in these situations, and drafting emergency action plans to respond to a wide variety of natural disaster situations. The requirements for starting this specialized consulting service are numerous, including first-aid training, disaster response training, and knowledge of natural disaster situations and how to create proactive response and action plans. Given the frequency and widely publicized severity of many natural disasters, successfully marketing this type of business should not prove difficult.

Federal Emergency Management Agency, www. fema.gov: FEMA has disaster preparation and relief information, programs, education, training, resources, and links.

16. Gift Baskets Sales

Gift baskets are extremely easy to assemble. Simply select items such as specialty foods, flowers, or personal health products and arrange them in attractive wicker baskets or similar containers, wrap in foil or colored plastic, and the gift basket is complete. The real secret to success in operating a homebased gift basket service is not so much in the gift basket, but in the sales and marketing of the baskets. I suggest that you concentrate your marketing efforts on gaining repeat corporate clients, professionals, small business owners, and sales professionals, such as realtors. Basically, individuals or companies that would have reason to regularly send out gift baskets to existing and new clients. Promote the business using a direct mail brochure, e-mail broadcasting, and networking with your target audience at business and social functions. Also be sure to provide clients with free local delivery of the gift baskets and to arrange delivery for baskets that are being sent outside the local area.

Gift Basket Review Magazine Online, www.festivities-pub.com: Print and electronic magazine serving the gift basket industry with information, resources, and links.

17. Kitchen Facelift Service

Not every homeowner can afford to shell out $25,000 or more for a new kitchen, yet many can and will gladly part with a few thousand dollars to get the next best thing: a professional kitchen facelift. Leaving the wall and floor cabinets in place, install new doors, countertops, hardware, and trim to make even the dullest kitchen look new and exciting, for a fraction of the cost of a total replacement kitchen. You will need carpentry skills and equipment in order to start and operate this business with success. If these are available, market your business at home and garden shows with the aid of a before and after kitchen facelift display and through traditional advertising in newspapers, on radio, and via direct mail.

Kitchens Online, www.kitchens.com: Industry information, resources, links, and kitchen professionals' directory.

18. Piñata Manufacturing and Sales

What a great home business opportunity and concept—unique, low overhead, minimal start-up costs, virtually no competition, and no limitations on growth and expansion. Thousands of children's parties take place every day, and tapping into this very lucrative marketplace is easy. Simply get started by developing piñata samples and knocking on doors or perspective bulk purchasers. I will guarantee that you will find little resistance to your product, and chances are the biggest business challenge you will face is trying to keep up with the demand. Consider focusing on the wholesale market and try to secure accounts with retail children's stores, party planners, restaurants, and, of course, online sales. Strive to get the piñatas into as many print

and electronic mail order catalogs as possible. There are few requirements for starting and operating this home business. The largest will be creativity, both in how you manufacture and how you market the finished piñatas. Keep safety in mind, and be sure to put prizes inside that cannot harm, spoil, or create potential liability for you.

Piñatas, www.pinatas.com: Retail and wholesale piñata buying opportunities and information.

19. Party Tent Rentals

A party tent rental business can be started as a stand-alone home-managed business, or it can make a great add-on to existing homebased rental businesses, focusing on camping equipment, recreational vehicles, or movie props. Potential clients include wedding planners, catering companies, event and corporate planners, charity organizations, retailers hosting under-the-tent sales and clearance events, and sports teams and clubs. New large party tents retail for $3,000 to $5,000 or more, while secondhand party tents can generally be found in good condition for about half that cost. As a rule of thumb, party tents require about one hour for two people to set up and about the same time to disassemble. Currently, party tent rental rates are in the range of $200 to $400 per day, depending on tent size. Additional revenues can also be earned by renting tables, chairs, lighting, and PA systems.

FS Tents Inc., www.fstents.com: Manufacturers and distributors of custom made-to-order and standard party tents.

20. Embroidery Services

Recent technology changes in the embroidery industry have made it very easy for even a novice to start an embroidery service. Embroidery machines are now available in single or multihued units enabling the operator to embroider six items at a time or more. Modern embroidery equipment is computer assisted. Designs can be created using specialty software and then automatically transferred to the embroidery machine to complete the stitching of the design onto the chosen garment. The business can easily be operated from a homebased location.

However, there should be a small showroom established, even if it is in the home, to display items that can be embroidered as well as samples of embroidery options and designs. Marketing is as easy as creating a product catalog and marketing brochure and distributing the promotional package to potential customers, such as sports associations, schools, corporations, government agencies, organizations, and charities. Consider hiring a subcontract, commission salesperson to solicit or cold-call for new business, preferably one with existing contacts that can be capitalized upon.

Embroidery Monogram Business Magazine Online, www.embmag.com: Print and electronic magazine serving the embroidery industry with information, resources, and links.

21. Cartridge Recycling

Ink and toner cartridges used in most photocopiers, fax machines, and laser and inkjet printers can be recycled by simply replenishing the ink or toner supply. This fact creates a wonderful home business opportunity for energetic entrepreneurs to start toner cartridge recycling businesses. Requirements are basic: simple tools, reliable transportation, and the ability to refill cartridges with new ink, which is easily learned. Your competitive advantage over retail operations selling new ink and toner cartridges is the fact that you can offer clients fast and free delivery of recycled cartridges right to their office or home. In addition, clients can save as much as 50 percent by purchasing recharged ink and toner cartridges, as opposed to the cost of new cartridges.

Recharger Magazine Online, www.rechargemag.com: Print and electronic magazine serving the cartridge recycling industry with information, resources, and links.

22. Mobile Boat Broker

In most area of North America, certification is not required to start a professional boat brokerage business, and that is good news if this is the type of business venture that gets you thinking "what if?" Thousands of pre-owned motorboats, sailboats, and personal watercrafts are bought and sold annually in

this country. Securing just a tiny portion of this very lucrative market may be easier than you think, especially when you consider that you can operate from home and travel to numerous marinas to show clients boats for sale. The business could be a general boat brokerage business or you can specialize in one particular type of boats, such as wooden sailboats or commercial fishing boats and equipment. Generally, boat brokerage or boat sales consultants charge the owner of the boat a 10 percent commission fee upon the successful sale and transfer of the boat. However, the commission rate can be as high as 25 percent for boats with a value of less than $5,000 and as low as 3 percent when selling boats in the million-dollar price range.

United States Boat Brokers Association, www.usboat brokers.com: Members receive industry information, advice, and support.

23. Handyperson Service

Handyperson services require little explanation in terms of the business opportunity. The main requirement for starting such a service is, of course, that you are handy with tools and have a good understanding and working knowledge of many trades, that is, be a jack-of-all-trades. Currently, handyperson billing rates are in the range of $25 to $40 per hour, plus materials and a markup on material cost to cover the costs associated with handling and delivery. The service can be promoted and marketed to both residential and commercial clients through traditional advertising and marketing means such as the Yellow Pages, newspaper advertisements, fliers and door hangers, site and vehicle signage, door knocking, home and garden shows, and word-of-mouth referrals.

Case Handyman Inc., www.casehandyman.com: National handyman franchise opportunities.

24. Trophy and Award Sales

Millions of trophies and custom-engraved awards are given to winning sports teams, game MVPs, and to people being recognized for outstanding achievement in sports, work, and community participation every year. Consumer demand for trophies and awards is a proven winner, making this an excellent choice as a home business venture. The business can be started for less than $5,000, and purchasing trophies and awards on a wholesale basis should not prove difficult, as there are hundreds of trophy and award manufacturers worldwide. Of course, ingenious entrepreneurs could also design and manufacture their own custom trophies and awards to separate their products from competitors. Furthermore, the equipment needed for engraving name plaques for the trophies is inexpensive and available at most building supply centers.

Awards and Engravers Magazine Online, www. nbm.com: Print and electronic magazine serving the trophy and award industry with information, resources, and links.

25. Party Balloon Service

Less than a $1,000 investment will adequately get you started in your own party balloon service. The demand for this service is endless and certainly not limited only to children's birthday parties. Marketing a party balloon service is best achieved by creating a basic, yet colorful brochure that can be distributed to local party and event planners, children's stores, restaurants and banquet facilities, day-care centers, catering companies, and wedding planners. Attending business networking meetings and chamber of commerce functions is also a fantastic way to network and get the word out about your service. A small amount of research into your local market will assist in establishing pricing and demand. Great add-on services can include a party cleanup service, streamer and decoration supplies, and event planning services, especially for children's birthday parties. This is a business that can easily be managed from a homebased location, but reliable transportation will be needed to move equipment and supplies to the party site or to deliver the balloons.

Balloon Basics Inc., www.balloonbasics.com: Wholesale distributor of balloons and related supplies and equipment.

26. Homebased Manufacturing Business

Your options are endless in terms of what can be easily manufactured from a simple homebased workshop—picnic tables, birdhouses, picture frames, wind chimes, custom furniture, or specialty soaps and candles, just to get you thinking. Of course, a wee bit of creative design and handyperson skills will be needed as well as basic tools and equipment to ensure the products you manufacture are quality and become sought after. Depending on what you manufacture you can sell the end products at crafts shows, through retailers on a consignment or wholesale basis, directly to commercial users, or directly to consumers via trade shows, mail order, and online sales. However, careful consideration will have to be taken to ensure your workshop meets zoning codes and that all fire and safety precautions have been taken for your and your neighbor's safety.

American Home Business Association, www.home business.com: Members receive home business information, access to specific products and services, advice, and support.

27. Dog Walking Service

A dog walking service is perfectly suited for the person who has the time, patience, and love for dogs. Best of all, a dog walking service can be launched for a few hundred dollars. There are various styles of multilead dog walking collars and leashes available that will allow three or more dogs to be walked at the same time without becoming tangled in the leash. Acquiring this equipment is important because it will reduce frustration and enable you to walk multiple dogs at the same time, and so increase revenues and profits. To secure clients for the service, simply design a promotional flier that explains your dog walking service and qualifications. Distribute the fliers to businesses that are frequented by dog owners, such as grooming locations, kennels, pet food stores, community animal shelters, and town halls. Once word is out about your dog walking service, it should not take long to establish a base of 20 or 30 regular clients.

National Association of Professional Dog Walkers, www.napdw.com: Members receive industry information and support.

28. Home Office Planner

Functional room design is more important for a home office than you might think. "Where is my. . . ?"

"I can't work with all this noise. . . ." Many first time attempts to work or operate a business from home meet with frustration and a feeling of "what do I need and where do I start?" These very common problems are the basis of starting a home office planning service with the focus on assisting employees or business owners to establish, or make the transition to, a homebased office. You will work one on one with clients to develop successful work and organization plans and programs that are tailored to specific needs. The home office planning service can include assisting employees and business owners with homebased office solutions, such as office layout design, ergonomics, security systems and devices, storage solutions, recycling programs, work routine schedules, computer and technology integration, communications systems, and suitable equipment and supplies requirements. Remember not to forget to market this service to corporations because many are now having key employees work from homebased office, as telecommuters.

Organize Tips Online, www.organizetips.com: Web site offering visitors hundreds of home office planning and organization tips and ideas.

29. Mobile Car Wash

A mobile car wash service is perfectly suited for the entrepreneur who is seeking a simple, profitable, and low-investment opportunity. The business requires only basic equipment and supplies and can be operated from a van, pick-up truck, or enclosed trailer. The market potential is enormous with more than 130,000,000 vehicles registered in the United States. However, the real target market for this service is to establish monthly car and truck washing and cleaning accounts with companies, organizations, and government agencies that have a fleet of automobiles. It is way easier to land one repeat customer than it is to find new customers all the time.

Car Wash Equipment Directory, www.car-wash-equipment.net: Online car wash equipment manufacturers and suppliers directory.

30. Home Inspection Service

Providing you have construction experience and are prepared to invest some money and time in a training course that will qualify you as a certified home and property inspector, you can earn a very good living from owning and operating your own home and property inspection service. Millions of homes and properties are bought and sold each year in North America. As a condition of sale, most of these homes have to be inspected by a professional home inspector to make sure the building does not have major structural or mechanical problems. Currently, home and property inspection rates range from $150 for a small and basic residential home to more than $1,000 for larger commercial buildings and complexes. A home and property inspection service can be managed from a home office with minimal monthly overhead costs, making this business start-up a wise choice.

National Association of Home Inspectors, www.nahi.org: Home inspectors association in the United States.

Canadian Association of Home and Property Inspectors, www.cahi.ca:. Home inspectors association in Canada.

31. Disc Jockey Service

Not only are mobile disc jockey services in high demand, the business can also be launched on a modest investment, often less than $10,000, and the monthly operating overheads are virtually nonexistent. But there are still a few basic ingredients required to start and successfully operate a mobile disc jockey service. These include an excellent and varied music selection, DJ equipment and reliable transportation, and an outgoing personality and talent for public speaking. Clients can include event and wedding planners, tour operators, restaurant and nightclub owners, and individual consumers seeking to secure disc jockey services for a celebration or special event. Disc jockeys routinely charge $200 to $400 per event and as an added bonus, generally fare quite well in the tips department.

Disc Jockey Online, www.discjockeyonline.com: Web site serving the professional mobile disc jockey industry with information, resources, and links.

32. Online Researcher

Do you spend hours every day surfing the Web? If so, why not start an Internet research service and get paid for surfing? This business opportunity was once called information brokering, but, with the introduction of the Internet, the name has changed. The business remains the same, however, as the information that was once researched and compiled from newspapers, trade magazines, and business and industry journals can now be found on the Internet. In a nutshell, an Internet research service operates in two fashions. The first is to collect data and facts relevant to a specific topic and then sell the compiled data to individuals and businesses that require this information. Business owners also enlist the services of an Internet researcher to source specific data and facts relevant to their particular business, industry, or market. In both cases, clients pay for information they are seeking. Billing rates for the services vary, depending on how much research time is required to compile the data; however, many Internet research services have base billing rates of $25 to $35 per hour.

Association of Internet Researchers, www.aoir.org: Industry information, resources, and links for professional researchers.

33. Promotional Product Sales

The business world spends billions of dollars annually on embossed and printed promotional items such as T-shirts, pens, hats, and calendars as promotional giveaways to customers and potential clients. Securing just a small portion of this very lucrative market can make you rich. The key to success in the promotional products marketing industry for the small or homebased operator is not to manufacture and print the items yourself, but simply to market them enlisting the services of existing manufacturers and printers to fill the orders. This is a business opportunity that requires excellent sales and marketing abilities, and is definately not suited to someone who is afraid to knock on doors and ask for business. Aim to achieve yearly sales of $300,000 with a 50 percent markup on all products sold and the end result will be a homebased advertising business that generates a pretax and expense earnings of $100,000.

Promotional Products Online, www.promotional products.com: Directory service listing promotional product manufacturers, printers, and distributors.

34. Errand Service

Busy lifestyles dictate that most working folk just don't have time for even the simplest of errands, like taking the family dog to the veterinarian for a routine check up or picking up the dry cleaning. An errand service can be set up for peanuts and operated with the aid of a cellular telephone. Creating a marketing brochure that explains your service can be your best tool for attracting new clients. A few promotional items such as pens and memo pads emblazoned with your company logo, name, and telephone number will go a long way as a gentle reminder of your fast, reliable, and affordable service. Attending just a few local business networking meetings can also secure new clients for the service, enough so that with providing good service, word-of-mouth advertising will kick in. This is the kind of business where growth is fuelled by referrals. Therefore, customer satisfaction is the number-one goal. That is what you will really be selling.

International Concierge and Errand Association, www.iceaweb.org: Members receive industry information, advice, and support.

35. Marketing Consultant

Without marketing, a business cannot survive. Top-notch marketing consultants are in high demand across North America. Many specialize in one particular marketing discipline, while the more experienced consultants tackle the full range of marketing activities for clients. Securing clients for the service can be accomplished by promoting the service at business networking meetings, initiating a direct-mail advertising campaign, or simply working the telephone and setting appointments with business owners and professionals to present and explain the benefits of your services. If you possess skills and experience marketing products or services via the Internet, be sure to capitalize on this ability. Marketing constants with proven results in Internet marketing are earning as much as $100 an hour.

The Direct Marketing Association, www.the-dma.org: The association services the direct marketing industry, including mail order, telemarketing, and direct sellers.

36. Homebased Delivery Service

"Have car will deliver" could become your corporate motto if you start a homebased delivery service. Armed with a cell phone to handle incoming and outgoing customer calls, you can offer clients delivery and or pick up of dry cleaning, spirits, fast foods, medications, event tickets, groceries, pet foods, or just about anything else imaginable. Expand the business by concentrating on promoting the service and hiring subcontracted drivers with their own cars to handle the deliveries. Maximize efficiency by installing two-way radios in each. Strike deals with local restaurants, grocery stores, pharmacies, liquor stores, and other retailers to handle their delivery services. And if they do not presently offer their customers fast and convenient delivery, explain the benefits of doing so and why your delivery service is the right outfit for the job.

Entrepreneur Online, www.entrepreneur.com: Online resource and information center for small business.

37. Retail Display Specialist

Retailers often must rely on an elaborate window displays to grab the attention of passing consumers and draw them into the store. Once in, exciting in-store displays create desire and buying urgency for their goods. Starting a business that specializes in creating effective window and in-store merchandise displays for retailers is the focus of this home business opportunity. Marketing the service can be as easy as approaching local retailers and offering a free trial period so the owners realize the benefits and increased sales from a well-designed product display. The free display you create can also be used as a powerful marketing tool to present to other shop owners. Be sure to build an inventory of interesting props, signage, and lighting so that you can provide clients with an all-inclusive display service.

National Retail Federation, www.nrf.com: Association serving retailers and shop owners' nationwide.

38. Cosmetics Retailing

For the innovative entrepreneur, there are numerous ways to sell cosmetics and make a profit, including home cosmetics parties, online sales, mail order, temporary kiosks set up in malls and fashion shows, and in-home personal sales visits. The first step to getting started in cosmetics sales is to source a quality and reputable supply. You can create your own cosmetics brand and have it manufactured under a private labeling agreement. Or, you can strike a deal with an existing cosmetics manufacturer and distributor, marketing its line in an exclusive territory of your choosing. In both cases, information about cosmetic manufacturers and distributors can be found online or through the Independent Cosmetics Manufacture and Distributors Association. Expand the business by hiring cosmetic sales representatives that are paid by way of a commission on sales they generate. This home business is easy to set up and has the potential to earn huge profits.

Independent Cosmetic Manufacturers and Distributors Inc., www.icmad.org: Directory service listing cosmetic manufacturers and distributors, as well as industry information, resources, and links of interest.

39. Window Cleaning Service

Window washing is perhaps the granddaddy of all home-managed service businesses. The advantages are apparent:

- Proven consumer demand with millions of potential clients
- Low start-up investment and low fixed operating overheads
- No special skills or business experience required
- Flexible operating hours
- No need to stock or warehouse costly inventory
- Year-round operation by offering interior and exterior window cleaning
- Potential to generate a fantastic income
- Unlimited growth potential and can even be franchised

Promoting a window washing service is just as easy as starting one: print and distribute fliers detailing your service, run low-cost classified ads under home services, network with potential customers at business association functions and social events, and piggyback your service with existing businesses such as house painters, window installers, property managers, real estate agents, and renovation contractors.

Window Cleaning Net Online, www.window-cleaning-net.com: Window washing information, resources, and links, as well as a directory of window washing equipment suppliers.

40. Valet Parking Service

Starting a valet parking service is very easy. Basically, if you have a driver's license and can secure third-party and automobile liability insurance, you are in business. A valet parking service can be marketed directly to consumers. However, a more logical approach is to offer the service to entertainment industry professionals, such as event and wedding planners, trade show organizers, and charity groups and organizations for their special functions. The business can be started with a minimal capital outlay. The profit potential is also excellent, as current rates for valet parking services are in the range of $50 to $70 per hour for a two-to three-person valet crew, and the cash tips can really add up.

Valet Park, www.valetpark.net: Web site serving the valet parking industry with information, resources, and links.

41. Label and Electronic Mailing Lists

Good up-to-date and well-targeted mailing lists, both label and electronic, can rent for as much as $1 per name, and herein lies an exciting home business. The main requirements for getting the business rolling are to have great marketing skills, a computer, and entry management software. The mailing lists you compile should be categorized by industry and target market, as well as being available for companies or direct marketers to rent in electronic and mailing label formats. Marketing mailing lists can be as easy as conducting your own e-mail or fax blast campaign to advertise your lists for rent. Or you can opt to let a mailing list broker or manager with a existing client base rent your list on a profit share or commission basis.

Info USA, www.infousa.com: Billed as the world's largest suppler of mailing lists, which are indexed by consumer, business, industry, hobby, geographic, and demographic classifications.

42. Mystery Dinner Party Organizer

Organizing mystery dinner parties is not only a sensational new venture to get rolling, but it could also prove to be a whole lot of fun. "Who done it?" or murder mystery dinner parties have become an extremely popular entertainment service in the past few years, resulting in lots of new mystery dinner party services springing up. But don't worry, there is room for a lot more. The business can be managed from a home office and started for less than a few thousand dollars. The demand for the service is excellent, and clients can include individuals wanting to host an interesting dinner party, corporations seeking a fun social function for their employees or customers, and event planners searching for something out of the ordinary in terms of a unique entertainment experience for their clients. The theme of the party can be created, or you can use a popular mystery theme or story people are familiar with. Currently, mystery dinner party services are charging rates starting at $25 per person plus the cost of a catered dinner.

Killer Scripts, www.killerscripts.com: Company that offers license rights to murder mystery dinner scripts.

43. Human Billboard Advertising

Sometimes in wacky costumes, human billboards are simply people that hold signs or banners emblazoned with promotional messages in high-traffic areas of the community—usually outside, in front of, or in close proximity to the business they are promoting. They advertise everything from new housing developments to car dealerships to restaurant openings and are really catching on as a highly effective, cost-efficient method of promoting services and products. The objective of a human billboard is to grab the attention of passing motorists and pedestrians and get them to visit the business being promoted. Your human billboard staff can include homemakers, students, actors, musicians, and retirees, basically anyone that is available to work on a part-time, as-needed basis. Marketing the service can be as easy as setting appointments with local business owners to explain and promote the benefits of your service. Joining local business networking clubs is also a good way to get the word out. Rates for human billboards vary based on factors such as the number of people (billboards), the length of the promotion, and other items like signage and special costumes.

American Association of Advertising Agencies, www.aaaa.org: Members receive industry information, business advice, and support.

44. Product Demonstration Service

We have all seen people in grocery stores offering free samples of food or cleaning products to shoppers. These people are generally not employed by the supermarket, but by a product demonstration company. The concept behind this type of marketing is to get consumers to like and therefore start to purchase and use these products on a regular basis. Typically, product demonstration services are awarded to operators on a contract basis and include a certain number of demonstration hours and outlets in the contract. Currently product demonstration rates range from a low of $7 per hour to as much as $15 per hour, with employee demonstrators paid 75 percent. It will, therefore, be vital to the survival of the business that a lot of product demonstration contracts are secured in order to realize substantial revenues and profits.

Thomas Register, www.thomasregister.com: Online and print manufacturers directories.

45. Cloth Diaper Service

Ah, the not-so-sweet smell of success. Disposable diapers are not environmentally friendly and can often irritate a baby's skin. The solution? Environmentally friendly cloth diapers made of natural fibers. A baby can go through as many as 4,000 diapers before being fully toilet trained, which creates an outstanding home business opportunity. Depending on your business start-up budget, there are two methods of pursuing this venture. You can offer a complete service, including diaper supply, delivery, pickup, and cleaning. Or you can simply supply delivery and pickup services of the diapers and have an established commercial laundry clean them at a reduced or bulk rate. If start-up capital is plentiful, the first

option is probably more profitable than the second over the long term. Word-of-mouth marketing will be your main promotional weapon, so be sure to get out and start the promotional train rolling by talking with as many new parents as you can.

Diaper Pin Online, www.diaperpin.com: Extensive online directory serving the cloth diaper industry with information, products, services, resources, and links.

46. Instruction Classes

Capitalize on your knowledge, experience, and special skills by starting your own homebased instruction business. Depending on your skills, you could offer clients instruction classes on cooking, gardening, home improvement, dog training, self defense, survival training, music lessons, language training, sewing, or anything you have mastered yourself. Classes can be conducted at your home if suitable, or you can arrange to teach at your client's locations or rent space as needed. Market the classes by running print advertisements, distributing promotional fliers, and via word-of-mouth networking. Specialized instruction training is one of the best home businesses to start because in most cases the product (your skill) helps others to solve a problem, improve themselves, or both. However, remember to charge for what the service is really worth. In most cases it will be higher than what you think.

National Tutoring Association, www.ntatutor.org: Members receive industry information, advice, and support.

47. Business Plan Service

Did you know that a recent survey of new business owners revealed that less than 25 percent of the 250 owners surveyed had created a business plan for their new venture? When asked why they had not, the number-one reason was that they simply did know how. According to the Small Business Administration, approximately 750,000 new businesses are started each year in the United States. This creates an outstanding opportunity for the ingenious entrepreneur to capitalize by starting a business that researches and creates business plans for owners of new and existing businesses. Market your business plan service by attending business networking meetings; also attempt to obtain a list of all new and renewal business registration licenses through your local business service center.

Business Plan Writer Online, www.business-plan-writer-online.com: Web site dedicated to the business plan writer, including information, resources, and links.

48. Recycling Consultant

Taking the time to educate yourself in the subject of recycling industrial and household materials can really pay off, especially if you apply that knowledge and become a recycling consultant. Millions of homeowners and companies now recycle waste materials. However, millions more could. But what can be recycled, and where do you start? This is the point where you put your recycling knowledge to work by teaching homeowners, business owners, and employees how to recycle, what to recycle, and where it can be recycled. Charge corporations and homeowners a fee to design a specially created recycling plan for their particular needs. In addition to creating the recycling program, you can also give a brief instructional course on the recycling program that you have created for them, as well on the topic of recycling in general. The timing has never been better because the need for every person on the planet to practice recycling measures has never been more apparent. Potential income ranges from $50 to $70 per hour plus markup on products sold.

Solid Waste Association of North America, www.swana.org: Recycling and environmental issues, information, education, training, resources, and links.

49. Bartender for Hire

Starting a bartender-for-hire service is a fantastic way to get into business for yourself, without breaking the bank. You can market your services as an independent bartender to catering companies, event and wedding planners, hotels, and pubs for relief duties. The business only requires a few hundred dollars of seed capital to initiate and can return $150 to $200 per day plus gratuities. Ideally, the entrepreneur who starts a bartender-for-hire service will be an experienced one with outstanding social skills. Employing other bartenders on an as-needed, on-call basis can generate additional revenue. A bartender-for-hire service has the potential to generate annual revenues that can easily top $50,000.

Bartender Online, www.bartender.com/link-trade.html: Directory service listing industry information, resource, and links for bartenders.

50. Property Manager

Here is the perfect new business venture for someone who wants to get started on a limited budget and manage his or her new business enterprise from the comforts of a home office. Becoming a property manager is relatively straightforward. Find residential and commercial landlords who are seeking the services of a property management firm, negotiate a service contract, and start the business. The duties of a property manager include, but are not limited to, organizing tradespeople to conduct repairs, receiving and answering to tenant and owner inquiries, leasing or renting vacant units, and negotiating lease terms and details. A property management service is ideally suited to a person with a real estate background. However, anyone can start this venture on a small or part-time basis and gain valuable on-the-job experience, which can be leveraged to grow the business into a large and profitable concern.

National Property Managers Association, www.npma.org: Members receive industry information, advice, and support.

51. Flier Distribution Service

Small business owners, salespeople, and marketers of all sorts have utilized promotional fliers for decades as a fast and frugal, yet highly effective, method of advertising their products and services. A homebased flier delivery service is easy to start and operate, yet it also has the potential to generate a great full-time or part-time income and requires no more than a telephone and a good pair of walking shoes to get started. Currently, flier delivery services are charging in the range of 5 cents to 10 cents for each flier individually hand delivered, and as much as $1 for each flier that is posted (pinned) onto community notice and bulletin boards commonly found at supermarkets, laundromats, and schools. As a method of increasing revenues, consider hiring students or retirees to deliver fliers during busy times.

Corel Inc., www.corel.com: Corel is a leading software development company with numerous desktop publishing products available for a wide variety of user applications.

Adobe Inc., www.adobe.com: Adobe is a leading software development company with numerous desktop publishing products available for a wide variety of user applications

52. Bed and Breakfast

Providing you don't mind sharing your home with overnight guests, you stand to profit substantially by turning your home into a bed-and-breakfast operation. Use the money you generate renting out rooms to travelers for living income, to pay down the mortgage, or to save for retirement. B & B rates are in the range of $40 to $100 per night per person and include a light breakfast. Promote your bed and breakfast through local tourist associations, via online directories, and by establishing alliances with independent travel agents and brokers. Of course, the obstacle to overcome in terms of turning your home into a B & B will be zoning regulations. Some municipalities encourage B & B's, while others prefer to keep guest accommodations within the confines of an established a hotel zone. So a trip to the city hall planning and zoning department will be your first stop.

American Bed and Breakfast Association, www.abba.com: Members receive industry information, advice, and support.

Canadian Bed and Breakfast Directory Online, www.bbcanada.com: Bed and breakfast directory serving the Canadian market, indexed geographically.

53. Rubbish Removal Service

It isn't pretty, but trash could put you on the road to riches. A secondhand truck or trailer, shovels, rakes, and a few garbage cans are all you need to start a rubbish removal service. Rubbish removal rates can be charged by the hour, truckload, or by a quotation. And by offering home and business owners fast and convenient rubbish removal services at competitive prices, I will guarantee word of mouth advertising will generate more work than you can handle. Also be sure to build alliances with people that can refer your business to their customers and clients. These people will include real estate agents, residential and commercial cleaners, home service companies such as carpet cleaners, and property managers. In terms of a low-cost home business start-up that requires little in the way of skills or experience, a rubbish removal service is one of the better choices.

Entrepreneur Online, www.entrepreneur.com: Online resource center for small business.

54. Boat Cleaning Service

Don't want to compete in the highly competitive residential or commercial cleaning industry, but would like to start a cleaning service? Why not consider a boat cleaning service? The competition is minimal and providing the cleaning service is established in the right area, the number of potential customers is nearly unlimited. Starting a boat cleaning service could not be easier, as there are no special skills or equipment required to operate the business and marketing the service requires no more then some printed fliers and a little bit of leg work to distribute them at marinas and boating clubs. Considering a boat cleaning service can be started on an initial investment of less than $1,000, the income potential at $20 to $30 per hour is excellent. Additionally, if you have the equipment and necessary skills, you could also expand the business and offer clients additional services including in-the-water bottom cleaning, sailboat rigging, haul-out bottom painting, and woodwork or brightwork refinishing.

Mer-Maids Inc., www.mermaid.com: Manufacturers and distributors of boat cleaning products and supplies.

55. Bicycle Repair Service

Consider all of the advantages of starting a home-based bicycle repair service:

- Low initial start-up investment and minimal monthly operating overheads
- Proven consumer demand for repairs in an industry that is experiencing double-digit growth annually
- Potential to earn $30 per hour and more
- Part-time or full-time opportunity that has flexible working hours
- Repair skills needed to operate the business are minimal and can be learned quickly on the job or through specialty training courses

One key aspect of marketing is making sure that you establish alliances with bicycling clubs and organizations in the community because the membership of these clubs can become customers with a little promoting by you. Also work for established bike retailers and repair shops on a subcontract basis to handle their overflow work in the busy season.

United Bicycle Institute, www.bikeschool.com: Oregon-based training school offering students certification courses in bicycle mechanics.

56. Medical Billing Service

The medical billing industry is extremely competitive. However, for the determined entrepreneur, there is still a good opportunity to earn $40,000 or more per year operating a medical claims billing service from a home office location. All medical claims billing is processed electronically and sent directly to Medicare clearinghouses, so computer equipment and the ability to use computer hardware and medical billing software programs are required. Additionally, you will need to familiarize yourself with the diagnostic and procedure coding system used by doctors and health-care professionals on medical claim forms to indicate the type of service being billed. Currently, medical billing services charge clients in the range of $2 to $3 per claim processed, and the overall profit potential for the service is good, providing you can process medical claims on a volume basis. There is a fairly steep leaning curve for operating this service and careful research and planning techniques must be practiced to ensure initial and continued success.

American Association of Medical Billers, www.billers.com: Members receive industry information, advice, and support.

57. Proposal Writer

Government agencies on the federal, state, and local levels put thousands of RFPs (requests for proposals) out for bid annually. Proposals can range from construction of new buildings to supplying computer equipment for government offices, and just about anything in between. Although these proposals can be very lucrative for the company or individual that successfully bids for the contract, many small- to medium-sized contractors simply do not complete the proposal and bid forms. Because the process is extremely involved and usually requires technical drawings, action plans, and contingency plans, business owners and managers often have neither the time nor abilities to complete them. A proposal writer compiles and completes the proposal documents on behalf of the contractor. It's as simple as that. Proposal writers charge fees based on the amount of time it takes to complete the proposal, typically in the range of $30 to $40 per hour; some will even charge a commission based on the value of the contract should their client win it. Furthermore, most proposal writers specialize in one area, such as nonperishable goods, construction, services, or maintenance. A proposal writer must also have access to a wide range of research resources and in almost all cases a technical writing ability and knowledge.

Association of Proposal Management Professionals, www.apmp.org: Members receive industry information, advice, and support.

58. Independent Sales Consultant

Some of the highest earning professionals in any industry are independent sales consultants working on a freelance basis for clients. Freelance sales consultants represent companies that sell products and services ranging from manufactured goods to home improvement services. Securing clients to represent is easy, simply because freelance sales consultants generally supply all the tools of the trade—transportation, communications requirements, and computer hardware. Many independent sales consultants also generate and qualify their own sales leads. To put it differently, clients have little to lose by having a freelance sales consultants representing their business. Remuneration for products and services sold is always by way of commission, which will range between 10 and 25 percent of the total sales value depending on what is being sold.

Entrepreneur Online, www.entrepreneur.com: Online resource center for small business owners and sales professionals.

59. Budget Decorating Service

Popular television programs like "Trading Spaces," "While You Were Out," and "The Designer Guys" have fired up people's imaginations about how they can dramatically change the look of their homes on a relatively small budget. But there is a hook; in order to do so, someone involved with the budget decorating makeover must have a creative flair for decorating and design and the skills necessary to pull it all together, leaving out many homeowners. However, if these are skills you possess, then operating a budget decorating service might be right up your alley. Spend time at garage and estate sales, scrounge through flea markets, and scan local newspaper classified ads for wacky decoration items, recycled building materials, and unique home furnishing, all of which can be purchased and resold to clients for a profit while you redecorate rooms or their entire home. Market your service through home and garden shows and by creating colorful before-and-after brochures that illustrates your decorating talents.

International Interior Design Association, www. iida.org: Members receive industry information, advice, and support.

60. Office Protocol Consultant

The time has never been better to start a business as an office protocol consultant. Disputes between employees or between employees and management based on allegations of sexual harassment, racism, and abusive behavior within the office environment can bankrupt a business, morally and financially. The business concept is very straightforward. As an office protocol consultant, you can advise clients on issues pertaining to these subjects as well as create a training program for employees and management on how to avoid, or react, if necessary, to any potentially unfavorable situations that arise in the office environment. The demand for this type of consulting service is gigantic, as thousands of corporation rush to retain the services of protocol consultants as a proactive measure to ensure they are not caught in politically and socially inappropriate situations, reflecting negatively on corporate image.

The Protocol School of Washington, www.psow. com: Etiquette and protocol training and certification courses.

61. Public Opinion Survey Service

Businesses often rely on public opinion surveys to discover more about their products, services, and customers. Politicians rely on opinion polls to gauge what voters feel are the most important issues. And just about every level of government agency relies on public opinion polls to find out what services taxpayers want and need. Public opinion polls and surveys can be conducted on the telephone, by mail, or by way of personal interview, making this service a great candidate for a new home business start-up. Capitalizing on your communications, organizational, and marketing skills will be your main weapons to make this business successful. To get started, create and conduct a few of your own public opinion polls on topics that would be interesting to the public at large. Send local media the results in the form of a press release or media alert, and use the media coverage as a marketing tool to secure paying customers for the business.

Marketing Research Association, www.mra-net. org: Members receive industry information, advice, and support.

62. Mobile Dog Wash Service

The purchase of a secondhand van or enclosed trailer is the first step toward starting a mobile dog wash service. You will have to outfit the truck or trailer with a water tank and some other basic equipment such as a hose and brushes. You can market a mobile dog wash service by creating promotional fliers and displaying them at pet-related retail shops, vet offices, and the local SPCA. Establish the business in a densely populated urban center where many people live in apartments and condominiums. These people with dogs have limited ways to wash their pets and, therefore, are your primary target audience. Like many pet-related services, word-of-mouth advertising will be your main marketing tool, so be sure that you provide a quality service with excellent customer relations.

Wag 'n Tails Inc., www.wagntails.com: Mobile pet grooming and washing equipment.

63. Interior and Exterior House Painting
Heights, ladders, and slow, tedious labor-intensive work are enough reasons to scare off even the most hardcore do-it-yourself homeowners and make a house painting service a wise start-up for entrepreneurs with the required skills. House painting is a very simple business to set in motion and only requires a small investment. Like most labor-intensive business ventures, you can pretty much be guaranteed work, regardless of economic conditions. Providing free value-added services such as cleaning the rain gutters or windows while on the job site is a great way to separate your company from the competition. Often free value-added services will increase the number and the quality of referrals your business receives.

Painting and Decorators Contractors Association, www.pdca.org: Members receive industry information, advice, and support.

64. Silk-Screening Service
Silk-screen printing equipment can be set up in your garage, basement, or any spare room and used for printing logos and images on a wide variety of products, such as T-shirts, mouse pads, bumper stickers, hats, sweatshirts, heat transfers, shower curtains, binder covers, furniture, and sports and corporate uniforms. Best of all, the profit potential is great. For example, basic T-shirts can be purchased in bulk for less than $5 each and the ink used to print the image adds up to only a few cents per printed item. Securing orders for 500 printed T-shirts a week and charging only $10 each for the shirt and printing can generate gross profits in excess of $100,000 per year! It's more than compelling reason to start a homebased, silk-screening business, wouldn't you agree?

United States Screen Printing Institute, www.usscreen. com: Online screen printers portal and billed as the global meeting place for screen printers, including industry information, resources, and links.

65. Employee Training
The demand from employers for specialized employee training is enormous, and starting a homebased employee-training service is a terrific new business venture to set in motion. The key to success in this business is specialization, and your service should focus on one particular training style or method that you have mastered or can quickly master. Popular employee training course topics include computer and software training, customer service, working without distraction, multi-tasking, money handling, sales, theft-reduction, and coping with stress. The training course can be conducted on the client's site and marketing the service can be accomplished through networking meetings and a direct mail program explaining the service and course curriculum.

National Training Registry, www.trainingreg istry.com: Online directory listing professional business, management, and employee training consultants, as well as training courses and training products, all indexed geographically and by topic.

66. Romantic Catering
Who needs cupid when they can hire your romantic catering service and surprise that someone special in their lives with a unique and unforgettable romantic dinner for two? Romantic catering is just that. You plan and play host to a memorable dining experience for clients. The evening could start with a romantic ride in a horse-drawn carriage through a park, complete with wine, roses, and mood-setting

music. The ride could end on a secluded beach under the stars where the client would dine on lobster and caviar picnic-style. Of course, your service would provide the gourmet meal, make all the arrangements, supply the transportation, and even serve the meal on the finest china while dressed in exquisite formal wear. Best of all, you do not need to be a chef, have the horse-drawn carriage, or even have the ability to serve the meal. All of these can be contracted to qualified people who posses these abilities and equipment. What is required, however, is the ability to market the service and have the creative imagination to plan the best romantic dinner adventure possible.

Romantic Tips Online, www.romantic-tips.com: Web site listing hundreds of romantic tips and ideas making it a great place to get started on your quest to start a romantic catering business.

67. Deck Building

One of the fastest growing segments of the home improvement industry is designing and building custom sundecks that can retail for as much as $20,000 and include features such as built-in planters, hot tub gazebos, glass or cast iron handrails, atmosphere lighting, and custom manufactured wood patio furniture to match the deck's design. The most profitable way to operate the business is to sell the sundecks directly to the consumer. However, this method is also the most expensive to start and market. Additional ways to get started include subcontracting for established building and renovation companies, establishing alliances with landscape designers and architects, and marketing your sundecks directly to consumers via home and garden shows. In most areas of the country, the installation of a sundeck requires a building permit, which must be issued prior to installation. There are also building codes in place for the construction specifications of sundecks that must be met. Starting this business requires construction experience and skills, as well as creative design abilities. Equipment such as table saws, miter saws, drills, and a host of hand tools will also be required, but much of this can be rented at first to keep start-up costs to a minimum.

Deck Industry Association, www.deckindustry.org: Members receive industry information, advice, and support.

68. Collectible Clothing Sales

The value and popularity of collectible clothing has been on a steady increase for the past decade, and the demand for collectible clothing from the 1940s to the 1980s shows no signs of diminishing. Working full-or part-time from home, you simply cannot go wrong buying collectable and vintage clothing and reselling it for a profit. Collectible clothing can be purchased at garage sales, auctions, estate sales, and by placing classified ads in newspapers and online. The same clothing can then be sold for a profit to collectors through vintage clothing shows and fashion events, in home collector clothes parties, and via online malls and collector clothing Web sites. Of course you can also establish and promote your own collector clothing Web site to sell your full product line.

Collecting Network, www.collectingnetwork.com: Directory listing antiques and collectibles information, resources, valuation guides, and links.

69. Temporary Health Agency

Ideally, your homebased temporary help agency should specialize in supplying qualified workers on a temporary basis in one particular industry or area of expertise, such as the construction industry, home care workers, domestic help, office workers, or warehouse staff. Recruiting workers prepared to work on a temporary basis should not prove difficult, just target students, early retirees, homemakers, and even other homebased business owners seeking to gain additional income periodically. Marketing the service can be as easy as creating an information package describing the service and your available workforce and distributing the packages to businesses and companies that occasionally rely on temporary workers. The billing rate for the workers supplied is based on market value of the work being performed, with the agency generally retaining 10 percent to 15 percent of the workers' earnings.

American Staffing Association, www.staffingto day.net: Members receive industry information, advice, and support.

70. Web Site Design and Maintenance

More than 1,000 Web sites a day are being posted to the Internet, and here is your chance to cash in by starting a Web site design service. Fear not if you do not know how to design a highly effective Web site. You can take a crash course in Web site design at your local community college or, failing that, you can hire a high-tech wizard to design the sites while you concentrate your efforts on sales and marketing. Online competition in Web site design and service is steep; thus you may want to take a more hands-on approach to marketing the service right in your own city or local community. Start by designing a few sample sites—one in an e-commerce format and one as an information portal. The next step is to initiate a letter, telephone, and e-mail direct marketing campaign to introduce yourself and your service to small business owners in your community that currently do not have a business Web site or have one that you know that can be improved. The goal is to get a presentation appointment at their place of business. Finally, armed with a notebook computer, you can meet with business owners, present your sample sites, and explain the benefits of your Web site design service. Additional revenues can be generated by hosting sites, maintaining sites, providing content, and by creating online marketing programs to meet individual client needs.

The International Association of Web Masters and Designers, www.whosontheWeb.com: Members receive industry information, advice, and support.

71. Vending Routes

The snack vending business is a multibillion-dollar industry in North America and continues to grow year-after-year. Getting started in the vending industry is very easy. Simply purchase a few vending machines, stock and locate them, and you're in business, right? Wrong. The vending industry also has one of the highest failure rates due to heavy competition, which in turn can make it difficult for new operators to secure high-traffic and potentially profitable locations to install the machines. Therefore the key to success in vending is the same as opening a retail store: location, location, location. Research and source the right location and a vending machine will not only make money, it will be profitable for many years.

National Automatic Merchandising Association, www.vending.org: Members receive industry information, advice, and support.

72. Homebased Rental Business

One of the best aspects about starting a homebased rental business is the flexible hours. Depending on the item most often your busy rental times will be nights and weekends, enabling you to keep your job or even operate another business. Good products to rent include recreational vehicles and trailers, canoes, kayaks, trade show displays, props for film production, musical instruments, camping equipment, office equipment, store displays and fixtures, and portable signage. Of course, you will want to choose only one or two and specialize in short-and long-term rentals of that item. Market your rental items by advertising in local newspapers, printing and distributing two-for-one rental coupons, networking at business and social functions, and being in Yellow Pages telephone directories.

American Home Business Association, www.home business.com: Members receive home business information, access to specific products and services, advice, and support.

73. Awning Cleaning Service

In the past decade, more and more business owners have been switching to commercial awning signs, as opposed to traditional box signs, to advertise their businesses and brand their operating locations. All of these awnings have one thing in common. They all have to be cleaned on a regular basis to project a good corporate image for the businesses they are promoting. This creates a great opportunity for the enterprising entrepreneur to cash in and profit, by starting an awning cleaning service. The best way to gain clients is simply to put on some comfortable walking shoes and start knocking on doors. Visit all the shops and offices in your area that have awning signs and present your service. Explain about the benefits of first impressions. This may seem to be an old-fashioned and time-consuming way to promote the business. However, if you set objective of talking with ten potential customers a day and can close two of these presentations, you will then have 40 new clients in a month's time, and be well on your way to establishing a solid and profitable business.

National Register of Professional Awning Cleaners, www.awningpro.com: Members receive industry information, advice, support, and a listing in the association's online consumers guide.

74. Landscaping Service

A basic one-or two-person landscaping service can be set in motion for less than $10,000, and much of the skills and experience needed to run it successfully can be learned on the job. However, operating a landscaping service still requires some past landscaping experience to give clients peace of mind. Potential customers for a landscaping service include commercial property owners, residential property owners, contractors, and property developers. While an established landscaping service can compete for work in all categories, a new landscaping service should focus on one particular type of customer until the business has established a successful track record. Most landscaping contracts are completed on an estimate basis prior to starting the work, so be sure to practice your estimating skills, as it is easy to underbid and overbid, both of which can be very costly in terms of bottom-line profits.

Associated Landscape Contractors of America, www.alca.org: Members receive industry information, advice, and support.

75. Independent Record Label

The rise in numbers of independent music labels rests solely on the commercialization and subsequent popularity of the Internet. Independent music labels and artists now have the ability to level the playing field with their larger and generally much better financed competition by using the Internet to reach a global audience of music lovers. In fact, never in the history of music has there been such a wide variety of musical styles available—everything from jazz to hip-hop and back to good old rock 'n roll. The key to successfully starting and operating an independent music label will rest on your ability to secure the right musical acts and performers to sign, market, and promote. The start-up costs are high for this unique home business venture, but the profit potential justifies the risk.

Association for Independent Music, www.afim.org: Members receive industry information, advice, and support.

76. Mobile Screen Repair

Starting a mobile screen repair and replacement business could put you on the road to riches, especially in the light of the recent mosquito-spread West Nile virus and ever-present threat of killer bees. Getting started will require basic tools and materials, such as a miter saw, screen rollers, various screen replacement parts, and a selection of fiberglass and aluminum screen rolls in various widths. The business can be operated from an enclosed trailer or van to provide protection from inclement weather. In terms of marketing, a mobile screen repair service should try to establish alliances with companies and individuals that require screen repairs and replacements on a regular basis. These include residential and commercial property management firms, condominium strata corporations, apartment complexes, government institutions, and renovation contractors. The profit potential is excellent, as there is limited competition and consumer demand for screen repairs and replacements is proven.

The Blue Book, www.thebluebook.com: Directory service listing manufactures and distributors of screening materials, parts, and equipment.

77. Used Fitness Equipment Sales

The time has never been better than now to start a home business that buys and resells for a profit previously owned fitness equipment. Millions of people across North America are striving to become more fit, and obviously fitness equipment such as treadmills, steppers, elliptical trainers, and exercise bikes play a major role in this pursuit. Fitness equipment can be purchased at garage sales, gym closeouts, auction and estate sales, and via newspaper classified ads. Reselling the fitness equipment for a profit is also very easy because it can be advertised for free in many community newspapers, on community bulletin boards, and through flier distribution. This is a business that will be promoted by word-of-mouth, and it won't take long until the telephone is ringing off the hook with people calling about what they want.

Fitness Equipment Trader, www.fitnessequipment trader.com: Online fitness equipment auction and classified ads service bringing buyers and sellers of fitness equipment and related equipment together.

78. Draft Proofing Service

Save homeowners money. Help the environment by reducing energy consumption. Create a more comfortable living environment for homeowners. Build a successful and profitable homebased business. You can accomplish all this and more by starting your own residential draft proofing service. Create a report to present homeowners that explains the recommended draft-proofing measures that could save them money on heating and cooling energy costs. These repairs could include increased insulation and ventilation, caulking, installation of door and window weather striping, replacement of electrical wall receptacles to draft proof versions, and even replacement of old doors and windows to new high-efficiency models. Providing you have the experience and tools required, you can carry out these repairs. If not, the repairs could be contracted to qualified local handyman or renovation contractor. Ideally, draft-proofing services are best marketed by establishing working relationships with utility companies, real estate brokers, home inspectors, renovation contractors, and property management firms, all of which can recommend your service to their clients.

Building Performance Contractors Association, www.home-performance.org: Members receive industry information, advice, and support.

79. Equities Day Trader

With the advent and wide use of the Internet, an entirely new homebased self-employment opportunity has surfaced. This business has the potential to generate six figure incomes for everyday Americans as day traders of equities and commodities. However, this opportunity is certainly has a risky downside, as the potential is also great to lose money, especially for the novice and inexperienced trader. The key to successfully earning an income as an equity day trader is to gain as much knowledge about the industry as possible. Specialize in a specific type of stock or commodities trading, have considerable investment capital to get rolling, and, most importantly nerves of steel and an understanding of what goes up must come down. Remember, most day traders go for short gains, buy early and sell out the same day. Holding overnight is too much risk, especially for heavily invested traders in unstable market conditions. Of course, also never forget the golden rule of stock and commodities trading: Never risk more than you can afford to lose.

Electronic Traders Association, www.electronic-trader. org: Members receive industry information, advice, and support.

80. Pool and Hot Tub Service

There are millions of swimming pools and hot tubs in North America, and they all have one thing in common—they must be cleaned and maintained on a regular basis in order to work properly and be safe for the occupants to use. A pool and hot tub maintenance service can be marketed in all traditional advertising mediums and by all promotional methods. However, as a fast start method to secure paying customers quickly, consider distributing fliers or coupons throughout your local community. The fliers or coupons should feature free pool and hot tub water safety tests for owners. The safety test would simply be checking the water for toxins and recommending any corrective measures that can be taken to fix the problem. The true purpose of the free water safety test is, of course, to gain clients for the service on a regular monthly basis.

Pool and Spa Online, www.poolandspa.com: Swimming pool and spa supplies, chemicals, industry information, resources, and links.

81. For-Sale-by-Owner Consultant

Many people attempt to sell their own homes, properties, and cottages every year. While some are successful, many are not. This fact creates a fantastic opportunity to start a for-sale-by-owner consulting business to assist these people in selling their homes quickly and for top dollar. Your duty is to instruct clients how to prepare their home for listing, help them establish a value, teach them how to market their property, instruct them on the finer points of hosting an open house, and provide them with template forms that can be used to write an offer and sale agreement. Ideally, the venture is suited for those with a real estate or sales background. Securing clients is as easy as calling people that currently have their homes for-sale-by-owner and by advertising locally in the newspaper in the Real Estate section. Charge clients a flat fee for providing the service, and charge separately for extras like printing fliers, creating for-sale and open-house signs, and listings on your homes for-sale-by-owner Web site and in any for-sale-by-owner publications that you print and distribute.

Entrepreneur Online, www.entrepreneur.com: Online resource center for small business.

82. Mail Order Sales

Mail order sales is still one of the best home business opportunities to get started and the best products to sell mail order are those that fill a niche in the marketplace and are typically not readily available at local bricks and mortar retailers. The products should have high profit margins, pack and ship well, have mass appeal within the niche target market, and preferably be a product that unlocks a mystery or helps people to attain a goal. Good products include building plans, how-to reports, herbs and home remedies, fishing lures and products, books, music, kitchen items, and special recipes. You can reach your target audience for your products by launching a direct mail campaign, advertising in

publications read by your target audience, and promoting your goods on Web sites that are visited by your target audience—and of course by establishing your own mail order product catalog and building a mailing list for it.

Info USA, www.infousa.com: Billed as the world's largest suppler of mailing lists, all of which are indexed by consumer, business, industry, hobby, geographic, and demographic classifications.

Publicly Accessible Mailing Lists, www.paml.net: Directory service listing information about 6,900 public mailing lists.

83. Home Crafts Business

Calling all crafts enthusiasts, put your creative artistic skills to work for you by creating a multitude of nifty craft items that can be sold for big profits to those of us who are less than crafty. From a simple home workspace, you can create craft items like specialty soaps, scented candles, pottery, woodcarvings and turnings, Christmas decorations, woven baskets, or stained glass items. Once completed, these craft items and decorations can be sold online, through mail order, at craft shows, and by renting kiosk space in malls during the holidays. Invest the profits you earn into more equipment and inventory so that you can grow your part-time crafts business into a full-time, profitable business concern.

Crafts Reports Magazine Online, www.craftsreport.com: Print and electronic magazine serving the crafts industry by providing information, products, services, resources, and links.

84. Packing Service

Let's face, it the worst aspect of moving is packing and unpacking—slow, tedious, and back-breaking work. And that's great news if you're the kind of person that is not afraid of a little hard work and looking for a simple home business venture. Moving companies will be your main source of work because they can subcontract you to provide packing services or refer you to their clients. Regardless, your billing rate should be in the range of $15 to $20 per hour, and you can earn additional money by selling packing supplies and by hiring additional people to work as packers.

Entrepreneur Online, www.entrepreneur.com: Online resource center for small business.

85. Online Sales

The real question is not what can be sold online for a profit, but what can't be sold online for a profit. The answer, not much. New, used, overstocked, slightly damaged, or one of a kind, just about anything can be sold online, confirmed by eBay, which has already turned out hundreds of new millionaires and thousands more that are making six figure incomes selling everything from boats to little knickknacks on the wildly popular shopping and auction site. But just like in the bricks-and-mortar shopping world, to truly succeed what you are selling will have to fill a niche, be highly desirable or collectable, or be priced low enough to spur impulse buying. Other considerations will be whether or not to create your own shopping Web site, open a storefront in an existing online shopping mall or auction, or strictly rely on e-mail marketing to promote your goods and reach your target audience.

eBay, www.ebay.com: Online auction and retail cyber storefronts offering every imaginable product available. Offers entrepreneurs selling opportunities.

Amazon, www.amazon.com: Online retailer of books, music, clothes, and lots more. Offers entrepreneurs selling opportunities.

86. Hand Painted Products

Capitalize on your artist abilities by starting a home business that involves hand painting various products for resale in the retail and corporate gifts industry. You can specialize in watercolor, acrylics, oils, or all paint mediums and depict landscapes, people, abstracts, or any subject that tickles your fancy. Products that can be hand painted include calendars, greeting cards, report covers, flowerpots, wood and metal crafts, and glassware. Painted household, craft, and garden items can be placed on consignment with local retailers or sold to retailers on a bulk and wholesale basis. These same products can be sold to consumers directly at craft shows, through

mail order, and via online malls. Hand painted items that are specific to the corporate gift market can be promoted through business networking meetings and by launching a direct marketing campaign aimed squarely at companies and professionals that routinely send out gifts to clients. The main requirement to ensure success is, of course, artistic ability.

Create for Less, www.createforless.com: Wholesale craft supplies, industry information, resources and links.

87. Yard Maintenance Service

Offer clients a host of yard and property clean-up and maintenance services by starting a general yard maintenance service. Cut grass, provide rubbish removal, trim trees and hedges, and offer lawn aeration and garden tilling. Concentrate your marketing efforts at securing customers that are prepared to sign up for a regular service and offer financial incentives to persuade them to do so. Most of the equipment needed to operate a yard maintenance service is relatively inexpensive to purchase, and to keep start-up costs to a minimum this equipment can be purchased secondhand or rented on an as needed basis. Averaged out, you should have no problem charging in the range of $20 to $30 per hour. Yard maintenance can be hard work, so there should be no shortage of homeowners prepared to part with a few dollars per month to have their yards professionally maintained and kept in tip-top condition, providing you offer great service at fair rates.

Home Contracting Directory, www.home-contracting.com: National online referral service indexed geographically matching consumers with qualified yard maintenance contractors.

88. Wood Floor Sanding and Repairs

Many do-it-yourself homeowners are more than happy to stain and finish hardwood floors. However, when it comes to sanding off old finishes, repairing, and fixing deep scratches on hardwood floors, that's another story entirely. Let's face it, sanding hardwood floors can be a back-breaking task, and it also requires a certain amount of experience and skill to do the job right. These are good reasons for starting your own hardwood floor sanding service. Of course, there is the skill requirement to take into account, but with practice on your own, family, and friends' hardwood floors, this skill can definitely be learned in a relatively short period of time. To keep start-up costs to a minimum, you can rent the required floor sanding equipment as needed until the business is established and generating revenues. Floor sanding is billed on a per square foot basis, so you will want to call around to find out rates in your area.

Floor Sanding Online, www.floorsanding.com: Floor sanding equipment and supplies for sale, as well as, floor sanding industry information, resources, and links.

89. Power Washing Service

A power washing service can be extremely profitable. The only fixed costs are a telephone, liability insurance, transportation, and the occasional equipment repair. The income that can be achieved will depend on how much power washing is completed, but there are hundreds of items that can be cleaned using power washing equipment, including:

- Concrete, pavement, and paving stone driveways, walkways, and parking lots
- Recreational vehicles, mobile homes, cars, trucks, and boats
- Store signs, awnings, and outdoor furniture
- Decks, patios, siding, and metal roofs
- Construction and farm equipment

The true key to success will lie in your ability to secure repeat clients. It costs 100 times as much to find 100 clients as opposed to finding one client and selling them 100 times. Focusing marketing efforts on companies and individuals that could become regular customers is by far the best approach.

Carved Stone, www.carvedstone.com: Web site dedicated to serving professionals within the power washing industry with information, products, services, support, resources, and links of interest.

90. Computer Specialist

It's time for you to get in on the multi-billion dollar, ever-growing computer industry. Working from home you can buy and sell new and used computers for a profit or rent specialized computer equipment such as notebooks to consumers and businesses. Call on businesses of all sizes and offer computer cleaning and installation of security devices. Start a homebased or mobile computer repair and software trouble-shooting business. Or team with computer retailers and offer their customer computer delivery, set-up, and instructional training. In terms of computer-related businesses, the sky really is the limit. Of course, all of the above will require training and experience to pull together, as well as a cash investment in equipment in order to establish yourself properly. But the future for computer-related businesses could not look brighter, and earnings in the six-figure range are certainly attainable for determined entrepreneurs.

National Association of Computer Consultant Businesses, www.naccb.org: Members receive industry information, advice, and support.

91. Small Business Advertising Agency

Put your advertising skills and experience to good work by starting an advertising agency focused on assisting home business and small business owners create knockout advertising campaigns that get results. Creating cost-effective advertising campaigns is one of the toughest challenges that most new and existing small business owners face because advertising is an all-encompassing task that requires experience and creative skills that most small business owners do not have. Small business owners are bombarded daily by salespeople with the greatest advertising offer to date. Where does the average small business owner even learn to get started and what is right for their specific business? Capitalizing on your advertising experience, you can create specialized advertising campaigns for clients that will directly reach their target market and within their budget. Advertising is costly, and small business owners cannot waste money on advertising that does not hit the target.

American Association of Advertising Agencies, www.aaaa.org: Members receive advertising industry information, advice, and support.

92. Photography Service

Providing you have the skills and equipment necessary there are a multitude of photography-related home businesses that can be started and operated with success—commercial photography, aerial photography, portrait photography, weddings and special events photographer and videogapher, pet photography, extreme sports videographer, actors and models portfolios, video editing service, and a security photo identification service. Market your photography service by networking at business and social functions, advertising in your local newspaper and telephone directory, and by establishing alliances with like-minded business people such as wedding and event planners, and small business owners that can help spread the word. Full-time photographers that become known in their field of expertise routinely earn six figure incomes.

Advertising Photographers Association of America, www.apanational.com: Members receive industry information, advice, and support.

Wedding and Event Videographers Association International, www.weva.com: Members receive industry information, advice, and support.

International Freelance Photographers Organization, www.aipress.com: Members receive industry information, advice, and support.

93. Home Security

Much like a photography business, home security also offers innovative entrepreneurs a nearly unlimited number of related start-ups, such as sales and installations of window security bars and rollshutters, home alarm sales and installations, locksmith, crime prevention training, security engraving service, or closed circuit surveillance camera sales and installations. Of course, the prerequisites for most will be training, experience, and in some instances, certification. Home security is one of the fasted growing segments of the home services and home products industry and for good reason. Property and violent crime is a fact of life in our society and people want their families to be safe. Market your home security business through traditional forms of advertising, as well as offering free security seminars in your field of expertise to secure sales leads. Also

consider writing a home security column for your local newspaper because the weekly exposure is great publicity for your business and positions you as an expert in the industry.

The International Association of Professional Security Consultants, www.iapsc.org: Members receive industry information, advice, and support.

94. Fashion Design and Manufacturing

Independent fashion designers, manufacturers, and merchandisers have been springing up all over the country in the past few years. Much of this growth can be attributed to the Internet—now these junior fashion houses have a way to get their designs in front of a global audience, leveling the playing field with their larger competitors. From a homebased design and manufacturing workspace (e.g., spare bedroom), you can design, manufacture, and market custom handbags, hats, jackets, bathing suits, belts, costume jewelry, shoes, shirts, elegant formal wear, business wear, or casual social wear. Remember, at the root of the fashion industry is buzz. Therefore, spend considerable time figuring out how you will get your fashion creations, be they clothes or accessories, to someone that can create the buzz. These someone's should be entertainment or sports celebrities and fashion writers and editors. As much as the fashion industry is about creating great fashions, it is equally about creating great publicity.

National Association of Fashion and Accessory Designers, www.nafad.com: Members receive industry information, advice, and support.

95. Antique Furniture Sales

Dig through garage sales, attend estate sales, and scan your local newspaper classifieds to find truly outstanding antique and collectibles bargains. Resell these same items for a profit by placing selected ads in antique-related magazines and newspapers, creating your own Web site, listing the antiques in other Web sites, and by consigning your best items to well-attended antique and collectibles auctions. Antique furniture and collectibles sales is a fantastic home business venture to get rolling. Work your own hours. Keep your present job. Investments are minimal and so is the operating overhead. It's the perfect home business for people that know antique bargains when they find them. You will need suitable transportation like a truck or van to pick up and delivery inventory, but secondhand trucks in good condition can be bought for a few thousand dollars. And if you have the credentials, skills, and equipment, extra revenue can also be earned by providing antique and collectibles appraisals and antique restorations.

Antique and Collectibles Dealers Association, www.acda.org: Members receive industry information, advice, and support.

96. Cleaning Service

Cleaning services still rank as the most common new home business start-ups and with good reason. They're cheap to get going, easy to operate, able to generate excellent revenues and profits, easy to expand, in high demand in a growth industry, and light on special skills to master. You can operate a residential cleaning service focused on homes and apartments or a commercial cleaning service focused on stores and offices. Or you can offer a more specialized cleaning service providing any number of options from carpet cleaning to ceiling cleaning to blind cleaning and construction site clean-up. Your options are wide open. On average, most cleaners charge in the vicinity of $20 per hour and more for specialized services like floor stripping and waxing and restaurant hood cleaning. Promoting the business requires no more than knocking on doors and asking for business with commercial clients. Residential cleaners can rely on print ads, fliers, and coupons to get the word out.

Cleaning and Maintenance Management Magazine Online, www.cmmonline.com: Print and electronic magazine featuring cleaning industry information, resources, and links.

97. Specialty Travel Agent

Heli-skiing, ice climbing, deep sea diving, dude ranch, or a Mayan ruins tour, arrange the adventure of a lifetime for clients by starting a specialty travel agency. Forget boring cruise ships and forgettable all-inclusive hotels on the Mexican Riviera, and concentrate instead on seeking out and offering clients

the most unique vacation adventures available. Market your adventure vacation packages through company newsletters, online in chat rooms and forums, and by e-mail broadcasting. Remuneration can be earned by charging clients a fee for making arrangements and organizing the vacation or by charging host companies and accommodation providers a fee for marketing their accommodations and activities to your clients. Either way, once established, a substantial living can be earned by arranging an adventure vacation for people that are seeking something out of the ordinary.

The National Association of Commissioned Travel Agents, www.nacta.com:. Represents independent homebased travel agents and members receive industry information, advice, and support.

98. Freelance Writer

Some writers' Web sites peg the number of freelance writers in the United States at more than 100,000 at any given time, and while the competition certainly is steep, the rewards can be great financial compensation and a fulfilling career for those that make it. When asked, most successful freelancers will tell you that if you want to make it, you must specialize. Pick a writing topic that you know, practice, and keep submitting. You could specialize in business, sports, entertainment, real estate, financial, health, retirement, travel, or venture into more well-defined niche markets. Rates can be based on a per word scale or per feature article, and expect to write a few freebies to get your name out there and have publication credits. The best paying markets tend to be major monthly magazines. The least attractive pay is usually for content for Web publishing.

Freelance Online, www.freelanceonline.com: Online resource center for freelance writers.

99. Event Planner

Attention to detail, well-organized, good communicators, and creative—all personality traits shared by event planners. If this describes you, perhaps you should consider starting your own event planning service. In a nutshell, event planners are responsible for organizing and hosting special events for their clients, and duties can include creating and sending out invitations, selecting the event location, decorations, and props, arranging entertainers and speakers, selecting caterers and creating menus, and just about every thing else that is required to pull a special event together and put it on without a hitch. You can specialize in planning social events like wedding anniversaries, birthdays, graduations, and award ceremonies. Or you can focus on corporate event planning including luncheons, parties, grand openings, investor meetings, and trade shows. Networking, networking, and more networking will be your main marketing tool for attracting and securing new business.

Event Planner Online, www.event-planner.com: Directory service listing event planners, information about how to start and market an event planning service, and industry information and links.

ENTREPRENEUR MAGAZINE'S ULTIMATE START-UP DIRECTORY

Additional home business start-up ideas can be found in *Entrepreneur Magazine's Ultimate Start-Up Directory* by James Stephenson (Entrepreneur Press). The *Ultimate Start-Up Directory* features 1,350 great business start-up ideas representing more than 30 industries, such as retail, manufacturing, advertising, sports, recreation, travel, and transportation and includes hundreds of home business opportunities. *The Ultimate Start-Up Directory* is available online from Entrepreneur Press, www.entrepreneurpress.com; Amazon, www.amazon.com; Barnes and Noble, www.barnesandnoble; and at bookstores nationwide.

GETTING STARTED WITH 99 HOME FRANCHISE OPPORTUNITIES

The following 99 home franchise opportunities represent various industries, budgets, and skill levels. You will find the name of the franchise followed by complete contact information, including telephone numbers and Web sites, along with a brief description of the business activity the franchise is engaged in. The majority of the homebased franchises featured here are well-known operations with many years of experience and multiple operating units.

However, this list does not endorse any one specific franchise. As is true of any new business start-up, it is your responsibility to apply for and receive a business license or permit, as well as register or incorporate your business at the local, state, or federal level. A major component of starting a home business is to research all the legal elements and aspects of the business venture, including, but not limited to, the franchisor, licenses and permits, liability insurance, zoning and building-use codes, fire and health regulations, employee regulations, and certificates of training. A successful entrepreneur is one who carefully researches and plans every aspect of a new business venture, including the financial investment needed to start the home business and the working capital required to achieve positive cash flow. The following are 99 home franchise opportunities.

1. Budget Blinds Inc.
733 W. Taft Avenue
Orange, CA 92865
(800) 420-5374
www.budgetblinds.com
Budget Blinds provides custom window coverings sales and installations.

2. Wee Watch Private Home Day Care
105 Main Street
Unionville, ON L3R 2G1
(800) 663-6072
www.weewatch.com
Wee Watch provides in-home day care services catering to children of all ages.

3. Racing Limos
8242 Laurel Lakes Boulevard
Naples, FL 34119
(866) 746-5466
www.racinglimos.com
Racing Limos provides unique race car themed limousine services for all special occasions.

4. Maui Wowi Smoothies
5601 S. Broadway, Suite 200
Littleton, CO 80121

(888) 862-8555
www.mauiwowi.com
Maui Wowi Smoothies sells all-natural specialty fruit beverages on a mobile basis.

5. House Doctors

6355 Kemper Road, Suite 250
Cincinnati, OH 45241
(800) 319-3359
www.housedoctors.com
House Doctors provides handyman and home repair services for residential clients.

6. Safe Kids Cards

17100B Bear Valley Road, Suite 238
Victorville, CA 92392
(909) 496-9982
www.safekidscard.com
Safe Kids Cards specializes in child, adult, and pet identification cards, using CD-ROMs the size of business cards with digital photos, fingerprints, and information, for use in emergency.

7. Have Signs Will Travel

1595A Ocean Avenue, Suite 5
Bohemia, NY 11716
(631) 567-6801
www.gethswt.com
Have Signs Will Travel designs and sells vinyl signs and banners for clients onsite from a mobile sign factory.

8. Wag 'n' Tails

12634 Industrial Park Drive
Granger, IN 46530
(800) 513-0304
www.wagntails.com
Wag 'n' Tails provides mobile on-site dog grooming services from specially equipped vans.

9. Greenland Irrigation

150 Ambleside Drive
London, ON N6G 4R1
(800) 661-0221

www.greenlandirrigation.com
Greenland Irrigation sell, installs, and services lawn sprinklers and irrigation systems for commercial and residential clients.

10. Oil Butler International

1599 Route 22 West
Union, NJ 07083
(908) 687-3283
www.oilbutlerinternational.com
Oil Butler provides mobile on-site automotive oil change services.

11. Complete Music

7877 L Street
Omaha, NE 68127
(800) 843-3866
www.cmusic.com
Complete Music provides mobile disc jockey services for all special occasions and events.

12. Chem-Dry Carpet and Upholstery Cleaning

1530 N. 1000 West Street
Logan, UT 84093
(877) 307-8233
www.chemdry.com
Chem-Dry provides unique carpet and upholstery cleaning services on a mobile basis from specially equipped service vehicles.

13. Checkmate Systems

661 St. Andrews Boulevard
Charleston, SC 29407
(800) 964-6298
www.checkmatepeo.com
Checkmate Systems offers clients employee leasing programs.

14. Bark Busters

5901 Vine Street S.
Greenwood Village, CO 80121
(877) 280-7100
www.barkbusters.com
Bark Busters provides in-home and on-site dog training programs for all dog breeds.

15. Jani-King
16885 Dallas Parkway
Addison, TX 75001
(800) 552-5264
www.janiking.com
Jani-King provides professional commercial cleaning services.

16. Christmas Décor
PO Box 5946
Lubbock, TX 79408-5946
(800) 687-9551
www.christmasdecor.net
Christmas Décor provides holiday and special event interior and exterior decorating services.

17. Weed Man
11 Grand Marshall Drive
Scarborough, ON M1B 5N6
(416) 269-5754
www.weed-man.com
Weed Man provides lawn maintenance services.

18. Internet Marketing Group
1470 Jamboree Road, Suite 107
Newport Beach, CA 92660
(877) 803-3003
www.imgfranchises.com
Internet Marketing Group provides Web site development and Internet marketing services for small business owners and professionals.

19. Ledger Plus
401 St. Francis Street
Tallahassee, FL 32301
(888) 643-1348
www.ledgerplus.com
Ledger Plus provides tax and bookkeeping services for individuals, organizations, and small business owners.

20. Impressions on Hold
4880 S. Lewis Avenue, Suite 200
Tulsa, OK 74105-5100
(800) 580-4653
www.impressionsonhold.com
Impressions on Hold offers clients professionally produced and recorded telephone on-hold advertising message services.

21. Property Damage Appraisers
6100 Southwest Boulevard, Suite 200
Fort Worth, TX 76109-3964
(800) 749-7324, ext 23
www.pdahomeoffice.com
Property Damage Appraisers provides appraisal services to insurance companies.

22. Stretch-n-Grow
9190 Oakhurst, Suite 3A
Seminole, FL 33776
(727) 596-7614
www.stretch-n-grow.com
Stretch-n-Grow provides on-site fun fitness programs and activities for kids.

23. ATM Franchise
3100 Steeles Avenue, Suite 201
Toronto, ON L3R 8T3
(866) 557-5505
www.atmfranchise.com
ATM Franchise installs and services automated teller machines within retail outlets.

24. Pop-a-Lock
101 Harding Street, Suite 205
Lafayette, LA 70503
(337) 233-6211
www.pop-a-lock.com
Pop-A-Lock provides roadside assistance services, car door unlocking, and general locksmith services on a mobile basis.

25. Pets Are Inn
5100 Edina Boulevard, Suite 206
Minneapolis, MN 55439
(800) 248-7387
www.petsareinn.com

Pets Are Inn provides business travels and vacationers with in-home pet boarding services.

26. Snap-On Tools

PO Box 1410
Kenosha, WI 53141-1410
(800) 775-7630
www.snapon.com
Snap-On Tools sells tools and equipment to the automotive repair industry from specially equipped mobile showroom vans.

27. United States Seamless

2001 First Avenue N.
Fargo, ND 58102-2426
(800) 615-9318
www.usseamless.com
United States Seamless sells and installs seamless steel siding and gutters, as well as vinyl replacement windows on site.

28. Kitchen Tune-Up

813 Circle Drive
Aberdeen, SD 57401
(800) 333-6385
www.kitchentuneup.com
Kitchen Tune-Up provides kitchen cabinet, door, and countertop repairs and facelifts.

29. Chips Away

1536 Sawmill Run Boulevard
Pittsburgh, PA 15210
(800) 837-2447
www.touchup.biz
Chips Away provides on-site automotive paint touch up and repair services.

30. The Mad Science Group

8360 Bouganville, Suite 101
Montreal, Quebec H3R 2E8
(514) 344-4181
www.madscience.org
The Mad Science Group hosts on-site interactive science shows for children.

31. Jet-Black

25 Cliff Road W., Suite 103
Burnsville, MN 55337
(888) 538-2525
www.jet-black.com
Jet-Black provides residential and commercial asphalt driveway repair and sealing services.

32. Full Circle Image

6256 34th Avenue, NW
Rochester, MN 55901
(800) 584-7244
www.fullcircleimage.com
Full Circle Image sells and delivers remanufactured laser toner, ink jet, and printer ribbon cartridges directly to businesses and individuals.

33. Worldwide Express

2501 Cedar Springs Road, Suite 450
Dallas, TX 75201
(800) 758-7447
www.wwex.com
Worldwide Express provides discounted airfreight services to businesses and individuals.

34. Rezcity.com

560 Sylvan Avenue
Englewood Cliffs, NJ 07632-3104
(201) 567-8500
www.rezcity.biz
Rezcity.com is an e-regional city guide providing visitors with travel products and services.

35. Video Masters

2200 Dunbarton Drive, Suite D
Chesapeake, VA 23325
(800) 836-9461
www.videomasters.info.com
Video Masters provides video photography services to businesses and consumers, as well as film-to-tape transfers and editing services

36. The Screenmobile

72050 Corporate Way

Thousand Palms, CA 92276

(866) 540-5800

www.screenmobile.com

The Screenmobile builds new window and door screens, as well as repairs existing window and door screens on-site for residential and commercial customers.

37. Homewatch Caregivers

2865 S. Colorado Boulevard

Denver, CO 80222

(800) 777-9770

www.homewatch-intl.com

Homewatch Caregivers provides in-home, non-medical care services for the elderly, disabled, and people recovering from illness and injuries.

38. Mr. Plant

1106 Second Street

Encinitas, CA 92024

(888) 974-0488

www.mrplant.com

Mr. Plant sells and rents indoor plants, as well as offers interior plant maintenance services for consumers and businesses.

39. Cruise Planners

3300 University Drive, Suite 602

Coral Springs, FL 33065

(888) 582-2150

www.cruiseagents.com

Cruise Planners is a homebased cruise-only travel agency.

40. The Buyer's Agent

1255A Lynnfield Road, Suite 273

Memphis, TN 38119

(800) 766-8728

www.forbuyers.com

The Buyer's Agent provides homeowners with information and services to help them sell their homes and properties.

41. Happy and Healthy Products

1600 S. Dixie, Suite 200

Boca Raton, FL 33432

(800) 764-6114

www.fruitfull.com

Happy and Healthy Products sells frozen fruit bars to retailers on a wholesale basis.

42. Furniture Medic

860 Ridge Lake Boulevard

Memphis, TN 38120

(901) 820-8600

www.furnituremedicfranchise.com

Furniture Medic provides on-site residential and commercial furniture repair services.

43. The Visual Image

100 East Brockman Way

Sparta, TN 38583

(800) 344-0323

www.thevisualimageinc.com

The Visual Image is a full-service mobile portrait photography service.

44. Candy Bouquet

423 E. Third Street

Little Rock, AR 72201

(877) 226-3901

www.candybouquet.com

Candy Bouquet designs and sells specialty candy gift baskets and bouquets.

45. The Perfect Wedding Guide

1206 N C.R., Suite 427

Longwood, FL 32750

(888) 222-7433

www.thepwg.com

The Perfect Wedding Guide publishes regional buyers guides featuring wedding and honeymoon information, and products and services advertisements.

46. Aloette Cosmetics

4900 Highlands Parkway

Smyrna, GA 30082

(800) 256-3883

www.aloette.com

Aloette Cosmetics sells Aloe Vera-based skin care products directly to consumers.

47. Posi Grip
7411 East Sixth Avenue, Suite 205
Scottsdale, AZ 85251
(800) 847-9605
www.posigrip.com
Posi Grip provides residential and commercial clients with anti-slip surface coatings.

48. Ductbusters
3054 Weaver Park Drive
Clearwater, FL 33761-2400
(800) 786-3828
www.ductbusters.com
Ductbusters provides on-site residential and commercial duct-cleaning services.

49. Tax Recovery Group
1880 Office Club Pointe
2nd Floor, South Wing
Colorado Springs, CO 80920
(800) 714-3504
www.trginc.com
Tax Recovery Group helps individual and business clients to recover overpaid taxes.

50. Computer Moms International
537 Woodward Street, Suite D
Austin, TX 78704-7324
(866) 447-3666
www.computermoms.com
Computer Moms provides on-site, one-on-one computer training and support for individuals and business owners.

51. i9 Sports
1463 Oakfield Drive, Suite 135
Brandon, FL 33511
(813) 662-6773
www.i9sports.com/corporate
i9 Sports organizes amateur sports events, including sports leagues, tournaments, and clinics in various sports.

52. Outdoor Connection
10W. Rutledge
Yates Center, KS 66783
(316) 625-3466
www.outdoor-connection.com
Outdoor Connection organizes hunting and fishing trips for companies and for individual sportsmen.

53. Perma-Glaze
163S. Research Loop Road, Suite 160
Tucson, AZ 85710
(800) 332-7397
www.permaglaze.com
Perma-Glaze provides on-site bathroom sink, tub, and shower restoration services from a mobile work van.

54. Dent Doctor
11301 W. Markham Street
Little Rock, AR 72211
(800) 946-3368
www.dentdoctor.com
Dent Doctor provides on-site paintless automotive dent and ding repair services for consumers and car lot owners.

55. Lil Angels Photography
6080 Quince Road
Memphis, TN 38119
(800) 358-9101
www.lilangelsphoto.com
Lil Angels Photography provides full service on-site children's photography services.

56. Archadeck
2112 W. Laburnum Avenue, Suite 100
Richmond, VA 23727
(800) 789-3325
www.archadeck.com
Archadeck designs and installs custom decks, sunrooms, and gazebos.

57. Grand Gatherings
417 Commercial Court
Venice, FL 34292

(941) 484-1312
www.aboutgrandgatherings.com
Grand Gatherings provides no-fee, all-occasion event planning services for consumers and corporate clients.

58. Mr. Appliance
1020 N. University Parks Drive
Waco, TX 76707
(800) 290-1422
www.mrappliance.com
Mr. Appliance provides mobile household appliance repair services.

59. Palm Beach Specialty Coffee
3965 Investment Lane, Suite A-8
West Palm Beach, FL 33404
(800) 291-5722
www.palmbeachcoffee.com
Palm Beach Coffee provides coffee machines and specialty coffee sales.

60. Elephant House
160 Pine Knoll Drive
Austin, TX 7875
(800) 276-2405
www.elephanthouse.com
Elephant House distributes a custom greeting card line to retail accounts.

61. Dr. Vinyl and Associates
821 NW Commerce
Lee's Summit, MO 64086
(800) 531-6600
www.drvinyl.com
Dr. Vinyl provides on-site automotive and boat leather, fabric, and vinyl repair services.

62. Shield Security Systems
1690 Walden Avenue
Buffalo, NY 14225
(716) 681-6677
www.shieldsecurity.net
Shield Security Systems sells, installs, and monitors home and commercial alarm systems.

63. Great Gumballs
11081 Zaring Court
Cincinnati, OH 45241
(513) 205-4887
www.greatgumballs.com
Great Gumballs vending machines.

64. Bevinco Bar Systems
505 Consumers Road, Suite 510
Toronto, ON M2J 4VCanada
(888) 238-4626
www.bevinco.com
Bevinco Bar Systems provides on-site liquor inventory control services to commercial clients.

65. Stork News of America
1305 Hope Mills Road
Fayetteville, NC 28304
(800) 633-6395
www.storknews.com
Stork News provides newborn announcement and yard display services.

66. Adventures in Advertising
400 Crown Colony Drive
Quincy, MA 02169
(800) 432-6332
www.advinadv.com
Adventures in Advertising sells advertising specialties and promotional items.

67. Permacrete Systems
21 Williams Avenue
Dartmouth, NS B3B 1X3
(800) 565-5325
www.permacrete.com
Permacrete Systems restores concrete surfaces and structures for residential and commercial customers.

68. Sunbelt Business Advisors
474 Wando Park Boulevard, Suite 204
Mt. Pleasant, SC 29464
(800) 771-7866
www.sunbeltnetwork.com

Sunbelt Business Advisors is a full-service business brokerage company.

69. Showhomes of America
5460 McGinnis Village Place, Suite 104
Alpharetta, GA 30005
(770) 391-0852
www.showhomes.com
Showhomes of America supplies people and furniture to occupy vacant home listed for sale.

70. The Entrepreneur's Source
900 Main Street S. Building 2
Southbury, CT 0648
(800) 289-0086
www.theesource.com
The Entrepreneur's Source provides consulting and guidance to people seeking self-employment opportunities.

71. Window Genie
350 Gest Street
Cincinnati, OH 45203
(800) 700-0022
www.windowgenie.com
Window Genie provides window washing and pressure cleaning services from mobile, fully equipped service vehicles.

72. Two Men and a Truck
3400 Belle Chase Way
Lansing, MI 48911
(800) 345-1070
www.twomenandatruck.com
Two Men and a Truck provides local residential and commercial packing and moving services.

73. American Leak Detection
88 Research Drive, Suite 100
Palm Springs, CA 92262
(800) 755-6697
www.leakbusters.com
American Leak Detection provides water, gas, and oil leak detection services.

74. Jazzercise
2460 Impala Drive
Carlsbad, CA 9200
(760) 476-1750
www.jazzercise.com
Jazzercise is the founder of the original dance for fitness programs.

75. Coffee News
PO Box 8444
Bangor, ME 04402-8444
(207) 941-0860
www.coffeenewsusa.com
Coffee News publishes a free regional entertainment newsletter supported by advertising sales.

76. Superglass Windshield Repair
6101 Chancellor Drive, Suite 200
Orlando, FL 32809
(407) 240-1920
www.sgwr.com
Superglass provides on-site windshield repair services.

77. Aire-Master of America
PO Box 2310
Nixa, MO 65714
(800) 525-0957
www.airemaster.com
Aire-Master provides odor control and restroom fixture cleaning services and products.

78. Critter Control
9435 E. Cherry Bend Road
Traverse City, MI 49684
(231) 947-2400
www.crittercontrol.com
Critter Control provides wildlife control services.

79. Sandler Sales Institute
10411 Stevenson Road
Stevenson, MD 21153
(800) 669-3537
www.sandler.com
Sandler Sales Institute provides on-site sales and management training.

80. Quik Internet

170 E. 17th Street, Suite 101
Costa Mesa, CA 92627-3701
(949) 548-2171
www.quik.com
Quik Internet provides Web design, Internet access, and online marketing services to small business customers.

81. Pressed 4 Time

124 Boston Post Road
Sudbury, MA 01776
(800) 423-8711
www.pressed4time.com
Pressed 4 Time provides dry cleaning pick-up and delivery services.

82. Cartex

42816 Mound Road
Sterling Heights, MI 48314
(586) 739-4330
www.fabrion.net
Cartex provides leather and fabric repairs and restoration services for residential and commercial customers.

83. Border Magic

1503 Country Road, 2700 N.
Rantoul, IL 61866-9705
(877) 892-2954
www.bordermagic.com
Border Magic sells and installs seamless concrete landscape, parking lot, and walkway edging.

84. U-Build-It

12006 98th Avenue, NE, Suite 200
Kirkland, WA 98034
(425) 821-6200
www.ubuildit.com
U-Build-It provides homeowners with remodeling project management services.

85. WSI Internet

5915 Airport Road, Suite 300
Toronto, ON L4V 1T1 Canada
(905) 678-7588
www.wsicorporate.com
WSI Internet provides Internet consulting services for business clients.

86. Colors on Parade

642 Century Circle
Conway, SC 29526
(800) 726-5677
www.colorsfranchise.com
Colors On Parade provides mobile automotive detailing services for consumers and business.

87. Drama Kids

3225-B Corporate Court
Ellicott City, MD 21042
(410) 480-2015
www.dramakids.com
Drama Kids provides on-site drama classes for kids.

88. Interiors by Decorating Den

19100 Montgomery Avenue
Montgomery Village, MD 20866
(800) 686-6393
www.decoratingden.com
Decorating Den provides mobile on-site interior decorating services for residential customers.

89. Amerispec Home Inspection Services

889 Ridge Lake Boulevard
Memphis, TN 38120
(800) 426-2270
www.amerispecfranchise.com
AmeriSpec provides residential home inspection services.

90. Val-Pak Direct Marketing Systems

8605 Largo Lakes Drive
Largo, FL 33773
(800) 237-6266
www.valpak.com
Val-Pak provides small business owners and professionals with direct mail marketing and coupon delivery services.

91. American Pool Players Association

1000 Lake Boulevard, Suite 325
St. Louis, MO 63367
(636) 625-8611
www.poolplayers.com
American Pool Players Association provides pool tournament and pool association management services.

92. Energy Wise

215 Dutton Ave.
Sebastopol, CA 95472
(800) 553-6800
www.energywiseinc.com
Energy Wise provides homeowners with an annual major appliances preventive maintenance program, and sells air and water quality products.

93. Merry Maids

860 Ridge Lake Boulevard
Memphis, TN 38120
(800) 798-8000
www.merrymaids.com
Merry Maids provide residential cleaning services.

94. Enchanted Honeymoons

2927 S. 108th Street
Omaha, NE 68144
(800) 253-2863
www.enchantedhoneymoons.com
Enchanted Honeymoons provides unique honeymoon and leisure travel services.

95. Hydro Physics Pipe Inspection

1855 W. Union Avenue, Unit N
Englewood, CO 80110
(800) 781-3164
www.hydrophysics.com
Hydro Physics specializes in the video inspection of underground pipes for residential and commercial clients.

96. Wheelchair Getaways

PO Box 605
Versailles, KY 40383-0605
(800) 536-5518
www.wheelchairgetaways.com
Wheelchair Getaways rents wheelchair-accessible vans by the day, week, month, or year.

97. Mr. Rooter

1020 N. University Park Drive
Waco, TX 76707
(800) 298-6855
www.mrrooter.com
Mr. Rooter provides plumbing and drain cleaning services.

98. Proforma

8800 E. Pleasant Valley Road
Cleveland, OH 44131
(216) 520-8400
www.connectionwithproforma.com
ProForma sells specialty printing and promotional products.

99. Marad Fine Art

992 High Ridge Road
Stamford, CT 06905
(203) 322-7666
www.maradfineart.com
Marad Fine Art sells high-end, reproduction art directly to consumers.

Home Business Resources

UNITED STATES GOVERNMENT AGENCIES AND BUSINESS ASSOCIATIONS

United States Small Business Administration (SBA)
409 Third Street SW
Washington, DC 20416
(800) 827-5722
www.sba.org
The U.S. Small Business Administration provides new entrepreneurs and existing business owners with financial, technical, and management resources to start, operate, and grow a business. To find the local SBA office in your region, log on to www.sba.org/regions/states.html.

SBA Services and Products for Entrepreneurs
    U.S. SBA Small Business Start-Up Kit, www.sba. gov/starting/indexstartup.html.
    U.S. SBA Business Training Seminars and Courses, www.sba.gov/starting/indextraining.html.
    U.S. SBA Business Plan: Road Map to Success, www.sba.gov/indexbusplans.html.
    U.S. SBA Business Financing and Loan Program, www.sba.gov/financing

United States Patent and Trademark Office
Commissioners of Patents and Trademarks
PO Box 9
Washington, DC 20231
(800) 786-9199

www.uspto.gov
United States Copyright Office
Library of Congress
101 Independence Avenue SE
Washington, DC 20559-6000
(202) 707-3000
www.loc.gov/copyright

Internal Revenue Service (IRS)
United States Department of the Treasury
1111 Constitution Avenue NW
Washington, DC 20224
(202) 622-5164
www.irs.ustreas.gov

U.S. Department of Labor
200 Constitution Avenue NW Room S-1032
Washington, DC 20210
(202) 219-8211
www.dol.gov

Service Corps of Retired Executives (SCORE)
409 Third Street SW, 6th Floor
Washington, DC 20024
(800) 634-0245
www.score.org
SCORE, the Service Corps of Retired Executives is a nonprofit association in partnership with the Small Business Administration to provide aspiring entrepreneurs and business owners with free business counseling and mentoring programs.

The association consists of more than 11,000 volunteer business councilors in 389 regional chapters located throughout the United States. The SCORE team is comprised of seasoned professionals, mostly retired, representing a wide range of business experiences and backgrounds—from bank executives to CEO's of major international corporations. In addition to joining up for one or more of the many workshops SCORE hosts monthly you can also educate yourself though SCORE publications. Member coaches can even help you directly with a one-on-one coaching session to answer specific business questions and problems. SCORE is not limited to business management and operations information and help. Its members are also well versed in all sales and marketing methods. SCORE has many publications and training programs focused on ways to increase revenues and profits by utilizing various marketing techniques. By tapping into the SCORE network, you will be tapping into a wealth of free business knowledge and experience.

U.S. Chamber of Commerce
1615 H Street NW
Washington, DC 20062-2000
(202) 659-6000
www.uschamber.com
The U.S. Chamber of Commerce represents small businesses, corporations, and trade associations from coast to coast. Log on to its Web site to locate a regional branch office.

National Business Incubation Association (NBIA)
20 E. Circle Drive, Suite 190
Athens, OH 45701-3571
(704) 593-4331
www.nbia.org
In the United States, there are more than 900 business incubation programs and NBIA provides links to them. Additionally, NBIA assists entrepreneurs with information, education, and networking resources to help in both the early stages of business start-ups and the advanced stages of business growth.

National Association of Women Business Owners (NAWBO)
830-1100 Wayne Avenue
Silver Spring, MD 20910
(301) 608-2590

www.nawbo.org
NAWBO provides women business owners support, resources, and business information to help them grow and prosper in business.

American Association of Home Based Businesses (AAHBB)
PO Box 10023
Rockville, MD 20849
www.aahbb.org
Formed in 1991, the AAHBB is a nonprofit organization that provides members with support and networking opportunities. All members operate their businesses from a homebased location, and the organization provides services and products that can be utilized by the home business owner.

American Home Business Association
4505 Wasatah Boulevard S.
Salt Lake City, UT 84124
(800) 664-2422
www.homebusiness.com

National Association for the Self-Employed
PO Box 612067
DFW Airport
Dallas, TX 75261-2067
(800) 232-6273
www.nase.org

SOHO America (Small Office Home Office)
PO Box 941
Hurst, Texas 76053-0941
(800) 495-SOHO
www.soho.org

Home Office Association of America
PO Box 51
Sagaponack, NY 11962-0051
(212) 588-9097
www.aahbb.org

International Franchise Association (IFA)
1350 New York Avenue NW, Suite 900
Washington, DC 20005-4709
(202) 628-8000
www.franchise.org
International Franchise Association members include franchisors, franchisees, and service and product suppliers for the franchising industry.

CANADIAN GOVERNMENT AGENCIES AND BUSINESS ASSOCIATIONS

Canadian Business Service Centers (CBSC)
The CBSC offers a wide range of products and services to assist Canadian, American, and international entrepreneurs to start, grow, and manage their businesses. The federal government of Canada has partnered with provincial governments and private industry to develop Business Service Centers in all Canadian provinces and territories. CBSC products, services, and publications can be accessed on the CBSC Web site located at www.cbsc.org, or at any Provincial Business Service Center location. Some of the services offered to entrepreneurs include:

Interactive Business Planner (IBP)
IBP is an online interactive software application that will let you develop and prepare a comprehensive business plan.

Online Small Business Workshops
CBSC online small business workshops have been developed to assist entrepreneurs in starting, financing, and marketing new business ventures, or to improve existing businesses.

Info-Guides
CBSC info-guides are available free of charge at www.cbsc.org or at Provincial Business Service Centers. Info-guides are brief overviews and are industry specific, such as retailing, manufacturing, or exporting.

Business Information System (BIS)
BIS is a business resource databank containing more than 1,200 documents pertaining to business programs, services, and specific regulations. BIS documents are free and can be accessed at www.cbsc.org or at any Provincial Business Service Center.

CBSC Provincial Office Locations
Alberta Business Link
100-10237-104th Street NW
Edmonton, AB T5J 1B1
(800) 272-9675
www.cbsc.org/alberta

British Columbia Business Service Center
601 West Cordova Street
Vancouver, BC V6B 1G1
(604) 775-5525
www.smallbusinessbc.ca

Manitoba Business Service Center
250-240 Graham Avenue
Winnipeg, MB R3C 4B3
(800) 665-2019
www.cbsc.org/manitoba

New Brunswick Business Service Center
570 Queen Street
Fredericton, NB E3B 6Z6
(506) 444-6140
www.cbsc.org/nb

Newfoundland and Labrador Business Service Center
90 O'Leary Avenue
St. John's, NF A3I 3T1
(709) 772-6022
www.cbsc.org/nf

Northwest Territories Business Service Center
PO Box 1320
Scotia Center, 8th Floor
Yellowknife, NT X1A 2L9
(800) 661-0599
www.cbsc.org/nwt

Nova Scotia Business Service Center
1575 Brunswick Street
Halifax, NS B3J 2G1
(902) 426-8604
www.cbsc.org/ns

Nunavut Business Service Center
PO Box 1000, Station 1198
Parnaivik Building
Iqaluit, Nunavut X0A 0H0
(877) 499-5199
www.cbsc.org/nunavut

Ontario Business Service Center
North York Civic Center
500 Young Street
Toronto, ON M2N 5V7
(800) 567-2345
www.cbsc.org/ontario

Prince Edward Island Business Service Center
75 Fitzroy Street
Charlottetown, PEI C1A 7K2

(902) 368-0771
www.cbsc.org/pe

Quebec Business Service Center
5 Place Ville Marie, Suite 12500
Montreal, Quebec H3B 4Y2
(800) 322-4636
www.infoentrepreneurs.org

Saskatchewan Business Service Center
122 Third Avenue N.
Saskatoon, SK S7K 2H6
(800) 667-4374
www.cbsc.org/sask

Yukon Business Service Center
101-307 Jarvis Street
Whitehorse, Yukon Y1A 2H3
(800) 661-0543
www.cbsc.org/yukon

Canadian Intellectual Property Office (CIPO)
Patents, Trademarks & Copyrights
Industry Canada, Place Du Portage
50 Victoria Street, 2nd Floor
Hull, Quebec K19 0C9
(819) 997-1936
www.cipo.gc.ca

Canada Customs and Revenue Agency
333 Laurier Avenue W.
Ottawa, ON K1A 0L9
(800) 959-2221
www.ccra-adrc.ga.ca
Information and resources pertaining to small business taxes, corporate tax, tax rebates and programs, payroll deductions, and goods and services tax/harmonized sales tax (GST/HST).

Business Development Bank of Canada (BDC)
150 King Street W. Suite 100
Toronto, ON M5H 1J9
(416) 395-9014
www.bdc.ca
BDC provides financial services and programs to Canadians seeking to start or grow a business. Loan applications can be ordered by calling the BDC or by visiting the Web site.

The Canadian Chamber of Commerce
BCE Place, 181 Bay Street, Heritage Building

Toronto, ON M5J 2T3
(416) 868-6415
www.chamber.ca
The Canadian Chamber of Commerce represents small businesses, corporations, and trade associations from coast to coast. Log on to its Web site to locate a regional branch office.

Small Office Home Office Business Group (SOHO)
2255B Queen Street E., Suite 3261
Toronto, ON M4E 1G3
(800) 290-7646
www.soho.ca
SOHO is a nonprofit small business organization founded in 1995, which provides members with networking, education, and incentive programs and opportunities.

Young Entrepreneurs Association (YEA)
720 Spadina Avenue, Suite 300
Toronto, ON M5S 2T9
(888) 639-3222
www.yea.ca
Young Entrepreneurs Association of Canada provides members with peer support, networking opportunities, and business and entrepreneur resources.

Canadian Franchise Association (CFA)
300-2585 Skymark Avenue
Mississauga, ON L4W 4L5
(800) 665-4232
www.cfa.ca

Women Business Owners of Canada
20 York Mills Road, Suite 100
York Mills, ON M2P 2C2
www.wboc.ca

BUSINESS MAGAZINES

Entrepreneur
2445 McCabe Way
Irvine, CA 92614
(800) 274-6229
www.entrepreneur.com

Business 2.0
One California Street, 29th Floor
San Francisco, CA 94111

(415) 293-4800
www.business2.com

Fast Company
77 N. Washington Street
Boston, MA 02114
(800) 688-1545
www.fastcompany.com

Home Business
9582 Hamilton Avenue, PMB 368
Huntington Beach, CA 92646
(714) 968-0331
www.homebusinessmag.com

Franchise Times
2500 Cleveland Avenue N.
Roseville, MN 55113-2728
(800) 528-3296
www.franchisetimes.com

My Business Magazine
3322 West End Avenue, Suite 700
Nashville, TN 37203
(615) 690-3450
www.mybusinessmagazine.com

Profit
777 Bay Street, 8th Floor
Toronto, ON M5W 1A7
(416) 596-5523
www.profitguide.com

Forbes
60 Fifth Avenue
New York, NY 10011
(800) 888-9896
www.forbes.com

eCompany Now
One California Street, 29th Floor
San Francisco, CA 94111
(800) 317-9704
www.ecompany.com

PC Magazine
2East 28th Street
New York, NY 10016-7930
(212) 503-3500
www.pcmag.com

Small Business Opportunities
1115 Broadway

New York, NY 10010
(202) 807-7100
www.sbomag.com

Marketers Forum
3E. Main Street
Centerport, NY 11721
(800) 635-7654
www.forum123.com

Barter News
PO Box 3024
Mission Viejo, CA 92690
(949) 831-0607
www.barternews.com

Family Business
PO Box 41966
Philadelphia, PA 19101-1966
www.familybusinessmagazine.com

Inc.
100 First Avenue, 4th Floor
Building 36
Charlestown, MA 02129
(800) 234-0999
www.inc.com

Female Entrepreneur
1420 Fifth Avenue, Suite 2200
U.S. Bank Center
Seattle, WA 98101
(800) 663-2400
www.female-entrepreneur.com

Black Enterprise
130 Fifth Avenue, 10th Floor
New York, NY 10011-4399
(212) 242-8000
www.blackenterprise.com

Home Business Report
2625 Alliance Street, Suite A
Abbottsford, BC V2S 3J9
(800) 672-0103
www.homebusinessreport.com

Hispanic Business
425 Pine Avenue
Santa Barbara, CA 93117-3709
(805) 964-4554
www.hispanicbusiness.com

eBusiness Advisor
PO Box 49002
San Diego, CA 92142-9002
(858) 278-5600
www.advisor.com

American Demographics
PO Box 10580
Riverton, NJ 08076-0580
(800) 529-7502
www.demographics.com

World Trade Magazine
755 W. Big Beaver Road, Suite 1000
Troy, MI 48084
(248) 362-3700
www.worldtrademag.com

Small Business Canada Magazine
PO Box 31010
Barrie, ON L4N 0B3
(705) 722-9692
www.sbcmag.com

Business Travel News
770 Broadway
New York, NY 10003
(646) 654-4500
www.btnonline.com

BUSINESS NEWSPAPERS

U.S. *Wall Street Journal,* www.wsj.com
Washington Business Journal, www.washington.bizjournals.com/washington
San Francisco Business Journal, www.sanfrancisco.bizjournal.com/sanfrancisco

Canada *Financial Post,* www.canoe.ca/FP
Business In Vancouver, www.biv.com
Ottawa Business Journal, www.ottawabusinessjournal.com

WEB SITES OF INTEREST

American Teleservices Association, www.atacontact.org: Representing the call centers, trainers, consultants, and equipment suppliers that initiate, facilitate, and generate telephone, Internet, and e-mail sales, service, and support.

Association of Coupon Professionals, www.couponpros.org: Industry trade organization for marketing professionals who work or have interests in the consumer promotion business.

Biz Buy Sell, www.bizbuysell.com: Billed as the Internet's largest business-for-sale site, with over 20,000 listings.

Brian Tracy International, www.briantracy.com: Sales and motivational expert. Provides coaching, information, products, programs, and services.

Business Know-How, www.businessknowhow.com: Small business information, advice, and links.

Business Marketing Association, www.marketing.org: BMA develops and delivers benefits, services, information, skill enhancement, and networking opportunities that help its members grow, develop, and succeed in their business-to-business careers.

Business Network International, www.bni.com: Billed, as the world's largest referral organization comprised of more than 2,600 chapters worldwide with thousands of members.

Canadian Home & Micro Business Federation, www.homebiz.ca: Non profit Canadian home business association providing members with information, support, and business growth networking opportunities.

Entrepreneur Online, www.entrepreneur.com: Small business information, products, and services portal.

Franchise Online, www.franchise.com: Franchise and franchisee information and services and directory service of franchise opportunities.

Franchise Works, www.franchiseworks.com: Online directory of franchise opportunities, business opportunities, franchises, home business franchise opportunities, and franchise information.

Guerrilla Marketing Online, www.gmarketing.com: Small business marketing tips, information, seminars, books, and links.

Home Working Moms, www.homeworkingmoms.com: Information and advice for parents working from a home office.

Independent Computer Consultants Association, www.icca.org: Members are computer and software experts who have practical experience with the industry's rapidly changing technology.

International Business Brokers Association, www. ibba.org: Links to more than 1,100 business brokers in North America, Asia, and Europe.

International Customer Service Association, www.icsa.com: Offering members information, products, services, and education aimed at improving customer service skills and relationship building.

Licensing Industry Merchants' Association, www. licensing.org: Representing 1,000 member companies and individuals engaged in the marketing of licensed properties, both as agents and as property owners: manufacturers, consultants, publications, lawyers, accountants, and retailers in the licensing business.

Market Research, www.marketresearch.com: Billed as the most comprehensive collection of published market research available on demand.

Marketing Source, www.marketingsource.com: Fee-based directory service listing more than 5,000 associations.

National Mail Order Association, www.nmoa.org: Members receive and keep up to date on information, products, and services affecting the mail order and direct marketing industries.

National Venture Capital Association, www.nvca. org: Association membership consists of venture capital firms and organizations that manage pools of risk equity capital designated to be invested in young, emerging companies.

News Link, www.newslink.org: An online newspaper directory serving the United States, Canada, Mexico, and South America, indexed geographically and by type of newspaper.

Nolo, www.nolo.com: Online legal self-help information, products, services, resources, and links for consumers and business owners.

Power Home Biz, www.powerhomebiz.com: Home business information portal.

Small Business Loans Online, www.smallbusiness loans.com: Online loan applications for financing new business start-ups and for financing existing businesses to help growth.

Smart Biz, www.smartbiz.com: Small business information.

Trade Show Exhibitors Association, www.tsea.org: Online news and information about marketing products and services at trade shows and special events.

V Finance, www.vfinance.com: Directory of venture capital firms and angel investors.

Work At Home Parent, www.work-at-home-parent. com: Information and advice for parents working from a home office.

HOME OFFICE ONLINE BUYERS GUIDE
Business Books

Amazon, www.amazon.com: Retailer of new and used books.

Barnes and Noble, www.barnesandnoble.com: Retailer of new and used books.

Chapters/Indigo, www.chapters.indigo.ca: Canadian bookseller.

Entrepreneur Press, www.entrepreneurpress.com: Small business and management books, start-up guides, and business software.

Half Price Computer Books, www.halfpricecomputer books.com: Selling business and computer books at 50 percent off retail.

Powell's Books, www.powells.com: Retailer of new and used books.

Small Business Books, www.smallbizbooks.com: Industry and business specific start-up guides, manuals, and software.

Office Supplies

Staples, www.staples.com
Office Depot, www.officedepot.com
Office Max, www.officemax.com
Business Supply, www.business-supply.com

Desktop and Notebook Computers

Dell Computers, www.dell.com
IBM Computers, www.ibm.com
Apple Computers, www.apple.com

Gateway Computers, www.gateway.com
Toshiba, www.toshiba.com
Hewlett Packard (HP) Compaq, www.hp.com

Inkjet and Laser Printers
Hewlett Packard, (HP) www.hp.com
Epson, www.epson.com
Canon, www.usa.canon.com
Lexmark,www.lexmark.com

Business Software, Shareware, and Downloads
Download Superstore, www.downlaodsuperstore.com
Find Accounting Software, www.findaccounting software.com
CNET Shareware, www.shareware.com
Biz Rate, www.bizrate.com

Promotional Products
Promomart, www.promomart.com
Café Press, www.cafepress.com
Branders, www.branders.com
Killer Promotions, www.killerpromotions.com

Custom Printing
Print USA, www.printusa.com
Printing For Less, www.printingforless.com
Quebecor, www.quebecorworldinc.com
The Print Guide, www.theprintguide.com

Home Office Furniture
Ikea, www.ikea.com
Office Furniture, www.officefurniture.com
By Design, www.officebydesign.com
Home Office Direct, www.homeofficedirect.com

Index

equipment, 120–125, 128
furniture and equipment costs worksheet, 121
furniture, equipment and supplies checklist, 129–130
Online buyers guide for home office, 398–399
Online selling, 344–350. *See also* Internet, Web site
Options, home-based business, 26–28
Organized, getting, 13

P

Part-time business, 27, 206–207
Partnerships, 75–76
Patent protection, 80
Payment terms, 197–201
Permits, 77–78
Personal
assets and liabilities worksheet, 54–55
goals, defining, 22
savings, 56–57
situation, taking stock of your, 16–26
worksheet, 17
Pets and the home based business, 137–138
Planning, business, 6
Presentations, winning, 294–297
Press release
creating a, 269–272
sample, 273
Pressure, handling, 187–189
Pricing, 153–164
basics, 154–157
information for service providers, 160–163
resources, additional, 164
strategy, 157–160
Print identity package, 131–132
Professional service providers, 146–148
Promissory note, sample of, 59
Property insurance, 87
Prospect
management database, 288–292
qualifying the potential, 292–294

Public relations, 265–282
media contact form, example of, 272
media kit, 272–274
press release, 269–272
press release, sample of, 273
resources, 282
strategy, 267–269
the basics, 266–267
tips, techniques and great ideas, 274–279
Public speaking, 321–322

R

Radio advertising, 247–248
Realtors, 32
Referral form, sample of, 307
Referrals, 185, 306–308
Renovation
costs worksheet, 118
workspace, 116–119
Rental insurance, 88–89
Reputation, building a solid, 11
Residence, suitability of yours for business purposes, 18
Resource checklist, 24
Resources, home business, 392–399
Retail financing/leasing services, 63
Retirement, starting a home business in your, 28

S

Safe, home office, 62, 127
Safety
home office, 125–128
issues, 139
Sale, always ask for "the," 7
Sales, 283–310
closing techniques, 301–303
communications, 284–287
identifying buying signals, 300–301
negotiations, 303–306
online, 344–350
overcoming objections, 298–300
presentations, 294–297
prospecting, 287–294
resources, 309–310
tax, 65, 78
through the Internet, 344–350

trial closing, 297–298
SBA (Small Business Administration) loan programs, 57
Schools, networking with local, 151
Search engine, 332–336
directory tracking form, 333
Seasonal home business, 27–28
Self promotion, shameless, 7–8
Selling
preparation as starting point for, 283–284 (See also Sales)
Selling your business, 205–206
Seminars, 318–321
Seriousness of purpose, 5–6
Signage, 138, 260–261
Slogans, 131
Small claims court, 201
Sole proprietorship, 74–75
Special skills checklist, 20–21
Sponsorship opportunities, 150, 324–326
Start-up
capital, 56
costs, estimator/calculator for home business, 40–46
ideas, "99 great home business and franchise," 355–381
ideas, resources for, 29–30
Starting a new business from scratch, 26, 30–31
Successful entrepreneurs, 25 common characteristics of, 4–5
Suppliers and associates, establishing favorable credit terms with, 61
SWOT analysis and action plan, 219–220

T

Taxes, 64–67, 78
Technology, leveling the playing field with, 8–9
Telemarketing, 254–255
Telephones, 123–124
Television advertising, 248–250
Time management, 189–196
decision matrix, 190
Time off, importance of taking, 13–14